Greenhill Books

A HISTORY
OF THE
PENINSULAR
WAR

A HISTORY OF
THE PENINSULAR WAR

A HISTORY
OF THE
PENINSULAR
WAR

Emery Walker Ph.Sc.

Duke of Wellington
From a portrait in the Hope Collection
(1813)

A HISTORY
OF THE
PENINSULAR WAR

Volume III:
September 1809 to December 1810
Ocaña, Cadiz, Bussaco, Torres Vedras

SIR CHARLES OMAN

Greenhill Books, London
Stackpole Books, Pennsylvania

Greenhill Books

This edition of *A History of the Peninsular War*, volume III
first published 2004 by
Greenhill Books, Lionel Leventhal Limited, Park House,
1 Russell Gardens, London NW11 9NN
and
Stackpole Books, 5067 Ritter Road, Mechanicsburg,
PA 17055, USA

British Library Cataloguing in Publication Data
Oman, Sir Charles, 1860–1946
A history of the Peninsular War. – Vol. 3: September 1809 –
December 1810, Ocaña, Cadiz, Bussaco, Torres Vedras. –
(Greenhill military paperback)
1, Peninsular War, 1807–1814
I. Title
940.2'7
ISBN 1-85367-617-9

Library of Congress Cataloging in Publication Data
available

PUBLISHING HISTORY
A History of the Peninsular War, volume III, was first published
in 1908 (Oxford), and is reproduced now exactly as the original
edition, complete and unabridged. The original maps have been
re-presented by John Richards, in the interests of clarity.

Printed and Bound by CPD, Ebbw Vale

PREFACE

THIS, the third volume of the History of the Peninsular War, covers a longer period than either of its predecessors, extending over the sixteen months from Wellington's arrival at Badajoz on his retreat from Talavera (Sept. 3, 1809) to the deadlock in front of Santarem (Dec. 1810), which marked the end of Masséna's offensive campaign in Portugal. It thus embraces the central crisis of the whole war, the arrival of the French in front of the Lines of Torres Vedras and their first short retreat, after they had realized the impossibility of forcing that impregnable barrier to their advance. The retreat that began at Sobral on the night of Nov. 14, 1810, was to end at Toulouse on April 11, 1814. The armies of the Emperor were never able to repeat the experiment of 1810, and to assume a general and vigorous offensive against Wellington and Portugal. In 1811 they were on the defensive, despite of certain local and partial attempts to recover their lost initiative. In 1812 they had to abandon half Spain—Andalusia, Estremadura, Asturias, La Mancha, and much more, —despite of Wellington's temporary check before Burgos. In 1813 they were swept across the Pyrenees and the Bidassoa; in 1814 they were fighting a losing game in their own land. Rightly then may Masséna's retreat to Santarem be called the beginning of the end—though it was not for a full year more that Wellington's final offensive commenced, with the investment of Ciudad Rodrigo on Jan. 8, 1812.

The campaign of Bussaco and Torres Vedras, therefore, marked the turning-point of the whole war, and I have endeavoured to set forth its meaning in full detail, devoting special care to the explanation of Wellington's triple device for arresting the French advance—his combination of the system of devastation, of the raising of the *levée en masse* in Portugal, and of the construction of great defensive lines in front of Lisbon. Each of these three measures would have been incomplete without the other two. For the Lines of Torres Vedras might not have saved Portugal and Europe from the domination of Napoleon, if the invading army had not been surrounded on all sides by the light screen of irregular troops, which cut its communications, and prevented it from foraging far afield. Nor would Masséna have been turned back, if the land through which he had advanced had been left unravaged, and if every large village had contained enough food to subsist a brigade for a day or a battalion for a week.

The preparations, the advance, and the retreat of Masséna cover about half of this volume. The rest of it is occupied with the operations of the French in Northern, Eastern, and Southern Spain—operations which seemed decisive at the moment, but which turned out to be mere side-issues in the great contest. For Soult's conquest of Andalusia, and Suchet's victories in Aragon, Catalonia, and Valencia only distracted the imperial generals from their central task —the expulsion of Wellington and his army from the Peninsula. Most readers will, I think, find a good deal of new information in the accounts of the siege of Gerona and the battle of Ocaña. The credit due to Alvarez for the defence of the Cata-

Ionian city has never been properly set forth before
in any English history, nor have the details of
Areizaga's miserable campaign in La Mancha been
fully studied. In particular, the composition and
strength of his army have never before been
elucidated, and Appendices V, VI of this volume
consist of absolutely unpublished documents.

I have to offer my grateful thanks to those who
have been good enough to assist me in the writing
of this book, by furnishing me with stores of private
papers, or hitherto unknown official reports. Two
of the kind helpers who put me on the track of
new information for the compiling of Volume II
have passed away while Volume III was in progress.
I bitterly regret the loss of my friends General
Arteche and Colonel F. A. Whinyates. The former,
with his unrivalled knowledge of the contents of the
historical department of the Madrid War Office, had
enabled me to discover many a lost document of
importance. The latter had placed at my disposal
his copious store of papers, letters, and diaries
relating to his old corps, the Royal Artillery. In
this present section of the history of the war I
am still using much of the material which he
lent me.

But new helpers have come to my aid while
this volume was being written. To three of them
I must express my special gratitude. The first is
Mr. W. S. M. D'Urban, of Newport House, near Exeter,
who has furnished me with copies of a collection
of papers of unique interest, the diary and correspondence of his grandfather, Sir Benjamin D'Urban,
who served as the Quartermaster-General of the
Portuguese army, under Marshal Beresford, during

the two years covered by this section of my history. Thanks to the mass of documents furnished by Mr. D'Urban's kindness, I am now in a position to follow the details of the organization, movements, and exploits of the Portuguese army in a way that had hitherto been impossible to me. Moreover, Sir Benjamin's day by day criticisms on the strategy and tactics both of Masséna and of Wellington have the highest interest, as reflecting the opinions of the more intelligent section of the head-quarters staff. It is noteworthy to find that, while many of Wellington's chief subordinates despaired of the situation in 1810, there were some who already felt an enthusiastic confidence in the plans of their leader, so much so that their criticisms were reserved for the occasions when, in their opinion, he showed himself over-cautious, and refused to take full advantage of the uncomfortable positions into which he had lured his enemy.

The second mass of interesting private papers placed in my hands of late is the personal correspondence of Nicholas Trant and John Wilson, the two enterprising leaders of Portuguese militia forces, to whom Wellington had entrusted the cutting off of Masséna's communication with Spain, and the restriction of his raids for sustenance to feed his army. These letters have been lent me by Commander Bertram Chambers of H.M.S. *Resolution*, a collateral relative of Wilson. They fill up a gap in the military history of 1810, for no one hitherto had the opportunity of following out in detail the doings of these two adventurous soldiers and trusty friends, while they were engaged in the difficult task that was set them. For a sample of Trant's breezy style

of correspondence, I may refer the reader to pages
399–400 of this volume. Unfortunately, when the
two militia generals were in actual contact, their
correspondence naturally ceased, so that the series
of letters has many *lacunae*. But they are nevertheless of the highest value.

Thirdly, I have to thank Sir Henry Le Marchant
for a sight of the private papers of his grandfather,
the well-known cavalry brigadier, General John Gaspar
Le Marchant, who fell at Salamanca. He did not
land in the Peninsula till 1811, but during the
preceding year he was receiving many letters of
interest, some from his own contemporaries, officers
of high rank in Wellington's army, others from
younger men, who had been his pupils while he
was in command of the Military College at High
Wycombe. Some of the seniors, and one especially,
were among those downhearted men—of the opposite
type to Benjamin D'Urban—who were consistently
expecting disaster, and looked for a hasty embarkation
at Lisbon as the natural end of the campaign of 1810.
The younger men took a very different view of
affairs, and invariably sent cheerful accounts of the
doings of the army.

I must mention, once more, kind assistance from
the officials of the Historical sections of the War
Ministries at Paris and at Madrid. My friend
Commandant Balagny, who gave me so much help
during the compilation of my second volume, has
unfortunately been absent on a military mission to
Brazil during the last three years. But the kind
offices of M. Martinien have continually aided me
in getting access to the particular sections of the
Paris archives with which I was from time to time

concerned. I must here take the opportunity of
expressing once more my admiration for his colossal
work, the *Liste des officiers tués et blessés pendant
les Guerres de l'Empire*, which, on the numberless
occasions when no casualty-return appears in the
Paris archives, enables one to determine what
regiments were present at any action, and in what
proportion they suffered. At Madrid Captain
Emilio Figueras has continued his kind services,
offered during the compilation of my second volume,
and was indefatigable in going through the papers
of 1810 with me, during my two visits to the Spanish
capital.

Among my English helpers I must cite with
special gratitude four names. The first is that of
Mr. C. T. Atkinson, Fellow of Exeter College,
Oxford, who has read the proofs of the greater part
of this volume, and given me many valuable correc-
tions and pieces of information, from his wide knowledge of British regimental history. The second is
that of Major John H. Leslie, R.A., who has compiled
the Artillery Appendix to this section, corresponding
to that which Colonel Whinyates compiled for the
last. I am also most grateful to him for an early
view of the useful 'Dickson Papers,' which he is
publishing for the Royal Artillery Institution. The
third is that of the Rev. Alexander Craufurd, who
has continued to give me notes on the history of the
Light Division, while it was commanded by his
grandfather, the famous Robert Craufurd. The
fourth is that of Mr. C. E. Doble of the Clarendon
Press, who has again read for errors every page of
a long volume.

Lastly, the indefatigable compiler of the Index

must receive once more my heartfelt thanks for a labour of love.

The reader will find several topographical notes appended at the end of chapters, the results of my first and second tours along the borderland of Spain and Portugal. Two long visits to the battlefield of Bussaco, and some days spent between the Coa and the Agueda, and behind the Lines of Torres Vedras, gave me many new topographical facts of importance. Drives and walks in the Badajoz–Elvas country, and about Coimbra, also turned out most profitable. But my notes on the battlefields of Fuentes d'Oñoro and Albuera can only be utilized in my next volume, which I trust may not be long in following its predecessor into print.

The spelling of many of the Spanish, and more especially the Portuguese, names may appear unfamiliar to some readers. But I believe that correctness should be studied above all things, even though the results in cases like Bussaco with the double s, Golegão, or Santa Comba Dao, may produce a momentary shock to the eye. Portuguese spelling, both in personal names and in topography, was in a state of flux in 1810. For example, the General commanding the Artillery always appears as da Rosa in the official army lists, yet signed his name da Roza; countless other instances could be produced. Where it was possible I have followed the individual's own version of his name: he ought to have known best. There are still, no doubt, errors of spelling surviving: no man is infallible, but I have done my best to reduce them to a minimum.

C. OMAN.

Oxford :
March 1, 1908.

CONTENTS

SECTION XXI

Bussaco and Torres Vedras (Sept.–Dec. 1810)

SECTION XXII

The End of the Year 1810

APPENDICES

MAPS AND PLANS

ILLUSTRATIONS

NOTES ON THE ILLUSTRATIONS
I. SPANISH INFANTRY 1808
This shows the old uniform of Charles IV. The Line regiments had white, the Foreign and Light regiments blue, coats. Both wore white breeches and black gaiters: the plume and facings varied in colour for each regiment.

II. SPANISH INFANTRY 1810
Under the influence of the immense quantity of British materials supplied, the uniform has completely changed since 1808. The cut is assimilated to that of the British army—the narrow-topped shako, and long trousers have been introduced. The coat is dark blue, the trousers grey-blue, the facings red. Grenadiers have the grenade, light companies the bugle-horn on their shakos.

ERRATA
Page 264, *line* 13, *for* 318 *read* 333
Page 277, *line* 20, *for* 1811 *read* 1810
Page 335. Lord Blayney's force had only a half-battalion, not a whole battalion of the 89th, but contained 4 companies of foreign chasseurs, not mentioned in the text. [See his Memoirs, i, pp. 5–6.]

SECTION XVII
FROM TALAVERA TO OCAÑA

CHAPTER I

INTRODUCTORY. THE CENTRAL JUNTA. WELLESLEY AND WELLINGTON

BETWEEN the 20th of August, 1809, when Robert Craufurd's Light Brigade[1] withdrew from the Bridge of Almaraz, to follow the rest of the British army across the mountains to the neighbourhood of Badajoz, and February 27, 1810, when part of that same brigade was engaged in the first skirmish of Barba del Puerco, not a shot was fired by any of Wellington's troops. This gap of over six months in his active operations may appear extraordinary, and it was bitterly criticized at the time. Between August and March there was hard fighting both in the south of Spain and along the north-eastern frontier of Portugal; but the British army, despite many invitations, took no part in it. Wellington adhered to his resolve never to commit himself again to a campaign in company with the Spaniards, unless he should be placed in a position in which he could be independent of the freaks of their government and the perversity of their generals. Two months' experience of the impracticability of Cuesta, of the deliberate disobedience of Venegas, of the fruitless promises of the commissary-general Lozano de Torres, of the insane demands and advice sent in by the Central Junta, had convinced him that he dare not risk his army in a second venture such as that which had led him to Talavera. If he were made commander-in-chief by the Spanish Government, and granted a free hand in the direction of the Spanish armies, matters would look different[2]. But

[1] Not, it must be remembered, to become the Light *Division* till March 1810.

[2] See Wellington to Canning, Sept. 5, 1809, in *Dispatches*, v. 123–4.

there was at present no chance whatever that he would receive
such a mark of confidence.   Only a small minority of the
leading men at Seville could endure with patience the idea
of a British commander-in-chief.   Wellington himself had long
dismissed the project—which Frere had broached in the spring[1]—
as impracticable.

Meanwhile the French advance had no sooner ceased—after
the rather objectless combat of Arzobispo—than the Junta
began to press upon the British general schemes for a resumption of the offensive and a second march toward Madrid.
The political situation, and not any military considerations, was
the originating cause of their untimely activity.   They felt
that their authority was waning, that their popularity had
vanished, that their critics were daily growing more venomous,
and they saw that success in the war would be the only possible
way out of their difficulties.   Hence at the very moment when
Wellington was withdrawing his half-starved army from the
Tagus, and impeaching in letters of stinging irony the conduct
of the Junta's mendacious commissaries, he was being pressed
to resume the offensive.   Countless appeals were made to him.
Both formal and argumentative invitations from the ministers
at Seville, and private remonstrances by individuals, Spanish
and English, were showered upon him [2].   The Junta even went
so far as to offer him command of the Spanish troops in
Estremadura, though this offer was qualified by their statement
that they intended to reduce those troops to 12,000 men, the
larger half of the army being under orders to march eastward
into La Mancha and join the force of Venegas.   This proposal
did not in the least meet Wellington's main objection to
resuming active operations; viz. that he could not trust the
Spanish Government to feed his army, nor the Spanish generals
to carry out with punctual accuracy any scheme for a joint
campaign which might be laid before him.   He put the matter
very plainly—' till the evils of which I think that I have reason
to complain are remedied: till I see magazines established

[1] See vol. ii. pp. 465–6.

[2] See *Dispatches*, v. 168, for an account of an interview with the
Marquis of Malaspina and Lord Macduff, who had come to Badajoz to
make personal representation, which Wellington much resented.

for the supply of the troops, and a regular system adopted
for keeping them filled: till I see an army upon whose exertions
I can depend, commanded by officers capable and willing to carry
into execution the operations which have been planned by mutual
agreement, I cannot enter upon any system of co-operation with
the Spanish armies [1].' This statement was for publication:
in private correspondence with his brother, the ambassador at
Seville, he added still more cogent reasons for declining to
take the field with Venegas or Eguia. He had witnessed with
his own eyes the panic of Portago's division on the night before
Talavera, ' when whole corps threw away their arms and ran
off in my presence, while neither attacked nor threatened with
attack, but frightened (I believe) by their own fire ': he had
seen Albuquerque's cavalry, the day after the combat of Arzobispo, lurking in every village for twenty miles round, and 'had
heard Spanish officers telling of nineteen or twenty actions
of the same description as that of Arzobispo, an account of
which (I believe) has never been published.' The army of
Estremadura consisted, he concluded, ' of troops by no means
to be depended upon'—on every ground, therefore, he ought
to avoid 'risking the King's army again in such company [2].'

There was no getting over this fundamental objection of
Wellington's, and his brother, therefore, was placed in a very
uncomfortable position. During all his negotiations with the
Central Junta, Lord Wellesley's task indeed was a most invidious one. He had been directed by his government to
profess an earnest desire to aid the Spaniards in bringing
the war to a successful conclusion, and to pledge the aid of
Great Britain, yet he was forced to refuse every definite proposal
made to him by the Junta. On the other hand, there were
clauses in his instructions which provoked the most openly-
displayed suspicion and resentment, when he touched upon them
in his conversations with Martin de Garay and the other Spanish
ministers. Such were the proposal to place the whole Spanish
army under a British commander (i. e. Wellington), the attempt

---

[1] Wellington to Wellesley, Oct. 30 : *Dispatches*, v. 213. For stronger
language about the rash folly of Spanish generals, see Wellington to
Beresford, ibid. 179.

[2] Wellington to Wellesley, Aug. 24, from Merida.

to open up the subject of a certain measure of free trade with Spanish America, and—most of all—the offer to send British troops to garrison Cadiz. For despite the fiasco of the preceding winter, the Portland ministry were still harping on this old string, and allusions to it occur in nearly every dispatch sent from London to the ambassador at Seville [1].

Wellesley's position was made even more difficult by the fact that all the Spanish factions opposed to the Central Junta tried to draw him into their schemes, by making lavish professions of what they were ready to do if only the present government were evicted from office. Of these factions there were many: the old 'Council of Castile,' which the Junta had superseded, still clung together, making protests as to the legality of their successor's position. The local assemblies were equally jealous of the central authority — the Juntas of Estremadura and Valencia, in especial, were always intriguing behind its back, and the former at least made many tempting proposals both to Wellesley and to Wellington. But the most dangerous enemies of the existing government were the malcontents close at its gates—the Andalusian conspirators, led by the members of the old Junta of Seville, and by the intriguers like the Conde de Montijo, the dukes of Infantado and Ossuna, and Francisco Palafox. The dissatisfaction caused by the incapacity, indecision, and—as it was openly said—the nepotism and venality of the Junta was so general, that a plan was formed in Seville to seize them, deport them all to the Canaries, and proclaim a Regency. The troops in the place were tampered with, some demagogues were ready to raise the mob, and Infantado [2], who was in the thick of the plot, came to Wellesley one night to divulge the arrangements for the 'Pronunciamento' and to bespeak his aid. Much as he disliked the Junta and its methods, the Ambassador scornfully refused to make himself a member of a conspiracy, and after warning Infantado of his intention, went straight to the Secretary Garay and gave him all the information as to the project, though without divulging

---

[1] See Canning's instruction to Wellesley of June 27, 1809, on pages 186–91 of Wellesley's *Dispatches and Correspondence*, Lond. 1838.

[2] See Baumgarten, *Geschichte Spaniens*, i. 408, and Toreno, vol. ii. p. 72. Wellesley only calls the Duke 'a person' : *Dispatches*, p. 160.

any names.   Some of the plotters fled, others were arrested.
' For the last two days,' writes Wellesley to his brother, ' I have
been employed in endeavouring to save the necks of these caitiffs
from the just fury and indignation of the people and soldiery,
and I have succeeded.   A regular plot was formed to seize (and
I believe to *hang*) them all.   But I could not suffer such outrages
under my nose, so I interfered and saved the curs from the rope.
They were all gratitude *for an hour* [Wellesley was offered and
refused the Order of the Golden Fleece next morning], but now
that they think themselves secure they have begun to cheat me
again[1].'

Much as every patriot should deprecate the employment of
coups d'état while a foreign war is on hand, there was much
to excuse the conduct of the enemies of the Junta.   That body
was now more than a year old; it had been from the first
regarded as a stop-gap, as a provisional government which was
destined to give place to something more regular and constitutional when occasion should serve.   A ' Committee of Public
Safety ' which fails to preserve the state stands self-condemned,
and the history of the Central Junta had been one record of
consistent disaster.   A body of over thirty persons is too large
for a ministry, too small for a representative assembly.   Every
intelligent Spaniard, whatever his politics, was desirous of seeing
it give place to a regular government.   The Conservatives and
bureaucrats would have been contented if it had appointed
a Regency of four or five persons, and then abdicated.   The
Liberals demanded that it should summon the national Cortes,
and leave to that body the creation of an executive.   Pamphlets
were showered by dozens from the press—now more or less free,
for the first time in Spanish history—to advocate one or other
of these courses.   The Junta, however, had no intention of surrendering its power, whatever pretence of disinterestedness it might
assume and proclaim.   Its first attempts to put off the evil day
when it must yield to public opinion were ingeniously absurd.   It
issued, as early as May 22, a proclamation acknowledging the
advisability of summoning a Cortes, and then invited all well-
thinking Spaniards to send in schemes and suggestions during the

---

[1] Wellesley to Wellington, Sept. 19, 1809.   Wellington, *Supplementary
Dispatches* vi. 372.

next two months concerning the best way in which the national
assembly could be organized, and the reforms and constitutional
improvements which it should take in hand.   These documents
were to be read and pondered over by a Commission, mainly
composed of members of the Junta, which was to issue a report
in due time, embodying the best of the suggestions and the
results of its own discussion [1].   This was an admirable device for
wasting time and putting off the assembly of the Cortes.   The
Commission finally decided, on September 19, after many weeks
of session, that a supreme Executive Council of five persons
should be appointed, carefully avoiding the name of Regency.
But only existing members of the Central Junta were to be
eligible as Councillors, and the Council was to be changed at
short intervals, till every member of the Junta had taken a turn
in it [2].   The only laudable clause of this scheme was one
providing that Spanish America should be represented in the
Junta, and therefore ultimately in the Executive Council.   The
arrangement satisfied nobody—it merely substituted a rapidly
changing committee of the Junta for the whole of that body
as the supreme ruling power : and it was clear that the orders
of the Council would be those of the Junta, though they might
be voiced by fewer mouths.   The assembly of the Cortes would
be put off *ad infinitum*.

Any effect which the report of the Commission might have
had, was spoilt by the fact that it was followed by a minority
report, or manifesto, drawn up by the Marquis of La Romana,
who had been one of the Commissioners.   The Junta had
called him back from Galicia, and compelled him to surrender
the army that he had re-formed, under the pretext that he
had been co-opted as a member of their own body.   A death-
vacancy had been created in the representation of the kingdom
of Valencia : he had been named to fill it, summoned to Seville,
and placed on the constitutional Commission.   Dissenting from
every word of the report of the majority, he published on
October 14 a counter-scheme, in which he declared that the

---

[1] For the text of this wordy proclamation see Wellesley's *Spanish
Dispatches,* pp. 135–9.

[2] Note the extraordinary similarity of this plan to that produced by the
Athenian oligarchs in 411 B. C.   Had some one been reading Thucydides?

venality, nepotism, and dilatory incapacity of the Junta made it necessary for Spain to seek a new executive which should be wholly independent of that body. Accordingly he suggested that a Regency of five members should be constituted, as the supreme governing body of the realm. No member of the Junta was to sit therein. It was to be assisted, for consultative purposes, by a body of six persons—one of whom was to be a South American. This second committee, to be called 'the Permanent Deputation of the Realm,' was to be considered to represent the Cortes till that assembly should meet. It was not to meddle with executive matters, but was to devote itself to drawing up the details of the constitution of the future Cortes, and to suggesting practical reforms.

So far as the declaration in favour of a Regency went, most sensible Spaniards liked La Romana's scheme, and it obtained Wellesley's approval also. But the idea of the 'Permanent Deputation' frightened the Liberals, who feared that its existence would be made the excuse for putting off the summoning of the Cortes for an indefinite time. Moreover it was rumoured that La Romana intended to resign his seat in the Junta, and to become a candidate for the position of Senior Regent, so that his proposals must be intended to benefit himself. The suspicion that his personal ambitions inspired his patriotic denunciation of the Junta's misdoings was made the more likely by events that occurred at the same moment in Valencia. There the leading personage of the moment was the governor, General José Caro, the younger brother of La Romana, who had complete control of the local Junta, and exercised what his enemies called a tyranny in the province. He and his following were already on the worst terms with the Seville Government, and now took the opportunity of bursting out into open rebellion. They issued a sounding manifesto against the Supreme Junta, declared their intention of refusing to obey it any longer, and republished and sent in all directions to the other local Juntas La Romana's report in favour of a Regency, of which Caro had struck off 6,000 copies. They threatened to turn back by force General Castro whom the Supreme Junta had sent to supersede Caro, and declared their second representative in that body, the Conde de Contamina, deposed for 'disobedience to the will of the people.' It looked as if La Romana might be intending to overthrow the central government by means of his brother's Valencian army. Apparently he must be acquitted of this charge, his fiery and ambitious kinsman having gone far beyond his intentions.

In the midst of all these intrigues, plots, and manifestos the Central Junta had only one hope—to rehabilitate themselves by means of a great military success. With ruinous consequences they tried to direct the course of the war with political rather than strategical ends in view. Of the unhappy autumn campaign which their rashness precipitated we shall speak in its proper place ; but before narrating the disasters of Ocaña and Alba de Tormes, we must turn back for some months to consider the situation of Eastern Spain, where the continuous chronicle of events has been conducted no further than Blake's rout at Belchite in June, and St. Cyr's victory of Valls in February 1809. Much had happened in Catalonia and Aragon even before the day of Talavera. Much more was to take place before the ill-judged November campaign of the Junta's armies in New Castile and Leon had begun.

N.B.—This is a military history : for the war of pamphlets and manifestos, plots and intrigues, between the Seville Government and its adversaries, the reader who is anxious to master the disheartening details may consult Toreno's Tenth Book ; Schepeler, iii. 460–86 ; Baumgarten, vol. i. chapter viii ; Arteche, vol. vii. chapter vi, and above all the volume of the Marquis of Wellesley's *Spanish Dispatches* (London, 1838). There is a good and lively description of the chief members of the Junta and the ministry, and of the intrigues against them, in William Jacob's *Travels in the South of Spain* (London, 1811).

SECTION XVII: CHAPTER II

EVENTS IN EASTERN SPAIN DURING THE SUMMER AND
AUTUMN OF 1809. THE SIEGE OF GERONA BEGUN

In the spring of 1809 the theatres of operations of the two
French army-corps entrusted with the reduction of Aragon and
of Catalonia were still divided by a broad belt of territory
which was in the hands of the Spaniards, around the fortresses
of Lerida, Mequinenza, and Tortosa. Only once had communication been opened between Suchet and St. Cyr, and then
the force which had crossed from Aragon into Catalonia found
itself unable to return. The only way of getting a dispatch
from Saragossa to Barcelona was to send it by the circuitous
road through France. Co-operation between the 3rd and the
7th Corps would have been difficult in any case; but since each
of the two corps-commanders was interested in his own problems
alone, and found them all-absorbing, the war in Catalonia and
the war in Aragon went on during 1809 and the first half of
1810 as separate affairs from the French point of view. It was
otherwise with the Spaniards: Blake had been placed in command of the whole of the *Coronilla*, the three provinces of
Valencia, Aragon, and Catalonia which had formed the ancient
kingdom of Aragon [1]. He had Suchet on his left and St. Cyr
on his right, was equally interested in the operations of each,
and might, so far as the rules of strategy go, have turned his
main force against whichever of the two he might please,
leaving a comparatively small force to 'contain' the other.
Unfortunately he proved unable to make head against either
of his adversaries. We have already seen how, in the early
summer, he threw himself upon Suchet, and was beaten off at
Maria and routed at Belchite. In the later months of the
year it was mainly with St. Cyr that he had to deal, and his

[1] Catalonia had been added to his command after Reding died of
wounds received at the battle of Valls.

efforts were equally unsuccessful. It would seem that he found it very difficult to concentrate any preponderant portion of his troops for a blow to either side: very few battalions from Catalonia accompanied his Valencians and Aragonese to Maria: very few Valencians were brought up to aid the Catalans in the operations about Gerona. The prcblems of food and transport had something to do with this, but the main difficulty was that the armies of both provinces, more especially the Catalans, were essentially local levies, and disliked being drawn far from their homes. There was always some threatening danger in their own district which made them loath to leave it unguarded, while they were taken off on some distant expedition. The complaints and arguments of the Juntas, the manifest unwillingness of the officers and men, fettered the hands of the commander-in-chief, whenever he strove to accomplish a general concentration. Hence it came to pass that for the most part St. Cyr was opposed by Catalan troops only, Suchet by Valencians and Aragonese only, during the campaigns of 1809.

The tasks of the commander of the 3rd Corps in the months that followed his victories over Blake were both less interesting and less important than those imposed upon his colleague in Catalonia. They were however laborious enough; after having driven the Spanish regular armies out of Aragon, Suchet had now to tame the country-side. For even after Belchite he held little more than the towns of Saragossa and Jaca, and the ground on which his camps were pitched from day to day. When he had concentrated his corps to fight Blake, the rest of the province had slipped out of his hands. Its reconquest was a tedious matter, even though he had only to contend with scattered bands of peasants, stiffened by stragglers from the army that had dispersed after Belchite. The plain of the Ebro, which forms the central strip of Aragon, was easily subdued, but the mountains to the north and south were well fitted to be the refuge of insurgents. The Aragonese, along with the Galicians, were the first of the Spaniards to take to systematic guerrilla warfare. Undismayed by the fate of Blake's army, they had resolved to defend themselves to the last. There was more than one focus of resistance: a colonel Renovales, who had been one of the defenders of Saragossa, and had escaped after the capitulation, was at the head of the bands of the north-western mountains, in the vale of Roncal and on the borders of Navarre. In the north-eastern region, about the upper waters of the Cinca and the hills beyond Jaca, two local chiefs named Perena and Sarasa kept the war on foot, getting their stores and ammunition from the Catalans on the side of Lerida. In an entirely distinct part of the province, south of the Ebro, lay Gayan and Villacampa, whose centres of activity were Daroca and Molina, mountain towns from which they were often driven up into that central ganglion of all the ranges of Spain, the Sierra de Albaracin, from which descend in diverging directions the sources of the Tagus, the Guadalaviar, and the Xucar. Both Gayan and Villacampa were officers of the regular army, holding commissions under Blake : the band of the former had as its nucleus the regiment of La Princesa, whose extraordinary escape across northern Spain after the combat of Santander has been told in another place [1].

Suchet's work, during the later summer and the autumn of 1809, was to break up and as far as possible to destroy these bands. His success was considerable but not complete : in July he stormed Gayan's stronghold, the mountain sanctuary of Nuestra Señora del Aguila, captured his magazines, and drove him up into the mountains of Molina. Continuing his campaign south of the Ebro, he sent the Pole Chlopiski against Villacampa, who abandoned Calatayud, Daroca, and the other hill towns, and retired into the Sierra de Albaracin, where he took refuge at the remote convent of El Tremendal, one of the most out-of-the-way spots in the whole Peninsula. Here, nevertheless, the partisan was followed up on Nov. 23-4 by a column under Colonel Henriot, who manœuvred him out of his position, surprised him by a night attack, and drove him over the Valencian border. The convent was blown up, the dependent village of Origuela sacked, and the French withdrew [2].

---

[1] See vol. ii. p. 387.

[2] For an excellent personal diary of all these operations see General Von Brandt's *Aus meinem Leben,* pp. 100–12. He accuses Suchet of grossly exaggerating, both in his dispatches and his memoirs, the difficulty and importance of these mountain raids (see Suchet's *Memoirs,* i. pp. 40–

These operations had been carried out by Musnier's division; but meanwhile movements of a very similar sort were being undertaken by another division, that of Laval, on the other side of Aragon, along the slopes and gorges of the Pyrenees[1]. In the end of August a column of 3,000 men stormed the convent of San Juan de la Peña, close to Jaca, which Sarasa and Renovales were wont to make their head quarters. It was an ancient building containing the tombs of the early kings of Aragon, who reigned in the mountains before Saragossa had been recovered from the Moor ; it had never seen an enemy for eight hundred years, and was reputed holy and impregnable. Hence its capture dealt a severe blow to the confidence of the insurgents. Renovales, however, held out in the western upland, continuing to defend himself in the valley of Roncal, till he was beset on all sides, for Suchet had obtained leave from Paris to call up the National Guards of the Ariége, Basses Pyrénées and Haute Garonne, and their *bataillons d'élite* attacked the insurgents in the rear from across the high mountains, while the 3rd Corps advanced against them from the front. After much scattered fighting Renovales capitulated, on condition that he should be allowed a free departure. He retired to Catalonia with some of his men : the rest dispersed for the moment, but only to reassemble a few weeks later, under another and a more wary and obstinate chief, the younger Mina, who commenced in this same autumn to make the borders of Aragon and Navarre the theatre of his hazardous exploits. But the region was comparatively quiet in September and October, and Suchet transferred the activity of his movable column further to the eastward, where he drove some *partidas* out of the valleys of the Cinca and Essera, and tried to open up a new line of

74, for a highly picturesque narrative). The insurgents were still unskilled in arms, shot very poorly, kept bad watch, and were given to panic. That there is something in Brandt's criticism seems to be shown by the fact that the whole division of Musnier lost between July 1 and Dec. 31, 1809, only three officers killed and eight wounded out of 200 present with the eagles in six months of incessant raids and skirmishes (see Martinien's *Liste des officiers*, often quoted before).

[1] Suchet's third division, that of Habert, was lying out in the direction of the Cinca and the Guadalupe, watching lest Blake might make a new sally from Tortosa or Lerida.

communication with France by way of the valley of Venasque.
This was accomplished, for a moment, by the aid of national
guards from beyond the Pyrenees, who entered the valley from
the north while the troops of Suchet were operating from the
south.   But the road remained unsafe, and could only be used
for the passage of very large bodies of troops, so that it was
practically of little importance.

In December Suchet completed the formal conquest of Aragon,
by moving up the whole of Laval's division into the high-lying
district of Teruel, in the extreme south-east of the province, the
only part of it that had never yet seen the French eagles.
The Junta of Aragon fled from thence over the border of the
kingdom of Valencia, but Villacampa and his bands remained
in the mountains unsubdued, and while they continued to exist
the conquest of the upland was incomplete.   The moment that
its towns ceased to be held by large garrisons, it was clear that
the insurgents would descend to reoccupy them.   Nevertheless
Suchet had done much in this year: besides the crushing of
Blake he had accomplished the complete subjection of the
plains of Central Aragon, and had obtained a grip upon its two
mountain regions.   He had fortified Monzon, Fraga, Alcañiz,
and Caspe as outposts against the Catalans, and, having received
large drafts from France in the autumn, was on the last day of
the year at the head of a fine corps of 26,000 men, from which
he might hope to produce in the next spring a field army
sufficient for offensive operations against Catalonia or Valencia,
after providing garrisons for his various posts of strength[1].
The weak point of his position was that the guerrilleros had
learned caution, refused for the future to fight save under the
most favourable conditions, and devoted themselves to the safe

---

[1] The 3rd Corps which had gone down to little over 10,000 men in
May 1809, counted on Jan. 1, 1810, the following force :

Division Laval	5,348	Garrisons of Alcañiz, Jaca,	
,, Musnier	8,465	Monzon, Saragossa, Tudela	3,110
,, Habert	4,757	' Chasseurs des Montagnes'	
Cavalry Brigade	2,172	[permanently embodied Py-	
Artillery and Engineers	928	renean National Guards]	1,425
		Total	26,205

Of these 23,074 were effectives present with colours, the remainder were
in hospital or detached.

and vexatious policy of intercepting communications and cutting up small parties and stragglers. They were much harder to deal with, when once they had learnt that not even in fastnesses like El Tremendal or San Juan de la Peña was it wise to offer the French battle. Unless Suchet left a garrison in every town, nay, in every considerable village, of the sierras, the insurgents dominated the whole region. If he did take such measures for holding down the upland, he was forced to immobilize a very large proportion of his army. We shall note that in 1810 he was only able to draw out 12,000 of his 26,000 men for the invasion of Western Catalonia.

While the commander of the 3rd Corps was making steady progress with the conquest of Aragon, the fortunes of his colleague of the 7th Corps had been far more chequered. Indeed for the greater part of 1809 St. Cyr was brought to a complete standstill by the unexpected obstinacy of the gallant garrison of Gerona, who for no less than eight months kept the main body of the army of Catalonia detained in front of their walls.

When last we dealt with the operations in this region we left St. Cyr victorious at the well-contested battle of Valls, after which he advanced into the plain of Tarragona, made some demonstrations against that fortress, but returned after a few weeks to Barcelona (March 18) without having made any serious attempt to turn his victory to practical account. This retreat after a brilliant success may be compared to Victor's similar evacuation of Southern Estremadura after Medellin, and was brought about, in the main, by the same cause, want of supplies. For when he had consumed the resources of the newly-subdued district between Valls and Tarragona, St. Cyr had no means of providing his army with further subsistence. Barcelona, his base, could not feed him, for the city was itself on the edge of famine: it was still beset to north and west by the local miqueletes, who had returned to their old haunts when the main French army had gone off southward on the campaign of Valls. It was stringently blockaded on the sea side by the British Mediterranean fleet, and it could not draw food from France by land, because the high-road to Perpignan passed through the fortress of Gerona, which was still in

Spanish hands. St. Cyr himself, it will be remembered, had only reached Barcelona by turning off on to side tracks through the mountain, and winning his way down to the shore by the hard-fought battle of Cardadeu. Till Gerona should fall, and the garrison of Barcelona be placed in direct communication with France, there was little use in making ambitious offensive movements against Tarragona or any other point in Southern or Central Catalonia. It was absolutely necessary to reduce Gerona, and so to bring the division left behind under Reille, in the Ampurdam and on the frontier of Roussillon, into free communication with the remainder of the 7th Corps. From the moment when St. Cyr passed the mountains during the winter Reille had been fighting out a petty campaign against the northern Catalans, which had no connexion whatever with his superior's operations at Molins de Rey and Valls, and had little definite result of any kind.

No one saw more clearly than Napoleon the need for the reduction of Gerona: as early as January he had issued orders both to St. Cyr and to Reille to prepare for the enterprise. But St. Cyr was now out of touch, and Reille was far too weak in the early spring to dream of any such an adventure: he had been left no more than seven depleted battalions to maintain his hold on Northern Catalonia, when St. Cyr took the rest of the army across the hills to Barcelona. The Emperor was not slow to realize that the 7th Corps must be reinforced on a large scale. He did so by sending thither in the spring of 1809 a brigade of Berg troops (four battalions), the regiment of Würzburg (two battalions), and a division (seven battalions) of Westphalians: it will be noted that now, as always, he was most chary of drafting native French troops to Catalonia, and always fed the war in that direction with auxiliaries in whose fate he was little interested: the campaign in eastern Spain was, after all, but a side issue in the main struggle [1]. When these reinforcements had arrived Reille began to collect material at Bascara on the Fluvia, to which siege-guns laboriously dragged across the Pyrenees were added: several companies of heavy artillery and sappers were brought up from France.

[1] Cette portion de l'Espagne reste, d'ailleurs, isolée, et sans influence sur le reste de la Péninsule. Imperial Minute of Dec. 1, 1809.

St. Cyr meanwhile, four weeks after his retreat from the plain of Tarragona, moved on to Vich upon April 18, with the divisions of Souham, Pino, Lecchi, and Chabot, leaving Duhesme with his original French division, which had held Barcelona since the outbreak of the war, in charge of his base of operations.   His departure was partly designed to spare the stores of Barcelona, where the pinch of famine was beginning to be felt ; for he intended to subsist his army on the upland plain of Vich, a rich corn-bearing district hitherto untouched by the war.   But a few days after he had marched forth Barcelona was freed from privation, by the lucky arrival of a squadron of victuallers from Toulon, convoyed by Admiral Cosmao, which had put to sea in a storm and eluded the British blockading squadron (April 27).   The position of Vich, however, had been chosen by St. Cyr not only for reasons of supply, but because the place was happily situated for covering the projected siege of Gerona against any interruption by Blake.   If the Spanish commander-in-chief brought up the wrecks of the old Catalan army from Tarragona, with his Valencian levies added, he would almost certainly take the inland road by Manresa and Vich, since the coast-road was practically barred to him by the French occupation of Barcelona. As a matter of fact the commencement of the leaguer of Gerona was not vexed by any such interruption, for Blake had his eyes fixed on Saragossa in May and June, and was so far from dreaming of an assault on St. Cyr, that he drew off part of the Catalan army for his unhappy invasion of Aragon, which finished with the disaster of Belchite.   During the early months of this long siege the only external helpers of the garrison of Gerona were the small force of regulars under the Swiss Wimpfen, and the miqueletes of Claros and Rovira from the Ampurdam, Reille's opponents during the spring.   At Tarragona the Marquis of Coupigny, the senior officer now in Catalonia, had no more than 6,000 men left of Reding's old army, and was helpless to interfere with St. Cyr who had some 20,000 men concentrated at Vich.

The preparations for the siege therefore went on in the end of April and the beginning of May without any hindrance, save from the normal bickerings of the French outlying detachments with the local *somatenes*, which never ceased.   Around

Vich matters were particularly lively, for the whole population
of the town and the surrounding plains had gone up into
the hills, where they wandered miserably for three months,
much hunted by French foraging parties, which they occasionally
succeeded in destroying. St. Cyr opened up his communications
with Reille by sending to him Lecchi's Italian division, which
cut its way amid constant skirmishes along the banks of the
Ter to Gerona, and met the troops from the Ampurdam under
its walls. Reille had moved forth from Bascara on May 4,
and on the eighth expelled the Spanish outposts from all the
villages round the fortress, not without some lively skirmishing.
He had brought up some 10,000 infantry—including his own
old division and all the newly arrived Germans—with some
1,300 artillerymen and engineers. Almost at the same moment
arrived dispatches from Paris, announcing that the Emperor,
just before departing for the Austrian war, had superseded
both St. Cyr and Reille, being discontented with their handling
of affairs in Catalonia. It is unfortunate that no statement
in detail of his reasons appears in the *Correspondance* [1], but
it would seem that he thought that the victories of Molins
de Rey and Valls should have had greater results, disapproved
of St. Cyr's retreat from in front of Tarragona, and thought
that Reille had shown great weakness in dealing with the
insurgents of the Ampurdam. He ignored the special difficulties of the war in Catalonia, thinking that the 30,000 men
of the 7th Corps ought to have sufficed for its complete
conquest. Indeed he showed his conception of the general state
of affairs by recommending St. Cyr in March to undertake simultaneously the sieges of Gerona, Tarragona, and Tortosa [2]. The
leaguer of one, and that the smallest, of these places was
destined to occupy the whole army of Catalonia, when largely
reinforced, for eight months. If it had been cut up according
to the imperial mandate, it is probable that at least one of
its sections would have been destroyed. St. Cyr wrote in his
memoirs that his master was jealous of him, and wished to see
him fail, even at the cost of wrecking the 7th Corps. This is
of course absurd; but there can be no doubt that the Emperor

---

[1] There is only a short note in Dispatch no. 16,004. See p. 63 of this vol.
[2] See St. Cyr to Berthier, March 6, 1809, and St. Cyr's *Memoirs*, p. 130.

disliked his lieutenant, all the more because of the long string
of complaints, and of demands for more men, money, and stores,
which he was now receiving week by week from Catalonia.   He
loved generals who achieved the impossible, and hated grumblers
and *frondeurs*, a class to which St. Cyr, despite all his talents,
undoubtedly belonged.   It is possible that Napoleon's determination to replace him may have been fostered by intrigues on
the part of the officer to whom the 7th Corps was now turned
over.   Marshal Augereau had served with great credit in
the old republican campaign in Catalonia during 1793 and
1794, imagined himself to have a profound knowledge of the
country, and was anxious to try his hand in it.   It was many
years since he had been trusted with an independent command ;
both in the wars of 1806–7 and in that of 1809 he had been
lost in the ranks of the Grand Army.   His nomination to
supersede St. Cyr was made early in May, but on his way
to the seat of war he was seized with a fit of the gout, and was
detained in bed at Perpignan for many weeks.   Thus his
predecessor, though apprised of his disgrace, was obliged to
continue in command, and to commence the operations of
which the Marshal, as he well knew, would take all the credit.
At the same moment Reille was displaced by Verdier, the
general who had conducted the first unlucky siege of Saragossa
—an experience which seems to have made him very cautious
when dealing with Spaniards behind walls.

Lecchi's division forced its way back to St. Cyr on May 18,
bringing him the intelligence of his supersession, but at the
same time apprising him that Augereau would not arrive as
yet, and that the duty of commencing the siege of Gerona
would still fall to his lot.   At the same time Verdier sent
letters urging that his 10,000 infantry formed too small a force
to surround such a large fortress, and that he must ask for
reinforcements from the covering army.   If they were denied
him, he should refuse to begin the siege, throwing the responsibility for this disobedience of the Emperor's commands on his
superior: he had reported the situation to Paris.   St. Cyr was
incensed at the tone of this dispatch[1], above all at the fact

---

[1] It may be found printed in full in the Appendix to the narrative of
the siege of Gerona in Belmas's *Sieges*, vol. ii. pp. 660–1.

that Verdier was appealing straight to the Emperor, instead of corresponding through his hierarchical superior, according to the rules of military etiquette.   But he saw that Verdier had a good case, and he had just learnt that Blake had turned off against Aragon, so that no trouble from that quarter need be feared.   Accordingly he, very grudgingly, sent back Lecchi's division to Gerona.   It was the worst that he possessed, being composed of no more than four Neapolitan and three Italian battalions, with a strength of little over 3,000 bayonets [1].   He added to it a regiment of Italian light horse, several of his own batteries, and nearly all the engineers and sappers of his corps, so that the total reinforcement sent to Verdier consisted of more than 4,000 men.

Having received these succours, which brought up his total force to 14,000 infantry and cavalry, and 2,200 artillerymen, sappers and engineers, Verdier commenced on May 24 his operations against Gerona: on that day Lecchi's division took its post in the plain of Salt, on the west of the town, while the French and Westphalian divisions were already close to the place on its eastern and northern sides.   The head quarters and the French brigades of Joba and Guillot lay by Sarria and the bridge of Pont-Mayor, where the magazines were established, while the Germans had been sent up on to the heights east of the fortress and held the plateaux of Campdura, San Medir, and Domeny.   The rocky southern side of Gerona, in the direction of the gorge of the Oña, was not yet properly invested.

Something has already been said, in an earlier volume of this work, concerning the situation of Gerona, when its two earlier sieges by Duhesme were narrated [2].   It must suffice to repeat here that the town is built on the steep down-slope of two lofty heights, with the river Oña at its foot: the stream is crossed by two bridges, but is fordable everywhere save in times of spate. Beyond it lies the suburb of the Mercadal, surrounded by fortifications which form an integral part of the defences of the

---

[1] 3,116 bayonets and two squadrons of Italian light horse by the return of May 15.   The Neapolitans were bad troops, deserting whenever it was safe to do so.

[2] See vol. i. pp. 317–29.

city. The river Ter, coming from the west, joins the Oña at
the north side of the Mercadal and washes the extreme north-
western corner of the walls of the city proper. The two heights
upon whose lower slopes Gerona is built are separated from
each other by a deep ravine, called the Galligan, down which
run an intermittent watercourse and a road, the only one by
which approach to the city from the east is possible. The
northern height is crowned by the strong fort of Monjuich, the
most formidable part of the city defences, with its three outlying redoubts called San Narciso, San Luis and San Daniel.
The crest of the southern height is covered in a similar fashion
by the three forts of the Capuchins, Queen Anne, and the
Constable, with the Calvary redoubt lower down the slope
above the Galligan, facing San Daniel on the other side of
the ravine. Two other small fortifications, the redoubts of
the ' Chapter' and the ' City,' cover the path which leads down
from the forts to Gerona. Neither the Monjuich nor the
Capuchin heights are isolated hills; each is the end of a spur
running down from the higher mountains. But while the
southern summit rises high above the hilly reach which joins it
to the mountain of Nuestra Señora de los Angeles, the northern
summit (where lies Monjuich) is at the end of a plateau extending far to the north. The Capuchin heights, therefore, can only
be attacked uphill, while Monjuich can be assailed from ground
of a level little inferior to itself. But except on this point both
heights are very strong, their slopes being in many places
absolutely precipitous, especially towards the Galligan, and
everywhere steep. Nevertheless there are winding paths leading
up both, from Sarria and Pont-Mayor in the case of Monjuich,
from Casa de Selva and other villages towards the east and the
sea in the case of the Capuchin heights. All the ground is
bare rock, with no superincumbent soil.

All the fortifications were somewhat antiquated in type,
nothing having been done to modernize the defences since the
war of the Spanish Succession [1]. Ferdinand VI and Charles III
had neglected Gerona in favour of the new fortress of Figueras,
nearer to the frontier, on which large sums had been expended

---

[1] For a good historical study of the fortifications of Gerona and their
history, see Vacani, vol. iii. pp. 245–55.

—for the benefit of the French who seized it by treachery in 1808, and were now using it as their base of operations. The actual wall of enceinte of the city was mediaeval—a plain rampart twenty-five feet high, too narrow for artillery and set thickly with small towers; only at its two ends, on the Oña and the Ter, two bastions (called those of La Merced and Santa Maria) had been inserted, and properly armed. This weakness of the walls went for little so long as Monjuich, the Capuchins, and the other forts held firm, since the enemy could only approach the town-enceinte at its two ends, where the bastions lay. Far more dangerous was the feebleness of the Mercadal, whose ramparts formed the southern section of the exterior defences of the place. Its circuit had five plain bastions, but no demi-lunes or other outer defences, no covered way nor counterscarp: its profile, only some eighteen or twenty feet high, was visible, across the flat ground which surrounds it, from the foot to the summit of the wall, for want of ditch or glacis. The ground leading up to it was favourable for siege approaches, since the soil was soft and easy to dig, and was seamed with hollow roads and stone walls, giving much cover to an assailant. Aware of the defects of the fortifications of the Mercadal, the Spaniards had prepared a line of defence behind it, along the further bank of the Oña. They had made the river-front of the city proper defensible to a certain extent, by building up the doors and windows of all the houses which abut upon the water, mining the two bridges, and fixing a stockade and entanglements in the bed of the Oña, along the considerable space, where it is fordable in dry weather[1]. They had indeed repaired the whole circuit of the defences since Duhesme's sieges of 1808, having cleared out the ditches of Monjuich and of the bastions of La Merced and Santa Maria, walled up many posterns, and repaired with new and solid

---

[1] This last was done by public subscription, when the engineers pointed out the danger of the city being stormed across the river-bed. See Arteche, vii. 151. Belmas and Vacani do not seem to have known of this fact, as each of them makes the remark that if the Mercadal had been taken, a sudden rush might have taken the assailants across the shallow river and into the old town. It may be remarked that there had once been a river-wall, but that most of it had been allowed to fall into decay when the Mercadal was taken into the city defences.

masonry all the parts of the walls that had been dilapidated at the moment of the first siege. They had also pulled down many isolated houses outside the walls, and demolished the nearer half of the suburban village of Pedret, which lies (most inconveniently for the defence) along the bank of the Ter between the water and the slopes of Monjuich.

All these precautions must be put to the credit of the governor, Mariano Alvarez de Castro, a man to be mentioned with all honour and respect, and probably the best soldier that Spain produced during the whole Peninsular War. He was a veteran of the Revolutionary and Portuguese wars, and had a good reputation, but no special credit for military science, down to the moment when he was put to the test. He had been the officer in charge of the castle of Barcelona on the occasion when it was seized by Duhesme in March 1808 : his spirit had been deeply wounded by that vile piece of treachery, and he had at once adhered to the national cause. Since then he had been serving in the Ampurdam against Reille, till the moment when he was appointed governor of Gerona. Alvarez is described by those who served under him as a severe, taciturn man of a puritan cast of mind. ' I should call him,' wrote one of his brigadiers, ' an officer without the true military talents, but with an extreme confidence in Providence—almost, one might say, a believer in miracles. His soul was great, capable of every sacrifice, full of admirable constancy ; but I must confess that his heroism always seemed to me that of a Christian martyr rather than of a professional soldier [1].' General Fournas, who wrote this somewhat depreciatory sketch of his chief, was one of those who signed the capitulation while Alvarez was moaning *no quiero rendirme* on his sick-bed, so that his judgement is hardly to be taken as unprejudiced ; but his words point the impression which the governor left on his subordinates. The details of his defence sufficiently show that he was a skilful and resourceful as well as an obstinate general. His minute care to utilize every possible means of defence prove that he was no mere waiter on miracles. That he was a very devout practising Catholic is evident from some of his doings ; at the opening of the siege a great religious ceremony was held, at which the local

[1] Manuscript notes of General Fournas, quoted by Arteche, vii. 458.

patron saint, Narcissus, was declared captain of the city and presented with a gold-hilted sword. The levy *en masse* of the citizens was called ' the Crusade,' and their badge was the red cross. The ideas of religion and patriotism were so closely intertwined that to the lay companies of this force were afterwards added two clerical companies, one composed of monks and friars, the other of secular priests : about 200 of these ecclesiastics were under arms [1]. Even the women were organized in squads for the transport of wounded, the care of the hospitals, and the carrying of provisions to the soldiery on the walls : about 300 served, under the command of Donna Lucia Fitzgerald and Donna Maria Angela Bibern, wives of two officers of the regiment of Ultonia. Five of this ' company of St. Barbara ' were killed and eleven wounded during the siege.

The garrison at the moment of Verdier's first attack consisted of about 5,700 men, not including the irregulars of the Crusade. There were seven battalions of the old army, belonging to the regiments of Ultonia [2], Borbon, and Voluntarios de Barcelona, with three battalions of miqueletes, two local corps, 1st and 2nd of Gerona, and the 1st of Vich. Of cavalry there was a single squadron, newly levied, the ' escuadron de San Narciso.' Of artillery there were but 278 men, a wholly insufficient number : the officers of that arm were given 370 more to train, partly miqueletes of the 2nd Gerona battalion, partly sailors having some small experience of gunnery. It was difficult to make proper use of the great store of cannon in the fortress, when more than half the troops allotted to them had never before seen, much less served, a heavy gun of position. To the above 5,700 men of all arms must be added about 1,100 irregulars of the ' Crusade '—seven lay and two clerical companies of fusiliers and two more of artificers. But these were

---

[1] The bishop gave his sanction to the formation of this strange corps ; see his proclamation in Arteche's Appendix vii. p. 539, dated June 9.

[2] Ultonia, the regiment of Ulster, still contained many officers of the old Jacobite strain, as may be seen by consulting the list of killed and wounded, where such names as O'Donnell, Macarthy, Nash, Fitzgerald, Pierson, Coleby, Candy, occur : but it had just been raised from 200 to 800 bayonets by filling the depleted *cadre* with Catalan recruits, and all the junior lieutenants, newly appointed, were Catalans also. So there was little Irish about it save the names of some of its senior officers.

set to guard almost unapproachable parts of the wall, or held in reserve: most of the stress fell upon the organized troops. The defence was altogether conducted on scientific principles, and had nothing in common with that of Saragossa. Here the irregulars formed only a small fraction of the garrison [1], and were never hurled in senseless fury against the French batteries, but used carefully and cautiously as an auxiliary force, capable of setting free some part of the trained men for service on the more important points of the enceinte [2].

For the first two months of the siege Alvarez received no help whatever from without: in May the central government of Catalonia had been left in a perfectly paralysed condition, when Blake went off himself and took with him the best of the regular troops, in order to engage in the campaign of Alcañiz and Maria. Coupigny, the interim commander at Tarragona, had only 6,000 organized men, and he and the Catalan provincial junta were during that month much engrossed with an enterprise which distracted them from the needs of Gerona. A widespread conspiracy had been formed within the walls of Barcelona, with the object of rising against the garrison in St. Cyr's absence. A secret committee of priests, merchants, and retired officers had collected all the arms in the city, smuggled in many muskets from without, and enlisted several thousand persons in a grand design for an outbreak and a sort of 'Sicilian Vespers' fixed—after two postponements—for the 11th of May. They opened communication with Coupigny and with the captains of the British frigates blockading the port. The one was to bring his troops to the gates, the others to deliver an attack on

[1] For the details of the composition of the Gerona garrison, see Appendix no. 1.

[2] I know not why Napier, contrasting Gerona with Saragossa (ii. 251), says that at the former place the regular garrison was 3,000, the armed multitude 'less than 6,000.' When it is remembered that its total popula- was 14,000 souls—of whom some fled to places of safety before the siege began—and that it had already raised two battalions of miqueletes with 1,360 bayonets out of its able-bodied male inhabitants, it is difficult to see how more than 5,000 armed irregulars are to be procured, for in a population of 14,000 souls there cannot be more than some 3,000 men between eighteen and forty-five. As a matter of fact (see documents in Arteche, vii. Appendix 5), the 'Crusade' was about 1,100 strong at most.

the port, upon the appointed night. No Spaniard betrayed the plot, though 6,000 citizens are said to have been in the secret, but it was frustrated by two foreigners. Conscious that the town could not be freed if the citadel of Monjuich was retained by the French, the conspirators sounded two Italian officers named Captain Dottori, fort adjutant of Monjuich, and Captain Provana, who was known to be discontented and thought to be corruptible. They offered them an immense bribe—1,000,000 dollars, it is said—to betray the postern of Monjuich to the troops of Coupigny, who were to be ready in the ditch at midnight. But they had mistaken their men : the officers conferred with Duhesme, and consented to act as *agents provocateurs* : they pretended to join the conspiracy, were introduced to and had interviews with the chiefs, and informed the governor. On the morning before the appointed date many of the leaders were arrested. Duhesme placed guards in every street, and proclaimed that he knew all. The citizens remained quiet in their despair, the chiefs who had not been seized fled, and the troops on the Llobregat retired to Tarragona. Duhesme hanged his captives, two priests named Gallifa and Pou, a young merchant named Massana, Navarro an old soldier, and four others. 'They went to the gallows,' says Vacani, an eye-witness, 'with pride, convinced every one of them that they had done the duty of good citizens in behalf of king, country, and religion [1].'

Engrossed in this plot, the official chiefs of Catalonia half forgot Gerona, and did nothing to help Alvarez till long after the siege had begun. The only assistance that he received from without was that the miqueletes and *somatenes* of the Ampurdam and the mountain region above Hostalrich were always skirmishing with Verdier's outposts, and once or twice cut off his convoys of munitions on their way from Figueras to the front.

The French engineers were somewhat at variance as to the right way to deal with Gerona. There were two obvious alternatives. An attack on the weak front of the Mercadal was certain to succeed : the ground before the walls was suitable for trenches, and the fortifications were trifling. But when

[1] Vacani, iii. 211.

a lodgement had been made in this quarter of the town it would be necessary to work forward, among the narrow lanes and barricades, to the Oña, and then to cross that river in order to continue similar operations through the streets of Gerona. Even when the city had been subdued, the garrison might still hold out in the formidable works on the Monjuich and Capuchin heights. The reduction of the Mercadal and the city, moreover, would have to be carried out under a continuous plunging fire from the forts above, which overlooked the whole place. This danger was especially insisted upon by some of the engineer officers, who declared that it would be impossible for the troops to work their way forward over ground so exposed. As a matter of fact it was proved, after the siege was over and the forts had been examined by the captors, that this fear had been exaggerated; the angle of fire was such that large sections of the town were in no way commanded from the heights, and the streets could not have been searched in the fashion that was imagined. But this, obvious in December, could not have been known in May [1]. The second alternative was to commence the attack on Gerona not from the easiest but from the most difficult side, by battering the lofty fort of Monjuich from the high plateau beside it. The defences here were very formidable: the ground was bare exposed rock: but if Monjuich were once captured it was calculated that the town must surrender, as it was completely overlooked by the fort, and had no further protection save its antiquated mediaeval wall. The deduction that it would be cheaper in the end to begin with the difficult task of taking Monjuich, rather than the easier operations against the Mercadal, seemed plausible: its fault was that it presupposed that Alvarez and his garrison would behave according to the accepted rules of siegecraft, and yield when their situation became hopeless. But in dealing with Spanish garrisons the rules of military logic did not always act. Alvarez essayed the impossible, and held out behind his defective defences for four months after Monjuich fell. The loss of men and time that he thereby inflicted on the French was certainly no less than that which would have been suffered if the besiegers had begun with the Mercadal, and worked upwards by incessant

[1] See Belmas, iii. 516.

street fighting towards the forts on the height.   But it is hard to say that Verdier erred: he did not know his adversary, and he did know, from his experiences at Saragossa, what street fighting meant.

It may be added that Verdier's views were accepted by the engineer-general, Sanson, who had been specially sent from France by the Emperor, to give his opinion on the best mode of procedure.   The document which Verdier, Sanson, and Taviel (the commanding artillery officer of the 7th Corps) sent to Paris, to justify their choice of the upper point of attack, lays stress mainly on the impossibility of advancing from the Mercadal under the fire of the upper forts [1].   But there were other reasons for selecting Monjuich as the point of attack.   It lay far nearer to the road to France and the central siege-dépôts beside Sarria and the Pont Mayor.   The approaches would be over highly defensible ground where, if a disaster occurred, the defeated assailant could easily recover himself and oppose a strong front to the enemy.   The shortness of the front was suitable for an army of the moderate strength of 14,000 men, which had to deal with a fortress whose perimeter, allowing for outlying forts and inaccessible precipices, was some six miles.   Moreover, the ground in front of the Mercadal had the serious inconvenience of being liable to inundation; summer spates on the Ter and Oña are rare, but occur from time to time; and there was the bare chance that when the trenches had been opened all might be swept away by the rivers [2].

Verdier's opinion was arrived at after mature reflection: the French had appeared in front of Gerona on May 8: the out-lying villages on the east had been occupied between the twelfth and eighteenth: Lecchi's Italians had closed the western exits by occupying the plain of Salt on the twenty-fourth: the inner posts of observation of the Spaniards had been cleared off when, on May 30, the Italians seized the suburban village of Santa Eugenia, and on June 1 the Germans took possession of the mountain of Nuestra Señora de los Angeles.   But it was only on June 6 that the besiegers broke ground, and commenced their trenches and batteries on the

---

[1] See their letter in Appendix V to Belmas's account of the siege.

[2] Note, ibid., ii. p. 502.

plateau of Monjuich. It was necessary to make a beginning
by subduing the outer defences of the fort, the towers or
redoubts of San Luis, San Narciso, and San Daniel : two
batteries of 24-pounders were constructed against them, while
a third battery of mortars on the 'Green Mound' by the Casa den
Roca on the west bank of the Ter, was to play upon the north
end of the town : Verdier hoped that the bombardment would
break the spirit of the citizens—little knowing the obstinate
people with whom he had to deal. Five thousand bombs
thrown into the place in June and July produced no effect
whatever. More batteries on the heights were thrown up upon
the 13th and 15th of June, while on the former day, to distract
the attention of the Spaniards, Lecchi's division, in the plain
below, was ordered to open a false attack upon the Mercadal.
This had good effect as a diversion, since Alvarez had expected
an assault in this quarter, and the long line of trenches thrown
up by the Italians in front of Santa Eugenia attracted much of
his attention. Three days of battering greatly damaged San
Luis and San Narciso, which were no more than round towers
of masonry with ditches cut in the rock, and only two or three
guns apiece. The French also took possession on the night of
the fourteenth and fifteenth of the remains of the half-destroyed
suburb of Pedret, between Monjuich and the Ter, as if about to
establish themselves in a position from which they could attack the
low-lying north gate of the town and the bastion of Santa Maria.

Hitherto the defence had seemed a little passive, but at dawn
on the morning of the seventeenth Alvarez delivered the first of
the many furious sallies which he made against the siege lines.
A battalion of Ultonia rushed suddenly downhill out of Monjuich and drove the French, who were taken completely by
surprise, out of the ruins of Pedret. Aided by a smaller
detachment, including the artificers of the *Crusade*, who came
out of the Santa Maria gate, they destroyed all the works and
lodgements of the besiegers in the suburb, and held it till they
were driven out by two French and one Westphalian battalion
sent up from Verdier's reserves. The Spaniards were forced
back into the town, but retired in good order, contented to
have undone three days of the besiegers' labour. They had lost
155 men, the French 128, in this sharp skirmish.

Two days later the towers of San Luis and San Narciso, which had been reduced to shapeless heaps of stone, were carried by assault, with a loss to the French of only 78 men; but an attempt to carry San Daniel by the same rush was beaten off, this redoubt being still in a tenable state. Its gorge, however, was completely commanded from the ruins of San Luis, and access to or exit from it was rendered so dangerous that Alvarez withdrew its garrison on the next night. The possession of these three outworks brought the French close up to Monjuich, which they could now attack from ground which was favourable in every respect, save that it was bare rock lacking soil. It was impossible to excavate in it, and all advances had to be made by building trenches (if the word is not a misnomer in this case) of sandbags and loose stones on the surface of the ground. The men working at the end of the sap were therefore completely exposed, and the work could only proceed at a great expense of life. Nevertheless the preparations advanced rapidly, and on the night of July 2 an enormous battery of sandbags (called the *Batterie Impériale*) was thrown up at a distance of only four hundred yards from Monjuich. Next morning it opened on the fort with twenty 16- and 24-pounders, and soon established a superiority over the fire of the defence. Several Spanish pieces were dismounted, others had to be removed because it was too deadly to serve them. But a steady fire was returned against the besiegers from the Constable and Calvary forts, on the other side of the Galligan ravine. Nevertheless Monjuich began to crumble, and it looked as if the end of the siege were already approaching. On July 3 there was a breach thirty-five feet broad in the fort's north-eastern bastion, and the Spanish flag which floated over it was thrown down into the ditch by a chance shot. A young officer named Montorro climbed down, brought it up, and nailed it to a new flagstaff under the fire of twenty guns. Meanwhile long stretches of the parapet of Monjuich were ruined, the ditch was half-filled with débris, and the garrison could only protect themselves by hasty erections of gabions and sandbags, placed where the crest of the masonry had stood.

By this time St. Cyr and the covering army had abandoned the position in the plain of Vich which they had so long occupied. The general had, as it seems, convinced himself at last that Blake, who was still engaged in his unlucky Aragonese campaign, was not likely to appear. He therefore moved nearer to Gerona, in order to repress the efforts of the local *somatenes*, who were giving much trouble to Verdier's communications. On June 20 he established his head quarters at Caldas de Malavella, some nine miles to the south-east of Gerona. That same evening one of his Italian brigades intercepted and captured a convoy of 1,200 oxen which the Governor of Hostalrich was trying to introduce into the beleaguered city along one of the mountain-paths which lead to the Capuchin heights from the coast. St. Cyr strung out his 14,000 men in a line from San Feliu de Guixols on the sea to the upper Ter, in a semi-circle which covered all the approaches to Gerona saving those from the Ampurdam. He visited Verdier's camp, inspected the siege operations, and expressed his opinion that an attack on the Mercadal front would have been preferable to that which had been actually chosen. But he washed his hands of all responsibility, told Verdier that, since he had chosen to correspond directly with Paris, he must take all the praise or blame resulting from his choice, and refused to countermand or to alter any of his subordinate's dispositions. On July 2 however he sent, with some lack of logic, a summons of his own to Alvarez, inviting him to surrender on account of the desperate state of his defences : this he did without informing Verdier of his move. The Governor returned an indignant negative, and Verdier wrote in great wrath to complain that if the siege was his affair, as he had just been told, it was monstrous that his commander should correspond with the garrison without his knowledge [1]. The two generals were left on even worse terms than before. St. Cyr, however, gave real assistance to the siege operations at this time by storming, on July 5, the little fortified harbour-town of Palamos, which lies on the point of the sea-coast nearest to Gerona, and had been hitherto used by the miqueletes as a base from which they communicated by night with the fortress, and at the same time

---

[1] See St. Cyr to Alvarez and Verdier to the Minister of War at Paris, nos. 9 and 11 of Belmas's Appendices in his second volume, pp. 677 and 678.

kept in touch with Tarragona and the English ships of the blockading squadron.

On the night of the 4th and 5th of July the defences of Monjuich appeared in such a ruinous condition that Commandant Fleury, the engineer officer in charge of the advanced parallel, took the extraordinary and unjustifiable step of assaulting them at 10 P.M. with the troops—two companies only— which lay under his orders, trusting that the whole of the guards of the trenches would follow if he made a lodgement. This presumptuous attack, made contrary to all the rules of military subordination, was beaten off with a loss of forty men. Its failure made Verdier determine to give the fort three days more of continuous bombardment, before attempting to storm it : the old batteries continued their fire, a new one was added to enfilade the north-western bastion, and cover was contrived at several points to shelter the troops which were to deliver the assault, till the actual moment of the storm arrived[1]. But three hundred yards of exposed ground still separated the front trenches from the breach—a distance far too great according to the rules of siegecraft. The Spaniards meanwhile, finding it impossible under such a fire to block the breach, which was now broad enough for fifty men abreast[2], threw up two walls of gabions on each side of it, sank a ditch filled with chevaux-de-frise in front of it, and loopholed some interior buildings of the fort, which bore upon its reverse side.

Monjuich, however, looked in a miserable state when, just before sunrise on July 7, Verdier launched his columns of assault upon it. He had collected for the purpose the grenadier and *voltigeur* companies of each of the twenty French, German, and Italian battalions of the besieging army, about 2,500 men in all[3]. They were divided into two columns, the larger of

---

[1] Napier says (ii. 250) that 'the breaching fire ceased for four days before the assault,' and that this caused the failure. The statement is in direct contradiction of Vacani (iii. 277) who states that Verdier on the contrary ' prosegui per tre giorni il vivo fuoco della sua artilleria,' and of Belmas (ii. 530) who makes the same statement.

[2] See Alvarez's letter in Belmas's Appendix, no. 15, where he says that the breach had this breadth since July 3.

[3] This seems a low estimate of Belmas, as the *compagnies d'élite* formed a third of each battalion.

which went straight at the breach, while the smaller, which was furnished with ladders, was directed to escalade the left face of the demi-lune which covers the northern front of Monjuich. The troops passed with no great loss over the open space which divided them from the work, as its guns had all been silenced, and the fire from the more distant forts was ineffective in the dusk. But when they got within close musketry range they began to fall fast; the head of the main column, which was composed of some sapper companies and the Italian Velites of the Guard, got up on to the face of the breach, but could never break in. Every officer or man who reached the cutting and its chevaux-de-frise was shot down; the concentric fire of the defenders so swept the opening that nothing could live there. Meanwhile the rear of the column was brought to a stand, partly in, partly outside, the ditch. The Spaniards kept playing upon it with musketry and two or three small 2- and 4-pounders, which had been kept under cover and reserved for that purpose, firing canister into it at a distance of twenty or thirty yards. Flesh and blood could not bear this for long, and the whole mass broke and went to the rear. Verdier, who had come out to the *Batterie Impériale* to view the assault, had the men rallied and sent forward a second time: the head of the column again reached the breach, and again withered away: the supporting mass gave way at once, and fell back much more rapidly than on the first assault. Yet the General, most unwisely, insisted on a third attack, which, made feebly and without conviction, by men who knew that they were beaten, only served to increase the casualty list. Meanwhile the escalade of the demi-lune by the smaller column had been repelled with ease: the assailants barely succeeded in crossing the ditch and planting a few ladders against the scarp: no one survived who tried to mount them, and the troops drew off.

This bloody repulse cost the French 1,079 casualties, including seventy-seven officers killed or wounded — much more than a third of the troops engaged. It is clear, therefore, that it was not courage which had been lacking: nor could it be said that the enemy's artillery fire had not been subdued, nor that the breach was insufficient, nor that the 300 yards of open ground crossed by the column had been a fatal obstacle;

indeed, they had been passed with little loss. The mistake of
Verdier had been that he attacked before the garrison was
demoralized—the same error made by the English at Badajoz
in 1811 and at San Sebastian in 1813. A broad breach by
itself does not necessarily make a place untenable, if the spirit
of the defenders is high, and if they are prepared with all the
resources of the military art for resisting the stormers, as were
the Geronese on July 7–8. The garrison lost, it may be
remarked, only 123 men, out of a strength of 787 present in
the fort that morning. The casualty list, however, was somewhat increased by the accidental explosion, apparently by
a careless gunner, of the magazine of the tower of San Juan,
alongside of the Galligan, which was destroyed with its little
garrison of twenty-five men.

The repulse of the assault of Monjuich thoroughly demoralized
the besieging army : the resistance of the Spaniards had been
so fierce, the loss they had inflicted so heavy, that Verdier's
motley collection of French, German, Lombard, and Neapolitan
regiments lost heart and confidence. Their low spirits were
made manifest by the simultaneous outbreak of desertion and
disease, the two inevitable marks of a decaying morale. All
through the second half of July and August the hospitals
grew gradually fuller, not only from sunstroke cases (which were
frequent on the bare, hot, rocky ground of the heights), but
from dysentery and malaria. The banks of the Ter always
possessed a reputation for epidemics—twice in earlier centuries
a French army had perished before the walls of Gerona by
plagues, which the citizens piously attributed to their patron,
San Narciso. It was mainly because he realized the depression
of his troops that Verdier refrained from any more assaults,
and went on from July 9 to August 4 battering Monjuich
incessantly, while he cautiously pushed forward his trenches, till
they actually reached the ditch of the demi-lune which covers
the northern front of the fort. The garrison was absolutely
overwhelmed by the incessant bombardment, which destroyed
every piece of upstanding masonry, and prevented them from
rebuilding anything that was demolished. They were forced to
lurk in the casemates, and to burrow for shelter in the débris
which filled the interior of the work. Three large breaches had

been made at various points, yet Verdier would never risk
another assault, till on August 4 his approaches actually
crowned the lip of the ditch of the demi-lune, and his sappers
had blown in its counterscarp. The ruined little outwork was
then stormed with a loss of only forty men. This put the
French in the possession of good cover only a few yards from
the main body of the fort. Proceeding with the same caution
as before, they made their advances against Monjuich by
mining: on the night of the 8th-9th August no less than
twenty-three mines under the glacis of the fort were exploded
simultaneously. This left a gaping void in front of the original
breach of July 7, and filled up the ditch with débris for many
yards on either side : part of the interior of the fort was clearly
visible from the besiegers' trenches.

Only one resource for saving Monjuich remained to Alvarez
—a sortie for the expulsion of the enemy from their advanced
works. It was executed with great courage at midday on
August 9, while at the same time separate demonstrations to
distract the enemy were made at two other points. The column
from Monjuich had considerable success ; it stormed two
advanced batteries, spiked their guns, and set fire to their
gabions ; the French were cleared out of many of their trenches,
but made head behind one of the rear batteries, where they were
joined by their reserves, who finally thrust back the sallying
force into the fort. The damage done, though considerable,
could be repaired in a day. Verdier gave orders for the storm
of the dilapidated fort on the night of August 11, and
borrowed a regiment from St. Cyr's covering army to lead the
assault, being still very doubtful of the temper of his own
troops. But at six on the preceding afternoon an explosion
was heard in Monjuich, and great part of its battered walls
flew up into the air. The Spaniards had quietly evacuated it
a few minutes before, after preparing mines for its demolition.
The French, when they entered, found nothing but a shapeless
mass of stones and eighteen disabled cannon. The garrison
had lost, in the sixty-five days of its defence, 962 men killed
and wounded ; the besiegers had, first and last, suffered something like three times this loss.

While the bombardment of Monjuich was going on, the

Spanish generals outside the fortress had at last begun to make serious efforts for its assistance. Not only had the *somatenes* redoubled their activity against Verdier's convoys, and several times succeeded in destroying them or turning them back, but Coupigny had at last begun to move, for he saw that since Blake's rout at Belchite on June 18 he, and he alone, possessed an organized body of troops on this side of Spain, small though it was. Unable to face St. Cyr in the field, he tried at least to throw succours into Gerona by the mountain paths from the south, if he could do no more. The first attempt was disastrous: three battalions started from Hostalrich under an English adventurer, Ralph Marshall, whom Alvarez had suggested for the command of this expedition. They evaded the first line of the covering army, but at Castellar, on July 10, ran into the very centre of Pino's division, which had concentrated from all sides for their destruction. Marshall escaped into Gerona with no more than twelve men: 40 officers and 878 rank and file laid down their arms; the rest of the column, some 600 or 700 men, evaded surrender by dispersion.[1]

Equally disastrous, though on a smaller scale, was another attempt made on August 4 by a party of 300 miqueletes to enter Gerona: they eluded St. Cyr, but on arriving at the entry of the Galligan, close under the forts, made the unfortunate mistake of entering the convent of San Daniel, which the garrison had been compelled to evacuate a few days before. It was now in the French lines, and the Catalans were all taken prisoners. It was not till August 17, six days after the fall of Monjuich, that Alvarez obtained his first feeble reinforcement: the miquelete battalion of Cervera, with a draft for that of Vich already in the garrison, altogether 800 bayonets, got into the city on the west side, by eluding Lecchi's Italians in the plain and fording the Ter. They were much needed, for Alvarez

[1] St. Cyr, Vacani, and Belmas all say that Marshall escaped by hoisting the white flag, and taking to the hills while terms of capitulation were being arranged. Coupigny on the other hand (see his letter in Belmas's Appendix no. 18) says that Marshall behaved admirably, but was not seconded by his men, who flinched and abandoned him. Rich, the officer who failed to guide the column aright, was not, as Napier supposed (ii. 236), an Englishman, but a Catalan, as is shown by his Christian name Narciso. Ric or Rich is a common name in Catalonia.

was complaining to the Catalan Junta that he had now only 1,500 able-bodied men left of his original 5,000 [1].

Verdier had written to his master, after the capture of Monjuich, to announce that Gerona must infallibly surrender within eight or ten days [2], now that it had nothing but an antiquated mediaeval wall to oppose to his cannon. So far, however, was he from being a true prophet that, as a matter of fact, the second and longer episode of the siege, which was to be protracted far into the winter, had only just begun.

---

[1] This must have been an exaggeration, as 2,000 men under arms of the old garrison survived to surrender in December. See Alvarez's letter, on p. 686 of Belmas's Appendix.

[2] See Verdier's letter of August 12, in Belmas's Appendix no. 11, p. 700.

SECTION XVII: CHAPTER III

WHEN Monjuich had been evacuated, the position of Gerona was undoubtedly perilous: of the two mountain summits which command the city one was now entirely in the hands of the French; for not only the great fort itself but several of the smaller works above the ravine of the Galligan—such as the fortified convent of San Daniel and the ruined tower of San Juan—had been lost. The front exposed to attack now consisted of the northern section of the old city wall, from the bastion of Santa Maria at the water's edge, to the tower of La Gironella, which forms the north-eastern angle of the place, and lies further up the slope of the Capuchin heights than any other portion of the enceinte. The space between these two points was simply covered by a mediaeval wall set with small round towers: neither the towers nor the curtain between them had been built to hold artillery. Indeed the only spots on this front where guns had been placed were (1) the comparatively modern bastion of Santa Maria, (2) a work erected under and about the Gironella, and called the 'Redoubt of the Germans,' and (3, 4) two parts of the wall called the platforms[1] of San Pedro and San Cristobal, which had been widened till they could carry a few heavy guns. On the rest of the enceinte, owing to its narrowness, nothing but wall-pieces and two-pounders could be mounted. The parts of the curtain most exposed to attack were the sections named Santa Lucia, San Pedro, San Cristobal, and Las Sarracinas, from churches or quarters which lay close behind them. With nothing but an antiquated wall, seven to nine feet thick, thirty feet high, and destitute of a ditch, it seemed that this side of Gerona was doomed to destruction within a few days.

But there were points in the position which rendered the

---

[1] Some call them bastions, but they are too small to deserve that name.

attack more difficult than might have been expected.   The
first was that any approaches directed against this front would
be exposed to a flanking fire from the forts on the Capuchin
heights, especially from the Calvary and Chapter redoubts.
The second was that the greater part of the weak sections
of the wall were within a re-entering angle; for the tower of
Santa Lucia and the 'Redoubt of the Germans' by the Gironella
project, and the curtains between them are in a receding sweep
of the enceinte.   Attacks on these ill-fortified sections would
be outflanked and enfiladed by the two stronger works.   The
only exposed part of the curtain was that called Santa Lucia,
running from the tower of that name down to the bastion of Santa
Maria.   Lastly, the parallels which the French might construct
from their base on Monjuich would have to be built on a down
slope, overlooked by loftier ground, and when they reached the
foot of the walls they would be in a sort of gulley or bottom,
into which the defenders of the city could look down from
above.   The only point from which the north end of Gerona
could be approached from flat ground and without disadvantages
of slope, is the short front of less than 200 yards breadth
between the foot of Monjuich and the bank of the Ter.   Here,
in the ruins of the suburb of Pedret, there was plenty of cover,
a soil easy to work, and a level terrain as far as the foot of the
Santa Maria bastion.   The engineers of the besieging army
selected three sections of wall as their objective.   The first was
the 'Redoubt of the Germans' and the tower of La Gironella,
the highest and most commanding works in this part of the
enceinte : once established in these, they could overlook and
dominate the whole city.   The other points of attack were
chosen for the opposite reason—because they were intrinsically
weak in themselves, not because they were important or
dominating parts of the defences.   The curtain of Santa Lucia
in particular seemed to invite attack, as being in a salient
angle, unprotected by flanking fire, and destitute of any
artillery of its own.

Verdier, therefore, on the advice of his engineers, set to work
to attack these points of the enceinte between La Gironella and
Santa Maria.   New batteries erected amid the ruins of Monjuich
were levelled against them, in addition to such of the older

batteries as could still be utilized.   On the front by Pedret
also, where nothing had hitherto been done, works were
prepared for guns to be directed against Santa Maria and
Santa Lucia.   Meanwhile a perpetual bombardment with shell
was kept up, against the whole quarter of the town that lay
behind the selected points of attack.   Mortars were always
playing, not only from the Monjuich heights but from two
batteries erected on the so-called 'Green Mound' in the plain
beyond the river Ter.   Their effect was terrible: almost every
house in the northern quarter of Gerona was unroofed or
destroyed: the population had to take refuge in cellars, where,
after a few days, they began to die fast—all the more so that food
was just beginning to run short as August advanced.   From the
14th to the 30th of that month Verdier's attack was developing
itself: by its last day four breaches had been established: one,
about forty feet broad, in the curtain of St. Lucia, two close
together in the works at La Gironella [1], the fourth and smallest
in the platform of San Cristobal.   But the approaches were
still far from the foot of the wall, the fire of the outlying
Spanish works, especially the Calvary fort, was unsubdued, and
though the guns along the attacked front had all been silenced,
the French artillery had paid dearly both in lives and in
material for the advantage they had gained.   Moreover sickness
was making dreadful ravages in the ranks of the besieging
army.   The malarious pestilence on which the Spaniards had
relied had appeared, after a sudden and heavy rainfall had
raised the Ter and Oña beyond their banks, and inundated
the whole plain of Salt.   By malaria, dysentery and sunstroke
Verdier had lost 5,000 men, in addition to his casualties in the
siege.   Many of them were convalescents in the hospitals of
Perpignan and Figueras, but it was hard to get them back to
the front; the *somatenes* made the roads impassable for small
detachments, and the officers on the line of communication,
being very short of men, were given to detaining drafts that
reached them on their way to Gerona [2].   Hence Verdier, including

---

[1] Belmas, for convenience' sake, distinguishes these two breaches by
calling the northern one the breach in the Barracks, the southern the
breach in the Latrines of the 'German Redoubt.'

[2] Between Gerona and Perpignan, for the defence of communications

his artillerymen and sappers, had less than 10,000 men left for the siege, and these much discouraged by its interminable length, short of officers, and sickly.   This was not enough to guard a periphery of six miles, and messengers were continually slipping in or out of Gerona, between the widely scattered camps of the French.

On August 31 a new phase of the siege began.   In response to the constant appeals of Alvarez to the Catalan Junta, and the consequent complaints of the Junta alike to the Captain-General Blake, and to the central government at Seville, something was at last about to be done to relieve Gerona.   The supreme Central Junta, in reply to a formal representation of the Catalans dated August 16[1], had sent Blake 6,000,000 reals in cash, and a peremptory order to march on Gerona whatever the state of his army might be, authorizing him to call out all the *somatenes* of the province in his aid.   The general, who had at last returned to Tarragona, obeyed, though entirely lacking confidence in his means of success ; and on the thirty-first his advance guard was skirmishing with St. Cyr's covering army on the heights to the south of the Ter.

Blake's army, it will be remembered, had been completely routed at Belchite by Suchet on June 18.   The wrecks of his Aragonese division had gradually rallied at Tortosa, those of his Valencian divisions at Morella : but even by the end of July he had only a few thousand men collected, and he had lost every gun of his artillery.   For many weeks he could do nothing but press the Junta of Valencia to fill the depleted ranks of his regiments with recruits, to reconstitute his train, and to provide him with new cannon.   Aragon had been lost—nothing could be drawn from thence : Catalonia, distracted by Suchet's demonstration on its western flank, did not do as much as might have been expected in its own defence.   The Junta was inclined to favour the employment of miqueletes and

and the garrisoning of Figueras, there were at this time the Valais battalion, one battalion of the Confederation of the Rhine (Waldeck-Reuss-Schwarzburg), one battalion each of the French 7th and 113th—not more than 2,300 bayonets in all.   See Returns of the Army of Spain for Sept. 15, 1809.

[1] For this correspondence see the Appendices nos. 16 and 24–5 in vol. ii of Belmas.

somatenes, and to undervalue the troops of the line: it forgot
that the irregulars, though they did admirable work in
harassing the enemy, could not be relied upon to operate in
large masses or strike a decisive blow. Still, the regiments
at Tarragona, Lerida, and elsewhere had been somewhat
recruited before August was out.

Blake's field army was composed of some 14,000 men: there
were five Valencian regiments—those which had been least
mishandled in the campaign of Aragon—with the relics of
six of the battalions which Reding had brought from Granada
in 1808 [1], two of Lazan's old Aragonese corps, and five or six
of the regiments which had formed the original garrison of
Catalonia. The battalions were very weak—it took twenty-
four of them to make up 13,000 infantry: of cavalry there
were only four squadrons, of artillery only two batteries.
Those of the rank and file who were not raw recruits were
the vanquished of Molins de Rey and Valls, or of Maria and
Belchite. They had no great confidence in Blake, and he had
still less in them. Despite the orders received from Seville,
which bade him risk all for the relief of Gerona, he was
determined not to fight another pitched battle. The memories
of Belchite were too recent to be forgotten. Though much
obloquy has been poured upon his head for this resolve, he
was probably wise in his decision. St. Cyr had still some
12,000 men in his covering army, who had taken no share in the
siege: their morale was intact, and they had felt little fatigue
or privation. They could be, and were in fact, reinforced by
4,000 men from Verdier's force when the stress came. Blake,
therefore, was, so far as regular troops went, outnumbered by
the French, especially in cavalry and artillery. He could not
trust in time of battle the miqueletes, of whom some 4,000
or 5,000 from the Ampurdam and Central Catalonia came to
join him. He thought that it might be possible to elude or

---

[1] See the 'morning state' given in Arteche, vii. pp. 565–6. The
Valencian regiments were Savoya, Orihuela, Voluntarios de Valencia,
and Almanza, with about 5,000 bayonets. Of Reding's old troops from
the south there were Almeria, Baza, Santa Fé, 1st of Granada (otherwise
called Iliberia), and two battalions of Provincial Grenadiers, something
over 3,000 men. The rest were mainly Catalans.

outflank St. Cyr, to lure him to divide his forces into scattered
bodies by threatening many points at once, or, on the other
hand, to induce him to concentrate on one short front, and so to
leave some of the exits of Gerona open.   But a battle with the
united French army he would not risk under any conditions.

St. Cyr, however, was too wary for his opponent : he wanted
to fight at all costs, and he was prepared to risk a disturbance
of the siege operations, if he could catch Blake in the open and
bring him to action.   The moment that pressure on his outposts, by regular troops coming from the south, was reported,
he drew together Souham's and Pino's divisions on the short
line between San Dalmay on the right and Casa de Selva on
the left, across the high road from Barcelona.   At the same
time he sent stringent orders to Verdier to abandon the unimportant sections of his line of investment, and to come to
reinforce the field army at the head of his French division,
which still counted 4,000 bayonets.   Verdier accordingly
marched to join his chief, leaving Lecchi's Italians—now little
more than 2,000 strong—to watch the west side of Gerona, and
handing over the charge of the works on Monjuich, the new
approaches, and the park at Pont Mayor, to the Westphalians.
He abandoned all the outlying posts on the heights, even the
convent of San Daniel, the village of Campdura, and the peak
of Nuestra Señora de los Angeles.   Only 4,600 infantry and
2,000 gunners and sappers were left facing the garrison : but
Alvarez was too weak to drive off even such a small force.

On September 1 Blake ostentatiously displayed the heads of
his columns in front of St. Cyr's position ; but while the French
general was eagerly awaiting his attack, and preparing his
counter-stroke, the Spaniard's game was being played out in
another quarter.   While Rovira and Claros with their miqueletes made noisy demonstration from the north against the
Westphalians, and threatened the park and the camp at Sarria,
Blake had detached one of his divisions, that of Garcia Conde,
some 4,000 strong, far to the left beyond St. Cyr's flank : this
corps had with it a convoy of more than a thousand mules
laden with provisions, and a herd of cattle.   It completely
escaped the notice of the French, and marching from Amer at
break of day came down into the plain of Salt at noon, far in

the rear of St. Cyr's army. Garcia Conde had the depleted Italian division of the siege corps in front of him: one of the brigadiers, the Pole Milosewitz, was in command that day, Lecchi being in hospital. This small force, which vainly believed itself covered from attack by St. Cyr's corps, had kept no look-out to the rear, being wholly intent on watching the garrison. It was surprised by the Spanish column, cut into two halves, and routed. Garcia Conde entered the Mercadal in triumph with his convoy, and St. Cyr first learnt what had occurred when he saw the broken remnants of the Italians pouring into the rear of his own line at Fornells.

That night Gerona was free of enemies on its southern and eastern sides, and Alvarez communicated freely with Rovira's and Claros's irregulars, who had forced in the Westphalian division and compelled it to concentrate in Monjuich and the camp by the great park near Sarria. The garrison reoccupied the ruined convent of San Daniel by the Galligan, and placed a strong party in the hermitage on the peak of Nuestra Señora de los Angeles. It also destroyed all the advanced trenches on the slopes of Monjuich. On the next morning, however, it began to appreciate the fact that the siege had not been raised. St. Cyr sent back Verdier's division to rejoin the Westphalians, and with them the wrecks of Lecchi's routed battalions. He added to the force under Verdier half Pino's Italian division—six fresh battalions. With these reinforcements the old siege-lines could be reoccupied, and the Spaniards were forced back from the points outside the walls which they had reoccupied on the night of September 1.

By sending away such a large proportion of the 16,000 men that he had concentrated for battle on the previous day, St. Cyr left himself only some 10,000 men for a general action with Blake, if the latter should resolve to fight. But the Spanish general, being without Garcia Conde's division, had also no more than 10,000 men in line. Not only did he refuse to advance, but when St. Cyr, determined to fight at all costs, marched against him with offensive intentions, he hastily retreated as far as Hostalrich, two marches to the rear. There he broke up his army, which had exhausted all its provisions. St. Cyr did the same and for the same reasons; his men had to

disperse in order to live. He says in his memoirs that if Blake
had shown a bold front against him, and forced him to keep
the covering army concentrated for two more days, the siege
would have had to be raised. For the covering army had
advanced against the Spaniards on September 2 with only two
days' rations, it had exhausted its stores, and eaten up the
country-side. On the fourth it would have had to retire, or to
break up into small fractions, leaving the siege-corps unprotected. St. Cyr doubted whether the retreat would have ceased
before Figueras was reached. But it is more probable that
he would have merely fallen back to join Verdier, and to live
for some days on the dépôts of Pont Mayor and Sarria. He
could have offered battle again under the walls of Gerona, with
all his forces united. Blake might have got into close touch
with Alvarez, and have thrown what convoys he pleased into
the town ; but as long as St. Cyr and Verdier with 22,000 men
lay opposite him, he could not have risked any more. The
situation, in short, would have been that which occurred in
February 1811 under the walls of Badajoz, when Mortier faced
Mendizabal, and would probably have ended in the same
fashion, by the French attacking and driving off the relieving
army. Blake, then, may be blamed somewhat for his excessive
caution in giving way so rapidly before St. Cyr's advance : but
if we remember the quality of his troops and the inevitable
result of a battle, it is hard to censure him overmuch.

Meanwhile Garcia Conde, whose movements were most happy
and adroit, reinforced the garrison of Gerona up to its original
strength of 5,000 bayonets, by making over to Alvarez four
whole battalions and some picked companies from other corps,
and prepared to leave the town with the rest of his division and
the vast drove of mules, whose burden had been discharged into
the magazines. If he had dedicated his whole force to strengthening the garrison, the additional troops would have eaten up
in a few days all the provisions that the convoy had brought in [1].

---

[1] The reinforcements left behind by Garcia Conde consisted of two
battalions of Baza (one of Reding's old Granadan regiments), with 1,368
bayonets, two Catalan ' tercios,' 1st and 2nd of Talarn, with 716 bayonets,
and select companies of 1st of Granada (Iliberia), 2nd of Vich, and Voluntarios de Tarragona—in all apparently about 2,707 men.

Accordingly he started off at two a.m. on September 4 with some 1,200 men, by the upland path that leads past the hermitage of Los Angeles: St. Cyr had just placed Pino's troops from the covering army to guard the heights to the south-east of Gerona, but Garcia Conde, warned by the peasants of their exact position, slipped between the posts and got off to Hostalrich with a loss of no more than fifty men [1].

Before he could consider his position safe, Verdier had to complete the lines of investment: this he did on September 5 by driving off the intermediate posts which Alvarez had thrown out from the Capuchin heights, to link the town with the garrison in the hermitage of Nuestra Señora de los Angeles. Mazzuchelli's brigade stormed the hermitage itself on the following day, with a loss of about eighty men, and massacred the greater part of the garrison. On that same day, however, the French suffered a small disaster in another part of the environs. General Joba, who had been sent with three battalions to clear the road to Figueras from the bands of Claros and Rovira, was beaten and slain at San Gregorio by those chiefs. But the miqueletes afterwards retired to the mountains, and the road became intermittently passable, at least for large bodies of men.

It was not till September 11, however, that Verdier recom-

The table on p. 375 of Arteche's vol. vii seems to err in crediting the Cervera 'tercio' to Garcia: this had come in on Aug. 17, as described on p. 35. On the other hand the company of Voluntarios de Tarragona should be credited to him.

[1] St. Cyr tells a story to the effect that he had placed Mazzuchelli's brigade of Pino's division in ambush behind the hill of Palau to intercept Garcia Conde, and that the Spaniards would have marched right into the trap on Sept. 3, if the Italians had not been stupid enough to sound the *réveil* at dawn, and so warn the enemy of their existence. But the Spanish accounts of Minali and Claros are quite different (see Arteche, vii. 377); they are to the effect that Garcia Conde had intended to start *at dusk* on the third, but, hearing firing on the side of Palau, deferred his exit and took another road. If he was starting at 7 or 8 o'clock at night on the third, he cannot have been warned by the morning bugles at 4 o'clock on the previous morning. See St. Cyr, p. 234, and Napier, ii. 245, for the French story, which the latter takes over whole from the former. Belmas and Vacani do not give the tale, though they have a full narration of the escape of Garcia Conde.

menced the actual siege, and bade his batteries open once more upon Gerona. The eleven days of respite since Blake interrupted the bombardment on September 1 had been invaluable to the garrison, who had cleared away the débris from the foot of the breaches, replaced the damaged artillery on the front of attack, and thrown up interior defences behind the shattered parts of the wall. They had also destroyed all the advanced trenches of the besiegers, which had to be reconstructed at much cost of life. In four days Verdier had recovered most of the lost ground, when he was surprised by a vigorous sally from the gate of San Pedro: the garrison, dashing out at three P.M., stormed the three nearest breaching batteries, spiked their guns, and filled in all the trenches which were advancing towards the foot of the walls. Four days' work was thus undone in an hour, and it was only on September 19 that Verdier had reconstructed his works, and pushed forward so far towards his objective that he considered an assault possible. He then begged St. Cyr to lend him a brigade of fresh troops, pleading that the siege-corps was now so weak in numbers, and so demoralized by its losses, that he did not consider that the men would do themselves justice at a storm. The losses of officers had been fearful: one battalion was commanded by a lieutenant, another had been reduced to fifty men; desertion was rampant among several of the foreign corps. Of 14,000 infantry [1] of the French, Westphalian, and Italian divisions less than 6,000 now remained. So far as mere siegecraft went, as he explained to St. Cyr, 'the affair might be considered at an end. We have made four large practicable breaches, each of them sufficient to reduce the town. But the troops cannot be trusted.' St. Cyr refused to lend a man for the assault, writing with polite irony that 'every general has his own task: yours is to take Gerona with the resources placed at your disposal by the government for that object, and the officers named by the government to conduct the siege.' [2] He added that he considered, from its past

---

[1] Verdier did not exaggerate: see Appendix no. 2 at end of this volume, showing that his three divisions had lost 8,161 men out of 14,044 by September 15.

[2] See the acrid correspondence between St. Cyr and Verdier in Appendices nos. 37-8, 40-6 of Belmas, vol. ii.

conduct, that the morale of the siege-corps was rather good than bad.   He should not, therefore, allow the covering army to join the assault; but he would lend the whole of Pino's division to take charge of Monjuich and the camps, during the storm, and would make a demonstration against the Mercadal, to distract the enemy from the breaches.   With this Verdier had to be content, and, after making two final protests, concentrated all his brigades save those of the Westphalian division, and composed with them four columns, amounting to some 3,000 men, directing one against each of the four breaches.   That sent against the platform of San Cristobal was a mere demonstration of 150 men, but the other three were heavy masses : the Italians went against Santa Lucia, the French brigade against the southern breach in the 'Redoubt of the Germans,' the Berg troops against the northern one.   A separate demonstration was made against the Calvary fort, whose unsubdued fire still flanked the breaches, in the hope that its defenders might be prevented from interfering in the main struggle.

Alvarez, who had noted the French columns marching from all quarters to take shelter, before the assault, in the trenches on the slopes of Monjuich and in front of Pedret, had fair warning of what was coming, and had done his best to provide against the danger.   The less important parts of the enceinte had been put in charge of the citizens of the 'Crusade,' and the picked companies of every regiment had been told off to the breaches.   The Englishman, Ralph Marshall, was in charge of the curtain of Santa Lucia, William Nash, the Spanish-Irish colonel of Ultonia, commanded at the two breaches under La Gironella : Brigadier Fournas, the second-in-command of the garrison, had general supervision of the defences; he had previously taken charge of Monjuich during the great assault in August.   Everything had been done to prepare a second line of resistance behind the breaches; barricades had been erected, houses loopholed, and a great many marksmen disposed on roofs and church towers, which looked down on the rear-side of the gaps in the wall.

At four o'clock in the afternoon of September 19 the three columns destined for the northern breaches descended from Monjuich on the side of San Daniel, crossed the Galligan, and plunged into the hollow at the foot of the 'Redoubt of the Germans.' At the same moment the fourth column started from the ruins of the tower of San Juan to attack the curtain of Santa Lucia. The diversion against the Calvary fort was made at the same moment, and beaten off in a few minutes, so that the fire of this work was not neutralized during the assault according to Verdier's expectation. The main assault, nevertheless, was delivered with great energy, despite the flanking fire. At the two points of attack under La Gironella the stormers twice won, crossed, and descended from the breach, forcing their way into the ruined barracks behind. But they were mown down by the terrible musketry fire from the houses, and finally expelled with the bayonet. At the Santa Lucia curtain the Italians scaled the breach, but were brought up by a perpendicular drop of twelve feet behind it—the foot of the wall in this quarter chancing to be much higher than the level of the street below. They held the crest of the breach for some time, but were finally worsted in a long and furious exchange of fire with the Spaniards on the roofs and churches before them, and recoiled. The few surviving officers rallied the stormers, and brought them up for a second assault, but at the end of two hours of hard fighting all were constrained to retire to their trenches. They had lost 624 killed and wounded, including three colonels (the only three surviving in the whole of Verdier's corps) and thirty other officers. The Spanish loss had been 251, among them Colonel Marshall, who was mortally wounded at his post on the Santa Lucia front.

Verdier accused his troops of cowardice, which seems to have been unjust. St. Cyr wrote to the Minister of War to express his opinion that his subordinate was making an excuse to cover his own error, in judging that a town must fall merely because there were large breaches in its walls.[1] 'The columns stopped for ninety minutes on the breaches under as heavy a fire as has ever been seen. There was some disorder at the end, but that is not astonishing in view of the heavy loss suffered before the

---

[1] ' Il paraît que l'on a employé la ressource, malheureusement trop usitée en pareil cas, de dire que les troupes n'ont pas fait leur devoir, ce qui produit de justes réclamations de leur part.' (St. Cyr to the Minister, Sept. 24, 1809.)

retreat. I do not think that picked grenadiers would have done any better, and I am convinced that the assault failed because the obstacles to surmount were too great.' The fact was that the Spaniards had fought with such admirable obstinacy, and had so well arranged their inner defences, that it did not suffice that the breaches should have been perfectly practicable. At the northern assault the stormers actually penetrated into the buildings behind the gaps in the ruined wall, but could not get further forward.[1] In short, the history of the siege of Gerona gives a clear corroboration of the old military axiom that no town should ever surrender merely because it has been breached, and justifies Napoleon's order that every governor who capitulated without having stood at least one assault should be sent before a court martial. It refutes the excuses of the too numerous commanders who have surrendered merely because there was a practicable breach in their walls, like Imaz at Badajoz in 1811. If all Spanish generals had been as wary and as resolute as Mariano Alvarez, the Peninsular War would have taken some unexpected turns. The moral of the defences of Tarifa, Burgos, and San Sebastian will be found to be the same as that of the defence of Gerona.

The effect of the repulse of September 19 on the besieging army was appalling. Verdier, after writing three venomous letters to the Emperor, the War Minister, and Marshal Augereau, in which he accused St. Cyr of having deliberately sacrificed the good of the service to his personal resentments, declared himself invalided. He then went off to Perpignan, though permission to depart was expressly denied him by his superior: his divisional generals, Lecchi and Morio, had already preceded him to France. Disgust at the failure of the storm had the same effect on the rank and file: 1,200 men went to the hospital in the

---

[1] The not unnatural suggestion that the German and Italian troops may have failed to display such desperate courage as the native French in the assault seems to be refuted by their losses, which were hardly smaller in proportion. Of 1,430 native French of the 7th and 56th Line and 32nd Léger, 328 were put out of action ; of 1,400 Berg, Würzburg, and Italian troops, 296. The difference in the percentage is so small that it is clear that there was no great difference in conduct.

[2] See especially Verdier to Augereau, no. 53, and to the Minister, no. 61, of Belmas's Appendices.

SIEGE OF GERONA

1. Redoubt of the Germans
2. San Christobal
3. San Pedro
4. Tower of Sta.Lucia

Battery .... 🏰
10 Metres between contours
Breaches ⌐ₘₘ

Sta.Eugenia

S ——————➤ N

GERONA

to Barcelona

River Ter

Mercadal

La Marina

La Merced

R. Oña

La Gironella

City Redoubt

Chapter Redoubt

Constable Fort

Ravine

St.Dani Conven

Queen Anne Fort

Calvary Redoubt

Capuchin's Fort

B.V.Darbishire, Oxford, 1907

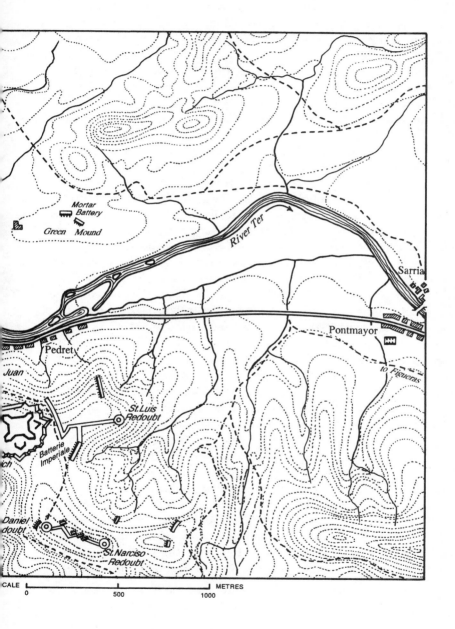

Mortar Battery

Green Mound

River Ter

Sarria

Pontmayor

to Figueras

Pedret

Juan

St. Luis Redoubt

Batterie Imperiale

Daniel doubt

St. Narciso Redoubt

SCALE

0   500   1000   METRES

fortnight that followed the assault, till by October 1 the three
divisions of the siege-corps numbered little more than 4,000
bayonets—just enough to hold Monjuich and the camps by the
great dépôts at Pont Mayor and Sarria.   The store of ammunition in the park had been used up for the tremendous bombardment poured upon the breaches from the 15th to the 17th of
September.   A new supply was wanted from Perpignan, yet no
troops could be detached to bring it forward, for the miqueletes
were again active, and on September 13 had captured or destroyed
near Bascara a convoy guarded by so many as 500 men.

St. Cyr, left in sole charge of the siege by Verdier's departure,
came to the conclusion that it was useless to proceed with the
attack by means of trenches, batteries, and assaults, and frankly
stated that he should starve the town out, but waste no further
lives on active operations.   He drew in the covering corps
closer to Gerona, so that it could take a practical part in the
investment, put the wrecks of Lecchi's troops—of whom less
than 1,000 survived—into Pino's division, and sent the French
brigade of Verdier's old division to guard the line between
Bascara and the Frontier.   Thus the distinction between the
siege-corps and the covering troops ceased to exist, and St. Cyr
lay with some 16,000 men in a loose circle round Gerona, intent
not on prosecuting advances against the walls, but only on
preventing the introduction of further succours.   He was aware
that acute privations were already being suffered by the
Spaniards: Garcia Condé's convoy had brought in not much
more than eight days' provisions for the 5,000 men of the reinforced garrison and the 10,000 inhabitants who still survived.
There was a considerable amount of flour still left in store,
but little else: meat, salt and fresh, was all gone save horseflesh,
for Alvarez had just begun to butcher his draught horses and
those of his single squadron of cavalry.   There was some small
store of chocolate, tobacco, and coffee, but wine and aguardiente
had run out, so had salt, oil, rice, and—what was most serious
with autumn and winter approaching—wood and charcoal.   All
the timbers of the houses destroyed by the bombardment had
been promptly used up, either for fortification or for cooking [1].

[1] The very interesting list of the prices of commodities at the commencement and the end of the siege, drawn up by Dr. Ruiz, one of the Gerona

Medical stores were wholly unobtainable: the chief hospital
had been burnt early in the siege, and the sick and wounded,
laid in vaults or casemates for safety, died off like flies in the
underground air. The seeds of pestilence were spread by the
number of dead bodies of men and animals which were lying
where they could not be reached, under the ruins of fallen houses.
The spirit alike of garrison and troops still ran high : the
repulse of the great assault of September 19, and the cessation
of the bombardment for many days after had encouraged them.
But they were beginning to murmur more and more bitterly
against Blake: there was a general, if erroneous, opinion that
he ought to have risked a battle, instead of merely throwing
in provisions, on September 1. Alvarez himself shared this
view, and wrote in vigorous terms to the Junta of Catalonia,
to ask if his garrison was to perish slowly by famine.

Blake responded by a second effort, less happily planned than
that of September 1. He called together his scattered divisions,
now about 12,000 strong, and secretly concentrated them at
La Bispal, between Gerona and the sea. He had again got
together some 1,200 mules laden with foodstuffs, and a large
drove of sheep and oxen. Henry O'Donnell, an officer of the
Ultonia regiment, who had been sent out by Alvarez, marched
at the head of the convoy with 2,000 picked men ; a division
of 4,000 men under General Wimpfen followed close behind to
cover its rear. Blake, with the rest, remained at La Bispal: he
committed the egregious fault of omitting to threaten other

diarists, may be found on p. 579 of Arteche's vol. vii. Note the following
—the real (20 to the dollar) = $2\frac{1}{2}d$. :—

	Reals.				Reals.	
	In June.	In Sept.			In June.	In Sept.
Wheat flour, the qr. .	80	112	Wood, the arroba (32			
Barleymeal, the qr. .	30	56	lb.).	5	48
Oatmeal, the qr. . .	48	80	Charcoal, ditto. . .	$3\frac{1}{2}$	40
Coffee, the lb. . . .	8	24	Tobacco, the lb. . .	24	100
Chocolate, the lb.. .	16	64	A fowl	14	320
Oil, the measure . .	$2\frac{1}{2}$	24	Rice, the lb. . . .	$1\frac{1}{2}$	32
Salt fish, the lb. . .	$2\frac{1}{4}$	32	Fresh fish from the		
Cheese, the lb. . .	4	40	Ter, the lb.. . .	4	36

Thus while flour and meal had not doubled in value, coffee had gone up
threefold, chocolate and tobacco fourfold, cheese and fuel tenfold, and the
other commodities far more.

parts of the line of investment, so as to draw off St. Cyr's
attention from the crucial point.   He trusted to secrecy and
sudden action, having succeeded in concentrating his army
without being discovered by the French, who thought him still
far away beyond Hostalrich.   Thus it came to pass that though
O'Donnell struck sharply in, defeated an Italian regiment near
Castellar, and another three miles further on, and reached the
Constable fort with the head of the convoy, yet the rest of
Pino's division and part of Souham's concentrated upon his
flank and rear, because they were not drawn off by alarms in
other quarters.   They broke in between O'Donnell and his
supports, captured all the convoy save 170 mules, and destroyed
the leading regiment of Wimpfen's column, shooting also,
according to the Spanish reports, many scores of the unarmed
peasants who were driving the beasts of burden[1].   About 700
of Wimpfen's men were taken prisoners, about 1,300 killed or
wounded, for little quarter was given.   The remnant recoiled
upon Blake, who fell back to Hostalrich next day, September 27,
without offering to fight.   The amount of food which reached
the garrison was trifling, and Alvarez declared that he had no
need for the additional mouths of O'Donnell's four battalions,
and refused to admit them into the city.   They lay encamped
under the Capuchin fort for some days, waiting for an opportunity to escape.

After having thus wrecked Blake's second attempt to succour
Gerona, and driven him from the neighbourhood, St. Cyr betook
himself to Perpignan, in order, as he explained to the Minister
of War[2], to hurry up provisions to the army at the front, and
to compel the officers at the base to send forward some 3,000
or 4,000 convalescents fit to march, whose services had been persistently denied him[3].   Arrived there he heard that Augereau,
whose gout had long disappeared, was perfectly fit to take the
field, and could have done so long before if he had not preferred to shift on to other shoulders the responsibility for the
siege of Gerona.   He was, on October 1, at the baths of Molitg,
' destroying the germs of his malady' as he gravely wrote to

---

[1] See Toreno, ii, and Arteche, vii. 412.
[2] See St. Cyr to the Minister, Belmas, ii, Appendix no. 67.
[3] Augereau to the Minister, ibid., Oct. 8.

Paris,—amusing himself, as St. Cyr maintains in his memoirs. Convinced that the siege had still a long time to run, and eager to do an ill turn to the officer who had intrigued to get his place, St. Cyr played on the Marshal precisely the same trick that Verdier had played on himself a fortnight before. He announced that he was indisposed, wrote to congratulate Augereau on his convalescence, and to resign the command to his hands, and departed to his home, without waiting for an answer, or obtaining leave from Paris—a daring act, as Napoleon was enraged, and might have treated him hardly. He was indeed put under arrest for a short time.

From the first to the eleventh of October Souham remained in charge of the army, but on the twelfth Augereau appeared and took command, bringing with him the mass of convalescents who had been lingering at Perpignan. Among them was Verdier, whose health became all that could be desired when St. Cyr had disappeared. The night following the Marshal's arrival was disturbed by an exciting incident. Henry O'Donnell from his refuge on the Capuchin heights, had been watching for a fortnight for a good chance of escape. There was a dense fog on the night of the 12th–13th : taking advantage of it O'Donnell came down with his brigade, made a circuit round the town, crossed the Oña and struck straight away into the plain of Salt, which, being the most open and exposed, was also the least guarded section of the French lines of investment. He broke through the chain of vedettes almost without firing, and came rushing before dawn into Souham's head-quarters camp on the heights of Aguaviva. The battalion sleeping there was scattered, and the general forced to fly in his shirt. O'Donnell swept off his riding-horses and baggage, as also some prisoners, and was out of reach in half an hour, before the rallying fractions of the French division came up to the rescue of their chief. By six o'clock the escaping column was in safety in the mountains by Santa Coloma, where it joined the miqueletes of Milans. For this daring exploit O'Donnell was made a major-general by the Supreme Junta. His departure was a great relief to Alvarez, who had to husband every mouthful of food, and had already put both the garrison and the townsfolk on half-rations of flour and horseflesh.

Augereau was in every way inferior as an officer to St. Cyr. An old soldier of fortune risen from the ranks, he had little education or military science; his one virtue was headlong courage on the battlefield, yet when placed in supreme command he often hesitated, and showed hopeless indecision. He had been lucky enough to earn a great reputation as Napoleon's second-in-command in the old campaigns of Italy in 1796–7. Since then he had made his fortune by becoming one of the Emperor's most zealous tools and flatterers. He was reckoned a blind and reckless Bonapartist, ready to risk anything for his master, but spoilt his reputation for sincerity by deserting him at the first opportunity in 1814. He was inclined to a harsh interpretation of the laws of war, and enjoyed a doubtful reputation for financial integrity. Yet he was prone to ridiculous self-laudatory proclamations and manifestos, written in a bombastic strain which he vainly imagined to resemble his master's thunders of the *Bulletins*. Scraps of his address to the citizens of Gerona may serve to display his fatuity—

'Unhappy inhabitants—wretched victims immolated to the caprice and madness of ambitious men greedy for your blood— return to your senses, open your eyes, consider the ills which surround you! With what tranquillity do your leaders look upon the graves crammed with your corpses! Are you not horror-struck at these cannibals, whose mirth bursts out in the midst of the human hecatomb, and who yet dare to lift their gory hands in prayer towards the throne of a God of Peace? They call themselves the apostles of Jesus Christ! Tremble, cruel and infamous men! The God who judges the actions of mortals is slow to condemn, but his vengeance is terrible. . . . I warn you for the last time, inhabitants of Gerona, reflect while you still may! If you force me to throw aside my usual mildness, your ruin is inevitable. I shall be the first to groan at it, but the laws of war impose on me the dire necessity. . . . I am severe but just. Unhappy Gerona! if thy defenders persist in their obstinacy, thou shalt perish in blood and flame.

(Signed) AUGEREAU.'

Stuff of this sort was not likely to have much effect on fanatics like Alvarez and his 'Crusaders.' If it is so wrong to cause the deaths of men—they had only to answer—Why has Bonaparte sent his legions into Spain? On the Marshal's line of argument, that it is wrong to resist overwhelming force, it is apparently a sin before God for any man to attempt to defend his house and family against any bandit. There is much odious and hypocritical nonsense in some of Napoleon's bulletins, where he grows tender on the miseries of the people he has conquered, but nothing to approach the maunderings of his copyist.

Augereau found the army about Gerona showing not more than 12,000 bayonets fit for the field—gunners and sappers excluded. The men were sick of the siege, and it would seem that the Marshal was forced, after inspecting the regiments and conferring with the generals, to acquiesce in St. Cyr's decision that any further assaults would probably lead to more repulses. He gave out that he was resolved to change the system on which the operations had hitherto been conducted, but the change amounted to nothing more than that he ordered a slow but steady bombardment to be kept up, and occasionally vexed the Spaniards by demonstrations against the more exposed points of the wall. It does not appear that either of these expedients had the least effect in shaking the morale of the garrison. It is true that during October and November the hearts of the Geronese were commencing to grow sick, but this was solely the result of starvation and dwindling numbers. As to the bombardment, they were now hardened to any amount of dropping fire: on October 28 they celebrated the feast of San Narciso, their patron, by a procession all round the town, which was under fire for the whole time of its progress, and paid no attention to the casualties which it cost them.

Meanwhile, when the second half of October had begun, Blake made the third and last of his attempts to throw succours into Gerona. It was even more feebly carried out than that of September 26, for the army employed was less numerous. Blake's force had not received any reinforcement to make up for the men lost in the last affair, a fact that seems surprising, since Valencia ought now to have been able to send him the remainder of the regiments which had been reorganized since the disasters of June. But it would seem that José Caro, who was in command in that province, and the local Junta, made excuses for retaining as many men as possible, and cared little

for the danger of Gerona, so long as the war was kept far from
their own frontier. It was, at any rate, with no more than
10,000 or 12,000 men, the remains of his original force, that
Blake once more came forward on October 18, and threatened
the blockading army by demonstrations both from the side of
La Bispal and that of Santa Coloma. He had again collected
a considerable amount of food at Hostalrich, but had not yet
formed a convoy: apparently he was waiting to discover the
weakest point in the French lines before risking his mules and
his stores, both of which were by now very hard to procure.
There followed a fortnight of confused skirmishing, without
any battle, though Augereau tried with all his might to force
on a general engagement. One of his Italian brigades was
roughly handled near La Bispal on the twenty-first, and another
repulsed near Santa Coloma on the twenty-sixth, but on each
occasion, when the French reinforcements came up, Blake gave
back and refused to fight. On November 1 the whole of
Souham's division marched on Santa Coloma, and forced Loygorri
and Henry O'Donnell to evacuate it and retire to the mountains.
Souham reported that he had inflicted a loss of 2,000 men on
the Spaniards, at the cost of eleven killed and forty-three
wounded on his own side! The real casualty list of the two
Spanish divisions seems to have been somewhat over 100 men [1].

Nothing decisive had taken place up to November 7, when
Augereau conceived the idea that he might make an end of
Blake's fruitless but vexatious demonstrations, by dealing a sudden
blow at his magazines in Hostalrich. If these were destroyed
it would cost the Spaniards much time to collect another store
of provisions for Gerona. Accordingly Pino marched with three
brigades to storm the town, which was protected only by a dilapidated mediaeval wall unfurnished with guns, though the castle
which dominated it was a place of considerable strength, and
proof against a *coup de main*. Only one of Blake's divisions, that
of Cuadrado, less than 2,000 strong, was in this quarter, and
Augereau found employment for the others by sending some
of Souham's troops against them. The expedition succeeded:
while Mazzuchelli's brigade occupied the attention of Cuadrado,

[1] See Souham's dispatch, striving to make the combat into a very big
business, in Belmas, ii, Appendix no. 72, and cf. Arteche, vii. pp. 430–1.

the rest of the Italians stormed Hostalrich, which was defended
only by its own inhabitants and the small garrison of the castle.
The Spaniards were driven up into that stronghold after a lively
fight, and all the magazines fell into Pino's hands and were
burnt. At a cost of only thirty-five killed and sixty-four
wounded the food, which Blake had collected with so much
difficulty, was destroyed [1]. Thereupon the Spanish general gave
up the attempt to succour Gerona, and withdrew to the plain
of Vich, to recommence the Sisyphean task of getting together
one more convoy. It was not destined to be of any use to
Alvarez and his gallant garrison, for by the time that it was
collected the siege had arrived at its final stage.

The Geronese were now reaching the end of their strength:
for the first time since the investment began in May some of the
defenders began to show signs of slackening. The heavy rains
of October and the commencement of the cold season were
reducing alike troops and inhabitants to a desperate condition.
They had long used up all their fuel, and found the chill of
winter intolerable in their cellars and casemates. Alvarez,
though reduced to a state of physical prostration by dysentery
and fever, was still steadfast in heart. But there was discontent
brewing among some of his subordinates: it is notable, as showing
the spirit of the time, that the malcontents were found among
the professional soldiers, not among the citizens. Early in
November several officers were found holding secret conferences,
and drawing up an address to the local Junta, setting forth the
desperate state of the city and the necessity for deposing the
governor, who was represented as incapacitated for command by
reason of his illness: it was apparently hinted that he was going
mad, or was intermittently delirious [2]. Some of the wild sayings
attributed to Alvarez during the later days of the siege might
be quoted as a support for their representations. To a captain
who asked to what point he was expected to retire, if he were
driven from his post, it is said that he answered, 'to the
cemetery.' To another officer, the first who dared to say that

---

[1] See Pino's and Augereau's dispatches in Belmas's Appendices, nos.
73 and 74.

[2] Alvarez's letter to Blake of Nov. 3 printed in Arteche's Appendix,
no. 18 of his vol. vii, gives this account of the first discovery of plots.

capitulation was inevitable because of the exhaustion of the
magazines, he replied, ' When the last food is gone we will start
eating the cowards, and we will begin with you.' Though aware
that their conspiracies were known, the malcontents did not
desist from their efforts, and Alvarez made preparations for
seizing and shooting the chiefs. But on the night of November 19
eight of them, including three lieutenant-colonels [1], warned by
a traitor of their approaching fate, fled to Augereau's camp.
Their arrival was the most encouraging event for the French
that had occurred since the commencement of the siege. They
spoke freely of the exhaustion of the garrison, and said that
Alvarez was mad and moribund.

It was apparently this information concerning the desperate
state of the garrison which induced Augereau to recommence
active siege operations. He ordered up ammunition from Perpignan to fill the empty magazines, and when it arrived began
to batter a new breach in the curtain of Santa Lucia. On
December 2 Pino's Italians stormed the suburb of La Marina,
outside the southern end of the town, a quarter hitherto unas-
sailed, and made a lodgement therein, as if to open a new point
of attack. But this was only done to distract the enemy from
the real design of the Marshal, which was nothing less than to
cut off the forts on the Capuchin heights from Gerona by seizing
the redoubts, those of the 'Chapter' and the 'City,' which
covered the steep upward path from the walls to the group of
works on the hill-top. At midnight on December 6 the voltigeur
and grenadier companies of Pino's division climbed the rough
southern face of the Capuchin heights, and surprised and escaladed
the 'Redoubt of the City,' putting the garrison to the sword.
Next morning the batteries of the forts above and the city below
opened a furious fire upon the lost redoubt, and Alvarez directed
his last sally, sending out every man that he could collect to
recover the work. This led to a long and bloody fight on the
slopes, which ended most disastrously for the garrison. Not only
was the sortie repulsed, but in the confusion the French carried
the Calvary and Chapter redoubts, the other works which guarded
the access from Gerona to the upper forts. On the afternoon

---

[1] Of whom two, strangely enough, had been specially mentioned for
courage at the September assault.

of December 7 the communication with them was completely cut off, and as their garrisons possessed no separate magazines, and had been wont to receive their daily dole from the city, it was clear that they must be starved out. They had only food for forty-eight hours at the moment [1].

The excitement of the sally had drained away the governor's last strength : he took to his bed that evening, was in delirium next day, and on the morning of the ninth received the last sacraments of the Church, the doctors having declared that his hours were numbered. His last conscious act was to protest against any proposal to surrender, before he handed over the command to the senior officer present, General Juliano Bolivar. Had Alvarez retained his senses, it is certain that an attempt would have been made to hold the town, even when the starving garrisons of the forts should have surrendered. But the moment that his stern hand was removed, his successor, Bolivar, called together a council of war, to which the members of the Junta, no less than the officers commanding corps, were invited. They voted that further resistance was impossible, and sent out Brigadier-General Fournas, the man who had so well defended Monjuich, to obtain terms from Augereau. On the morning of the tenth the Marshal received him, and dictated a simple surrender, without any of the favourable conditions which Fournas at first demanded. His only concession was that he offered to exchange the garrison for an equal number of the unhappy prisoners from Dupont's army, now lying in misery on the pontoons at Cadiz, if the Supreme Junta concurred. But the bargain was never ratified, as the authorities at Seville were obdurate.

On the morning of December 11 the survivors of the garrison marched out, and laid down their arms on the glacis of the Mercadal. Only 3,000 men came forth ; these looked like living spectres, so pale, weak, and tattered that 'the besiegers,' as eye-witnesses observed, 'felt ashamed to have been held at bay so long by dying men.' There were 1,200 more lying in the

---

[1] Napier (ii. 249) says that the sortie was so far successful that the Geronese opened the way for the garrison of the Constable fort to escape into the city. But I can find no authority for this in either the French or the Spanish narratives, see especially Vacani.

hospitals. The rest of the 9,000 who had defended the place from May, or had entered with Garcia Conde in September, were dead. A detailed inspection of figures shows that of the 5,723 men of Alvarez's original command only 2,008 survived, while of the 3,648 who had come later there were still 2,240 left: i.e. two-thirds of the old garrison and one-third of the succours had perished. The mortality by famine and disease far exceeded that by the sword: 800 men had died in the hospitals in October, and 1,300 in November, from mere exhaustion. The town was in a dreadful state: about 6,000 of the 14,000 inhabitants had perished, including nearly all the very young and the very old. 12,000 bombs and 8,000 shells had been thrown into the unhappy city: it presented a melancholy vista of houses roofless, or with one or two of the side-walls knocked in, of streets blocked by the fallen masonry of churches or towers, under which half-decayed corpses were partially buried. The open spaces were strewn with broken muskets, bloody rags, wheels of disabled guns and carts, fragments of shells, and the bones of horses and mules whose flesh had been eaten. The stench was so dreadful that Augereau had to keep his troops out of the place, lest infection should be bred among them. In the magazines nothing was found save a little unground corn; all the other provisions had been exhausted. There were also 168 cannon, mostly disabled; about 10,000 lb. of powder, and a million musket cartridges. The military chest handed over contained 562 reals—about 6*l.* sterling.

Augereau behaved very harshly to the garrison: many feeble or diseased men were made to march to Perpignan and perished by the way. The priests and monks of the 'Crusade' were informed that they were combatants, and sent off with the soldiery. But the fate of the gallant Governor provokes especial indignation. Alvarez did not die of his fever: when he was somewhat recovered he was forwarded to Perpignan, and from thence to Narbonne, where he was kept for some time and seemed convalescent. Orders then came from Paris that he was to be sent back to Spain—apparently to be tried as a traitor, for it was alleged that in the spring of 1808 he had accepted the provisional government installed by Murat. He was separated from his aide-de-camp and servants, and passed on from dungeon to dungeon till he reached Figueras. The day after his arrival at that place he was found dead, on a barrow—the only bed granted him—in the dirty cellar where he had been placed. It is probable that he perished from natural causes, but many Spaniards believed that he had been murdered [1].

Great as the losses of the garrison of Gerona had been, they were far exceeded, both positively and proportionately, by those of the besieging army. The French official returns show that on June 15 the three divisions charged with the attack, those of Verdier, Morio, and Lecchi, had 14,456 bayonets, and the two divisions of the covering army, those of Souham and Pino, 15,732: there were 2,637 artillerymen and engineers over and above these figures. On December 31, twenty days after the surrender, and when the regiments had been joined by most of their convalescents, the three siege-divisions counted 6,343 men, the covering divisions 11,666, and the artillery and engineers, 2,390.

This shows a loss of over 13,000 men; but on examination the deficit is seen to be even larger, for two new battalions from France had just joined Verdier's division in December, and their 1,000 bayonets should be deducted from his total. It would seem, then, that the capture of Gerona cost the 7th Corps about 14,000 men, as well as a whole campaigning season, from April to December. The attack on Catalonia had been brought to a complete standstill, and when Gerona fell the French occupied nothing but the ruined city, the fortresses of Rosas and Figueras hard by the frontier, and the isolated Barcelona, where Duhesme, with the 6,000 men of his division, had been lying quiescent all the summer and autumn. Such a force was too weak to make detachments to aid St. Cyr or Augereau, since 4,000 men at least were needed for the garrison of the citadel and the outlying forts, and it would have been hopeless for the small remainder to take the field. Duhesme only conducted

---

[1] For details of this disgraceful cruelty, see Arteche's ' Elogio ' on Alvarez in the proceedings of the Madrid Academy. The Emperor Napoleon himself must bear the responsibility, as it was by orders from Paris that Alvarez was sent back from France to Figueras. Apparently he was to be tried at Barcelona, and perhaps executed. There is no allusion to the matter in the *Correspondance de Napoléon*.

one short incursion to Villafranca during the siege of Gerona.
In the last months of the year Barcelona was again in a state
of partial starvation: the food brought in by Cosmao's convoy
in the spring had been exhausted, while a second provision-fleet
from Toulon, escorted by five men-of-war, had been completely
destroyed in October.   Admiral Martin surprised it off Cape
Creus, drove ashore and burnt two line-of-battle ships and
a frigate, and captured most of the convoy.   The rest took
refuge in the harbour of Rosas, where Captain Halliwell attacked
them with the boats of the squadron and burnt them all [1].

While Gerona was enduring its last month of starvation,
those whose care it should have been to succour the place at all
costs were indulging in a fruitless exchange of recriminations,
and making preparations when it was all too late.   Blake, after
retiring to Vich on November 10, informed the Junta of Catalonia that he was helpless, unless more men could be found, and
that they must find them.   Why he did not rather insist that
the Valencian reserves should be brought up, and risk stripping
Tarragona and Lerida of their regular garrisons, it is hard to
say.   This at any rate would have been in his power.   The
Catalan Junta replied by summoning a congress at Manresa on
November 20, to which representatives of every district of the
principality were invited.   The congress voted that a levy
en masse of all the able-bodied men from seventeen to forty-five
years of age should be called out [2], and authorized a loan of
10,000,000 reals for equipping them.   They also wrote to
Seville, not for the first time, to demand reinforcements from
the Central Junta.   But the battle of Ocaña had just been
fought and lost, and Andalusia could not have spared a man,
even if there had been time to transport troops to Tarragona.
All that the Catalans received was honorary votes of approval
for the gallant behaviour of the Geronese.   The levy *en masse*
was actually begun, but there was an insuperable difficulty in
collecting and equipping the men in winter time, when days
were short and roads were bad.   The weeks passed by, and
Gerona fell long before enough men had been got together to

---

[1] For details, see James's *Naval History*, v. pp. 142–5.

[2] The Proclamation of Nov. 29 ordering this levy, written in a very
magniloquent style, may be found in Belmas, Appendix no. 81.

induce Blake to try a new offensive movement. Why was the congress not called in September rather than in November? Blake had always declared that he was too weak to risk a battle with the French for the raising of the siege, but till the last moment the Catalans contented themselves with arguing with him, and writing remonstrances to the Central Junta, instead of lending him the aid of their last levies.

One or two points connected with this famous siege require a word of comment. It is quite clear that St. Cyr during its early stages did not try his honest best to help Verdier. During June and July his covering army was doing no good whatever at Vich: he pretended that he had placed it there in order to ward off possible attacks by Blake. But it was matter of public knowledge that Blake was far away in Aragon, engaged in his unhappy campaign against Suchet, and that Coupigny, left at Tarragona with a few thousand men, was not a serious danger. St. Cyr could have spared a whole division more for the siege operations, without risking anything. If he had done so, Gerona could have been approached on two sides instead of one, the Mercadal front might have been attacked, and the loose blockade, which was all that Verdier could keep up, for want of more men, might have been made effective. But St. Cyr all through his military career earned a reputation for callous selfishness and habitual leaving of his colleagues in the lurch. On this occasion he was bitterly offended with Verdier, for giving himself the airs of an equal, and corresponding directly with the Emperor. There can be no doubt that he took a malicious pleasure in seeing his failures. It is hardly disguised in his clever and plausible *Journal des Opérations de l'Armée de Catalogne en 1808-1809* [1].

---

[1] Napoleon's comments on the operations of his generals are always interesting, though sometimes founded on imperfect information, or vitiated by predispositions. Of St. Cyr's campaign he writes [Disp. no. 16,004] to Clarke, his Minister of War:

'Il faut me faire un rapport sérieux sur la campagne du général Gouvion Saint-Cyr en Catalogne: (1) Sur les raisons qui l'ont porté à évacuer cette province, lorsque Saragosse était prise et sa jonction faite avec le maréchal Mortier. (2) Sur ce qu'il s'est laissé attaquer par les Espagnols, et ne les a jamais attaqués, et sur ce que, après les avoir toujours battus par la valeur des troupes, il n'a jamais profité de la

Verdier, on the other hand, seems to have felt all through that he was being asked to perform a task almost impossible, when he was set to take Gerona with his own 14,000 men, unaided by the covering army.   His only receipt for success was to try to hurry on the matter by delivering desperate blows.   Both the assault on Monjuich on July 8 and that on the city on September 19 were premature ; there was some excuse for the former : Verdier had not yet realized how well Alvarez could fight.   But the second seems unpardonable, after the warning received at Monjuich.   If the general, as he declared before delivering his assault, mistrusted his own troops, he had no right to order a storm at all, considering his experience of the way in which the Spaniards had behaved in July.   He acted on the fallacious theory that a practicable breach implies a town that can be taken, which is far from being the case if the garrison are both desperate and ingenious in defending themselves.   The only way to deal with such a resolute and capable adversary was to proceed by the slow and regular methods of siegecraft, to sap right up to the ditch before delivering an assault, and batter everything to pieces before risking a man.   This was how Monjuich was actually taken, after the storm had failed. Having neither established himself close under the walls, nor subdued the flanking fires from the Calvary and Chapter redoubts, nor ascertained how far the Spaniards had prepared inner defences for themselves, he had no right to attack at all.

As to Blake, even after making all possible allowances for the fact that he could not trust his troops—the half-rallied wrecks of Maria and Belchite—for a battle in the field, he must yet be pronounced guilty of feebleness and want of ingenuity. If he could never bring up enough regulars to give him a chance of facing St. Cyr, the fault was largely his own : a more forcible

victoire. (3) Sur ce qu'il a, par cet esprit d'égoïsme qui lui est particulier, compromis le siège de Gérone : sur ce qu'il n'a jamais secouru suffisamment l'armée assiégeante, l'a au contraire attirée à lui, et a laissé ravitailler la ville. (4) Sur ce qu'il a quitté l'armée sans permission, sous le vain prétexte de maladie.'

The first point seems unjust to St. Cyr.   From his position in front of Tarragona, after Valls, he had no real chance of combining his operations with the army of Aragon.   But the other three charges seem well founded.

general would have insisted that the Valencian reserves should march [1], and would have stripped Lerida and Tarragona of men : it could safely have been done, for neither Suchet nor Duhesme was showing any signs of threatening those points. He might have insisted that the Catalan Junta should call out the full levy of *somatenes* in September instead of in November. He might also have made a better use of the irregulars already in the field, the bands of Rovira, Milans, and Claros. These miqueletes did admirable service all through the siege, by harassing Verdier's rear and cutting off his convoys, but they were not employed (as they should have been) in combination with the regulars, but allowed, as a rule, to go off on excursions of their own, which had no relation to the main objects of Blake's strategy. The only occasion on which proper use was made of them was when, on September 1, they were set to threaten Verdier's lines, while Garcia Conde's convoy was approaching Gerona. It may be pleaded in the Spanish general's defence that it was difficult to exact obedience from the chiefs : there was a distinct coolness between the regulars and the irregulars, which sometimes led to actual quarrels and conflicts when they met. But here again the reply is that more forcible captain-generals were able to control the miqueletes, and if Blake failed to do so, it was only one more sign of his inadequacy. It is impossible to avoid the conclusion that he mismanaged matters, and that if in his second and third attempts to relieve Gerona he had repeated the tactics of his first, he would have had a far better chance of success. On September 1 only did he make any scientific attempt to distract the enemy's attention and forces, and on that occasion he was successful. Summing things up, it may be said that he was not wrong to refuse battle with the troops that he had actually brought up to Gerona : they would undoubtedly have been

---

[1] The Valencian troops at Maria were eleven battalions, viz. Savoia (three), 1st and 3rd Cazadores de Valencia (two), America (two), Voluntarios de Valencia (one), 1st of Valencia (three). Of these only Savoia (now two batts. only) and Voluntarios de Valencia turned up for the relief of Gerona. Along with them came two fresh regiments, 2nd Cazadores of Orihuela, and Almanza, which had not been at Maria. But these were Murcian, not Valencian, troops.

routed if he had risked a general engagement. His fault was that he did not bring up larger forces, when it was in his power to do so, by the exercise of compulsion on the Catalan and Valencian Juntas. But these bodies must share Blake's responsibilities: they undoubtedly behaved in a slack and selfish fashion, and let Gerona perish, though it was keeping the war from their doors for a long eight months.

All the more credit is due to Alvarez, considering the way in which he was left unsuccoured, and fed with vain promises. A less constant soul would have abandoned the defence long before: the last two months of resistance were his sole work: if he had fallen sick in October instead of December, his subordinates would have yielded long before. But it is not merely for heroic obstinacy that he must be praised. Every detail of the defence shows that he was a most ingenious and provident general: nothing was left undone to make the work of the besiegers hard. Moreover, as Napier has observed, it is not the least of his titles to merit that he preserved a strict discipline, and exacted the possible maximum of work from soldier and civilian alike, without the use of any of those wholesale executions which disgraced the defence of Saragossa. His words were sometimes truculent, but his acts were just and moderate. He never countenanced mob-law, as did Palafox, yet he was far better obeyed by the citizens, and got as good service from them as did the Aragonese commander. He showed that good organization is not incompatible with patriotic enthusiasm, and is far more effective in the hour of danger than reckless courage and blind self-sacrifice.

SECTION XVII: CHAPTER IV

THE AUTUMN CAMPAIGN OF 1809: TAMAMES, OCAÑA, AND ALBA DE TORMES

As early as August 30, when Wellington had not fully completed his retreat from Almaraz and Jaraicejo to Badajoz and Merida, the central Junta had already begun to pester him and his brother, the Ambassador at Seville, with plans for a resumption of the offensive in the valley of the Tagus. On that day Martin de Garay, the Secretary of State, wrote to represent to Wellesley that he had good reason to believe that the troops of Victor, Mortier, and Soult were making a general movement to the rear, and that the moment had arrived when the allied armies in Estremadura and La Mancha should 'move forward with the greatest activity, either to observe more closely the movements of the enemy, or to attack him when circumstances may render it expedient[1].' The French movement of retreat was wholly imaginary, and it is astonishing that the Spanish Government should have been so mad as to believe it possible that 'their retrograde movement may have originated in accounts received from the North, which compel the enemy either to retire into the interior of France, or to take up a position nearer to the Pyrenees.' On a groundless rumour, of the highest intrinsic improbability, they were ready to hurl the newly-rallied troops of Eguia and Venegas upon the French, and to invite Wellington to join in the advance. Irresponsible frivolity could go no further. But the Junta, as has been already said, were eager for a military success, which should cause their unpopularity to be forgotten, and were ready to seize on any excuse for ordering their troops forward. This particular rumour died away—the French were still in force on the Tagus, and, as a matter of fact, the only movement northwards on their part had been the return of Ney's corps

[1] De Garay to Wellesley in *Wellesley Dispatches*, p. 92.

F 2

to Salamanca. But though the truth was soon discovered, the
Junta only began to look out for new excuses for recommencing
active operations.

Wellington, when these schemes were laid before him,
reiterated his refusal to join in any offensive campaign, pointed
out that the allied forces were not strong enough to embark
on any such hazardous undertaking, and bluntly expressed his
opinion that 'he was much afraid, from what he had seen of
the proceedings of the Central Junta, that in the distribution
of their forces they do not consider military defence and military
operations so much as political intrigue, and the attainment
of petty political objects.' He then proceeded to make an
estimate of the French armies, to show their numerical superiority
to the allies ; in this he very much under-estimated the enemy's
resources, calculating the whole force of the eight corps in Spain
at 125,000 men, exclusive of sick and garrisons not available
for active service. As a matter of fact there were 180,000 men,
not 125,000, with the Eagles at that moment, after all deductions
had been made, so that his reasoning was far more cogent than
he supposed [1]. But this only makes more culpable the obstinate
determination of the Junta to resume operations with the much
inferior force which they had at their disposal.

Undismayed by their first repulse, the Spanish ministers were
soon making new representations to Wellesley and Wellington,
in order to induce them to commit the English army to a
forward policy. They sent in repeated schemes for supplying
Wellington with food and transport on a lavish scale [2]; but he
merely expressed his doubts as to whether orders that looked
admirable on paper would ever be carried out in practice. He
consented for the present to remain at Badajoz, as long as he
could subsist his army in its environs, but warned the Junta
that it was more probable that he would retire within the
Portuguese border, for reasons of supply, than that he would
join in another campaign on the Tagus.

Despite of all, the government at Seville went on with its
plans for a general advance, even after they recognized that
Wellington was not to be moved. A grand plan of operations

---

[1] Wellington to Wellesley, from Merida, Sept. 1, 1809.
[2] See the details in Wellesley to Canning, Sept. 2, 1809.

was gradually devised by the War-Minister Cornel and his advisers. Stated shortly it was as follows. The army in La Mancha, which Venegas had rallied after the disaster of Almonacid, was to be raised to a strength of over 50,000 men by the drafting into it of a full two-thirds of Cuesta's old army of Estremadura. On September 21 Eguia marched eastwards up the Guadiana, with three divisions of infantry and twelve or thirteen regiments of cavalry, to join Venegas [1]. The remaining force, amounting to two divisions of infantry and 2,500 cavalry, was left in Estremadura under the Duke of Albuquerque, the officer to whom the government was obliged to assign this army, because the Junta of Badajoz pressed for his appointment and would not hear of any other commander. He was considered an Anglophil, and a friend of some of the Andalusian malcontents, so the force left with him was cut down to the minimum. All the old regular regiments were withdrawn from him, save one single battalion, and he was left with nothing save the newly-raised volunteer units, some of which had behaved so badly at Talavera [2]. His cavalry was soon after reduced by the order to send a brigade to join the Army of the North, so that he was finally left with only five regiments of that arm or about 1,500 sabres. Of his infantry, about 12,000 strong, over 4,000 were absorbed by the garrison of Badajoz, so that he had only 8,000 men available for service in the field.

Eguia, on the other hand, carried with him to La Mancha some 25,000 men, the picked corps of the Estremaduran army; and, as the remains of Venegas's divisions rallied and recruited after Almonacid, amounted to rather more than that number, the united force exceeded 50,000 sabres and bayonets. With this army the Junta intended to make a direct stroke at Madrid, while Albuquerque was directed to show himself on the Tagus, in front of Almaraz and Talavera, with the object of detaining

[1] His head quarters moved from Truxillo on the seventeenth, were at La Serena on the twenty-first, and joined the army of La Mancha about October 1.

[2] See the list of Albuquerque's army in Appendix no. 2. There had been twenty-one regular battalions in Cuesta's army in June. Twenty of these marched off with Eguia, leaving only one (4th Walloon Guards) with Albuquerque.

at least one of the French corps in that direction. It was
hoped, even yet, that Wellington might be induced to join
in this demonstration. If once the redcoats reappeared at the
front, neither Soult nor Mortier could be moved to oppose the
army of La Mancha. Meanwhile Ney and the French corps
in Leon and Old Castille were to be distracted by the use
of a new force from the north, whose composition must be
explained. The Junta held that the last campaign had failed
only because the allies had possessed no force ready to detain
Soult and Ney. If they had not appeared at Plasencia, Wellington, Cuesta, and Venegas would have been able to drive
King Joseph out of his capital. Two months later the whole
position was changed, in their estimation, by the fact that Spain
once more possessed a large ' Army of the Left,' which would
be able to occupy at least two French corps, while the rest of
the allies marched again on Madrid. That such a force existed
did indeed modify the aspect of affairs. La Romana had
been moved to Seville to become a member of the Junta, but
his successor, the Duke Del Parque, was collecting a host very
formidable as far as numbers went. The old army of Galicia
had been reformed into four divisions under Martin de la Carrera,
Losada, Mahy, and the Conde de Belveder—the general whose
name was so unfortunately connected with the ill-fought combat
of Gamonal. These four divisions now comprised 27,000 men,
of whom more than half were newly-raised Galician recruits,
whom La Romana had embodied in the depleted cadres of his
original battalions, after Ney and Soult had evacuated the
province in July. A few of the ancient regiments that had
made the campaign of Espinosa had died out completely—their
small remnants having been drafted into other corps [1]. On the
other hand there were a few new regiments of Galician volunteers
—but La Romana had set his face against the creation of such
units, wisely preferring to place his new levies in the ranks of
the old battalions of the regular army [2]. In the main, there-

---

[1] The only regiments of Blake's original army that seem to be completely dead in October 1809 are 2nd of Catalonia, Naples, Pontevedra,
Compostella. Naples had been drafted into Rey early in 1809. Of the
others I can find no details.

[2] The new Galician regiments which appear in the autumn of 1809 are

fore, the new 'Army of the Left' represented, as far as names
and cadres went, Blake's original 'Army of Galicia[1].' It had
the same cardinal fault as that army, in that it had practically
no cavalry whatever: the single dragoon regiment that Blake
had owned (La Reina) having been almost completely destroyed
in 1808[2]. Each division had a battery; the guns, of which
La Romana's army had been almost destitute in the spring,
had been supplied from England, and landed at Corunna during
the summer.

But the Galician divisions, though the most numerous, were
not the only units which were told off to the new 'Army of the
Left.' Asturias had been free of invaders since Ney and Bonnet
retired from its borders in June 1809. The Central Junta
ordered Ballasteros to join the main army with the few regular
troops in the principality, and ten battalions of the local
volunteers, a force of over 9,000 men. The Asturian Junta,
always very selfish and particularist in its aims, made some
protests but obeyed. Nine of its less efficient regiments were
left behind to watch Bonnet.

Finally the Duke Del Parque himself had been collecting
fresh levies about Ciudad Rodrigo, while the plains of Leon lay
abandoned by the French during the absence of Ney's corps
in the valley of the Tagus. Including the garrison of Rodrigo
he had 9,000 men, all in new units save one old line battalion
and one old militia regiment[3]. Deducting the 3,500 men which
held the fortress, there were seven battalions—nearly 6,000
bayonets—and a squadron or two of horse available for the
strengthening of the field army. These were now told off as
the '5th Division of the Army of the Left'; that of Ballasteros
was numbered the 3rd Division.

The Galician, Asturian, and Leonese divisions had between
them less than 500 horsemen. To make up for this destitution
the Central Junta directed the Duke of Albuquerque to send off
to Ciudad Rodrigo, via the Portuguese frontier, a brigade of his

Monforte de Lemos, Voluntarios de la Muerte, La Union, Lovera, Maceda,
Morazzo.

[1] For the full muster-roll of Del Parque's army in October, see
Appendix no. 4.

[2] Some small fraction of it reappeared in the campaign of 1809.

[3] One battalion of Majorca, and the Militia battalion of Segovia.

cavalry. Accordingly the Prince of Anglona marched north with three regiments [1], only 1,000 sabres in all, and joined Del Parque on September 25. Thus at the end of that month the 'Army of the Left' numbered nearly 50,000 men—all infantry save 1,500 horse and 1,200 gunners. But they were scattered all over North-Western Spain, from Oviedo to Astorga, and from Astorga to Ciudad Rodrigo, and had to be concentrated before they could act. Nor was the concentration devoid of danger, for the French might fall upon the Asturians or the Leonese before they had joined the Galician main body. As a matter of fact the 50,000 never took the field in one mass, for Del Parque left a division under Mahy to protect Galicia, and, when these regiments and the garrison of Rodrigo were deducted, he had but 40,000 in all, including sick and men on detach-ment. This, nevertheless, constituted a formidable force—if it had been in existence in July, Soult and Ney could never have marched against Wellington with their whole strength, and the Talavera campaign might have had another end. But the troops were of varying quality—the Leonese division was absolutely raw: the Galicians had far too many recruits with only two months' training in their ranks, the Estremaduran cavalry had a bad record of disasters. A general of genius might have accomplished something with the Army of the Left—but Del Parque, though more cautious than many of his compeers, was no genius.

The Junta had a deeply-rooted notion that if sufficient pres-sure were applied to Wellesley and Wellington, they would permit Beresford's Portuguese army, now some 20,000 strong, to join Del Parque for the advance into the plains of Leon. They had mistaken their men: Wellington returned as peremp-tory a refusal to their request for the aid of the Portuguese troops as to their demand that his own British army should advance with Albuquerque to the Tagus [2].

Nothing could be more hazardous than the plan finally formulated at the Seville War Office for the simultaneous advance

[1] Borbon, Sagunto, and Granaderos de Llerena, 1,053 sabres in October. These regiments had newly rejoined the Estremaduran army from the rear.

[2] See Wellington to Wellesley, from Badajoz, Oct. 30, 1809.

of the armies of La Mancha, the North, and Estremadura. Even if it had been energetically supported by Wellington and Beresford, it would have been rash : converging operations by several armies starting from distant bases against an enemy concentrated in their midst are proverbially disastrous. In this particular plan three forces—numbering in all about 110,000 men, and starting from points so far apart as Ciudad Rodrigo, Truxillo, and the Passes by La Carolina, were to fall upon some 120,000 men, placed in a comparatively compact body in their centre. A single mistake in the timing of operations, the chance that one Spanish army might outmarch another, or that one of the three might fail to detain any hostile force in its front (as had happened with Venegas during the Talavera Campaign) was bound to be ruinous. The French had it in their power to deal with their enemies in detail, if the least mischance should occur : and with Spanish generals and Spanish armies it was almost certain that some error would be made.

Meanwhile the Junta made their last preparation for the grand stroke, by deposing Venegas from the command of the united army in La Mancha. Eguia held the interim command for a few days, but was to be replaced by Areizaga, an elderly general who had never commanded more than a single division, and had to his credit only courage shown in a subordinate position at the battle of Alcañiz. He was summoned from Lerida, and came hastily to take up his charge.

The sole advantage which the Spaniards possessed in October 1809 was that their enemy did not expect to be attacked. A month after Talavera matters had apparently settled down for the whole autumn, as far as the French generals could calculate. With the knowledge that the Austrian War was over, and that unlimited reinforcements could now be poured into Spain by his brother, King Joseph was content to wait. He had refused to allow Soult to make his favourite move of invading Portugal in the end of August, because he wished the Emperor to take up the responsibility of settling the next plan of campaign, and of determining the number of new troops that would be required to carry it out. The French corps, therefore, were in a semi-circle round Madrid: Soult and Mortier in the central Tagus Valley at Plasencia and Talavera, Victor in La Mancha, with

Sebastiani supporting him at Toledo and Aranjuez, Ney at Salamanca, Dessolles and the Royal Guard as a central reserve in the capital. This was a purely defensive position, and Joseph intended to retain it, till the masses of troops from Germany, with the Emperor himself perchance at their head, should come up to his aid. It does not seem to have entered into his head that the enemy would again take the offensive, after the fiasco of the Talavera campaign, and the bloody lesson of Almonacid.

In September and the early days of October the French hardly moved at all. Ney left his corps at Salamanca, and went on a short leave to Paris on September 25, so little was any danger expected in the plains of Leon. The charge of the 6th corps was handed over to Marchand, his senior divisional general. There was an even more important change of command pending—Jourdan had been soliciting permission to return to France ever since July. He had been on excellent terms with King Joseph, but found it hard to exact obedience from the marshals—indeed he was generally engaged in a controversy either with Victor or with Soult. The Emperor was not inclined to allow him to quit Spain, but Jourdan kept sending in applications to be superseded, backed by medical certificates as to his dangerous state of health. Finally he was granted leave to return, by a letter which reached him on October 25, just as the new campaign was beginning to develop into an acute phase. But he gladly handed over his duties to Soult, who thus became 'major-general' or chief of the Staff to King Joseph, and departed without lingering or reluctance for France, glad to be quit of a most invidious office [1].

Before Jourdan's departure there had been some small movements of the French troops: hearing vague rumours of the passage eastward of Eguia's army, King Joseph ordered a corresponding shift of his own troops towards that quarter. Soult and the 2nd Corps were ordered from Plasencia to Oropesa and Talavera, there relieving Mortier and the 5th Corps, who were to push up the Tagus toward Toledo. This would enable Victor to call up Sebastiani's cavalry and two of his infantry divisions from Toledo into La Mancha. Having thus got

[1] For Jourdan's personal views, see his *Mémoires*, ed. Grouchy, p. 282.

together some 25,000 men, Victor advanced to Daimiel, and
pressed in the advanced posts of the main Spanish army on
October 15. Eguia, who was still in temporary command,
since Areizaga had not yet arrived, made no attempt to stand,
but retired into the passes of the Sierra Morena. This apparent
timidity of the enemy convinced the Marshal that nothing
dangerous was on hand in this quarter. He drew back his army
into cantonments, in a semicircle from Toledo to Tarancon,
leaving the cavalry of Milhaud and Paris out in his front.

Nothing more happened in La Mancha for a fortnight : but
on the other wing, in the kingdom of Leon, matters came to
a head sooner. About the middle of September the bulk of
the Galician army, the divisions of Losada, Belveder and La
Carrera, had moved down the Portuguese frontier via Alcanizas,
and joined Del Parque at Ciudad Rodrigo. On the twenty-fifth
of the same month the Prince of Anglona, with the cavalry
brigade from Estremadura, also came in to unite himself to
the Army of the Left. Del Parque had thus 25,000 infantry
and 1,500 horse concentrated. He had still to be joined by
Ballasteros and the Asturians, who had to pick their way with
caution through the plains of Leon. Mahy and the 4th division
of the Galicians had been left in the passes above Astorga, to
cover the high-road into Galicia. He had a vanguard in
Astorga, under Santocildes, and the town, whose walls had
been repaired by the order of La Romana, was now capable
of making some defence.

Facing Del Parque and his lieutenants there were two distinct
forces. The 6th Corps, now under Marchand, was concentrated
at Salamanca. Having received few or no drafts since its return
from Galicia it was rather weak—its twenty-one battalions and
four cavalry regiments only counted at the end of September
some 13,000 bayonets and 1,200 sabres [1] effective—the sick
being numerous. In the north of Leon and in Old Castile
Kellermann was in charge, with an independent force of no great
strength : his own division of dragoons, nearly 3,000 sabres,
was its only formidable unit. The infantry was composed of
three Swiss battalions, and four or five French battalions,
which had been left in garrisons in Old Castile when the

[1] See the table given by Sprünglin on p. 366 of his *Mémoires*.

regiments to which they belonged went southward in the preceding winter [1]. The whole did not amount to more than
3,500 bayonets. The dragoons were very serviceable in the
vast plains of Leon, but it was with difficulty, and only by
cutting down garrisons to a dangerous extent, that Kellermann
could assemble a weak infantry brigade of 2,000 men to back
the horsemen.

It was nevertheless on Kellermann's side, and by the initiative
of the French, that the first clash took place in north-western
Spain. Hearing vague reports of the movement of the Galician
divisions towards Ciudad Rodrigo, Kellermann sent General
Carrié, with two regiments of dragoons and 1,200 infantry, to
occupy Astorga, being ignorant apparently that it was now
garrisoned and more or less fortified. Carrié found the place
occupied, made a weak attack upon it on October 9, and was
beaten off. He was able to report to his chief that the
Spaniards (i. e. Mahy's division) were in some force in the passes
beyond.

At much the same moment that this fact was ascertained Del
Parque began to move : he had been lying since September 24
at Fuente Guinaldo in the highland above Ciudad Rodrigo.
On October 5 he made an advance as far as Tamames, on the
by-road from Rodrigo to Salamanca which skirts the mountains,
wisely avoiding the high-road in the more level ground by San
Martin del Rio and Castrejon. He had with him his three
Galician divisions and his 1,500 horse, but he had not brought
forward his raw Leonese division under Castrofuerte, which still
lay by Rodrigo. On hearing of the duke's advance Marchand
sent out reconnaissances, and having discovered the position of
the Spaniards, resolved at once to attack them. On October 17
he started out from Salamanca, taking with him his whole corps,
except the two battalions of the 50th regiment, which were left
to garrison the town.

On the afternoon of the next day Marchand came in sight
of the enemy, who was drawn up ready to receive him on the
heights above Tamames. The French general had with him

---

[1] Apparently Kellermann had at this moment a battalion each of the
2nd, 3rd, and 4th Swiss, a battalion of the Garde de Paris, one each of
the 12th Léger and 32nd Line, and one or two of the 122nd.

nineteen battalions, some 12,000 bayonets—his 1,200 horse, and
fourteen guns. Del Parque had 20,000 Galician infantry,
Anglona's cavalry, and eighteen guns: his position was so
strong, and his superiority in infantry so marked, that he was
probably justified in risking a battle on the defensive.

Tamames, an unwalled village of moderate size, lies at the
foot of a range of swelling hills. Its strategical importance
lies in the fact that it is the meeting-place of the two country
roads from Ciudad Rodrigo to Salamanca *via* Matilla, and from
Ciudad Rodrigo to Bejar and the Pass of Baños *via* Nava
Redonda. Placed there, Del Parque's army threatened Salamanca, and had a choice of lines of retreat, the roads to Rodrigo
and to the passes into Estremadura being both open. But
retreat was not the duke's intention. He had drawn up his
army on the heights above Tamames, occupying the village
below with a battalion or two. On the right, where the hillside
was steeper, he had placed Losada and the 2nd Division: on
the left, where the ridge sinks down gently into the plain, was
Martin de la Carrera with the Vanguard Division. The Conde
de Belveder's division—the third—formed the reserve, and was
drawn up on the reverse slope, behind La Carrera. The Prince
of Anglona's cavalry brigade was out on the extreme left, partly
hidden by woods, in the low ground beyond the flank of the
Vanguard.

Marchand, arriving on the ground in the afternoon after
a march of fourteen miles from Matilla, was overjoyed to see the
enemy offering battle, and attacked without a moment's hesitation. His arrangements much resembled those of Victor at
Ucles—though his luck was to be very different. It was clear
that the Spanish left was the weak point, and that the heights
could be turned and ascended on that side with ease. Accordingly
Maucune's brigade (six battalions in all)[1] and the light cavalry,
strengthened by one regiment of dragoons, were ordered to
march off to the right, to form in a line perpendicular to that
of Del Parque, and break down his flank. When this movement
was well developed, Marcognet's brigade (six battalions)[2] was

---

[1] 6th Léger (two batts.), 69th Line (three batts.), and one battalion of
voltigeurs réunis.

[2] 39th and 76th of the Line.

to attack the Spanish centre, to the east of the village of Tamames, while the 25th Léger (two battalions) was to contain the hostile right by a demonstration against the high and difficult ground in that direction. Marchand kept in reserve, behind his centre, the 27th and 59th of the Line (six battalions) and his remaining regiment of dragoons. The vice of this formation was that the striking force—Maucune's column—was too weak: it would have been wise to have strengthened it at the expense of the centre, and to have made a mere demonstration against the heights above the village of Tamames, as well as on the extreme French left.

Maucune accomplished his flank march undisturbed, deployed in front of La Carrera's left and advanced against it. The Spanish general threw back his wing to protect himself, and ordered his cavalry to threaten the flank of the advancing force. But he was nearly swept away: when the skirmishing lines were in contact, the French brigadier ordered his cavalry to charge the centre of the Spanish division: striking in diagonally, Lorcet's Hussars and Chasseurs broke La Carrera's line, and captured the six guns of his divisional artillery. Almost at the same moment Anglona's cavalry came in upon Maucune's flank; but being opposed by two battalions of the 69th in square, they received but one fire and fled hastily to the rear. Maucune then resumed his march up the hill, covering his flank with his horsemen, and pushing La Carrera's broken line before him. But at the head of the slope he met Belveder's reserve, which let the broken troops pass through their intervals, and took up the fight steadily enough. The French were now opposed by triple numbers, and the combat came to a standstill: Maucune's offensive power was exhausted, and he could no longer use his cavalry on the steep ground which he had reached.

Meanwhile, on seeing their right brigade opening the combat with such success, the two other French columns went forward, Marcognet against the Spanish centre, Anselme of the 25th Léger against the extreme right. But the ground was here much steeper: Losada's Galician division stood its ground very steadily, and Marcognet's two regiments made an involuntary halt three-quarters of the way up the heights, under the full fire of the two Spanish batteries there placed and the long line of infantry. The officers made several desperate attempts to induce the columns to resume their advance, but to no effect. They fell in great numbers, and at last the regiments recoiled and descended the hill in disorder. Losada's battalions pursued them to the foot of the slope, and the Spanish light troops in the village sallied out upon their flank, and completed their rout. Marcognet's brigade poured down into the plain as a disordered mass of fugitives, and were only stayed when Marchand brought up the 27th and 59th to their rescue. Del Parque wisely halted the pursuing force before it came into contact with the French reserves, and took up again his post on the heights.

Meanwhile the 25th Léger, on the extreme French right, had not pressed its attack home, and retreated when the central advance was repulsed. Maucune, too, seeing the rout to his left, withdrew from the heights under cover of his cavalry, carrying off only one of the Spanish guns that he had taken early in the fight, and leaving in return a disabled piece of his own on the hill.

The battle was fairly lost, and Marchand retired, under cover of his cavalry along the Salamanca road. The enemy made no serious attempt to pursue him in the plain, where his horsemen would have been able to act with advantage. The French had lost 1,300 or 1,400 men, including 18 officers killed, and a general (Lorcet) and 54 officers wounded [1]. Marcognet's brigade supplied the greater part of the casualties; the 76th lost its eagle, seven officers killed and fifteen wounded: the 39th almost as many. The cavalry and Maucune's brigade suffered little. The very moderate Spanish loss was 713 killed and wounded, mostly in La Carrera's division.

This was the first general action since Baylen in which the Spaniards gained a complete victory. They had a superiority of about seven to four in numbers, and a good position; nevertheless the troops were so raw, and the past record of the Army

---

[1] Marchand in his dispatch says 1,300 men in all were lost, and a gun ; he makes no mention of the eagle. His aide-de-camp, Sprünglin, who has a good account of the battle in his *Mémoires* (pp. 370–1), gives the total of 1,500. The Spaniards exaggerated the loss to 3,000.

BATTLE OF TAMAMES, Oct.18.1809

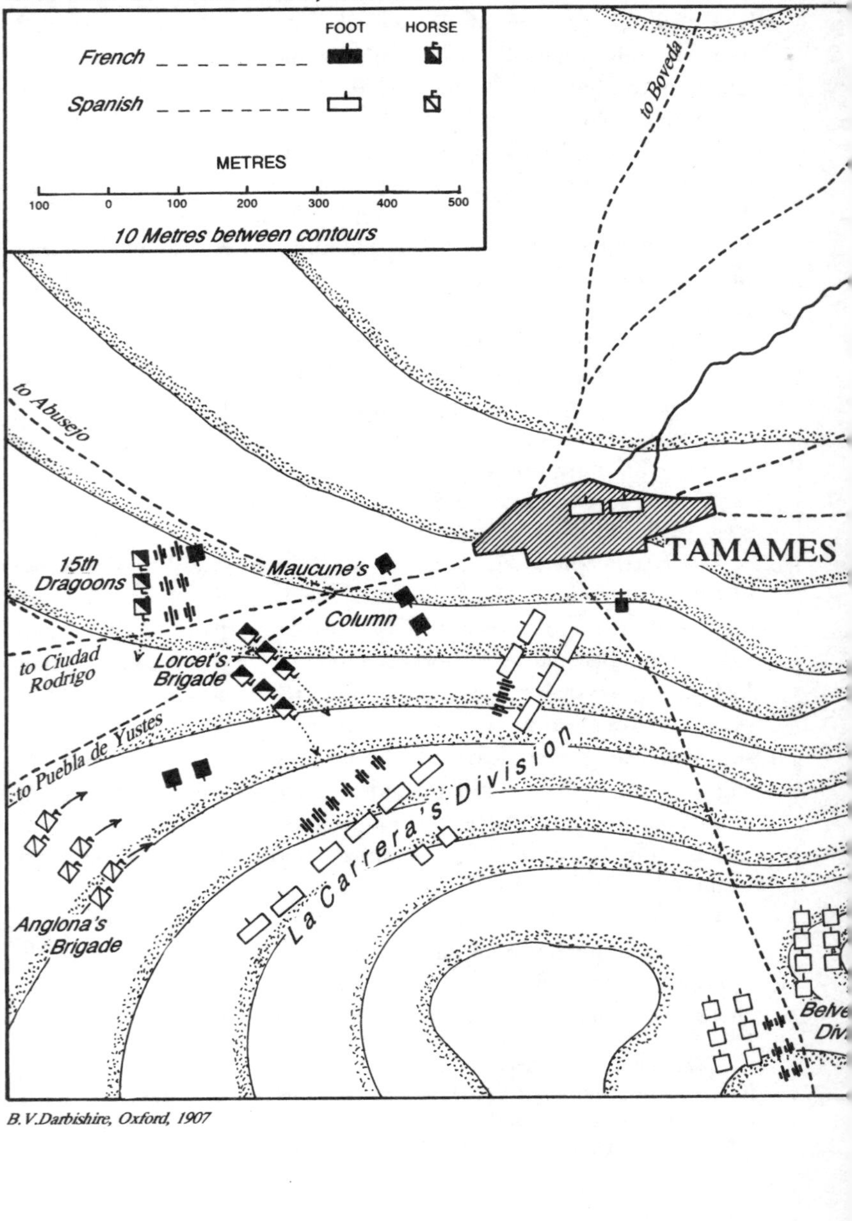
FOOT
HORSE
French
Spanish
METRES
100 0 100 200 300 400 500
10 Metres between contours
to Boveda
to Abusejo
TAMAMES
15th Dragoons
Maucune's Column
Lorcet's Brigade
to Ciudad Rodrigo
to Puebla de Yustes
La Carrera's Division
Anglona's Brigade

B.V.Darbishire, Oxford, 1907

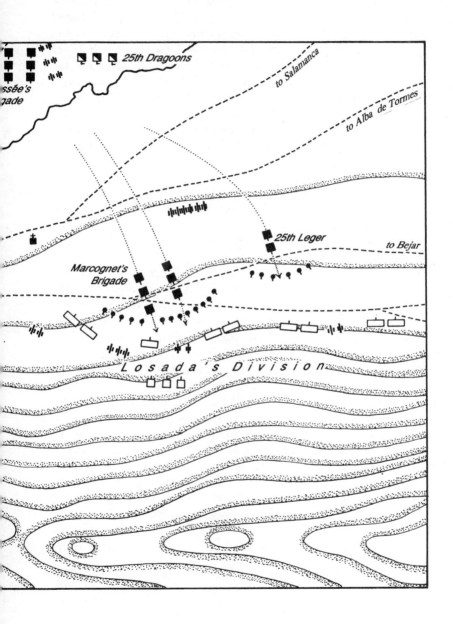

25th Dragoons

ssée's
gade

to Salamanca

to Alba de Tormes

to Bejar

25th Leger

Marcognet's
Brigade

Losada's Division

of the Left was so disheartening, that the victory reflects considerable credit on the Galicians.   The 6th Corps was reckoned the best of all the French units in Spain, being entirely composed of old regiments from the army of Germany.   It is not too much to say that Ney's absence was responsible for the defeat of his men.   Marchand attacked at three points, and was weak at each.   The Marshal would certainly have massed a whole division against the Spanish left, and would not have been stopped by the stout resistance made by Belveder's reserve. A demonstration by a few battalions would have 'contained' Losada's troops on the left, where the ground was too unfavourable for a serious attack [1].

On the 19th of October the beaten army reached Salamanca by a forced march.   Marchand feared that the enemy would now manœuvre either by Ledesma, so as to cut him off from Kellermann and the troops in the north, or by Alba de Tormes, so as to intercept his communication with Madrid.   In either case he would have to retreat, for there was no good defensive ground on the Tormes to resist an army coming from the west. As a matter of fact Del Parque moved by Ledesma, for two reasons : the first was that he wished to avoid the plains, fearing that Kellermann might have joined the 6th Corps with his cavalry division.   The second was that, by moving in this direction, he hoped to make his junction with Ballasteros, who had started from the Asturias to join him, and had been reported to have moved from Astorga to Miranda del Duero, and to be feeling his way south-eastward.   The juncture took place : the Asturian division, after an unsuccessful attempt to cut off the garrison of Zamora on the seventeenth, had marched to Ledesma, and met the main army there.   Del Parque had now 28,000 men, and though still very weak in cavalry, thought himself strong enough to march on Salamanca.   He reached it on October 25 and found it evacuated.   Marchand, learning that Kellermann was too far off to help him, and knowing that no reinforcements from Madrid could reach him for many

---

[1] ' La perte de cette affaire fut entièrement due à la faute que fit le Général Marchand de multiplier ses attaques, et de s'engager par petits paquets.   Tout le monde se mêlait de donner son avis, et on remarquait l'absence de M. le Maréchal,' says Sprünglin in p. 371 of his *Mémoires*.

days, had evacuated the town on the previous evening. He retired towards Toro, thus throwing up his communications with Madrid in order to make sure of joining Kellermann. This seems doubtful policy, for that general could only aid him with 4,000 or 5,000 men, and their joint force would be under 20,000 strong. On the other hand, by retiring on Peñaranda or Medina de Campo, and so approaching the King's army, he could have counted on picking up much larger reinforcements, and on resuming the struggle with a good prospect of success.

As a matter of fact Jourdan, on hearing of the disaster of Tamames, had dispatched, to aid the 6th Corps, Godinot's brigade of Dessolles' division, some 3,500 bayonets, from Madrid, and Heudelet's division of the 2nd Corps, about 4,000 strong, from Oropesa, as well as a couple of regiments of cavalry. He made these detachments without scruple, because there was as yet no sign of any activity on the part of the Spanish armies of La Mancha and Estremadura. A week later he would have found it much more hazardous to weaken his front in the valley of the Tagus. These were the last orders issued by Jourdan, who resigned his post on October 31, while Soult on November 5 arrived at Madrid and replaced him as chief of the staff to King Joseph.

Del Parque, not unnaturally elated by his victory, now nourished ambitious ideas of clearing the whole of Leon and Old Castile of the enemy, being aware that the armies of La Mancha and Estremadura ought now to be on the move, and that full occupation would be found ere long for the French corps in the valley of the Tagus. He ordered up his 5th Division, the raw Leonese battalions of Castrofuerte, from Ciudad Rodrigo, and made vehement appeals to the Portuguese Government to lend him the whole of Beresford's army for a great advance up the Douro. The Regency, though much pressed by the Spanish ambassador at Lisbon, gave a blank refusal, following Wellington's advice to have nothing to do with offensive operations in Spanish company [1]. But part of

---

[1] Del Parque's demands had begun as early as the end of September, see Wellington to Castlereagh, Badajoz, Sept. 29, *Dispatches*, v. 200–1, and cf. Wellington to Forjaz, Oct. 15, ibid. 223.

Beresford's troops were ordered up to the frontier, not so much to lend a moral support to Del Parque's advance [1] as to be ready to defend their own borders in the event of his defeat. Showing more prudence than Wellington had expected, Del Parque did not push forward from Salamanca, when he became certain that he would have to depend on his own forces alone. Even after the arrival of his reserves from Rodrigo he remained quiet, only pushing out reconnaissances to discover which way the enemy had gone. He had, in fact, carried out his part in the Central Junta's plan of campaign, by calling the attention of the French to the north, and distracting troops thither from the King's army. It was now the time for Albuquerque and Areizaga to take up the game, and relieve him. Marchand meanwhile had retired across the Douro, and taken up an extended line behind it from Zamora to Tordesillas—a front of over forty miles—which it would have been impossible to hold with his 13,000 men against a heavy attack delivered at one point. But he was hardly in position when Kellermann arrived, took over the command, and changed the whole plan of campaign (November 1). He had left two battalions to guard Benevente, two to hold Valladolid, and had only brought up his 3,000 dragoons and 1,500 infantry. Seeing that it was absolutely necessary to recover the line of communication with Madrid, he ordered the 6th Corps to leave Zamora and Toro, mass at Tordesillas, and then cross the Douro to Medina del Campo, the junction point of the roads from Madrid, Segovia, Valladolid, and Toro. To this same place he brought up his own small force, and having received Godinot's brigade from Madrid, had thirty-four battalions and eighteen squadrons concentrated—about 23,000 men. Though not yet joined by the other troops from the south—Heudelet's division—he now marched straight upon Salamanca in two columns, one by Cantalapiedra, the other by Fuente Sauco, intending to offer battle to Del Parque.

But the duke, much to the surprise of every one, utterly refused to fight, holding the plain too dangerous for an army so weak in cavalry as his own, and over-estimating the enemy's

[1] Wellington to Beresford, Nov. 16, 1809.

force at 36,000 men [1]. He retired from Salamanca, after having held it less than a fortnight, on November 5, and took not the road to Ciudad Rodrigo but that to Bejar and the Pass of Baños, as if he were about to pass the mountains into Estremadura [2]. This was an excellent move: the French could not pursue him in force without evacuating Old Castile and Leon, which it would have been impossible for them to contemplate. For when Kellermann had concentrated his troops to strike at Salamanca, there was nothing left behind him in the vast upland save a battalion or two at Benevente, Valladolid, and Burgos. Mahy, from Galicia, and the Asturians might have overrun the whole region unopposed. As it was, the whole of the provinces behind the Douro showed signs of bursting out into insurrection. Julian Sanchez, the Empecinado, and other guerrillero chiefs, whose names were soon to be famous, raised large bands during the absence of the normal garrisons, and swept the country-side, capturing convoys and cutting the lines of communication between Vittoria, Burgos, and Valladolid. Porlier came down with a flying column from the Asturias, assaulted Palencia, and threatened Burgos. The French governors on every side kept reporting their perilous position, when they could get a message through to Madrid [3].

Realizing that he must cover his rear, or the whole of Old Castile would be lost to the insurgents, Kellermann, after occupying Salamanca on November 6, left the 6th Corps and Godinot's brigade distributed between Ledesma, Salamanca, and Alba de Tormes, watching Del Parque, and returned in haste with his own troops to the Douro. He commenced to send out flying columns from Valladolid to deal with the guerrilleros, but did not work too far afield, lest he might be called back by a new forward movement on the part of the Army of the Left. But in a few days he had to recast all his arrangements, for—as

---

[1] He sent this estimate to Wellington, see the latter to Beresford, Badajoz, Nov. 16.

[2] The Junta afterwards contemplated bringing him down to join Albuquerque, via Plasencia, which was free of French troops, since Soult had moved to Oropesa. But this does not seem to have been thought of so early as Nov. 5.

[3] See Soult to Clarke, from Madrid, Nov. 6, for these movements.

Del Parque had calculated—the campaign in La Mancha had just opened, and the position of the French in Leon and Old Castile was profoundly affected by the new developments.

In the south, as we have already explained, the Junta designed Albuquerque's army of Estremadura to be a mere demonstrating force, while Areizaga's 55,000 men were to strike the real blow. The Estremaduran troops, as was proper, moved early to draw the attention of the enemy. Albuquerque's first division under Bassecourt— 6,000 infantry and 600 horse—was on the Tagus from Almaraz to Meza de Ibor : his second division under St. Juan and the rest of his cavalry—some 4,000 in all—were moving up from Truxillo. Bassecourt began by sending a small force of all arms across the river at Almaraz, to drive in Soult's outposts and spread reports abroad in all directions that he was acting as the vanguard to Wellington's army, which was marching up from Badajoz. Unfortunately the full effect that he desired was not produced, because deserters informed Soult that the British Army was still quiescent on the Guadiana[1]. The French made no movement, and left the 2nd Corps alone to watch Albuquerque.

Meanwhile Areizaga, within a few days of assuming the command of the army of La Mancha, commenced his forward movement. On November 3, having concentrated his eight divisions of infantry and his 5,700 horse at Santa Cruz de Mudela, at the foot of the passes, he gave the order to advance into the plains. The head quarters followed the high-road, with the train and three divisions : the rest, to avoid encumbering the *chaussée*, marched by parallel side-roads, but were never more than ten miles from their Commander-in-chief : at any rate Areizaga avoided the sin of dispersion. His army was the best which had been seen under the Spanish banners since Tudela. The men had all been furnished with new clothes and equipment since August, mainly from English stores landed at Cadiz. There were sixty guns, and such a body of cavalry as had never yet been collected during the

---

[1] Soult to Clarke, from Madrid, Nov. 6. The deserters were a body of twenty-one men of the Walloon Guards, who had enlisted from Dupont's prisoners in order to get a chance of escaping : they reached Oropesa on Oct. 25.

war. The value of the troops was very unequal; if there were many old battalions of the regular army, there were also many new units composed of half-trained Andalusian levies. The cavalry included the old runaways of Medellin, and many other regiments of doubtful value. The morale was on the whole not satisfactory. 'I wish I had anything agreeable to communicate to you from this army' wrote Colonel Roche, a British officer attached to Areizaga's staff, to Wellington. 'The corps which belonged to the original army of La Mancha are certainly in every respect superior to those from Estremadura, and from everything that I can learn none of those abuses which were to be lamented in the army of Estremadura existed here—or, at least, in a much less degree. But nothing can exceed the general discontent, dissatisfaction, and demoralization of the mass of the people and of the army. How can anybody who has the faculty of reason separate the inefficiency, intrigue, bad organization, and consequent disasters of the army from the source of all those evils in the Junta? There is not a man of the least reflection who, as things now stand, has a hope of success; and this is the more melancholy, because the mass of the people are just as inveterate in their resentment and abhorrence of the French as at the first hour of the revolution[1].' The fact seems to have been that the superior officers doubted the wisdom of taking the offensive according to the Junta's orders, and had no confidence in Areizaga, who was only known as a fighting general, and had no reputation for skill. The rank and file, as Arteche remarks, were disposed to do their duty, but had no confidence in their luck [2]. Their government and not their generals must take the major part of the blame for the disaster that followed.

Areizaga was well aware that his best chance was to strike with extreme boldness and vigour, and to dash into the midst of the French before they could concentrate. Hence his march was at first conducted with great rapidity and decision; between the 3rd and the 8th of November he made nearly fifteen miles a day, though the roads were somewhat broken up by the autumn

---

[1] Roche to Wellington, from Santa Cruz de la Mudela, *Wellington Supplementary Dispatches*, vi. 394. Cf. also the same to the same, vi. 414.

[2] *Historia de la Guerra de la Independencia*, vii. 283.

rains. On the eighth he reached La Guardia, eighty miles from his starting-point, and his advanced cavalry under General Freire had its first skirmish with a brigade of Milhaud's dragoons at Costa de Madera, near Dos Barrios. The Spanish horse deployed in such numbers that the French were compelled to move off in haste and with some loss, though they had beaten off with ease the first two or three regiments which had gone forward against them.

The Spanish advance had been so rapid and so unexpected that Soult and King Joseph had been taken completely by surprise. On November 6 the Marshal had reported to Paris that 'the troops on the Tagus and in La Mancha are up to the present unmolested, and as, from all I can learn, there is no prospect of the enemy making any offensive movement on that side, I intend to form from them a strong flying column to hunt the brigands in the direction of Burgos[1].' Only four days later he had to announce that an army of at least 40,000 men was close in front of Aranjuez, and not more than thirty-five miles from Madrid, and that he was hurrying together troops from all quarters to make head against them. At the moment indeed, there was nothing directly between Areizaga's vanguard at La Guardia and the Spanish capital, save the Polish division of the 4th Corps stationed at Aranjuez, and Milhaud's five regiments of dragoons at Ocaña. If the Spaniard had pushed on for three days more at his starting pace, he might have crossed the Tagus, and have forced King Joseph to fight, close in front of Madrid, with an imperfectly assembled army. On the ninth and tenth Leval's Germans were in march from Toledo to Aranjuez to join Sebastiani's Poles : Mortier's first division was hurrying from Talavera to Toledo, and his second division was making ready to follow. The 2nd Corps, despite Albuquerque's demonstration in front of Almaraz, was preparing to quit Oropesa, in order to replace Mortier's men at Talavera. Victor, in the meanwhile, with the First Corps, was lying in front of Toledo at Ajofrin, with his cavalry at Mora and Yebenes : he reported that no hostile force had come his way, but that he had ascertained that a large army had marched past his front along the great *chaussée* from Madridejos to Aranjuez. He was

---

[1] Soult to Clarke, Madrid, Nov. 6.

in a position to attack it in rear and flank, if there was a sufficient force gathered in its front to justify him in closing[1].

But on reaching La Guardia, Areizaga seemed suddenly to
realize the dangers of his movement. No doubt it was the
news that Victor was almost in his rear that paralysed him, but
he halted on the ninth, when a bold advance would certainly
have enabled him to seize Aranjuez, by evicting the small
force under Milhaud and Sebastiani. For three fatal days,
the 9th, 10th, and 11th of November, the Spanish main body
remained halted in a mass at La Guardia, as if for the special
purpose of allowing the enemy to concentrate. On the eleventh
Areizaga at last began to move again : he sent forward the
whole of his cavalry, supported by Zayas and his Vanguard
division, to press back the force in his front. They found
Milhaud's five regiments of dragoons ranged in line of battle
before the small town of Ocaña, and supported by Sebastiani's
Polish infantry. Freire advanced, using his triple superiority
of numbers to turn both flanks of the French cavalry ; Milhaud,
after some partial charges, retired behind the Poles, who formed
a line of six battalion squares. The Spanish horse made a
half-hearted attempt to attack them, but were repelled by their
rolling fire before they came to close quarters, and drew back.
It was now four o'clock in the afternoon, and the Spanish
infantry was only just beginning to come up. Zayas and
Freire agreed that it was too late to begin a second attack, and
put off fighting till the next morning. But during the night
the French evacuated Ocaña and retired to Aranjuez, wisely
judging that it would be insane to wait for the arrival of the
Spanish main body. They had lost about fifty men, Freire's
cavalry just over two hundred.

Next day [November 12], Areizaga brought up the whole of
his army to Ocaña, and his cavalry reconnoitred up to the gates
of Aranjuez and the bridge of Puente La Reyna. Sebastiani
made ready to defend them, and having been joined by the
German division from Toledo, wrote to Soult to say that he
would resist to the last extremity, in order to gain time for
the arrival of Victor's corps and the other troops which were

---

[1] Soult to Clarke, Madrid, Nov. 10.

marching up from the west and north[1]. The attack which he
expected was never delivered. Areizaga, nervous about the
presence of the 1st Corps on his flank, had resolved to shift his
army eastward to get further away from it. Abandoning his
line of communication by La Guardia and Madridejos, he
marched his whole force by cross-roads parallel to the Tagus up
to La Zarza, and seized the fords of Villamanrique, twenty-five
miles above Aranjuez, on the Madrid-Albacete road. If Victor,
as he supposed, had been manœuvring on his flank, this movement would have cut him off from his base in Andalusia, and
have left him only the mountains of Murcia as a line of retreat.
But, as a matter of fact, the 1st Corps was no longer at Ajofrin
or Mora, but had been called behind the Tagus, so that his
retreat was safer than he supposed.

Soult and King Joseph, meanwhile, had been completing their
concentration. They had written to Kellermann, ordering him
to send back to Madrid without delay the brigade of Dessolles'
division under Godinot which had been lent him, and to spare
them as well one infantry brigade of the 6th Corps. These
troops were too far off to be available at once; but of the
remainder of their units the Royal Guard and Spanish battalions
of King Joseph, with Dessolles' remaining brigade, were moved
out to support Sebastiani. Victor had been brought back across
the Tagus, and was also marching on Aranjuez. Mortier's corps
was concentrated at Toledo, while the 2nd Corps was in motion
from Oropesa to Talavera, having discovered no signs of a serious
advance on the part of Albuquerque. The care of Madrid was
handed over to the incomplete French division of the 4th Corps[2],
some of whose battalions were dispersed at Guadalajara, Alcala,
Segovia, and other garrisons. Paris's light cavalry of the same
corps was also at this moment watching the roads to the east of
Madrid.

On the twelfth Areizaga threw Lacy's division across the
Tagus, and laid down two pontoon bridges near Villamanrique,
so as to be able to bring over his whole army in the shortest
possible time. But the thirteenth, fourteenth, and fifteenth

[1] Sebastiani to Soult, night of the twelfth–thirteenth, from Aranjuez.
[2] It had still no divisional general, and was officially known by the
name of 'Sebastiani's division'—regiments 28th, 32nd, 58th, 75th.

were days of storm, the river rose high, and the artillery and
train stuck fast on the vile cross-roads from Ocaña over which
they were being brought.   In consequence less than half the
Spanish army was north of the Tagus on November 15, though
the advance cavalry pushed on to the line of the Tajuna, and
skirmished with Paris's *chasseurs* about Arganda.   It seemed
nevertheless that Areizaga was committed to an advance upon
Madrid by the high-road from Albacete, wherefore Soult blew
up the bridges of Aranjuez and Puente la Reyna, and ordered
Victor to march from Aranjuez on Arganda with the 1st Corps,
nearly 20,000 men, purposing to join him with the King's
reserves and to offer battle on the Tajuna, while Mortier and
Sebastiani's Poles and Germans should fall upon the enemy's
flank.   But this plan was foiled by a new move upon Areizaga's
part; he now commenced a retreat as objectless as his late
advance.   Just as Victor's cavalry came in touch with his front,
he withdrew his whole army across the Tagus, destroyed his
bridges, and retired to La Zarza on the seventeenth, evidently
with the intention of recovering his old line of communication
with Andalusia, via Ocaña and Madridejos.

The moment that this new departure became evident, Soult
reversed the marching orders of all his columns save Victor's, and
bade them return hastily to Aranjuez, where the bridge was repaired in haste, and to cross the Tagus there, with the intention
of intercepting Areizaga's line of retreat and forcing a battle
on him near Ocaña.   Victor, however, had got so far to the east
that it would have wasted time to bring him back to Aranjuez,
wherefore he was directed to cross the river at Villamanrique and
follow hard in Areizaga's rear.

On the morning of the eighteenth Milhaud's and Paris's
cavalry, riding at the head of the French army, crossed the Tagus
at Aranjuez, and pressing forward met, between Ontigola and
Ocaña, Freire's horsemen moving at the head of Areizaga's
column, which on this day was strung out between La Zarza
and Noblejas, marching hastily westward towards the high-
road.   The collision of Milhaud and Freire brought about
the largest cavalry fight which took place during the whole
Peninsular War.   For Milhaud and Paris had eight regiments,
nearly 3,000 men, while three of Freire's four divisions were

present, to the number of over 4,000 sabres.   On neither side
was any infantry in hand.

Sebastiani, who had come up with the light cavalry of his
corps, was eager for a fight, and engaged at once.   Charging
the Spanish front line with Paris's light horse, he broke it with
ease : but Freire came on with his reserves, forming the greater
part of them into a solid column—an odd formation for cavalry.
Into this mass Milhaud charged with four regiments of dragoons.
The heaviness of their formation did not suffice to enable the
Spaniards to stand.   They broke when attacked, and went to
the rear in disorder, leaving behind them eighty prisoners and
some hundreds of killed and wounded.   The French lost only
a few scores, but among them was Paris, the not unworthy
successor of the adventurous Lasalle in command of the light
cavalry division attached to the 4th Corps.

Moving forward in pursuit of the routed squadrons, Sebastiani
approached Ocaña, but halted on discovering that there was
already Spanish infantry in the town.   The head of Areizaga's
long column had reached it, while the cavalry combat was in
progress : the rest was visible slowly moving up by cross-roads
from the east.   Soult was at once apprised that the enemy's
army was close in his front—so close that it could not get away
without fighting, for its train and rearguard were still far
behind, and would be cut off if the main body moved on
without making a stand.

Areizaga, though he had shown such timidity when faced by
Sebastiani's 9,000 men at Aranjuez, and by Victor's 20,000 on
the Tajuna, now offered battle to the much more formidable
force which Soult was bringing up.   He was indeed compelled
to fight, partly because his men were too weary to move forward
that night, partly because he wished to give time for his train to
arrive and get on to the *chaussée*.

On the morning of the nineteenth his army was discovered
drawn up in two lines on each side of the town of Ocaña.   There
were still some 46,000 infantry and 5,500 cavalry under arms
despite of the losses of the late week[1].   The oncoming French army

---

[1] Colborne, in a letter dated December 5, says ' we had 46,100 infantry
and nearly 6,000 cavalry drawn out, in a very bad position.'   He was
present all through the campaign, but wrote no full report.

was smaller; though it mustered 5,000 horse it had only 27,000 foot—the Germans and Poles of Sebastiani, Mortier with nearly the whole of the 5th Corps, a brigade of Dessolles' division, the King's guards, and the cavalry of Milhaud, Paris, and Beauregard [1]. Victor was too far off to be available; having found the flooded Tagus hard to cross, he was on this day barely in touch with the extreme rearguard of Areizaga's army which was escorting the train. Being nearly twenty miles from Ocaña, he could not hope to arrive in time for the general action, if it was to be delivered next morn. If Areizaga stood firm for another day, Victor would be pressing him from the flank and rear while the main army was in his front: but it was highly probable that Areizaga would not stand, but would retreat at night; all his previous conduct argued a great disinclination to risk a battle. Wherefore Soult and the King, after a short discussion [2], agreed to attack at once, despite their great numerical inferiority. In the open plain of La Mancha a difference of 16,000 or 17,000 infantry was not enough to outweigh the superior quality and training of the French army.

There is, so to speak, no position whatever at Ocaña: the little unwalled town lies in a level upland, where the only

---

[1] Viz. Mortier's Infantry Divisions (Girard and Gazan),

twenty-two batts. [one regiment deducted] about	12,000	men
Sebastiani's Polish Division and German Division (under Werlé and Leval)	,, 8,000	,,
Rey's Brigade of Dessolles' Division of the Central Reserve	,, 3,500	,,
The King's Reserves, viz. four guard battalions and three others	,, 3,500	,,
Milhaud's Dragoons, five regiments . .	,, 1,800	,,
Paris's Light Cavalry, attached to 4th Corps, three regiments	,, 1,000	,,
Beauregard's Cavalry of the 5th Corps, four regiments	,, 1,500	,,
The King's Cavalry, one regiment of the Guards, one of Chasseurs . . .	,, 700	,,
Artillery, Sappers, &c.	,, 1,500	,,

Total about 33,500 men

[2] Joseph declared that he urged instant attack when Soult advised waiting for Victor. See his letter in vol. vii of Ducasse's *Life and Correspondence of Joseph Napoleon*.

natural feature is a ravine which passes in front of the place ;
it is sufficiently deep and broad at its western end to constitute
a military obstacle, but east of the town gradually grows
slighter and becomes a mere dip in the ground.   Areizaga had
chosen this ravine to indicate the line of his left and centre ;
but on his right, where it had become so shallow as to afford
no cover, he extended his troops across and beyond it.   The
town was barricaded and occupied, to form a central support to
the line.   There were olive-groves in the rear of Ocaña which
might have served to hide a reserve, or to mark a position for
a rally in case a retreat should become necessary.   But Areizaga
had made no preparation of this sort.   His trains, with a small
escort, had not arrived even on the morning of the nineteenth,
but were still belated on the cross-roads from Noblejas and
La Zarza.

The order of the Spanish army in line of battle is difficult
to reconstruct, for Areizaga uses very vague language in the
dispatch in which he explained his defeat, and the other documents available, though they give detailed accounts of some of
the corps, say little or nothing of others.   It seems, however,
that Zayas, with the vanguard division, formed the extreme
left, behind the deepest part of the ravine, with a cavalry
brigade under Rivas on its flank and rear.   He had the town
of Ocaña on his right.   Then followed in the line, going from
left to right, the divisions of Vigodet, Giron, Castejon, and
Lacy.   Those of Copons, Jacomé, and Zerain appear to have
formed a second line in support of the other four[1].   Vigodet's
left was in the town of Ocaña and strongly posted, but the
other flank, where Lacy lay, was absolutely in the air, with no
natural feature to cover it.   For this reason Areizaga placed

[1] This order seems the only one consistent with the sole sentence in
Areizaga's dispatch to the Junta in which he explains his battle-array :
' Inmediatamente formé por mí mismo la primera linea en direccion de
Ocaña, colocando por la izquierda la division de Vigodet, defendida por la
frente de la gran zanja, y por su derecha las divisiones de Giron, Castejon
y Lacy : la de Copons formaba martillo, junta á las tapias de la villa,
inmediata á la de Giron, y las demás la secunda linea á distancia
competente para proteger á la primera.'   The unnamed divisions which
must have lain beyond Copons in the right of the second line are Jacomé
and Zerain.

beyond it Freire, with the whole of the cavalry except the brigade on the extreme left under Rivas. Unfortunately the Spanish horse, much shaken by the combat of the preceding day, was a weak protection for the flank, despite its formidable numbers. The sixty guns of the artillery were drawn out in the intervals of the infantry divisions of the first and second line.

Soult's plan of attack was soon formed. The ravine made the Spanish left—beyond Ocaña—inaccessible, but also prevented it from taking any offensive action. The Marshal therefore resolved to ignore it completely, and to concentrate all his efforts against the hostile centre and right, in the open ground. The scheme adopted was a simple one : Sebastiani's Polish and German divisions were to attack the Spanish right wing, and when they were at close quarters with the enemy the main mass of the French cavalry was to fall upon Freire's horse, drive it out of the field, and attack on the flank the divisions already engaged with the infantry. For this purpose Milhaud's, Paris's, and Beauregard's regiments, more than 3,500 sabres, were massed behind the Poles and Germans. For a time their march would be masked by olive-groves and undulations of the ground, so that they might come in quite suddenly upon the enemy. Mortier with his first division—that of Girard—and a regiment of Gazan's, followed in the rear of the Polish and German infantry, to support their frontal attack. Dessolles, with his own brigade and Gazan's remaining one, took post opposite Ocaña, ready to fall upon the Spanish centre, when the attack to his left should have begun to make way. He had in his front the massed artillery of the 4th and 5th Corps, thirty guns under Senarmont, which took ground on a low knoll above the great ravine, from which they could both play upon the town of Ocaña and also enfilade part of the Spanish line to its immediate right—Vigodet's division and half of Giron's. Finally the King, with his guards and other troops, horse and foot, were placed to the right rear of Dessolles, to act as a general reserve, or to move against Zayas if he should attempt to cross the ravine and turn the French right.

The plan, despite of some checks at the commencement, worked in a satisfactory fashion. The German and Polish

divisions of Leval and Werlé attacked Lacy's and Castejon's
divisions, which gave back some little way, in order to align
themselves with Vigodet who was sheltered by the slight eastern
end of the ravine. The enemy followed and brought up six guns
to the point to play upon the new position which the Spaniards
had taken up. The forward movement was continuing, when
suddenly to the surprise of the French, Lacy's, Castejon's, and
Giron's men, leaving their places in the line, made a furious
counter-charge upon the Poles and Germans, drove them back for
some distance, and threw them into disorder. This movement was
no result of Areizaga's generalship: he had betaken himself to the
summit of the church-tower of Ocaña, an inconvenient place from
which to issue orders, and practically left his subordinates to fight
their own battle. Mortier was forced to bring forward Girard's
division to support his broken first line. It was hotly engaged
with Lacy and Giron, when suddenly it felt the Spaniards
slacken in their fire, waver, and break. This was the result of
the intervention of a new force in the field. The great mass of
French squadrons, which had been sent under Sebastiani to turn
the Spanish right, had now come into action. Arriving close to
Freire's cavalry before it was discovered, it fell on that untrustworthy corps, and scattered it to the winds in a few minutes.
Then, while three or four regiments followed the routed horsemen, the rest turned inwards upon the hostile infantry. The
flanks of the first and second lines of Areizaga's right were
charged simultaneously, and hardly a regiment had time to get
into square. Brigade after brigade was rolled up and dispersed
or captured; the mass of fugitives, running in upon the troops
that were frontally engaged with Girard, wrecked them completely. Of the five divisions of the Spanish left, a certain
number of steady regiments got away, by closing their ranks and
pushing ahead through the confusion, firing on friend and foe
alike when they were hustled. But many corps were annihilated,
and others captured wholesale. The last seems to have been the
fate of nearly the whole of Jacomé's division of the second line,
as hardly a single unit from it is reported as rallied a month
later, and the French accounts speak of a whole column of
6,000 men which laid down its arms in a mass before the light
cavalry of the 4th Corps. Just as the Spanish right broke up,

Dessolles with his two brigades, followed by the King's reserve, crossed the ravine and attacked the town of Ocaña, and the two divisions—Vigodet and Copons—which lay in first and second line immediately to the east of it. These retired, and got away in better order than their comrades to the right. Of all the Spanish army only Zayas's vanguard division, on the extreme left, now remained intact. Areizaga had sent it an order to cross the ravine and attack the French right, when he saw his army beginning to break up. Then, a few minutes later, he sent another order bidding it close to the right and cover the retreat. After this the Commander-in-Chief descended from his tower, mounted his horse, and fled. Zayas carried out the second order, moved to the right, and found himself encompassed by masses of fugitives from Giron's, Castejon's, and Lacy's broken divisions, mixed with French cavalry. He sustained, with great credit to himself and his troops, a rearguard action for some miles, till near the village of Dos Barrios, where his line was broken and his men at last mixed with the rest of the fugitives [1].

The whole routed multitude now streamed wildly over the plain, with the French cavalry in hot pursuit. Thousands of prisoners were taken, and the chase only ended with nightfall. The fugitives headed straight for the Sierra Morena, and reached it with a rapidity even greater than that which they had used in their outward march a fortnight before. Victor's cavalry arrived in time to take up the pursuit next morning: they had on their way to the field captured the whole of the trains of the Spanish army, on the road from Noblejas to Ocaña. The losses of Areizaga's army were appalling ; about 4,000 killed and wounded and 14,000 prisoners. Thirty flags and fifty out of the sixty guns had been captured. When the wrecks of the army had been rallied in the passes, three weeks after the battle, only some 21,000 infantry[2] and 3,000 horse were reported as

---

[1] The only detailed accounts of the Spanish movements that I have discovered are the divisional reports of Lacy and Zayas, both in the Foreign Office archives at the Record Office. Areizaga's dispatch is so vague as to be nearly useless.

[2] Viz. Zayas, Vigodet, and Castejon, about 4,000 men each, Copons 3,000, Giron 2,500, remains of the other three divisions about 3,500. From the returns in the Madrid War Office.

present.   The divisions of Lacy, Jacomé, and Zerain had practically disappeared, and the others had lost from a third to a half of their numbers.   The condition of the cavalry was peculiarly disgraceful ; as it had never stood to fight, its losses represent not prisoners, for the most part, but mere runaways who never returned to their standards.   The French had lost about 90 officers and 1,900 men, nearly all in the divisions of Leval, Werlé, and Girard[1].   The cavalry, which had delivered the great stroke and won the battle, suffered very little. Mortier had been slightly wounded, Leval and Girard severely.

Even allowing for the fact that Areizaga had been the victim of the Junta's insensate resolve to make an offensive movement on Madrid, it is impossible to speak with patience of his generalship.   For a combination of rashness and vacillation it excels that of any other Spanish general during the whole war.   His only chance was to catch the enemy before they could concentrate : he succeeded in doing this by his rapid march from the passes to La Guardia.   Then he waited three days in deplorable indecision, though there were only 10,000 men between him and Madrid.   Next he resumed his advance, but by the circuitous route of Villamanrique, by taking which he lost three days more.   Then he halted again, the moment that he found Victor with 20,000 men in his front, though he might still have fought at great advantage.   Lastly he retreated, yet so slowly and unskilfully that he was finally brought to action at Ocaña by the 34,000 men of Mortier and Sebastiani. He was sent out to win a battle, since Madrid could not be delivered without one, and knew that he must fight sooner or later, but threw away his favourable opportunities, and then accepted an action when all the chances were against him.   For he must have known by this time the miserable quality of his cavalry, yet gave battle in a vast plain, where everything depended on the mounted arm.   In the actual moment of conflict he seems to have remained in a hypnotized condition on his church-tower, issuing hardly an order, and allowing the fight to go as it pleased.   Yet he was, by all accounts, possessed

---

[1] Martinien's lists of officers killed and wounded show that the German division lost 19 officers, the Polish division 23, Girard's division 28— in all 70 out of the total of 94 officers hit in the whole army.

of personal courage, as he had proved at Alcañiz and elsewhere.
Apparently responsibility reduced him to a condition of vacil-
lating idiocy. Perhaps the most surprising fact of the whole
business is that the Junta retained him in command after his
fiasco, thanked him for his services, and sent him an honorary
present—as it had done to Cuesta after Medellin with somewhat better excuse. He was its own man, and it did not
throw him over, even when he had proved his perfect incom-
petence.

To complete the narrative of the deplorable autumn campaign
of 1809, it only remains to tell of the doings of Albuquerque
and Del Parque. The former played his part with reasonable
success ; he was ordered to distract the attention of the enemy
from the army of La Mancha, and did what he could. Having
got some 10,000 men concentrated at Almaraz, he sent one
column over the Tagus to demonstrate against the 2nd Corps
from beyond the river, and with another threatened the bridge
of Talavera from the near side. But Heudelet, now in command
of the 2nd Corps, soon found that there was no reality in his
demonstration, and that he was not supported by the English,
though he had given out that Wellington was close in his rear.
After skirmishing around Talavera from the 17th to the 22nd
of November, the Duke hastily recrossed the river on hearing the
news of Ocaña, and resumed his old positions.

Del Parque's campaign was more vigorous and more unfortunate. While he lay in the passes above Bejar and Baños, he
got early news of the withdrawal of Godinot's and Marcognet's
troops toward Madrid, when Soult summoned them off to
reinforce the main army. He reasoned that since he had now
only the 6th Corps, shorn of one of its brigades, in his front,
he might repeat the success of Tamames, for Marchand was
weaker than he had been in October, while he himself was far
stronger. Accordingly he disregarded an order from the Junta
to extend his operations southward, and to join Albuquerque in
the valley of the Tagus. Instead, he marched once more upon
Salamanca on November 18, the day before the disaster of
Ocaña. He drove in an outlying brigade of Marchand's
force from Alba de Tormes, and pressed it vigorously back
towards the main body. Conscious that with his 10,000 men

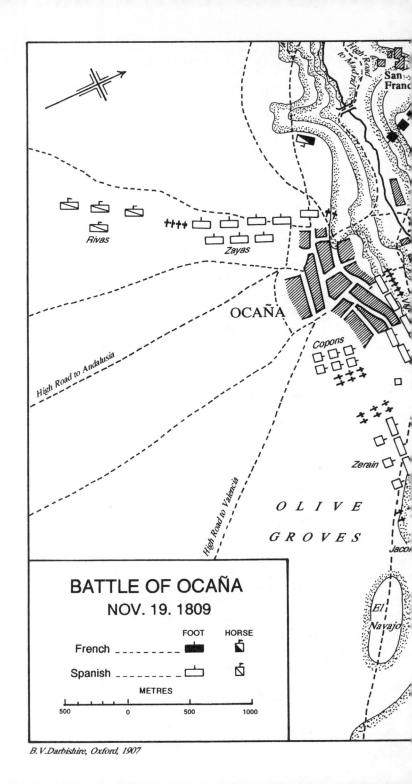

BATTLE OF OCAÑA

NOV. 19. 1809

French

Spanish

FOOT

HORSE

METRES

500   0   500   1000

Rivas

Zayas

OCAÑA

High Road to Andalusia

High Road to Valencia

Copons

Zerain

OLIVE

GROVES

El Navajo

San Franc

High Road to Madrid

Jaco

B.V.Darbishire, Oxford, 1907

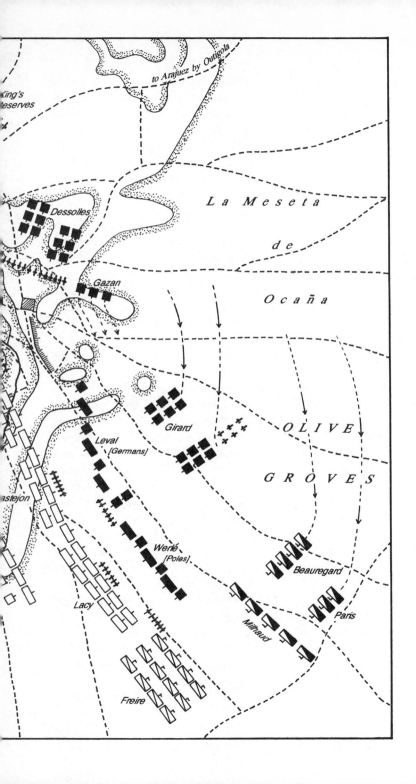

he could not hope to face 30,000, Marchand promptly evacuated Salamanca on December 19, and retired, just as he had done in October, behind the Douro, concentrating his whole corps at Toro. He sent urgent demands for help both to Kellermann at Valladolid, and to Soult at Madrid. By the time that they arrived Areizaga had been dealt with, and the army in New Castile could spare as many reinforcements as were required. Marcognet's brigade, the one which had been borrowed from the 6th Corps, was first sent back from Segovia, the point which it had reached in its southward march, and Gazan's division of the 5th Corps was ordered by Soult to follow.

Meanwhile Del Parque, still ignorant of the disaster in the south, had occupied Salamanca on November 20, and on the following day moved out towards Cantalapiedra and Medina del Campo, with the object of throwing himself between Marchand and Kellermann and the capital. This was an excellent move, and, but for what had happened at Ocaña, might have had considerable results, since the Army of the Left ought to have made an end of the small French force in Old Castile.

Kellermann, however, had seen the danger of Marchand's retreat to Toro, and had directed him to close in towards the east, and to occupy Medina del Campo, as the strategical point that must be held in order to maintain touch with Madrid. Thus it chanced that on November 23 Labassée's brigade and four regiments of cavalry, coming from Tordesillas, reached Medina del Campo just as Marcognet's brigade, returning from Segovia, came into the town from the other side. They had hardly met when the approach of Del Parque's army along the Salamanca road was reported. The two French brigadiers thought for a moment of fighting, and the cavalry was ordered to press back the Spanish advanced guard. They drove off with ease Anglona's horsemen, who rode at the head of the long column, but were repulsed by Ballasteros's infantry, which formed square in good style, and drove them off with a rolling fire of musketry. Seeing that the whole Spanish army was coming up, Marcognet and Labassée then evacuated Medina del Campo, and retired to Valdestillas. With one push more the Spaniards could have cut the line between Valladolid and Madrid.

On November 24 the whole 6th Corps and Kellermann's

dragoons, with a battalion or two from the garrisons of Old Castile, were concentrated at Puente de Duero, with their van at Valdestillas. If attacked, they must have gone behind the Douro and abandoned all touch with Madrid ; for there were not more than 16,000 men in line, and they were forced to take the defensive. But, to their surprise, Del Parque made no advance. He had heard on that morning of the disaster of Ocaña, and guessed that reinforcements for Kellermann must already be on the march. Wherefore he resolved to regain the mountains without delay, and to give up Salamanca and his other conquests. With this prudent resolve he broke up from Medina del Campo, and marched hastily away in retreat, making, not for Salamanca, which was too much in the plains to please him, but for Alba de Tormes. He had gained a day's start by his prompt action, but on the twenty-sixth Kellermann set off in pursuit, leaving orders for the troops that were expected from Madrid to follow him.

On the twenty-sixth and twenty-seventh the French cavalry failed even to get in touch with Del Parque's rearguard, and found nothing but a few stragglers on the road. But on the afternoon of the twenty-eighth the leading squadrons reported that they had come upon the whole Spanish army encamped in a mass around the town of Alba de Tormes. The duke had flattered himself that he had shaken off his pursuers, and was surprised in a most unfortunate position. Two of his divisions (Ballasteros and Castrofuerte) were beyond the Tormes, preparing to bivouac on the upland above it. The other three were quartered in and about the town, while the cavalry was watching the road, but had fallen in so close to the main body that its vedettes gave very short notice of the approach of the enemy. Kellermann was riding with the leading brigade of his cavalry— Lorcet's *chasseurs* and hussars ; the six regiments of dragoons were close behind him, so that he had over 3,000 sabres in hand ; but the infantry was ten miles to the rear. If he waited for it, Del Parque would have time to cross the river and take up a defensive position behind it. The French general, therefore, resolved to risk a most hazardous experiment, an attack with unsupported cavalry upon a force of all arms, in the hope of detaining it till the infantry should come up. The Spaniards

were getting into line of battle in a hurry, Losada's division
on the right, Belveder's and La Carrera's on the left, the cavalry
—1,200 sabres at most—in their front. The divisions beyond the
river were only beginning to assemble, and would take some
time to recross the narrow bridge : but 18,000 men were on the
right bank prepared to fight.

Without a moment's delay Kellermann ordered Lorcet's
brigade to charge the Spanish right and centre : it was followed
by the six regiments of dragoons in three successive lines, and
the whole mass came down like a whirlwind upon Del Parque's
front, scattering his cavalry to the winds, and breaking the
whole of Losada's and the right of Belveder's divisions. A
battery of artillery, and nearly 2,000 prisoners were taken.
The wrecks of the broken divisions fell back into Alba de
Tormes, and jammed the bridge, thus preventing the divisions
on the further side from recrossing it.   Kellermann then rallied
his squadrons, and led them against La Carrera's division and
the remaining battalions of that of Belveder. These troops,
formed in brigade-squares upon a rising ground, held out
gallantly and repulsed the charge.   But they were cut off from
the bridge, which they could only reach by a dangerous flank
movement over rough ground. By continually threatening to
repeat his attacks, Kellermann kept them from moving off, till,
two hours and a half after the action had begun, the French
infantry and guns commenced to come up. La Carrera saw
that it would be fatal to await them, and bade his division
retreat and reach the bridge as best it could. This was
naturally done in disorder, and with some loss ; but it was
already growing dusk, and the bulk of the Spanish left got
away.

While the Spaniards were defiling over the bridge, Marchand's
leading brigade attacked Alba, out of which it drove some
rallied troops of Losada's division, who held the town to cover
La Carrera's retreat.   This was done with ease, for Del Parque
had not brought over his two intact divisions, preferring to use
them as a second line behind which the others could retire.
Alba was stormed, and two guns, which had been placed behind
a barricade at its main exit, were taken by the French.

Here the fighting stopped : the Spaniards had lost five flags, nine guns, most of their baggage, and about 3,000 killed or taken—no very ruinous deductions from an army of 32,000 men. The French casualties were less than 300 in all [1]. Del Parque was determined not to fight again next morning, and bade his army make off under cover of the night. The disorder that followed was frightful : the three divisions that had been in the battle dispersed, and went off in all directions, some towards Ciudad Rodrigo, others towards Tamames, others by the hill-road that leads towards Tala and the Pass of Baños. Many of the raw Leonese troops, though they had not been engaged, also left their colours in the dark [2]. It was a full month before Del Parque could collect his whole army, which, when it had been reorganized, was found to number 26,000 men, despite all its misfortunes. It would seem, therefore, that beside the losses in the battle some 3,000 men must have gone off to their homes. The duke fixed his head quarters at San Martin de Trebejos in the Sierra de Gata, and dispersed his infantry in cantonments about Bejar, Fuenteguinaldo, and Miranda de Castanar. Having only the ruined region around Coria and Plasencia, and the small district about Ciudad Rodrigo, to feed them, these troops suffered dreadful privations during the winter, living on half-rations eked out with edible acorns. By the middle of January they had lost 9,000 men from fever, dysentery, and starvation.

Despite all this, it is fair to say that Del Parque's campaign contrasts most favourably with that of Areizaga. He showed a laudable prudence when he twice evacuated Salamanca rather than fight a battle in the plain. His victory of Tamames was most creditable, showing that when prudently conducted, and ranged in a well-chosen hill-position, his army could give a good account of itself. But for the disaster of Alba de Tormes his record might be considered excellent. There, it is true, he committed a grave mistake, by separating his army into two halves by the river when his enemy was in pursuit. But in his

[1] Martinien's lists show 4 officers killed and 14 wounded.

[2] There is a long report by Del Parque in the Record Office, in which he states that the panic was caused by a stray party of his own routed cavalry dashing in among the rearguard in the dark, and crying that the French were pursuing them. He afterwards court-martialled and shot some cavalrymen for cowardice.

defence it may be urged that his cavalry ought to have had vedettes out for ten or fifteen miles to the rear, and to have given him long warning of the approach of the French.   And when the enemy's horse did make its sudden appearance, it was contrary to the laws of probability that it would attack at once, without waiting for its infantry and guns.   Kellermann's headlong charge was a violation of all rules, a stroke of inspiration which could not have been foreseen.   If the Spanish cavalry had been of any use whatever, and if Losada's division had only known how to form square in a hurry, it ought to have been beaten off.   But the resisting-power of a Spanish army was always a doubtful quantity.   Kellermann resolved to take the risk of attacking, and was rewarded by a victory on which he was not entitled to reckon.   He would probably have justified his tactics by urging that failure could have no severe penalty, for the Spaniards could not pursue him if he were repulsed, while success would bring splendid results.   This was true : and if his infantry had been five miles more to the front, he might have captured the whole of La Carrera's division.

SECTION XVIII

THE CONQUEST OF ANDALUSIA

CHAPTER I

THE CONSEQUENCES OF OCAÑA. DECEMBER 1809— JANUARY 1810

THE news of the disaster of Ocaña gave a death-blow to the Central Junta. Its attempt to win back its lost credit by an offensive campaign against Madrid having ended in such a lamentable fashion, there was nothing left for it but to acquiesce in its own supersession by the oft-discussed national Cortes. But that assembly was not to meet till March 1, 1810 —a date still four months in the future,—and even its form and constitution had not yet been settled. For it would have been absurd to have called it together in the ancient and unrepresentative shape,—a legacy from the time of Charles V,— in which it had been wont to meet under the Bourbon kings. Many regions had few or no members; decayed mediaeval towns of Old Castile had more deputies than the most populous provinces. Moreover, it had yet to be settled how that larger half of the realm which was now occupied by the French was to elect its representatives. The commission was still sitting to determine these vital points, and in this moment of dismay the day of the assembly of the Cortes seemed very far distant. The French might be following hard on the heels of Areizaga's broken host, and might enter Seville, long before it had been decided what sort of a Cortes was to take over the power from the hands of the discredited Central Junta.

That most unhappy government, therefore, had to face both an acute constitutional crisis and an acute military crisis. Something had to be done without delay to satisfy public opinion concerning the convocation of the Cortes, or the revolution which had been checked by Wellesley's aid in September would certainly burst forth again. But even more pressing was the necessity for rallying and reinforcing the army which had been crushed at Ocaña, before the French should resume their advance. The actual administrative power was for the moment in the hand of the first of those temporary executive committees to which the Junta had agreed to delegate its authority by the decree of September 19. This body, composed of six members, among whom La Romana was numbered, had come into office on November 1. The rest of the Junta were only too eager to throw on their comrades the weight of the responsibility which should have fallen upon them all. The executive committee was accused on all sides of slow and feeble action. It published, as soon as possible, the details concerning the constitution of the forthcoming Cortes, which (in pursuance of the recommendation of the commission of inquiry) was to consist of two classes of members, elected representatives who were to be allotted in due proportion to all the provinces of the realm, and ' privilegiados ' or chosen individuals from the nobility and the higher clergy. The American colonies were to be given members no less than the mother country, but their numbers were to be small. Such an arrangement seemed to foreshadow a double-chambered legislature, resembling that of Great Britain, and British precedents had no doubt been running in the minds of the framers of the constitution. But—as we shall see—the Cortes, when it actually met, took no such shape. The mandate for the election of the assembly was duly published ; and so far public opinion was to a certain extent satisfied, for it was clear that the Central Junta was at last about to abdicate. But though the majority of the Spanish people were contented to wait, provided that the executive committee should show signs of rising to the occasion, and doing its best as an *interim* government, there were some politicians who saw in the crisis only an opportunity for pushing their private ambitions. Those veteran intriguers, the Conde de Montijo and Francisco Palafox, undismayed by the failure of the September plot, began to make arrangements with the Seville demagogues for a fresh attempt at a *coup d'état*. Their plots seem to have distracted Romana and his colleagues from their obvious military duties—the conspirator at home is always the enemy who looms most large before the eyes of a weak government. But after some search both were discovered, arrested and imprisoned.

Meanwhile the executive committee, with the Junta's approval, issued a long series of edicts concerning the reorganization of the army, and the defence of Andalusia from the French attack, which might at any moment begin. The 'Army of the Centre,' of which Areizaga was still, strange to say, left in command, was to be raised to 100,000 men by a strenuous conscription. The press was to be all-embracing, married men, novices in monasteries, persons in minor orders, only sons of widows, all the classes hitherto exempt, were to be subject to it. To provide funds the clergy were ordered to send in to the mint all church plate save such as was strictly necessary for the celebration of the sacraments, and all private citizens were bidden to contribute one half of their table-silver. In order to provide teams for the artillery—which had lost nearly all its horses and guns at Ocaña—a strict requisition for draught animals was begun all over Andalusia. Engineers were sent out to fortify all the passes of the Sierra Morena, with permission to exact forced labour from the peasantry of the hill country. Three members of the Junta—Rabe, Riquelme and Campo Sagrado—were sent to Areizaga's head quarters at La Carolina as 'field deputies,' to stir up or support the energy of the commander-in-chief. This was a device borrowed from the practice of the French Revolution, and had no better effect than might have been expected. As in 1793, the 'Representatives on Mission' were either useless or positively harmful. They either wished to thrust amateurish plans of their own upon the military men, or at least distracted them by constant inquisitorial supervision.

On the whole the effect of this volley of violent decrees was small. With six months to carry them out they might, no doubt, have produced great results. But within nine weeks after the disaster of Ocaña the French had commenced their attack, and in that space of time little had been accomplished. The money was beginning to come in, the recruits were being collected, but had not been armed or clothed, still less drilled. Of the fortifications in the passes many had been sketched out, but only a few had begun to take tangible shape. To man them there was still only the wrecks of Areizaga's old army, which had hardly begun to receive its drafts of conscripts. Its whole force at the New Year did not exceed 30,000 men, and these were distributed over a front of more than 150 miles, for not only the main group of passes in front of La Carolina had to be watched, but also the eastern ingress into Andalusia by Baeza and Ubeda, and the western defiles from Almaden and Benalcazar, which lead directly down on to Cordova. The whole country-side was in a state of desperate turmoil and excitement, yet very little in the way of practical defence had been completed by the middle of January.

Meanwhile, in accordance with the ridiculous constitution of the 'executive committee,' half of its members went out of office at the New Year, and were succeeded by other individuals of the Junta. Among those superseded was La Romana, who was now directed to go off to Valencia as captain-general. The Junta seems to have considered that he would be less dangerous in company with his brother Josè Caro in that province, than when posted at the seat of government, with his brother to back him by threats of Valencian military interference. Yet La Romana did not depart, and was still lingering at Seville when the French crossed the Sierra Morena.

There was a larger military problem before the Junta and the new 'executive committee' than the mere defence of Andalusia. The whole arrangement of the national armies had to be re-cast in consequence of the black day of Ocaña. The corps of Del Parque and Albuquerque, as well as all the smaller outlying bodies of troops, had to receive new orders. Above all it was necessary to discover what were the plans of Wellington, for the present position of the British army at Badajoz was the most important factor in the whole situation. As long as it remained there, in support of the small force under Albuquerque which was guarding the passages of the Tagus at Almaraz and Arzobispo, the western section of the front of Andalusia was secure. The defence of the eastern section, too, was in no small degree helped by the fact that Wellington's solid troops were in a position to march up the Guadiana, and to threaten the flank of any French army which might intend to attack the Despeña-Perros, or any other of the passes which lead from La Mancha down to the Andalusian plains.

It was a terribly disquieting fact for the Junta that, even

before Ocaña had been fought and lost, Wellington had begun to announce his intention of leaving Badajoz and retiring within the boundaries of Portugal. He had paid a flying visit to Seville on the 2nd–4th [1] of November, just as Areizaga's unhappy advance into La Mancha was commencing. The project had been concealed from him [2], and when he learnt of it he had expressed his entire disapprobation of it, and had refused to give any promise to support the Spanish armies in their offensive movements. For this reason he had been bitterly provoked when Areizaga and Albuquerque both wrote him, a little later, to say that they had been promised the assistance of his army by the Junta [3]. He had consistently prophesied ill of the adventure, and had recorded his opinion that both Del Parque and Areizaga would probably lose their armies. In a dispatch of November 20, six days before the news of Ocaña reached him, he had announced his definite intention of leaving Badajoz with the main body of his army, and transferring himself to the north of the Tagus, where, by posting himself in the Portuguese province of Beira, he would cover the high-roads to Lisbon from Old Castile. This decision was founded on his belief that when the French had made an end of Areizaga and Del Parque—a contingency which he regarded as almost certain [4]— they would strike at Lisbon and not at Seville. He had good reasons for holding this view; it was exactly consonant with

[1] He then pushed on to Cadiz, where he was on the 6th–7th, spent a night at Seville again on the 9th–10th, and was back at Badajoz on the 11th of November. At Cadiz he parted with his brother, who was just embarking for England, to take up his place in the new Ministry.

[2] As late as Oct. 28 he had written to Colonel Roche, the British officer attached to the staff of the Army of the Centre, to beg him to press on the newly-arrived Areizaga the necessity of adopting a defensive posture, and risking nothing. From the wording of the letter it is clear that no hint of the orders sent to Areizaga from Seville had reached Badajoz. *Wellington Dispatches*, v. 248–9, see also the dispatch to Castlereagh on p. 267.

[3] See Wellington to Roche, and to B. Frere, Badajoz, Nov. 19. *Dispatches*, v. 292–3 and 294.

[4] 'Nothing can save them save a victory by Areizaga, and the possession of Madrid, *which are the most improbable of events*. . . . If Del Parque and Albuquerque are destroyed, *which is not unlikely, indeed pretty certain* . . . we must make our arrangements for the defence of Portugal.' Wellington to Beresford, Nov. 20, 1809.

Napoleon's own plan, which was only abandoned by reason of King Joseph's pleadings with his brother. For, from the French standpoint, it was far more profitable to conquer Portugal and to expel the British army from the Peninsula, than to overrun Andalusia. Wellington and his troops formed the one solid nucleus of resistance which still remained ; it was clear that the dispersion of the miserable wrecks of Areizaga's host would present no difficulty. And not only was it advisable, from the Emperor's point of view, to destroy the most formidable hostile force still surviving, but the balance of strategical advantage was all in favour of subduing Portugal, before Andalusia should be invaded. For Portugal flanks the attack on southern Spain, and a good army based upon it could check the advance on Seville and Cadiz by demonstrations aimed at Valladolid or Madrid, which might wreck or delay the conquest of Andalusia. It may be objected that Andalusia also flanks the attack on Portugal ; but the objection had no validity since the day of Ocaña, as the Junta had now no longer any striking force in hand. It would be many months before Areizaga's host was in a proper condition for undertaking even cautious defensive operations. A French attack on Portugal, therefore, would be practically unmolested by external interference.

At the present moment the strength of the French troops in Spain was not sufficient to provide two armies for offensive purposes, the one destined to march on Seville, the other on Lisbon. The numbers at the front had not appreciably increased since the autumn, though already the reinforcements which the Emperor had set upon the march, after concluding his peace with Austria, had begun to appear at Bayonne, and to cross the Bidassoa. But in December and January the roads were bad, the days short, and provisions hard to procure. Hence Wellington reckoned that, till the spring should arrive, the allies would have to face no more than the forces which were already opposed to them. When, however, the campaigning season should have come round, and the reinforcements from Germany should have been incorporated with the old Army of Spain, he thought that Portugal would be the enemy's main objective. It was therefore his intention to withdraw his army, or at least the greater part of it, from Spanish Estrema-

dura, and to arrange it so as to cover Lisbon, even though by
making this movement he was weakening the left flank of the
defence of Andalusia. If he had to choose between the
interests of Portugal and those of Spain, he was prepared to
sacrifice the latter. His reasons were simple: (1) he considered
Portugal more important in the grand strategy of the defence
of the Peninsula than Andalusia; (2) he regarded it as more
defensible, and he had already—as we shall presently see—
sketched out and commenced the construction of his great
lines of Torres Vedras, in which his trust as a final impregnable
stronghold was already fixed; (3) he held that although Great
Britain was pledged to assist both Spain and Portugal, yet her
moral obligation to the latter was far more binding, since
Portugal had placed herself entirely in the hands of her allies,
had put her army at their disposal, and had contributed all her
resources to the common cause, while the Spanish Junta had
shown a jealous and suspicious spirit, had refused to show
confidence in Great Britain, and had persisted in carrying
out a military policy of its own, which led to a consistent
series of disasters; (4) the Portuguese army, though its
fighting power was not as yet ascertained, could be at least
relied upon for obedience; experience had shown that the
promises of the Spaniards could not be trusted, and that any
campaign undertaken in their company might be wrecked by
some incalculable piece of slackness or miscalculation [1].

Accordingly on November 20 Wellington declared his

---

[1] Wellington's arguments must be culled from his various dispatches to
Lord Liverpool and other ministers in November and December 1809.
For the first of the motives quoted above see Wellington to Liverpool
Dec. 9. 'The object in occupying this proposed position [in Beira] is to
be at the point of the defence of Portugal, to divert the attention of the
French from the South of Spain, when they shall receive their reinforcements, and thus to give time to the Spanish Government to repair their
losses. . . . It is absolutely necessary to cross the Tagus immediately, as it
may be depended upon that the enemy's first effort, after receiving his
reinforcements, will be upon the troops to the North of the Tagus.' Very
much the same opinion is expressed in the earlier dispatch to Lord Liverpool
of November 14. Expressions of Wellington's conviction that it was
impossible to co-operate with the Junta or the Spanish generals may be
found *passim* in all his confidential letters. See for example that to Sir J.
Anstruther, pp. 386-8 of *Supplementary Dispatches*, vol. vi.

intention of withdrawing his army—save one single division—
to the north of the Tagus, and of placing it at various points
in the province of Beira, so as to cover all the practicable
roads to Lisbon from the side of Old Castile.   On the
twenty-sixth he sent formal notice of his intentions to
Seville, well knowing the storm of indignation that would
be roused thereby.   At the same time he advised the Junta to
reinforce Albuquerque's army of Estremadura with troops
drawn from Del Parque, adding that to keep Albuquerque well
to the front, in his present positions at Almaraz and Arzobispo,
was the best means of protecting the western approaches of
Andalusia.   Del Parque's corps, whose reason for existence
was the 'containing' of the French troops in Old Castile,
would be able to spare troops to strengthen the army of
Estremadura, because the English host, in its new position,
would be behind it, and opposed to the forces under Kellermann
and Marchand, which had hitherto had nothing in their front
but the 'Army of the Left.'   Moreover, it would be an
appreciable relief to Del Parque, who was finding the greatest
difficulty in feeding his army in the thinly-peopled mountain
region between Ciudad Rodrigo and Bejar, to be freed from
the burden of maintaining one or two of his five divisions.

The Junta, as might have been expected, took Wellington's
determination to remove from Badajoz with the worst of graces.
They could hardly have failed to do so, when one of his main
reasons for departing, barely concealed in his dispatches to them,
was his fear of getting involved in their operations, and his
reluctance to place his troops in line with the Spanish armies.
Nor could they have been expected to agree with his strategical
view that Lisbon, not Cadiz, would be the main objective of
the grand advance of the French armies, when the spring
should come round.   To every man or body of men their own
possible dangers naturally seem more imminent and more
interesting than those of their neighbours.   The departure of
the English from Badajoz was formally announced to the
Junta on November 26, and began to be carried out on
December 8, when the brigade of Guards marched for Portalegre, and was followed on successive days by the other brigades
of the army.   By the 24th of December Wellington and his

staff alone were left in the Estremaduran fortress, and next day
his head quarters were at Elvas, across the frontier. The second
division, under Hill, halted at Abrantes, where Wellington
intended to leave it, as the nucleus of a covering force which
was to guard Lisbon from any possible attack from the south
side of the Tagus.   The rest of the army pursued its way
across the mountains of Beira, and by January 3, 1810, head
quarters were at Coimbra, and the main body of the British
troops was beginning to take up billets in the small towns of
the valley of the Mondego.

Convinced that no more was to be hoped from Wellington,
the Executive Committee issued their orders for a new arrangement of the line of defence of Andalusia.   Albuquerque was
ordered to leave no more than a small corps of observation on
the Tagus, in front of Almaraz, and to bring back the main
body of the army of Estremadura to the line of the Guadiana,
in order to link his right wing to the left of Areizaga's forces.
On December 24 his new head quarters were at Don Benito,
and he had some 8,000 men collected there and at the neighbouring town of Merida; the rest of his small army was
furnishing the garrison of Badajoz, and the detached force on
the Tagus, whose duty was to watch the movements of the French
2nd Corps, which still lay in its old post at Talavera, and
remained entirely quiescent.

From Albuquerque's post at Don Benito there was a gap of
seventy-five miles to the next force in the Spanish line. This
consisted of the wrecks of the two old divisions of Copons and
Zerain from the army of Areizaga, not more than 4,500 strong [1].
They were encamped at Pozo Blanco and at Almaden, the mining
town on the Alcudia, where the frontiers of Estremadura, Andalusia, and La Mancha meet.   This place lies near the northern
exit of the two passes, the Puerto Blanco and Puerto Rubio
which lead down from La Mancha on to Cordova, the one by
Villaharta, the other by Villanueva de la Jara and Adamuz.
Both are difficult, both pass through a desolate and uninhabited
country, but either of them might conceivably serve for the passage

---

[1] The papers in the Madrid archives show that Copons had about 3,000
men, Zerain (whose division had been almost entirely destroyed) about
1,500.

of an army.   Sixty miles east of Almaden was the main body
of the rallied Army of the Centre, occupying the group of passes
which lie around the high-road from Madrid to Andalusia.
Head quarters were at La Carolina, the central point upon
which the routes from most of these passes converge.   About
13,000 men were disposed in front, covering the main *chaussée*
through the Despeña-Perros, and the side defiles of the Puerto
del Rey and the Puerto del Muradal.   Here Areizaga had
concentrated the remains of the divisions of Zayas, Castejon,
Giron and Lacy, of which the last two were mere wrecks, while
the two former counted about 4,000 bayonets apiece.   Finally,
some fifteen miles off to the right, the remnants of the divisions
of Vigodet and Jacomé, perhaps 6,000 men in all, covered the
two easternmost passes from La Mancha, those of Aldea Quemada
and Villa Manrique, which descend not upon La Carolina,
but on Ubeda and Linares, the towns at the headwaters of the
Guadalquivir in the extreme north-eastern angle of the Andalusian plain.   Areizaga's artillery was all in the passes, placed in
the various new entrenchments which were being thrown up.
His cavalry had for the most part been sent back to recruit and
reform itself in the interior of the province, being useless in the
mountains.

The mere description of this disposition of forces is sufficient
to show the hopeless condition of the defence of Andalusia.
Areizaga was trying to cover every possible line by which the
French might advance, with the result that his army and
that of Albuquerque were strung out on a front of 150 miles,
and could not concentrate 15,000 men on any single point.
The passes which they were trying to guard were not only
numerous, but in several cases very practicable, where roads lay
not between cliffs or precipices, but over slopes which could be
ascended by infantry on each side of the pass.   The fortifications
and the troops holding them could be turned by enemies who
took the trouble to climb the side acclivities.   It was clear that
if the French chose to attack the Sierra Morena with no more
than the 60,000 men who had been concentrated after the
battle of Ocaña, they could bring an overwhelming force to
bear on any one or two of the passes which they might select,
while leaving the garrisons of the rest alone, or threatening them

Emery Walker Photo.

Spanish Infantry 1808
(showing the old Bourbon uniform.)

with trifling demonstrations. If the enemy should choose to
strike by Almaden at Cordova, the Spanish centre and right
wing would be cut off from their retreat on Seville, and would
have to take refuge in the kingdom of Murcia. If the Despeña-Perros and its neighbours should turn out to be the selected
objective, Areizaga's right wing must suffer the same fate. And,
if driven from the passes, the army would have to encounter, in
the broad plain behind, the overpowering force of French cavalry
which King Joseph could bring up. The problem set before
the defence was a hopeless one, and most of the generals under
Areizaga were aware of the fact—as indeed were the rank and
file. Disaster was bound to follow if the enemy managed his
business with ordinary prudence.

THE CONQUEST OF ANDALUSIA. KING JOSEPH AND HIS PLANS

WHEN considering the action of the French after the victory of Ocaña, it is necessary to remember that King Joseph and Soult were not in the position of ordinary invaders, who have just succeeded in demolishing the last army of their enemy. In wars of a normal type the victor knows that the vanquished will sue for terms when further resistance appears hopeless; he proceeds to dictate the cessions of territory or payments of indemnities that he thinks proper, as the price of peace. But it was not a profitable treaty which Napoleon desired: he had put it out of his own power to end the war in such a fashion, when he declared his brother King of Spain. For him there was no Spanish government in existence save that which he had set up at Madrid: the Central Junta, and the Cortes when it should meet, were mere illegal assemblies, with which he could not deign to enter into negotiations. It was now perfectly clear that the Spaniards would never submit of their own accord. Their position in December 1809, desperate as it might be, was no worse than it had been in the March of the same year. Areizaga's army had suffered no more at Ocaña than had those of Cuesta and Cartaojal nine months before, on the disastrous fields of Medellin and Ciudad Real. Indeed, there were probably more men actually in line to defend Andalusia in December than there had been in April. Moreover, in the early spring Soult had been in the full career of conquest in Portugal, and nothing save Cradock's insignificant force appeared to prevent his onward march to Lisbon. At midwinter, on the other hand, the flank of Andalusia was covered by Wellington's victorious army, and by the reorganized Portuguese host of Beresford. If the Junta had refused to listen to the insidious advances of Sotelo in April[1], there was no reason

[1] See vol. ii. pp. 168-9.

to suppose that it would lend a ready ear to any similar advocate of submission in December. Indeed, its every action showed a resolve to fight out the losing game to the end.

Joseph Bonaparte would never be King of Spain till every province was held down by French bayonets. Not only must each corner of the land be conquered, but after conquest it must be garrisoned. For, where there was no garrison, insurrection burst out at once, and the weary process of pacification had to be repeated.

It was this last fact that restrained King Joseph from following up his pursuit of the wrecks of the Spanish army to the Sierra Morena, and the gates of Seville, on the morning after Ocaña. To make up the host that had defeated Areizaga, and the other smaller force that was dealing with Del Parque in Leon, the King had been forced to concentrate all his divisions, and the consequence had been that the control of the broad tracts behind him had been lost. We have already had occasion to mention [1] that throughout Old Castile and Leon, the open country was now in the hands of the guerrilleros, who had been growing in force and numbers ever since the time of Talavera, and had risen to the height of their confidence after the day of Tamames, and Del Parque's repeated occupation of Salamanca. Navarre, and many parts of New Castile were equally disturbed, and Aragon, which Suchet had tamed during the autumn, was beginning once more to move. There were no French troops in the disturbed regions save scanty garrisons at Burgos, Valladolid, Benavente, Avila, Segovia, Guadalajara, Palencia, Tudela, Tafalla, and a few other strategic points. These were cut off from each other, and from Madrid, save when a governor sent out his messenger with an escort many hundreds strong, and even such a force had often to fight its way through half a dozen bands before reaching its destination. The garrisons themselves were not always safe : so powerful were the bands of some of the guerrillero chiefs that they aspired to waging regular war, and did not confine themselves to blocking the roads, or intercepting couriers and convoys. The Empecinado, whose sphere of activity lay on the borders of Old and New Castile, got possession of Guadalajara for a day, though he retired when

[1] See page 83.

reinforcements from Madrid were reported to be approaching. Somewhat later, the younger Mina—'the Student,' as he was called to distinguish him from his more celebrated uncle Espoz, stormed the town of Tafalla, and shut up the remains of its garrison in its castle, while the flying-columns of the governor of Navarre were seeking him in every other direction. He too, like the Empecinado, had to seek safety in retreat and dispersion, when his exploit drew in upon him forces sent from Suchet's army of Aragon.

The activity of the guerrilleros did not merely constitute a military danger for King Joseph. It affected him in another, and an equally vexatious, fashion, by cutting off nearly all his sources of revenue. While the open country was in the hands of the insurgents, he could raise neither imposts nor requisitions from it. The only regular income that he could procure during the later months of 1809 was that which came in from the local taxes of Madrid, and the few other large towns of which he was in secure possession. And save in the capital itself, his agents and intendants had to fight hard with the military governors to secure even this meagre pittance [1]. The King could not command a quarter of the sum which he required to pay the ordinary expenses of government. His courtiers and ministers, French and Spanish, failed to receive their salaries, and the Spanish army, which he was busily striving to form, could not be clothed or armed, much less paid. Nothing vexed Joseph more than this : he wished to make himself independent of his brother's generals, by raising a large force of his own, which should be at his personal disposition. He formed the *cadre* of regiment after regiment, and filled them with deserters from the foreign troops of the Junta, and with any prisoners who could be induced to enlist under his banners in order to avoid transportation to France. But the recruits, when sent to join the new regiments, disappeared for the most part within a few weeks. Joseph thought that it was from lack of pay and proper sustenance, and raged at the idea that, but for the want

---

[1] For a typical example of the relations of French governors and the King's officials see Thiebaud's account of his quarrel with Amoros in his autobiography, iv. 350-5. Cf. Miot de Melito, chapters xi–xii of vol. ii.

of money, he might have at his disposition a formidable army of his own.   But he deceived himself: the 'juramentados' had for the most part no desire save to desert and rejoin their old colours: the real renegades were few.   In the ranks of the Junta's army the soldier was even worse clothed, fed, and paid than in that of Joseph.   No amount of pampering would have turned the King's Spanish levies into loyal servants.

Pending the reduction to order of the country-side of the two Castiles, which he vainly hoped to see accomplished during the next six months, Joseph found only one expedient for raising money.   It was a ruinous one, and could not be repeated.   This was the confiscation of property belonging to all persons who were in the service of the Junta, and of all the religious orders. This would have given him vast sums, if only he could have found buyers.   But it was not easy to persuade any one to pay ready cash for lands overrun by the guerrilleros, or for houses in towns which were practically in a state of siege, and were also subject to a grinding taxation.   Property of immense value had to be alienated for wholly inadequate sums.   The *afrancesados*, whom Joseph was most anxious to conciliate, got such payment as he could afford, mainly in the form of vain grants of property which they could not turn to account.   The only ready money which was in circulation was that which came from the coining down, at the Madrid mint, of the considerable amount of plate belonging to the monasteries and the churches on which the King had laid hands.   Naturally, he was regarded as a sacrilegious robber by his unwilling subjects—though few, or none, murmured when the Central Junta filled its exchequer by similar expedients.   But the Junta had not decreed the abolition of the religious orders—it only purported to be raising a patriotic loan from their resources.   A minister of Joseph sums up the situation sufficiently well in three sentences. 'Spanish public opinion was inexorable : it rejected everything coming from us—even benefits : thus the King and his councillors spent themselves in fruitless labours.   Nothing answered their expectations, and the void in the Treasury, the worst danger, showed no sign of diminution.   On the contrary, the financial distress increased every day, and the unpleasant means which we were compelled to employ in order to supply the never-ceasing wants of the army completely alienated the nation from us [1].'

The orders issued by the King and Soult after the battle of Ocaña, show that they had no immediate intention of pursuing Areizaga's routed host, and entering Andalusia at its heels— tempting though such a policy might be from the purely military point of view.   After Victor and the 1st Corps had joined him, on the day following the battle, Joseph had nearly 60,000 men in hand.   But his first move was to disperse this formidable army : Gazan's division of Mortier's corps was at once hurried off towards the north, to reinforce Kellermann in Leon—for the battle of Alba de Tormes had not yet taken place, and it was thought that the 6th Corps needed prompt assistance.   Laval's division of Sebastiani's corps was detached in another direction, being told off to escort to Madrid, and afterwards to Burgos and Vittoria, the vast mass of prisoners taken at Ocaña.   Milhaud, with his own dragoons, and an infantry brigade taken from Sebastiani's corps, was directed to push eastwards by way of Tarancon, and then to march on Cuenca, where it was reported that many of the fugitives from Areizaga's army had rallied.   The brigade of Dessolles' division which had been present at Ocaña and Joseph's own troops returned to Madrid, in company with their master.   When the capital was again adequately garrisoned, numerous flying-columns were sent out from it, to clear the roads, and disperse the guerrilleros.   Mortier, with that part of the 5th Corps which had not been detached under Gazan, was drawn back to Toledo. Thus of all the troops which had been concentrated on November 20th, only Victor's corps and the Polish division, with the cavalry brigade of the 4th Corps, were retained in La Mancha, facing the Sierra Morena.   The 1st Corps was pushed forward to Ciudad Real and its neighbourhood, with its advanced cavalry watching the passes.   The Poles remained at Ocaña and La Guardia, with Perreymond's three regiments of light horse in front of them at Madridejos [2].

---

[1] Miot de Melito, ii. p. 351.

[2] For all these details see Soult's dispatches to the Minister of War at Paris, dated Nov. 21 and Nov. 24, from Aranjuez and Madrid. Perreymond had received the cavalry brigade of the 4th Corps when Paris fell in action.

In the dispatch which detailed to the Minister of War at Paris this disposition of the army, Soult explained his reasons for holding back.   It was a more pressing necessity to restore order in the provinces of the interior than to pursue the wrecks of Areizaga's force, which was so completely dispersed that no further danger need be feared from it.   Before undertaking any large general scheme of operation, the King thought it best to consult his imperial brother as to his wishes.   It was rumoured that Napoleon himself might appear on the scene within a few weeks, and it was certain that the first columns of reinforcements from Germany, which might prove to be the heralds of his approach, were just about to cross the Bidassoa. Moreover, it would be prudent to discover what had become of Albuquerque and of the English, before any great move to the southward was made, as also to make an end of the army of Del Parque, by means of the reinforcements which had just been sent to Kellermann[1].

Within three weeks the situation had changed, and many of the reasons which had induced the King and Soult to adopt a waiting policy had disappeared.   On November 28th, as we have already seen, Kellermann routed Del Parque at Alba de Tormes, though he had not yet received the succours which Gazan was bringing up to his aid.   The Army of the Left

[1] Soult to Clarke, Nov. 21 : 'Sa Majesté a pensé qu'il était inutile qu'elle s'engageât vers la Sierra Morena, à la poursuite des débris de l'armée de la Manche, qu'on ne pourra plus joindre, et qui se sauvent individuellement sur toutes les directions, d'autant plus que tout porte à croire qu'il y aura encore des mouvements sur la droite, et qu'il convient de se mettre en mesure de repousser les nouveaux corps [Albuquerque, Del Parque, and the English] qui pourraient se présenter pour la forcer.   Il est aussi pressant de prendre des dispositions pour rétablir l'ordre et la tranquillité dans les provinces de l'intérieur, et pour assurer la liberté des communications. Après la bataille d'Ocaña le roi a aussi en vue de se mettre en mesure d'attendre que Sa Majesté L'Empereur ait jugé à propos de faire connaître ses intentions sur les opérations ultérieures qui devront être faites.'   The entirely false supposition that Albuquerque and the English were on the move was, as Soult afterwards explained, due to a dispatch received from Heudelet at Talavera, who sent in an alarming report that Wellington was expected at Truxillo in a few days.   As to the idea that Del Parque might join Albuquerque, the Junta had actually given him an order to do so (see page 97), but he had ignored it, and marched on Salamanca.

being no longer a source of danger, Kellermann not only sent orders to Gazan—who had reached Segovia—to return to New Castile, since he was no longer wanted in the North, but presently sent back to the King Rey's brigade of Dessolles' division which had been lent him early in November.   Thus 10,000 men who had been detached came back under the King's control [1], and were once more available for offensive operations.

Still more important was the fact that in the first days of December the reinforcements from Germany had at last begun to cross the Pyrenees, and were arriving in Navarre and Biscay in enormous numbers.   Two strong divisions, commanded by Loison and Reynier and counting more than 20,000 bayonets, had already appeared, and the head of the interminable column which followed them had reached Bayonne.   It was certain that at least 90,000 men were on the march, to fill up the void in Old Castile which had been causing the King and Soult so much trouble.   The roads would soon be cleared, the isolated garrisons relieved, and the communications with Madrid made safe.   The newly arrived generals had received orders to sweep every valley on their southward march, and to disperse every band of guerrilleros [2].   Another possible source of danger, which had preoccupied the minds of Joseph and his Major-general after Ocaña, had also been removed.   The English had made no forward movement towards the Tagus ; they were reported to be still quiescent at Badajoz, and rumours (which afterwards turned out to be correct) had already reached the French head quarters, to the effect that Wellington was just about to retire into Portugal.   Moreover, Milhaud's expedition to Tarancon and Cuenca, and the excursions of the flying-columns sent out from Madrid, had all proved successful.   The insurgents had been dispersed with ease, wherever they had been met with.

Of all the reasons for delay which were valid on November 20th there was now none left unremoved save the most impor-

---

[1] At the New Year Gazan had 6,600 men present with the eagles, Rey 4,100.   See Tables at the end of this volume.

[2] See Orders for Loison (in Napoleon to Berthier of Dec. 9), and for Reynier (in Napoleon to Berthier, Dec. 14), in the *Correspondance*. Reynier was superseded by Lagrange, and sent to command the 2nd Corps a little later.

tant of all. The Emperor had not yet made his intentions known ; though pressed to declare his will by every letter sent by his brother or by Soult, he gave no answer as to a general plan of campaign. Several of his dispatches had reached Madrid : they were full of details as to the troops which he was sending across the Pyrenees, they contained some advice as to finance, and some rebukes for the King concerning petty matters of administration [1], but there was no permission, still less any order, to invade Andalusia or Portugal ; nor did Napoleon deign to state that he was, or was not, coming to Spain in person. It was only when Joseph received the first dispatch opening up the matter of the divorce of Josephine [2], that he was able to guess that, with such an affair on hand, his brother would not set out for the Peninsula during the winter or the early spring.

By the middle of December Joseph had made up his mind that it would be politic to attack Andalusia without delay. He had won over Soult to his ideas—the Marshal having now abandoned the plan, which he had urged so strongly in the autumn, that Lisbon not Seville should be the objective of the next French advance. It is easy to understand the King's point of view—he wished rather to complete the conquest of his own realm, by subduing its wealthiest and most populous province, than to do his brother's work in Portugal, where he had no personal interest. It is less obvious why Soult concurred with him—as a great strategist he should have envisaged the situation from the military rather than the political point of view. Apparently Joseph had won him over by giving him all that he asked, and treating him with effusive courtesy : their old quarrels of the preceding summer had been entirely forgotten. At any rate Soult had now become the ardent advocate of the invasion of Andalusia, though—as his predecessor Jourdan tersely puts it—' the English army being now the only organized force in a state to face the imperial troops, and its presence in the Penin-sula being the thing that sustained the Spanish government and

[1] The Emperor scolds his brother for not sending to Paris the flags taken at Ocaña, and for calling Sebastiani's 3rd Division ' the Polish division' instead of ' the division of the Grand Duchy of Warsaw ! '

[2] In a dispatch dated from the Trianon on Dec. 17.

gave confidence to the Spanish people, I imagine that we ought
to have set ourselves to destroy that army, rather than to have
disseminated our troops in garrisoning the whole surface of
Spain [1].' The same thought was in the Emperor's mind when
he wrote in January—too late to stop the Andalusian expedition—that ' the only danger in Spain is the English army ; the
rest are partisans who can never hold the field against us [2].'

On the 14th of December, 1809, Soult at last made a formal
appeal, in a dispatch to Berthier, for leave to commence the
march on Seville. ' At no time since the Spanish War began,'
he wrote, ' have circumstances been so favourable for invading
Andalusia, and it is probable that such a movement would
have the most advantageous results. I have already informed
your Excellency that preparations would be made for this
movement, while we waited for his Majesty to deign to
make known to us his supreme will.' Soult adds that if only
Loison's division of the reinforcements may be brought up
to Burgos, and a second division sent to Saragossa, in order
to free Suchet for field service, the invasion can be begun, as
soon as the army in New Castile has completed its equipment
and received its drafts.

No direct reply was received to this dispatch, nor to several
subsequent communications, in which Soult and Joseph set forth
the arrangements which they were making, always subject to
the Imperial approval, for concentrating an army for the
Andalusian expedition. Strange as it may appear, it was only
in a letter written on January 31, 1810, when the King had
already crossed the Sierra Morena, that Napoleon vouchsafed
a word concerning the all-important problem [3].' It is clear
that he had ample time to have stopped it, if such had been

[1] Jourdan, *Mémoires*, p. 294.

[2] Napoleon to Berthier, Jan. 31, 1810—giving directions which could
not be carried out, because the invasion of Andalusia had begun ten days
before the dispatch had been written.

[3] Soult writes plaintively to Berthier, from Madrid, on January 1, 1810 :
' Le Roi croit ne pouvoir différer davantage : ainsi il se met en mesure
d'exécuter les dispositions générales de l'Empereur, lorsque Sa Majesté aura
daigné les faire connaître ; et il est vraisemblable qu'avant que la Sierra
Morena soit passée, les ordres, qui ont été demandés depuis plus d'un
mois, seront parvenus.' But the order never came.

his will; the ultimate responsibility, therefore, lay with him.
But he refrained from ordering it, or from approving it, thus
reserving to himself all the possibilities of *ex-post-facto* criticism. Since no prohibition came, Joseph made up his mind
to strike; it was natural that he should be fascinated by the
idea of conquering in person the one great province of Spain
which remained intact. A brilliant campaign, in which he
would figure as commander-in-chief as well as king, might at
last convince the Spaniards of his capacity. He was prepared
to play the part of a merciful and generous conqueror. At
the worst the revenues of the wealthy Andalusia would be a
godsend to his depleted treasury.

Two plans were drawn up for the invasion. The first was
more cautious, and more consonant with the strict rules of
strategy. The second was bolder and promised more immediate
results. According to the first the King was to concentrate his
main army in La Mancha, and to threaten the passes, while two
great flanking columns carried out the preliminary conquest of
Estremadura and Valencia. Mortier was to march with the
5th and 2nd Corps upon Badajoz, to crush Albuquerque, and to
occupy the valley of the Guadiana. Simultaneously Suchet
was to make a push from Aragon into Valencia with the bulk of
his corps, while his place at Saragossa was to be taken by a large
force drawn from the newly-arrived reinforcements from France.
Only when Badajoz and Valencia had fallen, and Suchet and
Mortier could advance parallel with him on either flank, was
the King to march against Seville. The weak point of the
scheme was that either Badajoz or Valencia might make a long
resistance; if their garrisons fought like that of Gerona the
central advance on Andalusia might be delayed for an indefinite
time.

The second plan, the one that was adopted, was to leave the
2nd Corps alone to watch Albuquerque and Estremadura, to
order Suchet to advance against Valencia, but to strike straight
at Seville, without waiting for the completion of either the
Estremaduran or the Valencian operations. In the original
draft for this campaign [1], nearly the whole of the King's army

---

[1] It may be found set forth in full in Soult's dispatch to Berthier of
Jan. 1, 1810.

was to concentrate at Almaden and Ciudad Real, and from
thence to strike straight at Cordova, by the difficult and little-
used passes of the central Sierra Morena. Meanwhile
Sebastiani, with no more than a single infantry division and
Milhaud's dragoons, was to demonstrate against the main group
of passes in front of La Carolina, along the line of the high-
road from Madrid, so as to distract the attention of the
Spaniards from the real point of attack. More than 50,000
men were to descend suddenly on Cordova, for the whole of the
1st and 5th Corps, Dessolles' Reserve division, the King's
Guard, and Latour-Maubourg's dragoons, were to march in a
mass by the unexpected route via Almaden, Villanueva de la
Jara, and Adamuz. The Spanish centre would undoubtedly be
broken, and it was probable that Cordova, Seville, and Cadiz
would be carried by the first rush, for Areizaga's army would be
cut off from them and driven eastward towards Murcia.

The plan, an admirable one from the point of view of strategy,
had to be abandoned, for it was found that the country between
Almaden and Cordova was so absolutely barren and uninhabited,
and the roads so bad, that it would be impossible to carry a very
large body of troops across it at midwinter. It was doubtful
whether the passes were practicable for artillery ; it was certain
that no food could be obtained, and the train required to carry
rations for 50,000 men would be so large and heavy that it
would probably stick fast in the mountains.

On January 11, when Mortier, Dessolles, and the rest of the
army had already moved out of their cantonments and taken the
road for La Mancha, the revised draft of the plan of campaign
was issued. It was inferior in unity of conception to the first
plan, and did not seem likely to produce such good results ; but
it had the merit of being practicable. By this scheme Victor
alone was to march on Cordova, with the 22,000 men of the
1st Corps : he was to endeavour to take his artillery with him, but
if the passes proved too rough, he was to send it back by Almaden
to join the main army. Mortier, Dessolles, Sebastiani, Milhaud,
and the King's Reserves were to strike at the group of passes in
front of La Carolina, and to drive the Spaniards out of them :
it was hoped that they would thrust Areizaga's host into the
arms of Victor, who would be descending into the valley of the

Guadalquivir just in time to meet the enemy retiring from the
defiles. For this operation the King was to take with him rather
more than 40,000 men.

It may be remarked that this plan divided the French army
into two separate columns entirely destitute of lateral communications, and that, if the Spaniards had been stronger, considerable
danger would have been incurred. Areizaga might have concentrated every man against one or other of the columns, and
have brought it to a stand, while merely observing the other.
But to do so he would have required a far larger force than he
actually possessed : he had, as we have seen, only 23,000 men
under arms, and even if he collected every available bayonet in
one mass, either half of the French army was strong enough to
meet and to beat him. The King, therefore, was running no
real risk when he divided up his troops. As a matter of fact,
Areizaga had made matters easy for the enemy, by splitting his
small and dilapidated host into three sections—Zerain, with
4,500 men only, was on Victor's road; the head quarters, with
13,000 men, were at La Carolina opposite the King; Vigodet
with 6,000, was far to the right in the eastern passes[1]. Disaster
was inevitable from the first moment of the campaign.

On January 7 King Joseph and Soult moved out from Madrid
in the wake of the columns of Dessolles and the Royal Guard,
which had already started. On the 8th they were at Toledo,
on the 11th at Almagro, near Ciudad Real ; here they conferred
with Victor, and, in consequence of his reports concerning the
state of the passes in the direction of Cordova, recast their plans,
and adopted the scheme of operations which has just been
detailed. On the following day Victor and his corps marched
from Ciudad Real for Almaden, to carry out the great turning
movement. The main army waited for six days to allow him to
get far forward on his rugged route, and only on the 18th started
out to deliver the frontal attack on the Despeña-Perros and the
other passes in front of La Carolina.

It may be mentioned that Joseph had left behind him to
garrison Madrid the French division of the 4th Corps,[2] and not

---

[1] See for details pages 111-12.

[2] With the exception of the 58th Regiment, which went on with Sebastiani
to the front.

Dessolles' troops, who had been wont to occupy the capital during the earlier operations. Both Dessolles' and Joseph's own reserves, his Royal Guard and a strong brigade of his newly-raised Spanish army, joined in the invasion. Since the German division of the 4th Corps was still absent, escorting the prisoners of Ocaña,' it resulted that Sebastiani had with him only his Polish division, his cavalry, and some details sufficient to muster up a total of just 10,000 men. His corps was never properly reassembled during the whole of the rest of the war, as some of the regiments which he now left behind never rejoined him in Andalusia, but were left in garrison in New Castile till 1812, and practically became part of the 'Army of the Centre.'

Besides the garrison of Madrid, Joseph left to cover his rear the whole 2nd Corps, still under the provisional command of Heudelet, which lay at Talavera and was charged to watch Albuquerque. If the rumour of the departure of the English from Badajoz were true, there would be no danger in this quarter. But Joseph was not yet quite certain that Wellington had retired into Portugal. The only serious preoccupation which vexed his mind, at the moment when he was preparing to attack, was the idea that the English might still come up by Truxillo and join Albuquerque in a raid on Madrid. Heudelet, the constant purveyor of false information, did his best to scare his master on January 13, by sending him a report that Wellington was still at Badajoz with 23,000 men [1]. But later and more trustworthy news from other quarters, showing that the English army had marched off for Abrantes long before Christmas, at last set the King's mind at rest on this all-important topic.

There was nothing to be feared from the west when Wellington had taken his departure. Albuquerque's small force was powerless, and if Del Parque moved down from the Sierra de Francia into the valley of the Tagus, the 6th Corps could make a corre-

---

[1] Heudelet, writing from Talavera on Jan. 13, assured the King that he had certain information, by English deserters, that Wellington's army, 16,000 foot and 7,000 cavalry, was at Merida, Badajoz, and Elvas on Dec. 31. As a matter of fact, the army had marched off between Dec. 9 and Dec. 20, and Wellington himself had retired into Portugal on Christmas Eve. On the day when Heudelet wrote he and his head quarters were at Vizeu, in the Beira.

sponding movement. Ney had now returned to take command at Salamanca, and the confidence of his troops, shaken somewhat by Marchand's incapable leadership, was now restored. Behind Ney and Kellermann were the innumerable battalions of the new reinforcements from Germany, the head of whose column had now reached Burgos. The King's rear, therefore, was well guarded when he began his great offensive movement against Andalusia.

SECTION XVIII : CHAPTER III

On the 19th of January, 1810, the unfortunate Areizaga began to receive from all quarters dispatches which left him no doubt that the fatal hour had arrived, and that the whole of his line, from Villamanrique on the east to Almaden on the west, was about to be assailed by the enemy. From every point on his front of 150 miles, his subordinates sent him in reports to the effect that strong hostile columns had come up, and had thrust in their outposts. Indeed, Zerain, from his remote cantonment on the extreme left, had announced that an overwhelming force, coming from the direction of Ciudad Real, had beaten him out of the town of Almaden as early as the 15th, and had compelled him to retire towards the south-west, leaving the direct road to Cordova uncovered. This was, of course, the corps of Victor, whose flanking movement was already threatening to cut the line of communication between La Carolina and Seville. But it would take some days for the 1st Corps to pass the rugged defiles of the Sierra de Los Pedroches, which lie between Almaden and the valley of the Guadalquivir. An even more pressing danger seemed to be foreshadowed from the less-remote right of the Spanish line, where Vigodet reported, from the pass of Villamanrique, that he had been driven in to his final fighting position at Montizon, by a French column marching up from Villanueva de los Infantes. In the centre, the enemy had advanced to Santa Cruz de la Mudela, where the roads to all the group of passes about the Despeña-Perros branch off, but had not yet shown how many of them he intended to use. Areizaga could not determine whether some of the French movements were mere demonstrations, or whether every one of them portended a real attack on the morrow. Zerain was too far off to be helped ; but Vigodet's demands for assistance were so pressing that the Commander-in-Chief sent off to his aid,

on the night of the 19th, the one division which he had
hitherto kept in reserve at La Carolina, the 4,000 bayonets of
Castejon.   This left him only three divisions—those of Zayas,
Lacy, and Giron, not more than 9,000 men in all, to defend
the high-road to Madrid and the subsidiary passes on its
immediate flank.

As a matter of fact, the appearance of the French advanced
guards implied a genuine attack at every possible point of
access.   King Joseph had resolved to carry the whole of the
defiles by a simultaneous onslaught on the morning of the 20th.
His policy seems to have been one of very doubtful wisdom,
for it would have been as effective to pierce the Spanish line at
one point as at four, and he could have concentrated an overwhelming force, and have been absolutely certain of success, if
he had launched his main body at one objective, while demonstrating against the rest.   He had preferred, however, to cut
up his army into four columns, each of which assailed a different
pass.   Sebastiani, on the extreme French left, separated by a gap
of twenty miles from the main column, was the enemy who had
driven in Vigodet at the opening of the Villamanrique pass.
He had with him the remains of his own 4th Corps—of which
such a large proportion had been left behind in New Castile,—
a body of about 10,000 men [1].   His orders were to force the
defile in his front, and to descend into the plain in the rear of
the Spanish centre, by way of Ubeda and Linares, so as to cut
off the enemy's retreat towards Murcia, and to envelop him if
he should hold the Despeña-Perros too long.

Next to Sebastiani in the French line was a column composed
of Girard's division of the 5th Corps, the King's Guards, and
the Spanish regiments in Joseph's service [2].   It was nearly
14,000 strong, and advanced straight up the Madrid *chaussée*,
aiming at the Despeña-Perros and the Spanish centre.   If the
enemy should fight well, and if the flanking movements should

---

[1] Viz. by the ' morning states' of January 15, in the French War Office,
Sebastiani had : Polish Division, 4,809 men ; 58th of the Line, 1,630 men ;
Milhaud's Dragoons, 1,721 men ; Perreymond's Light Horse, 1,349 men ;
Artillery and Engineers, 569 men ; or a total of 10,078 sabres and bayonets.

[2] Strength apparently : Girard, 7,040 ; Royal Guards, about 2,500 ;
Spaniards, about 2,000 ; Cavalry, about 1,500 ; Artillery, &c., 800.

ANDALUSIA, to illustrate the Campaign of 1810

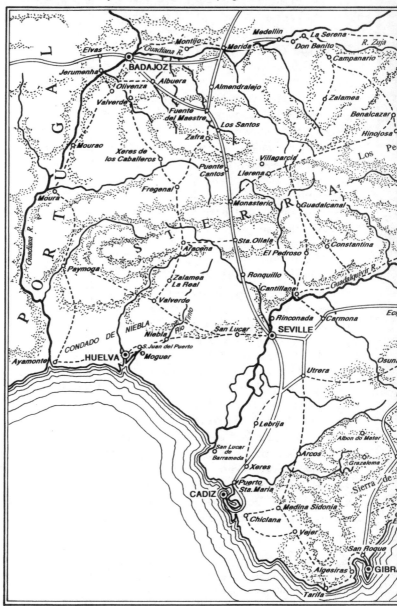

B.V.Darbishire, Oxford, 1907

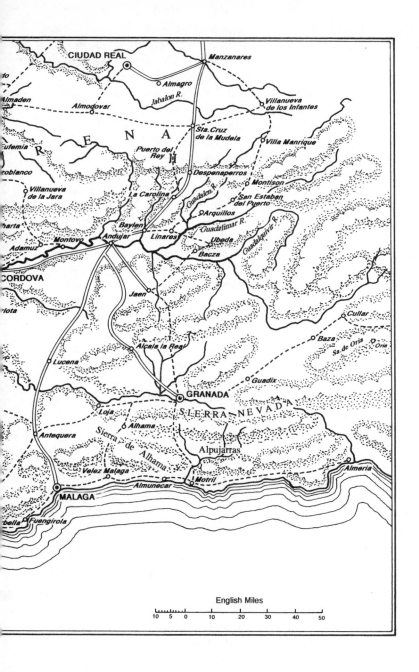

English Miles

10 5 0   10   20   30   40   50

fail, this column would have the hardest work before it: for, unlike the minor passes to east and west, the Despeña-Perros becomes in its central length a narrow and precipitous defile, easily capable of defence. The Spaniards had run entrenchments across it, and had mined the road at more than one point. But its fatal weakness lay in the fact that the by-paths from the western passes descend into it to the rear of the point where these obstructions had been placed. If they were seized by the advancing French, the fortifications across the *chaussée* would prove a mere trap for the troops which held them.

Mortier, with Gazan's division of the 5th Corps and Dessolles' troops, about 15,000 strong, was told off to assail these flanking defiles on the Spanish left[1]. The two passes are the Puerto del Rey and the Puerto del Muradal. The former got its name from Alfonso VIII, who in 1212 had turned the position of the Almohad Sultan Mohammed-abu-Yakub by this route, and so forced him to the decisive battle of Navas de Tolosa, a few miles to the rear. In 1810 it was a tortuous and rough road, but practicable for artillery: the slopes on either side of it, moreover, were not inaccessible to infantry. A mile or two to its left, nearer the Despeña-Perros, was the still rougher path of the Puerto del Muradal, which was practicable for infantry but not for guns. Between this defile and the entrenchments across the Madrid *chaussée*, the crest of the Sierra was accessible to troops advancing in loose order and prepared for a stiff climb: the Spanish engineers had therefore placed a large earthwork on its culminating point, known as the Collado de Valdeazores. Giron's weak division of no more than 3,200 bayonets was entrusted with the defence both of the Puerto del Rey and the Puerto del Muradal. Those of Lacy and Zayas, about 5,000 in all, held the Despeña-Perros and the entrenchments on each side of it. Areizaga lay behind them, with a reserve of 1,000 men at most—having sent off Castejon and his division to join Vigodet on the preceding night, he had no more with him than his personal guard, the 'Batallon del General', and some detached companies.

Mortier, like the good general that he was, did not confine

[1] Gazan's division, forming the third French column, had 6,414 bayonets ; Dessolles', the extreme right-hand column, 8,354.

his operations to an attack against the narrow fronts of the two passes, but assailed the rough hillside on each side of them, sending out whole battalions deployed as skirmishers to climb the slopes.   Of Gazan's division, one brigade marched against the Puerto del Muradal, but the other went up, in open order, on the space between the Puerto and the Spanish redoubt at the Collado de Valdeazores.   Similarly, Dessolles attacked the Puerto del Rey with a few battalions, but sent the rest up the less formidable portions of the flanking slopes.   Girard and the King's Reserves, meanwhile, did not press their attack on the Despeña-Perros, till the troops on their right had already begun to drive the enemy before them.

The results of these tactics might have been foreseen from the first: Giron's 3,200 men, attacked by 15,000, were driven in at a pace that ever grew more rapid.   They could not defend the passes, because the slopes on each side were turned by the enemy.   Their line was broken in two or three places, and they fled in haste down the rear of the Sierra, to escape being captured by flanking detachments which were pushing on at full speed to head them off.   The moment that the Despeña-Perros was turned by Mortier's movement, the troops occupying it had to retreat at headlong speed, just as Girard was commencing his attack on them.   All did not retire with sufficient promptness : the battalion in a redoubt on the Collado de los Jardines, on the right flank of the high-road, was cut off and captured *en masse*.   All the guns in the pass were taken, there being no time to get them away down the steep road in their rear.   After two hours of scrambling rather than fighting, the main passages of the Sierra Morena were in the hands of the French.   The mines on the high-road had been fired when the retreat was ordered, but did not wreck the *chaussée* in such a way as to prevent the enemy from pursuing.   The losses of the Spaniards were no more than a few hundreds killed and wounded, and 500 prisoners ; those of the French were less than 100 in all [1].   There had, in truth, been hardly the semblance of a battle.

[1] Soult's statement that he lost ' some 25 men ' (Soult to Berthier, Jan. 21) is no doubt a little exaggerated.   But Martinien's invaluable tables show that Mortier's corps, which did nearly all the fighting, lost only

The full results of the disaster were only developed next day : the troops which had defended the central passes escaped, though in dreadful disorder. But those further to their right were destined to a worse fate. While Mortier and the King were forcing the great defiles, Sebastiani had been fighting all day with Vigodet, in the defiles about Montizon and St. Esteban del Puerto. He had no such superiority in numbers over his enemy as had the King on the main field of operations [1], hence his progress was slower, and his victory, though complete, was not so prompt and crushing. Vigodet and his 6,000 men were dispersed by the afternoon, and fled down the valley of the Guadalen towards the plains, with Sebastiani's cavalry in pursuit. Having fought much longer than Lacy and Giron, their losses were heavier than those of the central division—probably 1,000 killed, wounded, or taken. Shortly after, there appeared on the scene, moving along the steep hill-path from La Carolina, the Spanish division of Castejon, which had been sent off on the previous night to support Vigodet. It found the St. Esteban position in the possession of the French, and turned hastily back to rejoin Areizaga. But, while it had been on the march, the Commander-in-Chief and his army had been routed, and La Carolina was in the hands of the French. Castejon found himself enclosed between Sebastiani and the King, in a most perilous position. On the morning of the 21st, he tried to escape by the by-path to Linares, but on arriving near that place found that Mortier's troops were already across his road. A brigade of Sebastiani's corps was in hot pursuit in his rear, and Castejon, seeing himself thus enclosed, surrendered at Arquillos, with his whole intact division of over 4,000 men and ten guns.

Already, before the capture of this Spanish corps, the King and Sebastiani had joined hands, their reconnoitring parties having met in the valley of the Guadalen. On learning of the complete success of both columns, Joseph and Soult resolved to urge the pursuit in two separate directions. Sebastiani was told

two officers out of 549 present, probably, therefore, it lost no more than forty men. Dessolles must have lost about the same.

[1] Of his whole 10,000 men only 6,400 were infantry, and Vigodet (with the wrecks of Jacomé's division) had nearly as many.

to push forward by way of Ubeda and Baeza to Jaen, while the main column marched by Baylen on Andujar and Cordova. It was hoped that news of Victor would soon be received : if all had gone well, he would have reached the Guadalquivir somewhere in the neighbourhood of Cordova, so as to be in the rear of any Spanish force that might have retreated from La Carolina in the direction of Seville.

As a matter of fact, however, both Vigodet and also Areizaga with the wreck of the troops from the central passes, had abandoned any hope of covering Seville, and had retreated southwards on Jaen. There was no force whatever left upon the Cordova road, and the King met no resistance upon the 22nd or the 23rd. On the latter day Sebastiani, arriving in front of Jaen, found the Spanish commander-in-chief with some 7,000 or 8,000 men prepared to defend the town. He attacked at once, and routed these dispirited troops, who made little or no show of resistance. Practically the whole force went to pieces : the French captured forty-six guns, mostly those of the reserve-park of the Army of Andalusia, which had been deposited in Jaen. Of the wrecks of that unhappy force, Areizaga carried off a small remnant to Guadix in the eastern mountains, near the borders of Murcia. Lacy, with another fraction, retired on Granada. But the large majority had left their colours, and dispersed to their homes.

King Joseph and Soult meanwhile, advancing unopposed along the high-road to Cordova and Seville, got into touch at Andujar with the advanced cavalry of Victor on the night of the 22nd of January. The march of the 1st Corps had been toilsome in the extreme, but almost unopposed save by the difficulties of the road. After driving Zerain's little detachment out of Almaden on the 15th, they had hardly seen an enemy. Zerain and his colleague Copons had retired by the road towards Seville south-westward. Victor, though he sent out flying parties of cavalry to threaten Benalcazar and Hinojosa, to his right, had really pushed further to the left, on the easternmost of the two rough passes which lead to Cordova. The day after leaving Almaden he had sent his artillery back to La Mancha, the dilapidated and abandoned road to which he had committed himself proving absolutely impracticable for anything that travelled on wheels. But he pushed on with his infantry and horsemen, and passing Santa Eufemia, Torrecampo and Villanueva de la Jara, came down into the plain of the Guadalquivir at Adamuz, fifteen miles to the east of Cordova, on January 21st, the day after Soult and King Joseph had forced the Despeña Perros and the Puerto del Rey. Wishing to get into touch with them before attacking Cordova, he halted his infantry, but sent out his cavalry to the gates of that city on the one side, and on the other to Montoro and Andujar, where they met the vedettes of the main army on the evening of the 22nd. Thus the French host was once more concentrated: the march on Seville could be continued without delay. Victor now became the advanced guard: he entered Cordova, which opened its gates without resistance, on the 24th. There was no Spanish force in front of the French army, since Zerain and Copons had retired towards Seville by a road far to the west, while the wrecks of Areizaga's army had been driven off in a southeasterly direction.

Soult and King Joseph, therefore, had leisure to plan out the remainder of their campaign without any disturbance from the enemy. On the 25th[1] they resolved to detach Sebastiani and his 10,000 men for the conquest of Granada, to leave Dessolles' division at Cordova and Andujar, but to march on Seville in a single mass with the remaining 50,000 sabres and bayonets of the Army of Andalusia. The desire to seize the capital from which the Junta had so long defied him, seems to have mastered every other idea in the mind of the intrusive King. The rebel government should be captured, or at least forced to take refuge in Portugal or the sea. Then at last the provinces would submit, the regular armies would lay down their arms, the guerrillero bands would disperse to their homes, and he might reign as a real king, not as the mere tool of his imperious brother. The capture of Seville would be the last act but one of the drama: after that he would become the national monarch of a submissive people, and carry out all the schemes of vague benevolence on which his mind was wont to dwell in his more hopeful hours. That the resistance would continue, even if Seville were his own

---

[1] For details of their plans see the dispatch of Soult to Berthier, from Andujar under the date of that day.

and the Junta were scattered and discredited, he did not dream. And Seville, he knew, must fall ; to defend it there could be, as he concluded, nothing but a half-armed mob, backed by the few thousand dispirited soldiers who had fled before Victor from the western section of the Sierra Morena. Even if the rebel capital made itself a second Saragossa, he had at his disposal an army double the strength of that which had reduced the obstinate Aragonese city.

In subsequent years critics, wise after the event, never tired of declaiming against the policy which Joseph and Soult approved on January 25, 1810. It was easy in 1811 or 1812 to point out that a division or two might have been spared from the victorious army to execute a march upon Cadiz, while the main force was dealing with Seville. The island-fortress, which was to defy the French during the next three years, might have been caught while it was still ungarrisoned and panic-stricken, if only the invaders had detached a column from Carmona, where the road from Cordova bifurcates to Seville on the right and Cadiz on the left. It is certain that, if any suggestion to that effect was made at the time, Soult, Mortier, and the other generals present at the council of war passed it over [1]. The fact was that Seville loomed large before the imaginations of them all : Cadiz seemed but a secondary affair at the moment. It appeared probable that the whole of the scattered forces of the enemy would mass themselves to defend the insurgent capital. On January 25th, when the original plan was drawn up, no one realized that there was a Spanish army approaching, whose presence in Andalusia had not yet become known, or that the general of that army

---

[1] There was a considerable controversy among French military writers as to whether the omission to march on Cadiz was the fault of Soult or of the King. The authors of *Victoires et Conquêtes*, having put all the blame on the latter (vol. xx, page 7), his friends hastened to reply. His aide-de-camp Bigarré, who was present with him at the time, explicitly says in his autobiography (pp. 265–6) that the King raised the point, but was talked down by Soult and Dessolles. Miot de Melito (ii. 385) bears witness to the same effect, saying that he heard Soult clinch his argument by crying ' Qu'on me réponde de Séville, moi je réponds de Cadix.' Both say that the final decision was made at Carmona. See also Ducasse's *Correspondance du roi Joseph*, vii. 142–3, and x. pp. 395–6, where the same story is given by the King himself.

would deliberately leave Seville to its fate, as incapable of defence and doomed to destruction, and hasten by forced marches to throw himself into the island-city which was destined to become the new capital of insurgent Spain. Unable to foresee such a development, Joseph wrote to his brother on January 27 that Seville would probably submit without fighting, and that he would then enter Cadiz 'sans coup férir.'

Albuquerque's operations, which ultimately turned out to be the most important section of the Andalusian campaign, need a word of explanation. It will be remembered that, early in January, he had assembled, at Don Benito and Medellin, the small field-force that he could command, after providing the garrison of Badajoz and leaving a detachment above Almaraz to watch the French 2nd Corps. It did not amount to more than 8,000 men, of which some 1,000 were cavalry. His position at Don Benito was intended to protect the flank of Zerain and Copons, who lay to his right, covering the passes that lead from Almaden on to Cordova. On January 15th he received from Zerain the news that he was about to be attacked at Almaden by a French column of at least 20,000 men. The Duke promptly began to march eastward to join his colleague, and reached Campanario on January 16th. Here he was met by the information that Zerain had been driven out of Almaden on the preceding day, and had drawn back by Benalcazar and Hinojosa on to the Seville road. Copons from Pozo Blanco was retiring in the same direction. The Duke thereupon concluded that his duty was to fall back by a route parallel to that of Victor's advance, and to draw nearer to Seville, strengthening himself as he approached that city by Zerain's and Copons' small corps.

Accordingly he sent off three of his weakest battalions to strengthen the garrison of Badajoz, which was very small at the moment, directed his artillery (with a cavalry escort) to take the good but circuitous high-road to Seville by Merida, Los Santos, and Santa Olalla, and started off across the mountains with his infantry and 500 horse. Marching very rapidly, though the roads were bad and the days short, he moved by Zalamea and Maguilla to Guadalcanal, on the borders of Andalusia, which he reached on January 18th. Here he received from the Central

Junta an absurd order, apparently based on the idea that he
was still at Campanario, which bade him stop Victor's advance,
by falling on his flank and rear by the road to Agudo and
Almaden. But since the marshal had seized Almaden on the
15th, and was known to have moved southward from thence, it
was clear that he must now be more than half-way to Cordova :
if the Army of Estremadura plunged back into the mountains
to seek Agudo and Almaden, it would only reach them on the
22nd or 23rd, and Victor would be at the gates of Cordova on
the 21st. The Junta's order was so hopelessly impracticable
that the Duke took upon himself to disobey it, and wrote in
reply that he should move so as to place himself between Victor
and Seville, and would cover the Andalusian capital ' so far as
was possible with the small force at his disposition.'

Accordingly Albuquerque, instead of returning northward
into the Estremaduran mountains, moved a stage further south,
to El Pedroso, on the road from Guadalcanal to Seville, and
sent orders to Copons and Zerain to join him with their small
divisions. Two days later he received the order which should
have been sent him on the 18th, instead of the insane directions
that were actually given ; by it he was directed to march on
Seville with all speed. On the 23rd, therefore, he arrived at
the ferry of Cantillana, twenty miles north of Seville : here he
received news that his artillery and its escort had safely completed its round, and were about to cross the Guadalquivir at
Rinconada, fifteen miles to the south. At Cantillana, however,
the Duke got the last dispatch which the Central Junta ever
issued ; it was dated on the 23rd, a few hours before the
members dispersed and fled. By this he was directed to march
not on Seville but on Cordova, which at the moment the
document came to hand—the morning of the 24th—had just
been occupied by Victor.

That day Albuquerque crossed the Guadalquivir and occupied
Carmona, where he was joined by his artillery, and by part of
Copons' division, but not (apparently) by Zerain's, which had
retired into Seville. He had now about 10,000 men, of whom
1,000 were horsemen, and 20 guns. From Carmona he threw
out a cavalry screen on all sides : his vedettes on the 27th struck
French cavalry at Ecija, and were driven in ; they reported that

the enemy was advancing in enormous force from Cordova—as was indeed the case. Meanwhile news had come up from Seville that the Junta had fled on the night of the 23rd–24th, that anarchy reigned in the city, and that a new revolutionary government had been installed. There was no longer any legitimate executive from which orders could be received. Albuquerque had to make up his mind whether he would retire into Seville, and put himself at the disposition of the mob and its leaders, or whether he should seek some safer base of operations. Without a moment's hesitation he resolved to leave the Andalusian capital to itself, and to retire on Cadiz, which he knew to be ungarrisoned, yet to be absolutely impregnable if it were properly held. This wise resolution, it may be said without hesitation, saved the cause of Spain in the south. If Cadiz had been left unoccupied there would have been no further resistance in Andalusia.

But we must return to the operations of the French. On the 25th Victor had advanced from Cordova, taking the direct road to Seville via La Carlota and Ecija, while Mortier and the Royal Guard followed him at short intervals. The Duke of Belluno occupied Ecija on the 27th and Carmona on the 28th. On these two days his advanced guard got into contact with Albuquerque's cavalry screen, and learnt from prisoners that the Army of Estremadura, whose presence in Andalusia thus became known, was in front of them [1]. On reaching Carmona Victor obtained the still more important news that Albuquerque, after staying in that place for two days, had not retired into Seville, as might have been expected, but had marched southward to Utrera on the road to Cadiz, leaving the greater city uncovered. On the night of the 29th the leading division of Victor's corps, the dragoons of Latour-Maubourg, appeared in front of Seville, and reported that works were being hastily thrown up around it on all sides [2], and that they had been fired

[1] See Soult to Berthier, from Carmona, Jan. 31.

[2] Soult, in his dispatch of Jan. 31, says that the advanced guard of the 1st Corps appeared before Seville *hier au soir*, i. e. on the 30th. But the Spanish authorities give the evening of the 29th as the true date, and seem to be correct. Possibly Soult is speaking of the first solid force of infantry, and does not count the cavalry as a real advanced guard, but

on by masses of armed irregulars at every point where they had pushed forward vedettes towards its suburbs [1].

Seville was at this moment, and had been now for six days, in a state of chaos. The Central Junta had absconded on the 23rd, taking along with it both its Executive Committee and the Ministers of State. The panic had begun on the 18th, when the news had come in that Victor's corps had thrust Zerain out of Almaden three days before, and was marching on Cordova. It had grown worse two days later, when Areizaga reported that another French army was marching against the Despeña-Perros. The Junta published a proclamation on the 20th, exhorting the Andalusians to have no fear, for Albuquerque had been directed to fall on Victor's flank, and Del Parque with the Army of Castile was on the march to join him, so that the enemy would be forced to turn back to guard himself. Such orders were indeed sent, but any man of sense could see that they must arrive too late. If Victor was at Almaden on the 15th, he might be at Cordova on the 21st: if King Joseph was at the foot of the passes on the 19th, he might be across them on the 20th. What use, therefore, would be a summons sent to Albuquerque in Estremadura, or to Del Parque in the mountains between Bejar and Ciudad Rodrigo? The French would be in the valley of the Guadalquivir long before Del Parque had even received his orders to move. As a matter of fact, that general got his dispatch on January 24, the day that Victor entered Cordova, and even Albuquerque

only as a reconnoitring force. As Latour-Maubourg was at Carmona on the 28th, it seems certain that he must have reached Seville (eighteen miles only from Carmona) on the 29th, not the 30th.

[1] Napier (ii. 298) seems unjust to the arrangements of the King and Soult when he writes : ' From Andujar to Seville is only 100 miles, and the French took ten days to traverse them, a tardiness for which there appears no adequate cause.' He then attributes it to King Joseph's wish to make spectacular entries, and to display his benevolence to the Andalusian towns. But the facts are wrong. Joseph reached Andujar late on Jan. 22 ; Victor's cavalry was in front of Seville on Jan. 29 : this makes seven, not ten, days : and the distance by the direct road via Ecija and Carmona is not 100, but 130 miles. A rate of eighteen miles a day is no bad record for an army advancing through a hostile country, even if it is meeting with no actual resistance. And January days are short, with sunrise late and sunset early.

was informed of the Junta's behests only on the 18th, when he reached Guadalcanal.

The obvious ineptitude which the Government had shown, and the imminent peril to which Seville was exposed, gave another chance to the local conspirators, who had already twice prepared a *pronunciamento* against the Junta. On the 22nd riots broke out, and demagogues were preaching at every street corner the necessity for deposing these incapable rulers, and substituting for them a regency of true patriots, and a Committee of Public Safety, which should show the energy in which the Junta had been so lacking. The people clamoured at the doors of the Arsenal, asking for muskets and cannon, they mustered outside the prisons where Palafox, Montijo, and other chiefs who had been arrested for their earlier plots, were still confined. Many of the members of the Junta left Seville on this and the following day, on the plausible pretext that it was necessary for them to betake themselves to Cadiz—which, by a decree of Jan. 13, had been designated as the meeting-place of the approaching National Cortes—in order to make preparations for the meeting of that august assembly. Indeed, the Junta had been directed to meet at Cadiz on February 1 for that purpose. The news that King Joseph had forced the passes of the Sierra Morena, which came to hand early on the 22nd, sufficed to make an end of any shadow of power which the Junta still possessed. Next day those members who had hitherto stuck to their post, and the Ministers, left the town with elaborately contrived secrecy. Seville fell into the hands of the mob, who, led by a Capuchin friar riding on a mule and brandishing a crucifix, burst open the prisons and the Arsenal, armed themselves, and nominated a new 'Supreme National Junta.' Its executive was to be composed of Palafox and Montijo, the Marquis of La Romana, General Eguia, and Francisco Saavedra, an aged and respectable person, who had been president of the old Junta of Seville, the original committee which had been suppressed by the Central Junta. He is said to have been used as a mere tool by Palafox and Montijo, and to have been disgusted by their acts. This new, and obviously illegal, Government issued decrees stigmatizing the fugitive 'Centralists' as cowards and traitors, and claiming authority not only over Andalusia, but over all Spain. They ordered the calling out of the levy *en masse*, and issued commissions displacing generals and governors in all the provinces. One of these documents declared Del Parque removed from the command of the Army of the Left, and named La Romana as his successor. The marquis, glad to escape from the tumult, rode off at once, presented himself at the head quarters of the Castilian army, and was recognized without difficulty as its chief—though his authority might well have been contested if any general had chosen to take up the cause of the discredited Central Junta.

But that unhappy body had no longer a single friend: its members were mobbed and arrested on their flight from Seville to Cadiz ; its President the Archbishop of Laodicea, its Vice-President the Conde de Altamira, and the War Minister Cornel were seized at Jerez by a frantic mob, and would have been murdered, if General Castaños, whom the Junta had treated so badly in December 1808, had not arrived in time to save their lives. Twenty-three members reached Cadiz, and there, by a proclamation dated January 29th, abdicated their authority, and nominated a Regency, to which they resigned their power, and the duty of receiving and welcoming the expected Cortes. The Regents were Castaños, the Bishop of Orense, Admiral Escaño, Saavedra—the president of the new and illegal Junta at Seville—and Fernandez de Leon, an American Treasury-official. who was to represent the Colonies [1]. It will be noted that the nominators were wise enough to refrain from appointing any of their own number to serve in the Regency.

Meanwhile, the duty of resisting the first shock of the French advance fell not on the Regency, but on the Revolutionary Government which had installed itself in power at Seville. These usurpers proved themselves quite as incapable as the men whom they had superseded. When once in possession of power, Palafox and his friends had to count up their resources : they had at their disposal an armed mob of 20,000 men, and a mere handful of regular troops, consisting of the regiments which had served as the guards of the late Junta, and four or

[1] After a very short tenure of office Fernandez de Leon was superseded by Lardizabal, another American.

five isolated battalions from the division of Zerain, which had finally sought refuge in Seville. These troops seem to have been about 4,000 strong at the most [1]. There was an immense quantity of artillery from the arsenal; it had been dragged out to line the new earthworks, on which the populace was busily engaged, but not two hundred trained gunners existed to man the batteries. It was hoped that Albuquerque's Estremaduran army would come to their aid, but—as we have already seen—the Duke deliberately refused to acknowledge the authority of the Seville Junta, and, instead of falling back upon the city, marched southwards to Utrera on the Cadiz road, leaving the great *chaussée* Ecija–Carmona–Seville open to the French.

On the 28th, the leaders of the Junta having taken stock of their position, and discovered its danger (for the lines which the people had thrown up would have required 50,000 men to man them, and not half that force was forthcoming even if every rioter armed with a musket was counted), copied in the most ignominious fashion the prudence or cowardice of the Central Junta, which they had so fiercely denounced five days before. Under the cover of the night Eguia, Montijo, Saavedra, and Palafox absconded from Seville without taking leave of their followers. Saavedra fled to Cadiz, where it is surprising to find that he was made a member of the new Regency, Palafox to Albuquerque's camp, Montijo to the southern mountains, where (as he announced) he was intending to collect an army of succour for Seville. When, therefore, on the next evening Latour-Maubourg's dragoons appeared before the entrenchments of the city, there was no longer any responsible government to turn the ardour of the multitude to account. Nevertheless, mobs, headed by frantic friars, ran to the entrenchments, and discharged musketry and cannon-shot at every French vedette that showed itself.

On the afternoon of the 30th, Victor appeared to reinforce Latour-Maubourg's cavalry, bringing with him the bulk of the

---

[1] It is difficult to make out what precisely were the battalions in Seville on January 23-29. But they certainly included a battalion of the 1st Walloon Guards [the Junta's old guard], with 1st and 2nd of España and Barbastro from Zerain's division. It is almost certain that most of Zerain's other battalions were with these three.

infantry of the 1st Corps. The King, Soult, and Mortier were close behind [1]. On this day it had been settled at a Council-of-War held at Carmona that the whole of the army should march on Seville, leaving Cadiz alone for the present, and detaching only a brigade of cavalry to pursue the army of Albuquerque. On the next morning Victor received assurances, from persons who had escaped from the city, that it was doubtful whether he would be opposed, since the mob was panic-stricken at the flight of its leaders, and the senior military officers were convinced that resistance was impossible. Certain that the defence would be feeble, if any were offered, Soult gave orders that the 1st Corps should storm the lines on February 1st. But no military operations were necessary : on the evening of January 31st the corporation of Seville had sent out a deputation to negotiate for surrender. They offered to admit the enemy, if they were guaranteed security of life and property for all who should submit, and a promise that no extraordinary war-contribution should be levied on their city. To this the King, who was anxious to enter the place as a pacific conqueror, without storm or bloodshed, gave an eager consent. While the civil authorities were treating with Victor, the small body of regular troops in Seville, under the Visconde de Gand, quietly left the place by the bridge leading to the western side of the Guadalquivir, and retreated in haste toward the Condado de Niebla and the borders of Portugal.

On the afternoon of February 1, Joseph entered Seville in triumph at the head of his Guard, and lodged himself in the Alcazar, the old residence of the Kings of Spain. He was welcomed by a deputation which comprised some persons of mark. The impression made on the citizens by the conduct of the two Juntas, and the turbulence of the mob which had ruled during the last eight days, had been so deplorable that a considerable number of the Sevillians despaired of the national cause, and rushed to acknowledge the usurper. Indeed, there were more 'Josefinos' found in this city than in any other

---

[1] Dessolles' division had been left behind at Cordova and Andujar, to garrison Upper Andalusia, and to extend a helping hand to Sebastiani, if he should meet with any resistance in his conquest of the kingdom of Granada.

corner of Spain. The 'intrusive king' released a number of political prisoners, whom the last Junta had arrested on suspicion of treason. Apparently this suspicion had been well grounded, as many of the captives, headed by the Swiss generals Preux and Reding [1], did homage to Joseph, and accepted office under him.

Encouraged by these defections to his cause, and by the fact that deputations had presented themselves from Cordova and Jaen to bespeak his protection, Joseph hastened to publish an absurd address to his army, couched in the magniloquent style which all French writers of proclamations at this time were wont to borrow from their Emperor. 'The barriers placed by Nature between the North and the South of Spain have fallen. You have met with friends only beyond the Sierra Morena. Jaen, Cordova, Seville have flung open their gates. . . . The King of Spain desires that between the Pillars of Hercules a third pillar shall arise, to recall to posterity, and to the navigators of both the new and the old world, the memory of the officers and men of that French army which drove back the English, saved thirty thousand Spaniards, pacified the ancient Baetica, and regained for France her natural allies.' The rather puzzling passage concerning the 'thirty thousand Spaniards saved' refers to the prisoners of Ocaña and the Sierra Morena, whom the French, according to the King, 'recognized as brethren led astray by the common enemy. You spared them, and I have received them as my children.'

Some elation in the King's language was, perhaps, pardonable at the moment. The moral effect of the surrender of Seville was considerable in France, England, and the rest of Europe, though less in Spain than elsewhere. The tangible trophies of the conquest were enormous—the place had been the central arsenal of Spain, and the amount of artillery, ammunition, and warlike equipment captured was very large. The cannon-foundry and other military factories were taken over in excellent condition, and kept the French army of Andalusia well supplied during the three years of its existence. Tobacco to the value, as it was said, of £1,000,000 was found in the great central magazine, and quinine, quicksilver, and other commodities of

[1] Younger brother of the victor of Baylen.

government monopoly to a considerable additional sum. Nothing had been done, since the news of the passage of the Sierra Morena had arrived, to destroy or remove all this valuable state property.

On the day following their entry into Seville, Joseph and Soult directed Victor to march in pursuit of Albuquerque, and to take possession of Cadiz. So complete had been the *débâcle* of the Spanish armies since the Andalusian campaign began, that it seems to have been supposed that the Army of Estremadura would offer no serious resistance, even if it should succeed in throwing itself into Cadiz before it was overtaken. Marching with laudable expedition, the Duke of Belluno covered the eighty-three miles between Seville and Cadiz in four days, and presented himself in front of the place on the evening of February 5th. But Albuquerque, unmolested in his march from Utrera, had arrived on the 3rd, bringing with him not only his own troops and those of Copons, but several recruit-battalions picked up at Xeres, Lebrija, San Lucar, and Puerto Santa Maria, where they had been organizing. He had some 12,000 men in all, not counting the civic militia of Cadiz, which had hitherto been its sole garrison.

Cadiz, in the days when the practicable range of the heaviest artillery did not exceed 2,500 yards, was one of the strongest places in the world. The town lies on the extreme point of a long sandy peninsula, which runs out into the sea from the Isla de Leon, a large island separated from the mainland of Andalusia by the salt-water channel of the Rio Santi Petri, an arm of the sea varying from 300 to 400 yards in breadth, and flowing through marshes which make access to its banks very difficult. The Isla, protected by this enormous wet ditch, has a front towards the continent of about seven miles, from the naval arsenal of La Carraca at its north end to the Castle of Santi Petri at its south. Batteries had already been thrown up at all the commanding points, and Albuquerque had broken the only bridge, that of Zuazo, which crossed the marsh and the Rio. It would be impossible to pass the channel save by collecting great quantities of boats, and these would have to move under artillery fire. Venegas, the military governor of Cadiz, had already ordered all the vessels, small and great, of

the villages round the bay to be destroyed or brought across to
the city. Moreover, there were a score of gunboats in the
channel, manned from the Spanish fleet, which could be used
to oppose any attempt to cross the Rio. Indeed, naval assistance to any amount was available for the defence of Cadiz:
there were a dozen Spanish and four English line-of-battle ships
in the harbour. All through the three long years while the
French lay in front of the Isla, no attempt was ever made to
throw a force in boats across the channel: the venture seemed
too hazardous.

If, however, Victor had, by some expedient, succeeded in
crossing the Rio, there were two lines of defence behind it, of
far greater strength than that formed by this outer ditch of the
Cadiz works. The triangular Isla de Leon forms with its apex
a long sand-spit, which projects for four miles into the Atlantic.
Half way along it the breadth of the spit is contracted to no
more than 200 yards, and here there was a continuous entrench-
ment from water to water, called the Cortadura, or the battery
of San Fernando, armed with many heavy guns. Supposing
this isthmus to have been passed, there lies, two miles further
along the sand-spit, the outer enceinte of Cadiz itself, with
a front of not more than 400 yards in breadth, and deep water
on either side.

Cadiz had been captured more than once in earlier wars, but
always by an enemy who could attack from the sea. Neither
the Isla de Leon nor the San Fernando line could be held against
an attack supported by a fleet which came close in shore, and
battered the works from flank and rear, or landed troops behind
them. The sea, it may be remarked, is four fathoms deep to
within a short distance (about 300 yards) of the shore, all along
the south front of the Isla and the Isthmus, so that there was
nothing to prevent a fleet coming close to the works. But
against any naval attack Cadiz was, in 1810, absolutely secured
by the predominance of the English fleet. There was no armed
French vessel nearer than Bayonne or Barcelona, nor any
possibility of bringing one round. All that was done by the
besiegers in a three years' leaguer was to build some gunboats
in the northern inlets of the bay, and these they never dared to
bring out into the open water.

The real danger to Cadiz lay not from the sea side, nor on the Isla front, but from the inner side of the harbour and the east. Here a long spit of land runs out from beside the town of Puerto Real in the direction of Cadiz. It is called the Trocadero, from a village situated on its south-eastern side. At its extreme point is a fort named San José, while another fort, named San Luis, lies alongside of the other on a low mud-island. In advance of both, built right in the marsh, and surrounded by water at high-tide, was a third called Matagorda. These three forts were the outer defences of the harbour against a naval attack, and could cross fires with the town batteries and a castle called Puntales, which lies on the easternmost point of the isthmus, a mile from the battery of San Fernando. Matagorda is only 1,200 yards from Puntales, and 3,000 yards from the eastern point of the city of Cadiz. If the French took possession of it, and of the neighbouring San José and San Luis, they could bombard the Puntales castle and all the neighbouring section of the Isthmus, to the grave danger and discomfort of all who had to pass between the city and the Isla de Leon. They would also be able to annoy ships lying in all the eastern reaches of the great harbour. But before Victor arrived in front of Cadiz, San José, San Luis, and Matagorda were blown up, with the leave of the governor Venegas, by a detachment of seamen from the British fleet. There could, therefore, be no trouble from this direction, unless the enemy succeeded in restoring and rearming the three forts,—no easy task under the fire of the Puntales castle and the fleet. It was not till some months had passed that the struggle began for these ruined works, the only points from which the defence could be seriously incommoded.

On his first arrival Victor summoned the town, and received a prompt and angry answer of refusal from the governor and the local Junta. The marshal inspected the city's outer defences, and was forced to report to the King at Seville that it seemed that nothing could be done against the place till he had brought up heavy artillery, and built himself boats. Joseph, unwilling to believe anything that contradicted the hopes of complete triumph that he had been nourishing ever since the passage of the Sierra Morena, came up to Puerto Santa Maria, on the bay of Cadiz, looked at the situation, did not find it reassuring, and wrote to his imperial brother to propose that he should send out his Toulon fleet to attack the place on the sea side [1]. Napoleon, still smarting under the memory of how Admiral Martin had destroyed an important section of that fleet in the preceding October, ignored this proposal. He did not forget, though his brother had apparently done so, the fact that the British Mediterranean fleet was still in existence.

Thus the position in front of Cadiz assumed the shape which it was to maintain for months, and even for years. Victor's corps could provide enough men to observe the whole shore of the bay, and to blockade the garrison. But the Spaniards recovered their courage when they saw the enemy reduced to inactivity, and began ere long to receive reinforcements. The first to arrive were 3,000 of the regular troops which had been at Seville. This corps, under the Visconde de Gand, had escaped westward after the capitulation, and, though pursued by a brigade of Mortier's corps, reached Ayamonte, at the mouth of the Guadiana, and there took ship for Cadiz. Somewhat later there arrived some troops sent by Wellington. The Spaniards in their day of disaster had forgotten their old jealousy about Cadiz, and asked for aid. Wellington, though loath to spare a man from Portugal, sent them in the early days of February three British [2] and two Portuguese battalions from Lisbon, under General William Stewart. So promptly were these troops shipped and landed, that they arrived at Cadiz between the 10th and the 15th of February, to the number of about 3,500 bayonets [3]. Thus the town was placed in security from any *coup de main* on Victor's part.

The internal situation in Cadiz, however, left much to be desired. The town had elected a local Junta of defence, of which the governor Venegas was made President, and this body

---

[1] ' Sire, il parait que Cadix veut se défendre. Nous verrons dans quelques jours ce qu'elle fera lorsque nous aurons quelques batteries montées. Si votre Majesté pouvait disposer de l'escadre de Toulon, l'occasion pourrait être bonne.' Joseph to Napoleon, Sta. Maria, Feb. 18.

[2] 79th, 2nd batt. 87th, and 94th regiments, and the 20th Portuguese line regiment.

[3] See Wellington to Bart. Frere and General Stewart, from Torres Vedras, Feb. 5th, and Vizeu, Feb. 27, 1810.

had frequent disputes with the new Regency, nominated by the
Central Junta at the time of its abdication, and also with
Albuquerque, whom Venegas did not wish to recognize as his
hierarchical superior. The local body could make a fair show
of objections to recognizing the legitimacy of the Regency : the
old Central Junta itself had a doubtful origin, and the government nominated by those of its members who had taken refuge
in Cadiz could not claim a clear title. But to raise the point
at this moment of crisis was factious and unpatriotic, and the
conduct of the local Junta became merely absurd when it tried
to arrogate to itself authority extending outside its own city,
and to issue orders to the outlying provinces, or the colonies of
America. Still worse, it refused to issue clothing and footgear
to Albuquerque's army, whose equipment had been worn out
by the long march from Estremadura, or to subsidize the
military hospitals, though it had a considerable stock both of
money and of military stores at its disposition. At the end of
February the Regency nominated Venegas Viceroy of Mexico,
and having bought him off with this splendid piece of prefer-
ment, made Albuquerque his successor in the governorship of
Cadiz. But even thus they did not succeed in getting proper
control over the city, for the Junta refused to allow the Duke
to place his head quarters within the walls, or to issue orders
to the civic militia. A *modus vivendi* was only reached
when the Regents made an ignominious pact with the local
oligarchy, by which the latter, in return for recognizing their
legitimate authority, and undertaking to pay and feed the
garrison, were granted the control of the port-revenues and
other royal taxes of Cadiz, as well as of all the subsidies arriving
from America. How the functions of government became still
further complicated, when the members of the long-expected
Cortes began to arrive, and to claim their rights as the sole
legitimate representatives of the nation, must be told in another
chapter [1].

Leaving matters at a deadlock in and about Cadiz, we must
turn back to the operations of the French in the outlying parts

---

[1] For a scathing account of the conduct of the Cadiz Junta and its
doings see Schepeler, vol. iii. 550-5. Napier very rightly calls it ' an
imperious body without honour, talents, or patriotism ' (ii. 334).

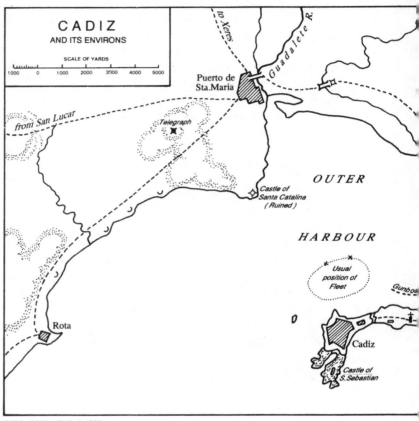

CADIZ
AND ITS ENVIRONS

SCALE OF YARDS

1000 0 1000 2000 3000 4000 5000

to Xeres

Guadalete R.

from San Lucar

Puerto de
Sta.Maria

Telegraph

Castle of
Santa Catalina
(Ruined)

OUTER

HARBOUR

Usual
position of
Fleet

Gunboa

Rota

Cadiz

Castle of
S.Sebastian

B.V.Darbishire, Oxford, 1907

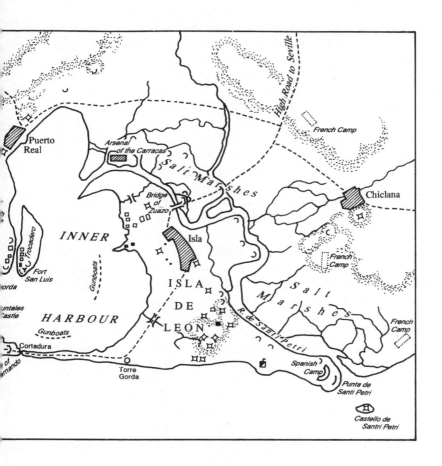

of Andalusia. Sebastiani, it will be remembered, had taken
Jaen on January 23rd. He was directed to march from thence
on Granada and Malaga, to scatter the remains of Areizaga's
army, and to subdue the valleys of the Sierra Nevada and the
long sea-coast below them. All this he accomplished with ease.
On the 28th he routed at Alcala la Real a force composed of
some of Areizaga's fugitives, which had been joined by Freire
and all the cavalry of the Andalusian army. These regiments,
which had been cantoned in the valley of the Guadalquivir, since
they were useless in the passes, had been collected by Freire to
the number of 2,000 sabres. They were routed and dispersed
by Milhaud's and Perreymond's dragoons and chasseurs, losing
over 500 men and the whole of their artillery. The survivors
dispersed, and retired in small parties eastward, only rallying in
the province of Murcia. That same evening Sebastiani pushed
on towards Granada, and was met by a deputation of its magistrates, who brought the keys of the city and a promise of
submission. The French vanguard entered it next day. Lacy,
who had taken refuge there with the small remains of his
division, retired to Guadix. Sebastiani levied a military contribution of 5,000,000 reals on the city, placed a garrison of
1,500 men in the Alhambra, and marched with a mixed force
on Malaga, the only place in this quarter where organized resistance showed itself. Here the local magistrates had been
deposed by a popular rising, and several thousand irregulars
had been collected by a Colonel Abello, a Capuchin friar named
Fernando Berrocal, and three brothers, notaries, of the name of
San Millan. They seized the passes of the Sierra de Alhama,
and called all the hill-country to arms. Sebastiani, marching by
Antequera, cleared the passes on February 5th, beat the half-
armed insurgent bands outside the suburbs of Malaga, and
stormed the town. He exacted a contribution of 12,000,000
reals, and hung the three San Millans and several other leading
insurgents. After this he extended his troops along the coast,
and occupied Velez Malaga, Motril, and Almunecar. The roads
and the towns were his, but many of the insurgents took
to the hills, and maintained a guerrilla warfare, which never
ceased throughout the next three years. There were always
bands on foot in the Alpujarras and the Sierra de Ronda,

though the 4th Corps expended much energy in hunting them down.

Meanwhile Giron, Lacy, Freire, and the rest of the fugitive generals had retired eastward. They had now come under the orders of Blake, who superseded Areizaga and took over charge of 3,000 or 4,000 dispirited men at Guadix on January 30th. He retired at once within the borders of the kingdom of Murcia. Small parties and stragglers continued to come in for many weeks, and by March there were 10,000 foot and 1,500 horse collected—all in the worst state of equipment, and thoroughly demoralized by their late disasters.

We must now turn to the other end of Andalusia: King Joseph, when departing to inspect the outworks of Cadiz, had left Mortier in command in this quarter. The Marshal, after hunting the little force of the Visconde de Gand out of the Condado de Niebla, had been directed to deal a stroke at Badajoz. Accordingly, leaving a brigade in Seville and another in the Condado, he marched with one infantry division and his light cavalry into Estremadura. He reached Olivenza with 9,000 men, and summoned Badajoz on February 12th, but he had arrived too late. A considerable Spanish force was now before him, the old host of Del Parque, which the Central Junta had called down to the Guadiana when the original Army of Estremadura marched under Albuquerque to succour Andalusia. How Mortier and La Romana, the successor of Del Parque, dealt with each other in the months of the spring must be told in a later chapter [1].

The King, meanwhile, spent the months of February and March in a circular tour through Andalusia, where he affected to perceive nothing but friendly feeling among the inhabitants. He visited Ronda, Malaga, Granada, Jaen, celebrating *Te Deums*, and giving bull-fights and banquets. It is certain that a sufficient show of submission was made to nourish his happy illusions as to the finality of his conquest. Threats or bribes induced many notables to present themselves at his receptions, and it seems that a considerable portion of the Andalusians hoped to save themselves from the rapacity of the military authorities by professing an enthusiasm for the King. He, for

[1] See Section xix, chapter iv of this volume.

his part, did his best to protect them—but he was soon gone, and the native officials whom he appointed were powerless against Sebastiani, the church plunderer, and Soult, the judicious collector of works of art. 'At the very moment when the King was lavishing assurances and promises,' writes his devoted servant Miot, 'and everywhere extolling the thorough disinterestedness of France, severe and crushing exactions were being laid on the provinces in our occupation. An iron hand was grinding them to the dust. The King was powerless to resist the open violation of the promises which he was daily giving[1].'

Open resistance, however, had ceased, save at Cadiz and in the inaccessible recesses of the Sierra Nevada. Andalusia had been subdued from end to end, and neither the King nor Soult yet realized that a lamentable strategic mistake had been made when 70,000 veteran troops had been pinned down to garrison the newly conquered realm, while Portugal and Wellington's army remained untouched. In their conception, as in that of the Emperor, the conquest of Portugal was to be sufficiently provided for by the new reinforcements which were now pouring over the Ebro, to the number of over 100,000 sabres and bayonets.

[1] Miot, ii. 432. Compare Joseph's hysterical letter to the Emperor (Ducasse, vii. 236) : ' La pacification générale de l'Andalousie sera opérée . . . Mais, sire, au nom du sang français et du sang espagnol rappelez Loison, Kellermann, Thouvenot ! Ces hommes nous coûtent bien cher ! ' It is curious that he, in the same letter, quotes as ' hommes honnêtes,' along with Mortier, Suchet, and Reynier, both Soult and Sebastiani, who were plunderers on as large a scale as Kellermann or Loison.

SECTION XIX

THE PORTUGUESE CAMPAIGN OF 1810.
THE PRELIMINARIES

CHAPTER I

THE MILITARY GEOGRAPHY OF PORTUGAL

THE continual existence of Portugal down to the present day in face of the persistent hostility and immensely superior force of its neighbour Spain seems at first sight to be one of the most inexplicable phenomena in modern history. It appears all the more astounding when we remember that the lesser kingdom was once conquered, and held down for sixty years, by the greater power. Few states have won back and maintained their independence in such masterful fashion as did Portugal, in the long 'War of Independence' that followed the insurrection of 1640 under the house of Braganza. But intense national spirit and heroic obstinacy on the part of the smaller people are not sufficient to account for the survival of the Portuguese kingdom as a separate entity. Its geography, which at the first sight seems hopelessly unfavourable to its defence, turns out on investigation to be eminently suitable for resistance against an attack from the east. On a first glance at the map it appears as if Portugal was composed of no more than the lower valleys of three great Spanish rivers, the Douro, the Tagus, and the Guadiana, so that the state which owns three-quarters of the course of each of these streams has but to send down its armies from the uplands of Leon and New Castile, to conquer the narrow land which lies about their estuaries. But nothing can be more deceptive than the map, when the Iberian Peninsula is in question. As we observed in our earlier volume [1], the rivers of Spain and Portugal are not highways, or lines of communication,

[1] See vol. i. pp. 75, 76.

but barriers—torrents sunk in gorges cut deep below the level of the face of the land.   The chief roads, with few exceptions, avoid, instead of courting, the neighbourhood of the great streams.   The leading routes which descend from Spain into Portugal in no case follow the lines of the Douro or the Tagus. Though the coast-plains, which form the heart of the kingdom of Portugal, its most wealthy and populous regions, lie about the mouths of those rivers, it is not by descending their banks that conquest or trade arrives most easily at its goal.   As a matter of fact, Spain and Portugal turn their backs upon each other: the smaller realm looks out upon the sea; her strength and wealth lie upon the Atlantic coast: the inland that touches Spain is rugged and unpeopled, in many parts a mere waste of rock and heath.   Nor, on the other hand, do Leon and New Castile look towards Portugal: the real ports of Madrid are Valencia and Alicante, not Lisbon, and that not from political reasons, but simply because those are the points where the sea can be reached with the minimum of mountain and desert to be passed through.   The way down from the central tableland of Spain to the Mediterranean is less difficult than the way down to the Atlantic.   Hence comes the fact that the high-roads leading from Spain into Portugal are so surprisingly few, and that the two main alternative routes from Madrid to Lisbon run, the one much further north, the other much further south, than might have been expected.   There is not now, and never has been, any straight road down the Tagus between the two capitals, obvious though the line looks upon the map.   The two main gates of Portugal are at Almeida and Elvas; at Alcantara, which appears the natural point of approach, there is but the most miserable of posterns—as Junot discovered in November 1807, much to his discomfiture.   Marshal Berwick had made the same experience in 1705, during the War of the Spanish Succession[1].

In the old wars between Spain and Portugal the whole land frontier of the smaller kingdom was exposed to attacks from the larger.   But the circumstances of 1810 differed from those of

[1] A student of the War of the Spanish Succession is always surprised to see how much fighting took place on fronts which were left severely alone by the English and French in 1809–12.

1705 or 1762 or 1801, in that the subsidiary campaigns in the
extreme north and south, which had always accompanied the
main clash along the frontiers of Beira and Alemtejo, could not
on this occasion take place. The French were no longer in
possession of Galicia, from which the Spaniards had been wont
to demonstrate against Oporto, nor, at the other extremity of
the line, had they a firm grip on Huelva, and the Condado de
Niebla, from which alone an attack could be directed against the
remote southern province of Algarve.

Portugal presents three sections of frontier to an invader
coming from the side of Spain. The northernmost, that from
the mouth of the Minho to Miranda-de-Douro, was not within
the scope of operations in 1810. It can only be approached
from Galicia ; that province was not subdued, nor had the
French any intention of dealing with it till after they should
have dealt with Portugal. An invasion of the Tras-os-Montes
and the Entre-Douro-é-Minho would have been an objectless
operation : they would fall of themselves if once Lisbon were
captured and the English expelled from the Peninsula. A
move against Oporto by some flanking division of the invading
army might have been conceivable, but such an attempt would
be made, if made at all, from the south of the Douro, through
northern Beira, and not through the mountains of the Tras-os-
Montes.

There remain two other sections of the Portuguese frontier : the
one from the Douro to the Tagus, and the other from the Tagus
to the Guadiana. Both of these were accessible to the French in
1810, since they were in possession alike of the plains of Leon and
of La Mancha, and of northern Andalusia. It was open to them
to choose one or the other front for attack, or to attack both at
once. Lisbon being the objective, it was clear that an attack
on the northern or Beira frontier possessed a paramount advantage
over an attack on the southern or Alemtejo frontier. A successful
advance north of the Tagus brings the invader directly to the
gates of Lisbon ; one south of the Tagus brings him only to the
heights of Almada, where he is separated from the Portuguese
capital by the broad estuary of the Tagus. Napoleon's power,
like that of the devil in mediaeval legends, ended at the edge
of the salt water ; and in face of the naval strength which the

English always maintained at Lisbon, a victorious French army camped on the heights of Almada would be almost as far from final success as when it started from Spain. The 1,900 yards of strait which protected the Portuguese capital could not be crossed. The most that the invader could accomplish would be to worry the ships in the port, and the lower quarters of the city, by a distant bombardment, if he could bring up heavy guns from Spain [1]. For nearly twenty miles inland from Lisbon the estuary of the Tagus expands into a broad brackish lagoon four to eleven miles broad, a complete protection against any attack from the east. Only at Alhandra does this inland sea contract, and for some further miles northward from that point the eastern bank of the Tagus is formed by broad salt-marshes (*lezirias*) cut up by countless channels of water, and practically inaccessible. It is only at Salvaterra, thirty miles north of Lisbon, that the Tagus assumes its ordinary breadth, and becomes an ordinary military obstacle. From that point upwards an invader from the Andalusian side might endeavour to cross it, and it presents no more difficulties than any other broad river. But, though even Rhines and Danubes may be passed in the face of an enemy, the operation is not one which a prudent general courts, and the Tagus is broad, absolutely bridgeless, and fickle in the extreme in its alternations of high and low water. To fight one's way from the valley of the Guadiana in order to meet such a problem at the end does not seem inviting. And even if the Tagus is passed, there are still thirty miles of road, including some formidable defensive positions, between the invader and Lisbon [2]. Yet there was one contingency under which an advance on the left bank of the river might be advantageous to the invader, and so possible was this contingency that Wellington from the very first had declared that he thought it probable that the French would move troops in that direction. If the

---

[1] See Map of the Lines of Torres Vedras, in Section xx of this volume, for the environs of Lisbon.

[2] Eliot, in his very judicious remarks on p. 100 of his *Defence of Portugal*, published just before Masséna's invasion, sums up the situation with—' a passage may without any difficulty be forced to the left bank of the Tagus : but then the enemy is as far from the accomplishment of his project as before, the river forming an insuperable barrier if well defended.'

Anglo-Portuguese army were drawn away to the Beira frontier, between Tagus and Douro, in order to resist a front attack delivered from the plains of Leon, and if it became involved in an active campaign somewhere far to the north, on the line of the Coa, or the Mondego, or the Alva, a subsidiary French force, striking south of the Tagus from the direction of Spanish Estremadura, might give dreadful trouble. If it could cross the Tagus anywhere between Abrantes and Salvaterra, it might get between the Anglo-Portuguese army and its base, and either fall upon its rear or capture Lisbon. For this reason Wellington, so far back as October 1809, had made up his mind that, if the French had an army on foot anywhere in the direction of Badajoz and Elvas, he must leave a considerable proportion of his own forces to watch them, and to defend, if need be, the line of the lower Tagus[1]. As long as the enemy had not yet subdued Badajoz and the neighbouring fortresses, and while there was still a strong Spanish army in that quarter, the need for precaution was not so pressing. Nevertheless, all through the summer of 1810 Wellington kept Hill with one English and one Portuguese division at Portalegre, south of the Tagus, though he withdrew this detachment when Masséna marched on Coimbra. Matters were much more perilous after the battle of the Gebora and the fall of Badajoz in February 1811. From that time onward, all through 1811 and 1812, nearly a third of the Anglo-Portuguese army was kept in the Alemtejo, first under

---

[1] Wellington to Col. Fletcher, commanding Royal Engineers, Oct. 20, 1809 (*Dispatches*, v. 235) : 'The enemy will probably attack on two distinct lines, the one south, the other north of the Tagus, and the system of defence must be founded upon this general basis. . . . His object will be, by means of the corps south of the Tagus, to turn the positions which we shall take up in front of the corps north of that river, to cut off from Lisbon the corps opposed to him, and to destroy it by an attack in front and rear. This can be avoided only by the retreat of the right, centre, and left of the allies to a point at which (from the state of the river) they cannot be turned, by the passage of the Tagus by the enemy's left corps.'

Six days later (*Disp.* v. 245) Wellington wrote to Admiral Berkeley in similar terms : ' It is probable that in the event of the enemy being enabled to invade this country in force, he will make his main attack by the right of the Tagus : but he will employ one corps on the left of the river, with the object of embarrassing, if not of preventing, the embarcation of the British army.'

Beresford, then under Hill, in order to guard against the possible stab in the back from the French army of Andalusia.

But the attack south of the Tagus was in Wellington's, and also, we may add, in Napoleon's conception [1], only a secondary operation. The main invasion was almost inevitably bound to take place on the Beira, not on the Alemtejo frontier. Between Fregeneda, where the Portuguese border line quits the Douro, to the pass of Villa Velha on the Tagus there is a distance of somewhat more than 100 miles. The division between Portugal and Spain does not lie along any well-marked natural feature, such as a mountain range or a broad river—though two small sections of the frontier are coincident with the insignificant streams of the Elga and the Agueda. It is rather drawn, in a somewhat arbitrary and haphazard fashion, through the midst of the desert upland, where Spain and Portugal turn their backs to each other. For the only piece of flat plain-land on the whole border is that from the Douro to Almeida, a mere ten or twelve miles, and immediately behind the Coa, only three or four miles from Almeida, the mountains begin. The rest of the frontier runs through thinly-peopled, barren highlands, from which the Coa, the Mondego, the Zezere, and the Ponçul fall away towards Portugal, and the Agueda and the Alagon towards Spain. The mountains are not, for the most part, very high—the culminating peak of the Serra da Estrella is only 6,540 feet—but they are singularly rugged and scarped, and much cleft by ravines, along whose sides the few roads crawl miserably, in constant precipitous dips and rises. This broad belt of upland, one long series of defiles for an invader, is some hundred miles broad, and does not cease till Coimbra, on the one side, or Abrantes, on the other, is reached: only then does the plain-land begin, and the country-side become fertile and thickly peopled. Only from those points onward is it possible for an army to live on the local produce: in the upland it must carry its food with it; for a single division would exhaust in a day the stores of the poor villages of the mountains; and the small

---

[1] So much so that in *Corresp.*, xx. p. 552, we find him informing Masséna that Badajoz and Elvas need not be touched till after Lisbon has fallen. The first contrary view, ordering a demonstration on the Lower Tagus, appears in the dispatch on p. 273 of vol. xxi.

poverty-stricken towns of Guarda, Celorico, Sabugal, Penama-cor, and Idanha have few resources. Castello Branco and Vizeu are the only two places in the upland where there is a valley of some breadth and richness, which can supply an army for many days. In this simple fact lies the explanation of the diffi-culties of the Portuguese campaigns of 1810 and 1811. Both the invader and the defender must bring their food with them, and protracted operations can only be kept up by means of incessant convoys from the rear. The campaign not infrequently became a starving-match, and the combatant who first exhausted his provisions had to retire, and to disperse his divisions in search of the wherewithal to live. Thanks to Wellington's providence it was always the French who were forced to this expedient.

The Beira frontier is divided into two sections by the range of mountains which crosses the border at right angles, half way between Douro and Tagus : it is known as the Sierras de Gata and de Jarama while in Spain, as the Serra da Estrella when it reaches Portugal. Its central ganglion lies between the high-lying towns of Sabugal and Penamacor in Portugal and the pass of Perales in Spain. From this point run off the great spurs which separate the valleys of the Ponçul, the Zezere, the Agueda, the Coa, and the Alagon. An invader must make his choice whether he will advance into Portugal south or north of the Serra da Estrella : to attempt to do so on both sides of the range would be risking too much, if there is an enemy of any strength in the field, since the columns to the right and to the left would be hopelessly separated, and liable to be beaten in detail. In the whole Peninsular War there was only one invasion made by the southern route, that of Junot in the winter of 1807–8. It was successful because it was absolutely unopposed. Nevertheless the French lost many men, had to leave their artillery behind them, and only arrived with the shadow of an army at Abrantes. It is true that Junot chose absolutely the worst path that could be found between the Serra da Estrella and the Tagus—the pass of Rosmarinhal, close above the latter river—and that he would have fared not quite so badly if he had marched from Zarza on Idanha and Castello Branco. But even at the best this region is most inhospitable : there are points where water is not pro-curable on stretches of eight or ten miles, others where the main

road is so steep that a six-pounder requires not only a dozen
horses but the assistance of fifty men to get it up the slope.
Except in the immediate neighbourhood of Castello Branco, the
country-side is almost uninhabited [1]. The whole ' corregidoria,'
which took its name from that town, and extended from the
Elga to the Zezere, had only 40,000 souls in its broad limits—
it was forty miles long by thirty broad, the size of a large English
county.   Junot's experiences served as a warning to his successors,
and no French army during the rest of the war endeavoured to
cross this corner of Portugal when advancing on Lisbon.   Castello
Branco was seized once or twice by a raiding force, but it was
never used as the starting-point of an army making a serious
attempt to advance towards the Portuguese capital.

    There remains to be considered only the section of the frontier
between the Douro and the Serra da Estrella, the front on which
Masséna's great blow was delivered in the autumn of 1810.   It
was a region which had from the earliest times been the battle-
ground of the Spanish and Portuguese.   Half a dozen times
since the Middle Ages armies from the plains of Leon had
invaded the Beira on this front.   Such campaigns always began
with a siege of Almeida, the sentinel-fortress pushed out in front
of the mountains to face the Spanish Ciudad Rodrigo.   Almeida
generally fell—it is too advanced a position for safety, and (as
Dumouriez remarked in his military study of Portugal) its value
would have doubled if it had only been placed upon the west
instead of the east bank of the Coa, close to the friendly mountains, and not on the outskirts of the perilous plain.   But rare,
indeed, were the occasions on which the Spaniard succeeded in
piercing the broad belt of tangled upland beyond Almeida, and
appearing at the gates of Coimbra or Oporto.

    There are four lines of further advance open to an invader
who has captured Almeida.   The first, a march on Oporto via
Pinhel and Lamego, may be mentioned only to be dismissed from
consideration.   It is of no use to an army which aims at Lisbon,
and proposes to conquer Portugal by a blow at its heart.   Masséna, whose directions were to drive the British into the sea in

---

[1] The above notes on the Castello Branco country and its roads are
mostly derived from Eliot's *Defence of Portugal*. Eliot has marched all
over the region ; see his pages 78-81.

the shortest and most effective fashion, could not have contemplated such a secondary object as the capture of Oporto for a moment. There remain three other roads to be investigated.

(1) The road north of the river Mondego, by Celorico, Vizeu, Bussaco, and Coimbra. (2) The corresponding and parallel road south of the Mondego, from Celorico by Chamusca, Maceira and Ponte de Murcella to Coimbra. (3) The road which, striking south from Celorico, crosses the headwaters of the Zezere, by Belmonte and Fundão, and then, climbing the Serra de Moradal, descends to Castello Branco, and from thence reaches Abrantes by the Sobreira Formosa. It may be remarked, by the way, that nothing in all the geography of Portugal seems more astonishing than that there should not be a fourth alternative road, one down the long valley of the Zezere, which, running in a straight line from Belmonte to Abrantes, looks on the map as if it ought to be a main artery of communication, and seems to indicate the obvious road to Lisbon from Almeida, since a straight line drawn between these points would run along the river for some forty miles. But as a matter of fact there was neither a first nor a second-rate road down the Zezere: the only towns on its course, Covilhão and Belmonte, lie hard by its sources, and its central reaches were almost uninhabited. The only good line of communication running near it is a by-road or duplication of the third route mentioned above, called the *Estrada Nova*, which, leaving the upper Zezere at Belmonte, keeps high up the side of the Serra de Moradal, and rejoins the Castello Branco road at Sobreira Formosa. This route was much employed by Wellington in later years, as a military road from north to south, usable even when Castello Branco was threatened by the French. But in 1810 he had ordered it to be rendered impassable, and this had been done by making several long cuttings at points where the track passed along precipices, the whole roadway being blown or shovelled down into the gulf below [1]. The French were, of course, unaware of this, and

---

[1] For the perilous adventure among these cuttings of a small French column which crossed the Estrada Nova, that which escorted Foy back to Santarem in Feb. 1811, see the autobiography of General Hulot, pp. 325–33. A considerable number of men and horses fell down these cuttings in a forced night-march, and in all several hundred men of Foy's

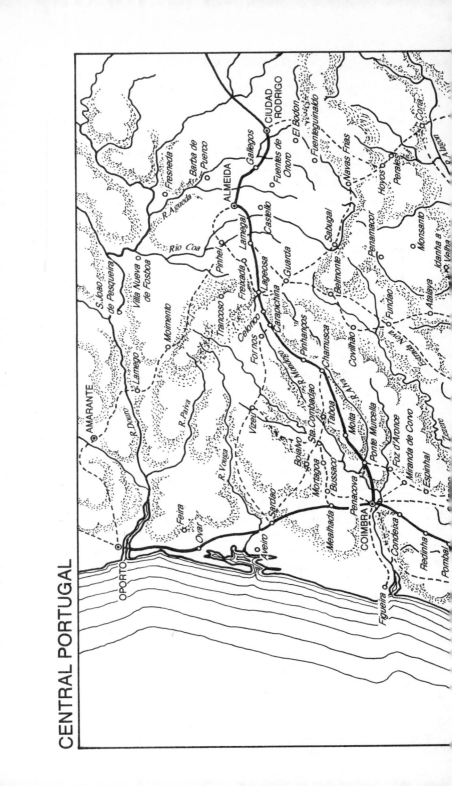

CENTRAL PORTUGAL

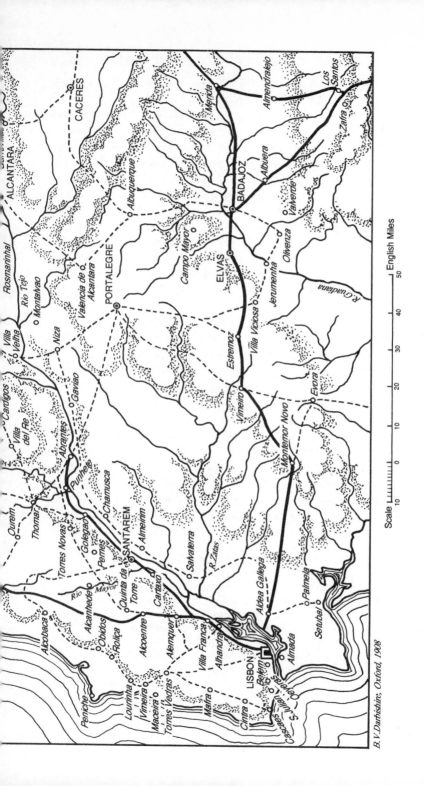

Scale |_____|_____|_____| English Miles

10   0   10   20   30   40   50

B.V.Darbishire, Oxford, 1908

Masséna is said by his confidant Foy to have taken the *Estrada Nova* into serious consideration, and to have decided against it because of the necessity for forcing the passage of the Zezere when the defiles were passed, and for laying siege to Abrantes [1]. A far more practical objection was its extreme wildness : it runs along an absolutely uninhabited mountain-side, and the neighbourhood is destitute not only of food but of water for great sections of its length. This Masséna ought to have known, if his Portuguese advisers had been competent. Apparently he was wholly unaware of its character, just as he was necessarily ignorant of the fact that his prescient adversary had blasted away huge sections of it, so that it was absolutely impassable for guns or wagons, as also that earthworks had been carefully constructed to cover the point where it debouches on to the Zezere.

The Castello Branco road, therefore, with this dependent by-road, the Estrada Nova, was practically left out of consideration by the Marshal. There remains the choice between the two northern routes, Celorico–Vizeu–Coimbra, and Celorico–Chamusca–Ponte de Murcella–Coimbra. Both traverse rough ground—but ground less rough than that to be found on some parts of the Castello Branco road. Along both there is an intermittent belt of cultivated land, and not unfrequent villages. Both are intersected by many good military positions, on which a defending army can offer battle to an invader with advantage. In especial, the northern road strikes and climbs the granite ridge of Bussaco with every disadvantage for the attacking side, and the southern road is contracted into a difficult defile at the passage of the Alva near Ponte de Murcella. On the whole,

---

column perished, starved and storm-beaten on this inhospitable road. The survivors only got through by cutting a slippery foot-track along the precipices : nothing on wheels could have passed that way.

[1] In Foy's interesting minute of his conversation with Napoleon about the invasion, on Nov. 23, 1810, when he had taken home Masséna's dispatches : ' Montrez-moi les deux routes de Ponte de Murcella et de Castello Branco,' says the Emperor. Then after a pause : ' Et l'Estrada Nova ? Pourquoi Masséna n'a-t-il pas débouché par l'Estrada Nova ?'— ' Sire, à cause d'Abrantès et du Zézère.' — ' Oui, Masséna a bien fait ; maintenant il faut prendre Abrantès : Elvas ne nous servirait de rien.' See Foy's *Mémoires*, p. 111.

however, this last is the better line for advance :—the strongest testimonial to the fact is that Wellington expected Masséna to take it, and erected at the passage of the Alva almost [1] the only earthworks, save those of the lines of Torres Vedras, which he constructed in his preparations for the reception of the invader. When he first heard that the Marshal was moving forward from Almeida to Celorico, and was clearly aiming at the Mondego valley, he announced that he should endeavour to stop the invader on the Alva [2], not apparently thinking it at all probable that Masséna would move by Vizeu and the north bank of the Mondego. On realizing that this was really his adversary's design, he observed with some exultation that, while there were certainly many bad roads in Portugal, the enemy had taken decidedly the worst of those open to him [3]; moreover, he had committed himself to attack the heights of Bussaco, the most formidable position in the whole of northern Portugal. How the French commander came to make this choice we shall discuss in its proper place. Suffice it to say that Wellington had not realized how bad was Masséna's information, how worthless his maps, and—what is most surprising of all—how entirely destitute of local knowledge were the Portuguese traitors—Alorna, Pamplona, and the other renegade officers—whom the Emperor had sent as guides and advisers to the Marshal. And in truth, the unsuspected ignorance of Masséna and his advisers added an incalculable element of chance to the problem set before Wellington. He was obliged to make his plans on the hypothesis that the enemy would make the correct move : and not unfrequently the enemy, for reasons which the English general could not possibly foresee, made the wrong one.

The French invasion was bound to commence with a preliminary clearance of the outlying fortresses still in the hands of the Spaniards. These to some extent protected the Portuguese frontier in 1810, though they had been built with the express purpose, not of protecting, but of threatening it, and had never

---

[1] There were some others thrown up on the extreme lower course of the Zezere, by Barca Nova and Punhete, to guard against a possible but unlikely use of the Castello Branco road by the enemy.

[2] Wellington to Hill (*Disp.*, vi. p. 441), Sept. 15.

[3] Wellington to Chas. Stuart, Sept. 18.

before been attacked by an enemy coming from the east. Only three of these fortresses were of any importance—Astorga, Ciudad Rodrigo, and Badajoz. The other strongholds of Spanish Estremadura, Alcantara (which had stood a siege in the War of the Spanish Succession), Albuquerque, Olivenza, were either not in a state of defence at all, or were hopelessly antiquated, and little suited to face modern artillery and modern siegecraft.

Astorga lies so far to the north that it might have been neglected without much peril to the French scheme of invasion. But the Emperor had ordered that it should be reduced before the great enterprise began : it gave the Spanish army of Galicia a foothold in the plains of Leon, from which it might operate against Masséna's rear, if he should pass it by. Its capture, too, was considered a matter of small difficulty, for it was but a mediaeval walled town, to which some hasty outworks had been added during the last year. It will be remembered that when Moore passed that way in January 1809, Astorga had been treated by both sides as an open town, and no attempt had been made to garrison or defend it. Since then La Romana had repaired its dilapidated enceinte, stockaded its suburbs, and armed it with guns brought from Ferrol. As late as January 11, 1810, Napoleon seems hardly aware of this fact : in a dispatch of that date he orders Loison to make his head quarters there, evidently under the impression that it is not held by the Spaniards, or at least that it is a place which they will evacuate at the first appearance of a serious attack [1]. It is only in March that he writes to Junot that Astorga must be besieged and taken, in order to occupy the attention of the Galicians and to thrust them back into their mountains [2].

Ciudad Rodrigo was a more serious business. It was a regular fortress, though only one of the second class ; its prestige, as the only Spanish stronghold on the Portuguese frontier, was great. It commands the whole southern stretch of the plains of Leon, being the only place out of the control of an invader who is superior in cavalry, and therefore master of the defenceless *Tierra de Campos*. There was also a small Spanish army depending upon it, and clinging to the skirts of the Sierra de Gata. This was the division

---

[1] *Nap. Corresp.*, xx. p. 117. Napoleon to Berthier.

[2] Ibid., p. 271.

of Martin de la Carrera, which had been left behind when the greater part of Del Parque's Army of the Left marched down into Estremadura in January 1810, in order to replace there the troops which had gone off to the defence of Cadiz. It was clear that Ciudad Rodrigo must be taken, and Martin de la Carrera brushed away or destroyed, before any serious attempt to invade Portugal was begun. If the Emperor thought that such a remote place as Astorga was worth his notice, it was obvious that he would regard Ciudad Rodrigo as absolutely indispensable to his designs. It was for its reduction that he gave Masséna the great battering train of fifty heavy guns, with 2,500 artillerymen and sappers, which was assigned to him, independent of the artillery of the three corps of the Army of Portugal.

Badajoz, far to the south, in Spanish Estremadura, stood to the defence of Southern Portugal exactly as Ciudad Rodrigo to the defence of Northern Portugal. It possessed also in Elvas a counterpart to Almeida. But Badajoz is immensely larger and stronger than Rodrigo, just as Elvas is infinitely more formidable than Almeida. The two fortresses on the frontier of Leon are small places crowning mere mounds set in a plain. Badajoz and Elvas have towering citadels set on rugged hills, and overlooking the whole country-side. They have also strong detached forts on dominant positions : the circuit of ground that must be taken up by an army that intends to besiege them is very large, and at Badajoz there is a first-class river, the Guadiana, which cuts in two the lines which the assailant must occupy. It may be added that based on Badajoz there was a whole Spanish army of 15,000 men, not a mere division of 3,000, like that which lurked in the mountains above Rodrigo. Noting the strength of Badajoz and Elvas, the Emperor had made up his mind that they should be observed and ' contained ' by troops from the Army of Andalusia, but not attacked till Lisbon had been conquered and the English expelled from Portugal. ' Les Anglais une fois battus et rembarqués, Badajoz et Elvas tombent d'eux-mêmes,' he wrote in a holograph minute addressed to Masséna, just before the advance across the Portuguese frontier began [1]. It was only when the invasion had been brought to a standstill before the lines of Torres Vedras, that he came to the conclusion that pressure must

[1] Napoleon to Masséna, July 29, 1810, *Corresp.*, xx. p. 552.

be applied south of the Tagus, to distract Wellington, and that Soult, as a preliminary to an attack on the Alemtejo, must capture Badajoz and Elvas, and disperse the Spanish Army of Estremadura. The idea came to him tardily: thanks to Wellington's careful starvation of the main French army, Massena was forced to retreat into Leon when Soult had only recently captured Badajoz, and had not yet shown a man in front of Elvas. The scheme was hatched, like so many of Napoleon's Spanish plans, about three months too late for effective realization. As late as November 1810 the orders to Soult are merely to demonstrate against Badajoz, and to hinder the departure of La Romana's army for the lines of Torres Vedras, but not to besiege the Estremaduran fortress. Probably it was Foy's information as to the existence and strength of the unsuspected lines of Torres Vedras, which reached him late in November, that made the Emperor realize the advisability of that secondary attack by the south bank of the Tagus which Wellington had foreseen and taken means to meet a full year before. Fortunately a capable general on the defensive always knows his own weak spots long before they are discovered by the enemy. By the time that Soult had at last captured Badajoz and the small dependent places—Olivenza, Albuquerque, Campo Mayor—Wellington had got rid of Masséna from the neighbourhood of Lisbon, and was preparing to chase him home across Northern Portugal. Within a few weeks of its surrender by the traitor Imaz, Badajoz was being besieged by a detachment of the British army, and Soult had his hands full, as he strove at once to hold down Andalusia and to relieve the beleaguered fortress.

SECTION XIX: CHAPTER II

WELLINGTON'S PREPARATIONS FOR DEFENCE

As far back as September 1809, while his army still lay at Badajoz and the Talavera campaign was hardly over, Wellington had foreseen the oncoming invasion of Portugal, which did not actually begin till August 1810 [1]. Writing to his brother, then on his special mission to Seville, he had laid down his conclusions. Bonaparte would, in consequence of the cessation of the Austrian war, be enabled to pour unlimited reinforcements into Spain. The British army, even if raised to 40,000 men, would not be strong enough to cover both Seville and Lisbon. Considering the temper of the Spanish government and the Spanish troops, he thought it would be most unadvisable to commit himself to the defence of Andalusia. But he was prepared to undertake the defence of Portugal. He implored the British Ministry not to sacrifice its strong position on the Tagus in order to embark upon a hazardous campaign in the South [2]. His views as to Portugal were simply the development of those which he had drawn up for Castlereagh's eye on his first sailing for the Peninsula [3]. Portugal though 'all frontier' might be defended against any French army of less than 100,000 men, if its resources were placed at his disposal, and he were given a free hand to utilize them according to his own plan. The Portland Cabinet, though much doubting whether Wellington could carry out his pledge, and though reluctant to abandon the idea that Andalusia might be defended and Cadiz made

[1] For his views just after Talavera see vol. ii. of this work, pages 609-10.

[2] ' I strongly recommend to you, unless you mean to incur the risk of the loss of your army, not to have anything to do with Spanish warfare, on any ground whatever, in the existing state of things. . . . If you should take up Cadiz you must lay down Portugal.' Wellington to Castlereagh, *Dispatches*, v. 90.

[3] See vol. ii. pages 286-8.

secure by British troops, finally yielded to the General's appeal.

But on December 2, 1809, the Portland Cabinet gave place to Spencer Perceval's new administration, and Wellington had to reiterate the arguments which he had used to Castlereagh and Canning to new correspondents, Lord Liverpool and Lord Bathurst. Fortunately the incoming ministers resolved to adhere to the promises made by their predecessors, and to persist in the defence of Portugal. It was of immense value to Wellington that his brother Wellesley soon replaced Lord Bathurst at the Foreign Office, so that he could command in this Ministry a supporter as firm as Castlereagh had been in the last. Nevertheless his position was not entirely fortunate : the new administration was being fiercely assailed by the Whigs over the general policy of risking British armies on the Continent. The calamities of the Walcheren expedition supplied a text on which the Opposition could preach interminable sermons. The men who were not ashamed to allege, for party reasons, that Wellington was a rash general, and that the Talavera campaign had been a disaster, were continually harassing the Ministry, by their suggestions that when the French Emperor marched in person to Spain the British army in the Peninsula must inevitably be destroyed. It was probably to aid them that Napoleon kept inserting in the *Moniteur* articles in which it was asserted that the maintenance of the incapable 'Sepoy General' at the head of the British forces was the thing which France must most desire. In Lord Liverpool's correspondence with Wellington it is easy to see that the idea that it might be necessary to evacuate Portugal, when the French attack was delivered, almost preponderated over that of preparing for the defence of that realm. While Wellington's whole mind is set on working out the details of a campaign from which he hopes great things, his correspondent is always thinking of the possibility of a disastrous embarkation at the end of it. The General could not pledge himself that Portugal might be defended against any odds whatever : it was possible that the Emperor might lead or send against him an army of absolutely overpowering strength, though he did not think such a contingency probable. But since he could not say that his

position was impregnable, he was being continually worried
with suggestions as to all the possible contingencies that might
occur to his discomfiture.   The ministers dreaded that the
Peninsular venture might end in a fiasco, like the Duke of York's
Dutch expedition of 1799, and thought that such a failure
would lose them their offices.   Hence they were nervous about
every false rumour that reached them from France concerning
the Emperor's approaching departure ; and the more certain
information about the immense numbers of troops that were
passing the Pyrenees filled them with dread.   It required all
Wellington's robust self-confidence to keep them reassured.   He
had to be perpetually repeating to them that all his preparations
for retreat and embarkation, if the worst should happen, had
been already thought out—they might make up their minds
that he would do nothing rash.   But he was inclined to think
that there would in the end be no need to depart.   ' I shall
delay the embarkation,' he wrote, ' as long as it is in my power,
and shall do everything that is in my power to avert the
necessity of embarking at all.   If the enemy should invade this
country with a force less than that which I should think so
superior to ours as to create a necessity for embarking, I shall
fight a battle to save the country, and for this I have made the
preparations.'   He did not think he could be beaten ; but if, by
some mischance, the fortune of war went against him, he had
still no doubt that he could bring off the army in safety.   ' If
we do go, I feel a little anxiety to go like gentlemen, out of the
hall door (particularly after all the preparations I have made to
enable us to do so), and not out of the back door or by the
area.'

It is curious to find that in this most interesting dispatch to
Lord Liverpool Wellington distinctly asserts that his worst
enemy was the ghost of Sir John Moore[1].   ' The great disadvantage under which I labour is that Sir John Moore, who
was here before me, gave his opinion that Portugal could not
be defended by the army under his command.   It is obvious that
the country was in a very different situation at that time from
what it is at present, and that I am in a very different situation
from that in which he found himself . . . , yet persons who ought

---

[1] See also vol. ii. page 286, of this book.

to be better acquainted with these facts entertain a certain prejudice against the adoption of any plan for opposing the enemy of which Portugal is to be the theatre.   I have as much respect as any man for the opinion and judgement of Sir John Moore, and I should mistrust my own if it were opposed to his in a case where he had had the opportunity of knowing and considering.   But he positively knew nothing about Portugal, and could know nothing about its existing state [1].'

The most vexatious thing for Wellington was that 'the persons who ought to have known better,' yet were perpetually uttering melancholy vaticinations as to the approach of disaster, included some of his own senior officers.   I have seen a letter from a general in Portugal to his friend in England containing such phrases as this: 'I most strongly suspect that before many months are over our heads there will be no opportunity for this employment (that of a cavalry brigadier) left to *any one*, on the Continent at least.   The next campaign will close the eventful scene in the Peninsula, as far as we are concerned; for I am decidedly of opinion that neither (Marshal) Wellington nor (Marshal) Beresford will prevent the approaching subjugation of Portugal.'   Or again: 'I am quite surprised at Lord W.'s pliant disposition.   I suspect he feels himself tottering on his throne, and wishes to conciliate at any sacrifice [2].'   The frequent complaints in Wellington's correspondence as to the sort of letters that were going home to England in the spring of 1810 sufficiently show that these down-hearted views were not uncommon among his subordinates.   If the generals on the spot foresaw disaster, it is no wonder that the ministers in London felt anxious, and refused to be comforted by the confident dispatches of the Commander-in-Chief.

[1] All these quotations are from Wellington to Lord Liverpool, April 2, 1810, a long dispatch written from Vizeu, every word of which is well worth study.

[2] I found these passages in letters to Sir John Le Marchant, then in command at the Staff College at High Wycombe, from a highly-placed friend in Portugal.   It is notable that other contemporary epistles from younger men, old pupils of Le Marchant, show a far more cheery spirit. The correspondence (from which I shall have many other passages to quote) was placed at my disposition by the kindness of Sir Henry Le Marchant, grandson of Sir John.

The preparations which Wellington was making during the winter of 1809–10 and the ensuing spring, for the reception of the inevitable French invasion, may be arranged, in the main, under three heads. We must first treat of the complete reorganization of the Portuguese military forces, not only the regulars but the militia, and the old *levée en masse* of the Ordenanza. Second come the elaborate plans for the construction of enormous field-works for the protection of Lisbon, the famous lines of Torres Vedras, and the fortification of certain other, and more advanced, points. The third, and in some ways the most important of all, was the arrangement of the great scheme for devastating the country-side in front of the invader, and fighting him by the weapon of starvation, a device new to the French, but not unprecedented in the earlier history of Portugal.

The Portuguese regular army had taken hardly any part in the campaigns of 1809. The only sections of it that had been under fire were Silveira's two regiments, the four battalions that marched with Wellington to Oporto in May, and Wilson's Loyal Lusitanian Legion, which had fought with more valour than success at the bridge of Alcantara and the Pass of Baños[1]. Beresford, with the greater part of the troops that were in a condition to take the field, had been out on the border in July, and had remained for some days in Spain, on the side of Coria and Zarza Mayor, but he had never been in contact with the enemy[2]. The fighting power of the reorganized Portuguese army was still a doubtful quantity.

The field-strength of the Portuguese regular forces should have been, according to its establishments, 56,000 men. In September 1809 there were only 42,000 men with the colours[3], and of these much more than half were recruits, who had recently been thrust into the depleted *cadres* of the old army. There were many regiments which had been practically destroyed by the French, and which showed, when Beresford first marched out to the frontier, only 200 or 300 men instead of their normal

[1] See vol. ii. pages 440–1 and 620.

[2] See vol. ii. pages 600–1. Beresford had some 18,000 men with him.

[3] See tables in vol. ii. pages 629–31.

1,500 [1]. Many others had less than half their complement.
The first thing that required to be done was to fill up the gaps,
and this was accomplished during the winter of 1809–10 by
a stringent use of the conscription law already existing.   The
line regiments in the Bussaco campaign showed, with hardly an
exception, 1,200 or 1,300 effectives present—i.e. if the sick and
'details' are added they were nearly or quite up to their
establishment of 1,500 [2].   The cavalry was less effective : the
number of men could be filled up, but horses were hard to
find, and in the end Wellington sent four of the twelve
regiments to do dismounted duty in garrison, and served out
their mounts to the remaining eight, which nevertheless could
never show more than 300 or 400 sabres present, out of
their nominal 594.   Portugal is not a horse-breeding country,
and the British cavalry was competing with the native for
the small supply of remounts that could be procured.   The
artillery, on the other hand, was high in strength and very
satisfactory.

Mere numbers are no test of the efficiency of a host.   The
weak point of the old national army had been—as we mentioned
in another place—the effete and unmilitary character of its
body of officers—more especially of its senior officers [3].   The
junior ranks, filled up since the French invasion with young
men who had taken up the military career from patriotic
motives, were infinitely better.   By the second year of the war
there were many admirable officers among them.   But it was
men capable of handling a battalion or a regiment that were
wanting.   We saw how Beresford had been forced to introduce
many British officers into the service, though he was aware that
the personal pride of the Portuguese officers was bitterly hurt
thereby.   His justification may be deduced from a confidential

---

[1] On Sept. 15, 1809, the 22nd, which had been destroyed by Soult at
Oporto, had only 193 men.   The 8th had but 369, the 15th 577, the 24th
505.

[2] Ten regiments present at Bussaco had over 1,100 men each, only one
less than 800.   This was the 22nd, mentioned above as practically non-
existent a year before.   It had only recruited up to the strength of one
battalion : all the rest had two.   The strongest regiment was the 11th
with 1,438 men.

[3] See vol. ii. pages 210–15.

memorandum written for him by his chief-of-the-staff, Benjamin D'Urban [1], which is well worth quoting :—

'There are yet among the field officers, captains, and older subalterns a number of incorrigible officers of the old school, who are a dead weight upon their respective regiments, and mischievous in the way of example. Whenever it may be thought expedient, from time to time, to get rid of them, there will be no difficulty in finding excellent young men to replace them from the ranks respectively below. . . . But I feel it incumbent upon me to give it you as my decided opinion, resulting from a close investigation into the causes of the defects of the Portuguese, that it will be utterly impossible either to make a regiment fit for service, or to preserve it when made so, without giving it an English commanding-officer and at least two English captains.

'The Portuguese soldier is naturally indolent. He falls with the greatest facility into slouching and slovenly habits, unless he is constantly roused and forced to exert himself. But many a Portuguese officer, if not constantly spurred and urged to do his duty, is at least as indolent as his men. Nothing (I am persuaded by experience) will counteract this, and create activity among the officers and consequent diligence and care among the men, but the strictness, energy and vigilance of an English commanding-officer.

'Even supposing a sufficient energy of character in the native officer, he does not and will not, if he be not a *Fidalgo* himself, exercise coercive or strong measures to oblige one of that class to do his duty. He is aware that in doing so he makes a powerful enemy, and all the habits of thought in which he has been educated inspire him with such a dread of this, that no sense of duty will urge him to encounter it. Thus, whenever a regiment is commanded by a non-Fidalgo, it never fails to suffer extremely : for the noblemen are permitted to do as they please, and afford a very bad example, for they are at least as indolent as the ordinary Portuguese.

[1] This unpublished document here quoted, along with the whole of Sir Benjamin's journal and correspondence, has been placed at my disposal by his grandson, Mr. D'Urban. They are invaluable for the Portuguese aspect of the War.

'The English captains will be found invaluable, especially in the hands of an English commandant. Their example is infinitely useful. The Portuguese captains are piqued into activity and attention, when they see their companies excelled in efficiency by those of the English, and they do from emulation what a sense of duty would perhaps never bring them to. There are a variety of by-paths and oblique means by which the parts of a Portuguese corps are constantly, and almost insensibly, endeavouring to return to the old habits that they are so much attached to. To nip this, from time to time, in the bud, it is necessary to be aware of it: without the faithful surveillance of English subordinate officers (who, ever mixing with the mass of the men, can't well be ignorant of what is going on) the commanding-officer can rarely be warned in time.'

Beresford replied that all this was true, but that 'the national feeling required management,' and that to place every regimental or brigade command in British hands would provoke such fierce jealousy that he was 'compelled to humour the prejudices and satisfy the pride of the nation.' His device for doing this was to make a general rule that wherever a Portuguese officer was in chief command he should have a British officer second in command under him, and vice versa [1]. When a brigade was given to a Portuguese, he managed that the two colonels of the regiments forming it should be Englishmen; similarly, if a Portuguese commanded a regiment his senior major was always an Englishman. By this means it was secured that a fair half of the higher pieces of promotion should be left to the native officers, but that every Portuguese placed in a responsible position should have a British officer at his back. In addition there were from two to four British captains in each battalion, but no subalterns; for, to encourage good men to volunteer into the Portuguese service, it was provided that all who did so should receive a step of promotion, and a British lieutenant became a Portuguese captain on exchange, and a British captain a Portuguese major. The system seems to have

---

[1] This rule I find definitely laid down in a letter of Hardinge, Beresford's Quartermaster-general, written as late as 1812, but the practice was already in full use by 1810.

worked well, and with far less friction than might have been expected[1]. The better class of native officers were piqued into emulation, just as D'Urban had expected; the worst was gradually eliminated[2]. It must be noted that to every battalion there were added one or two British sergeants, whose services were needed for the drilling of the men in the English exercises, which now superseded the old German system left behind by La Lippe, the last reorganizer of the Portuguese army. For the whole drill of the infantry was changed, and the British formations and manœuvres introduced. Dundas's 'Eighteen Manœuvres' were translated, and became the Bible of the Lusitanian no less than the British officer[3]. The employment of the two-deep line, the essential feature of the system, was made the base of all Portuguese drill; at Bussaco it justified itself. The Caçadores were trained on the 'Rifle Regulations' of Coote Manningham, and their uniform was modified in cut, though not in colour, to a close resemblance of that of the British rifleman[4]. The net result of all these changes was that for the future the British and Portuguese units of Wellington's army could be moved by the same words of command, and in the same formations, and that all the disadvantages resulting from the coexistence of two different systems of drill disappeared.

Two principal difficulties still remained in the administration of the Portuguese army. The first was, what to do with the few senior officers of undoubted patriotism but more doubtful capacity, who were too important and influential to be placed upon the shelf, yet might cause a disaster if placed in a critical position of responsibility. The most notable of them was Silveira, who had acquired much popularity by his obstinate, if ill-managed, resistance to Soult in the spring of 1809. Wellington, with many searchings of heart, placed him in com-

[1] For narratives of the daily life of a British officer in a Portuguese regiment see Bunbury's *Reminiscences of a Veteran*, and Blakiston's *Twelve Years of Military Adventure*. Both had their difficulties, but both, on the whole, got on well with their colleagues. D'Urban's correspondence supplies a frequent commentary on regimental problems.

[2] How this was done may be read in Blakiston.

[3] See Bunbury, p. 54.

[4] They were dressed in dark brown instead of in the rifle green. The shako, coat, and trousers were of the British model.

mand of the Tras-os-Montes, where it was most unlikely that
any serious irruption of the French would take place[1].   He had
a large force placed under him, but it did not include a single
regular regiment, and, with militia only at his disposition, it
was hoped that he would be discouraged from attempting any
hazardous experiments.   Moreover, he was given a British
second-in-command, first John Wilson and afterwards Miller,
to curb his eccentricities so far as was possible.   Baccelar,
another officer of doubtful merit, but more dangerous from
torpidity than from rashness, was given charge of the militia
of the three northern provinces, so that Silveira was techni-
cally under his orders—though the nominal subordinate would
seem to have paid little attention to his superior.   The most
important post, however, assigned to a Portuguese officer was
the governorship of Elvas, the strongest fortress of Portugal,
and one which would stand in the forefront of the battle if
the French made the subsidiary invasion south of the Tagus,
which Wellington was inclined to expect.   The command of
this great stronghold and the 6,000 men of its garrison (of
whom half were regulars) was given to General Leite, an active
and ingenious officer, and (what was more important) a man
who obeyed orders.   Of all the Portuguese he was the one
whom Wellington most trusted ; every British narrator of the
war who came in contact with him has a word of praise in
his behalf.   Of the other native generals, Lecor, in command
of a division, and Fonseca, in command of a brigade, were
with the field army.   Miranda was given charge of the militia
of Northern Estremadura, who were likely to be in the thickest
of the trouble.   But the other Portuguese units of the allied
host were under British officers : Pack, Archibald and Alexander
Campbell, MacMahon, Coleman, Harvey, Collins, and Bradford

---

[1] Silveira was the despair of Beresford and his chief-of-the-staff D'Urban.
The latter writes (Apr. 19, 1810) : ' This general is the most extraordinary
of all the people in this extraordinary country.   Perpetually fluctuating
—incapable of standing still—always wishing to move backward or forward
—all his movements to no purpose but that of harassing his troops.   The
man is either very weak or very designing—perhaps both.   Anyhow he is
a mischievous charlatan, and I wish the Marshal would not yield to the
prejudices of the people by employing him.'

had charge of the regular brigades of the field army. The native generals, save those above mentioned, were placed in administrative posts, or in charge of those sections of the militia which were probably destined to see no service.

The second point of difficulty in the organization of the Portuguese army was the commissariat. In the old days it had been a purely civilian branch of the service, non-military intendants dealing with contractors and merchants. For this had been substituted a *Junta de Viveres* mainly composed of officers, which proved as ineffective, if not as corrupt, as the body which had preceded it. The British government had taken over the responsibility of paying half the Portuguese army[1], but not that of feeding it, and despite of the handsome subsidies that it paid to the Regency for the general purposes of the war, the native troops, especially those quartered far from Lisbon, were often in a state of semi-starvation. 'The Portuguese corps ought to have a commissariat attached to them, and I believe each brigade has a commissary,' wrote Wellington, 'but they have no magazines and no money to purchase supplies[2].' One main difficulty arose from the fact that the Junta de Viveres shrank from the heavy expense of organizing a proper transport train, and tried to make shift with requisitioned carts and oxen, which were difficult to get (since the British army was competing with the Portuguese for draught animals) and still harder to retain—for the peasant driver always absconded with his beasts when he found an opportunity. Another difficulty was that the Junta tried to feed the troops with requisitioned corn, instead of paying for it with money down ; hence it got grudging service. 'I know from experience,' observes Wellington, ' that the Portuguese army could not be in the distress under which it suffers, from want of provisions, if only a part of the food it receives from the country were paid for.' And he suggested as a remedy that the British ministers should earmark part of the subsidy for use on the commissariat and no other purpose[3]. It was long before this

---

[1] Viz. the 1st, 2nd, 3rd, 4th, 7th, 10th, 11th, 13th, 14th, 15th, 16th, 19th of the line, and the 1st, 2nd, and 3rd Caçadores.

[2] Wellington to Hill, Jan. 24, 1810.

[3] Wellington to Villiers, Jan. 25, 1810.

matter was set to rights. Beresford's correspondence in 1810
bristles with complaints as to the inefficiency of the Junta de
Viveres[1].

If the regular army was badly fed, so that desertion and sickness were both too prevalent in some corps, it was not to be
expected that the militia would fare better. Wellington had
ordered, and Beresford had arranged for, the embodiment of every
one of the 48 militia regiments of the national establishment.
They should properly have given 70,000 men, but such a figure
was never reached. Some of the regimental districts were too
thinly peopled to give the full 1,500 men at which each was
assessed. In others the officers placed in charge were incapable,
or the local magistrates recalcitrant. Many regiments could
show only 500 or 600 bayonets in 1810, few over 1,000[2]. The
total number under arms at the time of Masséna's invasion may
have reached 45,000 bayonets. Of the 48 regiments eight
belonged to the lands south of the Tagus, and were never
brought up to the front; they furnished the garrisons of Elvas
and Campo Mayor, and a corps of observation on the lower
Guadiana, destined to watch the French in the direction of
Ayamonte and the Condado de Niebla, lest any unexpected
raid might be made in that quarter[3]. The five regiments
from the district immediately round the capital were at work on
the ever-growing lines of Torres Vedras. One regiment was in
garrison at Peniche, two at Abrantes, three at Almeida. The
main force, consisting of the remaining units contributed by the

---

[1] D'Urban writes, May 4, ' Such is the poverty, imbecility, and want of
arrangement of the Portuguese government, that any regular system of
supply is not to be expected. The whole civil branch of the army is in
such a state of confusion, that I hold it impossible to carry on active operations for more than a few weeks.'

[2] I note in D'Urban's diary, when he was making an inspection tour
with Beresford at the end of the winter, ' At Sardão a very good regiment
of militia, 1,100 strong, that of Maia.' ' Abrantes, two regiments of
militia, Lousão 1,035, Soure 1,035, all armed.' But, on the other hand,
' Vizeu, Arganil, Trancoso, ordered to be assembled at Almeida, have only—
the first 867, the second 600, the last 505 firelocks, and the description of
troops the very worst.' Of course the numbers were somewhat higher by
the next August.

[3] These regiments were Lagos, Tavira, Beja, Evora, Villaviciosa,
Portalegre, Alcazar do Sul, Setubal.

North and the Beira, was divided into five corps, destined partly
for active operations against the enemy's flanks and rear, when he
should enter Portugal, partly for the defence of Oporto and the
Tras-os-Montes, if any assault should be threatened in that
direction. These divisions stood as follows :—three regiments
under Lecor were left in the Castello Branco country, to protect
it against raids from Spanish Estremadura. Seven under Trant,
all corps from the coast-land between the Douro and the
Mondego, were to cover Oporto from the south, or to operate
against the rear of the invading army, if it should leave that
city alone and keep on the direct road to Lisbon. Six under
Silveira guarded the Tras-os-Montes, and watched the French
detachments in the northern part of the plains of Leon.
Eight under Miller lay around Oporto, ready to support
either Silveira or Trant if occasion should arise[1]. After the
campaign began, and Masséna's intention to leave the North

[1] It may be well to name, once for all, the composition of these Militia
Brigades. They were distributed as follows :—

Garrison of Abrantes :
  Lousão
  Soure
Garrison of Almeida :
  Vizeu
  Arganil
  Trancoso
In the Lines :
  1, 2, 3, 4 of Lisbon
  Torres Vedras
With Lecor about Castello Branco :
  Idanha
  Covilhão
  Castello Branco
Under Miller about Oporto :
  Guimaraens
  Viana
  Braga
  Basto
  Villa do Conde
  Arcos
  Barcellos
  Barco

With Trant, between the Douro and
the Mondego :
  Aveiro
  Feira
  Coimbra
  Porto
  Maia
  Penafiel
  Oliveira do Azemis
With Silveira about Braganza :
  Lamego
  Chaves
  Villa Real
  Braganza
  Miranda
  Moncorvo
With Miranda about Thomar :
  Tondella
  Santarem
  Thomar
  Leiria

Of Miller's division, I think, but am not sure, that the last four were those
detached under Wilson in September.

alone became evident, half Miller's division was placed under
John Wilson (who had originally been Silveira's chief-of-the-
staff and second-in-command) and sent south into the Beira
to co-operate with Trant. Finally, four regiments under the
Portuguese brigadier Miranda lay at Thomar, apparently for
the purpose of aiding Lecor or strengthening the garrison of
Abrantes. This division ultimately retreated into the lines
of Torres Vedras.

All these troops were entirely unfitted for a place in the
line of battle; Wellington refused to mix them with the
regular brigades, save in the garrisons of Almeida, Abrantes,
and Elvas. He directed the brigadiers never to risk them
in battle, even against a much inferior force of the French.
Their sole purpose was to cut lines of communication, to
render marauding by the enemy's small detachments impossible, and to restrict his power of making reconnaissances far
afield. They were told that they might defend a pass or a ford
for a time, so as to delay the advance of a hostile column,
but that they were never to commit themselves to a serious
combat with any considerable body. Convoys, stragglers,
small detachments, were the game on which they must prey.
The programme was not a brilliant one to lay down before an
ambitious officer, and more than once Silveira, Trant, and
Wilson disobeyed orders, and tried to withstand a full French
division in some chosen position. Such experiments almost
always ended in a disaster. It was not surprising, for the
militia were not troops from whom much could be expected.
The best men in every district had been taken for the regular
army; all the trained officers were also needed there. The
militia *cadres* were composed of civilians who had to learn their
duties just as much as the privates whom they were supposed
to instruct. All the patriotic and energetic young men of the
governing classes had sought commissions in the line; the less
willing and active were driven into the militia. Service therein
brought neither much credit nor much promotion. If the
Regency half-starved the regulars, it three-quarter-starved the
militia, which was normally in a state of destitution of clothing, shoes, and food. Hardly a regiment was provided with
uniforms; as a rule only the officers showed the regulation

blue and silver. As long as the corps was in its own district it was fed somehow, but when moved to some strategical point in the rugged mountains of the Beira, it was liable to go wholly to pieces from sheer privation. Fortunately the Portuguese peasant led a frugal life at all times, and expected little; the desertion, though large, was not nearly so great as might have been expected. The fact was that the men were essentially loyal, and hated the French with a perfect hatred. They might be very poor soldiers, but they were very bitter personal enemies of the invader. Nevertheless, they were liable to panics on very slight provocation. 'At the best they are a very daily and uncertain sort of fighting people[1],' remarked one of their leaders. Another wrote in a more forcible language, 'Scripture says, Put not your trust in princes—I say, Fool is the man who puts his trust in a damnable militia.' Each of these sentences was indited the day after a disastrous and wholly unnecessary rout.

Over and above the regular army and the militia, the Portuguese military system contemplated the utilization of the whole *levée en masse* of the nation under the name of the Ordenanza. This was no foreshadowing of the modern idea of universal service, but a survival of the mediaeval practice which, in Portugal as in England, made every freeman liable to be called out in time of extremity, at his own cost and with his own weapons. Every peasant between sixteen and sixty was theoretically supposed to be enrolled in one of the companies of 250 which each group of villages was supposed to possess. The organization had been effective enough in the old mediaeval wars with Castile: it had even proved serviceable in the 'War of Independence' that followed the successful rising of 1640. But against modern regular armies it was comparatively useless; when called out in the war of 1762 the Ordenanza had not justified its old reputation. Little could be expected of mobs armed with pikes and fowling-pieces, save that they should cut off a few convoys and stragglers, or occasionally obstruct a defile. A French officer who deeply studied this forgotten campaign

---

[1] D'Urban to Wilson, and Trant to Wilson, after two unfortunate incidents in 1812, when the militia had been more or less under arms for two whole years. The former are in D'Urban's the latter in Wilson's correspondence.

wrote that, 'whatever the Spaniards may say to the contrary, this war of the peasantry is by no means important, except against ignorant and undisciplined troops [1].'

When Wellington resolved to call out the Ordenanza in 1810 he was ignorant of none of these facts. Nevertheless, he insisted that the Regency should issue the old royal ' Ordinance ' to call out the levy. His object was threefold : from the political and moral point of view it was necessary to take this measure, because it was the ancient and established method of proclaiming that the country was in danger. It was so understood by the peasantry, in whose memories the traditions of the Spanish invasions were still fresh ; they expected to be summoned, and would have doubted the imminence of the emergency if they had not been. The call was at once an appeal to their patriotism, and equivalent to a proclamation of martial law. Secondly, Wellington hoped to find assistance to a certain degree for the work which he had set aside for the militia, by the aid of the Ordenanza. Pervading the whole country-side, and knowing every goat-track and inaccessible fastness, their motley companies would surround the invading army as it marched, prevent marauding by small parties, and render inter-communication between columns impossible, save by large detachments. French narrators of the campaign speak of ' the cruel callousness with which Wellington exposed these half-armed peasants to the wrath of the most efficient army in the world,' and wax sentimental over the miseries of the Portuguese. But sentiment from such a quarter is suspicious : it is absurd to find old soldiers writing as if the main duty of a general defending a country were to spare its peasantry as much inconvenience as possible. Did not Napoleon in 1814 make every endeavour to raise Lorraine and Champagne *en masse* in the rear of the Allies, and has any French critic ever blamed him for doing so ? Was the actual misery suffered by the inhabitants of Beira so much greater than what they would have endured if they had remained at home, and offered no resistance ? The country-side would have been stripped bare by an army forced to make ' war

[1] Dumouriez, *State of Portugal*, page 22. There was, however, one notable combat at Villa Pouca in the Tras-os-Montes where a whole Spanish column of 3,000 men was defeated by the Ordenanza.

support war,' and one can hardly believe, judging from parallel
incidents in Spain, that outrages would have been conspicuous
by their absence.

But it would seem that the third of Wellington's reasons for
calling out the Ordenanza was far more cogent, and lay nearer
to the heart of his scheme than the other two. Throughout
Portuguese history the summons to the levy *en masse* had always
been combined with another measure, from which indeed it
could not be disentangled—the order to the whole population
to evacuate and devastate the land in face of the advancing
enemy. The use of the weapon of starvation against the French
was an essential part of Wellington's plan for defending Portugal.
When he told the British Ministry that he would undertake the
defence of the realm, this was one of the main conditions of his
pledge.   He had realized the great fact that the conduct of the
war in the Peninsula depended on supplies : the old aphorism
that ' beyond the Pyrenees large armies starve and small armies
get beaten ' was at the back of all his schemes for the year 1810.
He calculated that the French would find the greatest difficulty
in accumulating stores sufficient to feed an army of invasion
large enough to attack Portugal, and that, even if such stores
could be gathered, there would be a still greater difficulty in
getting them to the front as they were needed.   For not only
would it be hard to collect the mass of transport required for
an army of 70,000, 80,000, or 100,000 men, but the convoys
which it formed would find it impossible to move over the vast
stretch of bad roads between Salamanca and Lisbon, when the
communications were cut and the Militia and Ordenanza were
infesting every pass and hillside.   It was almost certain that
the invaders would make no such attempt to feed themselves
from the rear, but would start with a moderate train, carrying
no more than provisions for a week or two, and hoping to subsist
(in the usual French style) on the resources of the invaded
country.   Such resources Wellington was determined that they
should not find.   They would ere long be starved out, and
forced to fall back on their magazines, certainly losing a large
proportion of their men from privations by the way.   If this
scheme had been carried out with rigid perfection, Masséna's
invasion would have amounted to no more than a promenade to

Torres Vedras, and a prompt return to the borders of Spain with a famished army. Unfortunately the device, though it worked well and was ultimately quite successful, was not perfectly executed in every corner and by every subordinate, so that the French, showing a magnificent obstinacy, and suffering untold privations, remained before the Lines for three months before they retired. But retire they did, and with a loss of a third of their army, and a deplorable decadence of their morale, so that Wellington's scheme was fully justified [1].

The plan for defeating the enemy by the system of devastation was neither 'dictated by the hard heart of a general trained in the atrocious wars of the East,' as certain French authors have written, nor was it (as some of the English authors have supposed) suggested to Wellington by the measures which had been taken in 1803–4 for withdrawing all food and transport from the south coast of England, if Napoleon should be successful in crossing from Boulogne. It was an ancient Portuguese device, practised from time immemorial against the Castilian invader, which had never failed of success. Nor had it come to an end with the War of Independence of 1640, or the war of the Spanish Succession of 1704. When Spain had made her last serious assault on Portugal in 1762 (Godoy's miserable mock-war of 1801 does not deserve to be counted), the plan had worked admirably. When the Conde d'Aranda invaded the Beira 'the country had been " driven" in the most systematic style, and everything that could not be carried off had been destroyed, so that the Spaniard found himself in a desert, being unable to discover either provisions, cars, or peasants: the inhabitants had abandoned their villages, and carried off everything. The enemy had to be supplied with every necessary from Spain: the infantry were harassed with fatigue in remaking the roads, and the cavalry-horses destroyed

---

[1] Unlike the many French writers who content themselves with denouncing Wellington's inhumanity, Pelet (Masséna's chief confidant) confesses that the English general's plan was perfectly logical. In his *Aperçu de la Campagne de Portugal*, he writes, ' On a critiqué sans raison son système de guerre. Il était à peu près infaillible contre un ennemi inférieur en nombre. Mais peu de généraux oseront " sauver un pays " d'une telle manière.'

in conducting provisions. At last d'Aranda retreated, leaving his sick and wounded at Castello Branco, with a letter commending them to the attention of the allies [1].' Of this same war Dumouriez wrote : ' As soon as the Spaniards enter Portugal the King publishes a declaration, by which he enjoins on his subjects to fall upon the invaders, and the national hatred always excites them to execute the "Ordinance." As the Spanish army pushes on, the villages are depopulated, and the inhabitants fall back on the capital. The peasantry arrive there in crowds with wives and children, so that the king at the end of three months has 200,000 or 300,000 extra mouths to feed [2].'

This sounds like a description of the great migration of 1810, but was actually written in 1766. It is clear, then, that Wellington did not invent the system of devastation, but simply utilized, and carried out to its logical end, an old custom essentially national, and familiar to the Portuguese from time immemorial. It was the regular device of the weak against the strong in the Middle Ages, and differed in nothing from ' Good King Robert's Testament,' the time-honoured system applied by the Scots to the English in the fourteenth and fifteenth centuries.

> ' In strait placis gar hide all store,
> And byrnen ye plaineland thaim before,
> Thanne sall thei pass away in haist,
> When that thai find na thing but waist,
> So sall ye turn thaim with gret affrai,
> As thai were chasit with swerd awai.'

Fortunately for himself, for England, and for Europe, Wellington had to deal with a peasantry almost as frugal, as tough, and as stubborn in their hatred as the mediaeval Scot. They saw nothing strange in the demand now made to them, and obeyed. The difficulty lay with the townsfolk of large places, such as Coimbra, Thomar, or Santarem, which lay far from the frontier, and had not the old traditions of the peasantry, since the Spaniards had never penetrated to their doors since the seven-

---

[1] Continuation of Vertot's *History of Portugal*, ii. 51.
[2] Dumouriez's *State of Portugal*, p. 21, *n.*

teenth century. Here there was much recalcitrance, as was but
natural; the burgher had much to abandon where the peasant
had little. Yet, as we shall see, the scheme was carried out in
the end, and those who stayed behind to greet the French could
be counted on one hand in places of the size of Vizeu, Coimbra,
or Leiria. That fanatical patriotism went far towards pro-
ducing such a result is true, but does not explain the whole
matter : quite as strong a motive was the unforgotten tale of
the horrors that had followed Soult's entry into Oporto. To
the Portuguese citizens the approach of the French meant
probable murder and rape, hence came the readiness that they
showed to depart. There were exaggerated rumours abroad
of the ruthlessness of the French: was not Loison, the ' Maneta '
of whom so many atrocious (and mostly false) stories were told,
known to be in high command ?

Wellington's scheme for the clearing of the country-side in
face of the enemy had long been thought out. It included
not merely the evacuation of the towns and villages, but the
destruction of bridges, mills, even ovens; the removal of all
animals and means of transport, the destruction of all food-stuff
that could not be carried off, the burning of all ferry-boats and
other small craft on the navigable rivers. 'The moment that
the enemy crosses the frontier,' he wrote to Beresford, ' the
governor of the province of Estremadura must be told that it
is necessary to order all carts, carriages, and other means of
conveyance, with all the provisions they can carry, away. He
ought to have all his arrangements prepared for ordering them
off as soon as the French approach. The Captains Mor [1] and
their Ordenanza must be prepared to give the enemy all the
opposition in their power, not by assembling in large bodies,
but by lying out in the mountains and the strong parts of the
roads, annoying their patrols and small parties, and interrupting
their communications [2].' This comes from an order of February :
by August, when a new harvest had been gathered in, the
question of the destruction of food stuffs became more difficult.
The peasantry, as was natural, persisted in hiding rather than

---

[1] For these officers and their duties see vol. ii. pp. 221-2.

[2] Wellington to Beresford, Vizeu, Feb. 28, 1810, long before the actual
invasion.

burning what could not be carried off. By one means or another a certain number of these concealed stores, even when buried in pits or removed to remote ravines, were discovered by the French, and enabled them to prolong their precarious stay in front of the Torres Vedras lines.

As to the displacement of the population, Wellington considered that in many parts it would be sufficient if it took to the hills for a few days, while the French army was passing. His military arrangements were such that he thought it impossible that the enemy would be able either to leave small posts behind him, or to maintain his lines of communication with Spain. It would suffice, therefore, that the peasantry in parts off the main roads, and remote from large towns or points of strategical importance, should make ready for a merely temporary migration. They must always, however, be ready to flit again, if fresh columns of the enemy, advancing or retreating, should come near their abodes. The townsfolk and the inhabitants of the fertile coast plains of Estremadura and Western Beira were recommended to retire either to Lisbon or to Oporto, according as they were nearer to one or to the other. It was clear that the problem of feeding them there would be a matter for the Government, for individuals of the poorer classes could not be expected to carry or to buy provisions for many weeks. Hence there was a need for the accumulation of immense stores, over and above those required for the army. The Portuguese Regency did what it could, but in its usual slip-shod and inefficient fashion, and there is no doubt that much misery and a certain amount of starvation fell to the lot of the unhappy emigrants. Fortunately Lisbon and Oporto were great ports and full of food; but despite of this, the position of the refugees became deplorable, when Masséna tarried at Santarem two months longer than Wellington had considered probable. But their suffering was not in vain: the French were starved out, even if it was a few weeks later than had been expected.

Having dealt with the organization of the military force of Portugal, and the arrangements for the depopulation of the country, we have still to explain the third section of Wellington's great scheme of defence—that consisting of fortifications. We have already mentioned that Almeida and Elvas had been

repaired and garrisoned, the former with 5,000 men, consisting
of one regiment of regulars and three of militia, under the
English general William Cox, the other by 8,000 men,—two
regiments of regulars and five of militia,—under General Leite.
These were the outer bulwarks of the realm.   Campo Mayor, a
small and antiquated fortress, a sort of outlying dependency of
Elvas, was held by one militia battalion under a Colonel Talaya,
a retired engineer officer. It was not expected to make a serious
resistance, but did so in the time of need, and detained a French
division before its walls for some precious days in the spring of
1811, to the great glory and credit of its governor.

Only two other of the ancient fortresses of Portugal were
placed in a state of defence, and made to play a notable part in
Wellington's general scheme for checking the French.   These
were Peniche and Abrantes.   The former is a very strong isolated
sea-fortress, on a projecting headland in the Atlantic, forty miles
north of Lisbon. It commands several good creeks and landing-
places, suitable for the embarkation and disembarkation of
troops, and is nearly impregnable, because of the narrowness
of the isthmus connecting it with the mainland.   Placed where
it is, just in the rear of the position which an enemy must take
who is meditating an attack on Lisbon, it offers unique opportunities for making incursions on his rear and his communications. Moreover, it afforded a refuge and a safe point of departure
by sea, for any section of the allied troops which might become
isolated, and be pressed towards the water by the advancing
enemy. Some of Wellington's officers considered that it was an
even better place for embarkation than Lisbon, if the French
should prove too strong, and the British should be compelled to
abandon Portugal. The Commander-in-Chief thought otherwise,
but caused its fortification to be carefully restored, and garrisoned
it with a picked regiment of militia [1].

---

[1] D'Urban says in his diary (Dec. 8, 1809) : ' Inspected Peniche. The
isthmus over which the peninsula is approached is covered with water at
high tide, and from the line of works describing a sort of arc, very powerful
cross-fires may be established upon every part of it.   There are nearly 100
good guns upon the work, the brass ones especially good.   This is the most
favourable position that can be conceived for embarking the British army,
should it ever be necessary to do so.   The circumference abounds with

Even more important than Peniche was Abrantes, the one
great crossing-place of the Tagus above Lisbon where there was
a permanent bridge, and free communication by good roads
between Beira and Alemtejo.   It lies at the point where the
road from Spain by way of Castello Branco crosses the road
from north to south down the Portuguese frontier, from Almeida
and Guarda to Evora and Elvas.   An invader who has advanced
towards Lisbon through Beira has it on his flank and rear,
equally so an invader who has advanced on the same objective
from Badajoz and the Guadiana.   It is the natural point at
which to move troops north and south along the frontier, though
Wellington had established an alternative temporary crossing-
point at Villa Velha, thirty miles higher up the river, by means
of pontoons.   But this secondary passage was inferior in safety,
since it was not protected by a fortress like Abrantes.   Orders
were given to burn the pontoons if ever a French force from the
East should came near.   At Abrantes, on the other hand, the
boat-bridge could be pulled up and stacked under the city walls in
the event of an attack, and did not need to be destroyed.   The
town is situated on a lofty eminence upon the north bank of the
Tagus.   Its fortifications were antiquated in 1809, but had been
for many months in process of being rebuilt and strengthened
by the English engineer Patton. With new earthworks and
redoubts it had been made a strong place, which could not be
taken without a regular siege and plenty of heavy artillery.
Here Wellington had placed a garrison of two militia regiments
under the Portuguese general Lobo, whose orders were to resist
to the last, and to make sure of burning the boat-bridge, down
to the last plank, before surrendering.   The French never put
him to the test, since they had no heavy guns with them, and

creeks and clefts in the rocks, inside which there is always smooth water,
and easy egress for boats.   They are out of the reach of fire from the
mainland : indeed, there is sufficient room to encamp a large force perfectly beyond the range of the enemy.   If it should be thought worth
while, this peninsula could be held by England, even if Portugal otherwise were in the power of the enemy.   There is abundance of water.   If it
be the wish of Lord Wellington he can retire upon Lisbon, give battle in
front of it, and, if the day go against him, retreat upon Peniche and defend
it so long as he pleases.'

therefore regarded it as hopeless to attempt an attack on the place [1].

Almeida and Elvas, Peniche and Abrantes, were regular fortresses with large garrisons. There were, however, other points where Wellington ordered fortifications of a less permanent kind to be thrown up, because he thought them of first-rate strategical importance. The two most important were one on the northern line of advance which the French might take, the other on the central or Castello Branco line. The first was a line of redoubts behind the river Alva, just where it joins the Mondego, on either side of the bridge and village of Ponte de Murcella. It was here, he thought, that Masséna would choose his road, along the south bank of the Mondego, if he marched on Lisbon by the Beira line. But the Marshal moved by Vizeu, partly (as it seems) because he had heard of the fortifications of this defile, and the works were never used. Equally unprofitable (so it chanced) was another important series of field-works, constructed to cover the lowest reach of the Zezere against an invader who should come by the Castello Branco road, and should have masked or taken Abrantes. This was a line of redoubts and trenches, almost a fortified camp, on the east bank of the river from Tancos to opposite Martinchel, blocking both the roads which lead from Castello Branco into Estremadura. Masséna, coming not by the route which was guarded against, but from Leiria and Thomar, took the lines of Zezere in the rear, and they proved useless.

Along with the precautions taken on the banks of the Alva and the Zezere, two other pieces of engineering must be mentioned. The one, the destruction of the *Estrada Nova*,—the mountain-road which leads from Fundão and Belmonte to the lower Zezere without passing through Castello Branco,—has already been noticed, when we were dealing with the possible lines of invasion in Portugal. The other move was constructive, not destructive, in character. Foreseeing that Abrantes might be masked, or besieged on the northern bank of the Tagus, and

---

[1] D'Urban has a long disquisition on Abrantes in his diary. Its weak points, he says, were an outlying hill on the Punhete road, which gave a favourable position for hostile batteries, and the friable nature of the gravelly soil, which did not bind well in trenches and outworks.

all the roads in that direction thereby blocked, while it might still be very profitable to have free communication between Lisbon and the Castello Branco region, he caused the road above the south bank of the Tagus, from opposite Abrantes to the flying-bridge at Villa Velha, to be thoroughly reconstructed. This route, by Gavião and Niza, was so much easier in its slopes than the old high-road Abrantes–Castello Branco, that, even when the latter was safe, troops moving from east to west, along the Tagus often used it during the next two years of the war, though it involved two passages of the river instead of one.

But all the matters of engineering hitherto mentioned were unimportant and merely subsidiary, when placed beside the one great piece of work which formed the keystone of Wellington's plan for the defence of Portugal. His whole scheme depended on the existence of an impregnable place of refuge, available both for his army, and for the emigrant population of the country-side which he was about to devastate. He must have a line on which the invader could be finally checked and forced to halt and starve. If such a line had not existed, his whole scheme would have been impracticable, and after a lost battle he might have been driven to that hurried embarkation which the ministers in London foresaw and dreaded. But his eye had been fixed upon the ground in front of Lisbon ever since his second landing in the Peninsula in April 1809, and there he thought that the necessary stronghold might be found. A full year before Masséna's invasion he had informed the British cabinet that though he could not undertake to defend all Portugal, ' for the whole country is frontier, and it would be difficult to prevent the enemy from entering by some point or other,' he yet conceived that he might protect the essential part of the realm, the capital, against anything save the most overwhelming odds[1]. The scheme had taken definite shape in his head when, on October 20, 1809, he wrote his famous dispatch to Colonel Fletcher, the commanding engineer at Lisbon, directing him to draw up without delay a scheme for the construction of two successive lines of trenches and redoubts, covering the whole stretch of country from the Atlantic to a point on the estuary of the Tagus twenty miles or more north of the capital. This

[1] For these views of Aug. and Sept. 1809, see vol. ii. p. 610.

was, in its essentials, the order for the construction of the lines of
Torres Vedras, for though the front designated does not exactly
tally with that ultimately taken up, it only differs from it in
points of detail.   Fletcher is directed to survey a line from the
mouth of the Castanheira brook to the mouth of the Zizandre,
and another, a few miles behind, from Alhandra on the Tagus by
Bucellas and Cabeza de Montechique towards Mafra.   These
roughly represent the two lines of defence ultimately constructed,
though in the end the extreme right flank was drawn back from
the Castanheira to the Alhandra stream.   Fletcher is told that
the works will be on the largest scale : the fortified camp above
Torres Vedras is to hold 5,000 men, the works at Cabeza de
Montechique alone will require 5,000 workmen to be set to dig
at once ; great operations, such as the damming up of rivers and
the creation of marshes many miles long, are suggested.

How the great scheme worked out, and how the works
stood when Masséna's long-expected army at last appeared in
front of them, will be told in a later chapter, in its due place.
Suffice it here to say that all through the spring and summer of
1810 they were being urged forward with feverish haste.

It must not be supposed that it was an easy matter to carry
out all these preparations.   The Portuguese government ended
by adopting all Wellington's suggestions : but it was not without
friction that he achieved his purpose.   While he was planning
works at the very gates of Lisbon, and making provisions for
the devastation of whole provinces in view of the approaching
invasion, he was often met by suggestions that it would be
possible to defend the outer frontiers of the realm, and that his
schemes were calculated to dishearten the Portuguese people,
rather than to encourage them to a firm resistance.   The Regency,
moreover, had enough national pride to resent the way in
which a policy was dictated to them, without any reference to
their own views.   The governing party in Portugal had accepted
the English alliance without reserve, but it often winced at the
consequences of its action.   There was a view abroad that the
little nation was being set in the forefront of the battle of
European independence mainly for the benefit of Great Britain.
Fortunately the memory of Junot's dictatorship and Soult's
ravages was still fresh enough to overcome all other considera-

tions. A moment's reflection convinced Wellington's most ardent critics that though the British yoke might sometimes seem hard, anything was better than a return to French servitude. The Regency murmured, but always ended by yielding, and issued the edicts necessary to confirm all the orders of the general.

The state of the Portuguese government at this moment requires a word of explanation. The original Regency confirmed by Sir Hew Dalrymple in 1808 had been somewhat changed in its personnel. It was now a more numerous body than at its first installation ; of the original members, only the Patriarch (Antonio de Castro, late bishop of Oporto), and the Marquez de Olhão (Francisco de Mello e Menezes, the Constable or Monteiro Mor, as he is more frequently called), now survived. But four new members had been appointed in 1810. The most important of them was José Antonio de Menezes e Sousa, generally known as the ' Principal Sousa,' an ecclesiastic who was one of the band of three Sousa brothers, who formed the backbone of the anti-French party in Portugal. The eldest of them, Rodrigo de Sousa Coutinho, Conde de Linhares, was prime minister of the Prince Regent at Rio de Janeiro. The third, Domingos Antonio de Sousa Coutinho, afterwards Conde de Funchal, was Portuguese minister in London. Thus when the Principal entered the Regency, this busy and capable family could pull the strings alike at Rio, London, and Lisbon, in the interests of their relations and dependants. This they did without scruple and without ceasing. Domestic politics in Portugal had always been a matter of family alliances, as much as of principles. They presented, indeed, a considerable resemblance to those of Great Britain during the Whig domination of the eighteenth century. Hence there was considerable danger that the policy of the alliance against Napoleon might become identified in the eyes of the Portuguese nation with the domination of the Sousa faction. That this peril was avoided was not their fault : they did their best to keep all promotion, civil and military, for their own adherents ; hence came interminable quarrels on petty personal questions both with Wellington and Beresford. Fortunately the two Marshals could generally get their way in the end, when large interests were at stake, because the Sousas were pledged to the British alliance, and dared not break with it. To do so would have brought other politicians to the front. But, meanwhile, unending controversies wasted Wellington's time and soured his temper: more than once he is found writing in his dispatches to Lord Liverpool that the 'impatient, meddling, mischievous'[1] Principal ought to be got out of the Regency and promoted to some foreign embassy, or great civil post, where he could do less harm. But the British government thought, and probably was right in thinking, that it was better to bear with known evils than to quarrel with the Sousa family, and thereby to break up the pro-British party in Portugal. Wellington had to endure the Principal's small intrigues and petty criticism till the end.

The other members who entered the Regency in 1810 were the Conde de Redondo, Fernando Maria de Sousa Coutinho— another of the Sousa clan—Doctor Raymundo Nogueira, a law professor of the University of Coimbra[2] and—far the most important of all—the newly appointed British Minister at Lisbon, Mr. Charles Stuart. The nomination of a foreigner to such a post touched Portuguese pride to the quick, and was looked upon by all enemies of the Sousa faction as an act of miserable weakness on the part of the Conde de Linhares and the Prince Regent. It was considered doubtful policy on the part of the Perceval Cabinet to consent to the appointment, considering the offence which it was certain to give. In their justification it must be pleaded that both the Patriarch and the Principal Sousa were men capable of causing any amount of difficulty by their ill-considered plans and their personal intrigues, and that a colleague who could be trusted to keep an eye upon their actions, and to moderate their ambitions was much needed. Stuart was a man of moderate and tactful bearing, but could be

---

[1] Wellington to Lord Liverpool, *Dispatches*, vi. p. 435.

[2] A man of whom all Portuguese writers speak with respect; even Napier notes him (ii. 386) as 'a man of talent and discretion.' But Wellington seems to have disliked him. 'The admission of Dr. Raymundo Nogueira to the Regency, and the reasons of his admission, were truly ludicrous. . . . his appointment is to be agreeable to the lower orders—from among whom he is selected!' (Wellington to Charles Stuart, Celorico, Aug. 4, 1810.)

neither cajoled nor overruled. It was on his influence in the
Regency that Wellington relied most for support. At this
moment there were two questions in process of discussion which
rendered it most necessary that the Portuguese government
should not be left entirely to its own guidance. Taking
advantage of the unhappy condition of Spain, and the weakness
of the newly appointed executive at Cadiz, the Portuguese were
pressing for the restoration of Olivenza, Godoy's old conquest of
1801, and for the recognition of the Princess Carlotta of Spain,
the wife of the Prince of the Brazils, as the person entitled to
act as Regent of Spain during the captivity of her brothers
at Valençay. Dom Pedro de Sousa Holstein, the Portuguese
minister at Cadiz—a kinsman of Linhares and the Principal—
was actively urging both these demands on the Spanish government. If he had succeeded in imposing them on Castaños
and his colleagues there would have been desperate friction
between the allies. But by promising the active support of the
Portuguese army within the Spanish frontiers—which he had
no power to guarantee, and which Wellington had absolutely
refused to grant—the minister won some support at Cadiz.
Extra pressure was brought to bear upon the Spaniards by the
massing of Brazilian troops on the South American frontier, on
the side of Rio Grande do Sul—a most unjustifiable act, which
might have led to an actual rupture, a thing which the British
government was bound to prevent by every means in its power.
The only way to prevent an open breach between Spain and
Portugal was to check the activity of Sousa Holstein, an end
which Stuart found much difficulty in accomplishing, because
the objects for which the minister was striving, and especially
the restoration of Olivenza to its old owners, were entirely
approved by his colleagues in the Regency. When it is added
that there were numerous other points of friction between the
British and the Portuguese governments—such as the question
of free trade with Brazil, that of the suppression of the slave
trade, and that of the form to be adopted for the payment of
the subsidies which maintained the Portuguese army—it is
easy to understand that Stuart's position on the Council of
Regency was no easy one. He often found himself in a minority
of one when a discussion started : he frequently had to acquiesce

in decisions which he did not approve, merely in order to avoid friction on matters of secondary importance. But in matters of really primary moment he generally succeeded in getting his way, owing to the simple fact that Portugal was dependent on Great Britain for the continuance of her national existence. Conscious of this, the other members of the Regency would generally yield a reluctant assent at the last moment, and Wellington's plans, when set forth by Stuart, though often criticized, delayed, and impeded, were in the end carried out with more or less completeness.

SECTION XIX: CHAPTER III

THE FRENCH PREPARATIONS: MASSÉNA'S ARMY OF PORTUGAL

DURING the summer campaign of 1809 the French Army of Spain had received hardly any reinforcements from beyond the Pyrenees. Every man that the Emperor could arm was being directed against Austria in May and June. But when Wagram had been won, and the armistice of Znaym signed, and when moreover it had been discovered that the British expedition to the Isle of Walcheren need not draw off any part of the Army of Germany, the Emperor began to turn his attention to the Peninsula. The armistice with Austria had been signed on July 12: only six days later, on the 18th of the same month, Napoleon was already selecting troops to send to Spain, and expressing his intention of going there himself to 'finish the business' in person [1]. But he had made up his mind that it was too late in the year for him to transport any great mass of men to the Peninsula in time for operations in the autumn, and had settled that the expulsion of the English and the conquest of Cadiz, Seville, and Valencia must be delayed to the spring of 1810. On September 7 he wrote [2] to approve King Joseph's decision that Soult should not be allowed to make any attempt on Portugal in the autumn, and a month later he advised his brother to defend the line of the Tagus, and drive back Spanish incursions, but to defer all offensive movements till the reinforcements should have begun to arrive [3].

The composition of the new army that was to enter Spain was dictated in a minute to the Minister of War on October 7, in

---

[1] 'Faites-moi connaître la marche que vous faites faire aux 66ᵉ, 82ᵉ, 26ᵉ, etc., etc. : *lorsque j'entrerai en Espagne* cela me pourra faire une force de 18,000 hommes.' Napoleon to Clarke, Schönbrunn, July 18.

[2] Napoleon to Clarke, Schönbrunn, Sept. 7.

[3] Napoleon to Clarke, memoranda for King Joseph, Oct. 3, 1809.

which the Emperor stated that the total force was to be about 100,000 men, including the Guard, that it was all to be on the roads between Orleans and Bayonne by December, and that he should take command in person [1]. It may be noted that the troops designated in this memorandum were actually those which took part in the campaign of 1810, with the exception of the Old Guard, which was held back when Napoleon determined to remain behind, and to send a substitute as commander-in-chief in Spain. Since the bulk of the immense column was only directed to reach Bayonne at the end of the year, it was clear that it would not be within striking distance of the enemy till March 1810.

Down to the month of December 1809, Napoleon's correspondence teems with allusions to his approaching departure for Spain. They were not merely intended to deceive the public, for they occur in letters to his most trusted ministers and generals. We might be inclined to suspect an intention to cajole the English Ministry in the magnificent phrases of the address to the Corps Législatif on December 3, when the Emperor declares that ' the moment he displays himself beyond the Pyrenees the Leopard in terror will seek the Ocean to avoid shame, defeat, and death.' But business was certainly meant when Berthier was advised to send forward his carriages and horses to Madrid, and when the Old Guard's departure for the frontier was ordered [2]. Suddenly, in the third week of December, the allusions to the Emperor's impending departure cease. It would appear that his change of purpose must be attributed not to the news of Ocaña, where the last great Spanish army had perished, but to a purely domestic cause : this was the moment at which the question of the Imperial Divorce came into prominence. It would seem that when Napoleon had conceived the idea of the Austrian marriage, and had learnt that his offers were likely to be accepted, he gave up all intention of invading Spain in the early spring in person. The divorce was first officially mooted when the ' protest ' was laid before a Privy Council on December 15 [3],

---

[1] Same to same, Oct. 7, 1809.

[2] Napoleon to Berthier, Nov. 28.

[3] Napoleon to Clarke, Dec. 5. Minute for the Privy Council dated Dec. 15, in the *Correspondance*.

and after that day there is no more mention of a departure for the South. All through January, February, and March the negotiations were in progress, and on April 1–2 [1] the Emperor married his new wife. The festivities which followed lasted many days, and when they were over the Emperor conducted his spouse on a long tour through the Northern Departments in May, and did not return to the vicinity of Paris till June, when the army of invasion, which had long since reached the Peninsula, had been already handed over to a new chief.

In the months during which the marriage negotiations were in progress, and the columns of reinforcements were pouring into Navarre and Old Castile, it is not quite certain what were the Emperor's real intentions as to the allocation of the command. Nothing clear can be deduced from an order given to Junot in the middle of February 'to spread everywhere the news of the arrival of the Emperor with 80,000 men, in order to disquiet the English and prevent them from undertaking operations in the South [2].' This is but a *ruse de guerre* ; the marriage project was so far advanced that the ratifications of the contract were signed only four days later than the date of the dispatch [3], and Napoleon must have known that he could not get away from Paris for another two months at the least. But it was only on April 17 that an Imperial Decree, dated at Compiègne, was published, announcing that not the whole French force in Spain, but three army corps (the 2nd, 6th, and 8th), with certain other troops, were to form the Army of Portugal and to be placed under the command of Masséna, Duke of Rivoli and Prince of Essling. After this it was certain that the Emperor would not cross the Pyrenees. Five days later this was made still more clear by an order to the Commandant of the Guard to recall the old Chasseur and Grenadier regiments of that corps from the various points that they had reached on the way to Bayonne, and to send on to Spain only the Tirailleur and Voltigeur regiments recently raised in 1809, and generally known as the

---

[1] The civil ceremony took place on the first, the religious on the second of these two days.

[2] Napoleon to Berthier, Paris, Feb. 12.

[3] On Feb. 16 : see Napoleon to King Joseph, Paris, Feb. 23.

'Young Guard'[1]. Napoleon never took the field in person without the veteran portion of his body-guard.

The non-appearance of the Emperor had one most important result. If he had taken the field, every marshal and general in Spain would have been subject to a single directing will, and would have been forced to combine his operations with those of his neighbours, whether he wished or no. On determining to devote the spring and summer of 1810 to nuptial feasts and state progresses, instead of to a campaign on the Tagus, he did not nominate any single commander-in-chief to take his place. Masséna, from his seniority and his splendid military record, might have seemed worthy of such promotion. He was not given it, but only placed in charge of three army corps, and of certain parts of Old Castile and Leon and the garrison troops there residing. This was a vast charge, embracing in all the command of 138,000 men. But it gave Masséna no control over the rest of the armies of Spain, and no power to secure their co-operation, save by the tedious method of appeals to Paris. Indeed, the Emperor had chosen the precise moment of King Joseph's conquest of Andalusia to break up such hierarchical organization of command as existed in the Peninsula. By a decree of February 8 he took the provinces of Aragon and Catalonia, with the army corps there employed, completely out of the sphere of the authority of King Joseph: Augereau and Suchet were forbidden to hold any communication with Madrid, and were directed to make every report and request to Paris. This would not have been fatal to the success of the main operations of the French army, for Aragon and Catalonia were a side-issue, whose military history, all through the war, had little connexion with that of Castile and Portugal. But their severance from the military hierarchy dependent on the King was followed by that of Navarre, the Basque provinces, Burgos, Valladolid, Palencia, and Toro, which were formed into four 'Military Governments' under Generals Dufour, Thouvenot, Dorsenne, and Kellermann. These governors were given complete civil and military autonomy, with power to raise taxes, administer justice, to name and displace Spanish functionaries, and to move their troops at

[1] Napoleon to Clarke, April 22, 1810. Not in the *Correspondance*, but given at length by Ducasse in his *Memoirs of King Joseph*, vii. 275.

their own pleasure, under responsibility to the Emperor alone. The '6th Government' (Valladolid, Palencia, Toro) was afterwards placed under the authority of Masséna; the others remained independent Viceroyalties.   Thus military authority in the Peninsula was divided up for the future between (1) the Commander of the Army of Portugal, who controlled not only his army but all the regions which it occupied—Leon, the greater part of Old Castile, and part of Estremadura; (2) the military governors of Catalonia, Aragon, Navarre, Biscay, Burgos; (3) the King, who practically controlled his Army of the Centre and the kingdom of New Castile alone, since Soult, in Andalusia, though not formally created a 'military governor,' practically acted on his own responsibility, without any reference to the King's wishes.   All the viceroys reported directly to Paris, and kept the Emperor fully employed with their perpetual bickerings. How Napoleon came to create and continue such a vicious system it is hard to conceive.   Apparently the explanation must be sought in the fact that he feared servants with too great power, and acted on the principle of *divide et impera,* despite of the fact that he knew, as a soldier, that the want of a commander-in-chief is ruinous in practical war.   At the bottom was the idea that he himself could manage everything, even when his armies were a thousand miles away, and when it took three weeks or a month to transmit orders to them.   He sometimes acknowledged in a moment of self-realization that this was a bad arrangement, and that it was impossible for him to conduct or criticize the details of strategy at such a distance, or under such conditions.   But after a lucid moment he would fall back into his usual ways of thought, and proceed to give orders and directions which were obsolete before the dispatches that conveyed them could be delivered to the hands of his marshals.

To proceed to details—the old Army of Spain had come to a standstill after it had overrun Andalusia in February 1810. Three corps under Soult were absorbed by that new conquest, some 73,000 men in all [1].   Suchet with his 3rd Corps, 26,000 men,

---

[1] Note that the 4th Corps had left behind in Madrid 6,000 men of its 1st division (the 28th Léger, 32nd and 75th Line) and taken on instead 8,000 men of the division Dessolles, properly forming part of the ' Army of the Centre.'

held Aragon; Augereau with the vast 7th Corps, 56,900 in all, did not hold down, but was executing military promenades in, the turbulent Catalonia. The 2nd and 6th Corps lay observing Portugal, the former with head quarters at Talavera, the latter with head quarters at Salamanca. Ney had now returned to take charge of the 6th Corps, and Reynier (an old enemy of the English, who had beaten him at Alexandria and Maida) was named chief of the 2nd Corps. This last had now been shorn of its third division,—that which had been composed of so many fractional units in 1809; these had been made over to the 6th Corps, which in 1810 possessed three divisions [1] and no longer two. Reynier had about 18,000 men, Ney no less than 33,000 after this rearrangement; he had been assigned Lorges' dragoon-division as well as the troops transferred from the 2nd Corps. The King had 14,000 men in Madrid and New Castile : the old garrisons of the Northern Provinces, excluding the newly arrived reinforcements, made up nearly 20,000 men more. This 237,000 sabres and bayonets represents the old army of 1809 [2]; the troops sent down by the Emperor after the termination of the Austrian War had not, for the most part, been absorbed into the old units, though they had crossed the Pyrenees in December and January.

It is now time to see what troops constituted these succours, the 100,000 men with whom the Emperor had originally intended to march in person to the conquest of the Peninsula. On looking through their muster roll the first thing that strikes the eye is that very little—almost nothing indeed—had been taken from the Army of Germany. The Emperor, though Austria was tamed and Prussia was under his feet, did not think it safe to cut down to any great extent the garrisons of Central Europe and Eastern France : (1) Of all the corps that had taken part in the Wagram campaign only one had been directed on Spain, and this was a force of the second line, a unit originally called

---

[1] Loison's division of the 6th Corps received these stray battalions, which were united to those of the same regiments which had crossed the Pyrenees with him. They consisted of a battalion each of the *Légion du Midi*, of the *Légion Hanovrienne*, the 26th, 66th, 82nd of the line, and the 32nd Léger.

[2] All these figures are *inclusive* of men sick and detached, the former about 16,000, the latter 44,000.

the ' Corps de Réserve de l'Armée d'Allemagne ' and afterwards the 8th Corps.   It had played only a small part in the late war, and was mostly composed of the newly raised 4th battalions of regiments serving elsewhere.   Recruited up to a strength of 30,000 men by the addition of some stray battalions from Northern Germany, it was the first of all the new reinforcements to reach Spain [1].   Indeed, the head of its column reached Burgos by the 1st of January, 1810.   It was assigned to the Army of Portugal.   By the drafting away of some of its 4th battalions to join the regiments to which they appertained it ultimately came down to about 20,000 men.

(2) Next in point of importance were the two divisions of the Young Guard under Generals Roguet and Dumoustier, nineteen battalions, with three provisional regiments of the Guard Cavalry, nearly 15,000 men in all.   These units had been formed in 1809, just in time for some of them to take their share in the bloody days of Essling and Wagram.   The Emperor did not make them over to the Army of Portugal, but retained them in Biscay and Navarre, close under the Pyrenees.   Apparently he disliked sending any of his Guards so far afield as to render it difficult to draw them back to France, in the event (unlikely as it was at this moment) of further troubles breaking out in Central Europe. The Guard divisions stayed in Spain two years, but were never allowed to go far forward into the interior.

(3) Deeply impressed with the danger and difficulty of keeping up the lines of communication between Bayonne and Madrid, since Mina and his coadjutors had set the guerrilla war on foot in Navarre and Old Castile, Napoleon had formed a corps whose special duty was to be the keeping open of the roads, and the policing of the country-side between the frontier and the Spanish capital.   This was composed of twenty squadrons of *Gendarmes,* all veterans and picked men, each with a total strength of seven officers and 200 troopers.   The decree ordering their selection

---

[1] Junot's original corps was reinforced by the 22nd of the line (4 batts.) drawn from the Prussian fortresses, and by some units which had hitherto been doing garrison duty in Navarrese and Biscayan fortresses, where they were now replaced by the Young Guard.   Among these were the Irish Brigade (2 batts.) and the Prussian regiment which had formed the original garrison of Pampeluna.

from among the *gendarmerie* of Southern and Central France was published on November 24, 1809 : but the first squadrons only began to pass the Pyrenees in February 1810, and many did not appear till April and May. Yet 4,000 men were in line by the summer [1].

(4) A few new regiments which had not hitherto been represented in the Peninsula were moved down thither. Among these were the Neuchâtel troops from Berthier's principality, a German division from the minor states of the Confederation of the Rhine under General Rouyer [2], which went to Catalonia, the 7th, 13th, and 25th *Chasseurs à Cheval*, with two battalions of Marines. The total did not amount to more than some 10,000 men.

(5) By far the largest item in the reinforcements was composed of the 4th battalions of wellnigh every regiment which was already serving in Spain. The army which had marched across the Pyrenees in 1808 had been organized on the basis of three field-battalions to the regiment, the 4th battalion being the dépôt battalion. But Napoleon had now raised the standard to four (or in a few cases more) field-battalions, over and above the dépôt. All the fourth battalions were now existing and available ; a few had served in the Austrian War, many of the others had been lying in the camps which the Emperor had formed at Boulogne, Pontivy, and elsewhere, to protect his coasts against possible English descents. Those belonging to 40 regiments already in Spain, with the full complement of 840 men each, were first ordered to cross the Pyrenees : they numbered 33,600 men : these were all at the front by May 1810. The Emperor somewhat later dispatched the fourth battalions of twenty-six regiments more to the Peninsula, giving to the temporary organization the name of the 9th Corps. This should have given another 21,840 men, and nearly did so ; their gross total, when all had reached Vittoria in September 1810, was 20,231. But the 9th Corps should not be reckoned in the first 100,000 men which the

[1] For details of this corps and its services see the monograph, *La Gendarmerie en Espagne et Portugal,* by E. Martin, Paris, 1898.

[2] Nine battalions as follows : Two of Nassau, the others from Gotha, Weimar, Altenburg, Waldeck, Reuss, Schwarzburg, Anhalt, and Lippe ; strength about 6,000 men.

Emperor set aside for the spring campaign of 1810, it was a supplementary addition [1].

(6) The Emperor dealt in a similar way with the cavalry; the regiments already in Spain had been reduced to a strength of two or three squadrons by the wear and tear of eighteen months of war. The dépôts had now got ready two squadrons fit for field service. Those belonging to sixteen regiments of dragoons, organized into eight provisional regiments, were sent early to the front, and were all in Spain by January 1810.

(7) In addition to units like 4th battalions and 3rd and 4th squadrons added to the strength of each dragoon or infantry regiment, the Emperor did not neglect to send drafts to fill up the depleted 1st, 2nd, and 3rd battalions and 1st and 2nd squadrons. In the early months of 1810, 27,000 men, in small drafts not amounting to the strength of a battalion or squadron were forwarded to recruit the old units. They went forward in ' régiments de marche,' which were broken up on reaching the head quarters of the corps to which each party belonged.

Adding together all the units, with an extra allowance of 3,500 artillery for the new batteries that came in with Junot's Corps, the Guard divisions, and the 9th Corps, we get as a total of the reinforcements poured into Spain between December 1809, and September 1810, the following figures :—

Junot's corps, at its final strength in June, infantry only	20,000
Young Guard divisions	15,000
Gendarmerie	4,000
New regiments	10,000
4th battalions, the first arrivals	33,600
4th battalions forming the 9th Corps . . .	20,000
Cavalry in organized squadrons	5,000
Artillery in complete batteries	3,500
Drafts, not in permanent units, for Infantry, Cavalry, and Artillery	27,000
	138,100

[1] The 4th battalions ultimately retained in Junot's corps did not for the most part belong to regiments of the Spanish army, but to regiments in Germany or the colonies. They are over and above the 66 fourth battalions accounted for in the list above. For details of the whole set of reinforcements see Tables in Appendix.

This total far exceeds the original 100,000 of which Napoleon had spoken in the autumn of 1809, but is certainly rather below the actual number of men received into the Peninsula ; the figure for drafts, in especial, is hard to verify.   But as the total strength of the Army of Spain in the autumn of 1809 was 237,000 men, and in September 1810, 353,000 men, while at least 25,000 had been lost in the interval [1], the figures cannot be far out.

Of this total, as we have already said, the 2nd, 6th, and 8th Corps and the troops under Kellermann and Bonnet occupying the provinces of Toro, Palencia, Valladolid, and Santander formed the ' Army of Portugal ' assigned to Masséna ; he was also given an extra unattached division under Serras [2], and promised the use of the 9th Corps when it should have crossed the Pyrenees.   The gross total of this force was in May, when the new Commander-in-Chief had taken up his post, about 130,000 men, of whom some 86,000 were effective and available for active operations at the moment.   Serras, Kellermann, and Bonnet were tied down to their local duties—the first had to look after the Spanish army of Galicia, the second to keep the plains of Valladolid quiet, the third to hold Santander and (when it was fully sub-dued) to enter and overrun the Asturias.   The 20,000 men of the 9th Corps were not yet arrived in Spain [3].   The troops in the provinces of Burgos, Biscay, and Navarre, though not placed under the Marshal's actual command, were yet in existence to cover his rear and his communications with France.   If they are added to the total of the force which, directly or indirectly, was employed for the conquest of Portugal, some 30,000 more must be taken into consideration.   But, though they were useful, indeed

[1] Over and above the ordinary death-rate for French troops quartered in Spain, which was very high, we have to allow for the losses at Tamames, Ocaña, the conquest of Andalusia, the sieges of Astorga, Gerona, Ciudad Rodrigo, and Almeida, and all smaller engagements.

[2] This division had charge of the Provinces of Leon, Zamora, and Sala-manca, which were not a ' military government.'

[3] Roughly, on May 15, 2nd Corps 20,000 men, 6th ditto 35,000, 8th ditto 26,000, Cavalry reserve 5,000, effectives present under arms, besides the sick, who made up about 12,000 more, and some 6,000 men detached.   See Tables in Appendix.

indispensable, for the conquest of Portugal, it is fairer to leave them out of consideration.

But the exact total of an army is, after all, less important than the character and capacity of its generals. The individuality of Masséna was the most important factor in the problem of the invasion of Portugal. He was fifty-two years of age— very nearly the eldest of all the Marshals—and he was the only one of those on active service, save Jourdan, who had achieved greatness in the days before Napoleon arrived at supreme power. He had led an army of 60,000 men when, of the three corps-commanders now under him, Ney was but a lieutenant-colonel, Junot a young captain, and Reynier a brigadier-general. Like nearly all the men of the Revolution he had risen from below ; he sprang from a poor family in Genoa : according to his enemies they were Jews, and his name was but Manasseh disguised. His personal character was detestable ; many of the marshals had an evil reputation for financial probity, but Masséna's was the worst of all. ' He plundered like a *condottiere* of the Middle Ages,' wrote one of his lieutenants. He had been in trouble, both with the Republican government and with the Emperor, for his shameless malversations in Italy, and had piled up a large private fortune by surreptitious methods[1]. Avarice is not usually associated with licentiousness, but he shocked even the easy-going public opinion of the French army by the way in which he paraded his mistress at unsuitable moments and in unsuitable company. He took this person, the sister of one of his aides de camp, with him all through the dangers of the Portuguese campaign, where her presence often caused friction and delays, and occasionally exposed him to insults[2]. Masséna was hard, suspicious, and revengeful ; an intriguer to the finger-tips, he was always prone to suppose

[1] The Emperor once confiscated 3,000,000 francs which Masséna had collected by selling licences to trade with the English at Leghorn and other Italian ports. See the Memoirs of General Lamarque, who carried out the seizure.

[2] See Thiébault, iv. 375 ; Marbot, ii. 380–1 ; Duchesse d'Abrantes, viii. 50. All these may be called scandal-mongers, but the lady's presence, and the troubles to which it gave rise, are chronicled by more serious authorities.

that others were intriguing against himself[1]. Though an old Republican, who had risen from the ranks early in the revolutionary war, he had done his best to make himself agreeable to Napoleon by the arts of the courtier. Altogether, he was a detestable character—but he was a great general. Of all the marshals of the Empire he was undoubtedly the most capable; Davoust and Soult, with all their abilities, were not up to his level. As a proof of his boldness and rapid skill in seizing an opportunity the battle of Zurich is sufficient to quote; for his splendid obstinacy the defence of Genoa at the commencement of his career has its parallel in the long endurance before the lines of Torres Vedras at its end. His best testimonial is that Wellington, when asked, long years after, which of his old opponents was the best soldier, replied without hesitation that Masséna was the man, and that he had never permitted himself to take in his presence the risks that he habitually accepted when confronted with any of the other marshals[2].

The fatigues of the late Austrian war, in which he had borne such an honourable part, had tried Masséna's health; it was not without difficulty that the Emperor had persuaded him to undertake the Portuguese campaign. When he first assembled round him at Salamanca the staff which was to serve him in the invasion, he astonished and somewhat disheartened his officers by beginning his greetings to them with the remark, 'Gentlemen, I am here contrary to my own wish; I begin to feel myself too old and too weary to go on active service. The Emperor says that I must, and replied to the reasons for declining this post which I gave him, by saying that my reputation would suffice to end the war. It was very flattering no doubt, but no man has two lives to live on this earth—the soldier least of all [3].' Those who had served under the Marshal a few years back, and now saw him after an interval, felt that there was truth in what he said. Foy wrote in his diary, ' He is no longer the Masséna of the flashing eyes, the mobile face,

---

[1] See Foy's complaints on p. 114 of his *Vie Militaire* (ed. Girod de L'Ain) as to the way in which the Marshal suspected him of undermining his favour with the Emperor.

[2] See Lord Stanhope's *Conversations with the Duke of Wellington*, p. 20.

[3] This comes from an eye-witness with no grudge against Masséna, Hulot, commanding the artillery of the 8th Corps. See his *Mémoires*, p. 303.

ANDRÉ

MASSÉNA,

DUC DE RIVOLI PRINCE D'ESSLING,

Né à Nice, en 1755,

Mort à sa Terre près Paris, en Avril 1817.

and the alert figure whom I knew in 1799, and whose head
then recalled to me the bust of Marius. He is only fifty-two,
but looks more than sixty ; he has got thin, he is beginning
to stoop ; his look, since the accident when he lost his eye by
the Emperor's hand[1], has lost its vivacity. The tone of his
voice alone remains unchanged.' But if the Marshal's bodily
vigour was somewhat abated, his will was as strong as ever. He
needed it at this juncture, for he had to command subordinates
who were anything but easy to deal with. Ney, though an
honest man and an admirable soldier, had the fault of insubordination in the highest degree. He never obeyed any one save
the Emperor in the true military fashion. He quarrelled with
every colleague that he met—notably with Soult—and had an
old and very justifiable personal dislike for Masséna. Even
before the latter appeared at the front, he had been heard to use
threatening language concerning him. Junot was almost as bad ;
having held the chief command in the last Portuguese expedition he had a strong, if a mistaken, belief that it was becoming
that he should be placed in charge of the second. His record
rendered the idea absurd, but this he was the last to understand,
being of an overweening and self-confident disposition. He was
stupid enough to regard Masséna as his supplanter, and to show
sullen resentment. . Of the three chiefs of the army corps about
to invade Portugal, Reynier was the only one on decent terms
with his Commander-in-Chief, but even he was not reckoned his
friend [2].

Masséna's chief of the staff was Fririon, a scientific soldier
and a man well liked by his colleagues ; but it is said that he
was not so much in the Marshal's confidence as Lieut.-Colonel

[1] Foy, p. 101. The Emperor, a notoriously bad shot, lodged some
pellets in the Marshal's left eye while letting fly at a pheasant. Napoleon
turned round and accused his faithful Berthier of having fired the shot : the
Prince of Neuchâtel was courtier enough to take the blame without a word,
and in official histories appears as the culprit (see e. g. Amic's *Masséna*,
p. 272) ; for other notes see Guingret, p. 250. What is most astonishing is
that Masséna was complaisant enough to affect to blame Berthier for the
disaster.

[2] See the admirable summary of all this in Foy's diary (Girod de L'Ain),
p. 101. Marbot gives the same views at bottom, but with his usual
exaggeration, and with ' illustrative anecdotes,' occasionally of doubtful
accuracy.

Pelet, the senior aide de camp of his staff. Complaints are found, in some of the letters and memoirs of the time, that Masséna would talk matters over with Pelet, and issue orders without letting even his chief of the staff know of his change of plan or new inspiration. Pelet's own indiscreet statements on this point seem to justify the complaints made by others against him [1]. There was friction, therefore, even within the staff itself, and all that the Marshal did, or said, was criticized by some of those who should have been his loyal subordinates, under the notion that it had been inspired by others, who were accorded a more perfect confidence by their common chief. Exact knowledge of the disputes in the *État Major* is hard to obtain, because, when the campaign was over, every man tried to make out that its failure had been due to the advice given to Masséna by those of whom he was jealous. At the bottom, however, all this controversy is not very important—there is no doubt that the Marshal himself was responsible for all that had happened— he was not the man to be led by the nose or over-persuaded by ambitious or intriguing underlings.

Failure or success is not the sole criterion of merit. Masséna's campaign was a disastrous business ; yet on investigating the disabilities under which he laboured, we shall be inclined in the end to marvel that he did so much, not that he did no more. The fundamental error was the Emperor's, who gave him too few men for the enterprise with which he was entrusted. Napoleon refused to take the Portuguese troops into considera-

---

[1] Note Pelet's *Aperçu sur la Campagne de Portugal,* nearly forty pages in the Appendix to *Victoires et Conquêtes,* vol. xxi : for his disputes with Baron Fririon see the *Spectateur Militaire* for 1841. Pelet says, ignoring the chief of the staff entirely, ' qu'il était investi de la confiance *absolue* du maréchal : qu'il faisait *seul* auprès de lui tout le travail militaire et politique, qu'il dirigeait la haute correspondance avec le major-général (Berthier) et les chefs de corps, etc., etc.' For Fririon's comparative impotence see a story on p. 387 of Marbot's vol. ii, which may or may not be true—probably the former.

Pelet's writings give a poor impression of his brain-power and his love of exact truth. He says, for example, in his *Aperçu* that Masséna had only 40,000 men in his army of invasion, when it is certain that he had 64,000. See Baron Fririon's remarks on him in *Spectateur Militaire,* June 1841, pp. 1–5.

tion, when he weighed the needs of the expedition. He repeatedly wrote that 'it was absurd that his armies should be held in check by 25,000 or 30,000 British troops,' as if nothing else required to be taken into consideration. He did not realize that Wellington had turned the Portuguese regular army into a decent fighting machine, capable of holding back French divisions in line of battle—as was shown at Bussaco. He had not foreseen that the despised militia required to be 'contained' by adequate numbers of troops on the line of communications. Still less had he dreamed of the great scheme for the devastation of Portugal, which was to be not the least effective of the weapons of its defender. But of this more will be said in the proper place.

THE MONTHS OF WAITING. SIEGE OF ASTORGA

MASSÉNA, as we have seen, was only appointed Commander-in-Chief of the Army of Portugal on April 17, 1810, and did not appear at Valladolid, to take up his charge, till May. The campaign, however, had begun long before under the Emperor's own directions. There were preliminary operations to be carried out, which could be finished before either the new General-in-Chief or the main body of the reinforcements from beyond the Pyrenees had arrived. These were the repression of the insurgent bands of Navarre, Biscay, and Old Castile, the firm establishment of the line of communications between Salamanca and Bayonne, and the capture of the outlying Spanish fortresses, Astorga and Ciudad Rodrigo, which served as external defences for the Portuguese frontier. ' Les besoins en Espagne sont successifs,' wrote the Emperor early in the winter of 1809–10 [1], ' il faut d'abord un corps qui soumette les derrières. Étant en Novembre il serait impossible de réunir tous les moyens avant du commencement de janvier. Et dans cette presqu'île coupée de montagnes les froids et les neiges de janvier ne permettront de rien faire.' All that he could do before spring would be to send forward Junot's corps, and the other earlier reinforcements, to positions from which they should be ready to strike, the moment that the fine weather began. With the coming of the new year, when these corps had reached their destined positions, the imperial orders begin to abound in elaborate directions for the extermination of the guerrillas of the Upper Ebro and the Upper Douro [2], orders which led to much marching and counter-marching of the newly arrived troops, but to little practical effect in the way of repression, for skilled leaders like Mina, the

---

[1] Napoleon to Clarke, Oct. 30, 1809.

[2] See for example Jan. 20, 1810, to Berthier ; Jan. 31, to same ; Feb. 12, to same.

Empecinado, and Julian Sanchez, nearly always slipped between the fingers of their pursuers, and on the few occasions when they were pressed into a corner, simply bade their men disperse and unite again at some distant rendezvous. These operations, however, were wholly subsidiary: the actual advance against Portugal only commences with the orders given to Junot in February to concentrate his corps at Valladolid, to hand over the charge of Salamanca and Old Castile to Kellermann's dragoons and the divisions of the 6th Corps, and then to subdue the whole of the plain-land of Leon, as far as the foot of the Asturian and Galician mountains, including the towns of Benavente, Leon, and Astorga. Bonnet and his division, now as always based on Santander, were already advancing to invade the Asturias, and to threaten Galicia from the east. Ney with the 6th Corps was ordered to draw near to the frontier of Portugal on the side of Ciudad Rodrigo, 'to inundate all the approaches to that kingdom with his cavalry, disquiet the English, and prevent them from dreaming of transferring themselves back to the south.' The news of the near approach of the Emperor himself with 80,000 men was to be spread in every direction [1].

Meanwhile the third great unit which was to form part of the projected Army of Portugal, the 2nd Corps (under the temporary command of General Heudelet [2]), was taking part in a separate and remote series of operations, far to the South. This corps, it will be remembered, had been left on the Tagus about Talavera and Oropesa, to protect the rear of Soult and King Joseph, when they marched in January with the 1st, 4th, and 5th Corps to conquer Andalusia. That exploit having been accomplished, Mortier went, with half of the 5th Corps, to attack Badajoz, and to subdue Estremadura, which Soult imagined to be defenceless, since Albuquerque had marched with the old Estremaduran army to save Cadiz. Mortier advanced unopposed to the walls of Badajoz, which he reached on February 12, but found himself unable to undertake its siege with his small force of 9,000 men, because a new Spanish host

[1] *Correspondance*, vol. xx, Napoleon to Berthier, Feb. 12, 1810.

[2] Soult had given up the 2nd Corps when he became King Joseph's Major-General : Reynier, appointed to command it, had not yet appeared.

had just appeared upon the scene. La Romana, with three of the divisions of the army that had been beaten at Alba de Tormes in November, had marched down the Spanish-Portuguese frontier by the Pass of Perales; and on the same day that Mortier appeared in front of Badajoz, his vanguard arrived at Albuquerque, only twenty miles away. These divisions were 13,000 strong: La Romana could add to this force a few thousands more left behind by Albuquerque. Mortier rightly felt that he dare not commence the regular siege of Badajoz when he had such superior numbers in his front. He therefore asked for reinforcements, both from Soult and from King Joseph. The former could spare nothing from Andalusia at this moment, but the 2nd Corps was ordered to leave the Tagus and place itself in communication with Mortier. Heudelet had other projects on hand at the moment: he had just seized Plasencia on February 10, and was engaged in bickering with Carlos d' España and Martin Carrera, whom La Romana had left in the Sierra de Gata. But, in obedience to his orders, he called in his detachments, and marched by Deleytosa and Truxillo into the valley of the Guadiana. This movement, from the French point of view, was a hazardous one; by the transference southward of the 2nd Corps, a long gap was left between Ney at Salamanca and Heudelet and Mortier in Estremadura. No troops whatever covered Madrid from the side of the south-west and the valley of the Tagus, and an irruption of the English on this line was one of the dangers which Napoleon most dreaded [1]. He was unaware of Wellington's deeply-rooted determination to commit himself to no more Spanish campaigns.

Long before Heudelet approached the Guadiana, Mortier had been compelled, partly by want of supplies, partly by the threatening attitude of La Romana, who began cautiously to turn his flanks, to retire from in front of the walls of Badajoz. He gave back as far as Zafra on the road to the south, and six days after marched for Seville, leaving only a rearguard at Santa Ollala, on the extreme border of Estremadura. Soult required his presence, for, on account of a rising in Granada, and a

[1] 'Il faut prévoir que les Anglais peuvent marcher sur Talavera pour faire diversion,' wrote Napoleon on Jan. 31 to Berthier. But Heudelet had been moved before his caution could reach Madrid.

threatening movement by the Spanish army of Murcia, the
French reserves in Andalusia had been moved eastward, and its
capital was almost stripped of troops. Hence when the 2nd
Corps reached Caçeres on March 8, and appeared in front of
Albuquerque on March 14, it found that the 5th Corps had
departed, and that it was nearly 100 miles from the nearest
friendly post. Heudelet, therefore, having all La Romana's
army in his front, and no orders to execute (since the junction
with Mortier had failed), retired to Merida, where Reynier
arrived from the north, superseded him, and took command.
Here the 2nd Corps remained practically passive for the rest
of the spring, keeping open, but with difficulty and at long
intervals, the communications between Madrid and Seville, by
means of detachments at Truxillo and Almaraz. To a certain
extent Reynier kept La Romana's army in check, but he did
not fully discharge even that moderate task, for the Spanish
general detached southward two of his divisions, those of
Contreras and Ballasteros, to threaten the frontiers of Andalusia
and stir up an insurrection in the Condado de Niebla and the
other regions west of Seville. Ballasteros surprised the cavalry
brigade of Mortier's corps at Valverde, at midnight on February
19, and scattered it, killing Beauregard, the brigadier. He
then advanced to Ronquillo, only twenty miles from Seville,
where, on March 25-6, he had an indecisive engagement with
one of Gazan's brigades, after which he retired into the Condado.
Mortier, thereupon, came out against him from Seville at the
head of a whole division. Unwisely offering battle at Zalamea,
on the Rio Tinto, on April 15, Ballasteros was beaten, and
retired into the mountains. Thither, after some time, he was
pursued by Mortier's columns, and again defeated at Araçena
on May 26. But he rallied his broken force in the Sierra de
Araçena, where he remained for long after, a thorn in the side
of the Army of Andalusia, always descending for a raid in the
plains of Seville when he was left unwatched. Soult was forced
to keep a considerable part of the 5th Corps in observation of
him—a detachment that he was loth to spare.

La Romana's central divisions, meanwhile, those of Charles
O'Donnell (brother of the Henry O'Donnell who had distinguished himself at Gerona in the previous autumn), Mendizabal,

and Contreras, bickered with the 2nd Corps in the direction of Caçeres and Torresnovas, without any notable advantage on either side. But as long as Reynier lay at Merida, and Mortier might at any moment come up from Seville to his aid, Wellington felt uneasy as to the possibility of a French advance between Tagus and Guadiana, and, regarding La Romana's army as an insufficient security on this side, moved Hill with a force of 12,000 men to Portalegre, close to the rear of Badajoz. Hill had with his own British division, now consisting of three brigades [1], another division composed of Portuguese, under General Hamilton [2], the English heavy cavalry brigade of Slade, a weak Portuguese cavalry brigade under Madden [3], and three batteries. He was ordered not to countenance any offensive movements on the part of La Romana, but to support him, and to endeavour to cover Badajoz, if the French should unite the 2nd and 5th Corps, and make a serious move westward. There was no need, as matters turned out, for any such support, for Reynier, though he executed some rather useless feints and counter-marches in April and May, undertook nothing serious. One of his demonstrations drew Hill to Arronches, close to Elvas, on May 14, but it turned out to be meaningless, and the British troops returned to their usual head quarters at Portalegre a few days later. There seems to have been some uncertainty of purpose in all this manœuvring of the French in Estremadura. Reynier was not strong enough to offer to fight La Romana and Hill combined ; he might have done so with good prospect of success if Mortier could have been spared from Andalusia ; but half the 5th Corps was usually detached far to the south, hunting the insurgents of the Sierra de Ronda, and the other half had to garrison Seville and watch Ballasteros. Hence Reynier, left to himself, did no more for the common cause of the French in Spain than detain Hill's two divisions in the Alemtejo. That Wellington was thus obliged to divide his army was no doubt

----

[1] Hill's division, two brigades strong at Talavera in August, had received a third brigade in September under Catlin Crauford, consisting of the 2/28th, 2/34th, and 2/39th.

[2] Composed of the 2nd, 4th, 10th, and 14th regiments, each two battalions strong, with 4,500 bayonets.

[3] 1st and 4th Portuguese cavalry.

a permanent gain to the enemy : yet they obtained it by the
very doubtful expedient of leaving nothing on the Tagus ; a
push in the direction of Plasencia and Almaraz by even
a small Spanish force would have been a very tiresome and
troublesome matter for King Joseph, who would have been
forced either to bring down Ney from Salamanca, or to call
Reynier back from the Guadiana, for Madrid was entirely
uncovered on the West. But nothing of the sort happened ; La
Romana kept his main body concentrated in front of Badajoz,
and had the full approval of Wellington for doing so.

At the extreme opposite flank of the French front, on the
shores of the Bay of Biscay, there was going on at this same
time a side-campaign conducted with a much greater degree of
vigour, but equally indecisive in the end. The Asturias had
been almost stripped of troops by Del Parque, in order to
reinforce the army that fought at Tamames and Alba de Tormes.
When the Duke moved his main force southward after the last-
named fight, he carried off with him the division of Ballasteros,
which had been the core of the old Asturian Army. General
Antonio Arce was left in the principality with some 4,000 men,
whom he kept at Colombres, behind the Deba, under General
Llano-Ponte, watching the French force in the province of
Santander. New levies, little more than 2,000 strong, were
being collected at Oviedo. In the end of January General
Bonnet, whose division at Santander had received its drafts, and
had been strengthened up to 7,000 men [1], thought himself strong
enough t o drive in Arce's weak line and to make a dash at
the Asturian capital. On the 25th he attacked the lines of
Colombres, and carried them with no difficulty. On the 31st
he captured Oviedo, which was evacuated by the Captain-General
Arce and the local Junta without serious fighting. But that
active partisan Juan Porlier at once cut off his communication
with Santander, by seizing Infiesto and Gijon. Bonnet at once
evacuated Oviedo, and turned back to clear his rear. Porlier
escaped along the coast to Pravia, and meanwhile the main body
of the Asturians, under General Barcena, reoccupied the capital.
Having driven off Porlier, the French general marched west-

[1] He had 7,094 men with the colours, besides sick and detached, by the
imperial muster rolls of Jan. 15, 1810.

ward once more, beat Barcena at the bridge of Colleto on
February 14, and again made himself master of Oviedo. The
Asturians rallied behind the Narcea, where they were joined by
a brigade of 2,000 men sent to their aid by Mahy, the Captain-
General of Galicia.

That province, like the Asturias, had been left almost
ungarrisoned by Del Parque, when he took the old 'Army of
Galicia' across the Sierra de Gata, and transferred it to Estremadura. Mahy had been left behind with the skeleton of one
division, which he was to recruit, as best he could, by new levies.
His main preoccupation at this moment was the defence of
the newly fortified stronghold of Astorga, which was already
threatened by the French troops in the plains of Leon. But
seeing his flank menaced by Bonnet's advance, he lent what men
he could spare to aid in the defence of the Asturias.

The Asturian junta, having deposed General Arce for incapacity and corruption, and appointed Cienfuegos to take over
his troops, ordered the resumption of offensive operations against
Bonnet in March. Porlier, their great partisan-hero, made
a circuit along the coast, and threatened the French communications with Santander. At the same time their main force
advanced against Oviedo by the valley of the Nalon. Bonnet's
advanced brigade was driven in, after a sharp skirmish at Grado
on March 19, and disquieted by Porlier's simultaneous attack
on his rear, he evacuated the Asturian capital for the *third*
time, and gave back as far as Cangas de Onis, in the valley of
the Ona. He then called up all the reinforcements that he
could obtain from Santander, and marched—for the fourth time
in three months!—on Oviedo with his whole division ; the
Spaniards retired without offering serious opposition, and took
up a line behind the Narcea [March 29]. This time Bonnet
left them no time to rally, but forced the passage of that river,
whereupon the Asturians ascended to Tineo in the mountains,
while the Galician succours gave back to Navia, almost on the
edge of their own principality [April 25–26]. After this,
Bonnet's offensive force was spent ; having to occupy Oviedo
and its ports of Gijon and Aviles, as well as all the central and
eastern Asturias, and, moreover, to defend his communication
with Santander from new attacks of Porlier, his strength

sufficed for no more. His 7,000 men were immobilized for the
rest of the year : he had conquered two-thirds of the Asturias,
and barely succeeded in keeping it down. But he was quite
unable to spare a man to aid in French operations in the plains
of Leon, or even to make a serious attempt to threaten Galicia.
Once or twice he succeeded in communicating with the forces
which Junot (and after him Kellermann and Serras) commanded
in the plains beyond the Cantabrian range, by expeditions
pushed down through the pass of Pajares on to Leon ; but the
road was always closed again by the guerrillas, and no co-operation
could take place. In short, the Spaniards lost the greater part
of the Asturias, and the French lost the further services of
Bonnet's division [1]. It had no power to threaten Galicia,
because it was forced to keep garrisons in Gijon, Aviles, Lastres,
Santona, and all the sea-ports, with a full brigade at Oviedo in
the centre, to support them. Any concentration of troops,
leading to the evacuation of the smaller garrisons, at once let
loose the guerrillas from their mountains. Bonnet had but
7,000 men in all : of these, not more than half could be used

---

[1] I cannot understand Napier's narrative of this little campaign, on
pages 352–4 of his vol. ii. It runs as follows, and seems to have no
relation to the facts detailed by Belmas, Toreño, Arteche, or any other
historian. No mention is made of the four captures of Oviedo !

‘ Mahy was organizing a second army at Lugo and in the Asturias. D'Arco
[Arce] commanded 7,000 men, 3,000 of whom were posted at Cornellana
under General Ponte. . . . Bonnet, from the Asturias, threatened Galicia by
the Concija d'Ibas : having destroyed Ponte's force at Potes de la Sierra
[30 miles from Colombres, where the actual fight took place], he menaced
Galicia by the pass of Nava de Suarna [a place which his vanguard did
not approach by a matter of 40 miles]. . . . But he did not pass Nava de
Suarna, and General D'Arco rallied the Asturian fugitives at Louarca. It
seems probable that while Bonnet drew the attention of the Galician army
towards Lugo [he was never within 100 miles of that place], Junot thought
to penetrate by Puebla Senabria. But finally Junot, drawing a reinforcement from Bonnet, invested Astorga with 10,000 infantry,' &c. [No troops
from Bonnet's force ever appeared before Astorga.]

This last blunder is apparently borrowed from *Victoires et Conquêtes*, xx.
12, which states that General Bonnet detached Jeannin's brigade, the 46th
and 65th, to Astorga. But these regiments did not belong to Bonnet,
but were, from the first to the last, parts of Junot's own corps, and never
entered the Asturias. Compare Napoleon, *Correspondance*, xx. 21, the
muster rolls of Jan. 1, Feb. 15, and Belmas, iii. p. 46.

for an expedition, and such a force was too small to have any practical effect on the general course of events in north-western Spain.

Bonnet's operations were, of course, wholly subsidiary; the really important movements that were on foot in the early spring of 1810 were those of Junot and Ney in the plains of Leon. In pursuance of the Emperor's orders to the effect that the whole plain-land of Leon was to be occupied, as a preliminary to the invasion of Portugal, Loison, who had re-entered Spain at the head of a number of battalions which were ultimately to join the corps of Ney, was ordered to move on from Valladolid and occupy the country about Benavente and Astorga. He was left free to select either of those towns as his head quarters, and was directed to communicate with Bonnet, when the latter should have entered the Asturias, so that their operations should threaten Galicia simultaneously [1]. Loison's expedition, however, proved a complete failure; he marched towards Astorga early in February with nearly 10,000 men. On the 11th he appeared before that town, and learnt that since Carrié's reconnaissance in October 1809 [2], it had been much strengthened. La Romana had repaired the breaches of its mediaeval walls. He had thrown up entrenchments round the suburb of La Reteibia, which occupies that part of the hill of Astorga, which is not covered by the town itself. He had also established outlying posts in the suburbs of San Andrés and Puerta del Rey, which lie at the foot of the hill, on its northern and eastern sides. Fourteen guns, only two of them 12-pounders, the rest light, had been mounted on the walls. The place, therefore, was a make-shift fortification of the most antiquated style. General Garcia Velasco, who had been left behind in Galicia with one division of the old Northern army when Del Parque marched for Estremadura, was in charge of this portion of the Spanish front, under the superintendence of Mahy, the Captain-General. He had placed half his troops—five battalions, or 2,700 men, in Astorga, while he himself with the remainder lay beyond the mountains, at Villafranca, in the Vierzo, with about the same force. The total of organized troops in Galicia

---

[1] Napoleon to Berthier, Jan. 11, 1810.

[2] See p. 76.

at this moment did not exceed 8,000 men, including the small brigade which Mahy sent to the Asturias, and a detachment under Echevarria at Puebla de Senabria. Astorga had not been expecting a siege at such an early date as February 11; it was only provisioned for twenty days, and the guns had not ammunition to last for even that short space of time. The governor, José Santocildes, was a man of courage and resource, who knew how to put on a bold face to an impossible situation, or instant disaster might have followed.

Loison was disconcerted to find that Astorga, his destined head quarters, was held and garrisoned against him. His engineers reconnoitred its walls, and informed him that it could not be taken without a regular battering-train. He had only field-pieces with him, the weather was abominable, and his troops—all conscript battalions from France—were suffering terribly from the continued rain and cold. Wherefore he contented himself with inviting Santocildes to surrender, promising him promotion at King Joseph's hands, if he ' would implore the clemency of a sovereign who treats all Spaniards like a father [1].' When the governor sent a curt reply, intimating that he and his people intended to do their duty, Loison retired to La Baneza, and reported to his chiefs that he was helpless for want of siege-guns. He announced at the same time that he had attempted to communicate with Bonnet at Oviedo, by sending two battalions to the foot of the pass of Pajares, but that the mountain roads were all blocked with snow, and that this detachment had been forced to fall back into the plains, without obtaining any news of what was afoot in the Asturias [2].

A few days later, the head of Junot's corps entered the province of Leon, and Loison was directed to move southward and join Ney at Salamanca. His place on the Esla and the Orbigo was taken by Clausel's division of the 8th Corps. The newly arrived general executed another reconnaissance to the neighbourhood of Astorga, and on February 26 sent Santocildes a second summons, in the name of Junot. It received the same answer that had been given to Loison. It was clear that Astorga

---

[1] For the letters of Loison to Santocildes and the reply of the Spanish brigadier, see the correspondence in Belmas, iii. pp. 53–6.

[2] Loison to Berthier, Feb. 16, from La Baneza.

must be besieged, and that a battering train must be placed at
the disposition of the force charged with the operation.   But
in the present state of the roads it would take some time to
bring heavy guns to the front.   Further operations had to be
postponed.   The 6th Corps, it may be remarked, had executed
at the same time that Loison appeared in front of Astorga,
a demonstration against Ciudad Rodrigo.   King Joseph had
written from Andalusia to beg Ney to threaten the place, while
the news of the French victories in the south were still fresh,
assuring him that the Spaniards were so cowed that a prompt
surrender was probable.   The Marshal, though doubting the
wisdom of these optimistic views, concentrated his corps,
advanced to San Felices, and on February 13 summoned Rodrigo.
He got from General Herrasti, the governor, an answer as bold
and confident as that which Loison received from Santocildes,
and returned to Salamanca to disperse his troops in cantonments
and ask for a battering-train[1].   His short and ineffective excursion
to the banks of the Agueda had taken him in sight of the
British outposts on the Spanish frontier, and had induced
Wellington for a moment to think that the invasion of Portugal
was at hand.   It was impossible that he should have guessed
that Ney's advance had no better cause than King Joseph's
foolish confidence.   Hence the withdrawal of the 6th Corps,
after the vain summons of Ciudad Rodrigo, was as inexplicable
as its advance.   'I do not understand Ney's movement,' he
wrote to his trusted subordinate, Robert Craufurd, 'coupled as
it is with the movement upon Badajoz from the south of Spain.
The French are not strong enough for the two sieges at the same
time, and I much doubt whether they are in a state to undertake one of them[2].'   The prompt retirement of Ney from before
Ciudad Rodrigo, and of Mortier from before Badajoz, completely justified his conclusions within a day or two of the
writing of his letter.

There was nothing for the French in the kingdom of Leon to
do, save to await the arrival of the great battering-train which

[1] For notes as to the cause and execution of this abortive movement,
see the diary of Ney's aide de camp, Sprünglin, pages 402–3.

[2] Wellington to Craufurd, Feb. 16.   Compare similar remarks in
Wellington to Beresford, from Vizeu, Feb. 21, 1810.

Napoleon had bestowed upon his Army of Portugal. It was far
to the rear: on February 20 its head was only beginning to
approach Burgos, and its tail had not quitted Bayonne. The
reason of this tardiness was the want of draught animals at the
southern dépôts of France. The equipment of the train and
the artillery of the 8th Corps, and the other great reinforcements which had just passed the Pyrenees, had exhausted the
available supplies of horses[1], and when the authorities at
Bayonne had to place the 'grand park' on a war footing there
was intolerable delay. Even when detachments of the park had
started, they made slow progress in Spain, for the French horses
died off rapidly in the bitter weather of the plateau of Old
Castile, and it was almost impossible to replace them by
requisition from the country-side. Junot, bold to the verge of
rashness, and feverishly anxious to remake the reputation that
he had lost at Vimiero, could not endure the delay. He sent to
requisition Spanish guns from the governors of Burgos and
Segovia, dispatched his own teams to draw them, and when he
heard that a small train was procurable, ordered the 8th Corps
towards Astorga on March 15, leaving the cannon to follow.
The month's delay in the investment had enabled Santocildes
to fill up the supply of food and ammunition which had been
so low in February; he had now got his fortress in as good
state as was possible, considering the intrinsic weakness of its
mediaeval walls, and had induced 3,000 of the 4,000 inhabitants
to retire to Galicia.

On March 21 Clausel's division invested Astorga, while
Solignac's came up to Leon and Benavente in support, and St.
Croix's division of dragoons took post in advance of La Baneza,
to observe the Spanish forces in southern Galicia and the
Portuguese of the Tras-os-Montes. Till the guns should
arrive, there was nothing to be done save to choose the point of
attack, prepare fascines and gabions, and open the first parallel,
out of harm's way from the small artillery of the garrison—
none of it heavier than a 12-pounder. Valazé, Junot's chief
engineer, opined that the low-lying suburbs at the foot of the
hill of Astorga might be neglected, and the newly entrenched

---

[1] Even the 8th Corps had to leave guns behind at Bayonne for want
of horses, Belmas, ii. 13.

Reteibia on the high ground masked by a false attack, while the projecting and unflanked north-west corner of the old walls of the city itself might be battered from the slopes below : here, as in all its circuit, the place had neither ditch nor glacis : there was simply the stout mediaeval wall, broken every 30 yards by a small square tower, which followed the sky-line of the plateau.

The first three weeks of the siege had an unusual character, since the French could build what works they pleased, but could not seriously batter Astorga with the sixteen field-guns of small calibre belonging to the division lying before the walls. The officer in temporary command of the artillery, Colonel Noël, contented himself with opening fire from various false attacks, from which the guns were repeatedly moved, in order to distract the attention of the enemy from the chosen front on the north-west, where the approaches were completed, and a great battery constructed, ready for the siege-guns when they should arrive. Meanwhile there was a good deal of infantry skirmishing in and about the lower suburbs, in whose outskirts the French ultimately established themselves, though they had no intention of pushing up to the walls either from Puerta del Rey or from San Andrés [1]. The garrison defended itself well, executed several vigorous sorties, and lost no post of importance, though the line of resistance in the suburbs was gradually thrust back. Santocildes received several encouraging messages from his chief Mahy, who announced that he was bringing up to the pass of Foncebadon, on the edge of the plain of Astorga, every man that Galicia could furnish. But even when the Captain-General had brought his reserves from Lugo to join Garcia's division, they had only 5,000 bayonets. To hold them off, Junot sent Clausel's division to the outposts, and replaced it in the trenches by Solignac's and one brigade of Lagrange's. Mahy, in face of such an accumulation of men, was absolutely helpless. Echevarria, with his weak brigade from Puebla de Senabria, had pushed a little forward, to give moral support to Mahy. He was surprised and routed near Alcanizas on April 10, by St. Croix's dragoons.

On the 15th the siege-train arrived from Valladolid ; it was

[1] There are good narratives in the autobiographies of Noël and Hulot of the artillery, beside the excellent account in Belmas, vol. iii.

small [1], but sufficient against an enemy so miserably provided
with guns as Santocildes. Junot himself came up on the 17th
to watch the effect of the attack. It was instant and overpowering. When once the artillery had been placed in the
works prepared for it, and had begun its fire, the old walls of
Astorga began to crumble. The light Spanish pieces on the
enceinte were overpowered, despite of the gallant way in which
the gunners stuck to their work [2]. By noon on the 21st of
April the north-western angle of the walls of Astorga had been
beaten down, and the fallen stones, there being no ditch, had
accumulated at the foot of the broad breach, so as to give an
easy entrance. Fortunately for the defence, there was a large
church just inside the angle : its roof and tower had been shot
down, but the garrison had made themselves strong in the lower
parts of the building, and threw up traverses from it to the
wall on each side of the breach. This gave them a second line
of defence, though but a weak one, and when Junot sent in
a summons in the afternoon Santocildes refused his offer. At
seven the French general bade 700 men storm the breach ; the
forlorn hope was composed of the voltigeur and grenadier
companies of the Irish Legion and the 47th of the Line. The
column penetrated to the foot of the breach without much
difficulty, though exposed to heavy musketry from the walls,
and a flanking fire from the suburb of the Reteibia. The breach
was carried, and, in addition, a house built with its back to the
ramparts just inside the enceinte. But the assailants could get
no further, owing to the murderous fire which the Spaniards
kept up from behind the ruined church and the traverses.
After an hour of desperate attempts to break in, they took
shelter, some in the house that they had captured, but the
majority behind the lip of the breach, where they covered
themselves as best they could, by piles of débris built in with
their haversacks, and even with the corpses of the fallen. Under

---

[1] Only consisting of four 24-pounders, one 16-pounder, four 12-
pounders, eight 6-inch howitzers, and one 6-inch mortar. See Belmas,
iii. 28.

[2] ' Les Espagnols rispostèrent avec vivacité ; on s'étonnait d'autant plus
que, le parapet étant en pierres sèches, chaque boulet qui le frappait en
faisait jaillir de nombreux éclats.' Belmas, iii. 34.

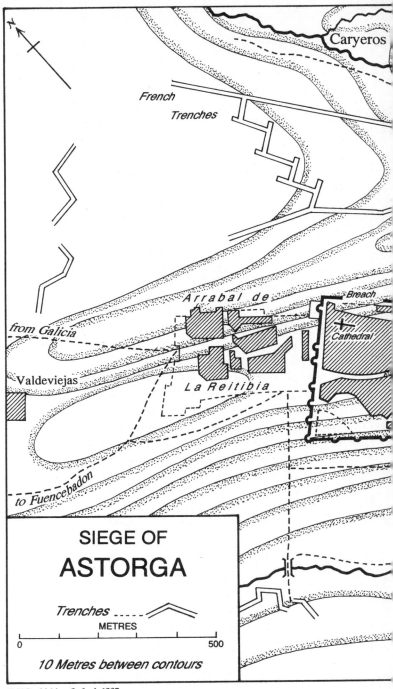

Caryeros

French
Trenches

Arrabal de

Breach

from Galicia

Cathedral

Valdeviejas

La Reitibia

to Fuencebadon

SIEGE OF
ASTORGA

Trenches ----- ⌒

METRES

0   500

10 Metres between contours

B.V.Darbishire, Oxford, 1907

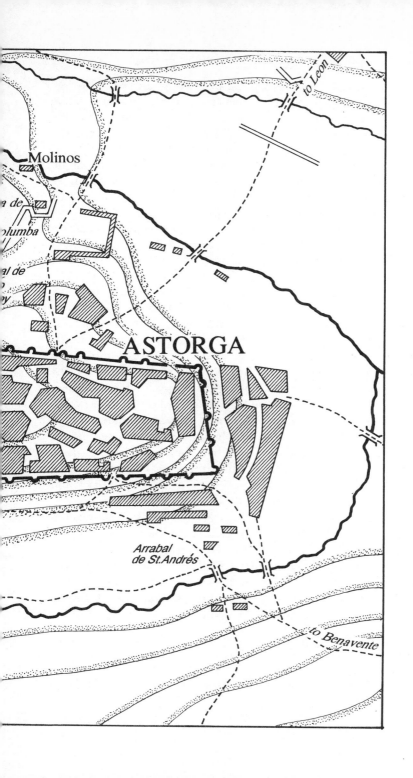

this poor shelter they lay till dark, suffering heavily. During the night the troops in the trenches ran out a line of gabions from the front works to the foot of the walls, and by dawn had opened a good communication with the men at the breach, though they had to work under a furious but blind fire from above.

At dawn on April 22, Santocildes surrendered. He might have held out some hours longer behind his inner defences, if he had not exhausted nearly all his musket ammunition in resisting the storm. There were less than thirty cartridges a head left for the infantry of the garrison, and only 500 pounds of powder for the artillery. The defence had been admirable, and, it may be added, very scientific, a fact proved by the low figures of the dead and wounded, which did not amount to 200 men [1]. The French, in the assault alone, lost five officers and 107 men killed, and eight officers and 286 men wounded [2]. Junot was thought to have been precipitate in ordering the storm : his excuse was that there were less than two hours of daylight left, and that, if he had deferred the attack till next morning, the Spaniards would have retrenched the breach under cover of the dark, and made it impracticable. The siege cost the 8th Corps in all 160 killed and some 400 wounded, a heavy butcher's bill for the capture of a mediaeval fortress armed with only fourteen light guns. Two thousand five hundred prisoners were taken, as shown by Santocildes' lists, but Junot claimed to have 'captured 3,500 fine troops, all with good English muskets, and well clothed in English great coats,' as well as 500 sick and wounded—impossible figures.

On the morning of the surrender Mahy made a feeble demonstration against the covering troops, on both the passes of Manzanal and Foncebadon, while Echevarria beat up the force at Penilla which lay facing him. All three attacks were checked with ease, the Galician army not being able to put more than 6,000 men in the field on the three fronts taken together. Its loss was heavy, especially at Penilla.

[1] Two officers and forty-nine men killed, ten officers and ninety-nine men wounded, according to his official report to the Junta, in which all details are duly given.

[2] See the figures in Junot's dispatch, given on pages 66–7 of Belmas, vol. iii.

After detaching the 22nd Regiment, which was ordered to endeavour to communicate with Bonnet in the Asturias, and garrisoning Astorga with two battalions, Junot drew back the greater part of his corps to Valladolid and Toro. He had been ordered to place himself near Ney, in order to aid and cover the 6th Corps in the oncoming siege of Ciudad Rodrigo. At the same time he received the unwelcome news that Masséna had been named Commander-in-Chief of the Army of Portugal, and that the 8th Corps was placed under his orders.

Masséna, as has been already mentioned, did not arrive at Salamanca till May 28th: he could not well have reached the front earlier, since the Emperor had only placed him in command in April. The long delay in the opening of the main campaign must, therefore, be laid to Napoleon's account rather than to that of his generals. If he had suspected that every day of waiting meant that Wellington had added an extra redoubt to the ever-growing lines of Torres Vedras, it is permissible to believe that he would have hurried forward matters at a less leisurely pace. But his determination to conduct the invasion of Portugal in what he called 'a methodical fashion' is sufficiently shown by the orders sent to Salamanca on May 29. 'Tell the Prince of Essling that, according to our English intelligence, the army of General Wellington is composed of no more than 24,000 British and Germans, and that his Portuguese are only 25,000 strong. I do not wish to enter Lisbon at this moment, because I could not feed the city, whose immense population is accustomed to live on sea-borne food. He can spend the summer months in taking Ciudad Rodrigo, and then Almeida. He need not hurry, but can go methodically to work. The English general, having less than 3,000 cavalry, may offer battle on ground where cavalry cannot act, but will never come out to fight in the plains [1].'

The Emperor then proceeds to add that with the 50,000 men of the 6th and 8th Corps, the cavalry reserve, &c., Masséna is strong enough to take both Rodrigo and Almeida at his ease: Reynier and the 2nd Corps can be called up to the bridge of Alcantara, from whence they can menace Central Portugal and cover Madrid. No order is given to bring up this corps

[1] Napoleon to Berthier, May 29, 1810.

to join the main army: it seems that the Emperor at this moment had in his head the plan, with which Wellington always credited him, of threatening a secondary attack in the Tagus valley. The 2nd Corps is treated as covering Masséna's left, while on his right he will be flanked by Kellermann, who is to add to the small force already under his command in Old Castile a whole new division, that of Serras, composed of troops just arrived from France[1]. This, added to Kellermann's dragoons, would make a corps of 12,000 men. In addition, as the Emperor remarks, by the time that the Army of Portugal is ready to march on Lisbon, it will have in its rear the 9th Corps under Drouet, nearly 20,000 men, who will be concentrated at Valladolid before the autumn has begun. There will be over 30,000 men in Leon and Old Castile when Masséna's army moves on from Almeida, and in the rear of these again Burgos, Navarre, and Biscay will be held by the Young Guard, and by twenty-six 4th battalions from France, which were due to start after the 9th Corps, and would have made their appearance south of the Pyrenees by August or September.

This document is a very curious product of the imperial pen. It would be hard to find in the rest of the *Correspondance* a dispatch which so completely abandons the 'Napoleonic methods' of quick concentration and sharp strokes, and orders a delay of three months or more in the completion of a campaign whose preliminary operations had begun so far back as February. We may reject at once the explanation offered by some of Napoleon's enemies, to the effect that he was jealous of Masséna, and did not wish him to achieve too rapid or too brilliant a success. But it is clear that a humanitarian regard for the possible sufferings of the inhabitants of Lisbon—the only reason alleged for the delay—is an inadequate motive. Such things did not normally affect the Emperor, and he must have remembered that when Junot occupied Portugal at the mid-winter of 1807–8

[1] Serras' division consisted of the 113th Line, a Tuscan regiment originally employed in Catalonia, which had been so cut up in 1809 that it had been sent back to refill its cadres; also of the 4th of the Vistula (two battalions), a Polish regiment raised in 1810, with four provisional battalions, and three stray battalions belonging to regiments in the South, which had not been allowed to go on to join Soult [4th battalions of the 32nd and 58th Line and of 12th Léger]: his total strength was 8,000 men.

famine had not played its part in the difficulties encountered
by the French.   Nor does it seem that an exaggerated estimate
of the enemy's strength induced him to postpone the attack
till all the reinforcements had arrived.   He under-estimates
Wellington's British troops by some 5,000, his Portuguese troops
by at least 15,000 men.   He is utterly ignorant of the works
of Torres Vedras, though six months' labour has already been
lavished on them, and by this time they were already defensible.
Three months seem an altogether exaggerated time to devote
to the sieges of the two little old-fashioned second-rate fortresses
of Ciudad Rodrigo and Almeida.   From whence, then, comes
this unprecedented resolve to adopt a 'methodical' system in
dealing with the invasion of Portugal?   It has been suggested
that the Emperor was very desirous to make sure of the absolute
suppression of the guerrilleros of the Pyrenees and the Ebro,
before pushing forward his field army to Lisbon.   Possibly he
was influenced by his knowledge of the infinite difficulty that
Masséna would find in equipping himself with a train, and more
especially in creating magazines during the months before the
harvest had been gathered in.   Some have thought that, looking
far forward, he considered it would be more disastrous to the
English army to be 'driven into the sea' somewhere in the
rough months of October and November rather than in the fine
weather of June—and undoubtedly no one who reads his dispatches can doubt that the desire to deal an absolutely crushing
blow to that army was his dominating idea throughout.   But
probably the main determining factor in Napoleon's mind was
the resolve that there should be no failure this time, for want
of preparation or want of sufficient strength; that no risks
should be taken, and that what he regarded as an overwhelming
force should be launched upon Portugal.   After Junot's disaster
of 1808 and Soult's fiasco in 1809, the Imperial prestige could
not stand a third failure.   The old pledge that 'the leopard
should be driven into the sea' must be redeemed at all costs
on this occasion.   Solid success rather than a brilliant campaign must be the end kept in view: hence came the elaborate
preparations for the sustaining of Masséna's advance by the
support of Drouet, Kellermann, and Serras.   Even Suchet's
operations in Eastern Spain were to be conducted with some

regard to the affairs of Portugal [1]. It was a broad and a formidable plan—but it failed in one all-important factor. Wellington's strength was underrated ; it was no mere driving of 25,000 British troops into the sea that was now in question, but the reduction of a kingdom where every man had been placed under arms, and every preparation made for passive as well as for active resistance. When Napoleon was once more foiled, it was because he had treated the Portuguese army —a ' *tas de coquins* ' as he called them—as a negligible quantity, and because he had foreseen neither that systematic devastation of the land, nor the creation of those vast lines in front of Lisbon, which were such essential features of Wellington's scheme of defence. The French attack was delivered by 65,000 men, not by the 100,000 whose advent the British general had feared : and precisely because the numbers of the Army of Portugal were no greater, the attack was made on the Beira frontier only. Masséna had no men to spare for the secondary invasion south of the Tagus which Wellington had expected and dreaded. The Emperor's plans went to wreck because he had underestimated his enemy, and assigned too small a force to his lieutenant. But it was no ordinary general who had so prepared his defence that Napoleon's calculations went all astray. The genius of Wellington was the true cause of the disastrous end of the long-prepared invasion.

[1] See the curious dispatch no. 16651, of July 14, directing Suchet to be ready to send half his corps to Valladolid after he should have taken Tortosa.

SECTION XIX: CHAPTER V

THE MONTHS OF WAITING. THE SIEGE OF CIUDAD RODRIGO

THE long months of delay that followed the first operations of the French in 1810 were a time of anxious waiting for Wellington. He had moved his head quarters to Vizeu on the 12th of January, and had been lying in that bleak and lofty town all through the rest of the winter. With him there had come to the North all the old British divisions save the 2nd, which had been left with Hill, first at Abrantes and then at Portalegre, to watch the French between the Tagus and the Guadiana. The 1st Division was placed at Vizeu, the 3rd at Trancoso and the neighbouring villages, the 4th at Guarda, while the cavalry wintered in the coast plain between Coimbra and Aveiro. Only the Light Brigade of Robert Craufurd, which takes the new style of the Light *Division* on March 1, was pushed forward to the Spanish frontier, and lay in the villages about Almeida[1], with its outposts pushed forward to the line of the Agueda. The Portuguese regular brigades, which were afterwards incorporated in the British divisions, were still lying in winter quarters around Coimbra and Thomar, drilling hard and incorporating their recruits. The militia were also under arms at their regimental head quarters, save the few battalions which had already been thrown into Elvas, Almeida, Peniche, and Abrantes.

Wellington's front, facing the French, was formed by Hill's corps in the Alemtejo, Lecor's Portuguese brigade in the Castello Branco district, and Craufurd's force on the Agueda. Neither Hill nor Lecor was in actual contact with the enemy, and La Romana's army, spread out from the Pass of Perales to

---

[1] The head quarters of the 43rd during January and February were at Valverde, above the Coa, those of the 52nd at Pinhel, those of the 95th at Villa Torpim.

Zafra and Aracena in a thin line, lay between them and Reynier's and Mortier's outposts. It was otherwise with Craufurd, who was placed north of La Romana's left division, that of Martin Carrera; he was in close touch with Ney's corps all along the line of the Agueda, as far as the Douro. Since the outposts of the 6th Corps had been pushed forward on March 9th, the Commander of the Light Division was in a most responsible, not to say a dangerous, position. The main army was forty miles to his rear in its cantonments at Vizeu, Guarda, and Trancoso. He had with him of British infantry only the first battalions of the 43rd, 52nd, and 95th, with one battery, and one regiment of cavalry, the 1st Hussars of the King's German Legion. His orders were to keep open the communication with Ciudad Rodrigo till the last possible moment, to cover Almeida as long as was prudent, and to keep the Commander-in-Chief advised of every movement of the enemy. It was clear that he might be thrust back at any moment: the 6th Corps, since Loison had joined it, was 30,000 strong: the Light Division had only 2,500 infantry with the 500 German light horse. On March 28th Wellington sent up to reinforce Craufurd two battalions of Caçadores, the 1st and 2nd. The latter of these units was afterwards changed for the 3rd[1], which, trained by Elder, the best of all the colonels lent to the Portuguese army, was reckoned the most efficient corps that could be selected from Beresford's command. But the two Caçador battalions only added 1,000 bayonets to the Light Division, and even after their arrival Craufurd's force was less than 4,000 strong.

Robert Craufurd, though only a brigadier, and junior of his rank, had been chosen by Wellington to take charge of his outpost line because he was one of the very few officers then in the Peninsula in whose ability his Commander-in-Chief had perfect confidence. Nothing is more striking than to compare the tone and character of the letters which Wellington wrote to him with those which he dispatched to most of his other

---

[1] On Craufurd's complaint that the 2nd Caçadores were badly commanded and too full of boys. He repeatedly asked for, and ultimately obtained, the 3rd battalion in place of the 2nd, because of his confidence in Elder.

general officers. Only with Craufurd, Hill, and Beresford, did he ever condescend to enter into explanations and state reasons. The rest receive orders without comment, which they are directed to carry out, and are given no opportunity to discuss[1]. The difference was noted and resented by the others: when on March 8th Craufurd was formally given charge of the whole outpost line of the army, and his seniors Picton and Cole were told to conform their movements to his, without waiting for orders from head quarters, some friction was engendered[2]. Picton and Craufurd, in especial, were for the rest of the campaign in a state of latent hostility, which more than once led to high words when they met—a fact which was not without its dangers to the welfare of the army[3].

The celebrated commander of the Light Division was at this time well known for his ability, but reckoned rather an unlucky soldier. He had entered the army so far back as 1779, and had seen service in every quarter of the globe, yet in 1809 was only a colonel. This was the more astounding since he was one of the few scientific soldiers in the British army when the Revolutionary War broke out. He had spent some time at Berlin in 1782, studying the tactics of the army of Frederick

---

[1] Note especially Wellington's explanatory dispatch to Craufurd of March 8, where he even goes so far as to give his subordinate a free hand as to the choice of his line : ' You must be a better judge of the details of this question than I can be, and I wish you to consider them, in order to be able to carry the plan into execution when I shall send it to you.' In another letter Wellington writes : ' Nothing can be of greater advantage to me than to have the benefit of your opinion on *any* subject.'

[2] ' I intend that the divisions of Generals Cole and Picton should support you on the Coa, without waiting for orders from me, if it should be necessary, and they shall be directed accordingly.' 8th March, from Vizeu.

[3] It should not be forgotten that Picton, no less than Craufurd, was at this time living down an old disaster. But Picton's misfortune had not been military. It was the celebrated case of *Rex* v. *Picton*. He had been tried for permitting the use of torture to extract evidence against criminals while governor of the newly conquered island of Trinidad, and convicted, though Spanish law (which was still in force in Trinidad) apparently permitted of the practice. After this Picton was a marked man. The story of Luisa Calderon, the quadroon girl who had been tortured by ' picketing,' had been appearing intermittently in the columns of every Whig paper for more than three years.

the Great, and had translated into English the official Prussian treatise on the Art of War. His knowledge of German, a rare accomplishment in the British army at the end of the eighteenth century, caused him to be given the post of military attaché at Coburg's head quarters in 1794, and he followed the Austrian army through all the disasters of that and the two following years. Again in 1799 he went out to take the same post at the head quarters of the army of Switzerland, but quitted it to serve on the staff of the Duke of York, during the miserable Dutch expedition of that same year. He seemed destined to witness nothing but disasters, and though he was known to have done his duty with admirable zeal and energy in every post that he occupied, promotion lingered. Probably his caustic tongue and fiery temper were his hindrances, but it seems astonishing that he took twenty-six years to attain the rank of colonel, though he was not destitute of political influence, having friends and relatives in Parliament, and even in the Ministry [1]. In 1801 he was a disappointed man, thought of retiring from the army, and, having accepted a nomination borough, sat in the Commons for five years. In 1805 he was at last made a colonel, and in the following year went on active service with the expedition which, sent originally to the Cape, was distracted in 1807 to the unhappy Buenos Ayres campaign. This was the zenith of his misfortunes; it was he who, placed in charge of a light brigade by the incapable Whitelocke, was thrust forward into the midst of the tangled streets of Buenos Ayres, surrounded in the convent of San Domingo, and forced to capitulate for lack of support. At the ensuing court-martial he was acquitted of all blame, but the fact that he had surrendered a British brigade rankled in his mind for the rest of his life. The unshaken confidence in his abilities felt by the Home authorities was marked by the fact that he was sent out in October 1808 with Baird's corps, which landed at Corunna, and again in June 1809 to Lisbon, each time in command of a brigade. But his bad luck seemed still to attend him: he missed the victory of Corunna because Moore

[1] His elder brother, Sir Charles Craufurd, was Deputy-Adjutant-General, and M.P. for Retford. Windham, the Secretary for War, was his devoted friend.

had detached his brigade on the inexplicable march to Vigo.
He failed to be present at Talavera, despite of the famous forced
march which he made towards the sound of the cannon.

In 1810 Craufurd was burning to vindicate his reputation,
and to show that the confidence which Wellington placed in
him was not undeserved. He still regarded himself as a man
who had been unjustly dealt with, and had never been given
his chance. He could not forget that he was four years older
than Beresford, five years older than Wellington, eight years
older than Hill, yet was but a junior brigadier-general in
charge of a division [1]. He was full of a consuming energy, on
the look-out for slights and quarrels, a very strict disciplinarian,
restless himself and leaving his troops no rest. He was not
liked by all his officers : in the Light Division he had many
admirers [2] and many bitter critics. Nor was he at first popular
with the rank and file, though they soon began to recognize the
keen intelligence that guided his actions, and to see that he was
a just if a hard master [3]. In the matter of feeding his troops,
the most difficult task imposed on a general of the Peninsular
army, he had an unparalleled reputation for accomplishing the
impossible—even if the most drastic methods had to be
employed. The famous old story about Wellington and the commissary had Craufurd (and not, as it is sometimes told, Picton) as

---

[1] Though senior in the date of his first commission to nearly all the
officers of the Peninsular army, Craufurd was six years junior to Picton,
and one year junior to Hope. Graham, much his senior in age, had only
entered the army in 1793.

[2] Such as Shaw-Kennedy, William Campbell, Kincaid, and Lord Seaton.

[3] For Craufurd's life and personality see his biography by his grandson
the Rev. Alex. Craufurd, London, 1890. The most vivid picture of him
is in Rifleman Harris's chronicle of the Corunna retreat, a wonderful piece
of narrative by a writer from the ranks, who admired his general despite
of all his severity, and acknowledges that his methods were necessary.
Though Napier as a historian is on the whole fairly just to his old commander, whose achievements were bound up indissolubly with the glories
of the Light Division, as a man he disliked Craufurd : in one of his
books which I possess (Delagrave's *Campagne de Portugal*) he has written
in the margin several bitter personal remarks about him, very unlike the
language employed in his history. The unpublished Journal of Colonel
McLeod of the 43rd is (as Mr. Alex. Craufurd informs me) written in the
same spirit. So is Charles Napier's *Diary*.

its hero.   As a sample of his high-handed ways, it may be mentioned that he once seized and impounded some church-plate till the villages to which it belonged found him some corn for his starving division.   Craufurd, on one of his happy days, and they were many, was the most brilliant subordinate that Wellington ever owned.   His mistakes—and he committed more than one—were the faults of an ardent and ambitious spirit taking an immoderate risk in the hour of excitement.

From March to July 1810 Craufurd, in charge of the whole outpost system of Wellington's army, accomplished the extraordinary feat of guarding a front of forty miles against an active enemy of sixfold force, without suffering his line to be pierced, or allowing the French to gain any information whatever of the dispositions of the host in his rear.   He was in constant and daily touch with Ney's corps, yet was never surprised, and never thrust back save by absolutely overwhelming strength; he never lost a detachment, never failed to detect every move of the enemy, and never sent his commander false intelligence. This was the result of system and science, not merely of vigilance and activity.   The journal of his aide de camp Shaw-Kennedy, giving the daily work of the Light Division during the critical months of 1810, might serve as an illustrative manual of outpost duty, and was ·indeed printed for that purpose in 1851[1].

Craufurd's one cavalry regiment, the German Hussars, had to cover a front of nearly forty miles, and performed the duty admirably;   it had been chosen for the service because it was considered by Wellington superior in scouting power to any of his British light cavalry corps.   'General Craufurd worked out the most difficult part of the outpost duty with them.   He had the great advantage of speaking German fluently, and he arranged for the outpost duties of the different parts of the long line that he had to guard by his personal communications with the captains of that admirable corps, men who were themselves masters of the subject.   They each knew his plan for the space that they covered, though not his general plan, and each worked out his part most admirably.   The General communicated with them direct.   He had the great advantage

[1] As an Appendix to Lord F. Fitz-Clarence's *Manual of Outpost Duties*.

of possessing, with his great abilities and energy, uncommon
bodily strength, so that he could remain on horseback almost
any length of time. . . . When his operations began, the point to
be observed was the line of the Agueda, extending for some
forty miles.   The country, although very irregular in its
surface, was quite open and unenclosed, and fit almost everywhere for the action of all three arms.   When he took up
the line he kept his infantry back entirely, with the exception
of four companies of the Rifles above the bridge of Barba del
Puerco, upon the *calculation* of the time that would be required
to retire the infantry behind the Coa, after he received information from the cavalry of the enemy's advance.   If we are
properly to understand Craufurd's operations, the *calculation*
must never be lost sight of, for it was on calculations that he
acted all along.   The hazarding of the four companies at Barba
del Puerco forms a separate consideration : it rested on the
belief that the pass there was so difficult, that four companies
could defend it against any numbers, and that, if they were
turned higher up the river, the Hussars would give the Rifles
warning in ample time for a safe retreat. . . . Special reports were
made of the state of the fords of the Agueda *every* morning,
and the rapidity of its rises was particularly marked.   An
officer had special charge of all deserters from the enemy, to
examine them and bring together their information[1].   Beacons
were prepared on conspicuous heights, so as to communicate
information as to the enemy's offensive movements.   To ensure
against mistakes in the night, pointers were kept at the stations
of communication, directed to the beacons. . . . As Napier has
remarked in his History, *seven minutes* sufficed for the division
to get under arms in the middle of the night, and a quarter of
an hour, night or day, to bring it in order of battle to its alarm-
posts, with the baggage loaded and assembled at a convenient
distance to the rear.   And this not upon a concerted signal, nor
as a trial, but at all times and certain [2].'

[1] One of the most curious points in Shaw-Kennedy's *Diary* [p. 218] is
that from the reports of deserters Craufurd succeeded in reconstructing
the exact composition of Ney's corps, in brigades and battalions, with a
final error of only one battalion and 2,000 men too few.

[2] Shaw-Kennedy, *Diary*, pp. 142 and 147.

To complete the picture it remains to be added that there were some fifteen fords between Ciudad Rodrigo and the mouth of the Agueda, which were practicable in dry weather for all arms, and that several of them could be used even after a day or two of rain.   The French were along the whole river; they had 3,000 horse available in March and April, 5,000 in May and June.   Their infantry at some points were only three or four miles back from the river: yet Craufurd's line was never broken, nor was even a picket of ten men cut off or surrounded. The least movement of the enemy was reported along the whole front in an incredibly short time, the whole web of communication quivered at the slightest touch, and the division was immediately ready to fight or to draw back, according as the strength of the French dictated boldness or caution.

During February Wellington had rightly concluded that Craufurd had nothing to fear; Ney's early demonstration against Ciudad Rodrigo had no more serious significance than Mortier's similar appearance in front of Badajoz.   But when March arrived, and the 8th Corps appeared in the plains of Leon and commenced the siege of Astorga, while Ney began to move up his cavalry to the line of the Yeltes, and Loison's division, coming from Astorga, established itself on the lower Agueda, it seemed likely that serious work would soon begin.   The first test of the efficiency of Craufurd's outpost system was made on the night of March 19–20, when Ferey, commanding the brigade of Loison's division which lay at San Felices, assembled his six voltigeur companies before dawn, and made a dash at the pass of Barba del Puerco.   He had the good luck to bayonet the sentries at the bridge before they could fire, and was half way up the rough ascent from the bridge to the village, when Beckwith's detachment of the 95th Rifles, roused and armed in ten minutes, were upon him.   They drove him down the defile, and chased him back across the river with the loss of two officers and forty-five men killed and wounded.   Beckwith's riflemen lost one officer and three men killed, and ten men wounded in the three companies engaged.   After this alarm Craufurd was in anxious expectation of a general advance of the 6th Corps, and made every preparation to receive them.   But Ferey's reconnaissance had no sequel, and a whole month passed by without any serious move on the part of the enemy. The Agueda was in flood for the greater part of April, owing to incessant rains, which made the outpost work simple, as the number of points to be observed went down from fifteen to three or four. It was not till the twenty-sixth that Maucune's and Ferey's brigades moved up close to Ciudad Rodrigo, drove in the Spanish outposts, and formed the blockade of the place on the east side of the Agueda. Even then its bridge remained unmolested, and Craufurd could communicate quite freely with the garrison, and did so till June 2nd. Masséna at a later date blamed Ney for having established this partial and useless blockade before he was ready to commence the siege in earnest. The two French brigades consumed, during the month of May, the whole of the local resources of the district around Rodrigo, so that, when the rest of the army came up, all supplies had to be brought up from a great distance. It may also be remarked that to advance a corps of no more than 7,000 men within striking distance of the British army would have been very hazardous, if Wellington had been entertaining any designs of taking the offensive—and Ney at this time could not have been sure that such a contingency was unlikely. The only advantage which the Marshal got from keeping his detachment so close to the fortress was that, in their month of waiting, the brigades were able to prepare a great store of gabions and fascines, and the engineers to make a thorough survey of the environs.

Ciudad Rodrigo stands on a single circular knoll of no great ·height, whose summit it exactly covers. It is a small place of some 8,000 souls, packed tight in narrow streets within a stout mediaeval wall thickly set with towers. A fourteenth-century castle, on which the houses press in too close for strength, fills its south-eastern corner: there is no other inner place of refuge. The Agueda, divided into several channels, runs under the southern side of the place; it is crossed by a bridge completely commanded by the fire of the walls. On the water-front the knoll is at its highest, on the opposite face it is much less steep, and only very slightly exceeds the level of the surrounding ground. Round the circuit of the mediaeval wall a low modern enceinte had been constructed, and served as an outer protection (*fausse-braye*); it was only twelve feet high, so did not shield more than a third of the inner wall, which could be battered over its summit. Its outline was zigzagged in the form of redans, and it was furnished with a dry ditch. Its glacis, owing to the rising of the knoll, gave it little protection, so that both the older and the modern wall could be searched, for the greater part of their height, by the artillery of a besieger. Outside the eastern gate of Rodrigo lies the straggling suburb of San Francisco, on very low ground. It was so large and so close to the walls that the governor Herrasti considered it absolutely necessary to take it inside the circuit of his defences. It had accordingly been surrounded by a strong earthwork, and the three great monasteries which it contains—San Francisco, San Domingo, and Santa Clara—had been strengthened and loopholed. The small suburb of La Marina, just across the bridge, was retrenched and manned, as was also the convent of Santa Cruz, which stands isolated 200 yards outside the north-west angle of the town. Other outlying buildings had been levelled to the ground, lest they should afford cover to the enemy.

These preparations were very wise and helpful, but they did not do away with the main weakness of Ciudad Rodrigo considered as a modern fortress. Like many other mediaeval strongholds it is commanded by outlying heights, which could be disregarded as an element of danger in the fourteenth or the sixteenth century, because of their distance, but became all-important with the improvement of artillery. In this case two knolls, considerably higher than that on which the place stands, lie outside its northern walls. The smaller, named the Little Teson, lies only 200 yards from the northern angle of the town ; it is some fifty feet higher than the base of the ramparts. Immediately behind it rises the Great Teson, which dominates the whole country-side, its broad flat top, three-quarters of a mile in diameter, being a hundred feet above the level of the plain. It was hopeless to think of holding the little Teson as an outwork, since the greater one looks down into it and searches it from end to end. The Great Teson, on the other hand, is so large—its circuit is about the same as the city itself—that it would be impossible to think of defending it, as when entrenched it would require a garrison of at least 3,000 men, and Herrasti had but 5,500 troops under his command. Its slopes, moreover, are gentle, and do not lend themselves to fortification. The southern edge of the plateau of the Great Teson being only 500 yards from the town wall, it was obvious that here was the place from which Rodrigo could best be assailed. Batteries on its skyline could breach both the inner and outer walls, and could command every square foot both of the town and of the fortified suburbs. Accordingly the brigades which lay before the place in May had encamped on and behind the Teson, and stored the gabions, fascines, and sandbags which they were making in a park, near the convent of La Caridad and the village of Pedro de Toro, on its further side.

Herrasti, as we have said, had a garrison of 5,500 men, composed of one line battalion, two militia battalions, three battalions of new levies from the town and its vicinity, called ' Voluntarios de Ciudad Rodrigo,' and one battalion of ' Urban Guards [1].' None of these troops, save the line battalion of Majorca (which had formed part of the old Army of Estremadura) had ever been under fire—a fact which makes their fine defence all the more creditable. There were only 11 officers and 37 men of the artillery of the line in the place : these had to train 350 men assigned to them from the infantry ; but fortunately the long delay in the opening of the siege had allowed the instruction to be thoroughly carried out. Of engineers there were only 4 officers and 60 sappers—of cavalry none—but the partisan chief Julian Sanchez with some 200 of his Lancers chanced to be in the place on the day when it was completely invested, and was forced to cut his way out when the bombardment began. Perhaps the main strength of Ciudad Rodrigo, as of Gerona, lay in the personality of its governor. General Andrès Herrasti, a veteran of nearly seventy years, was determined to do his duty, and showed as much ingenuity and readiness as obstinacy in his defence.

Though the French had appeared before the walls of Ciudad

---

[1] Herrasti's report gives 1st of Majorca 706 officers and men, Avila and Segovia militia 857 and 317 respectively, three battalions of volunteers of Ciudad Rodrigo 2,242, Urban guard 750, artillery 375, sappers 60 ; total, with some details added, 5,510, not including Sanchez's Partida. See Belmas, iii. 314.

SIEGE OF CIUDAD RODRIGO

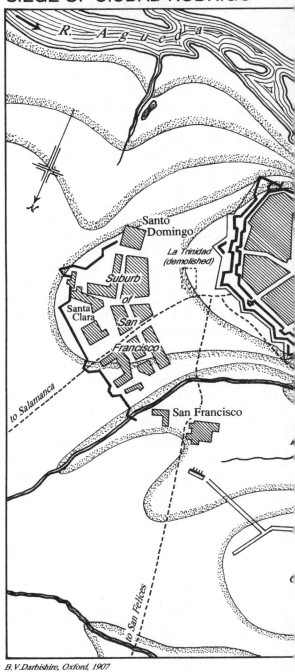

B.V.Darbishire, Oxford, 1907

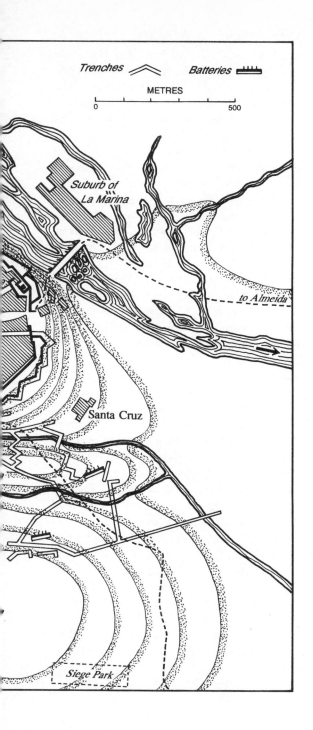

Rodrigo on April 26th, it was not till May 30th that Ney came up in person, with four brigades of infantry and Montbrun's division of reserve cavalry, to complete the investment. The main cause of the delay was, as usual, the lack of supplies. Ney had to levy and forward from Salamanca two months' rations for an army of 30,000 men, and could only do so after long and harassing preparation. He nearly came to actual blows with King Joseph over the matter, for he sent a cavalry brigade to raise requisitions in the province of Avila, which was outside his command, and General Hugo, the King's governor, put his troops under arms and refused to allow the dragoons to enter his district. An imperial rescript, however, soon arrived, which placed Avila at the disposition of the 6th Corps, and the royal authorities had to yield[1].

All Ney's troops were now concentrated for the siege, his outlying detachments in every direction having been relieved by Junot, who, at Masséna's orders, brought down the 8th Corps from the Douro, placed a brigade to watch the Pass of Baños, left garrisons in Zamora and Toro, and advanced with the remainder of his troops to the line of the Agueda. Clausel's division and St. Croix's division of dragoons took post at San Felices, in immediate touch with Craufurd's division. Solignac's division lay a march and a half to the rear at Ledesma. San Felices is only 20, Ledesma is 40 miles from Ciudad Rodrigo, so that the 8th Corps, deducting the outlying brigades, could have joined Ney in two days. These distances were the governing factor in Wellington's policy during the next month. Ney had 26,000 men of the 6th Corps and Montbrun's 4,000 dragoons in front of Rodrigo; Junot could join him with 8,000 infantry and 1,800 cavalry in a day; a second day would bring up Solignac with 7,000 men more. Unless the 6th Corps could be surprised in its camps, and forced to fight before it received its reinforcements, there would be 47,000 French to face. Of their numbers Wellington was roughly aware; the figures sent in to him by Craufurd were accurate to within a few thousands[2], and estimated the enemy at 40,000 men. The Commander-in-Chief's own calculation was even nearer the truth; early in May he reckoned

[1] See Sprünglin's *Journal*, p. 417.   [2] May 2, to Craufurd.

Ney, with Loison's division included, at 30,000 men, Junot and Kellermann at 30,000[1]. Early in June he made out that the two corps in his front, without Kellermann, amounted to 50,000 men,[2] which was only 3,000 over the true total. He himself had at this moment only 18,000 British troops under his hand, and within striking distance. He had on April 27th, brought up his head quarters and the 1st Division to Celorico, and moved forward Picton and the 3rd Division to Pinhel, while Cole with the 4th remained at Guarda, and the Light Division was, as usual, facing the Agueda. The cavalry had also come up from the Mondego valley, and lay behind Almeida. Moreover, the five Portuguese brigades of Harvey, Collins, Pack, Coleman, and Alex. Campbell were ordered up to the front[3], and joined the army in the first days of May. Wellington thereupon incorporated Harvey's brigade with the 3rd Division and Collins's with the 4th, a system which he afterwards carried out with nearly all the Portuguese units. The whole of this mass of troops came to some 15,000 men[4].

[1] On June 1 Craufurd calculated the troops in front of Ciudad Rodrigo, by counting regiments and battalions, at over 25,000 men. There were really 30,000, and the under-estimate came from allowing only 550 men to a battalion, while they really averaged 650. About the same time Craufurd estimated the parts of Junot's corps in the neighbourhood to be 13,000 men: they were really nearly 17,000. The cause of error was the same. See Shaw-Kennedy's *Diary*, pages 190–5. The estimates are corrected, on fuller information, early in July, see ibid., p. 220.

[2] To Charles Stuart, June 8, and to Hill, June 9.

[3] This movement, unchronicled elsewhere, appears in D'Urban's diary, April 26. 'The Portuguese ordered to the front, consisting of two brigades of artillery, 4th and 6th Caçadores, 1st and 16th (Pack), 7th and 19th (Coleman), 6th and 18th (Alex. Campbell), 11th and 23rd (Collins), 9th and 21st (Harvey) of the Line. They all go into march on the 28th, and will arrive by successive brigades at Celorico in four days.'

[4] At this moment the total force of the allied army was :—

1st Division (all British) .	6,000 bayonets.				
3rd ,, British	.	2,500 with Harvey's Portuguese .	1,800
4th ,, ,,	.	4,000 with Collins's ,,	. 2,500
Light ,, ,,	.	2,500 with 2 Caçador Batts.	. 1,000
Pack's, Campbell's, and Coleman's Portuguese brigades			. 8,000
Cavalry (British) .	. 2,100 .	Portuguese	. 700
Artillery ,, .	. 1,000 .	Portuguese	. 600
	18,100		14,600

These, with the British, making a total of 32,000 men, were
all that Wellington could count upon, for he could not dare
to move Hill's 12,000 men from the south, where they were
observing Reynier, nor to displace the small reserve, which lay
at Abrantes and Thomar to guard against a possible French
move along the Tagus by Castello Branco. Lisbon could not
be left unprotected on this side, so long as Reynier lay between
the Tagus and the Guadiana.

By bringing up every man Wellington could have attacked
Ney's 30,000 in front of Rodrigo with 33,000, of whom nearly
half would have consisted of the newly organised Portuguese
brigades, of which hardly a battalion had been under fire.
He would have had under 3,000 cavalry to face 5,000, and
a marked inferiority in artillery also. No practical assistance
could have been got by inviting the co-operation of Martin
Carrera's depleted Spanish division of 3,000 men, which lay
on the hills about the sources of the Agueda, watching Ney's
flank. If the first stroke should fail, and Ney were not surprised,
Wellington would have Junot's 17,000 men to count with
within forty-eight hours. Ciudad Rodrigo lies on a plain, a full
day's march from the hills, and by advancing to relieve it the
British army must commit itself to an action in the open.
It is no wonder then that Wellington refused to attempt the
movement ; weak in cavalry and with 15,000 troops of uncertain
value in his ranks, he would have been mad to embark upon
such an operation. It was most improbable that Ney could
have been surprised, and forced to fight without Junot's aid,
when he had 5,000 horsemen at hand, to discover and report
the first movement of the Anglo-Portuguese. Napoleon had
been right when he told Masséna that it was practically
impossible that Wellington would offer battle in the plains.
Herrasti had been sent assurances that the British army would
do anything that was feasible for his relief, but he was warned
in a supplementary letter of June 6th that it might be impossible to aid him. 'You will believe,' wrote Wellington, 'that
if I should not be able to attempt your relief, it will be owing
to the superior strength of the enemy, and to the necessity for my
attending to other important objects [1].' Notwithstanding this

---

[1] *Dispatches,* vi. p. 172.

caution it would appear that the Spanish governor still hoped for prompt assistance. It seemed to him, as it did to all Spanish and some English officers at the time [1], that Wellington would not be able to endure the spectacle of Ciudad Rodrigo being taken while his outposts were lying only six miles in front of it. Those who held such views little knew the inflexible character of the man with whom they had to deal, or his contempt for considerations of pride or sentiment. To take a great risk, when victory would mean only the raising of the siege of Rodrigo till Junot and Kellermann should have joined Ney, while defeat might mean the loss of Portugal, was not in consonance with Wellington's character. The possible gain and loss were too unequal, and he very rightly, and not without much regret, remained in observation at Celorico [2]. He sums up the matter thus :—' I must leave the mountains and cross the plains, as well as two rivers, to raise the siege. To do this I have about 33,000 men (including Carrera's Spaniards), of which 3,000 are cavalry [3]. Included are 15,000 Spaniards and Portuguese, which troops (to say the best of them) are of doubtful quality. Is it right, under these circumstances, to risk a general action to raise the siege of Ciudad Rodrigo ? I should think not [4].' And again, ' My object is to be able to relieve the place, if it should be advisable to attempt it, in consequence of any alteration in the enemy's force. This does not appear to be a very probable event at present, and ought not to be provided for according to the common rules of prudence, at any considerable risk [5].' Expressions of regret are added, ' I do not give the matter

[1] D'Urban, for example, wrote in his journal on June 18 that he took the daring step of suggesting a surprise attack on Ney to the General. No notice was taken of his suggestion.

[2] Picton summed up the situation in a letter to a friend [see Robinson's Life of Picton, i. 273] very clearly : ' If we attempt to relieve the place the French will drive us out of Portugal : while if they get possession of it, they will lose time, which is more important to them than Ciudad Rodrigo. But they have got to find this out.'

[3] A slight under-estimate, as it would seem, for with La Carrera's force the whole would have been 36,000 sabres and bayonets. Of the 3,000 cavalry 700 were Portuguese and 300 Spaniards.

[4] Wellington to Henry Wellesley, June 20

[5] Wellington to Craufurd, June 24.

up; if they hold out like men they are worth saving, and under
certain circumstances it might be possible to "incur the risk."'
But the 'certain circumstances' never came about; they seem
to have been the possibility either that (1) Ney or Junot might
make detachments, or move their corps into a less concentrated
position than they at present occupied, or (2) that they might
form a covering army, and advance to drive him off from his
present quarters, which were too close to Ciudad Rodrigo for
their comfort. This last contingency almost happened, as we
shall see; probably if the enemy had come out to attack him
Wellington would have accepted battle, in one of the defensive
positions that he knew so well how to select.

Ney, as has been already mentioned, arrived before the
fortress with some 20,000 men on May 30th. On June 1st he
threw a bridge across the Agueda, a mile and a half above
Rodrigo, but sent no troops across it. Two days later Masséna
came up from the rear, approved of the plan that had been
formed for breaching the city from the side of the two Tesons,
and, having reviewed the 6th Corps, took his way back to
Salamanca. At this moment he gave orders to Reynier and
the 2nd Corps to leave Truxillo and the valley of the Guadiana,
and to cross the Tagus to Coria and Plasencia, from whence they
could threaten Castello Branco and Abrantes. This was in accordance with the orders of the Emperor, who had bidden him call
up Reynier from the Guadiana, to cover his flank. Such a movement had been foreseen by Wellington, who as early as June 9th
had directed Hill to leave Portalegre with his 12,000 men, and
to cross the Tagus at Villa Velha the moment that Reynier
should have passed it at Almaraz[1]. Some days later the
Galician general Mahy sent to the British head quarters four
duplicates of Napoleon's dispatches to Masséna and King
Joseph, which had been intercepted by guerrillas on the way to
Salamanca[2]. They corroborated all Wellington's suspicions,

---

[1] Wellington to Hill, July 9.

[2] These were Napoleon's dispatches nos. 16,505, 16,519–20, and 16,504,
as is shown by the excellent analysis of them given by D'Urban in his
diary. He read them over with Beresford on July 1. No. 16,519 was
very valuable, as giving the exact strength of the 2nd, 6th, and 8th Corps
—the first absolutely certain analysis of them that Wellington obtained.

and enabled him to provide against the danger on this side
even before it had begun to arise.   Hill's route by Villa Velha
being appreciably shorter than that of Reynier, he was in
position beyond the Tagus before the 2nd Corps had reached
Coria.   Their cavalry met and skirmished at Ladoeiro on the
Zarza–Castello Branco road on July 22nd.   Thus the relative
position of the two hostile forces in the south was exactly
preserved : Wellington knew that he could call in Hill to join
his main army as quickly as Masséna could draw Reynier to
himself through the Pass of Perales—the only route possible for
him.   He felt all the more secure because he had now some
British troops at Abrantes ready to support Hill.   Three newly
arrived battalions [1], which landed at Lisbon early in April, had
been passed up the Tagus to Thomar and the line of the Zezere,
where, uniting with two Portuguese brigades, they formed
Leith's ' 5th Division,' a fresh factor in the situation.   This
detachment, with two batteries added, could assist Hill with
7,000 men, if Reynier should push forward in the direction of
Castello Branco.

Whether at this moment Masséna was proposing to order a
serious attack on this side, or whether he was from the first
intending to bring up the 2nd Corps to join the main army,
is not certain.   Napoleon in some of his dispatches seems to
recommend the rather hazardous 'attack on double external
lines'—a result of his general under-estimate of Wellington's
resisting power.   On May 29th he told his lieutenant that with
50,000 men of the 6th and 8th Corps he could capture both
Ciudad Rodrigo and Almeida, and then march ' methodically '
into Portugal, while Reynier at Alcantara could cover the communication with Madrid and menace Upper Beira ; ' le prince
le maintiendra dans cette position sans le laisser entamer.'
Masséna, however, did not think his main army strong enough,
and, being left a free hand by his master, ultimately called in
Reynier to join him, and so freed Wellington from the harassing
doubt as to whether he might not have to defend himself on the
Zezere and on the Mondego at the same moment.

[1] These were the 3/1st, 1/9th, 2/38th, which arrived at Lisbon April 1–8.
Leith's division was formally constituted only on July 15, but really
existed since June.

Long before the orders reached the 2nd Corps to move up from Truxillo to Coria and Zarza, the siege of Rodrigo had begun in earnest. On June 1st, as we have already seen, Ney had cast a bridge across the Agueda above the town ; four days later a second was constructed at the ford of Lora, below the place. The moment that it was completed, Marchand's division, half Mermet's, and the light cavalry brigade of Lamotte crossed the river and established camps on its western bank. The horsemen pushed back Craufurd's pickets to Marialva and Manzanilla, and completely cut his communication with Rodrigo, which had hitherto been intermittently open. The troops which had passed the river threw up redoubts to cover the bridge heads, and slightly entrenched their camps. On June 8th Ney received the first convoy of his siege train, which continued to come in by detachments during the next week, till he had fifty heavy guns in hand, with 700 rounds for each, and 2,000 gunners and sappers of the ' Grand Park [1].'

On the 15th the French opened their first parallel on the Great Teson, on a front of 1,500 yards ; it was only 500 yards from the glacis of the town. Herrasti kept up a furious fire upon it, and vexed the workmen by two sorties, which were not pressed home and did no harm. On the 19th six batteries on the Teson were commenced ; the work was easy owing to the great store of gabions and sandbags already in store, which the brigades of Maucune and Ferey had prepared in May. While the emplacements for the guns were being got ready, the sappers pushed forward zig-zags from the right end of the first parallel down the slopes on the flank of the Little Teson. One approach was directed toward the isolated convent of Santa Cruz, the other toward the extreme northern angle of the town. The Spaniards, though firing furiously day and night, could not prevent either the construction of the batteries or the advance of the approaches ; wherefore Julian Sanchez, seeing that his cavalry could not live under the oncoming bombardment, got leave from the governor to quit the town. On the night of the 21st–22nd he crossed the bridge, broke through the lines of Marchand's division, and escaped by the Fuente Guinaldo road with his 200 Lancers. He came into Craufurd's camp, and gave

[1] See the Emperor's dispatches to Berthier of May 27 and May 29.

a full report of the state of the garrison and the progress of the enemy's works.

It was impossible for the French to open their second parallel so long as the convent of Santa Cruz was held, for the fire of this outwork would have enfiladed its whole length. On the night of the 23rd–24th, therefore, Ney tried to storm the convent with a picked body of Grenadiers; they blew in its door with a petard, and set fire to its lower story, but were finally driven off. The convent was partially destroyed, but the garrison gallantly clung to its ruins, and covered themselves in the débris. The French lost fifteen killed and fifty wounded that night. On June 25th the batteries opened, without waiting for the reduction of Santa Cruz, with forty-six guns placed in six batteries along the crest of the Teson. The counter-fire of the besieged was very effective ; two expense magazines containing 9,000 lb. of powder were blown up in the trenches, many guns dismounted, and one battery silenced. The loss of the besiegers was heavy[1]. The Spaniards suffered less, but fires broke out in several quarters of the town from the shells thrown by the French mortars, and many houses were destroyed. The ruins of the convent of Santa Cruz, moreover, were so thoroughly battered to pieces that the garrison retired, when an assault was made upon it by 300 Grenadiers after nightfall. This enabled the French to push forward their works much nearer to the town.

Four days of furious artillery engagement followed, in which the besiegers, though suffering heavily, succeeded not only in setting more than half the town on fire, but, what was more serious, in making a breach in the fausse-braye, at the projecting angle of the north side of the city, on which four of the batteries had been trained, and in injuring the inner mediaeval wall at the back of it. Believing, wrongly as it seems, that the breach was practicable, Ney sent an officer to summon the town. Herrasti replied that he was still in a position to defend himself,

---

[1] Masséna came up from Salamanca this day to inspect the bombardment, and made (as was his wont) a rather mendacious report thereon to the Emperor, declaring that the French loss had been 12 killed and 41 wounded, whereas it had exceeded 100 [see Belmas, iii. p. 233], and that the defence of the place was seriously impaired—which it was not as yet.

and 'that after forty-nine years of service he knew the laws of
war and his military duty.' He made, however, the unusual
request that he might be allowed to send a letter to Wellington, and that a suspension of arms should be granted till the
return of his messenger. The Marshal, as was natural, sent
a refusal, and ordered the bombardment to recommence
(June 28th).

Up to this moment the French engineers had been under
the impression that Ciudad Rodrigo would probably surrender
when it had been breached, without standing an assault. Now
that they recognized that the governor intended to fight to
the last, and noted that he had spent the night following the
summons in clearing the ditch and repairing the damaged
fausse-braye with sandbags, they resolved that the breaching
batteries must be brought closer in, and the approaches pushed
up to the foot of the walls. Accordingly a second parallel was
opened along the front of the Little Teson, two hundred and
fifty yards in advance of the first, on the night of July 1st.
On the same night a column of 600 men stormed the convent
of San Francisco in the suburb, a post which would have
enfiladed the southern end of the new parallel in the most
dangerous fashion. Having obtained this lodgement in the
suburb the French set to work to conquer the whole of it,
and after some stiff street-fighting stormed Santa Clara, its
central stronghold. Herrasti thereupon evacuated the rest of
the scattered houses, and withdrew all his troops inside the
town (July 3rd).

The new battery on the Little Teson was costly to build and
maintain—on one night the French lost sixty-one men killed
and wounded in it [1]. But it was very effective; the original
breach was much enlarged, and the old wall behind it was
reduced to ruins. Meanwhile a mortar battery, placed in the
conquered suburb, played upon the parts of the town which
had hitherto escaped bombardment, and reduced many streets
to ashes. The position of the garrison was unsatisfactory, and
Herrasti sent out several emissaries to beg Wellington to help
him, ere it was too late. Most of these adventurers were
captured by the French, but at least two reached the British

---

[1] Belmas, iii. 245, July 2.

commander [1], who had recently come up to the front to observe for himself the state of the enemy's forces. He found them too strong to be meddled with, and sent back a letter stating that he was ready to move if he saw any chance of success, but that at present none such was visible. He then retired, after leaving Craufurd two squadrons of the 16th Light Dragoons to strengthen his thin outpost line. Herrasti, though much dispirited by Wellington's reply, continued to make a vigorous defence, but the town was now mostly in ruins, and the breach gaped wide.

On July 4th Masséna, who had again come up to visit the siege, obtained intelligence that Wellington had been with the Light Division at Gallegos, and determined to push back the British outposts, in order to discover whether the front line of his enemy had been strengthened by any troops from Portugal. It seemed to him likely enough that the British general might have massed his army for a bold stroke at the besiegers, now that the strength of Ciudad Rodrigo was running low. Accordingly St. Croix's division of dragoons, supported by a brigade of Junot's infantry, crossed the Azava brook and drove in Craufurd's cavalry pickets. They retired, skirmishing vigorously all the way, to Gallegos, where the five infantry battalions of the Light Division had concentrated. Craufurd, having strict orders from his chief that he was not to fight, fell back on Fort Concepcion, the work on the Spanish frontier half way to Almeida. Thereupon the French retired, having obtained the information that they wanted, viz. that Craufurd had not been reinforced by any considerable body of troops from the rear. The Light Division had manœuvred with its customary intelligence and alertness all day; its flanks were being continually turned by horsemen in overpowering numbers, but it beat them off with ease, and lost only five men wounded while falling back across ten miles of absolutely open country. The French lost five officers and over twenty men [2], mostly in combats with the German Hussars, who surpassed themselves on

---

[1] See Shaw-Kennedy's *Diary,* pp. 208–9 and 211.

[2] Belmas, iii. 250. For the conduct of the Hussars see Beamish's *German Legion,* i. pp. 274–6. Martinien's lists show that the 1st French dragoons lost one, the 2nd three, and the 4th one officer on this day.

this day, and repeatedly charged the heads of the hostile columns on favourable occasions. For the future Craufurd kept behind the Dos Casas, while the French took up his old line on the Azava. This move made any attempt to help Ciudad Rodrigo a harder business than before, since the British outposts were now fifteen instead of only six miles from the town. An attempt to storm by surprise the French camps on the near side of the place was for the future impossible.

Warned by this activity on the part of the enemy, Wellington again reinforced Craufurd's cavalry, giving him three squadrons of the 14th Light Dragoons, so that the Light Division had now some 1,200 horse to watch its long and much exposed front. But the French advance now halted again for a full fortnight, the demonstration of July 4th having had no other purpose than that of ascertaining the strength of the British observing force behind the Azava.

On the four days that followed Craufurd's retreat the French batteries were thundering against the northern angle of Ciudad Rodrigo, and had reduced it to one vast breach more than 120 feet broad. But Ney, more sparing of life than was his wont, refused to order an assault till the whole of the Spanish artillery on the neighbouring front should have been silenced, and till the engineers should have worked up to and blown in the counterscarp. This last preliminary was accomplished on the night of the eighth, when a mine containing 800 lb. of powder was exploded with success just outside the counterscarp, and cast down a vast amount of earth into the ditch, so that there was now an almost level road from the advanced trenches to the foot of the inner wall. The garrison repeatedly built up the lip of the breach with palisades and sandbags, under a heavy fire and at great expense of life. But their flimsy repairs were swept away again and again by the batteries on the Little Teson, and all their guns on this front of the walls were gradually disabled or destroyed. Early on the afternoon of July 9th the engineers informed the Marshal that Ciudad Rodrigo was untenable, and that a storm could not fail of success. Three battalions, composed of picked voltigeur and grenadier companies, were brought up to the advanced trenches, under the Marshal's personal superintendence. Before letting them loose

on the broad acclivity of rubble before them, Ney asked for
three volunteers who would take the desperate risk of climbing
up to the crest of the breach to see if it were retrenched behind.
A corporal and two privates made this daring venture, ran
lightly up to the summit, fired their muskets into the town,
and descended unhurt, under a scattering fire from the few
Spaniards who were still holding on to the ruins. On receiving
their assurance that nothing was to be feared, Ney ordered the
storming battalions to move out of the trenches, but ere they
had started an officer with a white flag appeared on the breach,
and descended to inform the Marshal that the Governor was
prepared to capitulate. Finding that Ney was immediately
below, Herrasti came out in person with his staff a few minutes
later, and settled the whole matter in a short conversation.
Ney congratulated the white-haired veteran on his handsome
defence, returned him his sword, and told him that he should
have all the honours of war.

Accordingly the garrison marched out next morning about
4,000 strong, laid down its arms below the glacis, and was
marched off to Bayonne. The Spaniards had lost 461 killed
and 994 wounded, just a quarter of their force, in their highly
honourable resistance. They had only a few days' provisions
left, and, though their munitions were by no means exhausted,
they would have been forced to yield for want of food, even if
the storm had failed, which was absolutely impossible. The
French captured 118 guns, most of them in bad order or
disabled, and 7,000 muskets. Not a house or church in the
place was intact, and a large majority were roofless or levelled
to the ground. There was no use whatever in protracting the
resistance, and it is clear that Herrasti had done all that a good
officer could. In his dispatch to the Junta he spoke somewhat
bitterly of the fact that Wellington had made no effort to
relieve the place, showing feeling natural enough under the
circumstances. Martin La Carrera, who had been commanding
the Spanish division that lay in the mountains south of the
town, expressed his wrath still more bitterly, and marched off
to Estremadura in high dudgeon, the moment that the news
of the surrender reached him.

The French had been forced to much greater exertions in

the siege of Rodrigo than they had expected when they first sat down before its walls. Their artillery had thrown 11,000 shells and 18,000 round shot into the place, which almost exhausted their store of munitions—only 700 rounds for each of their fifty guns having been provided. They had lost 180 killed and over 1,000 wounded, mainly in the costly work of pushing forward the approaches towards the wall, before the Spanish artillery fire had been silenced. Professional critics attributed the delays and losses of the siege entirely to the fact that the engineers believed, when they first planned their works, that the enemy would surrender the moment that a breach had been made, an idea which had never entered into Herrasti's head [1]. Masséna showed his ill-temper, when all was over, by sending the civilian members of the Junta as prisoners to France, and imposing a fine of 500,000 francs on the miserable ruined town. It is surprising to learn that he actually succeeded in extracting half that sum from the homeless and starving population.

On the day that the garrison of Rodrigo marched out (July 10) Craufurd had suffered a misadventure. Seeing that the French foragers were busy in the villages between the Azava and the Dos Casas, he had resolved to make an attempt to surprise some of their bands, and went out from Fort Concepcion with six squadrons of cavalry [2], six companies of the Rifles and the 43rd, a battalion of Caçadores and two guns. Coming suddenly upon the French covering party near the village of Barquilla, he ordered his cavalry to pursue them. The enemy, consisting of two troops of dragoons and 200 men of the 22nd regiment from Junot's corps, began a hasty retreat towards their lines. Thereupon Craufurd bade his leading squadrons, one of the German Hussars and one of the 16th, to charge [3]. They did so, falling upon the infantry, who halted and

[1] See the criticisms in Belmas, iii. 259. Compare the views of the artilleryman Hulot, pages 306–9 of his autobiography.

[2] Viz. three squadrons of the 14th, one (Krauchenberg's) of the 1st Hussars K.G.L., and two of the 16th. The other two squadrons of the hussars, and the 4th squadron of the 14th, were holding the outpost line to right and left.

[3] It is certain that both charged, and both were beaten off. But the regimental diarists of the two regiments each mention only the repulse

formed square in a corn-field to receive them. The charge, made
by men who had been galloping for a mile, and had been much
disordered by passing some enclosures, failed. The troopers,
opening out to right and left under the fire of the square, swept
on and chased the French cavalry, who were making off to the
flank. They followed them for some distance, finally overtaking
them and making two officers and twenty-nine men prisoners.
Meanwhile Craufurd called up the next squadron from the
road, the leading one of the 14th Light Dragoons, and sent
it in against the little square. Headed by their colonel Talbot
the men of the 14th charged home, but were unable to break
the French, who stood firm and waited till the horses'
heads were within ten paces of their bayonets before firing.
Talbot and seven of his men fell dead, and some dozen more
were disabled. Before another squadron could come up, the
French slipped off into the enclosures of the village of Cismeiro
and got away. It was said that no effort was made to stop
them because two outlying squadrons of British cavalry [1], which
had ridden in towards the sound of the firing, were mistaken
for a large body of French horse coming up to the rescue of
the infantry. Both Craufurd and the British cavalry were
much criticized over this affair [2]; but it was, in truth, nothing
more than an example of the general rule that horsemen could
not break steady infantry, properly formed in square, during
the Peninsular War. The instances to the contrary are few.
It was said at the time that Craufurd might have used his

of the squadron from the other corps. See Tompkinson (of the 16th),
Diary, p. 31, and Von Linsingen's letter (from the 1st Hussars), printed in
Beamish, i. 279–80.

[1] Von Grüben's squadron of the K.G.L. Hussars, and the fourth squadron
of the 14th Light Dragoons, neither of which formed part of Craufurd's
little expedition. The former had been watching Villa de Ciervo, the
latter was on outpost duty.

[2] Charles Napier in his diary [*Life*, i. p. 132] and Tomkinson [p. 31]
accuse Craufurd of reckless haste. Harry Smith, in his autobiography [i.
p. 22], holds that the Rifles could have got up in time to force the square
to surrender. Leach [p. 142] makes much the same comment. All these
were eye-witnesses. Yet it would have taken some time to bring up the
guns or the infantry, and the French were near broken ground, over
which they might have escaped, if not immediately assailed. See also
Craufurd's Life by his grandson, pp. 114–16.

leading squadrons to detain and harass the French till his guns or his infantry, which were a mile to the rear, could be brought up. This may have been so, but criticism after the event is easy, and if the guns or the riflemen had come up ten minutes late, and the French infantry had been allowed to go off uncharged, the General would have been blamed still more. He lost in all an officer and eight men killed, and twenty-three wounded, while he took thirty-one prisoners, but the defeat rankled, and caused so much unpleasant feeling that Wellington went out of his way to send for and rebuke officers who had been circulating malevolent criticism[1]. The French captain Gouache, who had commanded the square, was very properly promoted and decorated by Masséna: nothing could have been more firm and adroit than his conduct[2].

[1] Among these officers was General Stewart, the adjutant-general, see Wellington to Craufurd, from Alverca, July 23, a very interesting letter, commented on in the *Life of Craufurd*, pp. 117–20.

[2] Hulot (p. 36) says that he met the square retiring, and noticed that numbers of the bayonets and gun-barrels had been cut and bent by the blows of the English dragoons, as they tried to force their way in. See Masséna's dispatch to Berthier of Aug. 10, in Belmas's *Pièces Justificatives*.

SECTION XIX: CHAPTER VI

COMBAT OF THE COA. SIEGE OF ALMEIDA

On July 10th the French had entered Ciudad Rodrigo, but ten days more elapsed before they made any further advance. Masséna, who had returned to the front, was resolved to follow his master's orders and to act 'methodically.' It was clearly incumbent on him to begin the siege of Almeida as soon as possible, and, as that place is only twenty-one miles from Ciudad Rodrigo, one long march would have placed him before its walls. But since he had only a few thousand rounds of ammunition left for his heavy guns, he refused to move on till all the available reserves were on their way from Salamanca to the front, and requisition for a further supply had been sent to Bayonne. He had also to do his best to scrape together more food, since the magazines that Ney had collected were nearly exhausted when Rodrigo fell. Moreover, 1,500 draught animals had died during the late siege, and it was necessary to replace them before the Great Park could move forward.

On July 21st, however, some convoys having come up from Salamanca, Masséna directed Ney to advance with the 6th Corps and to drive Craufurd back on to Almeida. The main point that he was directed to ascertain on this day was whether the English intended to make a stand at Fort Concepcion, the isolated Spanish work which faces Almeida on the frontier, beyond the Turones. This was a solid eighteenth-century fort, covering the bridge where the high-road passes the river. It had lately been repaired, and could have resisted a bombardment for some days. But it would have required a garrison of 1,000 men, and, since it lies in the midst of the plain, there would be little chance of relieving it, if once it were surrounded. Wellington, therefore, gave orders that it should be blown up whenever the French should advance in force toward Almeida, and that Craufurd should make no attempt to defend the line of the Turones, and should send back his infantry to Junca, a village about a mile outside the gates of Almeida[1], keeping his cavalry only to the front.   On the 21st Ney advanced with the whole of Loison's division, and Treillard's cavalry brigade. Thereupon Craufurd, with some reluctance, retired and blew up Fort Concepcion as he went.   The French advanced, skirmishing with the 14th Light Dragoons and the German Hussars, but finally halted at Val de Mula, four miles from Almeida.   Craufurd established himself at Junca, only three miles from the enemy's line of pickets.   On the next evening he received a strong suggestion, if not quite an order, from his Chief to send his infantry across the Coa.   ' I am not desirous of engaging an affair beyond the Coa,' wrote Wellington.   ' Under these circumstances, if you are not covered from the sun where you are, would it not be better that you should come to this side of it, with your infantry at least ?[2] '   The tentative form of the note well marks the confidence that the Commander-in-Chief was wont to place in his subordinate's judgement.   This time that confidence was somewhat misplaced, for Craufurd tarried two days longer by the glacis of Almeida, and thereby risked a disaster.

It must be remembered that Almeida is not on the Coa, but two miles from it, and that its guns, therefore, did not cover the one bridge over which Craufurd could make his retreat. Indeed, that bridge and the river also are invisible from Almeida. The fortress is slightly raised above the level of the rolling plain, which extends as far as Ciudad Rodrigo : the river flows in a deep bed, so much below the plateau as to be lost to sight. Its ravine is a sort of cañon which marks the end of the plains of Leon.   It has often been remarked that Almeida's value would have been doubled, if only it had been on the near side of the Coa, and commanded its bridge.   But Portuguese kings had built and rebuilt the old fortress on its original site, with no regard for strategy.   Craufurd, then, should have remembered that, if he were suddenly attacked in his camp outside the gates, he risked being thrown back into the town (the last thing he would wish), or being hustled down to the bridge and forced to

---

[1] Wellington to Craufurd from Alverca, July 16.

[2] Wellington to Craufurd from Alverca, July 22, 8 p.m.

pass his division across it in dangerous haste. But he had so
often challenged, held back, and evaded Ney's and Junot's
advanced guards, that he evidently considered that he was taking
no very serious risk in staying where he was. He was, moreover,
discharging a valuable function by keeping Almeida from being
invested, as stores and munitions were still being poured into
the place. The only peril was that he might be attacked both
without warning and by overwhelming superiority of numbers,
with the defile at his back. Neither of these misadventures had
yet happened to him during the four and a half months while
he had been defying the 6th and the 8th Corps along the banks
of the Agueda. The French had never assailed him with much
more than a division, nor had they ever pressed on him with
headlong speed, so as to prevent an orderly retreat properly
covered by a moderate rearguard.

Now, however, Ney, untrammelled by any other operation,
had his whole corps concentrated behind Val de Mula, and
having learnt of the defile that lay in Craufurd's rear, thought
that he might be hurled into it and crushed or caught. Before
dawn he arrayed his whole 24,000 men in one broad and deep
column. Two cavalry brigades, Lamotte's 3rd Hussars and
15th Chasseurs, and Gardanne's 15th and 25th Dragoons, were
in front. Then came the thirteen battalions of Loison's division,
in a line of columns; behind them was Mermet with eleven
battalions more, while three regiments of Marchand's division
(the fourth was garrisoning Ciudad Rodrigo) formed the reserve.
In a grey morning, following a night of bitter rain, the French
horsemen rode at the British cavalry pickets, and sent them flying
helter-skelter across the three miles of rolling ground that lay
in front of the Light Division. On hearing the fire of the
carbines Craufurd's men turned out with their accustomed
celerity, and in a very short space were aligned to the right of
Almeida, with their flank only 800 yards from the glacis, and
their front covered by a series of high stone walls bounding
suburban fields. There would have been just enough time to
get cavalry, guns, and impedimenta across the bridge of the Coa
if the General had started off at once. But, not realizing the
fearful strength that lay behind the French cavalry advance,
he resolved to treat himself to a rearguard action, and not to

go till he was pushed. On a survey of the ground it is easy to understand the temptation, for it would be hard to find a prettier battlefield for a detaining force, if only the enemy were in no more than moderate strength. A long double-headed spur runs down from the high plateau on which Almeida stands to the Coa. Successive points of it can be held one after the other, and it is crossed by many stone walls giving good cover for skirmishers. With his left covered by the fire of the fortress, and his right 'refused' and trending back towards the river, Craufurd waited to be attacked, intending to give the leading French brigade a lesson. There was a delay of more than an hour before the French infantry was up, but when the assault came it was overwhelming. Craufurd's line of three British and two Portuguese battalions [1] was suddenly assaulted by Loison's thirteen, who came on at the *pas de charge* ' yelling, with drums beating, and the officers, like mountebanks, running ahead with their hats on their swords, capering like madmen and crying as they turned to wave on their men, " Allons, enfants de la Patrie, le premier qui s'avançera, Napoléon le recompensera [2]." ' The rolling fire of the British stopped the first rush, when suddenly a French cavalry regiment, the 3rd Hussars, charged across the interval between Craufurd's left and the walls of Almeida, braving the fire of the ramparts in the most gallant style. Some fell, but the gunners were flurried at this unexpected development, and fired wildly, so that the hussars swept down unchecked on the extreme flank of the Light Division, where a company of the 95th Rifles was annihilated [3], and began riding along the rear of the line and rolling it up. They were luckily checked for a moment by a stone wall, but Craufurd saw that he must retreat at once, since he was turned on the side where he had thought that he was safest. The cavalry and guns were ordered to gallop for the bridge, the

---

[1] The 43rd on the left, the two Caçador battalions in the centre, the 52nd on the right, while the Rifles were partly dispersed along the front, partly with the 43rd.

[2] Simmons's *Journal of a British Rifleman*, p. 77.

[3] Of this, O'Hare's Company of the 1/95th, sixty-seven strong, an officer and eleven men were killed or wounded and forty-five were taken prisoners.

Caçadores to follow them, and the rest of the infantry to fall back in échelon from the left, defending each enclosure and fold of the hillside as long as possible. But it is hard to make an orderly retreat when a foe with twofold strength in his fighting line is pressing hard. Moreover, the road to the bridge has an unfortunate peculiarity; instead of making straight for its goal it overshoots it, in order to descend the slope at an easy point, and then comes back along the river bank for a quarter of a mile. The cavalry and guns, forced to keep to the road because the hillside was too steep for them, had to cover two sides of a triangle with a sharp turn at the apex, which delayed them terribly. To add to the trouble an artillery caisson was upset at a sharp turn, and took much trouble to right and send forward. Thus it chanced that the covering infantry were driven down close to the bridge before the Caçadores and the last of the guns had crossed the river. The retreat of the three British battalions had been most perilous; at one moment a wing of the 43rd found themselves checked by a vineyard wall ten feet high, while the French were pressing hard on their rear. They only escaped by shoving a long part of it over by sheer strength—fortunately, like all other walls in this part of Portugal, it was made of dry flat stones without mortar. Finally the 43rd, the Rifles, and part of the 52nd were massed on a long knoll covered with pine-trees, which lies above the bridge and completely masks it against an attack from above. While they held firm, Craufurd ranged the guns and the Caçadores on the slopes upon the other side, so as to command the passage when the rest of the troops should have to cross. He then began to withdraw the 43rd, and part of that battalion had already crossed the water, when five companies of the 52nd, which had occupied the extreme right wing of the division, were seen hastening along the river bank some way above the bridge. They had held out a little too long on the slopes above, and seemed likely to be cut off, for the French, noting their position, made a vigorous effort, and carried the knoll which protected their line of retreat to the point of passage. This was a desperate crisis, but such was the splendid courage and initiative of the regimental officers of the Light Division that the disaster was averted. At one point Beckwith, colonel of the Rifles, at another Major McLeod of the 43rd, called on the disordered mass of men, who had been driven back to the bridge head, to charge again and save the 52nd. The soldiers grasped the situation, cheered and followed; they recaptured the knoll that they had just lost, and held it for ten minutes more, gaining time for the companies of the 52nd to pass behind and cross the bridge. 'No one present,' wrote an eye-witness, 'can fail to remember the gallantry of Major McLeod. How either he or his horse escaped being blown to atoms, while in this daring manner he charged on horseback at the head of some 200 skirmishers of the 43rd and 95th mixed together, and headed them in making a dash at the line of French infantry, whom we dislodged, I am at a loss to imagine. It was one of those extraordinary escapes which tend to implant in the mind some faith in the doctrine of fatality [1].'

The moment that the 52nd were safe, the troops on the knoll evacuated it, and crossed the bridge behind them at full speed, while the French reoccupied the wooded eminence. If Ney had been wise he would have stopped at this moment, and have contented himself with having driven in the Light Division with a loss of 300 men, while his own troops had suffered comparatively little. But, carried away by the excitement of victory, he resolved to storm the bridge, thinking that the British troops were too much shaken and disordered to make another stand, even in a strong position. There were plenty of examples in recent French military history, from Lodi to Ebersberg, where passages had been forced under difficulties as great. Accordingly he ordered the 66th, the leading regiment of Loison's division, to push on and cross the river. This was a dire mistake: Craufurd already had the Caçadores in position behind stone walls a little above the bridge, and Ross's guns placed across the road so as to sweep it from end to end. The British battalions were no sooner across the river than they began to string themselves out behind the rocks and walls, which lie in a sort of small amphitheatre on the slope commanding the passage. The bridge, a two-arched structure seventy yards long, crosses the Coa diagonally, at a point where it is narrowed down between rocks, and flows very fiercely: it was flooded at

---

[1] Leach's *Reminiscences*, pp. 149–50.

this moment from the rain of the previous night, and was swelling still, for a tropical storm had just begun and raged at intervals throughout the afternoon. The cavalry, useless at the bridge, was sent up-stream to watch some difficult fords near Alveirenos.

The French 66th, ordered by the Marshal to carry the bridge, formed its grenadiers on the knoll, to lead the column, and then charged at the passage. But the leading company was mown down, before it had got half way across, by a concentrated musketry salvo from the hillside in front, and the enfilading fire of the guns from the right. The column broke, and the men recoiled and dispersed among the rocks and trees by the bank, from whence they opened a fierce but ineffective fire upon the well-sheltered British battalions. Ney, who had now lost his temper, ordered up a *bataillon d'élite* of light infantry [1] which had distinguished itself at the siege of Ciudad Rodrigo, and told his aide de camp Sprünglin to take the command and cross at all costs [2]. There ensued a most gallant effort and a hideous butchery. The Chasseurs flung themselves at the bridge, and pushed on till it was absolutely blocked by the bodies of the killed and the wounded, and till they themselves had been almost literally exterminated, for out of a battalion of little more than 300 men 90 were killed and 147 wounded in less than ten minutes. A few survivors actually crossed the bridge, and threw themselves down among the rocks at its western end, where they took shelter from the British fire in a little corner of dead ground, but could of course make no further attempt to advance.

[1] The *Chasseurs de la Siège* formed of picked marksmen from all the regiments of the 6th Corps.

[2] That Ney himself was the person responsible for this mad adventure seems proved by the journal of Sprünglin, who writes 'A midi je reçus de M. le Maréchal lui-même l'ordre d'emporter *à tout prix* le pont de la Coa, d'où deux compagnies de Grenadiers venaient d'être repoussés. J'avais 300 hommes ; je formai mon bataillon en colonne et abordai les Anglais à la baïonnette, et au cri de *Vive l'Empereur.* Le pont fut emporté, mais j'eus 4 officiers et 86 soldats tués, et 3 officiers et 144 soldats blessés. Le 25 le bataillon, étant détruit, fut dissous.' That the bridge was ' emporté ' in any other sense than that a score or so of survivors got to the other side, and then returned, is of course untrue. Sprünglin, p. 439.

Ney, irritated beyond measure, now bade a mounted officer
sound for a ford at a spot above the bridge, where the river
spreads out into a broad reach. But horse and man were killed
by a volley from the British side, and floated down the swollen
stream [1]. Finding the river impracticable, the Marshal again
ordered the 66th to go forward: this third attack, delivered
without the dash and determination of the first two, was beaten
back with little trouble. The firing then died down, and
during one of the fierce rainstorms of the late afternoon the
few chasseurs who had crossed the bridge ran back and escaped
to their own bank. Craufurd held the position that he had
occupied till midnight, and then retired on Pinhel. He had
lost 318 men only [2], and was fortunate therein, for half his
division might have been destroyed if the officers had shown
less intelligence and the men less pluck. The French had 527
casualties, four-fifths of them in the mad attempt to force
the bridge, in which the colonel of the 66th and fifteen of his
officers had fallen, and the battalion of Chasseurs had been
practically exterminated [3]. Ney forwarded an honest chronicle
of the day's doings to his chief, which Masséna wrote up, and
sent to the Emperor turned into a work of fancy, in which he
declared that he had destroyed 1,200 of Craufurd's men (whom
he estimated at 2,000 horse and 8,000 infantry, double their
real strength), taken 300 prisoners, a colour, and two guns.
Making no mention of the complete check that Loison's division
had suffered at the bridge, he stated that 'the Imperial troops
have shown once again this day that there is no position which
can resist their intrepidity.' He added foolish gossip, 'Their
Estafete-Mor (chief Portuguese courier) has been captured with
all his dispatches, in which are several of the 25th and 26th
instant, which declare that the English army is in complete
rout, that its deplorable state cannot be exaggerated, that
the English have never been in such a hot corner, that they

---

[1] For an interesting description of this incident, see George Napier's
autobiography, p. 131.

[2] Thirty-six killed, 189 wounded, 83 missing. See Tables in Appendix.

[3] Martinien's invaluable lists show 7 officers killed and 17 wounded,
which at the normal rate of 22 men per officer, exactly corresponds to the
actual loss of 117 killed and 410 wounded (Koch, vii. 118).

have lost sixty officers, of whom they buried twenty-four on the battlefield, about 400 dead and 700 wounded [1].' Apparently these 'dispatches' are an invention of Masséna's own. It is incredible that any British officer can have written such stuff after a combat of which every man present was particularly proud, and in which the losses had been incredibly small, con-

[1] It is a curious fact that in the draft of Masséna's dispatch in the *Archives du Ministère de la Guerre*, we actually catch him in the act of falsifying returns. There is first written 'Nous leur avons pris 100 hommes et deux pièces de canon. Notre perte a été de près de 500 hommes tant tués que blessés.' Then the figures 100 are scratched out and above is inserted ' un drapeau et 400 hommes,' while for the French loss 500 is scratched out and 300 inserted. Ney, whose dispatch was lying before Masséna, had honestly written that Craufurd ' a été chassé de sa position avec une perte considérable de tués et de blessés, nous lui avons fait en outre une centaine de prisonniers.' Ney reported also a loss of about 500 men, which Masséna deliberately cut down to 300. Belmas (iii. 379) has replaced the genuine figures in his reprint of Masséna's dispatch, though both the draft in the *Archives* and the original publication in the *Moniteur* give the falsifications. Masséna says nought of the check at the bridge, though Ney honestly wrote ' au delà du Coa, une réserve qu'il avait lui permis de se reconnaître, et il continue sa retraite sur Pinhel la nuit du 24.' As to the guns captured, it was perfectly true that some cannon were taken that day, but not in fighting, nor from Craufurd. The governor of Almeida was mounting two small guns (4-pounders) on a windmill some way outside the glacis. They had not been got up to their position, but were lying below—removed from their carriages, in order to be slung up more easily on to the roof. The mill was abandoned when Ney came up, and the dismounted cannon fell into his hands. He said not a word of them, any more than he did of the imaginary flag alleged by Masséna to have been captured. But the Prince of Essling brought in both, to please the imperial palate, which yearned for British flags and guns. His dispatch, published some weeks later in the *Moniteur*, came into Craufurd's hands in November, and provoked him to write a vindication of his conduct, and a contradiction of ' the false assertions contained in Marshal Masséna's report of an action which was not only highly honourable to the Light Division, but positively terminated in its favour, notwithstanding the extraordinary disparity of numbers. For a corps of 4,000 men performed, in the face of an army of 24,000, one of the most difficult operations of war,—a retreat from a broken and extensive position over one narrow defile, and defended during the whole day the first defensible position that was to be found in the neighbourhood of the place where the action commenced.' For the whole letter see Alex. Craufurd's *Life of Craufurd*, pp. 140–1.

sidering the risks that had been run. Four officers, not twenty-four, had been killed, and one made prisoner. Instead of being in 'complete rout' the Light Division had retired at leisure and unmolested, without leaving even a wounded man or a single cart behind.

Wellington was justly displeased with Craufurd for accepting this wholly unnecessary combat: if the Light Division had been withdrawn behind the Coa on the 22nd, as he had advised, no danger would have been incurred, and the bridge might have been defended without the preliminary retreat to the water's edge. Yet so great was the confidence in which Craufurd was held by Wellington, that their correspondence shows no break of cordiality or tension of relations during the ensuing days[1], though unofficially the divisional general was aware that the Commander-in-Chief had disapproved his action, and felt the blame that was unspoken in the keenest fashion[2]. There was another British general involved in a serious degree of culpability on the 24th: this was Picton, who hearing at his post of Pinhel the firing in the morning, rode up to the bridge of the Coa; there he met Craufurd, who was just preparing to resist Ney's attempt to cross the river. Picton was asked to bring up the 3rd Division in support, which could have been done in less than three hours, but roughly refused, saying apparently that Craufurd might get out of his own scrape. The generals parted after an exchange of some hard words, and Picton rode back to order his division to get ready to retreat, having committed one of the greatest military sins, that of refusing to support a comrade in the moment of danger, because he did not choose to compromise his own troops[3].

---

[1] See the letter to Craufurd in the *Dispatches*, dated July 26 and 27. His letter to Lord Liverpool of July 25 offers, indeed, excuses for Craufurd. But in that to Henry Wellesley of July 27, and still more in that to his relative Pole of July 31, he expresses vexation. ' I had positively forbidden the foolish affairs in which Craufurd involved his outposts, ... and repeated my injunction that he should not engage in an affair on the right of the river. ... You will say in this case, " Why not accuse Craufurd ? " I answer, " Because if I am to be hanged for it, I cannot accuse a man who I believe has meant well, and whose error was one of judgement, not of intention." '   [2] See *Craufurd's Life*, pp. 149–50.

[3] This interview was denied by Robinson in his *Life of Picton* (i. 294)

Having cleared the country-side beyond the Coa by pressing back the Light Division, and having ascertained by a reconnaissance that Picton had evacuated Pinhel on the night of the 25th, Masséna was able to sit down to besiege Almeida at his leisure. The investment was assigned to Ney and the 6th Corps, while Junot and the 8th Corps were brought up from the Agueda, and placed in the villages behind and to the right of the besieged place, so as to be able to support Ney at a few hours' notice. The extreme steepness of the banks of the Coa during its whole course rendered it most unlikely that Wellington would attempt the relief of Almeida by a direct advance. He would have had to force a passage, and the Coa, unlike the Agueda, has very few fords. Its only two bridges, that opposite Almeida, and that higher up at Castello Bom, were held in force by the 6th Corps. The siege however might not improbably prove long. Almeida was in far better repair than Ciudad Rodrigo, and had less defects. The little town is situated on the culminating knoll of an undulating plateau, a very slight eminence, but one which was not commanded by any higher ground as Rodrigo was by the two Tesons. The outline of the place is almost circular, and exactly fits the round knoll on which it stands. It has six bastions, with demi-lunes and a covered way. There is a dry ditch cut in the solid rock, for Almeida lies on a bare granite plateau, with only two or three feet of earth covering the hard stratum below. It was well armed with over 100 guns, forty of which were 18-pounders or still heavier. It had casemates completely proof against bomb fire, and large enough to cover the whole garrison. This, as has been already said, consisted of one regular regiment, the 24th of the Line over 1,200 strong, and the three militia regiments of Arganil, Trancoso, and Vizeu—in all some 4,000 infantry, with a squadron of the 11th cavalry regiment and 400 gunners. The governor was William Cox—an English

on the mere allegation of some of Picton's staff that they had not heard of it, or been present at it. But the evidence of William Campbell, Craufurd's brigade-major, brought forward by Napier at Robinson's challenge, is conclusive. See Napier, vi. pp. 418–19, for the ' fiery looks and violent rejoinders ' witnessed by Campbell. Picton had been specially ordered to support Craufurd if necessary. See *Wellington Dispatches*, v. pp. 535 and 547.

colonel and a Portuguese brigadier; he had with him five other English officers, all the rest of the garrison being Portuguese. There was an ample store both of food and of ammunition, which Wellington had been pouring in ever since the siege of Ciudad Rodrigo began. Only two serious defects existed in the place: the first was that its glacis was too low, and left exposed an unduly large portion of the walls [1]. The second, a far worse fault, was that the grand magazine was established in a rather flimsy mediaeval castle in the centre of the town, and was not nearly so well protected as could have been desired. Nevertheless Wellington calculated that Almeida should hold out at least as long as Ciudad Rodrigo, and had some hope that its siege would detain Masséna so much that the autumn rains would set in before he had taken the place, in which case the invasion of Portugal would assume a character of difficulty which it was far from presenting in August or September.

For some days after the investment of Almeida had been completed the 6th Corps remained quiescent, and made no attempt to break ground in front of the place. Ney was waiting for the Grand Park and the train, which had now started in detachments from Ciudad Rodrigo, but were advancing very slowly on account of the lack of draught animals. For a moment Wellington thought it possible that the enemy was about to mask Almeida, and to advance into Portugal with his main army without delay [2]. This hypothesis received some support from the facts that Junot had moved up from the Agueda, and that Reynier had shown the head of a column beyond the Pass of Perales. This last appeared a most significant movement; for if the 2nd Corps was about to march up from the Tagus to

---

[1] This came from the extreme hardness of the soil, which induced the builders of the 18th-century enceinte to put less earth into the glacis than was needed, since it had to be scraped up and carried from a great distance, owing to the fact that the coating of soil all around is so thin above the rock.

[2] Wellington to Hill, Alverca, July 27, 'There is not the smallest appearance of the enemy's intending to attack Almeida, and I conclude that as soon as they have got together their force, they will make a dash at us, and endeavour to make our retreat as difficult as possible.'

join Masséna, the deduction was that it was required to join
in a general invasion, since it was clear that it was not needed
for the mere siege of Almeida. Wellington accordingly wrote
to urge Hill to keep a most vigilant eye on Reynier, and to be
ready to move up to the Mondego the moment that it was
certain that his opponent had passed the Sierra de Gata and
linked himself to the main French army. As a matter of fact
there was, as yet, no danger from Reynier. The advance of
one of his flanking detachments to Navas Frias beyond the
Pass of Perales, and a raid made upon Penamacor on July 31
and upon Monsanto on August 1, by another, were pure matters
of foraging and reconnaissance. Reynier had no orders to move
up his whole force to join Masséna, and was only amusing himself by demonstrations. His actions became most puzzling to
Wellington when, a few days later, he called back all the troops
that had moved northward, and concentrated his force at Zarza
la Mayor, on the road to Castello Branco, so as to threaten
once more to invade Central Portugal by the line of the Tagus.
This was no device of his own, but the result of a dispatch from
Masséna dated July 27, ordering him to keep more to the south
for the present, to threaten Abrantes, and to afford Hill no
chance of joining Wellington.

Reynier's feints meanwhile had given Hill some trouble; the
appearance of a northward move on the part of his adversary
had caused the British general to make ready for a parallel
march on Fundão and Guarda, so as to connect himself with
his chief. He transferred his head quarters first from Castello
Branco to Sarzedas, and then from Sarzedas to Atalaya, at the
foot of the pass that leads to the Mondego valley, intending
to cross the mountains the moment that Reynier had passed
over the Perales defiles with his main body. But seeing the
2nd Corps unexpectedly turning back and concentrating at
Zarza, Hill also retraced his steps, and lay at Sarzedas again
from August 3rd till September 21st, with his advanced guard
at Castello Branco and his cavalry well out to the front along
the Spanish frontier, watching every movement of the 2nd
Corps. During this time of waiting the Portuguese cavalry
of his division had two small but successful engagements with
Reynier's horse, of whom they cut up a squadron on the 3rd of

August near Penamacor and another on the 22nd at Ladoeiro, when two officers and sixty men of the Hanoverian *Chasseurs à Cheval* were killed or taken [1].

Wellington's doubts as to Masséna's intentions in the first days of August were provoked not merely by the movements of the 2nd Corps, but by a demonstration made on an entirely new front by General Serras, the officer who had been left with an unattached division to hold the plains of Leon, when Junot and the 8th Corps went off to join the main army on the Agueda. In obedience to Masséna's orders, on July 27 Serras collected at Benavente as much of his division as could be spared from garrison duty, and moved forward to threaten the frontier of the Tras-os-Montes, far to the north of Portugal. He advanced with some 5,000 men as far as Puebla de Senabria, from which on July 29 he drove out a small Spanish force under General Taboada—the weak brigade which Echevarria had formerly commanded. Silveira immediately collected all the Portuguese militia of his district at Braganza, and prepared to defend the frontier. But Serras unexpectedly turned back, left a battalion of the 2nd Swiss Regiment and a squadron of horse in Puebla de Senabria, and returned to Zamora. The moment that he was gone Silveira and Taboada united their forces, attacked this small detached force, routed it, and shut it up in the town on August 4. It was forced to surrender some six days later, about 20 officers and 350 men, all that remained of 600, being made prisoners. Serras, who had hurried back when he heard of Silveira's offensive movement, was too late by twelve hours to save his men, and found Puebla de Senabria empty, for the allies had gone off with their prisoners and taken to the mountains. He then retired to Benavente, and Taboada reoccupied Puebla de Senabria, where he was not again disturbed. Serras soon after was drawn away to the north-east by the demands of Bonnet, whose communications with Santander had once more been cut by Porlier's roving Asturian bands. He called on his colleague to attack this partisan force in the rear, and while Serras was hunting it at Potes and Alba, in the

---

[1] For details of this combat see Foy's observations on p. 97 of his *Vie Militaire*, ed. Girod de L'Ain.

Cantabrian hills, Northern Portugal and Galicia were left
undisturbed in September [1].

While glancing at the subsidiary operations in this remote
corner of Spain, it may be worth while to note, as a proof of
the slight hold which Bonnet and Serras possessed on their
allotted districts, that on June 7 Mahy threatened Astorga, while
the Asturian bands of Colonel Barcena, eluding Bonnet, came
down into the plains by the Pass of Pajares and surprised Leon [2].
They got into the town by escalade at night, held it for two
days, and only evacuated it when Serras came up in strength on
June 9. Provoked at this bold adventure, Bonnet made his last
attempt to conquer Western Asturias, and so to destroy the
indefatigable and evasive partisans in his front. He forced his
way across the Narcea and the Navia, and his vanguard had
reached Castropol, on the Galician border, upon July 5, when
he heard to his disgust that the enemy had slipped behind him.
Barcena was threatening his base at Oviedo, while Porlier's band,
carried round by English ships, had landed near Llanes and cut
the communication with Santander. These clever moves brought
Bonnet back in haste: he evacuated Western Asturias, called
up Serras to his aid, and was engaged in August and September
in the hunt after Porlier which we have already mentioned [3].

But to return to the main focus of the war in the North.
On August 15th Ney's troops, having at last received the siege-
train and a good supply of munitions from Ciudad Rodrigo and
Salamanca, broke ground in front of Almeida. Wellington was
much relieved at the news, as it was now clear that Masséna
was about to besiege the place, and not to mask it and march
forward into Portugal. The front which the engineers of the
6th Corps had chosen for attack was that facing the bastion of
San Pedro on the south-east front of the town. The first parallel
was drawn at a distance of only 500 yards from the walls; it was
found very difficult to complete, owing to the shallowness of the

[1] For a narrative of these obscure campaigns see Schaller's *Souvenirs d'un
officier Fribourgeois*, pp. 29–37.

[2] See ibid., pp. 32–3.

[3] For a narrative of these interesting but obscure movements, see
Schepeler, iii. 596–9. It is impossible to give a full account of them here,
but necessary to mention them, to show the Sisyphean character of
Bonnet's task.

earth, and had to be built with gabions and sandbags rather than to be excavated in the rocky subsoil. In many places outcrops of stone came to the surface, and had actually to be blasted away by the sappers, in order to allow of a trench of the shallowest sort being formed. It was clear that the construction of approaches towards the town would present the greatest difficulties, since there was little earth in which to burrow. Between the 17th and the 24th no less than eleven batteries were constructed along the first parallel. They were armed with more than fifty heavy guns, for there was artillery in abundance; in addition to the old siege-train many of the Spanish guns taken in Ciudad Rodrigo had been brought forward. The Portuguese kept up a vigorous but not very destructive fire all the time; but on the 24th they succeeded in preventing the commencement of a second parallel, driving out the workmen before they could cover themselves in the stony ground. At six o'clock on the morning of the 26th August the batteries were all completed and opened fire. Several quarters of the town were in flames before the afternoon, and the guns on the three bastions attacked were unable to hold their own against the converging fire directed on them. But no serious damage had been done to the defences, and the governor was undismayed. At seven o'clock in the evening, however, a fearful disaster occurred—one in its own way unparalleled in magnitude during the whole Peninsular War. The door of the great magazine in the castle had been opened, in order to allow of the sending out of a convoy of powder to the southern ramparts, where the artillery had been hard at work all day. A leaky barrel was handed out, which left a trail of powder behind it along the ground; it was being fixed to the saddle of a pack-ass when a French bomb fell in the courtyard of the castle. In bursting, the bomb chanced to ignite the train; the spark ran along it and exploded another barrel at the door of the magazine, which was still open[1]. This mischance fired the

---

[1] This version of the cause of the disaster is given by Soriano da Luz (iii. 73) from the mouth of an artillery officer (one José Moreira) who had it from the only man in the castle-yard who escaped. This soldier, seeing the train fired, jumped into an oven-hole which lay behind him, and chanced not to be killed.

whole store, and in two seconds the castle, the cathedral at its side, and the whole central portion of the town had been blasted out of existence. 'The earth trembled,' wrote a French eye-witness, 'and we saw an immense whirlwind of fire and smoke rise from the middle of the place. It was like the bursting of a volcano—one of the things that I can never forget after twenty-six years. Enormous blocks of stone were hurled into the trenches, where they killed and wounded some of our men. Guns of heavy calibre were lifted from the ramparts and hurled down far outside them. When the smoke cleared off, a great part of Almeida had disappeared, and the rest was a heap of debris [1].' Five hundred of the garrison perished, including nearly every man of the two hundred artillerymen who were serving the guns on the front of attack. Some inhabitants were killed, but not many, for the majority had taken refuge in the casemates when the bombardment began that morning. It was the unfortunate soldiers who were manning the walls that suffered.

Fearing that the French might seize the moment for an escalade, General Cox ran to the ramparts and, assisted by a Portuguese artillery officer, loaded and fired into the trenches some of the few guns on the south front which were not disabled. He turned out the whole garrison, and kept them under arms that night, lying behind the walls in expectation of an assault which never came. The morning light enabled him to realize the full extent of the disaster; the bastions and curtains had suffered little, the shell, so to speak, of the town was still intact, and the casemates had stood firm, but everything within the enceinte was wrecked. Only five houses in the place had kept their roofs: the castle was a deep hole, like the crater of a volcano: the streets were absolutely blocked with ruins, so that there was no going from place to place save along the ramparts.

There were still 4,000 men under arms; but the officer commanding the artillery reported that thirty-nine barrels of powder, and a few hundred rounds in the small expense-magazines on the ramparts, were all that had escaped the explosion. That is to say, there was not powder in the place to keep up a reply for one day to the batteries of the besieger. The infantry had 600,000 cartridges in their regimental stores

[1] Sprünglin's *Journal*, pp. 444–5.

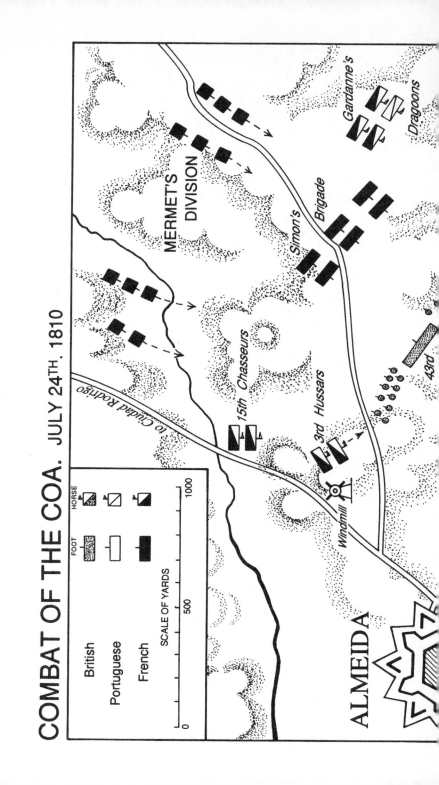

COMBAT OF THE COA. JULY 24TH. 1810

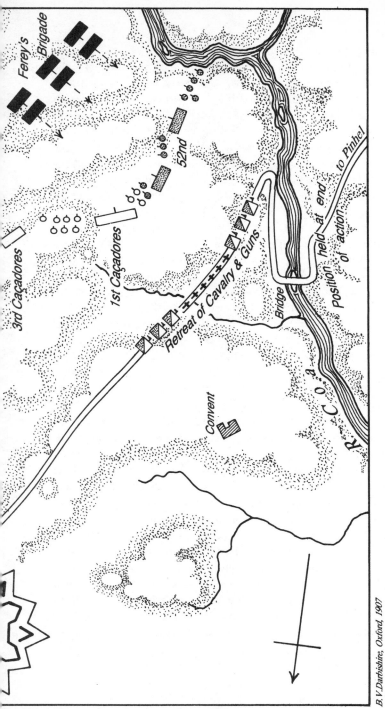

Fereys Brigade

3rd Caçadores

1st Caçadores

52nd

Retreat of Cavalry & Guns

Convent

Bridge

position held at end of action

to Pinhel

R. Côa

B.V.Darbishire, Oxford, 1907

(150 rounds per man) but that was of no use for the heavy guns. Moreover, more than half the gunners had perished in the disaster of the previous night—only 200 were left to man nearly 100 guns that were still serviceable. It was clear that Almeida was doomed, since it could not defend itself without powder : but there was a chance that Wellington, whose outposts must have heard and seen the explosion, might think it worth while to dash forward and endeavour to save the garrison during the next twenty-four hours. Therefore Cox resolved to protract his resistance as long as was possible, to give his chief the option of fighting if he should so please. But the defence could not be prolonged for more than a day or two at the most.

At nine on the morning of the 27th Masséna sent in his aide de camp Pelet to demand the surrender of the fortress. Cox had him blindfolded, and taken into a casemate for their interview, so that he might not be able to judge of the awful effects of the explosion. The usual haggling followed—the French officer threatened that the place should be escaladed at once, and the garrison put to the sword. The governor replied that his walls were intact, that he could still defend himself, and that the 'deplorable accident' had not appreciably diminished his resisting power[1]. But he finally consented to send out an officer to the French camp to negotiate for terms. All this was merely done to gain time, and the semaphore on the western ramparts was signalling desperate messages to Wellington all the morning.

Cox's attempt to gain time was fruitless, for a reason that he had not foreseen. The garrison was hopelessly demoralized, knew that it must surrender, and did not see why it should expose itself to another day's bombardment for a lost cause. During the conference in the casemate General d'Alorna and other Portuguese officers on Masséna's staff came out of the trenches, and boldly presented themselves at the foot of the walls, calling to their compatriots above and beseeching them to accept the good terms offered, and not to risk their lives for Wellington, who would abandon them just as he had abandoned Herrasti at Ciudad Rodrigo. The officers on the ramparts ought to have

---

[1] There is a good account of this interview in Sprünglin's *Journal*, p. 445, the diarist having accompanied Pelet into the town.

driven the renegades away, by shots if necessary ; but, far from doing so, they entered into long conversation with them and approved their arguments. D'Alorna recognized some old acquaintances among the regulars, and pledged his word to them that an assault was imminent, and that they were doomed if they made any resistance. What was still more unlucky for Cox was that the officer whom he sent out to the French camp to treat, Major Barreiros of the artillery, was one of those who were most convinced that further defence was fruitless ; he divulged the hopeless state of the place to the Marshal, and bade him press his attack without fear, for the garrison would not fight. He himself remained at the French head quarters, and did not return to Almeida. Masséna, therefore, sent back a blank refusal of all Cox's demands and conditions, and ordered the bombardment to recommence at seven in the evening, while approaches were thrown out from the second parallel towards the ramparts. A feeble musketry fire alone replied.

The renewal of the bombardment speedily brought matters inside the place to a head. A deputation of Portuguese officers, headed by Bernardo Da Costa, the second in command, visited Cox and informed him that further resistance was madness, and that if he did not at once hoist the white flag they would open the gates to the enemy. The Governor was forced to yield, and capitulated at eleven o'clock on the night of the 27th. Masséna granted him the terms that the regular troops should be sent as prisoners to France, while the three militia regiments should be allowed to disperse to their homes, on giving their parole not to serve again during the war.

On the morning of the 28th the garrison marched out, still 4,000 strong, its total loss during the siege having been some 600—nearly all destroyed in the explosion. The French had lost fifty-eight killed and 320 wounded during the operations. The capitulation was no sooner ratified than it was violated : instead of dismissing the militia and marching off the regulars towards France, Masséna kept them together, and set the rene-gades d'Alorna and Pamplona to tempt them to enter the French service. The officers were promised confirmation of their rank, the men were invited to compare the relative advantages of

prison and of joining the victorious side and keeping their
liberty. The arguments of the traitors seemed to prevail ;
almost the whole of the regulars and 600 of the militia signified
their consent to enlist with the enemy. The rest of the militia
were turned loose, but d'Alorna was able to organize a brigade
of three battalions to serve the Emperor as the 'Second
Portuguese Legion [1].' But the intentions of these docile recruits
were quite other than Masséna had supposed. They had
changed their allegiance merely in order to escape being sent to
France, and while left unguarded during the next three days,
absconded in bands of 200 or 300 at a time, officers and all, and
kept presenting themselves at Silveira's and Wellington's outposts, for a week. The French, undeceived too late, disarmed
the few men remaining in the camp, who were packed off to
France, to rejoin Cox and the half-dozen officers who had
loyally refused to accept D'Alorna's offers [2]. Wellington had
been somewhat alarmed when the first news of the adhesion of
the garrison to the French cause reached him, fearing that it
implied serious disaffection in the whole Portuguese army [3].
He was soon undeceived on this point, as the troops gradually
streamed in to his camp [4]. But he was then seized with grave
doubts as to whether he could, consistently with military honour,
accept the service of these perjured but patriotic people. ' It
was well enough for the private men, but highly disgraceful to
the character of the officers [5],' he observed, and was pondering
what should be done, and proposing to cashier the officers, when
he received a proclamation from the Regency approving the
conduct of the deserters and restoring them to their place in the
army. Finally he resolved that, since Masséna had obviously
broken the capitulation by his action, it might be held that

[1] The First Portuguese Legion, which served against Austria in 1809,
was composed of the troops drafted out of the Peninsula by Junot in 1808
during his domination at Lisbon.

[2] D'Urban's diary reports that 450 men and 18 officers of the 24th of
the Line came in between the 2nd and 4th of September to Silveira's outposts ; a still larger number reached Wellington's.

[3] D'Urban has most gloomy remarks on the subject in his diary, under
the date Aug. 30.

[4] To Chas. Stuart, from Celorico, Aug. 31.

[5] To Chas. Stuart, from Celorico, Sept. 11.

it was not binding on the prisoners, and ordered the 24th Regiment to be re-formed at its head quarters at Braganza. The militia he dismissed to their homes, on the scruple that the French had let some, though not all of them, go free after the capitulation [1]. There remained the problem of what was to be done with the Portuguese officers who had played a treacherous part on the 27th, especially Barreiros, the negotiator who had betrayed the state of the town to Masséna, and Da Costa, who had headed the mutinous deputation to Cox, which forced him to surrender. Finally, their names were included with those of the officers who had served on Masséna's Portuguese staff during the campaign, in a great indictment placed before a special commission on traitors (called a *Junta de Inconfidencia*), which sat at Lisbon during the autumn. All from D'Alorna downwards were declared guilty of high treason, and condemned to death on December 22, 1810, but only two were caught and executed—João de Mascarenhas, one of d'Alorna's aides de camp, and Da Costa, the lieutenant-governor of Almeida. The former was captured by the Ordenanza while carrying Masséna's dispatches in 1811, and the latter was apprehended in 1812 ; Mascarenhas died by the garotte, Da Costa was shot. Of the others, some never returned to Portugal, the others were pardoned at various dates between 1816 and 1820 [2].

During the siege of Almeida, the British army had been held in a position somewhat less advanced and more concentrated than that which it had occupied in July. Wellington had brought back his head quarters from Alverca to Celorico, where he had the Light Division under his hand. A few miles behind, on the high-road running down the south bank of the Mondego,

---

[1] Wellington to Masséna, Sept. 24. 'Votre excellence s'est engagée que les officiers et les soldats de la milice retourneraient chez eux : malgré cet engagement vous en avez retenu 7 officiers et 200 soldats de chaque régiment, pour en faire un corps de pionniers. La capitulation d'Almeida est donc nulle, et je suis en droit d'en faire ce que je voudrais. Mais je puis vous assurer qu'il n'y a pas un seul soldat de la milice qui était en Almeida au service.'

[2] For details of all this, including the curious terms of the Portuguese sentence for high treason, see Soriano da Luz, iii. 80–109, and 719–22. The attempts to exculpate Barreiros seem inadequate. Da Costa was shot, not for treason, but for cowardice and mutiny.

was the 1st Division, at Villa Cortes. Picton and the 3rd
Division had been drawn back from Pinhel to Carapichina, but
Cole and the 4th remained firm at Guarda. The Portuguese
brigades of Coleman and A. Campbell were at Pinhanços, that of
Pack at Jegua. The whole of the cavalry had come up from
the rear to join the brigade that had recently operated under
Craufurd's orders. They now lay in a thick line of six regiments from in front of Guarda, through Alverca and Freixadas
to Lamegal. Thus the whole army was concentrated on a short
front of fifteen miles, covering the watershed between the Coa
and the Mondego, and the bifurcation of the roads which start
from Celorico, down the two banks of the last-named river.
The French held back, close to Almeida, with a strong advance
guard at Pinhel, and occasionally raided the low country towards
the Douro, in the direction of Villanova de Fosboa and Castel
Rodrigo. About August 19 Wellington moved forward a
day's march, the front of his infantry columns being pushed up
to Alverca and Freixadas, on a false rumour that Masséna was
leaving the 6th Corps unsupported at Almeida, and had drawn
back Junot into the plains of Leon. If this had been the case,
Wellington intended to make a push to relieve the besieged
fortress. But he soon discovered that the report was baseless,
and that the 8th Corps was still on the Azava and the Agueda,
wherefore he halted, and was still lying twelve miles in front of
Celorico when the noise of the explosion at Almeida, and the
cessation of fire on the next day, betrayed the fact that the place
had fallen, and that there was no longer any reason for maintaining a forward position. On the night of the 28th, therefore,
the whole army was drawn back once more to the strong line
between Guarda and Celorico, and arrangements were made for
a further retreat, in case the French should follow up the
capture of Almeida by an instant and general advance. Masséna
seemed at first likely to make this move: on September 2 a
brigade of infantry and 1,200 horse drove in the British cavalry
outposts to Maçal de Chaõ only five miles in front of Celorico.
Looking upon this as the commencement of the serious invasion
of Portugal, Wellington sent back his infantry to Villa Cortes,
Pinhanços, and Moita, far down the high-road on the south of
the Mondego, and bade Cole draw in the 4th Division from

Guarda to San Martinho, under the north side of the Serra da Estrella. Only cavalry were left at, and in front of, Celorico and Guarda. This retreat shows that Wellington was fully convinced that the French would advance along the high-road to the south of the Mondego, where he intended to stand at bay on the Alva, behind the entrenchments of Ponte de Murcella.

The main point of interest at this moment was the movements of the French 2nd Corps, which still lay in cantonments at Zarza and Coria in front of Hill. Guarda being no longer held in force, it was clear that Hill could not safely join the main army by the road Atalaya–Fundão–Guarda, if Reynier moved up by the Pass of Perales to Alfayates and Sabugal. Wellington began an anxious daily correspondence with Hill, giving him a new line of march by Sobreira Formosa, Villa d'el Rei and Espinhal, for his junction, but ordering him to be sure that he did not move till Reynier had thoroughly committed himself to the transference of his whole force to the north of the Sierra de Gata. For it would be disastrous if feints should induce the British detaining force to leave Villa Velha and Abrantes uncovered, and Reynier should turn out to have selected them as his objective, and to be meditating an invasion along the Castello Branco line[1]. It was even possible, though not likely, that Masséna might bring up the 6th and 8th Corps to join Reynier, instead of bringing Reynier across the mountains to join them[2]. But every contingency had to be provided against,

[1] See Wellington to Hill of Aug. 31, Sept. 1, Sept. 4, Sept. 6. The Commander-in-Chief was much worried by a false rumour that Reynier was already in force at Sabugal on Aug. 31, and then by an equally false one that the whole 2nd Corps had marched south towards the Tagus, and was about to cross it near Alcantara (see the letter to La Romana of Sept. 6). As a matter of fact, Reynier made no definite move from Zarza till Sept. 10, though he had made feints, in both the directions indicated, with small forces.

[2] That this possibility was in Wellington's mind is shown by the letter to La Romana of Sept. 6, from Gouvea, in which he writes, ' Vous aurez appris les mouvements du corps de Regnier de la part du Général Hill. Ou l'ennemi va faire le mouvement sur notre droite (dont je vous ai écrit) ou il va faire le siège de Badajoz. On dit que du canon a passé d'Almeida à Sabugal, et de la vers Regnier, mais je ne sais pas si c'est vrai, ou si c'est du canon de siège. . . . Vous savez ce qu'il faut faire si on se met entre nous deux, en passant le Tage à Villa Velha, ou au-dessous de la jonction.

the unlikely ones as well as the likely.   As a corollary to Hill's march, that of Leith had also to be arranged; he must wait at Thomar till it was certain that the 2nd Corps had moved, but the moment that certainty was obtained, must march for Ponte de Murcella, and join the main army, if the French had gone north, but support Hill on the Castello Branco road if they had taken the other, and less probable, course.

NOTE ON ALMEIDA AND THE BRIDGE OF THE COA

THE small circular town of Almeida has never recovered from the disaster of 1810.   The population does not fill up the area within the walls : open spaces are frequent, and some of the more important buildings—especially the old palace of the governor—stand in ruins. Others show solid seventeenth- or eighteenth-century masonry on the ground floor, and flimsy modern repairs above, where the upper stories were blown away by the explosion. The cathedral has never been properly rebuilt, and is a mere fragment. The railway passes twelve miles south of Almeida, so that the place has had no chance of recovery, and remains in a state of decay. The walls stand just as they were left after Wellington's hasty repairs in 1811. The vast bomb-proof shelters repeatedly mentioned in narratives of the siege are still visible, damp but intact. The surrounding country-side is a low, rolling, treeless upland—the edge of the vast plains of Leon.   It contrasts very strongly with the hilly and picturesque scenery that is reached when once the Coa has been passed.

From Almeida the ground slopes down sharply to the place of Craufurd's celebrated skirmish.   The town is not visible after the first mile of the descent towards the deep-sunk gorge through which the Coa cuts its way. The high-road is very bad for artillery, being steep, filled with great stones, and in many places shut in by high banks, which tower above it and make it narrow.   The sharp turn at the end, where it descends to the river with a sudden twist, must have been specially tiresome to a force with cavalry and guns, compelled to a hasty retreat.   All the slopes about the road are cut up into small fields by high walls of undressed stone, without mortar, such as are seen on Cotswold.   The bridge is not visible till the traveller approaching from Almeida has got down to the level of the river : it is completely masked by the high fir-clad knoll described in the text, so long as he is descending the slope above.   From the point where the road swerves aside, to avoid this knoll, there is a rough goat-track down to the still invisible bridge, but this is not available for guns, horses, or *formed* infantry, only for men scrambling individually.

The two-arched bridge is seventy yards long; it crosses the Coa diagonally, with a curious twist in the middle, where there is a little monument recording the reparation of the structure by John VI, in the days after the war was over. There is no mention of Craufurd's fight in the inscription—only a laudation of the King. The bridge crosses the river at a sort of gorge—the place where the rocks on the two sides come nearest. Hence the stream runs under it very fiercely, being constricted to far less than its normal breadth. Up-stream the channel broadens and the passage looks much less formidable, but for some distance on each side of the bridge the river is very rapid, darting between rocks and boulders. The little corner where the few French who passed the bridge found a small angle of dead-ground can be easily identified. It was just to their right after crossing. All the rest of the ground on the west bank could be thoroughly searched by the British guns, which were placed a few hundred yards up the road on the left hand, as well as by the fire of the infantry ensconced among rocks and boulders above the bridge.

Of the French attacking force during the early part of the skirmish, those who were on their left, nearest the river and opposite the 52nd, had far easier ground to cover than those on the right, opposite the 43rd. It is not so high or rough, and less cut up by stone walls. Hence the stress on the 52nd ought to have been the heavier—yet they lost only 22 men to the 129 of the 43rd. The damage to the latter must have been caused partly when the cavalry got in among them, just as the retreat began, partly when they stormed the knoll to cover the retreat of the 52nd.

The scene of the fight is most picturesque on a small scale—one of the prettiest corners in Portugal, all rock, fir-trees, and rushing water.— [Notes made on the spot on April 14, 1906.]

SECTION XX

OPERATIONS IN THE EAST AND SOUTH OF SPAIN DURING THE SPRING AND SUMMER OF 1810

CHAPTER I

SUCHET AND AUGEREAU IN ARAGON, VALENCIA, AND CATALONIA

THOUGH Suchet had successfully pacified the plains of Aragon during the autumn of 1809, and though Augereau in the last month of that year had received the surrender of the much-enduring garrison of Gerona, the position of the French in North-Eastern Spain was still far from satisfactory. It was not yet possible for the 3rd and the 7th Corps to combine their operations. While the broad strip of territory in Western Catalonia reaching from the foot of the Pyrenees to the sea— whose places of strength were Lerida, Tarragona, and Tortosa— still remained intact, Augereau and Suchet could still communicate only by the circuitous route through France : a letter from Saragossa to Barcelona took a fortnight or more to arrive at its destination. It was high time that they should endeavour to get into touch with each other, by cutting through the Spanish line of defence. Both of the corps-commanders had now a comparatively free hand, and could assemble a considerable force for offensive operations. Suchet's position was the happier : he had no Spanish army opposed to him at the moment. His only opponents were—to the West the bold guerrillero Mina the Younger on the borders of Navarre; to the South Villacampa with the dilapidated remains of his band on the side of the Sierra de Albaracin and Molina; and to the East the governor of Lerida, who kept a flying force under Colonel Perena on foot between the Cinca and the Segre, for the encouragement of the insurgents of Eastern Aragon. None of

these three opponents could do any serious mischief to the
3rd Corps, which had risen by the New Year of 1810 to a
strength of 24,000 men [1], now that its drafts from France were
beginning to arrive. Mina was the most tiresome of the three :
he was a young man of untiring energy, and kept the borders of
Navarre in a perpetual ferment, till he was finally put down by
mere force of numbers. For while Suchet sent a number of
columns under General Harispe to hunt him, Lagrange's division
of the newly arrived 8th Corps came down from the side of
Pampeluna, and swept the valleys of the Arga and the Aragon
from the other quarter. Pursued from one refuge to another
by 12,000 men, Mina ended by bidding his followers disperse.
He did not appear again as a combatant till the 8th Corps had
passed on into Castile in the month of February 1810.

Villacampa and Perena being very weak adversaries, Suchet
could now dispose of the greater part of his corps for offensive
operations. Two lines of attack were open to him : the more
natural and obvious one was to attack Lerida or Tortosa, while
Augereau and the 7th Corps moved against them from the other
side. This was Suchet's own intention, and he had received dispatches from Paris which approved of the plan. But another
objective was pointed out to him from another quarter. It will
be remembered that while King Joseph and Soult were planning
the details of their Andalusian expedition, one of the schemes
which they discussed was the use of the 3rd Corps as a flanking
detachment to cover their attack on Seville [2] : it was to march
on Valencia while Mortier marched on Badajoz. The plan was
rejected in favour of the direct frontal march against the passes
of the Sierra Morena. Nevertheless, when the defiles had been
passed, and the King had entered Cordova in triumph, he
recurred to his original scheme, and on January 27 Soult sent
orders to Suchet directing him to make a dash at Valencia, and
assuring him that the demoralization of the Spaniards was so
great that he would probably enter the city without meeting
with much resistance. Similar orders, as we have already seen,

---

[1] Suchet in his *Mémoires* (i. 77) says that in Jan. 1810 his corps was only
20,000 strong. But the imperial muster-rolls show that it had 23,000
présents sous les armes, besides 1,819 men in hospital and 973 detached, in
that month.   [2] See p. 123 of this volume.

were sent to Ney, who was directed at the same moment to make himself master of Ciudad Rodrigo [1], which Soult and the King imagined to be likely to surrender at the first summons.

Suchet, though doubting (as he says) the wisdom of the plan of campaign imposed upon him, prepared to obey, and concentrated 8,000 men, consisting of Laval's division and half that of Musnier, at Teruel, on the borders of Valencia, while Habert, with six battalions more, was to move in a separate parallel column from Alcañiz, and to strike down on to the sea-coast of Valencia by way of Morella. On their way to Teruel some of Laval's columns made a side-stroke at Villacampa, and drove off his band into the mountains of New Castile.

The march on Valencia had already begun, when Suchet received at Teruel, on March 1, the dispatch from the Emperor which announced to him that the kingdom of Aragon had been made an independent 'military government' under his charge [2], and that he was for the future to take no orders from Madrid, but to seek all his instructions from Paris. By the same dispatch Suchet was informed that the Emperor approved of the plan for directing the 3rd Corps against Lerida and the rear of Catalonia which he had himself always advocated. But since Habert's column had already disappeared in the mountains, and could not be recalled, and since his own advanced guard had actually crossed the borders of Valencia, Suchet thought that it was now too late to turn back, and that he must endeavour to carry out Soult's orders, even though they were now countermanded by the Emperor. Accordingly he marched by Sarrion, on the road which leads from Teruel to Segorbe, and from thence to Murviedro on the Valencian coast, where Habert was to join him.

The force opposed to Suchet was that Valencian army which the governor—or rather the dictator—José Caro had so persistently refused to lend to Blake in the preceding autumn for the relief of Gerona. It was about 12,000 strong at the moment, and as some nine months had elapsed since the disaster of Belchite, where the Valencian troops had fared so badly, the regiments had been recruited up to their old strength, and had been thoroughly reorganized and re-equipped. Nevertheless,

---

[1] See p. 222.   [2] See p. 200.

Caro did not wish to risk them in the open field, and, when
Suchet's approach was reported to him, ordered the troops to
prepare to retreat within the walls of the city of Valencia,
which had been so successfully defended against Moncey two
years before. He was probably right in his decision : having
no great superiority of numbers over the French invading
columns, he would have been risking over much if he had
offered battle on the frontier, even in an advantageous position.
Behind the fortifications of Valencia, which had been improved
and enlarged during the last two years, he could at least be
certain of making a long and formidable resistance. If the
enemy appeared without a great battering-train, and unprepared
for a regular siege, the garrison would be absolutely safe.
Accordingly, Caro sent out only a single brigade to observe and
retard Suchet's advance : this force, assisted by some armed
peasants, tried to hold the defile of Alventosa against the
French (March 4), but was beaten out of the position with
ease, lost four guns, and retired by Segorbe and Murviedro on
to Valencia, without offering further resistance. Suchet, following in the wake of the Spanish detachment, reached Murviedro
on March 5, and there met Habert, whose march by Morella
and Castellon-de-la-Plana had been absolutely unopposed.

A day later the French appeared in front of the fortifications
of Valencia. Having surveyed the outworks, and summoned
the place in vain, Suchet found that there was no more to be
done. His bolt was shot : the city intended to defend itself :
it was full of troops, and the whole population had been armed.
Caro had given notice that the defence was to be conducted in
the style of Saragossa, and as a foretaste of his intentions court-
martialled and hanged several persons who were accused of
being traitors [1]. After lying four days in front of Valencia,
Suchet marched off again on the night of March 10–11, having

[1] Whether the Conde de Pozoblanco and the other persons executed
were really traitors is very doubtful. Napier takes them as such (ii. 303),
Suchet denies it (p. 100) ; Schepeler says (iii. 627) that proclamations of
King Joseph and treasonable letters were found in the Count's house.
Toreno (ii. 124) remains doubtful, but points out that Caro and Pozoblanco
were old enemies, and thinks that, at any rate, there was personal spite in
the matter.

convinced himself that he had been sent on a fool's errand by
Soult and King Joseph. For the expedition had only been
undertaken on the hypothesis that the enemy was demoralized
and ready to surrender—which was clearly not the case. No
siege train had been brought, and without heavy artillery
Valencia was impregnable. The retreat of the French was
hastened by the fact that their communications with Aragon
had already been cut off. Villacampa, undismayed by his defeat
in February, had returned to the front the moment that the
invading columns had passed on to the Valencian coast. He
had blockaded the garrison of Teruel, cut off two small columns
which were moving in its neighbourhood, and captured four
guns and some 300 prisoners. At the same moment, though
Suchet was unaware of the fact, Colonel Perena, with a detachment from Lerida, had made a demonstration against Monzon,
and when the garrison of Eastern Aragon concentrated to
defend it, had fallen on Fraga and burnt the bridge there—the
only crossing of the Cinca which was in French hands. Mina,
too, warned of the departure of the main body of the 3rd Corps
for the South, had reassembled some of his levies, and begun to
render the road from Saragossa to Pampeluna once more unsafe.

Suchet, therefore, on withdrawing from Valencia, found plenty
of occupation awaiting him in Aragon. Villacampa was once
more chased into the wilds of the Sierra de Albaracin : and
several columns were detached in pursuit of Mina. This time
the young partisan was unfortunate—he was caught between
one of Suchet's detachments and a party sent out by the governor
of Navarre, and taken prisoner on March 31, with some scores of
his followers. His place, however, was taken ere long by his
uncle Espoz y Mina, who rallied the remnant of the guerrilleros
of North-Western Aragon, and continued the struggle with an
energy as great, and a success far greater, than that of his
nephew.

Meanwhile, the months of February and March had been
wasted, so far as the 3rd Corps was concerned, and it was not
till April that Suchet was able to take in hand the enterprise
which he himself had approved, and to which the Emperor had
now given his consent—the siege of Lerida. A few weeks after
his return to Saragossa he received from Paris two imperial

letters denouncing his late campaign as presumptuous, objectless, and altogether deserving of high condemnation [1].

While the Valencian expedition had been in progress Marshal Augereau had been trying his hand at the Catalan problems which Verdier and St. Cyr had found so puzzling. His luck had been bad—and his faults had been many—for of all the commanders-in-chief who successively endeavoured to subjugate the untameable principality he was decidedly the least capable. When Gerona fell, the main body of his army was let loose for operations in the open field. But Verdier's divisions, on whom the burden of the siege work had fallen, were in much too dilapidated a condition for active service [2]. Leaving them to recover their strength and gather up their convalescents, in cantonments between Figueras and Gerona, Augereau moved southwards in January, at the head of the troops of Souham and Pino, whose two divisions still counted 12,000 bayonets with the eagles, though they left behind them 5,000 sick in the hospitals of Figueras and Perpignan.

The Marshal's main duty at this moment was to clear the road from Figueras to Barcelona, which the Spanish fortress of Gerona had so effectually blocked during the whole year 1809. All further advances were suspended till this operation should have been completed, by the Emperor's special orders. Duhesme, indeed, isolated in Barcelona with some 6,000 men, communicating with France only by sea, and surrounded by a discontented population, which was reduced to semi-starvation by the blockade kept up by the British fleet, was in a perilous condition. There had been many who thought that if Blake, in October 1809, had marched against Barcelona instead of trying to throw succours into Gerona, he would have forced Augereau to abandon the siege of the latter place. For Duhesme would have been in such danger, since he was neither strong enough to fight in the open nor to man efficiently the immense circuit of the walls of Barcelona, that Augereau might

---

[1] Dated from Compiègne on April 9 and April 20. See *Correspondance,* xx. 284 and 299.

[2] In January, Verdier's French and Westphalian divisions could only show 6,000 men in line and 7,000 in hospital. Muster roll of Jan. 15 in the *Archives Nationaux.*

probably have judged that it was better to save the capital of
Catalonia than to continue the interminable blockade of the
smaller town that was holding out so obstinately against him.
Be this as it may, Augereau set Souham's and Pino's columns
on the march early in January 1810, after having first executed
at their head a sort of *battue* of the *somatenes* of the mountains around Gerona, as far as Ripol and Campredon. His
progress was a reign of terror : he had issued on December 28th
a proclamation stating that all irregulars taken with arms in
their hands were to be treated as simple highway robbers, and
hung without any form of trial [1]. He was as good as his word,
and all the prisoners taken by the flying columns of Souham
and Pino were suspended on a line of gallows erected on the
high-road between Gerona and Figueras. These atrocities
turned the war in Catalonia into a struggle even more ferocious
than that of 1809, for the natives, very naturally, retaliated
upon every French straggler that they caught, and the Spanish
regular officers had great difficulty in saving the lives even of
large bodies who had laid down their arms upon formal terms
of surrender.

Two roads lead from Gerona and the valley of the Ter to
Barcelona—that by Vich and that by Hostalrich. They unite near
Granollers, twenty miles outside Barcelona. Augereau marched
with the Italian division of Pino by the second road, while he
sent Souham by the other. Both met with opposition : the
small castle of Hostalrich was still held by the Spaniards—it
was the only fortified place in central Catalonia which was now
in their hands, and commanded, though it did not actually block,
the main road to Barcelona. On arriving before it, the Marshal
ordered Mazzuchelli's Italian brigade to form the siege, trusting
that the place would fall in a few days ; but finding the resistance more serious than he had expected, he finally continued
his march, with the remainder of the Italian division, towards
Granollers and Barcelona. He had ordered Duhesme to come
out to meet him at the former place, with as many of his troops
as he could spare from garrison duty.

---

[1] The text of this bloodthirsty document may be found in Belmas, i. 429.
There are details of its execution in Barckhausen, who mentions that
several priests were among the victims.

Souham meanwhile, on the eastern road, had entered Vich on January 11.   He found that it had just been evacuated by the main body of the Spanish Army of Catalonia, whose head quarters had been maintained in that town all through the later months of the siege of Gerona.   This force, still number- ing about 7,000 men, was no longer under the command of its old general.   Blake had resigned at Christmastide, after a lively altercation with the Junta of Catalonia, who laid the blame for the fall of Gerona on his shoulders, while he maintained that they were to blame for not having ordered the general *levée en masse* of the principality at an earlier date [1].   The command then passed in quick succession to the two senior general officers of the Catalan army, first to the Marquis of Portago, and then, after he had fallen ill, to General Garcia Conde, Governor of Lerida.   But these interim commanders-in-chief were replaced in a few weeks by a younger and much more active leader, Henry O'Donnell—the man who had conducted the second convoy for Gerona, and had cut his way out of the place with such splendid address and resolution.   He had only just been raised to the rank of Major-General, yet was now entrusted by the Central Junta with the control of the entire army of Catalonia.   As he was setting to work to reorganize it, Souham arrived in front of his head quarters.   Judging it unwise to offer battle at the head of demoralized troops, O'Donnell eva- cuated Vich, and fell back to the mountains above it.   Souham followed him with an advanced guard as far as the pass called the Col de Suspina, where the Spaniard suddenly turned upon the pursuing force, and hurled it back with loss upon the main body of the division (January 12, 1810).   He refused, however, to face Souham next day, and retreated towards Manresa; there- upon the French general also turned back, thinking it profitless to leave the Vich–Barcelona road, and to plunge into the hills in pursuit of an evasive enemy.   He ended by making his way across the mountains to join the Marshal.

Meanwhile, Augereau, with Pino's Italian brigades, reached Granollers, and came into touch with Duhesme's troops, just in time to find that a disaster had preceded his arrival.   The Governor of Barcelona, in obedience to the orders sent him, had

---

[1] See pp. 62, 63 of this volume.

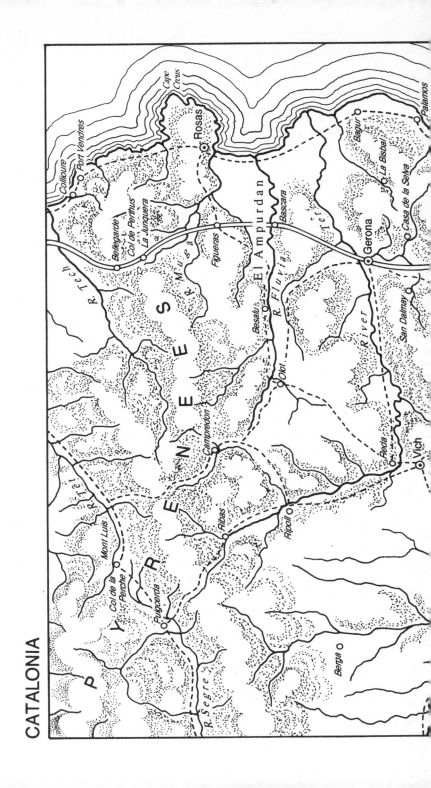

CATALONIA

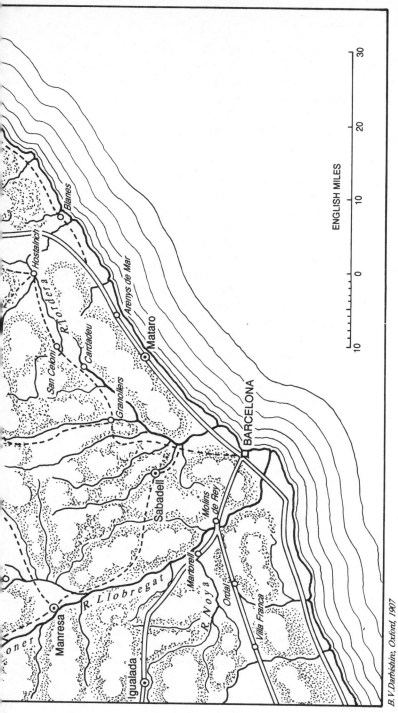

ENGLISH MILES

B. V. Darbishire, Oxford, 1907

marched out on January 16 with three battalions and 250 cuirassiers in order to meet the Marshal. He waited four days at Granollers, and then left the brigade under the charge of Colonel Guétry, and returned in person to Barcelona, recalled by rumours of a threatened attack from the side of Tarragona. On the morning after his departure Guétry's force, which believed itself in complete security, was suddenly surprised in its camps by a detachment sent out by O'Donnell.   That enterprising officer had heard that Augereau was still twenty miles away, and that Guétry had scattered his men in the three villages of Santa Perpetua, Mollet, and Granollers, in order to cover them from the bitter January weather.   Accordingly, he resolved to risk an attack on this unwary detachment.   Two brigades—about 4,000 men—under the Marquis of Campo Verde, made a forced march across the mountains, and fell upon the villages at dawn. The battalion of the 112th in Santa Perpetua was completely cut to pieces or captured—only two men are said to have escaped.   The 7th and the cuirassiers at Mollet fared somewhat better, but were driven back to Barcelona with heavy loss.   Part of the third battalion, one of the 5th Italian Line regiment, which was posted at Granollers, escaped destruction by throwing itself into a fortified convent, and held out for two days, till it was saved by the approach of Augereau along the high-road. Altogether, Duhesme's division was thinned by the loss of 1,000 men on January 21–22 : Guétry had been taken prisoner, with some 600 men more and two guns.   The Spaniards disappeared the moment that Augereau came in sight, and rejoined O'Donnell in the hills.

Augereau entered Barcelona on the twenty-fourth, and at once asserted his authority by deposing Duhesme from the governorship and sending him home to France.   They were old enemies, and the general's friends regarded his disgrace as a display of spite on the part of his superior [1]. But as all the Spanish narratives describe the eighteen-months' dictatorship of Duhesme as having been as much distinguished for private

---

[1] Duhesme, or the friend writing under his name, gives himself most handsome and unconvincing testimonials in the narrative printed in 1823, as part of the *Mémoires sur la Guerre d'Espagne*.   They contrast strangely with Arteche's quotations from Barcelonese local writers.

rapacity as for public oppression, it is probable that the Marshal's action was wholly justifiable. The Emperor, however, refused to sanction the prosecution of the general on the charges laid against him, remarking that such proceedings would give too much pleasure to the Catalans, 'il y avait bien autre chose à faire que de réjouir les Espagnols par cette réaction [1].'

Having concentrated Pino's and Souham's troops at Barcelona, Augereau would have proceeded to advance against the Catalans, and lay siege to Tarragona, but for one fact—the magazines of the city were almost empty, and no food could be procured for the army. Indeed, after a very few days it was necessary for the Marshal to retrace his steps, in order to bring up an enormous convoy for the revictualling of the place, which was being collected at Perpignan and Figueras. All that he had done by his march was to open up the road, and to muzzle the fortress of Hostalrich, which was still being blockaded by the Italians. Accordingly, on February 1 his two divisions marched back each by the way that it had originally taken—Souham to Vich, where he halted, Pino to Gerona, where the convoy began presently to gather, escorted thither in detachments by a large body of reinforcements which had just come up from France. For the Emperor had strengthened the Army of Catalonia by a division of troops of the Confédération of the Rhine, under General Rouyer, and by a Neapolitan brigade—some 8,000 men in all. But the long train of carts and mules came in slowly, and March began before Augereau was ready to move.

Meanwhile, his lieutenant Souham had been exposed to a sudden and unexpected peril. O'Donnell had discovered that the division at Vich was completely isolated and did not count much more than 5,000 sabres and bayonets. Having reorganized his own field army at Moya, near Manresa, and brought it up to a strength of 7,000 foot and 500 horse by calling a few troops from Tarragona, he directed the somatenes of Northern Catalonia to muster on the other side of Vich, so as to fall on Souham from the rear. The indefatigable miquelete leaders Rovira and Milans got together between 3,000 and 4,000 men, despite of all their previous losses and defeats. On February 19 these levies thrust in the pickets of the French division on the eastern

---

[1] Napoleon to Clarke, Compiègne, April 24, 1810.

side, but Souham did not see his danger till, on the following
morning, he found O'Donnell's regular troops pouring down into
the plain of Vich in three columns, and challenging him to a
battle in the open.   Since the day of Valls the Catalan army
had never tried such a bold stroke.

The French general was greatly outnumbered—he had but
4,000 infantry and 1,200 horse to oppose to O'Donnell's 7,500
regulars and the 3,500 miqueletes.   The action fell into two
separate parts—while Rovira and Milans bickered with two
battalions left to guard the town of Vich, Souham fought a
pitched battle against the Spanish main body with the eight
battalions and two and a half regiments of cavalry [1] which constituted the remainder of his force.   It was a fierce and well-
contested fight: O'Donnell took the offensive, and his men
displayed an unwonted vigour and initiative.   Unhappily for
this enterprising general his small body of horsemen was utterly
unable to restrain or to cope with the superior French cavalry.
Twice the battle was turned by the charge of Souham's
squadrons: after the first repulse O'Donnell rallied his beaten
right wing, threw in all his reserves, and tried to outflank the
shorter French line on both sides.   The enemy was losing
heavily and showing signs of yielding, when the whole of his
cavalry made a second desperate charge on the Spanish right.
It was completely successful; O'Donnell's turning column,
composed of the Swiss regiments of Kayser [2] and Traxler, was
broken, and the larger part of it captured.   Thereupon, the
Spanish general, who had displayed undaunted courage throughout the day, and headed several charges in person, thought it
time to retire.   He fell back on the mountains, leaving behind
him 800 killed and wounded, and 1,000 prisoners.   The French

---

[1] 1st Léger (three batts.), 42nd Ligne (three batts.), 93rd Ligne (one
batt.), and 7th Ligne (one batt.).   Meanwhile the other battalion of the 7th
Ligne and that of the 3rd Léger were holding back the miqueletes.   The
cavalry were the 24th Dragoons, 3rd Provisional Chasseurs (soon afterwards
rechristened the 29th Chasseurs), and half the Italian 'Dragoons of
Napoleon.'

[2] This regiment had been formed on the 'cadre' of the old Swiss
regiment of Beschard, by means of deserters from the German and Italian
troops of the French Army of Catalonia.

had suffered at least 600 casualties [1], including Souham himself, desperately wounded in the head, and had been within an ace of destruction : but for their superiority in cavalry, the day was lost.

On March 13, Augereau had at last collected his vast convoy at Gerona—there were more than a thousand waggons laden with flour, besides pack-mules, caissons, carriages, and other vehicles of all sorts. He marched in person to escort it, with the Italians—who were now under Severoli, Pino having gone home on leave,—and the newly arrived German division of Rouyer. Verdier was left behind—as in January - -to defend the Ampurdam from the incursions of the miqueletes of Rovira and Milans. Meanwhile, Souham's division, which had passed into the hands of General Augereau, the Marshal's brother, since its old chief had been invalided to France, pursued a line of march parallel to that of the main force. Moving from Vich by the Col de Suspina and Manresa, it came down into the valley of the Llobregat, on the same day that Pino's and Rouyer's troops reached it by the other route. The Marshal and the main column had made their way past Hostalrich, which was found still unsubdued, and still blockaded by Maz-zuchelli's brigade, which had been left opposite it in January. These troops were ordered to join their division, a mixed detachment under Colonel Devaux being left in their stead to watch the castle. The Marshal then took up his residence in the palace at Barcelona, and had himself proclaimed Governor of Catalonia with great state, in consonance with the imperial decree of February 8, which had taken the principality out of the hands of King Joseph, and made its administrator responsible to Paris alone, and not to Madrid.

Augereau established himself permanently at Barcelona, and proceeded during the next two months to act rather as a viceroy than as a commander-in-chief. The conduct of military operations he handed over to his brother, to the unbounded disgust of the other generals. In what proportions the responsibility

---

[1] Martinien's lists show 29 officers killed and wounded, which, at the usual rate, presupposes about 600 or 700 casualties. Napier, Schepeler, and Arteche all three state the French loss at 1,000 or 1,200—evidently too high.

for the disasters which followed should be distributed between
the two Augereaus it is hard to say.   But Napoleon, very
naturally and reasonably, placed it on the Marshal's shoulders,
and wrote that 'Ce n'est point en restant dans les capitales
éloignées de l'armée que des généraux en chef peuvent acquérir
de la gloire ou mériter mon estime [1].'   The force assembled on
the Llobregat was now a very large one, consisting of three
divisions, those of Augereau, Severoli, and Rouyer.   It numbered nearly 20,000 men, for along with the convoy there had
marched a mass of drafts for the old regiments of the 7th Corps,
which brought their battalions up to full strength [2].

There were only two rational plans of campaign open to the
French : the one was to march on Tarragona with a siege-train,
and to complete the conquest of Catalonia by the capture of
its greatest fortress.   The other was to mask Tarragona, and
to strike across the principality westward, in order to get into
communication with Suchet and the Army of Aragon, by way of
Igualada, Cervera, and Lerida.   If the two corps could meet,
Northern Catalonia would be completely isolated from Tarragona, Tortosa, and Valencia.   It was this latter plan which
Augereau had been ordered to carry out by his master.   He
was directed to march on Lerida, and to join Suchet before that
place.   By a dispatch of February 19 he had been informed
that on March 1 the Army of Aragon would have arrived
before Lerida, and would be forming its siege [3].   This prophecy
was false : for Suchet, as we have seen, had gone off on his
Valencian expedition, and was at Teruel on the appointed day.
It was impossible to direct from Paris a combined movement
depending on accurate timing for its success.   But Augereau
should have attempted to carry out the order sent him by his
master with proper zeal and dispatch.   This he failed to do :
his own inclination was to strike a blow at Tarragona, and the
movements of his corps show that this was the operation which
he had determined to carry out.   Instead of marching in person

---

[1] *Correspondance*, 16411.   From Compiègne, 24 April, 1810.

[2] Severoli's division alone numbered 6,900 foot and 900 horse at the
moment.

[3] Napoleon to Clarke, Feb. 19, from Paris.   Cf. another dispatch of
Feb. 26, no. 16294 of the *Correspondance*.

with his main body, on Cervera and Lerida, he directed his
brother to take his own and Severoli's divisions and to move by
Villafranca on Reus, a large town twelve miles to the north-west
of Tarragona, and suitable as a base of operations against that
city (March 29). A battalion and a half was dropped at Villafranca, to keep open the communications between Reus and
Barcelona, while a brigade of Rouyer's newly arrived Germans,
under the ever-unlucky Schwartz—the vanquished of Bruch and
Esparraguera [1]—was placed as a sort of flank-guard at Manresa.
On March 27 a summons was sent in to Tarragona demanding
surrender. This was, of course, refused—the town was full of
troops, for Henry O'Donnell had just strengthened its garrison
by retiring into it himself, with the 6,000 men who represented
the remains of his field army.

The Spanish general, contemplating the position of affairs
with a wary eye, had convinced himself that he could stop
General Augereau's further movements by striking at his line of
communication with Barcelona. This he proceeded to do in the
most skilful and successful fashion. Before the enemy closed in
upon Tarragona, he sent out a picked force under General Juan
Caro, with orders to attack Villafranca and Manresa without
a moment's delay. This daring stroke was completely successful :
Caro stormed Villafranca at dawn on March 30, and took or
captured the whole of the 800 men posted there. He was
wounded, and had to hand over his command to Campo Verde,
who, after some preliminary skirmishing lasting for three days,
completed the little campaign by driving Schwartz out of
Manresa, after a heavy fight, on April 5, in which the German
brigade lost 30 officers and 800 men [2]. The somatenes turned
out to hunt the routed force as it retired on Barcelona, and
inflicted many further losses, so that Schwartz only brought
back a third of his brigade to the Marshal.

The touch between the two divisions at Reus and the garrison
of Barcelona was thus completely severed. Moreover, Augereau

---

[1] See vol. i. pp. 309–11.

[2] The Lippe-Bückeburg officer Barckhausen says in his diary that only
20 officers and 620 men were lost. But Martinien's lists show 30 officers
of the Nassau, ducal Saxon, and Anhalt-Lippe regiments killed or wounded
at or near Manresa on the 2nd–5th of April.

feared lest the next move of the raiding force might be an attack on the isolated force under Colonel Devaux which was blockading Hostalrich.   He therefore sent out a brig with one of his aides-de-camp on board, bearing orders to his brother and Severoli to return at once to his head quarters with their troops.   By good fortune the messenger reached his destination without being intercepted by English cruisers, and the two divisions started on their march back to Barcelona on April 7. Only two days before, Severoli, more by luck than by skill, had got for a moment into touch with the Army of Aragon.   An exploring column of two battalions under Colonel Villatte, which he had sent out westward to Falcet, in the direction of the Ebro, met—entirely by chance—a similar detachment of Musnier's division of the 3rd Corps, which had advanced to Mora.   On interchanging news of their respective armies, Villatte learnt from his colleague that Suchet was at this moment marching on Lerida, where, according to the Emperor's instructions to Marshal Augereau, he ought to have arrived more than a month before.   Villatte brought back the information to Severoli, but the latter could make no use of it while he was under orders to return without delay to Barcelona [1].   He and General Augereau accomplished their retreat in three days, much harassed on the way, not only by the somatenes of the mountains but also by O'Donnell, who followed them with a detachment of the garrison of Tarragona.   They took some small revenge on him, however, at Villafranca, where they turned on the pursuers and inflicted a sharp check on their advanced guard, which was pressing in, with more courage than discretion, on a force which outnumbered it by four to one.   On April 9 the whole army was encamped outside the walls of Barcelona. Counting the garrison, Augereau had now more than 20,000 men in hand, but, not contented with this concentration, he sent orders back to the Ampurdam, ordering Verdier to bring forward as many troops as possible to Gerona, and from thence to push forward down the high-road as far as Granollers, so as to succour Devaux, if the Spaniards should show any intention of relieving Hostalrich.

The Marshal's next move lost him the favour of Napoleon,

[1] For details of Villatte's expedition see Vacani, iv. 140-1.

and led to his removal in disgrace to Paris. On April 11 he issued orders to Severoli to march on Hostalrich, and there to take over the conduct of the siege from Devaux, while at the same time he himself moved back to Gerona with his brother's French division, and an immense train, consisting partly of the empty carts of the convoy which he had brought south in March, partly of confiscated property of all sorts from Barcelona [1]. Augereau's excuse for this retrograde movement, which abandoned all Central Catalonia to the enemy, was that his army would have exhausted the magazines of Barcelona if he had kept it concentrated for ten days more, and that he had no other way of feeding it, since the activity of the somatenes made the dispatch of foraging detachments utterly impossible. The moral effect of the move was deplorable: after taking in hand an offensive movement against Tarragona, he had allowed himself to be checked by an enemy hopelessly inferior in numbers, had lost over 3,000 men in petty combats, and then had retired to the base from which he had started in January. Three months had been wasted, and nothing had been gained save that the small castle of Hostalrich was now in a desperate condition for want of food, and must fall if not speedily succoured. What rendered the position of Augereau the more shameful was that he had now in front of him only a skeleton enemy. For O'Donnell at this moment was distracted by the advance of Suchet against Lerida, and had been forced to draw off towards the borders of Aragon two of the four divisions into which he had reorganized his little field army. Facing Augereau there was only Campo Verde's division of regulars—not over 5,000 strong—and the bands of the mountains. It was against such an enemy that the Marshal had concentrated 25,000 men—including Verdier's force—between Hostalrich and Gerona.

The food-problem, on which those who defend Augereau lay all the stress possible [2], was no doubt a very real one.

---

[1] According to Spanish accounts this included much ill-gotten property belonging to the Marshal himself, and other superior officers. Ferrer (see Arteche, viii. 203) declares that Augereau carried off all the furniture of the Royal Palace.

[2] For a defence of the Marshal on these lines, see *Victoires et Conquêtes*, vol. xx. pp. 52–3.

The feeding of Barcelona, with its garrison and its large civil population, by means of convoys brought from France, was no easy task.   But it seems clear that with the large force at his disposition—the 7th Corps was over 50,000 strong [1]— Augereau could have organized convoy-guards sufficiently powerful to defy the Spaniards, without abandoning the offensive position in front of Barcelona, which was all-important to him.   He might have set aside 10,000 men for that purpose, and still have kept a strong field army together.   Had he done so, O'Donnell could not have dared to march with 8,000 men, the pick of the Catalan army, to relieve Lerida, while his old enemies were massed, awaiting an impossible attack, a hundred miles away.

Meanwhile, the one task which was completed by the 7th Corps during the months of April and May was the reduction of Hostalrich.   The little castle was a place of strength, perched high above the abandoned town to which it belonged.   It was garrisoned by two battalions, one of Granadan regulars from Reding's old division, the other of local Catalan levies [2], under Colonel Juliano Estrada, an officer of high spirit and commendable obstinacy.   To the first summons made to him in January by Augereau, he had replied that 'Hostalrich was the child of Gerona, and would know how to emulate the conduct of the mother-city.'   Nor was this high-flown epigram belied by the after-conduct of the garrison.   Hostalrich held out from January 16 to May 12 without receiving either a convoy from without or any reinforcements.   Twice the local miqueletes attempted to pass succours into the castle, but on each occasion they were driven off, after having barely succeeded in communicating with Estrada.   Their convoys never got close enough to enter the gates.   At last, on May 12, the provisions of the place were completely exhausted : thereupon Estrada took in hand a scheme which was only tried by one other governor during the whole Peninsular War—the Frenchman Brennier at Almeida in May 1811.   He put every ablebodied man of the garrison under arms at midnight, issued

---

[1] About 56,000 in all, but 10,000 were in hospital or detached.

[2] One battalion of Iliberia (or 1st of Granada) and one tercio of levies from the province of Gerona : total strength about 1,200 bayonets.

silently from the castle, and charged at the besiegers' lines, with the intention of cutting his way through to Campo Verde's head quarters in the mountains. He was fortunate enough to pierce the Italian outposts at the first rush. But two whole brigades were presently at his heels, his guides lost their way among cliffs and ravines, and he was overtaken. Turning back with his rearguard to fend off the pursuers, he was wounded and taken prisoner. Ten other officers and some 300 soldiers shared his fate : the rest of the garrison dispersed in the hills, and reached Vich in small parties to the number of 800 men. If only their gallant commander had escaped with them, the exploit would have been an exact parallel to the Almeida sortie of 1811.

The reduction of Hostalrich and of a small fort on the Isles of Las Medas near the mouth of the Ter, were the last achievements of the Army of Catalonia while it was under the command of Augereau. On April 24 the Emperor had resolved to remove him from his post, and had ordered Marshal Macdonald, Duke of Tarentum, to relieve him. In the *Moniteur* it was merely stated that the elder Marshal had been forced by ill-health to resign his charge. But the real causes of his displacement are plainly stated in Napoleon's letter to the Minister of War. They were the blow which he had given to the imperial prestige by his retreat to Gerona, and his disobedience in having failed to march on Lerida in aid of Suchet. It must be confessed that the wrath of the Emperor was justifiably roused. Its final manifestation took the shape of a minute directing that when the *Moniteur* published the news of the successes at Hostalrich and Las Medas, the name of Augereau was to be kept out of the paragraph, and only those of his subordinates mentioned [1].

While the new commander of the 7th Corps was on his way from Italy to Perpignan, and for some time after his arrival on May 22, there was a complete suspension of active operations. None of the French generals in the principality could do more than await orders, and keep the neighbourhood of his cantonments safe from the irrepressible miqueletes. The whole interest

[1] See *Correspondance*, 16411, Napoleon to Clarke, of April 24, and 16500, same to same of May 23.

of the French operations in North-Western Spain during this
period turns on the movements of the Army of Aragon.

On returning from his futile Valencian expedition, Suchet had
found awaiting him at Saragossa orders to commence without
delay the siege of Lerida, and promising that Augereau would
' contain ' the Spanish army of Catalonia, and would ultimately
open up communication with him by way of Cervera or Momblanch.   In obedience to the imperial mandate, the commander
of the 3rd Corps collected more than half his troops for the
expedition against Lerida.   This concentration entailed the
abandonment of the rough country of Southern Aragon to Villacampa and his bands ; for having determined to leave only
Laval's division behind him to protect the central parts of
the province, Suchet had to evacuate the region of Teruel,
Albaracin and Montalvan.   Laval's two brigades remained in the
valley of the Jiloca, between Saragossa and Daroca, watching the
debouches from the mountains.   The other two divisions of the
Army of Aragon were destined for the siege of Lerida.   Musnier,
with one column, marching down from Caspe and Alcañiz [1],
crossed the Ebro at Flix, and approached Lerida from the south.
Habert, with his division, coming from the side of Saragossa,
made for the same goal by way of Alcubierre and Monzon.   It
might seem a dangerous experiment to march the two isolated
columns across the Spanish front, for a junction at a point so
remote from their respective starting-points.   But, for the
moment, there was no hostile force of any importance in their
neighbourhood.   Severoli and Augereau being still at Reus,
when Musnier and Habert started on their way, O'Donnell could
spare no troops for the relief of Lerida.   It was not till they
had retired, and the Duke of Castiglione had withdrawn all his
forces to Hostalrich and Gerona, that the Captain-General found
himself free for an expedition to the West.   In front of Musnier,
while he was marching on Lerida, there were nothing but trifling
detachments sent out for purposes of observation by the Governor
of Tortosa.   In front of Habert there were only 2,000 men under
Colonel Perena, thrown out from Lerida to observe the open

---

[1] It was with a detachment of this column that Severoli's flanking party
under Villatte got into communication on April 4, as detailed above,
page 296.

country between the Segre and the Cinca. This was the sole field-force which remained from the old Spanish Army of Aragon, with the exception of the two dilapidated regiments that formed the nucleus of Villacampa's band.

On April 10, Suchet arrived at Monzon with a brigade of infantry, and the six companies of artillery and four of engineers which were destined for the siege of Lerida. On the thirteenth he was before the walls of the place on the west bank of the Segre, while on the next day Habert appeared on the other bank, driving before him Colonel Perena and his battalions. This second French column had passed the Segre at Balaguer, from which it had expelled the Spanish brigade. Perena, having the choice between returning into the mountains or strengthening the garrison of Lerida, had taken the latter alternative. On the same day Musnier came up from the South, and joined the army with the force that had started from Alcañiz and had crossed the Ebro at Flix. Suchet had now concentrated the whole of the 13,000 men [1] whom he destined for the siege.

The town of Lerida, then containing some 18,000 inhabitants, lies in a vast treeless plain on the western bank of the broad and rapid Segre. Its topography is peculiar : out of the dead level of the plain rise two steep and isolated hills. One of these, about 800 yards long by 400 broad, and rising 150 feet above the surrounding flats, is crowned by the citadel of the town ; the other, somewhat longer but rather narrower, is no other than the hill about which Caesar and Afranius contended in the old Civil Wars of Rome, when Lerida was still Ilerda. It lies about three-quarters of a mile from the first-named height. In 1810 its culminating summit was covered by a large work called Fort Garden, and its southern and lower end was protected by the two small redoubts called San Fernando and El Pilar. The town occupies the flat ground between the citadel-height and the river. It has no transpontine suburb, but only a strong

[1] For his strength at this moment, see the table which he gives in his *Mémoires*, vol. i, Appendix 4. His figures cannot always be trusted : for instance, purporting in this table to give his whole force, present at Lerida or detached in Aragon, he omits the six squadrons of gendarmerie which were guarding his rear [37 officers, 1,121 men] and the four battalions of *Chasseurs des Montagnes*, who were garrisoning Jaca, Venasque, &c. [about 2,000 men].

tête-du-pont on the other side of the Segre. The strength of the place lay in the fact that its whole eastern front was protected by the river, its whole western front by the high-lying citadel. The comparatively short southern front was under the guns of Fort Garden, which commanded all the ground over which an enemy could approach this side of the town. There only remained, unprotected by outer works, the northern front, and this was the point which a skilful enemy would select as his objective. Another fact which much favoured the defence was that the besieger was forced to make very long lines of investment, since he had to shut in not only the town, but the whole plateau on which lie Fort Garden and its dependent works. Moreover, he must keep a force beyond the Segre, to block the *tête-du-pont*, and this force must be a large one, because the east was the quarter from which succours sent from Catalonia must certainly appear. The garrison, on the other hand, was quite adequate to man the works entrusted to it ; the entry into the town of Perena's Aragonese battalions had brought it up to a strength of over 8,000 men. The artillery were the weak point—there were only 350 trained men to man over 100 pieces. The Governor was Major-General Garcia Conde, who owed his promotion to his brilliant achievements at Gerona in the preceding September.

Suchet's 13,000 men were insufficient for a close and thorough investment of such a large space as that covered by the Lerida-Garden fortifications. He was forced to leave a considerable part of its southern front watched by cavalry posts alone. Of his total force, Musnier, with six battalions and the greater part of the cavalry—about 4,000 men in all, was beyond the river. Three battalions blocked the *tête-du-pont*, the rest formed a sort of covering force, destined to keep off the approach of enemies from the side of Catalonia. On the hither side of the Segre the three brigades of Habert, Buget, and Vergès were encamped facing the western and north-western fronts of Lerida. They counted only thirteen battalions, being weakened by 1,200 men who had been detached to garrison Monzon and Fraga. The communication between Musnier's division and the rest of the army was by a flying bridge thrown across the Segre two miles above the town ; it was guarded by a redoubt. The artillery park was placed at the village of San Rufo, opposite the north-western angle of the town, from which it is distant about 2,500 yards. It was evident from the first that this would be the point of attack selected by the French engineers.

The army had barely taken up its position when, on April 19, rumours were spread abroad that O'Donnell was on his way to relieve Lerida. They must have been pure guesses, for the Spanish general on that day was still at Tarragona and had made no movement. They were, however, sufficiently persistent to induce Suchet to take off Musnier's covering corps, strengthened by three other battalions, on a mission of exploration, almost as far as Tarrega, on the Barcelona road. No Spanish force was met, nor could any information be extracted from the inhabitants. The absence of the troops on the left bank of the Segre was soon detected by Garcia Conde, who—to his great regret three days later—sent messengers to inform O'Donnell that the French lines to the east of the city were now almost unoccupied.

The fiery O'Donnell was already on his way when this news reached him. The moment that he was sure that Augereau had left Barcelona and was retreating northward, he had resolved to fly to the relief of Lerida with the two divisions of which he could dispose. On the twentieth he marched from Tarragona by Valls and Momblanch, with 7,000 regular infantry, 400 horse, a single battery, and some 1,500 miqueletes. On the twenty-third he had reached Juneda, twelve miles from Lerida, without having seen a French picket or having been detected himself. He intended to drive off the few battalions blocking the bridge-head, and to open up communication with the besieged town that same day. Unfortunately for him, Suchet and Musnier had returned on the previous night from their expedition to Tarrega, and were now lying at Alcoletge, three miles north of the bridge-head, with seven battalions and 500 cuirassiers.

Pushing briskly forward along the high-road, in a level tree-less plateau, destitute of cover of any kind, the leading Spanish division—that of Ibarrola—came into contact about midday with the small force guarding the bridge-head, which was now in charge of Harispe, Suchet's chief-of-the-staff. To the surprise of the Spaniards, who had expected to see these three battalions and two squadrons of hussars retire in haste, the French showed

fight. Harispe was aware that Musnier could come up to his
aid within an hour, and was ready for battle. His hussars
charged the leading regiment of Ibarrola's column, and threw it
into disorder, while his infantry formed up in support. At this
moment the Spanish general received news that Musnier was
moving in towards his flank ; he therefore retired, to get the
support of O'Donnell, who was following him with the second
division. But at the ruined village of Margalef, six miles from
Lerida, the column of Musnier came up with Ibarrola, and he
was so hard pressed that he formed line, with 300 cavalry on his
right wing and his three guns on his left. The position was as
bad a one as could be found for the Spanish division—a dead flat,
with no cover. Musnier, on reaching the front, flung his cavalry,
500 cuirassiers of the 13th regiment, at the Spanish right wing.
The horsemen placed there broke, and fled without crossing
sabres, and the French charge fell on the flank battalion of the
infantry, which was caught while vainly trying to form square.
It was ridden down in a moment, and the horsemen then rolled
up the whole line, regiment after regiment. A great part of
Ibarrola's corps was captured, and O'Donnell, who came on the
field with the division of Pirez just as the disaster took place,
could do no more than retire in good order, covering the scattered
remnants of his front line. A Swiss battalion, which he told off
as his rearguard, was pierced by the cuirassiers and for the most
part captured. In this disastrous affair the Spaniards lost 500
killed and wounded and several thousand prisoners [1], as also four
flags and the half-battery belonging to Ibarrola's division. The
French, of whom the cavalry alone were seriously engaged, are

---

[1] Suchet says that he took 5,600 prisoners, a figure that appears quite
impossible, as Schepeler rightly remarks (iii. 649). Ibarrola's division had
only 4,000 bayonets, and of that of Pirez only the one Swiss battalion was
seriously engaged. Moreover, Ibarrola's division was not absolutely
exterminated, for O'Donnell on April 26 issued an order of the day, in
which he thanks the division for its courage, and praises the battalions
which kept their ranks and re-formed behind those of Pirez, ' returning
in good order to occupy the position (Juneda), from which they had started
at dawn.' See the document, printed in Arteche's Appendix, no. 12 of
vol. viii. I should doubt if 2,000 prisoners were not nearer the mark
than 5,600.

said by Suchet to have had no more than 23 killed and 82 wounded [1].

It is clear that O'Donnell must take the blame for the ruin that fell upon his little field army. He should not have been caught with his two divisions marching with an interval of four miles between them. Nor ought he to have been ignorant of the return of Musnier's force, considering that he had 400 cavalry, who should have been exploring the whole country-side for miles around, instead of riding in a mass along with Ibarrola's infantry. The carelessness shown was unpardonable : relying, apparently, on Garcia Conde's dispatch—now two days old—concerning the weakness of the French beyond the Segre, the Spanish general was caught moving as if for an unopposed entry into Lerida, instead of in battle order. It may be added that he would have done well to collect more men before advancing against Suchet—8,000 bayonets and sabres were too small a force to tackle the main body of the 3rd Corps, even if they were aided by a sortie from Lerida, as O'Donnell had intended. It would have been well to make some endeavour to get troops from the Valencian army, whose 12,000 men were absolutely idle at the moment. It is true that José Caro and the Valencian Junta were very chary of sending their men outside their own border. But for such a great affair as the relief of Lerida a brigade or two might have been borrowed. There was a considerable Valencian force, at the moment, in the neighbourhood of Alcañiz.

After the combat of Margalef Suchet summoned Lerida for a second time, and offered to allow the Governor to see the prisoners and guns which he had taken from O'Donnell. Garcia Conde very rightly answered that he relied on his own forces alone, and should fight to the end. Accordingly, the regular siege began. The trenches were opened opposite the north front of the town on April 29 ; several days of heavy rain hindered the completion of the first parallel, but on May 7 the breaching batteries were ready and the bombardment began. The front attacked—the Carmen and Magdalena bastions—was weak : it was not protected by any flanking fires, and had neither a ditch

---

[1] Figures probably correct. Martinien's lists show one officer killed and two wounded ; of the latter, one was the cavalry general Boussard.

nor a covered way. It was bound to succumb before the very
heavy fire directed against it, unless the defence should succeed
in beating down the fire of the breaching batteries. The
Spaniards did their best, bringing up every gun that could be
mounted, and replacing each injured piece as it was disabled.
But the end was obvious from the first : the walls were not strong
enough to resist the attack.

Meanwhile, Suchet made two successive assaults on a part of
the defences very far distant from the main front of attack—the
two isolated redoubts which stood on the south end of the extra-
mural plateau, of which Fort Garden formed the main protection.
He wished to gain a footing on this high ground, both because
he could from thence molest the south front of the town, and
because he wished to prevent the Spaniards from using the
plateau as a place of refuge after the fall of the city, which he
regarded as inevitable. The first attempt to take the works by
escalade, on the night of April 23–24, was a disastrous failure :
the Pilar was occupied for a moment, but the attack on San
Fernando failed, and the dominating fire from it drove the
stormers out of the smaller work, after they had held it for
a few hours.

The second escalade was more successful : it was carried out
on the night of May 12–13, and ended in the storming of both
works. Only a small part of their garrison succeeded in escaping
into Fort Garden : the besieged lost 300 men, the successful
assailants only 120. The greater part of the plateau was now
in the hands of the French.

On the next day, May 13, the engineers announced that the
two breaches in the north front of the town walls were practicable,
and that same evening Lerida was stormed. The breaches were
carried with no great difficulty, but the garrison made a stubborn
resistance for some time, behind traverses and fortified houses in
the rear of them. When these were carried, the city was at
Suchet's mercy ; but it was not at the city alone that he was
aiming—he wished to master the citadel also. During the last
siege of Lerida, that by the Duke of Orleans in 1707, the high-
lying castle had held out for many days after the town had been
lost. Suchet's way of securing his end was effective but brutal.
On the whole, it was the greatest atrocity perpetrated by any

combatant, French, Spanish, or English, during the whole
Peninsular War.   When his troops had entered the streets, he
directed columns towards each gate, and having secured possession
of them all, so as to make escape into the open country impossible,
bade his troops push the whole non-combatant population of
Lerida up-hill into the citadel, where the beaten garrison was
already taking refuge.   'The soldiery,' as he writes, with evident
complacency and pride in his ingenuity, ' were set in a concentric
movement to push the inhabitants, along with the garrison,
towards the upper streets and the citadel.   They were dislodged
by musketry fire from street after street, house after house, in
order to force them into the castle.   That work was still firing,
and its discharges augmented the danger and the panic of the
civil population, as they were thrust, along with the wreck of
the garrison, into the ditch and over the drawbridge.   Pressed
on by our soldiers, they hastily poured into the castle yard,
before the Governor had time to order that they should not be
allowed to enter.'   The castle being crammed with some fifteen
thousand men, women, and children, Suchet gave orders to
bombard it with every available mortar and howitzer.   ' Every
shell,' he writes, ' that fell into the narrow space containing this
multitude, fell on serried masses of non-combatants no less than
of soldiery.   It had been calculated that the Governor and the
most determined officers would be influenced by the presence of
these women, children, old folk, and unarmed peasants.   As
General Suchet had flattered himself would be the case, the
scheme had a prompt and decisive effect.'   On the 14th at midday, Garcia Conde, unable to stand the slaughter any longer,
hoisted the white flag.

It is difficult to see how the forcing of thousands of non-
combatants, by means of musketry fire, on to the front of the
enemy's line of defence, differs in any way from the device, not
unknown among African savages and Red Indians [1], of attacking
under cover of captured women and children thrust in upon the
weapons of their fathers and husbands.   The act places that
polished writer and able administrator Louis-Gabriel Suchet on
the moral level of a king of Dahomey.   He acknowledges that
the plan was deliberately thought out, and that scores of his

[1] One or two cases can also be quoted from the European Middle Ages.

victims perished not in the subsequent bombardment, but by being shot down by his own men while the crowd was being collected and hunted forward [1]. Historians have denounced the atrocities committed by the French rank and file at Tarragona or Oporto, by the English rank and file at Badajos or St. Sebastian, but the cultured general who worked out this most effective plan for the reduction of a hostile citadel has never had his due meed of shame. Napier's remark that, ' though a town taken by assault is considered the lawful prey of a licentious soldiery, yet this remnant of barbarism does not warrant the driving of unarmed and helpless people into a situation where they must perish,' seems a sufficiently mild censure, when all the circumstances are taken into account [2].

The total number of Spanish troops surrendered by Garcia Conde in the Citadel and Fort Garden, or captured by the French during the storm, amounted to over 7,000 men, of whom about 800 were wounded lying in the hospital. It was calculated that 1,200 or 1,500 more had perished during the siege, and that about 500 of the civil population had fallen victims to Suchet's barbarous device. The French losses during the whole series of operations had been 1,100 killed and wounded. The Spaniards declared that Garcia Conde had betrayed Lerida, and ought never to have surrendered. But the only ground for this accusation was that, after a short captivity, he did homage to King Joseph, and became an *Afrancesado*. Though he had shown dash and courage at Gerona, it is clear that he lacked the firmness of governors such as Mariano Alvarez, or Andrés Herrasti. His defence of Lerida had not been particularly skilful nor particularly resolute : with over 8,000 men within the walls he ought to have been able to hold out longer against Suchet's 13,000. The most blameworthy part of his arrangements was his neglect to retrench the breaches, and to form a strong second line of temporary works behind them. Alvarez, under similar conditions, and with a garrison far less strong in comparison to the besieging army, held out for months after his walls had been breached, simply because he treated them only as an outer line of resistance, and was prepared to fight on behind his inner defences.

[1] Suchet, *Mémoires*, i. pp. 147–8.   [2] Napier, ii. 322.

After the fall of Lerida, Suchet, having received through France the news that the whole of Augereau's army was collected in the neighbourhood of Hostalrich and Gerona, made up his mind that he had better attempt nothing ambitious until the 7th Corps was in a position to help him. But there was a small task close to his hand, which was well worth undertaking in a moment of enforced leisure. This was the siege of Mequinenza, the only fortress left in Spanish hands on the eastern side of Aragon. It was a small place, but not without its strategic importance, for not only did it cover the junction of the Segre and the Ebro, but it was the highest point open for navigation on the last-named river. Any one holding Mequinenza can use the Ebro as a high-road, except in times of drought, and this was an advantage of no small importance, since the country from thence to the sea chances to be singularly destitute of roads of any kind. A few months later, Suchet found the place invaluable, as he was able to prepare his battering-train for the siege of Tortosa within its walls, and then to send all the heavy material down-stream with the minimum of trouble. Mequinenza was a small place, consisting of a few hundred houses along the river bank enclosed by a weak and old-fashioned wall, but dominated by a strong castle, which towers 500 feet above the water at the end of a spur of the Sierra de Montenegre. The garrison consisted of about 1,000 men, under a Colonel Carbon.

The very day after Lerida had fallen, Suchet sent a brigade to invest Mequinenza : more troops followed after an interval. It was clear that the taking of the town would offer small difficulty : but the castle was another matter. Its defences were independent of those of the place below, and its site was so lofty and rocky that it could not be battered from any ground accessible by existing roads. Indeed, it could only be approached along the crest of the Sierra, of which it forms the last lofty point. The main interest of the siege of Mequinenza lies in the fact that, in order to reduce the castle, the French engineers had to build a road practicable for heavy guns in zig-zags up the side of the Sierra. They had arrived in front of the place on May 15 : by June 1 the road was completed : it was a piece of hard work, as in order to utilize the easiest possible slopes it had been made no less than five miles long. But when the guns had once been

got up on to the crest of the mountain, Mequinenza—town and
castle alike—was doomed. The town was stormed on June 5 ;
it might have been captured long before, but there was little
use in taking possession of it until the attack upon the castle
had been begun. Before the storm, Colonel Carbon had wisely
ordered all the large river craft in the place, eleven in number,
to run down-stream to Tortosa ; he was well aware that Suchet
wanted to open up the navigation of the Ebro, and was resolved
that he should find no vessels ready for him. Two of the craft
ran ashore and were captured ; the other nine got off clear.

When the three batteries erected on the summit of the
Sierra opened on the castle, the walls began to crumble at once.
At the end of eight days its front towards the French trenches
was a mass of shapeless ruins. Carbon then surrendered, without waiting for an assault, which must undoubtedly have proved
successful. There was nothing particularly obstinate, or, on
the other hand, particularly discreditable, in the defence. The
castle was not a modern fortress; its sole strength had lain in
its inaccessible position ; and when the French had climbed up
on to a level with it, nothing more could be done.

Having mastered Lerida and Mequinenza, and obtained a
firm footing in the plain of Western Catalonia, Suchet had now
harder work before him. His first necessity was to clear the
country behind him of the insurgents, who had swarmed down
from the hills to attack the troops left behind in Central
Aragon, while the main army had been concentrated before
Lerida. Villacampa had half destroyed a column of 350 men
at Arandija on the Xalon on May 14. Catalan somatenes had
attacked the garrison of the valley of Venasque, on the very
frontier of France, on May 16. Valencian bands had besieged
the castle of Alcañiz for many days. But all the enemies of
Suchet had to fly, as soon as his main army became once more
free for field service. No attempt was made to oppose a serious
resistance to his movable columns : the insurgents fled to right
and left : the most extraordinary proof of their demoralization
was that, on June 13, General Montmarie, at the head of one of
these columns, found the strong fort of Morella, within the
Valencian border, absolutely unoccupied. He seized and
garrisoned it, knowing that this place, which commands the

mountain-road from Aragon to Valencia, was of immense strategical importance.

When June came round, Suchet had once more mastered all Aragon, and was free for work outside its borders. A march against Valencia, on the one side, or against Tortosa and Tarragona on the other, was equally possible. But at this moment Napoleon was set on proceeding ' methodically '—in Eastern Spain no less than in Portugal—and the orders issued to the Commander of the 3rd Corps were, to proceed against Tortosa, and cut off Valencia from Catalonia by its capture. The longer and more difficult advance against Valencia itself was relegated to a distant date ; there must be no more fiascos like that of February. Accordingly, Suchet was ordered to follow up the capture of Lerida and Mequinenza by the reduction of Tortosa [1]. He was informed at the same time that Macdonald, the new commander of the Army of Catalonia, was ordered to attack Tarragona. In this way, the restless O'Donnell would find his hands full at home, and would not be able to spare time or men for the relief of Tortosa. Only from the Valencian Army, which had always been badly led, and managed with the most narrow particularism by José Caro and his Junta, need Suchet expect any trouble.

But until Macdonald was prepared to lead down his corps to the neighbourhood of Tarragona and the lower Ebro, Suchet felt that his own enterprise must be held back, or at least conducted with caution. And although Macdonald had received his orders in May, on taking over Augereau's post, it was some time before he was able to execute them. June and July had passed, and August had arrived, before he appeared in the regions where Suchet had been told to expect him, and at last placed himself in communication with the Army of Aragon. This long delay was entirely due to the burden imposed upon him by the necessities of Barcelona, with its large garrison and its vast civil population. The provisions which Augereau had introduced into the city in the early spring were exhausted, and his successor was forced to replace them by escorting thither two new convoys of great size in June and July. So active were the miqueletes that Macdonald found himself obliged to

[1] Napoleon to Berthier, *Correspondance*, May 29, 1810,

take with him his French and his Italian division as escort on each occasion.   For a first-class convoy is a vast affair, stretching out to long miles in a mountain country, and requiring to be strongly guarded at every point of its unwieldy length.   The Emperor was bitterly disappointed at Macdonald's delays: it was hard to convince him that the problem of food-supply in Catalonia was almost insoluble, and that neither Barcelona nor the field army could be permanently fed by seizing the resources of the valley of the Llobregat, or the Campo of Tarragona, and making war support war in the regular style.   Catalonia had never fed its whole population even in time of peace, but had largely depended on corn brought up from Aragon or imported by sea.   But the British Mediterranean squadron now made the transport of food to Barcelona by water impossible, while, till the 3rd Corps and the 7th Corps should finally meet, it was impossible to supply the latter from the Aragonese base. While neither of the normal ways of procuring a regular supply of provisions was practicable, nothing remained but the weary task of escorting convoys from Perpignan and Figueras to Barcelona.   This Macdonald accomplished thrice, in June, July, and August : it was only after the third journey that he left the storeshouses of Barcelona so thoroughly replenished that he was able to think of further offensive operations, and to concert the long-delayed junction with Suchet and the 3rd Corps.   The Marshal in his autobiography confesses that he hated the task set him, and found it entirely out of the lines of his experience.   He began his career by repealing Augereau's hanging edicts, and endeavoured to introduce more humane methods of warfare.   But his own men were out of hand, and the Spaniards being as fierce as ever, his task was a very hard one.

Meanwhile, Henry O'Donnell was granted three months in which to reorganize the Catalan army, which had suffered so severely at Margalef.   His untiring energy enabled him to raise his force by the end of July to 22,000 men, organized in five divisions, with which he formed a double front, facing Suchet on the west and Macdonald on the east.   One division under Campo Verde lay northward in the mountains, with head quarters at Cardona, and detachments pushed forward as far as

Urgel and Olot : its main task was to harass the French
garrison of the Ampurdam, and to threaten Macdonald's rear
every time that he moved forward towards Barcelona.   A second
division lay facing that city, on the lower Llobregat, with
detachments at Montserrat and Manresa, which kept up the
communications with Campo Verde and the North.   Two more
divisions lay westward, in the direction of Falcet and Borja Blanca,
watching Suchet, and prepared to oppose any serious attempt on
his part to close in upon Tortosa.   The fifth division, or reserve,
formed a central mass of troops, ready to reinforce either the
detachments which watched Suchet or those which watched
Macdonald ; it lay south of Tarragona, at the Col de Alba.   Thus
posted O'Donnell waited for further developments, and continued
to drill and exercise his new levies, to dismiss inactive and incompetent officers, to collect magazines, and to quarrel with the
local Junta.   For this active and intelligent, if reckless and
high-handed, young officer was on even worse terms with the
Catalan authorities than his predecessor, Blake.   The main
cause of quarrel was that O'Donnell wished to strengthen his
regular troops, by drafting into the depleted *cadres* of Reding's
and Coupigny's old battalions every recruit that he could catch.
He held that the French could only be brought to a final
check by disciplined troops.   The Junta, on the other hand,
believed in guerrilla warfare, and preferred to call out from
time to time the miqueletes and somatenes, who drifted back
to their homes whenever a crisis was over.   Both sides had
much to say for themselves : the Catalans could point out
that the regular troops had been beaten times out of number,
while their own irregulars had achieved many small successes,
and done the French much harm.   O'Donnell, on the other
hand, was quite right in holding that guerrilla operations,
much as they might incommode the enemy, would never deal
him a fatal blow or finish the war.   He dreamed of recruit-
ing his army up to a force of 50,000 men at some happy
future date, and of delivering a stroke with superior numbers
which should destroy the French hold on Catalonia.   Meanwhile, much as they quarrelled, the Irish-Spanish general
and the local Junta were both too good haters of France to
allow their disputes to prevent a vigorous resistance from

being kept up in the principality.   O'Donnell carried his point
to the extent of persuading the Junta to allow him to form
many of the ever-changing tercios of miqueletes into 'legions,'
which were to be kept permanently embodied [1], and to count as
part of the regular army.   Hence came the large rise in his
muster-rolls.

[1] To please the Catalans, who hated the idea of long service, the
enlistment in the Legions was made for two years only, and the men
were to be entitled to fifteen days' leave during each half-year of service.

SECTION XX: CHAPTER II

OPERATIONS IN THE SOUTH OF SPAIN DURING THE
SPRING AND SUMMER OF 1810

THE situation which had been created by King Joseph's rapid conquest of the open country of Andalusia in January and February 1810, and by his failure to capture Cadiz, was destined to remain unchanged in any of its more important details for a full year. Soult, with the three corps of Victor, Sebastiani, and Mortier, was strong enough to hold the towns and plains, strong enough also to blockade Cadiz and to spare expeditionary forces at intervals for operations outside the limits of his own sphere of command. From time to time he sent the greater part of Mortier's corps against Estremadura, and the greater part of Sebastiani's corps against Murcia. But his 70,000 men were not sufficient to provide an army for the permanent conquest of either of these provinces. And every time that 10,000 or 15,000 sabres and bayonets were distracted to one of these raids, the total of troops left behind to watch Cadiz, to guard Seville, and to repress the interminable activity of the guerrilleros of the mountains was found to be dangerously small. Ere long the force that had marched out for external operations had to be called back in haste, to ward off some peril to one or other of the vital points of Andalusia.

Soult himself remained for the greater part of his time at Seville, occupied not only in keeping the movements of his three corps in unison—no easy task, for both Victor and Sebastiani had wills of their own, and even the placid Mortier occasionally murmured—but in superintending the details of civil administration. It was very seldom that he marched out in person at the head of his last reserves, to strengthen some weak point in his line of offence or defence. During the next two years he was quite as much the Viceroy as the Commander-in-Chief in Andalusia. Though the Emperor had refrained from naming that

kingdom one of the 'Military Governments,' which he had
created by his decree of Feb. 15, 1810, yet Soult made himself
in fact, if not in name, as independent as the governors of
Aragon or Navarre or Catalonia.   The bond of common interests
and desires which had united him to King Joseph during the
winter of 1809–10 was soon broken.   The monarch at Madrid
soon discovered that his presence was not desired in Andalusia—
some good military reason could always be discovered which
made it impracticable that he should revisit Seville.   Little or
no money was remitted to him from the South: rich as was
Soult's sphere of governance, it was always made to appear that
the expenses of the sustenance of the army and of the siege of
Cadiz were so great that no surplus remained for the central
government.   When the King murmured, and appealed to Paris,
his brother usually supported the Marshal [1]; it was Napoleon's
first maxim that war should maintain war, and he thought it of
far more importance that the army of Andalusia should pay
for itself, than that the bankrupt exchequer at Madrid should
be recruited [2].   As the months rolled on, and Joseph gradually
realized the position, his hatred for the plausible Marshal became
as bitter as it had been during their earlier quarrel in the summer
of 1809.   He had good reason to be angry, for Soult undoubtedly
sacrificed the interests of the King of Spain to those of the
Viceroy of Andalusia.   He played a selfish game, though he had
always a good military excuse for any particular refusal to fall
in with the King's plans or to obey his orders.   In 1810 his
conduct may be justified, but in 1811 and 1812 he undoubtedly
—as will be shown in chapters to come—ruined what small
chance there was of bringing the Peninsular War to a successful
termination, by pursuing a policy which made the maintenance
of the French authority in Andalusia its chief end, and not the
general good of the imperial arms in Spain.

Soult's conduct at Oporto in the days of his invasion of
Portugal must never be forgotten when his doings in Andalusia are discussed.   He undoubtedly yearned after supreme
power, and though the lesson which he had received after his

----

[1] Though not always.   See the case of the revenue from the quicksilver
mines, in *Correspondance*, no. 17,076.

[2] Cf. ibid., July 10, to Soult.

vain attempt to create himself king of 'Northern Lusitania'
had not been forgotten, his ambitions were as great as ever.
He suppressed his desire for the royal name, but gave himself
the reality of the royal power. He practically kept a court,
a ministry, and a revenue of his own [1], despite of all the angry
complaints of his immediate master at Madrid. Secure in the
support of the Emperor, who reckoned him the 'best military
head in Spain,' he ignored or disobeyed all such communication
from Joseph as did not suit his purpose. To a great extent he
justified his policy by success : the plain-land of Andalusia was
undoubtedly the part of the French holding in Spain where the
administration was most successful, and the occupation most
thorough. Soult not only built up, but kept together, an
Afrancesado party among the local population, which was
stronger and more compact than in any other part of the Peninsula. He even succeeded in raising a small permanent force of
Spanish auxiliaries, which was decidedly more trustworthy and
less given to desertion than the regiments of the same class which
King Joseph was perpetually creating in Madrid—only to see
them crumble away under his hand. The Army of Andalusia
was strengthened by two regiments of Chasseurs à Cheval, which
were attached to the 5th Corps [2], and some free companies of
infantry [3], which were used for garrison and blockhouse work.
But it was far more important that Soult succeeded in enlisting
many battalions of a sort of national guard, which he called
Escopeteros (fusiliers) ; with them he kept the peace of the larger
towns, such as Seville, Cordova, and Jaen. The very existence
of such a force, which King Joseph had vainly attempted to
establish in Madrid, was of evil omen for the patriotic cause in
Andalusia. On several occasions they fought well against the

---

[1] There was desperate quarrelling with Madrid when Soult tried to get
hold of the port-revenues—small as these were, owing to the English
blockade—and when he tried to nominate consuls on his own authority.
See Ducasse's *Correspondance du Roi Joseph*, vol. vii. p. 337.

[2] 3rd and 4th Chasseurs à Cheval, both present at Albuera and other
fights in Estremadura in 1810–12. They seem to have gone to pieces on
the evacuation of Andalusia in the autumn of 1812.

[3] Cazadores de Jaen, Francos de Montaña, &c. There was a company
of this sort in Badajoz when it was taken in 1812. The Spanish government shot the officers after trial by court martial.

guerrilleros, when the latter attempted raids dangerously close
to the great cities.   For the *Juramentado* was well aware that
if the national cause were at last to triumph an evil fate would
await him.   Having once committed himself to the French side,
he was forced to defend his own neck from the gallows.

Soult's civil government was conducted with a far greater
decency than that of Duhesme, Kellermann, and other noted
plunderers among the French governors.   But it involved, nevertheless, a considerable amount of more or less open spoliation.
The Marshal's own hands were not quite clean : his collection of
the works of Murillo and Velasquez, the pride of Paris in after
years, represented blackmail on Andalusian church-corporations,
when it did not come from undisguised confiscation.   Unless he
was much maligned by his own compatriots, no less than by the
Spaniards, hard cash as well as pictures did not come amiss to
him [1].   But his exactions were moderate compared with those of
some of his subordinates : though Mortier and Dessolles had
good reputations Sebastiani had an infamous one, and Perreymond, Godinot (who shot himself early in 1812 when called
to face a commission of inquiry), and certain other generals
have very black marks against them.   Still the machine of
government worked, if not without friction, at least with an
efficiency that contrasted favourably with the administration of
any other province of Spain save Suchet's domain of Aragon.

But it was only the valley of the Guadalquivir which lay
subdued beneath the feet of Soult.   Cadiz and the mountains had
yet to be dealt with, and, as the months went on, the difficulties
of the French Army of Andalusia became more and more evident.
It was only by degrees that the French generals came to comprehend the absolute impregnability of Cadiz, and the advantage
that the possession of the island-city and the fleet depending on
it gave to the Spaniards.   In the first months of the siege Victor's

---

[1] Cf. Observations by his aide-de-camp St. Chamans, in his *Memoirs*,
pp. 203–5, as to the Marshal's administration. It may serve as an example
of the liberal way in which the superior officers were allowed to draw in
money, that Soult gave his ex-aide-de-camp 1,500 francs a month, when
he was commanding in the town of Carmona, besides his pay and free food
and quarters. It is small wonder that he and other governors began, as
he said, 'à trancher du grand seigneur.' Cf. Arteche, viii. 109, for
Spanish views on Soult's administration.

engineers and artillerists had flattered themselves that something might be done to molest the place, if not to reduce it to surrender, by pushing batteries forward to the extreme front of the ground in their possession all around the harbour. Within the first weeks of his arrival in front of Cadiz, Victor made an attempt to push forward his posts along the high-road which crosses the broad salt-marshes of the Santi Petri. But the bogs and water-channels were found impracticable, and the Spanish works in front of the bridge of Zuazo too strong to be attacked along the narrow causeway. The French drew back to Chiclana, which became the head quarters of the left wing of the blockading force, and where Ruffin's division was permanently encamped. It was then thought that something might be accomplished further to the north, by working against the Arsenal of La Caracca, at the one end of the Spanish line, or the projecting castle of Puntales at the other. The struggle for the points of vantage from which Puntales could be battered formed the chief point of interest during the early months of the siege. The French, pushing down from the mainland on to the peninsula of the Trocadero, began to erect works on the ground most favourable for attacking the fort of Matagorda, which had once more become the outermost bulwark of Cadiz.

There was a bitter fight over this work, which stands on the tidal flats below the Trocadero, surrounded by mud for one half of the day, and by water for the other. It will be remembered that Matagorda had been blown up at the time of the first arrival of the French before Cadiz. But after a few days of reflection the English and Spanish engineer officers in command of the defence grew uneasy as to the possibilities of mischief which might follow from the seizure of the ruined fort by the enemy. Their fears, as it afterwards turned out, were unnecessary. But they led to the reoccupation of Matagorda on February 22 by a detachment of British artillery, supported by a company of the 94th regiment. The front of the work facing toward the mainland was hastily repaired, and heavy guns brought over the harbour from Cadiz were mounted on it. Moreover, it was arranged that it should be supported by a Spanish ship-of-the-line and some gunboats, as far as the mud banks permitted.

Victor took the reoccupation of the fort as a challenge, and thought that the Allies must have good reasons for attaching so much importance to it.   Accordingly he multiplied his batteries on the Trocadero, till he had got forty guns mounted in a dominating position, with which to overwhelm the garrison in their half-ruinous stronghold.   There was a long and fierce artillery contest, but the French had the advantage both in the number of guns and in the concentric fire which they could pour upon the fort.   The naval help promised to Matagorda proved of little assistance, partly owing to the impracticability of the mud flats when the tide was out, partly because the gunboats could not endure the fire of the French heavy artillery.   On April 22 General Graham, who had arrived at Cadiz and taken command of the British forces over the head of General Stewart, ordered Matagorda to be evacuated.   It was high time, for the fort was shot to pieces, and 64 men out of a garrison of 140 had been killed or wounded [1].   The enemy took possession of the ruins, and rebuilt and rearmed the fort ; they also re-established the ruined forts of San Luis and San José, on the firm ground facing Matagorda, to which they had not possessed a safe access till the outer work in the mud had been captured.   These were the most advanced points toward Cadiz which the French could hold, and here they mounted their heaviest guns, in the hope of demolishing the Castle of Puntales on the other side of the water, and of making the inner harbour useless for shipping.   Their purpose was only partly accomplished : the ships, it is true, had to move east or west, into the outer harbour or nearer to the Caracca and the Isla de Leon.   But Puntales was never seriously injured, and maintained an intermittent artillery duel with Matagorda across the strait as long as the siege lasted.   The occasional bombs that fell beyond Puntales, in the direction of the Cortadura, did not seriously incommode the garrison, and ships could always pass the strait between the two forts at night without appreciable risk.   Later on Soult caused mortars of unprecedented dimensions to be cast in the arsenal of Seville, on the designs presented to him by an artillery officer of the name

---

[1] There is a good account of the desperate life of the garrison of Matagorda during the bombardment in the *Eventful Life of a Scottish Soldier*, by Sergeant Donaldson of the 94th.

Spanish Infantry 1810
(showing the new uniform introduced under British influence)

Emery Walker Ph.sc.

of Villantroys. But even when these had been mounted on Matagorda no great damage was done, one bomb only—as a Spanish popular song recorded—ever touched Cadiz town, and that only killed a street dog.

After the fall of Matagorda, the next most notable event of the spring in front of Cadiz was a fearful hurricane, lasting from the 6th to the 9th of March, which caused grave losses to the vessels in the outer harbour. A south-wester from the Atlantic drove three Spanish line-of-battle ships, one of which, the *Concepcion*, was a three-decker of 100 guns, and a Portuguese 74, upon the coast about Puerto Santa Maria and Rota. The French opened upon them with red-hot shot, and destroyed them all, slaying a great part of the unfortunate crews, who had no thought of resistance, and were only trying to escape to land, where they were bound to become prisoners. More than thirty merchant ships, mostly British, were destroyed by the same storm. One was a transport containing a wing of the 4th regiment, which was coming to reinforce the garrison of Cadiz. Some 300 men from this unlucky vessel got ashore and were captured by the French.

A month after the loss of Matagorda the outer harbour of Cadiz again saw some exciting scenes. Moored beside the Spanish fleet were a number of pontoons, old men-of-war from which the masts and rigging had been removed, and which were used as prison-ships. On them there were still kept several thousands of French prisoners, mostly the men captured with Dupont in 1808. It is astonishing that the Regency had not ordered their removal to some more remote spot the moment that Victor's army appeared in front of Cadiz. Overcrowded, and often kept without sufficient food for days at a time, these unhappy captives were in a deplorable position. The sight of their fellow-countrymen in possession of the opposite coast drove them to desperation, and they were prepared to take any risks for a chance of escape. Having noted, during the hurricane of March 6th–9th, that every vessel which broke loose from its moorings had been cast by the set of the tide upon the coast in the direction of Rota, the prisoners on the *Castilla*, on which nearly all the officers were confined, waited for the next south-wester. When it came, on the night of the 15th–16th

May, they rose upon their small guard of Spanish marines, overpowered them, and then cut the cables of the pontoon, committing themselves to the perils of the sea as well as to the risk of being sunk by the neighbouring men-of-war. But it was supposed that they had got adrift by accident, and they had been carried by the tide almost to the opposite shore before it was realized that an escape was on foot. Two gunboats sent to tow the *Castilla* back met with resistance, the prisoners firing on them with the muskets taken from their guard, and throwing cold shot down upon the little vessels when their crews tried to board. Just as they were beaten off, the pontoon went ashore. The French garrisons of the neighbouring batteries ran down to help their countrymen to escape; at the same moment other gunboats, Spanish and English, came up, and began firing on the crowd, who strove to swim or scramble ashore. Some were killed, but over 600 got to land. It is surprising that after this incident the Spaniards did not take better care of the remaining pontoons, but ten days later the prisoners on the *Argonauta* were able to repeat the trick of their comrades. On this occasion the absconding vessel ran ashore upon a mud-bank some hundreds of yards from the shore of the Trocadero. The stranded vessel remained for hours under the fire of the gunboats which pursued it, and a large proportion of the men on board perished, for when the troops on shore brought out boats to save the survivors, many of them were sunk as they plied between the *Argonauta* and the land. Finally the pontoon was set on fire, and several wounded Frenchmen are said to have been burnt alive. The English seamen who were engaged in this distressing business were heartily disgusted with their share in it [1].

After this the Regency at last ordered the removal of the rest of the French prisoners from Cadiz. The few remaining officers were sent to Majorca, and afterwards to England. Of the men part were dispatched to the Canaries, part to the Balearic Islands. But the islanders protested against the presence of so

---

[1] See the letter of Charles Vaughan deploring the 'beastly necessity of firing into the poor devils' quoted by Napier in his Appendix, vol. ii. p. 482. For a narrative by one of the escaping French officers see the *Mémoires* of Colonel Chalbrand.

many French in their midst, raised riots, and killed some of
the prisoners. Thereupon the Regency ordered 7,000 of them
to be placed upon the desolate rock of Cabrera, where there were
no inhabitants and no shelter save one small ruined castle.
The wretched captives, without roofs or tents to cover them, and
supplied with food only at uncertain intervals and in insufficient
quantity, died off like flies. Once, when storms hindered the
arrival of the provision ships from Majorca, many scores
perished in a day of sheer starvation [1]. The larger half did not
survive to see the peace of 1814, and those who did were for
the most part mere wrecks of men, invalids for life. Even
allowing for the desperate straits of the Spanish government,
which could not feed its own armies, the treatment of the
Cabrera prisoners was indefensible. They might at least have
been exchanged for some of the numerous Spanish garrisons
taken in 1810–11; but the Regency would not permit it, though
Henry O'Donnell had arranged with Macdonald a regular
cartel for prisoners in the neighbouring Catalonia. This is
one of the most miserable corners of the history of the
Peninsular War.

But to return to Andalusia. By the month of May the
Regency at Cadiz had recovered a certain confidence, in view
of the utter inefficacy of Victor's attempt to molest their
city. From that month began a systematic attempt to organize
into a single system all the forces that could be turned to
account against Soult. There were now in the Isla some
18,000 Spanish troops, as well as 8,000 British and Portuguese.
This was a larger garrison than was needed, now that the
defences had been put in order; and it was possible to detach
small expeditionary corps to east and west, to stir up trouble in
the coastland of Andalusia, and serve as the nuclei round which
the insurgents of the mountains might gather. For the insurrection in the remoter corners of the kingdom of Granada had
never died down, despite of all the efforts of Sebastiani to
quell it. The Regency had now determined that an effort

---

[1] Nothing can be more distressing reading than the chronicles of the
Cabrera prisoners, Ducor, Guillemard, Gille and others. Actual canni-
balism is said to have occurred during the longest of the spells of fasting
caused by the non-arrival of provisions. [See Gille, p. 240.]

should be made to extend it westward—the Sierra de Ronda
being quite as well suited for irregular operations as the
Alpujarras. At the other end of the line, too, there were
opportunities in the Condado de Niebla and the lands by the
mouth of the Guadiana, which the French had hardly touched:
trifling detachments of the 5th Corps at Moguer and Niebla
observed rather than occupied that region. By means of the
large fleet always moored in Cadiz harbour, it was possible to
transfer troops to any point of the coast, for the French could
not guard every creek and fishing-village, and if an expedition
failed it had a fair chance of escaping by sea. Moreover any
force thrown ashore in the south had the option of retiring
into Gibraltar if hard pressed, just as any force sent to the
west might retire on Portugal.

In addition to the insurgents and the garrison of Cadiz there
were two regular armies whose energies might be turned against
Soult. The relics of Areizaga's unfortunate host, which had
fled into the kingdom of Murcia, and had been rallied by
Blake, were now 12,000 strong, and since Suchet's expedition
against Valencia had failed, and there was no danger from the
north, this force could be employed against Sebastiani and the
French corps in the kingdom of Granada. It was in a deplorable
condition, but was yet strong enough to render assistance to the
insurgents of the Alpujarras, by demonstrating against Granada,
and so forcing Sebastiani to keep his troops massed for a
regular campaign. Whenever the French general was threatened
from the east, he had to abandon his smaller posts, and to
desist from hunting the guerrilleros, who thus obtained a free
hand.

The Regency could also count to a certain extent upon aid
from La Romana and the Army of Estremadura. The Marquis
—it will be remembered—was now confronted in his own
province by Reynier and the 2nd Corps [1], but he had thrust his
flanking division, under Ballasteros, into the mountains of
North-Western Andalusia, where it had been contending with
Mortier's corps in the direction of Araçena and Zalamea, as
has already been recounted [2]. This outlying division was in

[1] See pp. 213–14 of this volume and p. 246.
[2] See pp. 215–16 of this volume.

communication with Cadiz, via Ayamonte and the lower Guadiana, and could always compel Soult to detach troops from Seville by descending into the plains. La Romana himself could, and occasionally did, provide further occupation for the 5th Corps by moving other troops southward, on the Seville high-road, when he was not too much engrossed by Reynier's demonstrations in his front.

Thus it was possible to harass the French troops in Andalusia on all sides. With the object of securing some sort of unity for their operations, the Regency made Blake Commander-in-Chief of the forces in Cadiz as well as of those in Murcia, declaring them parts of a single ' Army of the Centre.' Albuquerque's separate charge had come to an end when, after many quarrels with the Cadiz Junta, he resigned the post of governor, and accepted that of Ambassador to the Court of St. James's at the end of March. He died not long after his arrival in London, engaged to the last in a hot warfare of pamphlets and manifestos with the Junta, whose monstrous insinuations against his probity and patriotism are said to have driven him into the brain-fever which terminated his life. He was a man of unsullied honour and high personal courage, but not a lucky general, though his last military action, the direction of the Army of Estremadura on Cadiz, was a sound and meritorious piece of strategy. He and La Romana were the only Spanish officers with whom Wellington was able to work in concert without perpetual friction, but the British Commander-in-Chief had a greater respect for his allies' hearts than for their heads as may be gathered from constant references in the *Wellington Dispatches*, as well as from the confidential conversations of the Duke's later years [1].

Blake arrived in Cadiz on April 22, having turned over the temporary command of the Murcian army to General Freire, the ever-unlucky cavalry commander who had served under Venegas and Areizaga in the campaigns of Almonacid and Ocaña. He set himself to reorganize the various Estremaduran and other troops in Cadiz into one division of horse and three divisions of foot, which he numbered Vanguard, 2nd, and 4th of the Army

---

[1] See *Wellington Dispatches*, v. p. 292, &c., and Stanhope's *Conversations with the Duke of Wellington*, pp. 10 and 23.

of the Centre. The Murcian forces were distributed into the
1st, 3rd, and 5th infantry divisions of the same army, and two
small cavalry divisions. This reorganization of the regular
troops was followed by systematic attempts to foster the insurrection to right and left of Seville. General Copons was sent to
Ayamonte, at the mouth of the Guadiana, with 700 men, round
whom he collected a miscellaneous assemblage of peasantry,
which often descended from the hills to worry the French
garrisons of Moguer and Niebla. When chased by stronger forces
detached from Mortier's corps, he would retire into Portugal.
When unmolested he joined hands with Ballasteros and the
flanking division of the army of La Romana, or executed raids
of his own in the central plain of the kingdom of Seville.
Often chased, and sometimes dispersed, his bands were never
completely crushed, and kept Western Andalusia, or 'Spanish
Algarve,' as it was called in the old days when the boundaries
of Castile and Portugal had only just been fixed, in a state of
constant ferment.

The diversion which was prepared on the other flank by Blake
and the Regency was far more important. Their intention was
to wrest from the French the whole district of the Sierra de
Ronda, the mountain region between Gibraltar and Malaga, and
so to thrust in a wedge between Victor and Sebastiani. There
was already the nucleus of an insurrection in this quarter ; soon
after King Joseph's triumphal progress from Xeres by Ronda
and Malaga to Granada, the first small bands had appeared.
They were headed by local chiefs, such as Becerra, Ruiz, and
Ortiz—better known as El Pastor—whose original followers
were a party of the smugglers who, in times of peace and war
alike, had been wont to ply a contraband trade with Gibraltar.
In March and April they were not strong enough to do more
than molest the convoys passing from Malaga and Seville to the
French garrison of Ronda. But finding the enemy in their
neighbourhood weak and helpless—the bulk of the 1st Corps
was before Cadiz, and that of the 5th Corps was still watching
La Romana on the roads north of Seville—they multiplied
in numbers and extended their raids far afield. They asked for
aid both from the British Governor of Gibraltar and from the
Regency at Cadiz, promising that, if they were backed by regular

troops, they would easily expel the French and master the whole country-side. Already their activity had produced favourable results, for Soult sent down from Seville Girard's division of the 5th Corps, a detachment which left Mortier too weak for any serious operations on the side of Estremadura, and Sebastiani drew back from an expedition against Murcia, which might otherwise have proved most prejudicial to the Spanish cause.

This raid deserves a word of notice : just after Blake had left Murcia for Cadiz, Sebastiani (who had for the moment got the better of the insurgents in the Alpujarras) assembled at Baza, in the eastern extremity of the kingdom of Granada, the greater part of the 4th Corps, and marched with 7,000 men on Lorca. Freire, distrusting his troops, refused to fight, threw 4,000 men into the impregnable harbour-fortress of Cartagena, and retired with the rest of his army to Alicante, within the borders of Valencia. Thus, the rich city of Murcia, along with the whole of the rest of its province, which had never seen the French before, was exposed undefended to Sebastiani. He entered it on April 23, and commenced by fining the corporation 50,000 dollars for not having received him with a royal salute and the ringing of the bells of their churches. The rest of his behaviour was in keeping : he entered the cathedral while mass was in progress, and interrupted the service to seize the plate and jewels. He confiscated the money and other valuables in all the monasteries, hospitals, and banks. He permitted his officers to blackmail many rich inhabitants, and his rank and file to plunder houses and shops. Two days after his entry he retraced his footsteps, and retreated hastily towards Granada, leaving a ruined city behind him [1]. The cause of his sudden departure was the news that the insurgents of the Alpujarras, whom he had vainly imagined that he had crushed, were beleaguering all his small garrisons, and that Malaga itself had been seized by a large band of the Serranos, and held for a short space, though General Perreymond had afterwards succeeded in driving them out. But the whole of the Alhama and Ronda Sierras were up in arms, no less than the more eastern hills where the rising had begun. It would have been absurd for Sebastiani to proceed any further

---

[1] For strange and scandalous details of Sebastiani's doings in Murcia, see Schepeler, iii. pp. 566-7.

with the offensive campaign in Murcia, when Southern Andalusia was being lost behind his back.

Throughout the month of May Girard and Sebastiani, with some small assistance from Dessolles, who spared a few battalions from the kingdom of Cordova, were actively engaged in endeavouring to repress the mountaineers. The larger bands were dispersed, not without severe fighting—Girard's men had hot work at Albondonates on May 1, and at Grazalema on May 3[1]. But just as the main roads had been reopened, and the blockade of the French garrison of Ronda raised, the whole situation was changed by the landing at Algeciras of General Lacy, with a division of 3,000 regulars sent from Cadiz by the Regency (June 19). His arrival raised the spirits of the insurgents, and they thronged in thousands to his aid, when he announced his intention of marching against Ronda. Lacy, however, was both irresolute and high-handed—as he afterwards showed on a larger stage when he became Captain-General of Catalonia. On arriving before Ronda he judged the rocky stronghold too formidable for him to meddle with, and turned aside to Grazalema, to the disgust of his followers. He then fell into a quarrel with the Serranos, dismissed many of them—smugglers and others—from his camp, as unworthy to serve alongside of regular soldiers, and even imprisoned some of the more turbulent chiefs. At this moment Girard from the north and Sebastiani from the east began to close in upon him. Uneasy at their approach, Lacy fell back towards the coast, and after some insignificant skirmishes re-embarked his force at Estepona and Marbella, from whence he sailed round to Gibraltar and landed at the Lines of San Roque, under the walls of that fortress (July 12)[2]. Almost the only positive gain produced by his expedition had been the occupation of Marbella, where he left a garrison which maintained itself for a considerable time. It was no doubt something to have detained Girard and Sebastiani in the remote mountain

---

[1] Martinien's lists show that the 40th regiment of Girard's division lost four officers at Albondonates, and the 64th the same number at Grazalema —so the skirmishes must have been fairly vigorous.

[2] That Lacy's force was not so entirely destroyed as Napier implies is shown by the fact that many of the same regiments could be utilized for the subsequent expedition to the Condado de Niebla.

of the south for a full month, when they were much needed by
Soult in other directions. Yet the evil results of Lacy's timid
manœuvres and hasty flight upon the morale of the insurgents
might have been sufficiently great to counterbalance these small
advantages, if the Serranos had been less tough and resolute.
It is surprising to find that they did not lose courage, but kept
the rising afoot with undiminished energy, being apparently confirmed in their self-confidence by the poor show made by the
regular army, rather than disheartened at the ineffective succour
sent them from Cadiz. Despite of all the efforts of Soult's flying
columns, they could not be entirely dispersed, though they were
hunted a hundred times from valley to valley. The power of
the viceroy of Andalusia stopped short at the foot-hills, though
his dragoons kept the plains in subjection. Every time that
Ronda and the other isolated garrisons in the mountains had to
be revictualled, the convoy had to fight its way to its destination
through swarms of 'sniping' insurgents [1].

The Regency had not yet done with Lacy and his expeditionary
force. After they had lain for some time under the walls of
Gibraltar, they were re-embarked and taken back to Cadiz, from
where a short time after they were dispatched for a raid in the
Condado de Niebla. In this region, where Copons was already
in arms, the French forces, under Remond and the Duke of
Aremberg, were so weak that the Junta believed that Lacy's
division would easily clear the whole country-side of the enemy.
Its liberation would be most valuable, because Cadiz was wont
to draw both corn and cattle from the lands between the Rio
Tinto and Guadiana, and had felt bitterly the want of its
accustomed supplies since the war had been carried thither.

Lacy landed in the Bay of Huelva on August 23 with nearly
3,000 men. He had the good fortune to meet and to overcome
in succession two small French columns which marched against
him from Moguer and from San Juan del Puerto. Thereupon
the Duke of Aremberg—whose whole force in this region was less
than 1,500 men (two battalions of the 103rd of the line and
the 27th Chasseurs)—evacuated Niebla and fell back on Seville.

---

[1] For illustrative anecdotes of warfare in the Serrania de Ronda, see
the autobiography of Rocca of the 2nd Hussars, who was busy in this
region in the spring and summer of 1810.

Copons, who had been told to join Lacy but had failed to receive his instructions in time, pursued a separate French column under General Remond for some distance, but was soon stopped by the news that a large force was moving against him, to repair this check to the French arms.   Lacy, meanwhile, to the surprise and disgust of the inhabitants of the Condado, re-embarked on August 29 and went back to Cadiz, professing to regard the purpose of his expedition as completed.   He had this much justification, that the news of his raid had induced Soult to send out against him, at a most critical moment, the main body of Gazan's division, which marched to Niebla, vainly sought the expeditionary force, and returned to its base after wasting a fortnight.   But a larger garrison was now left in Western Andalusia, Copons was hunted more vigorously than before, and cruel reprisals were made on the inhabitants of Moguer and Huelva, who had aided Lacy.

Feeble as it had been, Lacy's raid on the Condado had staved off a serious danger to the Spanish Army of Estremadura, by forcing Soult to detach Gazan against him, at a moment when he was concentrating the 5th Corps for a blow at La Romana, and was already engaged in active operations against the Marquis. A complete change had taken place in the situation in Estremadura at the end of July, when Reynier, acting under orders from Masséna [1], had marched northward from his old base at Merida and Medellin, and crossed the Tagus at the ferry of Alconetar above the broken bridge of Alcantara [2] (July 16). This removal of the whole 2nd Corps to the north, followed (as we have already seen) by the corresponding transference of Hill's British force from Portalegre to the neighbourhood of Castello Branco, had left La Romana at Badajoz with no enemy in front of him, and had caused a complete rupture of communications between the French Army of Andalusia and the Army of Portugal, who could for the future only hear of each other by the circuitous route through Madrid, since that by Almaraz was closed.

[1] See pp. 246–7 of this volume.
[2] Not marked in any contemporary map that I have seen.   It is situated, however, opposite the junction of the River Almonte with the Tagus, about eighteen miles above Alcantara, near the ancient ruined bridge of Mantible.

Soult had now thrown upon his hands, to his immense disgust, the task of containing the whole of La Romana's force, which Reynier had been keeping in check from March till July. Accordingly he called back from the Sierra de Ronda the division of Girard, wishing to reunite the whole 5th Corps for the protection of the northern approaches to Seville. He was only just in time, for La Romana had seen his opportunity, and had resolved to concentrate his army for a demonstration against Andalusia, which seemed to offer great temptations while nothing but the solitary division of Gazan stood between him and Seville, and that division, moreover, was weakened by the detachments under Remond and Aremberg which lay in the Condado de Niebla. Accordingly the Marquis, leaving Charles O'Donnell to watch Reynier on the Tagus, and another division to guard Badajoz, marched with his cavalry and the infantry of La Carrera[1] and Ballasteros to invade Andalusia. He also told Copons to come up to reinforce him with his levies from the lower Guadiana. Even without the help of the latter, who never succeeded in reaching him, he had 10,000 foot and 1,000 horse. But La Romana was always unlucky when he fought: just as he started, Girard had returned from Ronda to Seville. On hearing that the Army of Estremadura was on the move, Soult pushed the newly returned division, strengthened by part of Gazan's regiments and a brigade of cavalry, out towards the passes of the Morena. On August 11, Girard, with about 7,000 bayonets and 1,200 sabres, encountered La Romana at Villagarcia, just outside the town of Llerena. The Spaniards were eager to fight, believing that they had only to deal with some fraction of Gazan's division; the news of Girard's return from Ronda had not yet reached them. They got involved in a severe combat, were beaten, and were forced back to Zafra and Almendralejo, with a loss of 600 men—triple that of the French.

Soult then strengthened Girard's column, placed Mortier in command, and bade him push for Badajoz. But just as the Duke of Treviso was preparing to advance, the news of Lacy's disembarkation at Moguer arrived. There were hardly any troops left in Seville, wherefore Soult hastily recalled from

---

[1] Which had just rejoined him from the north, after the fall of Ciudad Rodrigo. See p. 253.

Mortier such of Gazan's regiments as were with him, and nearly
all the cavalry, and sent them off against Lacy.   Girard's division retired from Zafra and took up a defensive position in the
passes covering Seville.   Thus a dangerous crisis was avoided,
for if the whole 5th Corps had marched on Badajoz in August,
and had driven back La Romana into Portugal, Wellington's
flank in the Alemtejo would have been left exposed.   There was
no longer a British division south of the Tagus to support the
Spanish Army of Estremadura, since Hill had transferred himself
to Castello Branco in order to 'contain' Reynier.   Of regular
troops, indeed, Wellington had nothing left on the Alemtejo
frontier save Madden's brigade of Portuguese horse, and the two
infantry regiments of the same nation, who formed part of the
garrison of Elvas.   Hence he was much troubled at La Romana's
tendency to take the offensive against Seville, and repeatedly
begged him to content himself with defensive operations, and
not to attract the notice of Soult.   For the Duke of Dalmatia,
if left alone, had enough to occupy his attention in Andalusia,
yet, if provoked, might abandon some outlying part of his viceroyalty, in order to concentrate a force which might crush the
Estremaduran army, and then execute that diversion against
Portugal south of the Tagus which Wellington so much dreaded[1].

Yet despite the warning that he had received at the combat
of Villagarcia, and, despite of his ally's entreaties, La Romana
renewed in September the project that had cost him so dear in
August.   Learning that the passes in front of Seville were once
more weakly held by the French, he began to move his army
southward in detachments, till he had gathered a heavy force at
Guadalcanal and Monasterio.   Attributing his misfortunes in
the last month to the weakness of his cavalry, he brought down
with him Madden's Portuguese horsemen, a weak brigade of 800
men[2], which Wellington had put at his disposition, not foreseeing

---

[1] See Wellington, *Dispatches*, vi. p. 343.   ' I am a little anxious about
Mortier's movement into Estremadura, not on account of the progress he
can make, but because I think that the Marquis de la Romana is inclined
to fight a battle.   If we could only avoid a disaster for some time, I hope
we may do some good at last.'   Cf. also vi. pp. 348 and 393.

[2] The brigade consisted of three squadrons each of the 5th and 8th
regiments, and two of the 3rd.   Beresford's report to Wellington speaks of
their behaviour in the highest terms.   See Soriano da Luz, vol. iii. pp. 66–7.

that its existence would add to the inclination which the Marquis felt for offensive demonstrations. The inevitable result followed. Disquieted by the activity of the Estremaduran army—its raiding parties had already pressed as far as Santa Olalla on the Seville road, and Constantina on the Cordova road—Soult ordered Mortier to concentrate the main body of the 5th Corps at Ronquillo, and to attack the enemy. La Romana gave back at once, evacuating the passes, but his rearguard was overtaken at Fuente Cantos, behind Monasterio, by the French horse (Sept. 15). His cavalry, under La Carrera [1], turned to bay to cover the retreat, but was charged and scattered with heavy loss by Briche's Chasseurs, who captured the battery that accompanied it, and enveloped a large mass of the beaten horsemen, who would have been forced to surrender if Madden's Portuguese, charging at the right moment, and with great vigour, had not checked the French advance, and given time for the routed brigades to save themselves in the hills. Madden, though pursued by the French reserves, made a steady and successful retreat, with small loss. The Spaniards, however, left behind them six guns and 500 killed and wounded, while the French loss had not exceeded 100.

Mortier then pursued La Romana to Zafra, and pushed his advanced cavalry as far as Fuente del Maestre, only thirty miles from Badajoz. Thus the situation which Wellington most dreaded had come into existence once again : a considerable French army was moving into central Estremadura, and threatening the Alemtejo frontier south of the Tagus, at a moment when every man of the Anglo-Portuguese field army was fully employed in Beira by the advance of Masséna. But again, as in August, Mortier did not push his advantage, though La Romana actually retired behind the Tagus to Montijo, after raising the garrison of Badajoz to its full strength, and left the Duke of Treviso the opportunity of laying siege either to that city, to Olivenza, or even to Elvas, if he should so please. But the governing fact in all the operations of Soult and his lieutenants at this period was, as we have already pointed out, that if any great concentration of the French for offensive purposes took place, it was only made

---

[1] Dissatisfied with all his cavalry officers, La Romana had removed La Carrera to the command of the horse, making over his old infantry division to Carlos D'España.

by withdrawing the garrison troops from some one of the many
disturbed regions of Andalusia. When the whole 5th Corps was
united, and had advanced to Zafra, Western Andalusia was
almost stripped of troops. Indeed, at Seville itself, Soult had
nothing but his new Spanish levies, and the convalescents from
his central hospital, together with some detachments escorting
convoys which happened to be passing through the city, and had
been detained in order to add a few hundred bayonets to its
garrison. When, therefore, Copons began to make himself felt once
more in the Condado de Niebla, and a second raiding expedition
from Cadiz landed at Huelva, Soult felt very uncomfortable.

His perturbation of mind was increased by news from the
East: Sebastiani at this moment had been molested by demonstrations of the Spanish Army of Murcia against his flank.
Blake had returned in August from Cadiz to inspect the section
of his forces which he had left behind under Freire, and which
he had not seen since April. He had pushed reconnaissances
to Huescar in the kingdom of Granada, had sent supplies to aid
the insurgents of the Alpujarras, and was beginning to stir up
a new rising on the side of Jaen. This provoked Sebastiani to
concentrate the larger part of the 4th Corps, and to march against
him with 8,000 men [1]. Blake gave back before his enemy as far
as the neighbourhood of Murcia, where he had prepared a fortified position by inundating the Huerta, or suburban plain, which
is watered by many canals drawn from the river Segura, and by
stockading all the villages. Fourteen thousand regulars, with
a powerful artillery, held the approaches, while a mass of armed
peasantry hung around Sebastiani's flanks. The French, however, only advanced as far as Lebrilla, twelve miles from Murcia,
and then halted (Aug. 28). Sebastiani, after reconnoitring
Blake's line, thought it too powerful to be meddled with, and
retired two days later towards his base, much harassed by the
peasantry on his way. But during the three weeks that it took
for the French general to concentrate his field-force, to march on
Murcia, and to return, all had gone to wrack and ruin behind

---

[1] The 4th Corps was now a little stronger than it had been in the
spring, the 32nd regiment, 2,000 strong, having joined from Madrid.
But it was still short of its German division, which now lay in La Mancha,
but had never crossed the Sierra Morena.

him. The insurgents of the Alpujarras had captured the
important seaport towns of Almunecar and Motril, and had
garrisoned their castles with the aid of English guns sent from
Gibraltar. The people of the Sierra de Alhama had cut the
roads between Malaga and Granada, and 4,000 mountaineers
had attacked Granada itself; they were defeated outside its
gates by the garrison on Sept. 4, but were still hanging about
its vicinity.

The news of all these troubles had reached Soult while
Sebastiani was quite out of touch, lost to sight in the kingdom
of Murcia. They undoubtedly had their part in inducing the
Marshal to recall Mortier and the 5th Corps from Estremadura.
He once more divided its two divisions, drawing back Gazan to
Seville to form his central reserve, while Girard watched the
passes as before. Meanwhile Copons had already been beaten
in the Condado by the column of General Remond (Sept. 15),
and Sebastiani on his return cleared the neighbourhood of
Granada and Malaga of insurgents, and drove the untameable
bands of the Alpujarras to take refuge in their mountains.
Motril and Almunecar were both recovered. Thus the storm
passed, as soon as the two French expeditionary forces under
Mortier and Sebastiani returned once more to their usual
garrison-posts.

Only two more incidents remain to be chronicled in the
Andalusian campaign of 1810. Campbell, the governor of
Gibraltar, had resolved—somewhat too late—to lend a small
detachment to aid the Granadan insurgents. The plan which
he concerted with the Spanish governor of Ceuta was that
Lord Blayney with two British battalions from the Gibraltar
garrison—the 82nd and 89th, and a Spanish regiment (Imperial
de Toledo) from Ceuta, 2,200 men in all, should be thrown on
shore at Fuengirola, twenty miles on the nearer side of Malaga,
where there was a small French garrison and a dépôt of stores,
which was serving for a brigade then engaged in the siege of
Marbella, the town which had been garrisoned by Lacy in
June [1], and which was still holding out gallantly in October.

It was calculated that, on hearing of a descent at Fuengirola,
Sebastiani would come with the larger part of the garrison

[1] See p. 328 of this chapter.

of Malaga to relieve the fort.   But the moment that he was known to be nearing the expeditionary force, Lord Blayney was to re-embark and to make a dash at Malaga itself, which he could reach more swiftly by water than Sebastiani by land. Secret partisans within the city were ready to take arms, and the peasantry of the Sierra de Alhama were also enlisted in the enterprise.   The scheme seems liable to many criticisms—the whole was at the mercy of the winds and waves of stormy October: what would happen if the weather was too rough to allow of re-embarkation, or of easy landing at Malaga?   And if Malaga were captured for the moment, for how long could 2,000 regulars, backed by a mass of undisciplined insurgents, hold it against the whole of Sebastiani's corps, which would be hurled upon it at short notice?   The expedition, however, was not actually wrecked on either of these dangers, but ruined by the folly of its chief.   Lord Blayney landed successfully on October 13, and laid siege to Fuengirola, which was held by 150 Poles under a Captain Milokosiewitz.   Instead of making the attack a mere demonstration, he brought some 12-pounders ashore, and set to work to batter the castle in all seriousness. Finding its walls commencing to crumble, he held on for two days, though, if he had reflected, he must have remembered that the garrison of Malaga might be with him at any moment. He was busily preparing for an assault, when Sebastiani suddenly fell upon him with 3,000 men from the rear.   Apparently the English commander had neglected to keep up any watch on the side of the inland, and the peasantry had failed to send any intelligence of the fact that the French were on the move. The besiegers, taken entirely by surprise, and distracted also by a sortie of the little garrison, were rolled down to the sea-shore in confusion.   Lord Blayney—a short-sighted man—rode in among some French whom he mistook for Spaniards, and was made prisoner in the most ignominious fashion.   The Spanish regiment got off with little loss: it had kept its ranks, and forced its way to the boats after beating off an attack.   The 82nd was partly on shipboard at the moment of the combat, and the companies which were on shore saved themselves by a steady rearguard action.   But the battalion of the 89th was half destroyed, losing over 200 prisoners besides some forty killed. The utter incapacity of the British commander was best shown by the fact that if he had but carried out the plan on which he was acting, he would certainly have captured Malaga—for Sebastian had left only 300 men in the city when he marched on Fuengirola, and, if the expeditionary force had re-embarked twenty-four hours before the disaster, it would have found the place practically undefended, and Sebastiani a long day's march away, and incapable of returning in time to save it [1].

The very last military event of the year 1810 on the Andalusian side was a disaster far worse than that of Lord Blayney —suffered by a general whose almost unbroken series of defeats from Medina de Rio Seco down to Belchite ought to have taught him by this time the advantages of caution, and the doubtful policy of risking a demoralized army in a fight upon open ground. When Sebastiani retired from the kingdom of Murcia in the first days of September, Blake had brought back his army to its old positions on the frontier of that realm. Seven weeks later, finding the French line in front of him very weak, he resolved to try a demonstration in force, or perhaps even a serious stroke against the force of the enemy in Granada. On November 2 he crossed the Murcian border, with 8,000 foot and 1,000 horse, and occupied Cullar.

On the next day he was at the gates of Baza, where there were four battalions of the French force which covered Granada [2]. But on the next morning General Milhaud rode up with a powerful body of horsemen, the greater part of his own division of Dragoons and the Polish Lancers from Sebastiani's corps-cavalry, some 1,300 men in all. Though he had only 2,000 infantry to back him, Milhaud determined to fight at once. Blake's army invited an attack ; it was advancing down the high-road with the cavalry deployed in front, one division of infantry supporting it, while a second division was some miles

---

[1] Lord Blayney, a humorous person save when the absurdities of his own generalship were in question, wrote an interesting narrative of his 'Forced Journey to France,' which contains one of the best accounts of the state of Madrid under King Joseph's government, as well as some curious notes on the state of the English prisoners at Verdun in 1811–13.

[2] From the 32nd and 58th Line, Rey's brigade of Sebastiani's corps. The 88th, in *Victoires et Conquêtes*, xx. 127, and Arteche is a misprint. That regiment was with Girard in the Sierra Morena, 150 miles away.

to the rear, on the hills which separate the plain of Baza from the upland of the Sierra de Oria. A rearguard of 2,000 men was still at Cullar, ten miles from the scene of action. The situation much resembled that of Suchet's combat of Margalef, and led to the same results. For Milhaud's squadrons, charging fiercely along and on each side of the road, completely routed Blake's cavalry, and drove it back on to the leading infantry division, which broke, and was badly cut up before its remnants could take shelter with the other division in reserve on the hill behind. Blake gave the order for an instant retreat, and Milhaud could not follow far among the rocks and defiles. But he had captured a battery of artillery and a thousand prisoners, and killed or wounded some 500 men more, in the few minutes during which the engagement lasted. The French cavalry lost no more than 200 men. The infantry had hardly fired a shot. Blake, not being pursued, retired only as far as the Venta de Bahul on the other side of Cullar, and remained on the Murcian border, cured for a time of his mania for taking the offensive at the head of a demoralized army.

Thus ended the inconclusive campaign of 1810 in Andalusia— the French on the last day of the year held almost precisely the same limits of territory that they had occupied on the 1st of March. They had beaten the enemy in four or five considerable actions, yet had gained nothing thereby. They were beginning to understand that Cadiz was impregnable, and that the complete subjection of the mountains of the South and East was a far more serious task than had been at first supposed. Things indeed had come to a deadlock, and Soult kept reporting to his master that another 25,000 men would be required to enable him to complete his task. Almost as many battalions belonging to the 1st, 4th, and 5th Corps as would have made up that force had been sent by the Emperor into Spain. They were intended to join their regiments in the end, but meanwhile they had been distracted into the 8th and 9th Corps, and were marching in the direction of Portugal, when Soult wished to see them on the Guadalquivir [1]. Very little of the mass of reinforcements which

---

[1] The 8th Corps had in its ranks the 4th battalions of the following regiments whose first three battalions were in the south of Spain, and belonged to the 1st, 4th, or 5th corps—the 28th, 34th, and 75th. But

had been poured into the Peninsula in the spring of 1810 had
come his way. While the whole battalions had been sent away
with Junot or Drouet, the drafts in smaller units had been
largely intercepted by the generals along the line of communication. There were 4,000 of such recruits detained in
New Castile alone, and formed into 'provisional battalions' to
garrison Madrid and its neighbourhood. King Joseph must
not be blamed too much for thus stopping them on their way :
he had been left with an utterly inadequate force, when the
Emperor turned off everything on to the direction of Portugal.
During the summer and autumn of 1810 there were with him
only two French infantry regiments [1], the same number of light
cavalry regiments [2], Lahoussaye's weak division of dragoons [3], and
the German division of the 4th Corps less than 4,000 strong,
over and above his own guard and untrustworthy 'juramentado'
battalions [4]. The royal troops numbered about 7,000 men, the
other units, including Soult's detained drafts, about 12,000 : with
them Joseph had to garrison Madrid, Avila, Segovia, Toledo, and
Almaraz, and hold down all New Castile and La Mancha—which
last province was described at the time as 'populated solely by
beggars and brigands '. He had the duty of maintaining the
sole and very circuitous line of communication between Soult
and Masséna, which, after Reynier went north in July, had to
be worked via Almaraz. He was frequently annoyed not only by
the Empecinado and other guerrilleros, but by Villacampa, who
descended from higher Aragon into the Cuenca region, and by
Blake's cavalry, which often raided La Mancha. But his great

the 9th Corps was almost entirely composed of 4th battalions of the corps
of Victor, Sebastiani, and Mortier, including those of the 8th, 24th, 45th,
54th, 63rd, 94th, 95th, 96th Line, and 16th and 27th Léger, of the 1st
corps, and of the 17th Léger, and 40th, 88th, 100th and 103rd Line of the
5th Corps.

[1] 28th and 75th, the remaining brigade of the 1st Division of the 4th
Corps, which never joined Sebastiani in Andalusia.

[2] 26th Chasseurs and 3rd Dutch Hussars.

[3] 17th, 18th, 19th, and 27th Dragoons, only two squadrons each—only
1,300 men.

[4] As a sample of their behaviour it may be mentioned that the whole
guard of the south gate of Toledo once marched off to join the insurgents,
officers and all.

fear was lest La Romana or Wellington should send troops
up the vast gap left between Reynier at Zarza and Coria
and Mortier in the Sierra Morena ; there was nothing but
Lahoussaye's dragoons and two infantry battalions in the whole
district about Almaraz and Talavera, where such a blow would
have fallen.   It was small wonder that he felt uncomfortable.

But military sources of disquietude formed only the smaller
half of King Joseph's troubles at this date.   His political
vexations, which engrossed a much larger portion of his time
and energy, must be dealt with elsewhere.   They will be
relegated to the same chapter which treats of the new development of Spanish politics consequent on the long-delayed meeting
of the Cortes in the winter of 1810–11.

SECTION XXI

BUSSACO AND TORRES VEDRAS

CHAPTER I

MASSÉNA'S ADVANCE TO BUSSACO

AFTER the fall of Almeida Masséna waited much longer than Wellington had anticipated. The reasons for his delay were the usual ones that were always forthcoming when a French army had to advance in the Peninsula—want of transport and penury of supplies. The Marshal had just discovered that the country-side in front of him had already been depopulated by Wellington's orders, and that the only inhabitants that were to be met would be the armed Ordenanza, who were already shooting at his vedettes and attacking his foraging parties. He was inclined to treat them as brigands; his Provost-marshal, Colonel Pavetti, having been surprised and captured along with five gendarmes of his escort by the villagers of Nava d'Avel on September 5, he caused the place to be burned, shot the one or two male inhabitants who could be caught, and issued a proclamation stating that no quarter would be given to combatants without uniforms. This provoked two stiff letters from Wellington [1], who wrote to say that the Ordenanza were an integral part of the Portuguese military forces, and that, if they wore no uniforms, the Marshal should remember that many of the revolutionary bands which he had commanded in the old war of 1792–7 were no better equipped: 'vous devez vous souvenir que vous-même vous avez augmenté la gloire de l'armée Française en commandant des soldats qui n'avaient pas d'uniforme.' If Ordenanza were shot as 'brigands and highway robbers' in obedience to the proclamation of September 7, it

---

[1] Wellington to Masséna, Sept. 9 and Sept. 24.

was certain that French stragglers and foragers would be knocked
on the head, and not taken prisoners, by the enraged peasantry.
At present the number of them sent in to the British head
quarters by the Portuguese irregulars proved that the laws of
war were being observed.   Masséna replied that Pavetti had
been ambushed by men who hid their arms, and ran in upon
him and his escort while he was peaceably asking his way.
His letter then went off at a tangent, to discuss high politics,
and to declare that he was not the enemy of the Portuguese
but of the perfidious British government, &c., &c.   Finally he
complained that the Arganil and Trancoso militia, whom he
had sent home after the fall of Almeida, had taken up arms
again ; if caught, 'leur sort sera funeste' [1].   The last statement
Wellington denied ; he said that the capitulation had been
annulled by the French themselves, when they debauched the
24th regiment, and detained 600 of the militia to form a
battalion of pioneers, but stated that as a matter of fact the
militia battalions had not been re-embodied.   The French
continued to shoot the Ordenanza, and the Ordenanza soon
began to reply by torturing as well as hanging French stragglers ;
Wellington forbade but could not prevent retaliation.

In his dispatch to Berthier of September 8 [2], Masséna explains
that the depopulation of the district in front of him, and the
fact that the Ordenanza had taken arms throughout the country-
side, have compelled him to make an enormous provision of
food for his army.   Since the land has been swept bare, he must
collect fifteen or twenty days' rations for the 6th and 8th Corps.
'Each day demonstrates the necessity of this more clearly, but
each day makes it more evident that we are not obtaining as
much as our activity deserves.   The small amount of transport
available, and the destruction by the Spanish brigands of several
convoys of corn which were coming up from the province of
Valladolid, have occasioned delay in the accumulation of the
stores.   An additional vexation is that while it was reported
that we had captured 300,000 rations of biscuit in Almeida,
there turn out really to be only 120,000 rations.'   But it was

[1] Masséna to Wellington, Sept. 14, from Fort Concepcion (*Archives du
Ministère de la Guerre*).
[2] In the *Archives du Ministère de la Guerre*, see Appendix to this vol.

the loss of draught-beasts that was the most serious trouble ;
to his great regret Masséna had to cut down the artillery of
each division from twelve to eight guns, for want of horses, with
a similar reduction of the caissons.   Every animal that could be
procured was given over to the train, yet it could not carry even
the fifteen days' food which the Marshal considered the minimum
that he could afford to take with him.   There was also a
deficiency in cartridges for the infantry, for whom 1,200,000
rounds were only procured by setting the artificers of the train
to make up as many as was possible from the powder captured
at Ciudad Rodrigo.   Finally Masséna explains that the losses
in the two late sieges, the necessity for garrisoning Almeida and
Rodrigo, and the effects of a sickly summer, have reduced the
two corps and the reserve cavalry under his hand to 42,000 or
45,000 men, so that he must incorporate Reynier with his main
army, in order to get a sufficient force concentrated for the
invasion.   When this has been done, he will have no force to
leave behind to guard his communications, and Kellermann and
Serras are too much occupied to spare a man for that purpose.
The Spaniards will press in between the army and Salamanca
the moment that the troops have entered the Portuguese mountains.   He will advance, therefore, on September 15, but only
with grave apprehension for his rear, and he begs that at all costs
a division of the 9th Corps should be brought up to Salamanca.
He had been promised long ago that this should be done, but
no signs of Drouet's arrival were yet visible.

Reynier accordingly was called up, at last, to join the main
army ; he left Zarza and Penamacor on the 10th of September,
crossed the Pass of Perales, and on the 12th was at Alfayates,
with cavalry in front at Sabugal.   Hill, always vigilant, perceived Reynier's movement as soon as it had taken place.   On
the 12th his corps quitted Sarzedas, leaving nothing behind in
the Castello Branco country save Lecor's Portuguese at Fundão,
who were ordered to follow, unless Reynier should send back
any detachments to the south side of the Sierra de Gata.   Leith
started from the banks of the Zezere three days later, and on
the 20th the two divisions were drawing near to Wellington's
rear in the valley of the Mondego, Hill being at Espinhal that
day, and Leith (who had less distance to cover) a march further

to the front, at Foz d'Aronce. Wellington's concentration on the Alva must obviously be completed before the French could strike.

On September 15, 1810, Ney and Junot broke up from the encampments in front of Almeida, while Reynier drew in close to the main body by marching up from Sabugal towards Guarda. It was clear that the attack of the French was to be delivered along the line of the Mondego, but whether by its southern or its northern bank Wellington could not yet be sure, though he was under the impression that the former would be the chosen route, since the *chaussée* from Almeida by Celorico and Ponte de Murcella is good for a Portuguese road, while the mountain track by Trancoso and Vizeu is abominable. Yet one of the three columns of the French pointed from the first towards the north bank: while Ney took his way by Freixadas and Alverca towards Celorico, Junot was reported to have turned off from the main road at Valverde, and to be marching by Pinhel westward or north-westward. What Reynier would do after reaching Guarda remained yet to be seen.

The total force which Masséna had drawn together for the invasion was 65,000[1] officers and men. He had left behind a regiment of dragoons and four battalions of infantry to take care of Almeida and Ciudad Rodrigo. In the latter place he had also deposited his siege-train, with the considerable body of artillerymen belonging to it. Brennier and Cacault commanded at the two places respectively. They had between them some 3,500 men, a force which perceptibly diminished the army of invasion, yet was insufficient to do more than to hold the two fortresses. Gardanne, with five squadrons of dragoons, was to maintain touch between them. Not a man would be available from the garrisons for service against Spanish or Portuguese insurgents—indeed both Almeida and Rodrigo were practically under blockade from the moment that the main army went forward, and were destined to learn nothing of its

---

[1] For details see the Tables in the Appendix. All the troops left behind have been rigidly deducted. The figures given by Fririon, 59,806, are not quite exact, see proofs in Appendix: he makes some troops enter Portugal which were left as garrisons, and on the other hand omits whole battalions which marched, as if they had never existed.

doings for many days. Wellington's *cordon* of Ordenanza proved perfectly efficient [1].

On the evening of the 15th the 2nd Corps had reached Guarda, from which it drove out a picket of the 16th Light Dragoons, who retired towards the Mondego. The 6th Corps bivouacked at Freixadas, having pushed back from it two squadrons of the 14th Light Dragoons and the German Hussars. The 8th Corps, which had to come up from the Azava, passed Almeida and slept beyond the Coa. In its rear was Montbrun's reserve cavalry division, and behind this again the reserve artillery of the whole army. This column, therefore, was by far the longest and (owing to the amount of guns and caissons) the most unwieldy of the three masses in which the French were marching.

On the 16th Wellington hoped to see Masséna's designs unmasked. But it proved a day of continued doubt: Reynier left Heudelet's division at Guarda, and moved on with Merle's and the cavalry to Celorico. Here he met Ney, who had marched from Freixadas to Celorico, and had pushed his light cavalry through it in advance. One body of horsemen took a hill road high up the side of the Serra da Estrella, and reached Linhares, another followed the great *chaussée* as far as Carapichina, and detached a squadron or two from that point to seize the bridge of Fornos d'Algodres, over which passes the bad side-road from Celorico to Vizeu. Was the enemy about to turn aside on this path, or to pursue the more probable policy of continuing along the *chaussée* to Ponte de Murcella? Nothing could yet be deduced from Junot's movements: his heavy column only reached Pinhel that day: from thence he might either come down to Celorico (the most probable course), or make a move towards Oporto, by the high-road Pinhel–Marialva–St. Joao da Pesqueira, or (what seemed least likely) follow the very bad mountain-road from Pinhel by Povoa d'el Rei to Trancoso and Vizeu. Meanwhile Wellington ordered

[1] The troops left behind were the fifth battalion of the 82nd, the fourth battalions of the 15th and 86th, and a provisional battalion of convalescents, or about 2,000 infantry; a squadron of the 3rd Dragoons (157 men), the whole of the 10th Dragoons (718 men) under Gardanne, and some 800 men belonging to the siege-train and park.

the continuation of the retreat of his army towards Ponte de
Murcella and the position behind the Alva.   The 1st, 3rd, and
4th Divisions retired at their leisure along the great *chaussée*, by
Saragoça and Chamusca : the Light Division moved parallel to
them by the mountain-road Gouvea–San Martinho–San Romão.
The appearance of Ney's cavalry at Linhares on this track made
the Commander-in-Chief anxious to have it watched, since it
was possible that the 6th Corps might use it.   The cavalry,
keeping the rear well guarded, lay this day at Pinhanços on
the *chaussée* and San Martinho on the hill-road.   Head quarters
were at Cea, on the latter line.   The only troops now left north
of the Mondego, on the route which Junot might possibly
follow from Pinhel, were a few cavalry-pickets, wherefore the Commander-in-Chief, conceiving it just possible that the 8th Corps
might be intending to make a dash at Oporto, while the other
two kept him in check, sent urgent letters to Trant, the officer
in charge of the militia of Northern Beira, and to Baccellar,
who lay at Oporto with the militia of the Entre-Douro-e-Minho,
to take precautions against this movement.   Trant, from
Moimento de Beira, was to feel for Junot's front and flank :
Baccellar was to send out some picked battalions, under
J. Wilson, to the line of the Vouga, and to get into touch with
Trant on his left.

On the 17th Masséna's intentions at last became clear to his
adversary.   The cavalry of the 6th Corps crossed the bridge
of Fornos, which it had seized on the previous night, and the
leading division of infantry followed it to Juncaes, on the
Mondego bank : nothing came along the *chaussée*, all the French
columns turning off it at Carapichina, and pursuing the cross-
road.   Ney's rear was still at Celorico, to which place the whole
of the 2nd Corps also came up that day.   In the evening the
head of the cavalry of the 6th Corps was near Mangualde, many
miles along the road north of the Mondego.   It seemed probable
therefore, that a transference of the whole French army to the
right bank, over the bridge of Fornos, was about to take place.
This became almost certain when the simultaneous news arrived
that Junot had marched that day from Pinhel not towards
Celorico, nor on the Oporto road (that by Marialva and St. Joao
da Pesqueira), but by the abominable cross-road by Povoa d'el

Rei to Trancoso. The 8th and 6th Corps therefore were showing a tendency to converge on Vizeu. If so, they must be aiming at reaching Coimbra without touching Wellington's chosen position of Ponte de Murcella, where he had hoped to fight. This deduction once made, the British commander had to recast his plans. 'The 2nd and 6th Corps came to Celorico yesterday,' he wrote to Leith that evening, 'and a part of them crossed the Mondego at Fornos. More have crossed this day, while no part of the enemy's army has moved this way [i. e. along the great *chaussée* south of the river]. It is generally understood that their whole army is between the Douro and the Mondego, and that they are about to move on Coimbra. I shall have troops in Coimbra to-morrow[1].' All the divisions were ordered back at once, so as to be ready on the Lower Mondego to resist the French, when they should appear from the direction of Vizeu. Only cavalry were left at Sampayo and Gouvea, to watch the passage of the Mondego by the French army, and to make certain that its rear (i. e. Reynier's corps) might not be about to use the main *chaussée*, a move which was even yet possible.

Masséna's resolve to use the route by the north bank of the Mondego surprised all British and some French observers at the time, and has been censured by most historical critics. He left a good for a bad road : he imposed two extra marches on his army at a moment when it was short of provisions. He gave Wellington ample time to call up Hill and Leith, and to select a new position for battle to replace that of Ponte de Murcella. The Bussaco hillsides, where the clash was to come, were as formidable as those behind the Alva. But these considerations were less obvious to Masséna in 1810 than they appear to the critic of 1907. It must first be remembered that his maps were abominable : the actual case of plans used by the staff of the Army of Portugal is preserved[2]: it is that issued by Lopez in 1778, which in the remoter parts of Portugal

[1] To Cotton and to Leith, both dated Sept. 17.

[2] For a most interesting article on these maps, and all that they show, see Mr. T. J. Andrews's article in the *English Historical Review* for 1901. The maps, captured at Vittoria, are now in the Library of Queen's College, Belfast.

not only offers a mere travesty of the natural features, but
actually marks as existing roads that never had been made,
and omits others that were actually available. It shows, moreover, no distinction between *chaussées*, country roads, and mere
mule tracts. Places of considerable importance are misplaced
by several miles, e. g. Almeida is placed on the Coa instead of
two miles from it : Vizeu is much too far north, as is also Bussaco.
As far as this map goes, the physical difficulties in the way
of an advance north of the Mondego look no greater than those
on the southern bank. But, it may be said, Masséna should
have supplemented the use of the map by collecting oral information, and by sending reconnaissances in every direction.
He did so, so far as was in his power. But exploration far
afield was only possible with large bodies of men, since the
Ordenanza blocked every road to the isolated staff-officer, and
the only oral information which was forthcoming was defective.
Masséna asked for it from Alorna, Pamplona, and the other
Portuguese officers on his staff—there were no less than eighteen
of them in all. They were absolutely ignorant of their own
country,—a normal thing in the military men of the old Portuguese army. Even Pamplona, whose estates lay in the neighbourhood of Coimbra, gave hopelessly erroneous information
about the routes leading into that town. But, from natural
amour propre they avoided confessing their ignorance, and, when
taken into council by Masséna, gave him copious but wholly
misleading details. They assured him that the roads Pinhel–
Trancoso-Vizeu and Fornos–Mangualde–Vizeu were no worse
than other lines of communication, and that the great *chaussée*
by Sampayo and Ponte de Murcella was crossed by so many
torrents and climbed so many slopes that it was not preferable
to the routes north of the river. The news that a formidable
position behind the Alva had been entrenched had reached the
French head quarters ; hence Masséna had fair reasons for
taking the route that he selected, so far as strategy went. It
undoubtedly enabled him to turn the line of the Alva. Moreover, on it lay a large town—Vizeu—from which it was hoped
that much food would be procured, for the invaders were still
ignorant of the thoroughness with which Wellington's plans for
devastating the country before them had been carried out. Even

after Celorico and Guarda had been found empty of inhabitants, they hardly believed that such a large place as Vizeu, a town of 9,000 souls, would be deserted.

Masséna's mistake became evident to his soldiers on the first day on which he ordered his columns to quit the main-roads and take to the by-paths. The infantry could still get forward, but the artillery and waggon-train began to drag behind, to lose horses, and to see vehicle after vehicle broken, disabled, or abandoned. On the 18th the infantry of the 6th Corps got as far as Mangualde on the north bank of the Mondego, but the artillery was so much delayed in the defile after passing Juncaes that it could not catch up the rear of the marching troops, and had to be parked at night not many miles beyond the bridge of Fornos. The 2nd Corps on reaching this spot found the road blocked, and bivouacked with one division beyond the Mondego, and one still in the rear of the bridge. But the troubles of this column were nothing to those of the 8th Corps on the miserable road from Pinhel to Vizeu. The journal of the commandant of the artillery of Junot's first division, Colonel Noël, may be quoted as giving a fair description of the marches of the 17th and 18th September :—

'After passing the little town of Trancoso, with its battlemented wall, all the country-side is mountain and rock. There is no road, only a stony narrow dangerous track, which the artillery had all the pains in the world to follow without meeting accidents. It is all steep ups and downs. I had to march with a party of gunners ahead of me, with picks and crowbars to enlarge the track. As each arm only looked out for itself, the artillery soon got left to the rear, and deserted by the infantry and cavalry. We only arrived at our halting-places late at night, utterly done up. The guns were almost always abandoned to themselves; we did not know what road to follow, having no one to give us information but a few infantry stragglers, who had themselves lost their way. At noon on the 18th I halted with my two batteries after two hours of incessant uphill, to find myself at the crest of a mountain, with a precipitous descent before me, and beyond that another ascent winding upwards, as far as the eye could reach. We were so exhausted that it was useless to go further that day, but on the 19th, with a party of gunners always working in front to enlarge the road, we moved over hill and vale, completely out of touch with the army. I had to ride out with four mounted men to hunt for any trace of it. At last, in a deserted village, we found an old peasant who pointed out the road to Vizeu. But it was only on the 20th that we got there.' Noël's batteries, it may be remarked, were moving all the time between the infantry, which was ahead, and the Grand Park which was behind them, with Montbrun's cavalry bringing up the rear. Yet they were absolutely lost and had to shift for themselves without orders or escort [1].

The Park fared even worse ; when nearing Sotojal, on the 20th, it was unexpectedly beset by Colonel Trant, who had come down from Moimenta with a brigade of his militia and two squadrons of Portuguese regular cavalry. The Park was escorted by one company of grenadiers, who marched at its head, and a battalion of the Irish Legion, who were far to the rear, while Montbrun's immense cavalry column was quite out of sight. Trant had a great opportunity, for the long file of vehicles and guns, caught in a narrow road, was almost helpless. But he failed to do all that was in his power ; his cavalry charged the company at the head of the column and was repulsed. He then filed his battalions along the hillside, opened fire on the horses and men of the train, and, descending into their midst, captured and destroyed some caissons and took some eighty prisoners. But when the escort-battalion came hurrying up from the rear, his levies were stricken with panic and hastily retired, though they were strong enough to have held off the five hundred Irish, and to have smashed or rolled over the precipices the greater part of the guns and waggons. Montbrun's cavalry did not get up till all was over, and would have been perfectly useless on the precipitous road, even if they had arrived earlier. If Trant's foray had been properly carried out, Masséna might have lost his reserve artillery and most of his provisions—a disaster which might have forced him to turn back to Almeida. He deserved such a punishment for having marched his all-important

<hr>

[1] *Mémoires* of Col. Noël, pp. 112–13.

train on the extreme flank of his army, with an insufficient escort[1].

Though Junot's infantry divisions reached the deserted walls of Vizeu on Sept. 19th and there met the corps of Ney, the divisional artillery did not arrive till next day, while the reserve artillery, the trains and the heavy cavalry were struggling in upon the 21st and 22nd by detachments. For Montbrun had halted the great convoy after Trant's attack, and parked it, fearing that the Portuguese might come back in greater numbers and give more trouble. When he started it again, on the 21st, he took care to give it better marching arrangements, and to attach cavalry escorts to each section. But this caused much delay, and meanwhile the 8th Corps waited at Vizeu 'marking time' and unable to move. Even the 6th Corps remained there two days, waiting while its gun-carriages and cannons were being repaired ; for the Fornos–Vizeu road, though infinitely less rough than that which the 8th Corps and the park had followed, was still bad enough to shake many vehicles to pieces. The Intendant-General reported that nineteen caissons carrying 2,900 rations of biscuit belonging to the 6th Corps broke down and had to be burnt ; the food was distributed among the regiments as they passed, with much consequent waste[2]. All that Ney could do between the 18th of September, when he reached Vizeu, and the 21st, was to push forward an advanced guard to Tondella, fifteen miles down the Vizeu–Coimbra road, with an infantry division in support at Fail. Meanwhile the 2nd Corps, following in the wake of the 6th, had also made its way to Vizeu. The bulk of Reynier's force took the Fornos–Mangualde–Lagiosa route, as Ney's had done. But an advanced guard of all arms descended the great *chaussée* south of the river as far as Taboa, driving in the pickets of the English cavalry, and then crossed the Mondego at the bridge of Taboa, and fell into the rear of the rest of the corps beyond Mangualde. This apparently was intended to keep Wellington uncertain, as long as possible, as to whether part

---

[1] A lively account of this affair may be found in Marbot, ii. 378 ; details may not be all trustworthy, but the general narrative agrees with Trant's report, printed in Soriano da Luz, vol. vii, Appendix.

[2] Report of Lambert, Intendant-General, dated Vizeu, Sept. 23.

of the French army was not intending, after all, to follow the
chaussée and present itself before the position on the Alva [1].
But it was executed by so small a force that the British general
was not for an hour deceived [2].   He was at this moment in a
cheerful frame of mind; Masséna had made a mistake in
choosing his route, and was merely wasting time when time
was most precious.   'There are certainly many bad roads in
Portugal,' he wrote, ' but the enemy has taken decidedly the
worst in the whole kingdom ' [3]; and again, 'I imagine that
Marshal Masséna has been misinformed, and has experienced
more difficulty in making his movement than he expected.
He has certainly selected one of the worst roads in Portugal
for his march [4].'   Owing to the necessary delays of the enemy
Wellington was now in a position as strong as that on the
Alva ; his head quarters were at the convent of Bussaco, his
divisions, including Leith and Hill, so placed that they could
be concentrated on the Serra de Alcoba, right across the Vizeu–
Coimbra road, long before the French could descend from Vizeu.
' We have an excellent position here, in which I am strongly
tempted to give battle [5],' he wrote on the evening of the 21st,
foreseeing six days ahead the probability of the engagement
which was to make Bussaco famous.   There was a road by
which his position might be turned, but it was doubtful
whether the enemy would discover it, and 'I do not yet give
up hopes of discovering a remedy for that misfortune [6].'

Masséna, meanwhile, was chafing at his self-imposed delays,
and writing querulous letters from Vizeu to Berthier.   'The
grand park and the baggage,' he wrote on the 22nd, ' are still
in the rear, and will only get up to-morrow.   It is impossible
to find worse roads than these ; they bristle with rocks ; the
guns and train have suffered severely, and I must wait for them.
I must leave them two days at Vizeu when they come in, to rest

---

[1] Wellington to Lord Liverpool, from Lorvão, Sept. 20.

[2] Indeed, an exploring party under Captain Somers Cocks, of the
16th Light Dragoons, had dogged the steps of the detachment, and counted
every battalion.   See Tomkinson's Diary, pp. 39–40.

[3] Wellington to Charles Stuart, Sept. 18.

[4] Wellington to Lord Liverpool, Sept. 20.

[5] Ibid., Sept. 20.

[6] Wellington to Stapleton Cotton, Sept. 21.

themselves, while I resume my march on Coimbra, where (as I am informed) I shall find the Anglo-Portuguese concentrated. Sir, all our marches are across a desert ; not a soul to be seen anywhere ; everything is abandoned. The English push their barbarity to the point of shooting the wretched inhabitant who tries to remain in his village ; the women, the children, the aged, have all decamped. We cannot find a guide anywhere. The soldiers discover a few potatoes and other vegetables ; they are satisfied, and burn for the moment when they shall meet the enemy.' The plan of devastation was already beginning to work ; Masséna had exhausted seven of the thirteen days' provisions which his army carried, and it was not with the potatoes gleaned in the fields of Vizeu, or the ripe grapes of its vineyards, that he could refill the empty store-waggons. He must push on for Coimbra as fast as possible ; this, no doubt, was why he made up his mind to march on that place, not by descending from Vizeu to Aveiro and entering the coast plain, but by taking the direct road by Santa Comba Dao, Mortagoa, and Bussaco. Even Lopez's faulty map shows the ridge of Bussaco as a serious physical feature, but the Marshal does not seem to have reflected for a moment that Wellington might choose to defend it. The orders drawn up on September 24th for the march on Coimbra presuppose an unobstructed progress [1]. Having met no active resistance as yet from the Anglo-Portuguese army, Masséna wrongly took it for granted that he might count on the prolongation of this good fortune.

Before moving on from Vizeu the organization of the French army was slightly modified. Junot's corps contained a number of fourth battalions, belonging to regiments whose three senior battalions were serving in the 2nd Corps. The two corps had never met till both lay at Vizeu. Masséna then ordered the fourth battalions of the 36th, 47th, 70th of the Line, and the 2nd and 4th Léger to join their regiments in Reynier's corps ; this reduced the 8th Corps by 2,850 men ; in return, however, Reynier was ordered to make over to Junot two regiments of old troops, the 15th and 86th of the line (each of three battalions)

---

[1] See the orders in the *Archives du Ministère de la Guerre.*

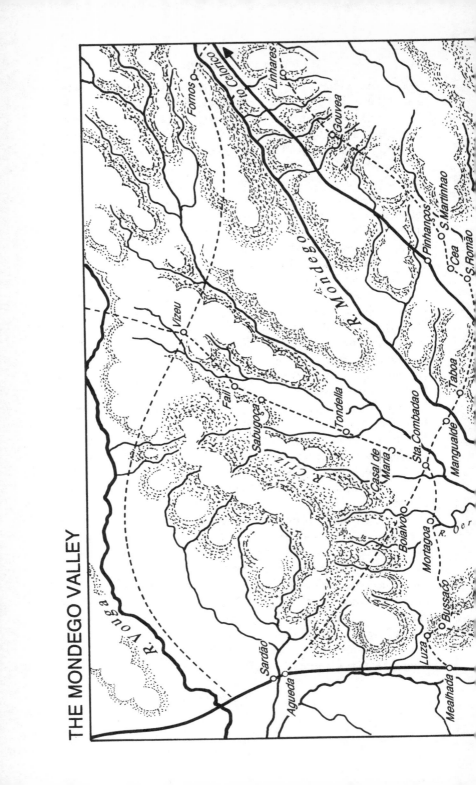

THE MONDEGO VALLEY

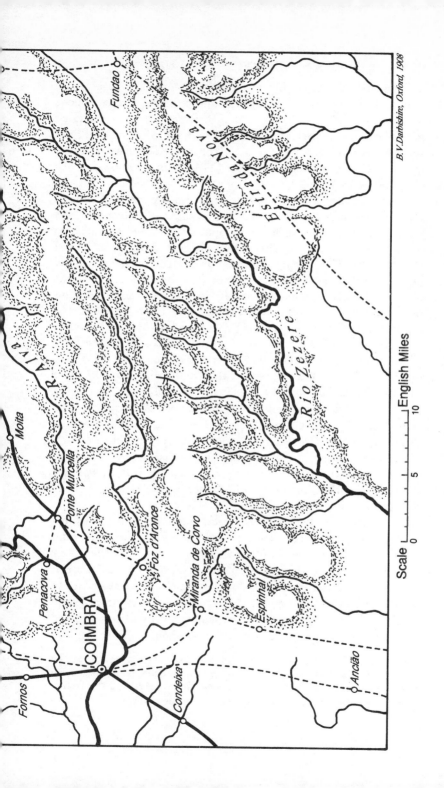

Scale
0   5   10
English Miles

B.V.Darbishire, Oxford, 1908

making in all 2,251 bayonets. Thus the two corps were somewhat equalized in quality, the 2nd receiving five battalions of recruits, while the 8th (in which there were too few veterans) got in return six battalions which had served in Spain since the commencement of the war. The net result was to make the 2nd Corps a little stronger (17,024 men) and the 8th Corps a little weaker (15,904 men) [1].

On September 21st the advance of the Army of Portugal was recommenced, though the train and heavy baggage was not yet prepared to start, and some of its rear detachments had not even reached Vizeu. But on that day the advanced guard of the 6th Corps advanced from Tondella, and found in front of it some light cavalry and two Portuguese regiments —the first hostile troops that the French had seen since the campaign began. The whole of the 2nd and 6th Corps followed behind, and bivouacked that night at Casal-de-Maria, Tondella, Sabugoça and other villages on the steep downward road from Vizeu to Coimbra. The 8th Corps still remained at Vizeu, guarding the belated reserve artillery and train. On the 22nd the 2nd Corps, passing the 6th, which had hitherto taken the lead, crossed the Criz and drove in the British outposts, who retired on Mortagoa. But Ney and the 6th Corps remained stationary, and the 8th did not even yet make a start. These delays seem extraordinary, but Masséna was still paying for his evil choice of roads ; the infantry had to wait for the guns, and the guns could only creep forward as the sappers enlarged and improved the roads for them.

Wellington, meanwhile, was recasting his dispositions at his leisure. When Masséna's march on Vizeu had become certain, the British Commander-in-Chief thought at first that the enemy would take the good *chaussée* Vizeu–Aveiro, so as to descend into the coast-plain and attack Coimbra from the easiest side. He therefore, on the 18th moved the 1st Division back from Ponte de Murcella to Coimbra, where it was joined by a new brigade from Lisbon, composed of the 1st battalions of the 7th and

---

[1] It is this interchange of troops which makes all the figures of the Army of Portugal so divergent. Fririon, for example, ignores it, as do most French statisticians. But see Masséna's orders (14), and the ' situations ' in the *Archives* of Sept. 14 and Sept. 27 respectively.

79th, newly landed. A. Campbell's and Coleman's Portuguese also moved to the same point. The 3rd and 4th Divisions remained at Ponte de Murcella in the entrenched position, with the Light Division and Pack's Portuguese in front of them at Venda do Porco and Sampayo.

But on the 20th, when Ney's advanced guard began to come out from Vizeu on the Santa Comba Dao road, not on the Aveiro road, Wellington discovered that it was on the mountain of Bussaco, and not on the plain in front of Coimbra, that he would next meet the enemy. Accordingly Pack's Portuguese and the Light Division forded the Mondego below Sampayo, as did the light cavalry, and a detaining force was thus thrown across the Vizeu–Coimbra road. The Portuguese brigade took post behind the Criz torrent, Craufurd's men a little to the rear at Mortagoa. At the same time the 1st Division and the troops attached to it moved out from Coimbra to Mealhada on the Aveiro road, a point from which they could easily be called up to the Bussaco position, if no French columns were discovered coming down the Aveiro road, as now seemed probable. This day, Leith's division, to Wellington's intense satisfaction, arrived at San Miguel de Payares behind the Alva, and so joined the main body. Hill was reported to be a day's march only to the rear, at Foz d'Aronce. Thus the whole of the Anglo-Portuguese regular forces between Douro and Tagus were neatly concentrated. At the same time Trant was told to bring the militia of Northern Beira down the Oporto–Coimbra road to Agueda and Sardão, and Baccellar was directed to support him with Wilson's militia brigade, in case Masséna should have some subsidiary operation against Oporto in his mind.

On the 24th the first skirmish of the campaign took place ; the 2nd Corps, advancing into the plain in front of Mortagoa, found Pack's Portuguese facing them on the right, and Craufurd's division on the left, with a screen of cavalry in front. They pushed in the horsemen upon the infantry, but halted when artillery opened upon them, and made no further advance. On this day the belated 8th Corps, with the reserve cavalry, at last started from Vizeu. Next morning Reynier pressed on in force with two heavy columns each formed by a division, and Craufurd was ordered by Wellington to retire, which he did with some reluctance by alternate échelons of brigades[1]. The 95th and 43rd had some sharp skirmishing with the French van, and made a stand by the village of Moura under the Bussaco heights, before retiring up the high-road, and taking position upon the crest of the great ridge [2], which they did at six o'clock in the evening.

While the advanced guards of Reynier and Ney were driving in Craufurd and Pack, the Anglo-Portuguese army was assembling on Wellington's chosen fighting-ground. Picton and Cole, with the 3rd and 4th Divisions, had already taken up their quarters on the Bussaco ridge on the 21st, the first across the road from San Antonio de Cantaro to Palheiros, the second across the *chaussée*, behind the spot to which the troops of Pack and Craufurd were retiring. Leith, who had been brought over the Mondego by the fords of Peña Cova on the 23rd, moved up on to the southern tract of the Bussaco heights on the 24th. Hill, who reached the line of the Alva on the 22nd, followed in Leith's wake, and on the 25th was at Peña Cova waiting for orders to cross. The 1st Division with Campbell's and Coleman's Portuguese alone were still absent, though not far off. They had started from Mealhada, when it became clear that no French force was coming by the Aveiro–Coimbra road, but on the night of the 25th were still some eight miles away, and did not get into position between Cole and Picton till between nine and ten o'clock on the morning of the 26th.

Nevertheless, nearly 40,000 men, composed of the Light, 3rd, 4th, 5th Divisions and their Portuguese auxiliaries, and of Hill on their flank, only four miles away, were concentrated on the night of the 25th, when Reynier's vanguard deployed in front of the heights. Before ten o'clock on the following morning Spencer had arrived, and Hill was over the fords and encamped along the rear slopes of the heights. There seems to be no truth whatever in the allegation that the British army was in a

---

[1] According to Napier (iii. 22–3) Craufurd risked his division somewhat in their skirmish. But this criticism is not made by D'Urban, Leach, and other eye-witnesses.

[2] The Light Division had been first divided into brigades on Aug. 8, when the 1st was constituted of the 43rd, four companies of the 95th, and the 1st Caçadores, under Beckwith : the 2nd of the 52nd, four companies of the 95th, and the 3rd Caçadores, under Barclay. See Atkinson's lists of the Peninsular Army in the *Eng. Hist. Rev.*

somewhat dangerous position on the evening of the 25th, for the French had only their vanguard up, and there were less than two hours of daylight left when Craufurd retired from Moura, and Reynier and Ney obtained their first view of the British position. Before the enemy could have collected in strength sufficient for an attack, night would have set in.

NOTE ON THE SITUATION ON SEPT. 25

Napier wholly misrepresents the state of affairs in vol. iii. pp. 22–3. He writes as follows : ' Before 3 o'clock 40,000 French infantry were embattled on the two points (the *chaussée* and the San Antonio de Cantaro road), their guns trying the range above, while the skirmishing clatter of musketry arose from the dark wooded chasms below. Ney, whose military glance was sure, instantly perceived that the mountain, a crested not a table one, could hide no great reserves, that it was only half occupied, and that the allies were moving with the disorder usual on the taking of unknown ground. He wished therefore to attack, but Masséna was ten miles to the rear, the officer sent to him waited two hours for an audience, and then returned with orders to attend the Prince's arrival. Thus a great opportunity was lost, for Spencer was not up, Leith's troops were only passing the Mondego, and Hill was still behind the Alva. Scarcely 25,000 men were in line, and with great intervals.'

Almost every statement here is incorrect. (1) The French did not reach the ground in front of the heights till 5 o'clock : they were not up at 3 p.m. [D'Urban's *Diary* : ' At noon, the heads of the French infantry columns having reached the lower falls leading from the Mortagoa Valley, he pushed forward his cavalry and began to skirmish with our pickets. It not being Lord Wellington's intention to dispute this ground, but rather to entice Masséna to follow and attack him in his position of Boçaco, the Light Division was gradually withdrawn, the 95th and 43rd covering the retreat and Ross's artillery playing upon the enemy's advance from hill to hill, till at 5 o'clock they were halted by the fire of the 43rd before the village of Sula. At about 6 the firing ceased, and our advance (heretofore at Moura and Sula) took up their ground (as well as General Cole's division) upon the heights of Boçaco.'] This diary, *written that same night*, cannot be wrong as to the dating of the hours. D'Urban was riding with Beresford at Wellington's side. Napier was writing from memory twenty years after.

(2) Ney did not ' perceive the mountain only half occupied, and wish to attack,' on the evening of the 25th. His reconnaissance was made on the morning of the 26th, and it was *then* that he expressed his wish to attack, when Wellington had every man in line. This is conclusively proved by the following note of Ney to Reynier, dated at 10.30 on the morning of the 26th, from his advanced posts, which lies in the French archives :—

' Je reçois à l'instant, mon cher général, votre lettre de ce jour. Je pense qu'une grande partie de l'armée anglo-portugaise a passé la nuit sur la crête des montagnes qui dominent la vallée de Moura. Depuis ce matin l'ennemi marche par sa gauche, et semble diriger ses colonnes principales sur la route d'Oporto. Cependant il tient encore assez de monde à la droite du parc, qui couvre le couvent de Minimes appelé Sako, et montre une douzaine de pièces d'artillerie. Le chemin de Coimbre passe tout près de ce couvent. Si j'avais le commandement j'attaquerais sans hésiter un seul instant. Mais je crois que vous ne pouvez rien compromettre en vous échellonant sur la droite de l'ennemi, et en poussant ses avant-postes le plus possible : car c'est véritablement par ce point qu'il faudrait le forcer à faire sa retraite.' What Ney had seen, and wrongly took for a general movement of the English army towards its left, was Cole taking ground to the left on the arrival of Spencer, who came up between 8 and 10 that morning, just before Ney was scribbling this hasty note to Reynier.

(3) The stretch of mountain opposite Ney and Reynier was *not* ' crested' but ' table '— so much so that Wellington took two squadrons of cavalry up to it, for use in the battle. The British general *never* took up a position where he had no space to hide his reserves.

(4) The time when Ney sent an officer to Masséna to ask leave to attack was the morning of the 26th, not the evening of the 25th. How could Ney have hoped to get the permission to fight and carry it out, when the time when he reached Moura was 5 o'clock, and dusk falls at 6.30? The messenger had twenty miles to ride, to Mortagoa and back. See Fririon's note in his ' Aperçu sur la Campagne de Portugal' in *Victoires et Conquêtes*, xxi. 320.

(5) Leith's troops, so far from being ' only passing the Mondego' on the afternoon of the 25th, had passed it on the 23rd [*Journal* of Leith Hay, aide-de-camp of Leith, i. 228]. On the night of the 22nd–23rd Wellington wrote to Hill, ' Leith's, Picton's, and Cole's divisions are now on the Serra de Busaco' [*Dispatches*, vi. 462]. Hill was not ' behind the Alva,' but massed at the fords of Peña Cova, only four miles from the battle-field. He crossed at dawn on the 26th, but could have been in action within two hours of the first shot, if the attack had been made on the 25th.

(6) Wellington, including Hill's division, had therefore 40,000 men, not 25,000. But the latter number would have sufficed, for Ney and Reynier had only their advanced guards up, and in the hour and a half before dusk could not have brought up their whole corps by the bad and narrow roads from behind. The *Diary* of the 6th Corps mentions that only the vanguard division (Loison) bivouacked in front of the heights. The rearguard was as far back as Barril that night.

(7) The exact moment of the arrival of the British 1st Division may be gauged from the fact that it passed Luzo, the village behind Bussaco, at 8 a.m. on the 26th—Diary of Stothert (3rd Foot Guards), p. 188. There is only two miles from Luzo to the position taken up by the 1st Division.

SECTION XXI: CHAPTER II

THE BATTLE OF BUSSACO

It remains that we should describe the ground which Wellington had chosen on the 21st, and on which he fought with such splendid success upon the 27th. The ridge which takes its name from the convent of Bussaco is one of the best-marked positions in the whole Iberian Peninsula. A single continuous line of heights covered with heather and furze, with the dull-red and dull-grey granite cropping up here and there through the soil, extends from the Mondego on the right—where it ends precipitously—to the main chain of the Serra de Alcoba on the left. The ridge is very irregular in its altitude : the two loftiest sections are one at a distance of two miles from the Mondego, and the other to the immediate right of the convent enclosure, where the original obelisk commemorating the battle was set up[1]. Between these two culminating summits the ridge sinks down, and is at its lowest where the country-road from San Antonio de Cantaro to Palheiros passes over it. There are three other points where it is crossed by lines of communication; two lie far to the east, not far from the Mondego, where bad paths from San Paulo to Palmazes and from Carvalhal to Casal exist. The third and most important is in its left centre, where (close to the convent) the *chaussée* from Celorico to Coimbra, the main artery of the local road-system, passes the watershed. It does so at a place which is by no means the least lofty point of the ridge ; but the line was obvious to the road-making engineer, because a spur (the only one of any importance in the heights) here runs gradually down from the Serra into the lower ground.

---

[1] There are two monuments : this simple weather-beaten obelisk on the culminating height where the 1st Division stood, a point where no fighting took place, and the modern column lower down and close to the high-road, behind the spot where Craufurd fought. Here the Portuguese to this day maintain a small military post, and hoist a flag to do honour to the victory.

To lead the *chaussée* up the side of this spur, past the village
of Moura, and so to the crest of the ridge on gentle slopes, was
clearly better than to make it charge the main range, even at
a less lofty point. The convent lies just to the right of the
spot where the *chaussée* passes the sky-line, a few hundred yards
off the road. It was a simple, low quadrangle, with a small
chapel in its midst, standing in a fine wood of pine and oak,
surrounded by a ten-foot wall. The wood is sprinkled with
hermitages, picturesque little buildings hewn in the rock, where
those of the monks who chose practised the anchorite's life. The
outer wall of the wood and the tops of its trees are just visible
on the sky-line of the main ridge : the convent is not, being
well down the reverse-slope. The point where the convent wood
tops the heights is the only section of them where trees are seen
on the summit : the rest of the line is bare heath, with occasional outbreaks of rock, falling in slopes of greater or lesser
steepness towards the broken wooded foot-hills, where the French
lay. On part of the left-centre there is ground which it is no
exaggeration to describe as precipitous, to the front of the
highest piece of the ridge, below the old obelisk. The effect
of the whole line of heights is not dissimilar to, though on a
smaller scale than, the Malvern Hills. The highest point on
the Serra is about 1,200 feet above sea-level— but much less,
of course, above the upland below.

The position of Bussaco is fully nine miles long [1] from end to
end, from the steep hill above the Mondego to Cole's western
flank : this was a vast front for an army of 50,000 men to cover,
according to the ideas of 1810. There were absolute gaps in the
line at more than one place, especially above Carvalho, where
about a mile separated Leith's left from his central brigade.
The defence of such a position could only be risked because of
two facts : one was that every movement of the enemy on the
lower ground before the ridge could be accurately made out from
above : he could not concentrate in front of any section of the
heights without being seen. His only chance of doing so would
have been to take advantage of the night ; but even if he had
drawn up for the attack before dawn—a thing almost impossible

---

[1] Which makes astounding Fririon's statement that it was only three-
quarters of a league long (p. 46).

in the broken, ravine-cut, wooded bottoms—he could not have moved till full daylight, because the face of the position presents so many irregularities, such as small gullies and miniature precipices, that columns climbing in the dark must undoubtedly have got lost and broken up on the wild hill-side. Moreover, there was a thick cordon of British pickets pushed forward almost to the foot of the ridge, which would have given warning by their fire and their preliminary resistance, if any advance had been attempted in the grey dawn.

The second advantage of the Bussaco position is that on its left-centre and right-centre the ridge has a broad flat top, some 300 or 400 yards across, on which all arms can move laterally with ease to support any threatened point. It is so broad that Wellington even ventured to bring up a few squadrons of dragoons to the summit, rightly arguing that a cavalry charge would be of all things the most unexpected reception that an enemy who had breasted such a hillside could meet at the end of his climb. As a matter of fact, however, this section of the heights was never attacked by the French. The right of the position is not flat-topped like the centre, but has a narrow saddle-back, breaking into outcrops of rock at intervals : but though here prompt motion from right to left, or left to right, is not possible on the crest, there is a rough country-path, good for infantry and available even for guns, a few hundred yards down the reverse side of the slope. Along this troops could be moved with ease, entirely out of sight of the enemy. It proved useful for Leith's division during the battle. Wellington calculated, therefore, with perfect correctness, that he could count on getting an adequate force of defenders to any portion of his long line before the enemy could establish himself on the summit. The extreme left, where Cole's division lay, was the hardest part of his line to reinforce, for want of good lateral communication : it was also a good deal lower than Craufurd's post ; here, therefore, Wellington had placed the main mass of his reserves ; the German Legion, and two Portuguese brigades were lying on his left-centre very close to the 4th Division, so that they would be available at short notice, though they would have a stiff climb if the French chose that section of the position as their objective, and it had to be strengthened in haste.

The distribution of the army remains to be described. On the extreme right, on the height of Nossa Senhora do Monte, just overhanging the Mondego, was a battalion of the Lusi-tanian Legion, with two guns. Next to them, on very high ground, lay Hill's division, three British and two Portuguese brigades[1], with a battery on each flank. Then came a slight dip in the ridge, where the road from San Paulo to Palmazes crosses it: athwart this path lay Leith's newly constituted 5th Division, consisting of three British and seven Portuguese battalions. The British brigade lay on the right, then came (after a long interval) two battalions of the Lusitanian Legion, the only troops guarding two miles of very rough ground. On Leith's extreme left, towards Picton's right, was Spry's Portuguese brigade, and three unattached battalions (8th Line and Thomar militia). Beyond the 8th regiment, where the watershed sinks again, and is crossed by the road from San Antonio de Cantaro to Palheiros, Picton's line began. On his right, across the road, was Arentschildt's Portuguese battery, supported by the 74th British regiment, and Champlemond's Portuguese brigade of three battalions. The 45th and 88th, the two remaining battalions of the brigade of Mackinnon, were placed to the left of the road, the former on the first spur to the north of it, the latter nearly a mile to the left. Lightburne's brigade, and Thompson's British battery were a short distance beyond the 88th. North of Picton's position the ridge rises suddenly again to its loftiest section; along this almost impregnable ground, with its precipitous front, were ranged the three British brigades of Spencer's 1st Division—the Guards on the right, Blantyre's on the left, Pakenham's in the centre, 5,000 bayonets dominating the whole country-side and the rest of the position. North of them again, where the ridge falls sharply along the back wall of the convent wood, was Pack's Portuguese brigade, reaching almost to the high-road. Along the curve of the high-road itself, in column, was Coleman's Portuguese brigade, and beside it A. Campbell's Portuguese, with

---

[1] Archibald Campbell's and Fonseca's brigades, forming Hamilton's Portuguese Division, which was attached to the British 2nd Division throughout the war, and shared with it the triumphs of Albuera, Vittoria, and St. Pierre.

the German Legion beyond them on the Monte Novo ridge. Coleman, Campbell, and the Germans were the main reserve of the army, and were in second line, for, far to the front of them, on a lower slope, along a curve of the *chaussée*, lay Craufurd and the Light Division, looking down on the village of Sula almost at the bottom of the heights. Between Craufurd and his next neighbour to the right, Pack, was a curious feature of the field, a long narrow ravine, with steep grassy sides, terraced in some places into vineyards [1]. This cleft, between Sula on the left and Moura on the right, cuts deep up into the hillside, its head almost reaching the crest of the watershed below the convent. In order to circumvent this precipitous gully, the *chaussée*, after passing through the village of Moura, takes a semi-circular curve to the right, and goes round the head of the cleft. For half a mile or more it overhangs the steep declivities on its right, while on its left at this point it is dominated by a pine wood on the upper slopes, so that it forms more or less of a defile. The gully is so narrow here that guns on Craufurd's position had an easy range on the road, and enfiladed it most effectively. The battery attached to the Light Division—that of Ross—had been placed in a sort of natural redoubt, formed by a semi-circle of boulders with gaps between; some of the guns bore on the village of Sula, on the lower slope below, others across the ravine, to the high-road. They were almost invisible, among the great stones, to an enemy coming up the hill or along the *chaussée*. Craufurd had got a battalion of his Caçadores (No. 3) in the village, low down the slope, with his other Portuguese battalion and the 95th Rifles strung out on the hillside above, to support the troops below them. His two strong Line battalions, the 43rd and 52nd, were lying far above, in the road, at the point where it has passed the head of the gully in its curve, with a little fir wood behind them and

---

[1] This is the feature which Napier, somewhat hyperbolically, describes as ' a chasm so profound that the naked eye could hardly distinguish the movement of troops in the bottom, yet so narrow in parts that 12-pounders could range across (iii. 21).' It does *not*, as he says, separate the Serra de Bussaco from the last ridge in front of it, that which the French held, as it only lay in front of Craufurd and Pack. There is no chasm between Spencer's, Picton's, Leith's, or Hill's position and the French knolls.

a small windmill in their front. The road being cut through the hillside here, they were screened as they stood, but had only to advance a few feet to reach the sky line, and to command the slope stretching upwards from the village of Sula.

To the left rear of Craufurd's position, and forming the north-western section of the English line lay Cole's 4th Division, reaching almost to the villages of Paradas and Algeriz. Its Portuguese brigade (11th and 23rd regiments) was thrown forward on the left under Collins, its two English brigades were at the head of the slope. The ground was not high, but the slope was very steep, and as a matter of fact was never even threatened, much less attacked.

Sixty guns were distributed along the line of the Serra. Ross's horse artillery troop were with Craufurd, Bull's with Cole ; of the field-batteries Lawson's was with Pack, Thompson's with Lightburne, Rettberg's [K.G.L.] with Spencer, Cleeves' [K.G.L.] with Coleman. There were also four Portuguese field-batteries ; Arentschildt's was on the high-road with Picton, Dickson's two batteries with Hill, Passos's with Coleman, alongside of Cleeves' German guns. Counting their artillerymen, and the two squadrons of the 4th Dragoons on the summit of the plateau, Wellington had 52,000 men on the field. Of the rest of his disposable army, the Portuguese cavalry brigade (regiments 1, 4, 7, 8 ; 1,400 sabres under Fane) and one British regiment (13th Light Dragoons) were beyond the Mondego, far to the south-east, watching the open country across the Alva as far as Foz Dao and Sobral. Their head quarters were at Foz de Alva. To defend the Ponte de Murcella position against any possible flanking force the French might have detached, Wellington had left Le Cor's Portuguese, two regular regiments (Nos. 12 and 13) and three battalions of the Beira militia. All these troops were ten or twelve miles from the nearest point at which a shot was fired, in a different valley, and were alike unseeing and unseen. In a similar fashion, far out to the west, on the other side of the watershed, in the low ground by Mealhada, was the English cavalry, with the exception of the one regiment at Foz de Alva and two squadrons on the Convent ridge.

Reynier's corps, pushing the English rearguard before it,

had arrived in front of the Bussaco position on the afternoon of
September 25th. When Ney's corps came up at dusk Reynier
edged away to the left, and established himself on the low hills
above the hamlet of San Antonio de Cantaro, leaving the ground
about the high-road to the 6th Corps. The 8th and Montbrun's
cavalry were still some way behind, beyond Barril. Masséna,
for reasons which it is hard to divine, had not come to the front,
though he must have heard the guns firing all through the afternoon, and had been informed by Reynier that the English were
standing at bay on the Bussaco ridge. He came no further to the
front than Mortagoa on the 25th. Ney on the morn of the next
day was busy reconnoitring the position ; he sent forward
tirailleurs to push in Craufurd's outposts, and ventured as far
to the front as was possible. So well hidden was Wellington's
line that the Marshal formed an entirely erroneous conception
of what was before him. At 10.30 in the morning he wrote
to Reynier to say that the whole English army seemed to be
moving to its left, apparently on the road towards Oporto,
but that it had still a rearguard, with a dozen guns, in position to the right of the park which covers the convent.
Apparently Cole's division, taking ground to its left on Spencer's
arrival, and Craufurd on the *chaussée* was all that he had
made out. He had not discovered Leith and the 5th Division,
and could not, of course, know that Spencer was at this
moment arriving at the convent, and that Hill was across
the Mondego at Peña Cova.

The Marshal added that if he had been in chief command
he should have attacked whatever was in front of him without
a moment's hesitation [1]. But things being as they were, he
thought that Reynier would risk nothing by pushing forward
on the English right, and thrusting back Wellington's outposts, for it was desirable to make him retreat towards his
left. It is clear that Ney, if he had possessed a free hand,
would have brought on a battle, when he was only intending
to drive in a rearguard. For by 10.30 on the 26th Wellington
had every man upon the field whom he intended to use in
the fight, and would have welcomed an assault. Of the French,
on the other hand, Junot's 8th Corps and the cavalry and

---

[1] See the letter quoted on page 358.

artillery were still far away to the rear. They only came up in rear of Ney on the night of the 26th–27th.

Masséna, on receiving Ney's report, rode up to the front at about two o'clock on the 26th—a late hour, but he is said to have been employed in private matters at Mortagoa[1]. When he had at last appeared, he pushed forward as near to the foot of the British position as was safe, and reconnoitred it with care. In the evening he drew up orders for attacking the Bussaco heights at their most accessible points—along the *chaussée* that leads from Moura up to the convent, and along the country-road from San Antonio de Cantaro to Palheiros.

The Prince of Essling had no hesitation whatever about risking a battle. He had never seen the English before, and held concerning them the same views as the other French officers who had no experience of Wellington's army. Some confused generalization from the misfortunes of the Duke of York's troops in 1794–5 and 1799 determined the action of all the marshals till they had made personal acquaintance with the new enemy. The English were to be dealt with by drastic frontal attacks pushed home with real vigour. It is curious, as Napoleon remarked soon after[2], that Reynier, who had been badly beaten by the English at Alexandria and Maida, had learnt no more than the others, and committed exactly the same errors as his colleagues. He, who had experience of his adversaries, and Ney, who had not, adopted precisely the same tactics. These, indeed, were indicated to them by Masséna's order to attack in columns, each at least a division strong, preceded by a swarm of *tirailleurs*. There was no question of a general advance all along the line; the two Corps-Commanders were directed to choose each his point, and to break through the British army at it, by force of mass and impact. Only two sections of Wellington's nine-mile position were to be touched, there being a long gap between the objectives assigned to Ney and to Reynier. But by throwing 13,000 or 14,000 men in close order at each of the two short fronts selected, Masséna thought that he could penetrate the thin line of the defenders.

---

[1] See Marbot, ii. p. 384—if that lively writer may be trusted.

[2] See Foy's account of his interview with the Emperor in his *Vie Militaire*, p. 108.

As none of the historians of the battle have thought it worth
while to give the Marshal's orders in detail, and many writers
have misconceived or mis-stated them, it is necessary to state
them [1]. The attacks of the 2nd and 6th Corps were not to be
simultaneous; Reynier, having the easier ground before him,
was told to move first. He was to select the most accessible
stretch of the hillside in his front, and to climb it, with his
whole corps in one or two columns, preceded by a skirmishing
line. Having gained the crest, and pierced the British line, he
was to re-form his men, and then drop down the reverse slope
of the heights on to the Coimbra road, along which he was
to press in the direction of the convent of Bussaco, toward the
rear of Wellington's centre.

Ney was directed not to move till he should have learnt that
Reynier had crowned the heights; but when he should see the 2nd
Corps on the crest, was to send forward two columns of a division
each against the British left-centre. One division was to follow
the *chaussée*, the other to mount the rough path up the spur on
which the village of Sula stands. Both columns, like those of
the 2nd Corps, were to be preceded by a thick line of skirmishers.
They were to halt and re-form when the crest of the English
position should be carried, and then to adapt their movements
to suit those of Reynier's corps.

Junot was to assemble his two infantry divisions behind
Moura, and to have them ready to reinforce either Ney or
Reynier as might be needed. His artillery was to be placed on
the knolls on each side of the *chaussée*, so as to be able to hold
back the allied army if, after repulsing Ney, it should attempt
a forward movement. Montbrun's cavalry and the reserve
artillery were to be placed on either side of the *chaussée* behind
Junot's centre [2].

The horsemen were obviously useless, save that in the event of
Wellington being defeated they could be sent forward in pursuit.
Nor were the guns much more serviceable : they could sweep
the lower parts of the slopes of Bussaco, but could not reach its
crest with their fire. Indeed, the only French artillery used

---

[1] This unpublished document from the *Archives du Ministère de la
Guerre* seems to have escaped all historians.

[2] These orders are printed in the Appendix.

successfully on the next day were two batteries which Ney's columns of attack took with them along the *chaussée*, as far as the elbow of road in front of Moura. These were in effective range of Craufurd's and Pack's troops, since the latter were on a level with them, and not on the highest crest of the British position. Reynier's guns could just reach the summit of the pass of San Antonio de Cantaro, but not so as to play upon it with any good result.

It is said that Junot and Reynier were in favour of trying the frontal attack which Masséna had dictated, as was also Laszowski, the Polish general who commanded the engineers of the army. Fririon, the chief of the staff, and Eblé, commanding the artillery, spoke against the policy of 'taking the bull by the horns.' Masséna, according to Fririon, turned on the doubters with the words 'You come from the old Army of the Rhine, you like manœuvring; but it is the first time that Wellington seems ready to give battle, and I want to profit by the opportunity [1].' Ney, too, as we read with some surprise, is said to have given the opinion that it would have been feasible to assault the heights yesterday, but that now, when Wellington had been given time to bring up his reserves and settle his army down into the most advantageous position, the policy of taking the offensive had become doubtful. He therefore advised that the army should turn aside and make a stroke at Oporto, which would be found unprotected save by militia. Masséna, according to his official biographer, announced 'that the Emperor had ordered him to march on Lisbon, not on Oporto. This was entirely correct : the capture of Lisbon would end the whole war, that of Oporto would prolong it, and bring no decisive result. Moreover, it was quite uncertain whether Wellington would not be able to prevent such a move. He has troops échelloned as far as the Vouga, and he could get to Oporto in three marches, because he possesses the Oporto-Coimbra *chaussée*, while the French army, moving by worse roads, would require five marches to reach it.' It is suggested that Ney's policy was

---

[1] So Fririon in his *Campagne de Portugal*, p. 47. But his enemy Pelet says (*Vic. et Conq.*, xxi. p. 321) that Ney, like Reynier, 'demanda la bataille à grands cris.' Cf., for what it is worth, Marbot's tale, ii. 384.

really to goad his superior into making the frontal attack at
Bussaco, by feigning to believe it dangerous and to counsel its
abandonment.   For he thought that Masséna would do precisely
the opposite of what he was advised, out of his personal dislike
for himself, and general distaste for having counsel thrust upon
him.   If this was so, the Duke of Elchingen carried his point—
to the entire discomfiture both of himself and his commander-
in-chief[1].

On the 26th, after Masséna had retired to his head quarters
at Mortagoa, there was a little skirmishing on the English
right-centre, where Reynier's advanced guard drove the light
company of the 88th off some knolls at the foot of the
heights, opposite San Antonio de Cantaro.   Much about the
same time there was some bickering on Ney's front : the pickets
of Pack's 4th Caçadores and Craufurd's 95th were attacked, but
held their ground.   The contest was never very serious and the
fire died down at dusk.   That evening the British army slept
in order of battle, 'each man with his firelock in his grasp at
his post.   There were no fires, and the death-like stillness that
reigned throughout the line was only interrupted by the
occasional challenge of an advanced sentry, or a random shot
fired at some imaginary foe.'   Below and in front, all the
low hills behind Moura and San Antonio were bright with the
bivouac fires of the French, of which three great masses could
be distinguished, marking the position of the 2nd, 6th, and
8th Corps[2].

The dawn of the 27th was somewhat misty, but as soon as
the light was strong enough Reynier commenced his attack.   He
had chosen for his objective, as was natural, the lowest point
of the ridge opposite him, the dip where the country-road from
San Antonio de Cantaro crosses the Serra.   His two divisions,
according to order, were drawn up in two heavy columns preceded by a dense swarm of *tirailleurs*.   Heudelet's division on
the left was across the high-road, with the 31st Léger in front,
then the two regiments of Foy's brigade, the 70th and 17th
Léger, with the 47th in reserve.   The whole made 15 battalions,

---

[1] All this is told at great length in Koch's *Vie de Masséna,* vii. p. 192,
where the Council of War is described with many details.

[2] Grattan's *Adventures with the 88th*, pp. 28–9, and Leith Hay, i. 231.

BATTLE OF BUSSACO Sep.27th 1810

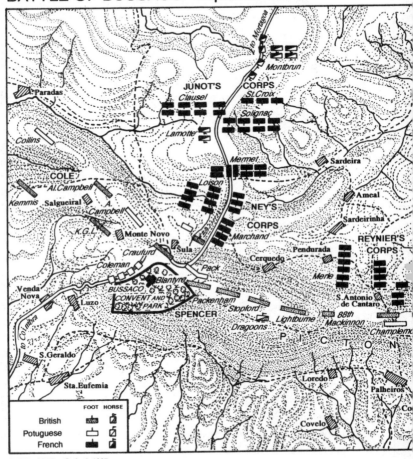

B.V.Darbishire, Oxford, 1907

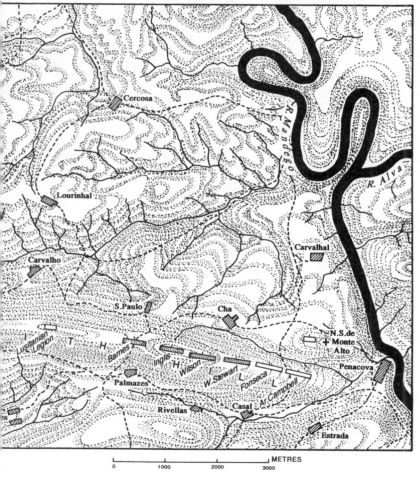

Cercosa

Lourinhal

Carvalho

S.Paulo

Cha

Carvalhal

R. Mandego

R. Alva

N.S.de
Monte
Alto

Penacova

Lusitanian
Legion

T   H

Barnes

Inglis   H   Wilson

W.Stewart

Fonseca

L

At Campbell

Palmazes

Rivellas

Casal

Estrada

METRES

| 0 | 1000 | 2000 | 3000 |

or 8,000 men.   Merle's division had the right, and was to attack
north of the road : of its eleven battalions, making 6,500 men,
the 36th of the Line led, the 2nd Léger followed, the 4th Léger
brought up the rear.   All the battalions were in serried column
with a front of one company only, and in each regiment the
three, or four, battalions were originally drawn up one behind
the other.   But the involuntary swerving of the attack soon
turned the two divisions into an irregular échelon of battalion-
columns, the right in every case leading.   And the roughness
of the hillside soon broke the ordered ranks of each column
into a great clump of men, so that to the British defenders
of the ridge the assault seemed to be delivered by a string of
small crowds crossing the hillside diagonally.   It is curious
that Reynier placed no troops to his left of the road ; a study
of his orders (as of those of Masséna[1]) leads to a suspicion
that they had failed to discover Leith's division, and still more
Hill's, and imagined that the road was on the extreme right,
not in the right-centre, of the British position.   Otherwise
Reynier would have taken some precaution to guard himself
from a flank attack from Leith, to which he was deliberately
exposing his left column.

There were, as has already been pointed out, several gaps in
the nine-mile British line.   One was between the 8th regiment
of Portuguese, on Leith's extreme left, and the rest of the 5th
Division.   Another was between Picton's troops at the pass
of San Antonio and his left wing—the 88th and Lightburne's
brigade.   Between the 45th and the 88th there was three-
quarters of a mile of unoccupied ground.   The first gap led to
no danger, the second caused for a moment a serious crisis.
Such was indeed almost bound to occur when a line so long was
held by such a small army.   But this morning there arose the
special danger that fog hid the first movements of the enemy
from the eye, if not from the ear.

Merle's division seems to have been the first of Reynier's two
columns to move : at dawn, with the mist lying thick on the
hillside, it began to move up the steep slope some three-quarters

---

[1] Masséna's orders for the battle call Reynier's attack one on 'la
droite de l'armée ennemie,' but it was really on the right-centre, Hill
and Leith extending for four miles south of the point assailed.

of a mile to the right of the San Antonio–Palheiros road. Here its *tirailleurs* came in contact with the light companies of the 74th, 88th, and 45th regiments, which were strung out along the front, and soon began to push this thin line up hill. For some reason undetermined—a trick of the mist, or a bend of the hillside—the three French regiments all headed somewhat to their left, so as to pass across the front of the 88th, and to direct their advance precisely to the unoccupied piece of crest between that regiment and the troops placed immediately above the pass of San Antonio. Their progress was slow : the *tirailleurs* left far behind them the eleven battalion-columns, which were trampling through the dense matted heather which here covers the hillside. Hearing the bicker of the skirmishing far to his left, Picton took the alarm, and though he could see nothing in the fog, detached first a wing of the 45th under Major Gwynne, and then the two battalions of the 8th Portuguese, to fill the unoccupied space which intervened between him and the 88th. If he had suspected the strength of the column that was aiming at it he would have sent more. But he was already distracted by the frontal attack of Heudelet's vanguard along the high-road. A column of four battalions— the 31st Léger—was pushing up the road, and driving in the skirmishers of Champlemond's Portuguese brigade. Just at this moment the mist began to lift, and Arentschildt's guns opened on the broad mass, and began to plough long lanes through it. It still advanced, but was soon brought to a stand-still by the fire of the British 74th and Portuguese 21st, which were drawn up in line to right and left, a little below the guns. The 31st Léger tried to deploy, but with small success, each section being swept away by the converging fire of the Anglo-Portuguese musketry, as it strove to file out of the disordered mass. Nevertheless, the French regiment gallantly held its ground for some time, shifting gradually towards its right to avoid the fire of the guns, and gaining a little of the hillside in that direction with its first battalion, while the other three were tending to edge away from the road, and to break up into a shapeless crowd [1].

[1] The *Mémoires* of Lemonnier Delafosse, a captain in the 31st Léger, give an excellent and clear account of its sufferings, see pp. 69–70 of his work.

Picton soon saw that there was no danger here, handed over the command at the Pass of San Antonio to Mackinnon, and started off towards his left, where the firing was growing heavier every minute, and the vast column of Merle's division, climbing the hillside diagonally, had become visible through the mist.

It was fortunate that the attack of Merle was made very slow by the steepness of the hillside and the heather that clung about the soldiers' stumbling feet. For the leading regiment reached the crest before there were any British troops yet established on the point at which it aimed. It was lurching over the sky-line on to the little plateau above, just as the defenders arrived—the 88th descending from the British left, the wing of the 45th and the two battalions of the 8th Portuguese coming along the hill-road from the right. If the French had been granted ten minutes to rest from the fatigue of their long climb, and to recover their order, they might have broken the British line. But Wallace, the commander of the 88th, was one of Wellington's best colonels, the very man for the emergency. Seeing that the French must be charged at once, ere they had time to make a front, he threw out three of his companies as skirmishers to cover his flanks, called to the wing of the 45th to fall in on his right, and charged diagonally across the little plateau on to the flank of the great disordered mass before him. At the same moment the 8th Portuguese, a little further along the hilltop, deployed and opened a rolling fire against the front of the enemy, while Wellington himself, who had been called down from his post of observation on the Convent height by the noise of the fighting, came up with two of Thompson's guns, and turned their fire upon the flank and rear of the climbing mass, which was still surging up the hillside. Apparently at the same instant the light companies of the 45th and 88th, which had been engaged in the earlier skirmishing with the French *tirailleurs*, and had been driven far away to their right, were rallied by Picton in person, and brought up along the plateau, to the right of the 8th Portuguese. They drew up only sixty yards from the flank of the leading French regiment, and opened a rolling fire upon it.

At any other juncture and on any other ground, four battalions would have been helpless against eleven. But Wal-

lace had caught the psychological moment: the French 36th,
dead beat from its climb, and in hopeless disorder, was violently
charged in flank by the Connaught Rangers and the wing of
the 45th, while it was just gathering itself up to run in upon
the Portuguese battalions that lay in its front. The French
had no time to realize their position, or to mark the smallness
of the force opposed to them, when the blow fell. The four
battalions of the 36th were rolled down hill and to their left
by the blasting fire of Wallace's little force, followed by a
desperate bayonet charge. They were thrust sideways against
the 2nd Léger, which was just reaching the sky-line on their left,
and was beginning to struggle in among some rocks which here
crown the crest of the heights. Then the whole mass gave way,
trampled down the 4th Léger in their rear, and rushed down the
slope. 'All was confusion and uproar, smoke, fire, and bullets,
French officers and soldiers, drummers and drums, knocked
down in every direction; British, French, and Portuguese mixed
together; while in the midst of all was to be seen Wallace
fighting like his ancestor of old, and still calling to his soldiers
to "press forward." He never slackened his fire while a Frenchman was within his reach, and followed them down to the
edge of the hill, where he formed his men in line waiting for
any order that he might receive, or any fresh body that might
attack him [1].' This was certainly one of the most timely and
gallant strokes made by a regimental commander during the
war, and the glory was all Wallace's own, as Picton very hand-
somely owned. 'The Colonel of the 88th and Major Gwynne
of the 45th are entitled to the whole of the credit,' he wrote to
Wellington, 'and I can claim no merit whatever in the executive
part of that brilliant exploit, which your Lordship has so highly
and so justly extolled [2].'

The victorious British troops followed the enemy far down
the hillside, till they came under the fire of Reynier's artillery,

---

[1] Grattan's *Adventure with the Connaught Rangers*, p. 35.

[2] Picton to Wellington, *Supplementary Dispatches*, vi. p. 635. I do not
know whether Wallace really descended from the famous Sir William,
but Craufurd of the Light Division (as his descendant and biographer
has pointed out to me) chanced to have a connexion with the Knight
of Ellerslie.

and were warned to retire to their former position. They thus
missed the last episode of Reynier's attack, which occurred along
the hillside just to the left of the point at which their collision
with Merle's battalions had taken place. The Commander of
the 2nd Corps, seeing his right column rolling down the slope,
while the 31st was melting away, and gradually giving ground
under the fire of the Anglo-Portuguese troops at the Pass of
San Antonio, hurried to Foy's brigade and started it up the hill
to the right of the 31st. Foy had been told to support that
regiment, but had taken Reynier's orders to mean that he was
to follow up its advance when it began to make headway. His
Corps-Commander cantered up to him shouting angrily, 'Why
don't you start on the climb? You could get the troops forward if you choose, but you don't choose.' Whereupon Foy
rode to the leading regiment of his brigade, the 17th Léger,
put himself at its head, and began to ascend the heights, his
other regiment, the 70th, following in échelon on his left rear.
At this moment Merle's division was still visible, falling back
in great disorder some way to the right, and pursued by Wallace
—a discouraging sight for the seven battalions that were about
to repeat its experiment. Foy chose as his objective the first
and lowest hilltop to the French right of the pass of San
Antonio, and took his string of columns, the right always leading, up towards it at such pace as was possible over the long
heather, and among the occasional patches of stones. The
troops which were in front of them here were those sections of
Picton's division which were neither far away on the English
left with Wallace and Lightburne, nor actively engaged on the
road against the 31st Léger, viz. the right wing of the British
45th under Colonel Meade, and the Portuguese 8th of the Line
which had just been aiding in the repulse of Merle. These were
soon afterwards joined by one battalion of the 9th Portuguese
from Champlemond's brigade, and the unattached battalion of
Thomar militia, which Picton sent up the hill. Yet this was
still far too small a force to resist Foy's seven battalions, unless
speedily supported.

But support in sufficient quantity was forthcoming. General
Leith had received orders from Wellington to close in to Picton's
right if he saw no hostile troops in his own front. As it was

clear that Reynier had kept no reserves or flanking detachments
to the south of the high-road, it was possible for the 5th Division
to move at once [1]. While the fog was still hanging thickly
along the crests of the Serra, Leith ordered a general move of
his brigades to the left, while Hill detached troops from the
southern end of the position to occupy the heights which the
5th Division was evacuating. This general move to the left
was carried out along the rough but serviceable country-road
which passes along the rear of the plateau, out of sight of the
French. At the moment when Foy's attack was beginning,
Leith had just reached the Pass of San Antonio, with Spry's
Portuguese brigade at the head of his column, then the two
battalions of the Lusitanian legion, and lastly, Barnes's British
brigade. One of Dickson's Portuguese batteries was also with
him. He dropped the guns at the pass to aid Arentschildt's
battery, whose fire was beginning to slacken from want of
ammunition, and left Spry in their rear and the Legionary
battalions on the country-road hard by, while he brought up
Barnes's brigade to the front, and reported his arrival to Picton.
The latter said, it appears, that he was strong enough at the
Pass, but would be obliged if Leith would attend to the attack
which was being made at this moment on the height to its
immediate left [2]. This movement of Foy's was now becoming

[1] Leith's nephew and aide-de-camp, Leith Hay, had explored all the
villages in this direction on the previous afternoon, with a squadron of
Portuguese horse, see his *Narrative*, i. 381.

[2] Picton and Leith each rather slur over the part taken by the
other in their parallel narratives of the crisis. Picton says that he
took command of Leith's troops : ' at this moment Major-General Leith's
aide-de-camp came up to report the arrival of that general and his
division, on which I rode from the post of San Antonio to the road of
communication, and directed the leading regiment of the brigade to
proceed without loss of time to the left, as I had no occasion for
assistance. General Leith's brigade, in consequence, moved on and
arrived in time to join the five companies of the 45th and the 8th Portuguese in repulsing the enemy's last attempt.' Leith, on the other hand,
speaks of having taken command of some of Picton's troops, as if the
latter had not been present, and says nought of their conversation. ' Major-
General Leith thereupon directed a movement of succession, ordering
Colonel Douglas with the right battalion of the 8th Portuguese to support
the point attacked. He also directed the 9th Portuguese under Colonel

dangerous: forcing his way to the summit under a destructive
fire, he had met on the edge of the plateau the three Portuguese
battalions and the wing of the British 45th, and had driven
the n back—the Thomar militia broke and fled down the rear
declivity of the heights, and the 8th Portuguese, though they
did not fly, gave way and fell back in disorder. Just at this
moment Leith, with Barnes's three battalions, came up along
the communication-road at the back of the plateau. 'A heavy
fire of musketry,' writes Leith, 'was being kept up upon the
heights, the smoke of which prevented a clear view of the state
of things. But when the rock forming the high part of the
Serra became visible, the enemy appeared to be in full possession
of it, and a French officer was in the act of cheering, with his
hat off, while a continued fire was being kept up from thence,
and along the whole face of the slope of the Serra, in a diagonal
direction towards its bottom, by the enemy ascending rapidly
in successive columns, formed for an attack upon a mass
of men belonging to the left battalion of the 8th and the
9th Portuguese, who, having been severely pressed, had given
way, and were rapidly retiring in complete confusion and
disorder. The enemy had dispersed or driven off everything
opposed to him—was in possession of the rocky eminence of the
Serra.' A few of his *tirailleurs* were even on the upper edge of
the rear slope.

Leith, realizing that there was still time to save the position
—for only the head of the French column had crowned the
rocky knoll,—deployed his leading battalion, the 9th, across the
summit of the plateau, while sending on his second, the 38th, to
get between the enemy and the reverse slope of the position.
This last move turned out to be fruitless, for the rear face of
the knoll is so steep and so thickly covered with large boulders [1],

Sutton (belonging to Major-General Picton's division) to move up to the
support of General Picton's division,' and again, ' He (General Leith)
ordered the 8th and 9th Portuguese to support the point attacked, and
where the enemy were fast gaining ground.' Each general speaks as if
he had been in command, and I fear that each is using undue reticence as
to the other's doings. See note at the end of this chapter.

[1] Napier calls it a ' precipice,' but this is not the right word. I found
that I could walk freely about on it, but no formed body of men could
have passed up the slope.

that the 38th was unable to climb it, and came back to fall in
on the right of the 9th. But before it could get back, the senior
regiment had done its work. Leith had led it diagonally across
the plateau, so as to place it along the flank of the leading
battalions of Foy's column, of which the first was now ensconced
on the summit of the heights, while the others were struggling
up to join it. The 9th opened with a volley at 100 yards, and
then advanced firing, receiving hardly any return from the
enemy, who seemed entirely disconcerted by the appearance of
a new force parallel with its flank. At twenty yards from the
French, the 9th lowered its bayonets and prepared to charge,
Leith riding at its head waving his plumed hat. Then the
enemy gave way. 'My heroic column,' writes Foy, 'much
diminished during the ascent, reached the summit of the plateau,
which was covered with hostile troops. Those on our left made
a flank movement and smashed us up by their battalion volleys;
meanwhile those on our front, covered by some rocks, were
murdering us with impunity. The head of my column fell
back to its right, despite my efforts; I could not get them to
deploy, disorder set in, and the 17th and 70th raced down-
hill in headlong flight. The enemy pursued us half-way to the
foot of the heights, till he pulled up on coming under effective
fire from our artillery [1].'

The battle was now over on this side : Reynier had in reserve
only one regiment, the 47th of the Line. His other twenty-
two battalions had all been beaten to pieces; they had lost
over 2,000 men, including more than half their superior officers :
Merle commanding the 1st Division was wounded, his junior
brigadier Graindorge was killed; Foy, commanding the first
brigade of the other division, was wounded. Of the six colonels
who had gone up the heights, those of the 31st Léger, 2nd Léger,
4th Léger, and 70th had been hit : of the twenty-three battalion
commanders four were killed, seven wounded. Of 421 officers
in all who went into action, 118—more than one in four—had
been disabled. Of the 2,023 casualties, 350 men and fifteen officers
were prisoners in the hands of the British. And these losses

---

[1] Foy's diary, pp. 103-4, tallies exactly with Leith's narrative in
Wellington Supplementary Dispatches, vi. 678, and Cameron's letter in
Napier, Appendix to vol. vi.

had been suffered without inflicting any corresponding loss upon
the defenders of the position : Picton's division had 427 killed
and wounded ; Leith's 160. The only regiments appreciably
diminished were the 45th, 88th, and Portuguese 8th—with 150,
134, and 113 casualties respectively. The only superior officers
hit were the Portuguese brigadier Champlemond, and a major
each in the 45th and 88th. Of the 3rd and 5th Divisions only
six British and five Portuguese battalions had been engaged [1]—
the superiority of force against them had been about two to one.
Yet Reynier complained in his dispatch to Masséna of being
crushed by 'a triple superiority of numbers'! As a matter of
fact, it was the position that beat him, not the imagined numbers
of the allies. Wellington could risk much in taking up a long
line, when he had a good road of communication along its rear,
to shift troops from point to point, and when he could descry
every movement of the enemy half an hour before it began to
take effect.

The other half of the battle of Bussaco was an even shorter
business than Reynier's struggle with Picton and Leith, but no
less bloody and decisive. Ney exactly obeyed Masséna's orders
to attack, with two divisions, the ground on each side of the
Coimbra *chaussée*, when he should see the 2nd Corps lodged on
the crest beside the pass of San Antonio de Cantaro. The many
reproaches heaped upon him, by critics who have not read his
orders, for attacking too late, and not at the same moment as
Reynier, are groundless : he was told to go forward only when
his colleague 'sera maître des hauteurs.' He moved precisely
when the dispersing mists showed Merle's great column massed
on the edge of the plateau. Of his three divisions he had, again
in exact obedience to orders, placed Loison on the right, Marchand on the left, while Mermet was in reserve, behind Moura.
The two fighting divisions were completely separated by the

---

[1] Viz. British : Mackinnon's 1/88th, 1/45th, 74th, Barnes's 3/1st, 1/9th,
2/38th. Portuguese : Champlemond's 9th Line (2 batts.) and 21st Line
(1 batt.), with the 8th from Leith's division (2 batts.). Spry's brigade
and the Lusitanian Legion from Leith were never under fire, and did not
lose a man. Picton's left brigade (Lightburne) was never engaged, save
that the light companies of the 5th and 83rd, far down the slope, lost
eight and four men respectively. The Thomar militia bolted before
coming under fire.

deep and steep ravine of which we have had occasion to speak.
The ground in front of them was very different: Marchand had
to advance, by rather gentle slopes, along the *chaussée*, which
curves up towards the convent of Bussaco.   Loison had to go
up a hillside of a very different sort, whose lower stretch, as far
as the village of Sula, is gentle, and much cut up by woods and
orchards, but whose upper half, beyond Sula, is extremely steep
and absolutely destitute of cover.   There was no road here, only
a rough mule-track.

Loison started a few minutes before Marchand : he had his
two brigades side by side, Simon's (six battalions) on the right,
Ferey's (also six battalions) on the left.   Both started from the
low ground in front of Sula, each with a strong chain of *tirailleurs*
covering an advance in serried battalion columns ; the 26th
regiment was the leading regiment in Simon's, the 66th in
Ferey's brigade.   On leaving the bottom, and advancing among
the trees on the lower slope, both brigades found their *tirailleurs*
at once checked by a very strong skirmishing line.   Pack
had spread out the whole of the 4th Caçadores on the hillside
in front of his line battalions.   Craufurd had thrown out the
95th—more than 700 rifles—and the 3rd Caçadores—600 rifles
more—into the enclosures in front of Sula.   The 43rd and 52nd,
with the 1st Caçadores, were lying down in the hollow road at
the head of the steep slope above that village, completely
concealed from sight.   Of formed troops, Loison could only see
the 1st Division far above him on the left on the highest plateau
of the Serra, and Cole far away to his right on the lower hillsides towards Paradas.   In order to press in the obstinate light
troops in front of him, Loison was compelled to push forward
whole battalions from his fighting-line : by a strenuous use of
these, the Caçadores and Rifles were evicted first from the lower
slopes, then from the village of Sula.   But when the latter had
been captured, the French found themselves under a heavy fire
of artillery : Ross's guns on the knoll above, between their
embrasures of rock, being carefully trained upon the exits of
the village, while Cleeves' German battery joined in from its
position at the head of the ravine, and took Ferey in flank.   It
was impossible to halt in Sula, and Loison ordered his brigadiers
to push forward the attack once more, taking Ross's guns and

the windmill near them as their objective. The slope was now much steeper, the British and Portuguese skirmishers had rallied once more above Sula, and Craufurd had sent down the 1st Caçadores to feed the fighting-line. It was only with a severe effort, and with much loss, that the French battalions won their way up the culminating slope. Simon's front regiment, the 26th of the Line, stuck to the mule-path up the hill from Sula, in one dense and deep column, with the front of a company only, and a depth of three battalions. Ferey's brigade, having no track to follow, seems to have moved in a somewhat less vicious formation along the slope further to the left, bordering on the northern edge of the funnel-like ravine which formed the boundary of Craufurd's position. Both were in a very disordered condition, owing to the fierce conflict which they had waged with the screen of Rifles and Caçadores all up the hillside.

Lying in the hollow road parallel with the head of the ravine were the two Line regiments of the Light Division, the 43rd on the right, the 52nd on the left. They were very strong battalions, despite their losses at the Coa, the one having 800 the other 950 bayonets. In front of them, on the skyline by the little windmill, to the right of Ross's guns, Craufurd had been standing all through the earlier stages of the engagement, watching the gradual progress of the French up the hillside. He waited patiently till the enemy's two columns, a few hundred yards apart, had reached the last steep of the hillside below him. His recoiling skirmishers were at last thrust in upon him —they passed, some to the flanks, some through the intervals between the battalions and the guns, and the front was clear.

Then came the opportunity: the French, pulling themselves together, were preparing to rush up the last twenty yards of the ascent and to run in upon the guns, when Craufurd waved his hat to the battalions lying in the road behind him, the appointed signal for action, and (it is said) called to the men behind him 'Now 52nd, revenge the death of Sir John Moore.' The crest was at once covered by the long red line, and the fronts of the French brigades received such a volley at ten paces as has been seldom endured by any troops in war. The whole of the heads of their columns crumbled away in a mass of dead and

dying. The centre and rear stood appalled for one moment ;
then Major Arbuthnot wheeled in three companies of the 52nd
upon the right flank of Simon's leading regiment, while Lloyd
of the 43rd did the same upon the extreme left, so as to produce
a semicircle of fire [1]. It was impossible to stand under it, and
the French broke and went hurtling down the hill, the wrecks
of the front battalions carrying the rear ones away with them.
So steep was the slope on their left that some are said to have
lost their footing and to have rolled down to the bottom of the
ravine before they could stop. The Light Division followed as
far as Sula, and beyond, not stopping till Loison's people had
taken refuge in the wooded ground beyond that village, and
the French guns by Moura had begun to play upon their
pursuers. The rush had carried away the whole of the enemy,
save one battalion upon Ferey's extreme left, which had moved
so far down in the slope of the ravine that it had become
separated from the rest. This solitary column, pressing forward,
came to the skyline not in front of Craufurd, but at the very
head of the ravine, below Cleeves' battery. Here it was dealt
with by the leading unit of Coleman's Portuguese brigade,
which was standing in line near the *chaussée*. The 1st battalion
of the 19th regiment, under Major McBean, charged it and rolled
it back into the cleft, down whose bottom it hastily recoiled,
and joined the rest of the flying division.

[1] A passage of Napier's account of the movements of the Light Division (iii. 27) has puzzled many readers. ' Eighteen hundred British
bayonets went sparkling over the brow of the hill. Yet so hardy were the
leading French that every man of the first section raised his musket, and
two officers and ten soldiers (of the 52nd) fell before them. Not a Frenchman had missed his mark ! ' This passage looks as if the whole French
division had been conceived by Napier as moving in a single column with
a front of only twelve men. An eye-witness, Sir John Bell, of the 52nd,
who owned the copy of the book which I now have before me, has written
Bosh ! in the margin against the words. Of course the enemy was
advancing with each battalion in column of companies, with a front of
thirty at least. What Napier seems to have had in his head was an
anecdote told by his brother George (*Autobiography*, p. 143). ' My company
met the very head of the French column, and immediately calling to my
men to form column of sections, in order to give more force to our rush,
we dashed forward. I was in front of my men a yard or two, when a
Frenchman made a plunge at me with his bayonet, and at the same time

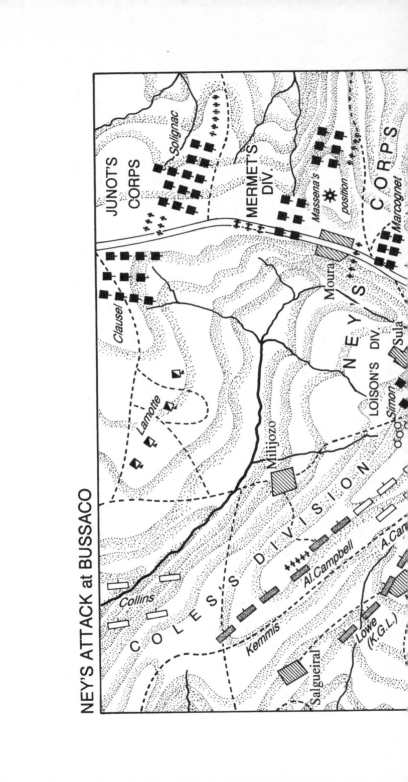

NEY'S ATTACK at BUSSACO

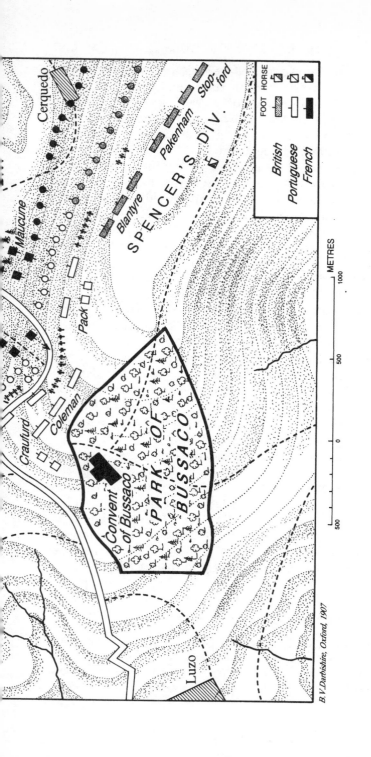

Cerquedo

Maucune

Blantyre

Pakenham

Stop-ford

SPENCER'S DIV.

Pack

Coleman

Crauford

PARK OF BUSSACO

Convent of Bussaco

Luzo

FOOT HORSE

British

Portuguese

French

METRES

1000   500   0   500

B.V.Darbishire, Oxford, 1907

This made an end of Loison's two brigades as a serious attacking force.   They reeled back to their original position, under cover of the 25th Léger, which Mermet sent out to relieve them.   But later in the day they pushed some skirmishers up the hill again, and bickered with Craufurd's outposts. Wellington, seeing that the Light Division was fatigued, sent the light companies of Löwe's German brigade and A. Campbell's 6th Caçadores, from the reserves, to take up the skirmishing.   It stood still about Sula, but the French got a few men into the village, whom Craufurd had to evict with a company of the 43rd.

Loison lost, out of 6,500 men used in the attack, twenty-one officers killed and forty-seven wounded, with some 1,200 men. His senior brigadier, Simon, was wounded in the face, and taken prisoner by a private of the 52nd.   The loss of the Light Division was marvellously small—the 3rd Caçadores and the 95th, who had fought through the long skirmish up the hill, had seventy-eight and forty-one casualties respectively, but the 43rd and 52nd had the astounding record of only three men killed, and two officers and eighteen men wounded.   McBean's Portuguese battalion lost one officer and twenty-five men : the German light companies had nearly fifty casualties, but this was later in the day.   Altogether, Loison's attack was repelled with a loss of only 200 men to the allies.

It only remains to tell of one more section of the Battle of Bussaco ; it was entirely independent of the rest.   When Ney started Loison to his right of the deep ravine, he had sent forward Marchand's division to his left of it, along the great *chaussée*.   On turning the sweep of the road beyond Moura, the leading brigade of this column (6th Léger and 69th Line, five battalions) came under a terrible artillery fire from the three batteries which Wellington had placed at the head of the ravine, those of Cleeves, Parros, and Lawson.   They, nevertheless, pushed along the road till they came level with a small pine wood on their left, which was full of the skirmishers of Pack's Portuguese

I received the contents of his musket under my hip and fell.   At the same instant they fired upon my front section, consisting of about nine men in the front rank, all of whom fell, four dead, the rest wounded.' But this does not imply that the French column was only twelve broad.

brigade—the whole of the 4th Caçadores had been sent down into it from the height above. The flanking fire of these light troops was so galling that the French brigade—apparently without orders and by an instinctive movement—swerved to its left, and went up the hillside to turn the Caçadores out of their cover. After a sharp bickering they did so, and then emerging from the wood on to the smooth slope of the height below the convent wall, got into a desperate musketry duel with Pack's four Line-battalions, who stood in front of them. They were now in disorder, and their brigadier, Maucune, had been wounded. But they made several attempts to storm the hillside, which were all beaten back by the Portuguese musketry and the fire of Lawson's artillery on the right. The second brigade of Marchand (that of Marcognet) pushed as far along the road as the preceding brigade had gone, but stopped when it came under the fire of Cleeves' and Parros's guns, to which that of Ross's (from across the ravine) was also added, when Loison's attack had been beaten off. Seeing that Marchand was making no headway, that Loison had been routed, and that Reynier's corps was out of action, Ney called back his column, which fell back behind Moura. Maucune's brigade had suffered severely—it had lost its brigadier, the colonel of the 6th Léger, and thirty-three other officers with some 850 men. The rear brigade (Marcognet's) had suffered less—its casualty list, however, was fully 300 killed and wounded. There had been a little skirmishing meanwhile opposite Wellington's centre, for during the main attack Ney had sent forward some voltigeur companies from his reserves to occupy the line of skirmishers at the foot of the heights, which Spencer's 1st Division had thrown out. These two thin screens of light troops paired off against each other, and contended all the morning with some loss, but no appreciable advantage on either side [1].

[1] Sprünglin, Ney's aide-de-camp, gives an account of his being detached with these voltigeurs, on p. 450 of his diary. He lost 142 men. It must have been in contending with these companies that the 1st Division (excluding the German brigade, occupied elsewhere) got the 89 casualties returned by Wellington, as also the 5/60 their 24 casualties. The only one of the British battalions in this quarter which had an appreciable number of men hurt was the 1/79th. Its regimental history says that its light company was almost cut off at the commencement of the day. The

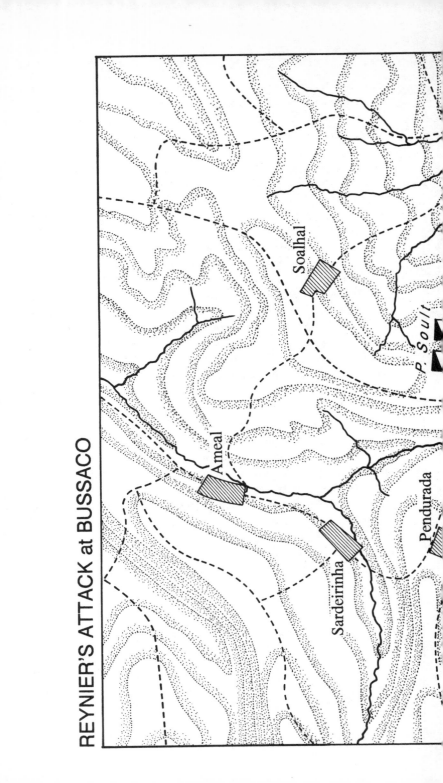

REYNIER'S ATTACK at BUSSACO

Soalhal

Ameal

Sardeirinha

Pendurada

P. Soult

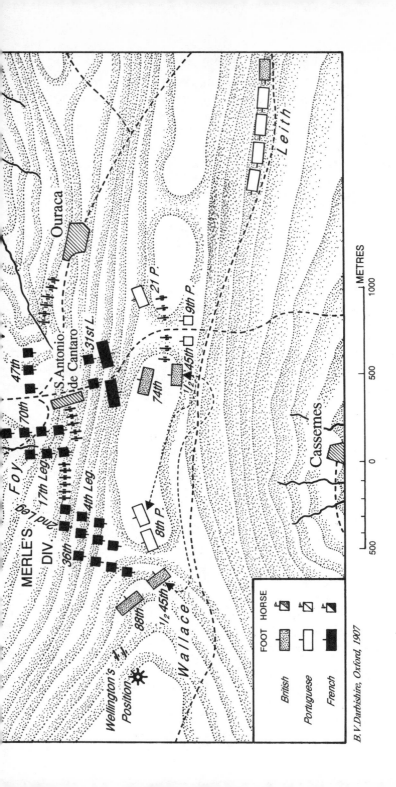

Ouraca

Leith

S.Antonio
de Cantaro

31st L.

21 P.

9th P.

47th

74th

½ 45th

70th

Foy.

17th Leg.

MERLE'S

DIV.

36th

4th Leg.

8th P.

Cassemes

88th

½ 45th

Wallace

Wellington's
Position

FOOT   HORSE

British

Portuguese

French

METRES

500   0   500   1000

B.V.Darbishire, Oxford, 1907

Masséna still had it in his power to attack again, for Mermet's division of the 6th Corps, and the whole of Junot's 13,000 infantry had not yet advanced and had hardly lost a man. But the result of Ney's and Reynier's efforts had been so disheartening that the Marshal refused to waste more lives on what was clearly a hopeless enterprise. He could now see Wellington's army concentrated on the two points that had been attacked. Hill's heavy column of 10,000 men had now lined the heights on Leith's right : Cole had edged the 4th Division close in to Craufurd's left, and Coleman and the Germans were visible in the rear. If Masséna had still 20,000 fresh infantry, the English general had 33,000 who had not yet come up into the fighting-line. It was useless to persist. Accordingly, the skirmishing along Ney's front was allowed to die down in the afternoon, and the French divisions retired to their camps.

The total loss of Wellington's army had been 1,252 officers and men, of whom 200 were killed, 1,001 wounded, and fifty-one missing. No officer over the rank of a major had been killed : and the only senior officers wounded were the Portuguese brigadier Champlemond and Colonel Barclay of the 52nd. Of the casualties, 626 were in the ranks of the British, 626 in those of the Portuguese regiments—a strange coincidence in the losses of the two allied armies. The Portuguese line, indeed, had done their fair half of the fighting, as the return showed—in no instance with discredit, in some with high merit. If the 8th and 9th Portuguese had broken before Foy's attack, it was under severe stress, and when attacked by superior numbers. On the other hand, Pack's brigade, Coleman's 19th, and the Caçadores of the Light Division won the highest praises from their commanders, and had taken a most distinguished part in the victory. Wellington now knew exactly how far they could be trusted, and could estimate at last the real fighting value of his army—at least, for a defensive battle in chosen and favourable ground. It would be another matter to calculate how far the allied host was capable of taking the offensive.

The total loss of the French, as shown by the return—which

captain was taken prisoner—being the only British officer captured that day—with six men, and there were over 40 other casualties. Stopford's brigade lost two men—Lord Blantyre's seven.

was not quite complete—presented to Masséna on October 1, was 4,498, of whom 522 were killed, 3,612 wounded, and 364 missing (i. e. prisoners). After his usual fashion he represented it to the Emperor as being 'about 3,000 [1].' One general (Graindorge), two colonels, and fifty-two other officers had been killed, four generals (Maucune, Foy, Merle, Simon) were wounded—the last was also a prisoner; five colonels and 189 other officers were wounded. The 2nd Corps in all had lost at least 2,043 officers and men, the 6th Corps at least 2,455 [2]. It may be remembered that of all the battles in the Peninsular War this was the one in which the proportion of officers to men hit on the French side was highest, one to sixteen—the average being one to twenty-two in ordinary engagements. The excessive proportion of casualties in the commissioned ranks bears witness to a desperate attempt to lead on the men to an impossible task, in which the officers sacrificed themselves in the most splendid style.

Masséna must not be too much blamed for his experiment. He had still to ascertain the fighting value of Wellington's army—and estimated it too low, because of the extreme prudence which his adversary had hitherto displayed. He was handicapped by the impossibility of using his artillery effectively, and the position in front of him was strong—even stronger than he guessed, because of the road of communication along the rear of the plateau—but not too strong to be forced, if the defenders did not fight well. Moreover, it was immensely long—nine miles from end to end, so that two blows delivered with a corps

[1] This too in a dispatch to Berthier dated Coimbra, Oct. 4, three days after the returns had been placed before him.

[2] For these returns, see Appendix, no. xiii. They are certainly incomplete, omitting (1) losses of the cavalry of the 2nd Corps (where Martinien's invaluable tables show that three officers were wounded), (2) losses of the 8th Corps, which caught a few shells as it stood on the heights by Moura and had (as again shown by Martinien's tables) six officers hit, which must imply some hundred men. (3) Some casualties in the infantry omitted in the returns, for while the report accounts for 253 killed and wounded officers, Martinien names 275. Deducting the cavalry and 8th Corps losses mentioned above, there are still fifteen officers (and therefore presumably 250 men) too few given in the reports sent in to Masséna; e.g. for the 2nd Léger the report has eighteen officers hit, Martinien gives the names of twenty-two.

each in the centre might have pierced the line before the enemy's distant reserves could get up. Favoured by the fog—as we have seen—Reynier actually won the heights for a moment, though Ney never got near the crest. The mistake lay not so much in making the trial as in under-rating the warlike efficiency of the enemy. Strokes like Wallace's charge with the 45th and 88th, or Craufurd's masterly advance with the 43rd and 52nd, are beyond the common experiences of war. Masséna put forty-five battalions [1] into his fighting-line—they were repulsed by twenty-four, for that was the number of Anglo-Portuguese battalions which engaged more than their light-companies [2]. This could not have been foreseen. But the lesson was learnt. Before the lines of Torres Vedras, a fortnight later, Masséna refused to take any more risks of the kind, and the campaign assumed a very different character, because the invader had learnt to respect his enemy.

[1] Viz. all Reynier's Corps, save the 47th, twenty-two battalions ; Marchand eleven battalions, Loison twelve battalions—total 26,000 men. See Tables in Appendix.

[2] Viz. the brigades of Mackinnon and Champlemond of the 3rd Division : the 1st, 9th, 38th, British, and the 8th Portuguese of Leith, Craufurd's five battalions, Pack's five battalions, three battalions of Coleman—total 14,000 men. See Tables in Appendix.

(1) NOTE ON THE TOPOGRAPHY OF BUSSACO

I spent two days in April 1904 and two days in April 1906 in going very carefully over the field—save that of its nine-mile length I did not investigate closely either Cole's position on the extreme north, or Hill's on the extreme south, no fighting having come near either of them. The ground is so minutely described in the preceding chapter that only a few additional points require notice.

(1) The ravine which lay between Pack and Craufurd, and between Marchand and Loison, is a feature which no map can properly express, and which no one who has not gone very carefully over the hillside can fully picture to himself. It produces an absolute want of continuity between the two fights which went on to its right and left.

(2) The Mondego is not visible from any point of the line of heights till Hill's position is reached. It is sunk far below the level of the upland.

(3) The San Antonio-Palheiros road is a mere country track, barely

deserving the name of road, though practicable for artillery and vehicles.
The *chaussée* Moura–Bussaco is a high-road of the first class, admirably
engineered. The paths across the Serra at Hill's end of it are wretched
mule-tracks, not suitable for wheeled traffic. So is the track from Sula
up the slope to Craufurd's standing-place.

. (4) The view from the summit of the Serra is very extensive, embracing
on the one side all the slopes of the Estrella as far as Guarda, and on the
other the whole coast-plain of Coimbra as far as the sea. But in each
direction there is so much wood and hill that many roads and villages are
masked. The French army, both in advance and retreat, was only intermittently visible. But enough could be made out to determine its general
movements with fair precision. When it reached the foot-hills before the
Serra every detail of its disposition could be followed by an observer on
any part of the crest, save that below Sula woods in the bottom hide the
starting-point of Loison's division.

(5) In the chapel by the side of the *chaussée*, just behind the sky-line of
the English position, the traveller will find a little museum, including a
very fine topographical map, with the position of the allied troops, and
more especially of the Portuguese regiments, well marked. There are a
few errors in the placing of the British battalions, but nothing of consequence. The French army is only vaguely indicated. But the map is a
credit to the Portuguese engineer officers who compiled it.

(6) As I have observed in the next chapter, the ground to the north,
along the Serras de Alcoba and de Caramula, is not so uniformly lofty, or
so forbidding in its aspect, as to cause the observer to doubt whether
there can be any pass across the watershed in that direction. Indeed, the
first idea that strikes the mind on reaching the summit of the Serra, and
casting a glance round the wide landscape, is that it is surprising that any
officer in the French army can have believed that the Caramula was
absolutely impracticable. Moreover it is far less easily defensible. than
the Bussaco ridge, because it is much more broken and full of cover. The
beauty of the Bussaco position is that, save on the Moura-Sula spurs, it
is entirely bare of cover on the side facing eastward. The smooth, steep
slope, with its furze and heather and its occasional out-crops of rock,
makes a splendid glacis. The reverse space would be a far worse position
to defend, against an enemy coming from Coimbra and the coast-plain,
because it is thickly interspersed with woods.

(7) With the possible exception of some of the Pyrenean fighting-
grounds, Bussaco gives the most beautiful landscape of any of the British
battlefields of the Peninsula. Albuera is tame, Talavera is only picturesque
at its northern end, Salamanca is rolling ground with uninteresting
ploughed fields, save where the two Arapiles crop up in their isolated
ruggedness. Fuentes d'Oñoro is a pretty hillside, such as one may see in
any English county, with meadow below and rough pasture above. Vimiero
is dappled ground, with many trees but no commanding feature. But
the loftiness, the open breezy air, the far-reaching view over plain, wood,

mountain, and distant sea, from the summit of the Bussaco Serra is unique
in its beauty.   It is small wonder that the modern Portuguese have turned
it into a health-resort, or that the British colony at Oporto have fixed on
the culminating plateau as the best golf-course in the Peninsula.

(2) NOTE ON THE CRISIS OF THE BATTLE
OF BUSSACO

While there is no point of dispute concerning that part of the Battle of
Bussaco in which Craufurd Pack, and Coleman were engaged against the
6th Corps, there was bitter controversy on the exact details of the repulse
of Reynier's corps by Picton and Leith.   Picton, and following him his
subordinates of the 3rd Division, thought that Leith's part in the action
was insignificant, that he merely repulsed a minor attack after the main
struggle was over.   Leith and his officers considered that they gave the
decisive blow, that Picton's line would have been broken and the battle
perhaps lost, if Barnes's brigade had not arrived at the critical moment
and saved the situation.   All- that Picton would allow was that Leith
'aided the wing of the 45th and the 8th Portuguese in repulsing the
enemy's last attempt.'   Grattan, who wrote an admirable narrative of
the defeat of Merle's division by the 88th and the neighbouring troops,
denied that the 3rd Division was ever pressed, says that he never saw
Leith's men till the action was over, and points out that Barnes's brigade,
out of 1,800 bayonets, lost but 47 men altogether, while the 45th
regiment alone lost thrice, and the 88th more than twice, as many killed
and wounded out of their scanty numbers (150 and 134 out of 560 and 679
respectively).   Other 3rd Division officers suggest (see the letters in the
Appendix to Napier's sixth volume) that Leith fought only with a belated
body of French skirmishers, or with men who had been cut off from the
main attacking column by the successful advance of Wallace.   On the
other hand Leith (see his letter in Wellington, *Supplementary Dispatches*,
vol. vi, p. 678) speaks of coming on the ground to find a large French
column crossing the Serra, and the Portuguese 8th and 9th broken, and
about to recoil down the rear slope.   His aide-de-camp, Leith-Hay, and
Cameron of the 9th bear him out.

Napier has failed to make the situation clear, from not seeing that
there were two completely separate attacks of the French, divided by
an appreciable interval.   He thinks that Foy was on the Serra as soon as
Merle, and calls his column (iii. p. 25) 'the French battalions which had
first gained the crest,' while as a matter of fact they had only started
after Wallace's repulse of Merle was long over.

· The real situation is made clear when Reynier's and Heudelet's dispatches in the French Archives and Foy's diary are studied.   From these
it is clear that there were *two* occasions on which the French got to the

top of the Serra, the first during Merle's attack, the second during Foy's. I have quoted Foy's narrative on p. 377 above ; but it may be well to give also his note showing the starting-time of his column. ' La première division (Merle) a gravi la montagne en se jettant à droite. Mais à peine les têtes arrivaient sur le plateau, qu'attaquées tout à coup par des troupes immensement supérieures en nombre, fraîches et vigoureuses, elles ont été culbutées en bas de la montagne dans le plus grand désordre. Ma brigade s'était portée au pied de la montagne, devant soutenir le 31e Léger. Au moment de l'échec de la 1re division j'ai fait halte un moment pour ne pas être entraîné par les fuyards.' It was only at this instant, when the fugitives from Merle's attack were pouring past him, that he got his orders from Reynier to attack, and started to climb the slope. There must, therefore, have been an interval of more than half an hour—possibly of an hour—between the moment when Wallace thrust Merle off the plateau, and that at which Foy crowned it, only to be attacked and beaten by the newly arrived Leith. For it took a very long time for the French 17th and 70th to climb the slope, and they only reached the top with difficulty, the skirmishers of the 8th and 9th Portuguese and of Meade's wing of the 45th having fought hard to keep them back.

Reynier's dispatch is equally clear as to his corps having made two separate attacks. He adds that some of Sarrut's men were rallied in time to support Foy, a statement for which I find no corroboration elsewhere.

Napier then has failed to grasp the situation, when he makes the French crown the crest above the pass of San Antonio and the crest opposite Wallace, 900 yards further north, at the same moment. And the statement that Leith's charge was directed against the other flank of the same mass that was beaten by the 88th and 45th is altogether erroneous.

Leith's narrative of the business, in short, fits in with the French story, and must be considered correct. Picton cannot be acquitted of deliberate belittling of the part taken by his colleague in the action. Foy's attack, though made by only seven battalions, while Merle had eleven, was the more dangerous of the two, and was defeated by Leith alone, after the small fraction of Picton's force in front of it had been broken and thrust back.

SECTION XXI: CHAPTER III

WELLINGTON'S RETREAT TO THE LINES OF TORRES VEDRAS

THE dawn of September 28 brought small comfort to Masséna. His desperate attacks of the preceding day had been repulsed with such ease and such heavy loss, that neither he nor any of his subordinates dreamed of renewing the attempt to force the line of the Serra. Only three courses were open to him—to retreat on Almeida, giving up the campaign as one too ambitious for the strength of his army, or to change his objective and strike backwards at Oporto,—if Lisbon were beyond his grasp,—or to endeavour to move Wellington out of his position by turning his flank, since a frontal attack had proved disastrous. The first course was advocated by more than one adviser, but presented no attractions to the Marshal: he was both obstinate and angry, and did not dream for a moment of spoiling his military reputation by retreating tamely after a lost battle. The blow at Oporto was equally unattractive: he had been told to drive the English out of Portugal, and to capture Lisbon, not to make a mere lodgement on the Douro. Moreover, as he had remarked to Ney before the battle, if he marched on Oporto by the bad road via Vizeu, he might find the British army once more in his front, when he drew nearer to the city, since the Coimbra–Oporto *chaussée* is both shorter and better than the by-roads which he would have to follow. There remained the third possibility—that of turning Wellington out of the Bussaco position by flanking operations. The country-side did not look very promising, but the attempt must be made.

Early on the 28th the French cavalry was sent out in both directions to explore the whole neighbourhood—a task which Masséna should have prescribed to it on the 25th and 26th, instead of keeping it massed in his rear. The reconnaissances sent southward by Reynier's light cavalry brought no encouraging report: if the French army crossed the Mondego, it would only run against Wellington's carefully prepared position behind the Alva. Fane's cavalry were out in this direction, and would give ample time of warning to allow the allied army to pass the fords of Peña Cova and man the long series of earthworks. Only a repetition of the Bussaco disaster could follow from an attempt to take the offensive on this side. From the north, however, Montbrun, who had ridden out with some of Sainte-Croix's dragoons, brought far more cheering news. This indeed was the flank where, on the first principles of topography, some hope of success might have been looked for. To any one standing either on the Bussaco heights or on the lower ridge in front of them, and casting an eye over the dappled and uneven country-side to the north, it seems incredible that there should be no route whatever across the Serra de Caramula. Both the seacoast-plain of Beira and the valley of the Oerins, the little river which drains the plain of Mortagoa, were thickly populated. Was it likely that there would be no means of getting from the one to the other save by the *chaussée* through Bussaco, or the circuitous road far to the north, from Vizeu to Aveiro via Feramena and Bemfeita? The maps, it is true, showed no other route: but every day that he remained in Portugal was proving more clearly to the Marshal that his maps, Lopez and the rest, were hopelessly inaccurate. The Serra de Caramula, though rugged, is not one continuous line of precipices, nor is it of any great altitude. On first principles it was probable that there might be one or more passages in this stretch of thirty miles, though it was conceivable that there might be no road over which artillery could travel [1].

There was, therefore, nothing astonishing in the fact that Montbrun discovered that such a track existed, nine miles north of Bussaco, running from Mortagoa, by Aveleira and Boialvo, to Sardão in the valley of the Agueda, one of the affluents of

[1] As a matter of fact, the modern railway from Coimbra and Pampilhosa to the upper Mondego does not use the pass of Bussaco, but goes north of it, round the left flank of Wellington's position, by Luso, far south of the Boialvo road to Mortagoa.

the Vouga. There was nothing particularly startling in the discovery, nor did it imply any special perspicacity in the discoverers, as many of the French narratives seek to imply. A peasant captured in one of the deserted villages high up the Oerins, and cross-questioned by Masséna's Portuguese aide-de-camp Mascarenhas, who accompanied Sainte-Croix on his reconnaissance, revealed the fact that this country-road existed. He even, it is said, expressed to his compatriot his surprise that the French had not taken it when first they arrived at Mortagoa, since it was unguarded, while the whole allied army was lying across the Bussaco *chaussée*. It was, he said, habitually used by the ox-waggons of the peasantry : it was not a good road, but was a perfectly practicable one.

With this all-important news Montbrun and Sainte-Croix returned to Masséna about midday. The Marshal at once resolved to make an attempt to utilize the Boialvo road. There was some danger in doing so, since it was possible that Wellington might wait till the greater part of the French army had retired from his front, and then descend upon the rearguard and overwhelm it. Or, on the other hand, he might have made preparations to hold the further end of the pass, so that when the vanguard of the invaders was nearing Boialvo or Sardão they might find 20,000 men, withdrawn from the Bussaco position in haste, lying across their path at some dangerous turn of the road. Indeed, we may confidently assert that if in 1810 the British general had possessed the army that he owned in 1813, Masséna would have had the same unpleasant experience that befell Soult at Sorauren, when he attempted a precisely similar manœuvre—a flank march round the allied army on the day after a lost battle.

But Masséna was prepared to take risks, and the risk which he was now accepting was a considerably less perilous one than that which he had incurred when he chose to make a frontal attack on the Bussaco position on the preceding day. For though flank marches across an enemy's front are justly deprecated by every military authority, this was one executed at a distance of nine or ten miles from the British line, and not in a level country, on to which Wellington might easily descend from his fastness, but in a broken wooded upland, full of ridges

on which the French might have formed up to fight if assailed.
If this fact did not remove the danger, it at any rate made it
infinitely less.　If one of the two possible contretemps should
happen—if Wellington should come down with a sudden rush
upon the rearguard—that force would have to fight a defensive
action on the ridges below Bussaco, till the main body could turn
back to help it.　In that case there would follow a pitched
battle upon rolling and uneven ground, which did not favour
one side more than the other; and this, at any rate, would be
a more favourable situation for the French than that in which
they had fought on Sept. 27.　If, on the other hand, Wellington
should send a strong detachment to hold the western debouch
of the Boialvo road, nothing would be lost—if nothing would be
gained.　It was improbable that there would be any position in
that quarter quite so strong as the tremendous slope of the
Serra de Bussaco.　The result of an attempt to force the defile
might be successful.

At any rate Masséna thought the experiment worthy of a
trial.　Accordingly, on the afternoon of the 28th, ostentatious
demonstrations were made against the front of the Bussaco position, which led to a good deal of objectless skirmishing [1].　Wellington was not for a moment deceived.　Indeed, the idea that
another assault was impending was negatived by the fact that
both Reynier's and Ney's men were seen to be throwing up
abattis and digging trenches on the flanks of the two roads on
which they lay.　These could only be meant for defensive use,
and presumably must be intended to help the French rearguard to hold the ridges, if the Anglo-Portuguese army should
descend upon them.　Late in the afternoon officers furnished
with good telescopes, and stationed on the highest point of the
Bussaco Serra, reported that they could detect columns in movement from the French rear in the direction of the north-west.
These were Sainte-Croix's cavalry and the baggage-trains of Ney
and Junot making their way to the rear, in order to get into the
Mortagoa–Boialvo road.　At six o'clock, dusk having still not
come on, it was reported that Ney's infantry reserves were
certainly moving in the same direction.　Only Loison's division
was still immovable on its old position opposite Sula.　At

---

[1] The firing commenced soon after 12 noon.　See Tomkinson, p. 44.

nightfall, therefore, the movement of the French was well ascertained. It might mean merely a general retreat on Mortagoa and an abandonment of the campaign [1], but this was most unlikely. Far more probable was some march to turn the allied flank by the passes of the Serra de Caramula. Wellington himself had no doubt whatever that this was the enemy's intention. As the dusk fell he stood for some time on the summit of the Serra, watching the French columns receding in the distance. He then rode back to his head quarters at the convent of Bussaco, and dictated without delay a series of orders which set his whole army in retreat for Coimbra and Lisbon. Before daylight the position was deserted, only a rearguard being left on it. He does not seem to have thought for a moment of attacking, on the following morning, the 2nd Corps and Loison's division, which had been left in his front, nor of directing his right wing to march on Sardão, which it could have reached long before the French arrived there. Each of these courses was so obvious that critics have lavished blame upon him for not adopting the one or the other [2].

The explanation of his conduct is neither that he failed to see the two alternatives which were in his power, nor that he showed (as several French writers maintain) an excessive timidity. Still less is it possible to urge, as some have done, that he was ruined by his own neglect to occupy the Boialvo road. He knew of that pass, had taken it into consideration, and in one of his dispatches speaks vaguely of a means which he was hoping to discover to render it useless to the enemy [3]. This remedy cannot mean, as some have supposed, the moving thither of Trant's corps of Portuguese militia. It is true that Wellington had ordered this force to occupy Sardão some days before. But it was neither large enough, nor composed of troops solid enough, to resist, even in a strong position, the attack of a single French brigade. Some other device must have been meant, though we

---

[1] This was imagined to be the case by some observers, who overrated Masséna's loss, and thought he had 10,000 casualties on the 27th.

[2] See, for example, Fririon, pp. 55–6, Toreno, ii. 164. Thiers, and even Napier, iii. 32–3.

[3] *Dispatches*, vi. 460. Had he proposed to blast away sections, so as to make it impassable for wheel traffic, as he did with the Estrada Nova?

cannot determine what it may have been. The true key to Wellington's action is to remember the immense pains that he had taken in building the Lines of Torres Vedras, and the elaborate arrangements that had been made during the last few weeks to complete the system for devastating Portugal in front of the enemy. It was by these means, and not by fights in the open, that he had from the first designed to defeat the invader. Bussaco had been an 'uncovenanted mercy': if Masséna chose to run his head against that stone wall, it was worth while to man it, and to permit him to break himself against its granite boulders. But such an operation as descending into the plain to attack the 2nd Corps on the 29th, or offering battle in front of Sardão on that same day, was not within the scope of Wellington's intentions. If he had wished to engage in that sort of fighting, he had already had ample opportunities to attack sections of the French army during the last two months. But to get engaged with one corps in a rolling upland, and then to have the other two converging on him while the fight was in progress, he had never intended—nor would he do so now. He gave his orders for the retreat of the army on Coimbra actually before the French had possession of their own end of the Boialvo pass, and at a moment when a single night march would have sufficed to place Cole, Craufurd, and Spencer across the western end of it, with ample time to choose a position before the enemy could arrive in front. He explains his refusal to do so in his 'Memorandum of Operations in 1810' in the following terms: 'It would have been impossible to detach a corps from the army to occupy the Serra de Caramula after the action of the 27th. That corps might have been hard pressed and obliged to retreat, in which case it must have retreated upon Sardão and the north of Portugal. It could not have rejoined the army, and its services would have been wanting in the fortified position in front of Lisbon. It was therefore determined to rely upon Colonel Trant alone to occupy the Serra de Caramula, as his line of operations and retreat was to the northward. Nothing could have been done, except by detaching a large corps, to prevent the French from throwing a large force across the Caramula. When, therefore, they took that road, there was nothing for it but to withdraw from Bussaco. And, after quitting

Bussaco, there was no position that we could take up with advantage, in which we could be certain that we could prevent the enemy from getting to Lisbon before us, till we reached the fortified positions in front of that place [1].' As to the other possibility, that of attacking the French rearguard below Bussaco instead of endeavouring to stop its vanguard at Sardão, Wellington only observes that 'they had at least 12,000 or 14,000 more men than we had, and good as our position was, theirs was equally good.' If he had fallen upon Reynier, the latter (he thought) could have detained him long enough to allow Ney and Junot to return, and so he would have found himself committed to an offensive action against superior numbers on unfavourable ground.

These arguments are unanswerable when we consider Wellington's position. He *might* have succeeded in checking Masséna at Boialvo or Sardão ; but, if he did not, ruin would ensue, since he might be cut off from the detached corps, and then would not have men enough to hold the Lines of Torres Vedras. He *might* have crushed Reynier before he was succoured, but if he failed to do so, and became involved in a general action, a disastrous defeat was possible. In short, considering what failure would mean—the loss of Lisbon, the re-embarkation of the army, probably the end of the Peninsular War—he rightly hesitated to take any risk whatever. At the same time, we may suspect that if the allied army of 1810 had been the army of 1813, Wellington might very possibly have played a more enterprising game. But the Portuguese still formed the larger half of his force, and though he had ascertained by their behaviour on the 27th that they were now capable of fighting steadily in a defensive action on favourable ground, it was nevertheless very doubtful whether he could dare to risk them in a battle fought under different conditions. One cheering example of the courage and discipline of these newly organized regiments did not justify him in taking it for granted that they could be trusted under all possible conditions, as if they were veteran British troops.

On the dawn of Sept. 29, therefore, the two armies were marching away from each other. On the Bussaco position there remained only Craufurd's Light Division, strengthened by

---

[1] *Dispatches*, vii. pp. 306-7

Anson's cavalry brigade, which was brought up behind the
Serra, to form the mounted section of the force which was for
the next ten days to act as the rearguard of the allied army.
Opposite them only Reynier remained, and he had drawn far
back on to the Mortagoa road, where he stood in a defensive
position in the morning, but retired, brigade after brigade, in
the afternoon. The main body of Wellington's army was
retiring in two columns: Hill, and Hamilton's Portuguese division crossed the fords of Peña Cova and marched for Espinhal
and Thomar. The force which had been left far out on the right
behind the Alva—Fane's cavalry and Lecor's Portuguese militia—
joined Hill and accompanied him to Lisbon. This column was
absolutely unmolested by the enemy during the whole twelve
days of the retreat to the Lines. The French did not so much
as follow it with a cavalry patrol. The other and larger column,
formed of Spencer, Cole, Leith, and Picton, with Pack's,
Coleman's, and Alex. Campbell's Portuguese, marched for
Mealhada and Coimbra. Craufurd and Anson started twelve
hours later to bring up the rear. During the hours while the
Light Division was waiting its orders to start, some of its officers
explored the evacuated French position, and found parked in an
enclosure 400 desperately wounded soldiers, whom Masséna had
abandoned to the mercy of the Portuguese peasantry. He had
used up all available carts and mules to carry his wounded, but
had been forced to leave the worst cases behind. They were
picked up and moved into the convent of Bussaco[1]; on what
became of them afterwards it is well not to speculate. No
friendly column came that way again[2], and the Ordenanza were
daily growing more exasperated at the conduct of the invading
army. The French were not only carrying out in an intermittent fashion Masséna's edict of Sept. 4, directing that all men
with arms but without uniforms were to be shot at sight, but
burning every village that they passed, and murdering nearly

---

[1] See Tomkinson, p. 44, and von Linsingen's Diary, in Beamish, i. 292.
Fririon and the other French narratives speak of the difficulties of trans-
porting the wounded, but do not mention that any were abandoned.

[2] Unless some of Reynier's rearguard cavalry may have looked in at
Bussaco on the 30th, when Craufurd had gone. This is possible. Trant's
Portuguese were back in the place on Oct. 4.

every peasant that they could hunt down, whether he was bearing arms or no [1].

Meanwhile, on the 29th and 30th of September, the French army was executing its flank march, practically unopposed, though not unobserved. Sainte-Croix's division of dragoons was at the head of the line of march: then came the infantry of the 8th Corps, which had been put in the vanguard because it had not suffered at Bussaco. Next came the reserve cavalry of Montbrun, followed by the Grand Park and the massed baggage of the 6th and 8th Corps, mixed with a convoy of over 3,000 wounded. Ney's troops brought up the rear of the main column. Reynier was a day's march to the rear; having spent the 29th opposite the Bussaco heights, he only reached Mortagoa that evening. Sainte-Croix's cavalry on this same day had passed the watershed and reached Avellans de Cima, where they met a patrol of De Grey's dragoons, who had sent parties out in all directions, from their head quarters at Mealhada in the coast-plain. From this time onward the French advanced guard was watched by the four regiments of Slade and De Grey, who were directed to hold back its exploring cavalry, and not to permit it to reach Coimbra an hour sooner than could be helped. There was also a clash on the afternoon of the 30th between part of Sainte-Croix's dragoons and the Portuguese militia of Trant in front of Sardão. Trant had been ordered to be at that place

---

[1] This seems proved by the 'Table of Damages committed by the French Army in 1810–11,' published by the Coimbra authorities in 1812, which gives the number of houses burnt and persons killed in each rural-deanery (arcyprestado) of the bishopric of Coimbra. Omitting the rural-deaneries south of the Mondego, where the damages were mainly done during the retreat of the French in March 1811, and taking only those north of the river, where no hostile column appeared after October 1810—the district having been protected by Trant and Wilson during Masséna's return march,—we find the following statistics :—

Deanery of Mortagoa	108 murders	19 villages and 47 isolated houses burnt.
,, Oliveirinha	102 ,,	100 houses burnt.
,, Arazede	99 ,,	124 ,,
,, Coimbra city	14 ,,	7 ,,

The figures for the deaneries south of Mondego (Soure, Arganil, Redinha, Miranda do Corvo, Sinde, Cea) are enormously higher. See Soriano da Luz, iii. 203.

on September 27 : he only arrived there on the afternoon of the
28th, not by his own fault, but because his superior officer
Baccellar, commanding the whole militia of the North, had
ordered him to move from Lamego to Sardão by the circuitous road along the Douro, and then from Feira southward, instead of taking the straight road across the mountains
north of Vizeu, where he might possibly have been stopped by
some outlying French detachment. Trant had at the moment
only a squadron of dragoons and four militia regiments with
him (Porto, Penafiel, Coimbra, and a battalion of light companies), and these, from hard marching, and from desertion, were
in all less than 3,000 strong. Knowing that he was expected to
hold the debouch of the Boialvo road against anything short of a
strong force, Trant made an attempt to stand his ground. But
his vanguard bolted at the first shot fired, and with the rest he
had to make a hurried retreat beyond the Vouga, leaving the
road free to the French [1]. Sainte-Croix had already pushed in

---

[1] I cannot resist quoting here Trant's account of the engagement. He
was a man of quaint humour, and the all too few letters from him to
General J. Wilson, which have come into my hands by the courtesy of
Wilson's representative, Captain Bertram Chambers, R.N., inspire me
with regret that I have not his whole correspondence. ' I have once more
been putting my fellows to a trial—my Caçadore battalion did not do as
it ought, and had about thirty killed, wounded, and prisoners, without
making scarcely any resistance—a pleasant business. On the 30th I was
still at Agueda (Sardão and Agueda are one village, properly speaking,
but divided by a bridge), though I was aware that the French principal
force of cavalry was at Boyalva, only a league from Agueda, and I was
completely cut off from the army. On that morning I had withdrawn the
infantry to the Vouga, but placed my dragoons close to Agueda to observe
the French, with the Caçadores at a half-way distance to support them. I
put them in the most advantageous possible position, protected by a close
pine wood, through which the French cavalry must pass. I had been
from three in the morning till one o'clock, making my arrangements, and
had just sat down to eat something, in a small village on the left of the
Vouga, when a dragoon came flying to inform me that the French were
coming on with two columns of cavalry in full speed. My coffee was not
ready, and remained for the French to amuse themselves with. I had
only time to get the Penafiel regiment over the bridge when the French
arrived—five minutes sooner and I had been nabbed ! I drew up in a good
position, but the French did not cross the Vouga, and I returned to
Oliveira without molestation—but not without a damned false alarm and

between him and the British cavalry, who now began to make a
slow retreat towards Mealhada. At that place, early on the 30th,
Slade and De Grey were joined by Anson's eight squadrons, who
had come in at the tail of Craufurd's division after the rearguard
evacuated the Bussaco position. On this day the main column
of the British infantry marched through Coimbra, leaving the
Light Division alone in the city. Wellington's head quarters that
night were at Condeixa six miles south of the Mondego. The
three cavalry brigades retired, bickering with the French advanced
guard all day, as far as Fornos, eight miles north of Coimbra.
Masséna's infantry, after emerging from the Boialvo pass, were
now pushing south, and bivouacked on the night of the 30th,
Ney and Junot's corps at Mealhada, Reynier's at Barreiro, ten
miles behind the others. The biscuit which the French army
had taken with it from Almeida was now almost exhausted, and
it was a great relief to the troops to find, in the deserted villages
of the plain of Coimbra, considerable quantities of maize and
rice, with which they could eke out or replace the carefully
hoarded rations.

Meanwhile the city of Coimbra was full of distressing scenes.
Though Wellington had ordered the whole population of Western Beira to leave their abodes as soon as the French reached
Vizeu, yet only the richest of the inhabitants of Coimbra had
departed. The bulk had still held to their houses, and the
news of the victory of Bussaco had encouraged them to hope
that no evacuation would be necessary. The Portuguese govern-

panic on the part of the dragoons who were covering my rear. They
galloped through the infantry, and carried confusion and all the comforts
of hell to Oporto ! Lieutenant-Colonel ' Bravoure Bombasto,' who commanded the Caçadores, ordered his men to fire, but thought that enough
for his honour, as he instantly left them to shift for themselves, and never
looked behind till he reached Oporto. I put this fellow, with four of the
leading dragoons, into the common dungeon of this place, and am about to
inflict some divisional punishment, for I daren't report such conduct to
the Marshal (Beresford), who does not punish by halves ! My regiments
of infantry—this is the brighter side of the picture—showed no agitation,
notwithstanding the attack on their nerves. The enemy's force, I now
ascertain, was 800 cavalry, two pieces, and two infantry regiments. The
cavalry alone would have done my business if they had crossed the Vouga !
But they contented themselves with driving in the dragoons and the
Caçadore battalion from Agueda. God bless you. N.T.'

ment, though it had consented to carry out Wellington's scheme of devastation, and had duly published proclamations commanding its execution, had taken no great pains to secure obedience to it.   The sacrifice, indeed, that was demanded of the citizens of a wealthy town such as Coimbra was a very great one—far more bitter than that imposed on the peasantry, who were told at the same moment to evacuate their flimsy cottages.   It was bitterly resented, and, despite of the proclamation, four-fifths of the 40,000 inhabitants of Coimbra were still in their houses when, on the night of the 28th–29th, arrived Wellington's dispatch stating that he was abandoning Bussaco, that the French would be in the city by the 30th or on the 1st of October, and that force would be used, if necessary, to expel people who still clung to their dwellings.   During the next two days the whole of the population of Coimbra was streaming out of the place by the roads to the south, or dropping down the Mondego in boats, to ship themselves for Lisbon at the little port of Figueira.   Even on the 1st of October, the day when the French were reputed to be facing Fornos, only eight miles away, all had not yet departed.   Many of the poor, the infirm, and the reckless remained behind to the last possible moment, and only started when the distant cannonade on the northern side showed that the British outposts were being driven in.   Twenty miles of road were covered by the dense column of fugitives, headed by those who had started on the 29th and brought up behind by those who had waited till the last moment.   There was a great want of wheeled conveyances : the richer folks had gone off with most of them, and others had been requisitioned for the allied wounded.   Hence, many could take off nothing but what they could carry on their persons.   An eye-witness writes that he saw the whole *chaussée* covered with respectable families walking on foot with bundles on their heads, while in the abandoned houses he noticed food of all sorts, table-linen, shirts, and all manner of other property, which was left behind in disorder because it was too heavy to be carried [1].   Another tells how ' the old and the infirm, no less than the young and robust, carrying with them all their more valuable effects, covered the fields as well as the road in every direction, and from time to

---

[1] Tomkinson, p. 47.

time the weary fugitives, unable to carry further the heavier
articles that they had endeavoured to save, dropped them by
the wayside and struggled onward, bereft of the remnant of
their little property[1].' Fortunately the weather for the first
eight days after the evacuation of Coimbra was warm and dry,
so that the unhappy multitude had almost reached Lisbon
before they began to suffer any inconvenience from the October
rains.

While this exodus was going on, Craufurd's Light Division
stood under arms on the northern side of the city, while the six
regiments of British horse, in the extreme rearguard, were bickering with Masséna's squadrons in the plain toward Fornos. On this
day the Marshal had strengthened his van with almost the whole
of his cavalry, having added to Sainte-Croix's division, which
had hitherto formed the advance, most of Montbrun's reserve of
dragoons, and Lamotte's light brigade from the 6th Corps.
This body of thirty-four squadrons was altogether too strong
for Stapleton Cotton's three brigades, who had to give way
whenever they were seriously pressed. Two miles outside
Coimbra the British horse was divided into two columns:
De Grey's heavy dragoons crossed the Mondego at a ford
opposite Pereira, Slade and Anson's light dragoons and hussars
by another at Alciada, nearer to the city. At the same moment
the Light Division, when the enemy's horse came in sight,
retired through Coimbra, crossed the bridge, and pressed up the
ascent towards Condeixa, thrusting before them the rearguard
of belated fugitives who had only made up their minds to depart
at the last possible moment. It is said that the block in front
of them was so great that Craufurd's regiments would have
been in a situation of some danger, if they had been closely
followed by French infantry, and forced to turn back to defend
themselves. But nothing more than a troop of dragoons
watched their passage of the bridge and their retreat to Condeixa, and not a shot had to be fired.

It was otherwise with the cavalry column composed of Slade's
and Anson's brigades: they were closely followed by the bulk
of the French cavalry, and had to turn at the ford to hold back
their eager pursuers. Two squadrons of the German Hussars

[1] Lord Londonderry, ii. p. 12.

and one of the 16th Light Dragoons charged in succession to
check the French vanguard, while a fire was kept up by a line
of dismounted skirmishers all along the river bank. The hussars
lost four men killed, and two officers and thirteen men wounded,
besides six prisoners ; the 16th, two wounded and one missing in
this skirmish. It could have been avoided, according to critics
on the spot, if the brigade had retreated a little faster in the
previous stage of its movement. But Stapleton Cotton, for-
getting the dangers of crossing such a defile as a narrow ford,
had been rather too leisurely in covering the last three miles,
considering that the French were so close behind him [1]. The
enemy's loss was insignificant [2].

That night the British rearguard lay at Soure and Condeixa,
while head quarters and the rear of the main army were at
Redinha. The French did not cross the Mondego with more
than a few cavalry patrols, and made no attempt to incommode
the retreating column. Indeed they were otherwise employed.
The entry of an army into a deserted town is always accompanied by disorders : that of the army of Masséna into Coimbra
was an exaggerated example of the rule—and for good reasons.
The men had been living on bare rations for a month, and
suddenly they found themselves in a town of 40,000 souls, where
every door was open, every larder garnished, and every cellar
full. The very quays were littered with sacks of flour torn open,
and puncheons of rum stove in, for Wellington's commissariat
officers had been to the last moment engaged in breaking up
and casting into the river the remains of the magazine which
had been feeding the army at Bussaco. The houses on every
side were full of valuable goods, for most of the inhabitants had
only been able to carry off their money and plate, and had left
all else behind them. The first division of the 8th Corps, the
earliest French troops to enter the place, consisted almost
entirely of newly-formed fourth battalions, composed of conscripts, and ill disciplined. They broke their ranks and fell

---

[1] See Beamish's *History of the King's German Legion*, i. 293–4, and
Tomkinson, p. 46.

[2] De Grey's brigade, though it had no regular fighting, lost five
prisoners and one trooper wounded in this same retreat. The total loss
of the cavalry that day was thirty-four men.

to plunder, only half-restrained by their officers, many of whom joined in the sport. A late comer from the artillery says that he saw one officer breaking open a door with a pickaxe, and another placing a sentry at the door of a shop which he wished to reserve for his own personal pillage [1]. There was widespread drunkenness, some arson, and an enormous amount of mischievous and wanton waste. It was afterwards said that Junot's corps destroyed in twelve hours an amount of food that would have sufficed to supply the whole army for three weeks. It is at any rate certain that Coimbra was full of provisions when the French arrived, and that, when order was tardily restored, only a few days' consumption could be scraped together to fill the empty waggons before the host marched on. Masséna raged against Junot for not having kept his men in hand, yet, if Portuguese narratives are to be trusted, he set as bad an example as any disorderly conscript, since he requisitioned for himself out of the University buildings all the telescopes and mathematical instruments, and distributed them among his staff [2]. The pillage was as wanton and objectless as it was thorough ; the tombs of the kings in the church of Santa Cruz were broken open, the University Museum and laboratories wrecked, and all the churches wantonly damaged and desecrated. There was no attempt to restore order, or to utilize the captured property for the general good of the army, till the 6th Corps marched in on the next day. Even these later comers, however, could not be restrained from joining in the plunder. The mob of soldiers threatened to shoot the commissary-generals Lambert and Laneuville, when they began to put guards over the nearly-emptied storehouses.

The state of his army on the 1st and 2nd October sufficiently explains the conduct of Masséna in refraining from the pursuit

---

[1] Colonel Noël's *Souvenirs Militaires*, pp. 120-1.

[2] The authority for this statement is the Portuguese renegade General Pamplona, who served on the Marshal's staff. See p. 155 of his *Aperçu sur les campagnes des Français en Portugal*. Pamplona adds that Ney refused to take the present of a large telescope, which Masséna sent him as a propitiatory gift. A less certain authority says that the Marshal caught in the street a plunderer with a barrel of butter, and another with a chest of wax candles, and let them off punishment on condition that they took them to his own quarters ! Soriano da Luz, iii. p. 198.

of Wellington's rearguard. But he was also somewhat puzzled to determine the policy which he must now adopt. Down to the last moment he had thought that Wellington would have fought at Fornos, or some other such position, to defend Coimbra. And even when Coimbra was evacuated, he had imagined that he might find the enemy drawn up to dispute the passage of the Mondego. But it was now clear that Wellington was in full retreat for Lisbon. Since the Marshal was still ignorant of the existence of the lines of Torres Vedras, which was only revealed to him four days later, he was somewhat uncertain how to interpret the conduct of his adversary. After the vigorous stand that Wellington had made at Bussaco, it seemed dangerous to argue that he must now be in headlong flight for his ships, and about to evacuate Portugal. Yet the rapidity of his retreat seemed to argue some such purpose. Ought he, therefore, to be pursued without a moment's delay, in order that his embarkation might be made difficult? This course, it is said, was advocated by Reynier, Montbrun, Fririon, and the Portuguese renegade d'Alorna. On the other hand, Ney and Junot both advised a stay at Coimbra, to rest the army, collect provisions, and, what was most important of all, to reopen communications with Almeida, Ciudad Rodrigo, and the 9th Corps, which was now due on the Spanish frontier. They pointed to the diminished strength of the army, which, having lost 4,600 men at Bussaco, and 4,000 more by the hard marching and poor feeding of the last month, was now reduced to some 57,000 men. The fighting-power of Wellington was formidable, as he had shown at Bussaco, where many of the French officers persisted in believing that he had shown numbers superior to their own—in which they erred. A hasty advance, it was urged, might bring the invaders in face of a second Bussaco, where there was no chance of a turning movement. Would the commander-in-chief wish to accept another battle of the same sort? It would be better to establish a new base at Coimbra, to bring up the 9th Corps from the rear, and only to move on when the army was thoroughly reorganized. Meanwhile a detachment might demonstrate against Oporto, to distract Wellington's attention [1]. This was

---

[1] Fririon, in his account of these debates (pp. 72-3), forgets that the existence of the Lines of Torres Vedras was still unknown both to Masséna

the policy that Napoleon, two months after, declared that Masséna should have adopted. 'Why,' he asked, 'did the Prince of Essling, after his failure at Bussaco, pursue the march on Lisbon, instead of taking up a position on the Mondego, and restoring his communications with Almeida? I had not burdened him with orders or instructions, and he could see that the English were not easy to beat.' Masséna's advocate, Foy, replied that 'if the Army of Portugal had been halted on the Mondego, your Majesty would have said to the Prince, Why did you not march on? The English would have re-embarked, if they had been pressed.' To which Napoleon, with a broad smile, answered, 'Very true; I probably should have said so [1].'

The problem presented to the Marshal, indeed, was not an easy one. If he remained at Coimbra, his enemies would delate him to the Emperor for timidity; if he advanced, he might find that he had undertaken a task too great for his strength. The personal equation settled the difficulty: Masséna was obstinate and enterprising to the verge of temerity. He resolved to go on, at the earliest possible moment, in the hope of forcing Wellington to a battle on ground less favourable than Bussaco, or of compelling him to embark without any general engagement at all. Two days only were spent at Coimbra. On October 3, Montbrun's cavalry, after making a reconnaissance as far as the sea and the port of Figueira, crossed the Mondego to Villa Nova de Ancos, while the 8th Corps, headed by Sainte-Croix's dragoons, occupied Condeixa: one division of Ney's corps followed them. The rest of the 6th Corps and Reynier made ready to resume their advance.

A minor problem remained to be resolved. Should a large garrison be left in Coimbra, and a new base for the army established there? The Marshal had shot into the convent of Santa Clara 3,000 Bussaco wounded, and 1,000 sick men. There was an accumulation of waggons of the corps-trains and the

and his subordinates. So does Delagrave (pp. 93–4). But Pelet, Masséna's confidant, is positive that they were first heard of from prisoners taken at Pombal on Oct. 5, two days after the advance had recommenced.

[1] Foy's minutes of his conversation with the Emperor on Nov. 22, sent by him to Masséna, in his letter of Dec. 4. See Appendix to Foy's *Vie Militaire* by Girod de L'Ain, p. 348.

Grand Park, which could push on no further, for want of draught beasts, and all manner of other impedimenta. If the army went on at full speed, in the hope of overtaking the English, all this must be left behind. But if left unguarded, wounded and all might become the victims of Trant's militia, which was known to have retired no further than the Vouga, or even of the Ordenanza of the hills. A strong garrison must be placed in Coimbra to make it safe: rumour had it on October 2 that Taupin's brigade and a regiment of dragoons were to be set to guard the city [1]. But rumour was wrong: Masséna, after some doubting, made up his mind that he could not spare even 3,000 men. Every bayonet would be wanted if Wellington once more turned to bay. Accordingly he took the extraordinary step of telling off only a single company, 156 men, of the 44th *Équipage de la Marine*—a naval unit which had been given him in order that he might have a nucleus of sea-going people, in case he succeeded in seizing the Portuguese arsenal at Lisbon. One would have thought that such men would have been so valuable, if only the enterprise had succeeded, that he would have chosen rather a company of ordinary infantry. These sailors, with two or three hundred footsore or convalescent men, organized into a couple of provisional companies, were all that the Marshal placed at the disposition of Major Flandrin, to whom he gave the high-sounding title of Governor of Coimbra. That officer was told that every day would increase his force, as more convalescents came out of hospital, and 3,500 muskets, belonging to the sick and wounded, were left with him. The whole mass of disabled men was concentrated in the convent of Santa Clara, a vast building outside the trans-pontine suburb of Coimbra, on the south side of the Mondego. The garrison was so weak that it could do no more than keep a guard at each of the exits of the town, which was destitute of walls, with a post of thirty men, all that could be spared, at Fornos, on the great north road facing Oporto. To abandon his wounded to almost certain destruction was a reckless act on the Marshal's part: probably he said to

[1] So Guingret, of the 6th Corps, who mentions that his own regiment received notice that no garrison was to be left, only just in time to enable it to pick up its slightly wounded and footsore men, who would otherwise have remained behind. (*Memoirs*, p. 79.)

himself that if he could but catch and beat the Anglo-Portuguese
army, a small disaster in his rear would be forgiven him.
Unlike Wellington, he was 'taking risks'[1].

On October 4 the French army made its regular start from
Coimbra ; the 6th Corps came out to Villa Pouca and Condeixa
on the Pombal road, the 2nd Corps to Venda do Cego on the
Ancião road, which runs parallel with the other, ten miles to
the east, and joins it at Leiria.   Montbrun's cavalry pushed
in from Soure, to place itself in front of the 8th Corps, which
now moved on from Condeixa as the head of the main infantry
column.   Its scouts that evening bickered in front of Pombal
with Anson's light cavalry, which was covering the retreat of
the allied army.   The two days which the French had spent in
plundering Coimbra had allowed the Anglo-Portuguese infantry
to get a start which they never lost : they never saw the enemy
again during the rest of the retreat.   That night Wellington's
head quarters were at Leiria, while Hill, unpursued by any
hostile force, was at Thomar.   For the next six days the British
pursued a leisurely course towards the Lines, along the three
roads Thomar-Santarem-Villafranca, which was taken by Hill ;
Alcobaça-Caldas-Torres Vedras, which was taken by Picton ;
and Leiria-Batalha-Alemquer, which was taken by Spencer,
Leith, and Cole.   It was along the last-named, the central,
road, that Craufurd's infantry and the three cavalry brigades
followed the main body, at the distance of a day's march.
Anson's light cavalry brought up the extreme rear, and was
almost the only unit which saw the enemy between the 4th
and the 10th of October[2].   The rest of the allied army had
completely outmarched Masséna.   Its retreat was marked by
some disorders : the sight of rich monasteries like Alcobaça and

---

[1] The best summing up of the Marshal's resolve may be found in Foy's
minute presented to Napoleon on Nov. 22 : ' Le prince n'a pas pu se
résoudre à faire un fort détachement lorsqu'il devait livrer sous peu de
jours une bataille décisive à une armée déjà victorieuse et deux fois plus
nombreuse [!] que la notre.   Les dangers que couraient ses malades ont
affligé son cœur, mais il a pensé que la crainte de perdre l'hôpital ne
devait pas arrêter la campagne.'   (Foy's *Vie Militaire*, Appendix, p. 348.)

[2] Though Slade's brigade had the rearguard on the 7th, and was
engaged on the 8th also, Anson's only was in touch with the French on
the 4th-6th, and again on the 9th-10th.

Batalha, and large towns, like Thomar and Leiria, standing
empty, yet left full of all such property as the inmates could
not easily carry off, proved as tempting to the British as the
sight of Coimbra had been to the French.   There was much
drunkenness,   much   looting,   and   some   wanton   mischief.
Wellington set himself to repress it by the strong hand.   He
hung at Leiria two troopers of the 4th Dragoon Guards, who
were caught plundering a chapel, and a man of the 11th
Portuguese infantry.   Some of the regiments which were found
specially addicted to pillage were ordered to bivouac in the open
fields every night, and never to be quartered in a village [1].

Anson's brigade, alone among the allied troops, had an adventurous career during the retreat to the Lines.   It was always in
touch with a pursuing force of immense strength, for Masséna
had constituted a flying vanguard under Montbrun, whose orders
were to push the enemy at all costs, and to try to come up with
his infantry.   This force consisted of Sainte-Croix's dragoons,
Pierre Soult's cavalry from the 2nd Corps, Lamotte's from the
6th Corps, one brigade (Ornano's) of the Reserve Cavalry, and
Taupin's infantry from the 8th Corps.   Lamotte's light horse
had the place of honour, and endured most of the hard knocks.
They had lively skirmishing with Anson's 1st German Hussars
and 16th Light Dragoons between Pombal and Leiria on the
5th October.   The British brigade turned back twice, and drove
their pursuers back on to Taupin's infantry, but always suffered
when it had to resume its inevitable retreat.   The French lost
eight killed, seventeen wounded (including five officers) and
twenty prisoners—the British fifty in all, including two officers
wounded, and one taken.   This combat would not have been
worth mentioning, but for the fact that it was from prisoners
captured in it that Masséna got his first news of the existence
of the Lines of Torres Vedras.   Some of the troopers spoke
freely of 'the Lines' as their point of destination, not guessing
that this was the first time that their captors had heard of them.
Hence the French generals learned that there were now fortifi-

---

[1] This was the case with Picton's division, despite its splendid services
and heavy loss at Bussaco, only ten days back.   Leith's British brigade
and the Lusitanian Legion are also specially upbraided for straggling.
See *General Orders* for 1810, pp. 173–4.

cations in front of Lisbon : but they had, of course, no knowledge of their extent or character, and only expected to find
some field-works on which Wellington would turn to bay. In
fact, Masséna was encouraged by the news, thinking that he was
now certain of the battle which he desired.

On the 7th October the French infantry was all concentrated
at Leiria, Reynier's corps having now rejoined the other two.
Montbrun's cavalry spread out so far as Alcobaça—whose
monastery it sacked—on the coast-road, and Muliano on the
central road. Vedettes were sent out on the cross-road to Thomar
also, but could find no trace of an enemy in that direction. On
the night that followed Masséna received the disquieting intelligence that his deliberate taking of risks with regard to
Coimbra had already been punished. A mounted officer, who
had escaped, brought him news that his hospitals and their
guard had been captured at a single blow by Trant's militia
that same afternoon.

That enterprising partisan, it will be remembered, had been
driven behind the Vouga by Sainte-Croix's dragoons on
September 30th. Since, however, none of the French turned
aside to molest him, and all marched across his front on the
Coimbra road, he was not forced to retire any further. And
having his orders from Wellington to follow the enemy with
caution, and pick up his stragglers and marauders, he came
southward again when Masséna's rearguard entered Coimbra.
He had advanced to Mealhada when it was reported to him, on
the 6th, that the rearguard of the French had left the city on
the preceding day. A few people who had returned from the
mountains to their homes, despite Wellington's proclamation,
sent him assurances that the numbers of the garrison were
absolutely insignificant, and that of the wounded enormous.
Judging rightly that it would have a splendid moral effect to
capture Masséna's hospitals, and the commencement of a base-
magazine which was being formed at Coimbra, Trant resolved
to strike at once. If he had waited a little he could have got
help from J. Wilson and from Miller, who had descended into
the Celorico–Vizeu country, each with his brigade. They had
been directed by Wellington to cut the French communications
with Almeida, and had already carried out their orders.

But Trant dreaded delay, thinking that Masséna might send back troops to Coimbra, when he found that Wellington was retiring as far as Lisbon. Without waiting for his colleagues, he marched at midday from Mealhada to Fornos on the 7th, and had the good fortune to surprise and capture the insignificant French post at that village : not a man escaped. He was now only eight miles from Coimbra, and was able to rush down into the city in the early afternoon before his arrival was known. He had with him one weak squadron of regular dragoons, and six militia battalions, having been joined since September 29th by all his stragglers and some outlying units. The whole made about 4,000 men [1]. Formed in two columns, they charged into Coimbra by its two northern entrances, sweeping away the small French guards at the gates. The squadron of cavalry then galloped along the street parallel with the river, and seized the bridge, thus cutting off the communication between the French in the town and those at the convent of Santa Clara, where the wounded lay. The small grand-guard, which the enemy kept inside the place, took refuge in the bishop's palace, but was forced to lay down its arms at the end of an hour. The men at the convent, joined by many of the convalescents, kept up a fire for a short time, but surrendered at discretion, on Trant's promise to protect them from the fury of his troops. He was, unfortunately, not entirely able to redeem his promise : the Coimbra local regiment was so enraged at the state in which it found its native town that it mishandled some of the prisoners—eight are said to have been slain [2]. The total loss of the Portuguese division was three killed and one officer and twenty-five men wounded.

Wilson and Miller came up next day, and sweeping the roads towards Condeixa and Pombal, picked up 300 more stragglers and marauders from the tail of Masséna's marching column. Trant handed over Coimbra to them, and escorted his prisoners to Oporto with his own division: there were 3,507 sick and

[1] The brigade was not complete, the Feira battalion having—somehow or other—got to Lisbon. But Porto, Penafiel, Coimbra, Aveiro, Maia, and a combined battalion of light companies were apparently present.

[2] See Trant's dispatch to Beresford in Soriano da Luz, vii, Appendix, p. 221.

wounded, of whom half could march, while the rest were taken off in carts. Of able-bodied men not more than 400 soldiers were taken : but some hundreds of commissariat and hospital employés and men of the train brought up the total figures of the prisoners to 4,500 men. Trant has been accused by some French writers [1] of deliberately exposing his captives to the fury of the peasantry, and parading the wounded in an indecent fashion through the streets of Oporto. But the handsome testimonial to his humanity signed by a committee of French officers, which Napier prints in the Appendix no. 5 to his third volume, is enough to prove that Trant did his best for his prisoners, and that the unfortunate incident which occurred just after the surrender must not be laid to his account [2].

Masséna's army received the news of the fall of Coimbra with indignation. It produced a painful impression on every mind ; and while the rank and file murmured at the Marshal's cruelty in abandoning their comrades to death— for it was falsely reported that the Portuguese had massacred them all—the officers blamed his blind improvidence, and observed that a brigade might well-have been spared to protect not only the hospitals but the invaluable base-dépôt behind them [3].

There was heavy skirmishing between the British rearguard cavalry and Montbrun's advance, both on the 8th and 9th of October. On the first of these days the horse-artillery troop attached to Anson's brigade was, by some extraordinary mistake, left encamped out in front of the squadrons which were told off as its escort, and was nearly surprised in Alcoentre by an

----

[1] As for example Delagrave, p. 197, and Fririon, p. 75.

[2] Trant delivered nearly 400 British and Portuguese wounded, whom Wellington had been obliged to leave behind at Coimbra, as non-transportable.

[3] Sprünglin writes, under Oct. 7, in his Diary : ' Lorsque le sort des malheureux abandonnés à Coimbre fut connu dans l'armée, on murmura hautement contre le Prince d'Essling. On qualifia de coupable entête-ment et de barbarie sa conduite à Busaco et l'abandon des blessés à Coimbre. Il faut avouer que le maréchal Ney, le général Reynier et le duc d'Abrantes ne firent rien pour faire cesser ces murmures. Dès lors l'armée perdit de sa force, parce que le général-en-chef n'avait plus la confiance de ses soldats.' Cf. Guingret, p. 79.

irruption of Sainte-Croix's dragoons in a storm of rain [1]. Somers Cocks's squadron of the 16th Light Dragoons charged just in time to save the guns, and to jam the head of the enemy's column, as it was crossing the bridge which leads into the village. Alcoentre was held till dusk, when Taupin's infantry came up, and Anson's brigade retired, having lost only one trooper wounded, while the French had sixteen disabled or taken.

From this day onward, the weather, which had been fine and dry since the army left Coimbra, broke up for the autumn rains, and the last three days of the retreat to the Lines were spent in torrential downpour. This had the advantage of delaying the French; for while the British infantry, who were two days ahead of them, reached their destined position on the 9th (with the exception of the Light Division and Pack's Portuguese), the enemy was marching on flooded roads from the 8th to the 11th.

On the 9th there was continual bickering in the rain, from Quinta da Torre as far as Alemquer, between Lamotte's light cavalry brigade, which had again replaced Sainte-Croix's dragoons at the head of the pursuing column, and Anson's two much-enduring regiments. On this day the 1st Hussars of the King's German Legion had the thick of the work: Linsingen's squadron of that admirable regiment, which formed the rear detachment of the whole army, turned back to charge no less than four times in five miles, and always with success. At dusk the French infantry got up, and the allied cavalry retired on to Alemquer after a fatiguing day of fighting, in which the hussars had lost two killed, two officers and nine men wounded, and seventeen missing; the supporting regiment, the 16th Light Dragoons, had one killed, three wounded, and four missing, and the Royals of Slade's brigade, who only got engaged in the late evening, one wounded and four missing. Lamotte's loss was a little more—six killed, twenty-two wounded, and twenty-one prisoners [2]. Three of his officers were hurt, one taken.

On the next day (Oct. 10) the whole of the British cavalry

---

[1] 'Rather a new style of war, to place guns in a village and the troops protecting them a mile in the rear.'—Tomkinson, p. 51.

[2] Readers interested in cavalry work should read Beamish, i. 298–301, and Tomkinson, 52–3, who have admirable accounts of this rearguard fighting.

marched from Alemquer to within the Lines, distributing themselves to the cantonments which had been arranged for them.
But Craufurd's and Pack's infantry, which had hitherto been
completely covered by the horsemen, did not follow their
example with quite sufficient promptitude, and got engaged
in an unnecessary skirmish. The Light Division should have
withdrawn at noon, but Craufurd, believing the French infantry
to be still far away, and despising the cavalry which hovered
around him, remained in Alemquer, intending to spend another
night in a dry cantonment, for the torrential rain which was
falling promised a fatiguing march to his men. At four o'clock
Taupin's infantry came up, and engaged the pickets of the Light
Division in a skirmish. Having been strictly forbidden by
Wellington to get entangled in a rearguard action, and remem-
bering perhaps his experience at the Coa, Craufurd tardily and
unwillingly moved off. But dusk coming on, his column missed
its road, and instead of retiring into the section of the Lines
which it was destined to occupy, between the Monte Agraça
and the valley of Calandriz, went too far to the west, and came
in upon the position of the 1st Division in front of Sobral.
This would have been dangerous if the French had had any
infantry to the front, to take advantage of the unoccupied gap
in the lines. But Montbrun's advanced guard had pressed more
than thirty miles in front of the main body of Masséna's army,
and this force contained nothing but cavalry, save the single
brigade of Taupin—less than 3,000 men [1]. This force, such as

---

[1] For this reason the dismal picture of the situation drawn by Napier
(iii. 38–9) must be considered exaggerated. The French main army was
further off than he imagines; it had not passed Alcoentre. The cavalry
could have done nothing against the heights, and Taupin's brigade would
have been crushed if it had endeavoured to enter the gap. But it never
came within ten miles of the exposed point on the 10th and 11th, not
having passed Alemquer. The Light Division diarists do not treat
seriously the position which Napier paints in such gloomy colours. See
Leach, p. 172, and Simmons, p. 111. The Light Division countermarched
from Sobral to Arruda and reached their proper post long before midnight.
There they picked up a detachment of 150 convalescents and recruits
from Lisbon, who had been waiting for them. Among these were
Harry Smith and Simmons, who have accounts of the arrival of the division
'after dark,' and of its relief at finding large fires already lighted and
provisions prepared by the draft.

it was, did not pass Alemquer that night—Craufurd, in his retreat on Sobral, was followed by cavalry alone. It was not till next morning, when Montbrun sent out reconnaissances in all directions, that he found himself in front of fortifications drawn across every road, and gradually realized that he was in front of the famous ' Lines of Torres Vedras.'

It must not be supposed that Wellington's final arrangements for the reception of the army of Masséna in front of Lisbon were made at leisure, or at a moment when he had nothing to distract him. Though the actual retreat of his army from the position of Bussaco to the position of Torres Vedras was conducted at an easy pace, and practically unmolested by the enemy, yet the days during which it was being carried out were a time of political, though not of military, storm and stress. Ever since the French had started from Almeida, and made their first advance into the mountains of Beira, Wellington had been engaged in an endless and tiresome controversy with the Portuguese Regency. Though they had assented, long before, to the scheme for devastating the country-side and bringing Masséna to a check only in front of Lisbon, yet when the actual invasion began, and the first hordes of fugitives were reported to be leaving their homes, and burning their crops, and taking to the mountains, several of the members of the Regency became appalled at the awful sacrifices which they were calling upon the nation to endure. The Principal Sousa put himself at the head of the movement, and was supported by the Patriarch, the Bishop of Oporto, so famous in 1808. Sousa brought before the Regency proposals that Wellington should be formally requested to try the chances of a pitched battle on the frontier, before retiring on Coimbra or Lisbon. In addition, he was always maintaining in private company that the people should not be required to take in hand the scheme of devastation and wholesale emigration, till it was certain the allied army was unable to stop Masséna somewhere east of the Serra da Estrella. He also laid before the Regency documents intended to prove that the system of devastation was physically impossible, and that it would prove incapable of stopping the advance of the French, owing to the difficulty that would be found in persuading the peasantry to destroy instead of hiding their

stores of food [1]. There was a certain modicum of truth in this
last argument, and the French did succeed in living for a longer
time in the evacuated districts than Wellington had considered
possible. On the other hand, the Principal was hopelessly
wrong in his contention that the French would suffer little
inconvenience. They were starved out of Portugal by
Wellington's device, even though it took longer to work out its
results than he had calculated. There is no reason to suppose
that Sousa was in any way treacherously inclined : he and his
whole family stood or fell with the English alliance, and the
victory of the French would mean ruin to them. But his
private and public utterances and those of his satellites had
a deplorable effect. In the mouth of the common people it
took the form of a widely-spread rumour that Wellington had
refused to fight at all, and intended to re-embark the British
army. This did not lead to any wish to submit to Napoleon,
but to a desperate determination to resist even if deserted.
Wellington's dispatches are full of a riot which took place in
Lisbon on September 7th, when the militia proposed to seize on
St. Julian's, the Citadel, and the Bugio fort because they were
informed that the English garrisons were about to evacuate them
and put to sea [2]. When Masséna had already passed Coimbra,
Sousa was mad enough to propose, at the Regency board, that
the Portuguese troops should not retire within the Lines, but
remain outside and offer battle in the open, even if the
British refused to stand by them. The nervous activity of
the government had been shown some three weeks before by
the sudden arrest and deportation of some fifty persons in
Lisbon, who were suspected, rightly or wrongly, of 'Jacobinism,'
and had been accused of having secret communication with
D'Alorna and the other renegades in Masséna's army. They
included a few officers, and a good many lawyers, doctors,
merchants, and minor officials, as well as some dependants and

[1] For Sousa's arguments, see Soriano da Luz, iii. pp. 130–44. That
author thinks the Principal's arguments weighty, and sees no harm in
the fact that he set them forth in public and private. Cf. Wellington,
Dispatches, vi. 430.

[2] See Wellington to Charles Stuart, Sept. 9, and to Lord Liverpool,
Sept. 13, 1810, *Dispatches*, vol. vi. pp. 420–30.

relatives of the exiles. The case against most of them was so weak that Wellington protested against their banishment, holding that the alarm caused by the arrests would make the people of Lisbon unreasonably suspicious, and give rise to a belief in wide-spread plots. But despite his letter to the Regency all were shipped off to the Azores[1]. Some were ultimately allowed to go to England, others to Brazil, but the majority were not allowed to return to Portugal till 1816.

'All I ask from the Government,' wrote Wellington, on October 6th, in the midst of the retreat, ' is tranquillity in the town of Lisbon, and provisions for their own troops[2].' These two simple requirements were precisely those which he did not obtain. The capital of Portugal was kept disturbed by arbitrary arrests, by proclamations which often contained false news, and sometimes pledged the Regency to measures which the Commander-in-Chief disapproved, and by senseless embargoes laid on vehicles and commodities, which were never turned to use[3]. At the same time the Portuguese troops were not fed, and the tents which had been ordered forward to the positions behind the lines never started from the magazines of Lisbon[4].

Wellington's temper, tried to the uttermost by these distractions, when his mind was entirely engrossed by military problems, grew sharp and irritable at this time. He went so far as to write to the Prince Regent at Rio de Janeiro, to declare that either he or Principal Sousa must leave the country. He suggested that some post as ambassador or special envoy should be found for the man who troubled him so. The Patriarch, as ' a necessary evil,' he did not wish to displace, but only to scare. Unfortunately, an appeal to Brazil was hopeless, since the Regent was entirely in the hands of the Principal's brother, the Conde de Linhares. Much acrimonious correspondence, delayed by the vast time which was consumed in getting letters

---

[1] See Soriano da Luz, iii. 90–9, for a list of them, and Wellington's *Dispatches*, vi. 433, for the protest against the deportation ; also ibid. 528–9.

[2] *Dispatches*, vi. p. 493.

[3] *Dispatches*, vi. 521. ' When they have got mules and carriages, by injudicious seizure, they do not employ them, but the animals and people are kept starving and shivering, while we still want provisions.'

[4] Ibid., vi. p. 506.

to and from Rio, only led in the end to a proposal from
Linhares that his brother should leave the Regency, if Charles
Stuart, the British Ambassador, was also withdrawn from it,
and if the War-Minister, General Miguel Forjaz, whom
Wellington considered a necessary person and the ablest man in
Portugal, should also be removed from his post[1]. To this
proposal neither Wellington nor the British government would
consent, and as it only came in when Masséna's invasion had
already been foiled, and the French had retired into Spain,
the crisis was over. The Principal remained at the Council
Board, to talk much impracticable and mischievous stuff, but to
do little positive harm. When the invasion was past Wellington could afford to disregard him.

[1] See Soriano da Luz, iii. p. 142. For text of it his *Appendix*, vii. 178–9.
The answer was only written on Feb. 11, 1811, and only got to Wellington
in April when the crisis was over.

WE have hitherto, when speaking of Wellington's immense
scheme for fortifying the position on which he intended to
bring his enemy to a standstill, refrained from entering into
the details of his plan. It is now time to describe it in full, and
to explain its design.

The character of the peninsula on which Lisbon stands lends
itself sufficiently well to defence. At a first inspection the
country-side offers a rather chaotic expanse of mountain and
valley, whose general features are hard to seize from any one
point. On further examination it appears that the whole
square mass of land between the Atlantic and the Tagus
estuary is nothing more than a continuation of the ridge of
the Serra de Monte Junta, the main mountain-chain of Estremadura. But from the backbone or central mass of the highland so many large spurs are thrown out to each side, and these
are themselves so high and steep, that the whole peninsula
seems more like a ganglion of mountains than a well-marked
chain. The two chief joints or vertebrae in the backbone are
the Monte Agraça above Sobral, and the Cabeça de Montechique six miles south of it, and these form the central points
respectively of the first and second lines of defence which were
finally laid out. Besides the outer defences there was in
Wellington's scheme, from the very start, an inner ring of
works, covering only a small area on the sea-shore, at the
southernmost point of the peninsula, to the west of Lisbon.
This was merely intended to cover an embarkation, if by any
unforeseen disaster the Lines themselves should be pierced.

It remains to speak of the system of defences in detail. In
October 1809, Wellington's plan had embraced no more than one
continuous line of works from Alhandra on the Tagus to the

mouth of the Rio São Lourenço on the Atlantic, with certain redoubts and fortified camps thrown out in front, at Torres Vedras, Monte Agraça, and other points. These latter fortifications were not intended to be held in permanence; but it was hoped that they might defer and hinder the enemy's attack on the main line in the rear. It was only the long delay in Masséna's advance, which gave Wellington five or six months on which he had not counted, that led to the ultimate strengthening of the scattered outer works, and their conversion into a continuous whole, capable of turning back, instead of merely detaining for a time, the invading army. Indeed, all across the peninsula, designs that were slight, isolated, and provisional when first drawn up, were in the end enlarged, and perfected into wholly different structures. For the engineers, having unlimited labour at their disposal, and much more time than had been promised them, could turn their attention, after the essential works had been completed, to devising all manner of additional improvements and securities for the chosen position.

The construction of the Lines was entrusted to Colonel Fletcher, Wellington's commanding engineer, who had as his chief assistant Major John Jones, the historian of the works, and in addition eleven British officers of the Royal Engineers, two from the King's German Legion, and three from the Portuguese regular army. Wellington himself, after making one all-embracing survey of the positions in Fletcher's company in October 1809, and another in February 1810, left all the rest to his subordinate, and refrained from worrying him with matters of detail, being satisfied that his own intentions had been thoroughly well grasped. The labour available was, firstly, that of the Lisbon militia regiments, who were brought up by alternate pairs, and paid an extra 4d. a day for their services[1]; secondly, that of hired volunteers from the peasantry of the district, of whom from 5,000 to 7,000 were generally in hand; they received 1s., afterwards 1s. 8d. a day[2]; and lastly of a conscription from the whole of southern Estremadura, for a circuit of forty miles around. The forced labour was paid at the same rate as

---

[1] Or two *vintems* Portuguese money.

[2] Or six, and afterwards ten, *vintems*. See Jones. *Lines of Torres Vedras*, p. 77.

that freely hired. On the whole, only about £100,000 was paid out between November 1809 and September 1810—so that the Lines of Torres Vedras may be considered one of the cheapest investments in history. The militiamen and peasantry were worked in gangs of some 1,000 or 1,500 men, each in charge of an engineer officer, who had a few English and Portuguese military artificers as his assistants : only 150 such were available, so short were both armies of trained men. ' In some districts a subaltern officer of engineers with a few English soldiers, utterly ignorant of the language, directed and controlled the labour of 1,500 peasantry, many of them compelled to work at a distance of forty miles from their homes, while their lands lay neglected. Nevertheless, during a year of this forced labour not a single instance of insubordination or riot occurred. The great quantity of work performed should, in justice to the Portuguese, be ascribed more to the regular habit of persevering labour in those employed than to the efficiency of the control exercised over them [1]. . . . Indeed, it is but a tribute of justice to the Portuguese of Estremadura to state that, during many months of constant personal intercourse, both private and public, the labouring classes ever showed themselves respectful, industrious, docile, and obedient, while the governing classes in every public transaction evinced much intelligence, patriotism, good sense, and probity. Secrecy with respect to the extent and nature of the works was enjoined, and it is highly creditable to all concerned that hardly a vague paragraph concerning the Lines found its way into the public prints. The French invaders remained ignorant of the nature of the barrier rising against them, till they found our army arrayed on it so as to stop their further advance [2].'

The total frontage of the southern and stronger series of lines, those which Wellington originally planned as his line of defence, was twenty-two miles from sea to sea. The outer and northern series of works, which was originally only a supplement and outer bulwark to the other, was longer, extending to twenty-nine miles, for it crosses the peninsula in a diagonal fashion and not on the shortest possible line that could be drawn. Lastly,

---

[1] Jones, p. 79. [2] Id., p. 107.

the small interior line round St. Julian's and Oyeras, which was prepared as the embarking-place of the army in the event of defeat, has a circumference of about two miles.   In all, therefore, fifty-three miles of defences were planned—a stupendous work, far exceeding, when its elaborate details are studied, anything that had been constructed in modern times in the way of field-fortification.

It must be remembered that the character of the Lines in no way resembles that of our own great Roman wall from Tyne to Solway, of the wall of China, or of any other long continuous stretch of masonry.   It is only on a few points that works of any great length are to be found.   The Lines are in essence a series of closed earthworks, dotted along the commanding points of the two ranges of hills which Wellington chose as his first and second fronts of resistance.   Some few of the earthworks rose to the dignity of fortified camps, armed with many scores of guns.   The majority of them were small redoubts, constructed to hold three to six guns and garrisons of two or three hundred men only.   But even the smallest of them were individually formidable from their structure : the normal ditch was 16 feet wide and 12 feet deep, the parapets 8 to 14 feet thick, and all were properly fitted with banquettes.   When it is remembered that they were well palisaded, and had outer hindrances of abattis, *chevaux de frise*, and *trous-de-loup* scattered in front, it is clear that they were forts requiring a regular attack, not mere lines of trench and mound.   The strength of the whole series was that they were placed in scientific fashion, so as to cross fires over all the ground on which an attacking force was likely to present itself.   No practicable point of assault could be found on which advancing columns would not be cut up by flanking fire for a very long distance, before they drew near to their objective.   Immense pains had been taken to make the more exposed sections of the country-side into one vast glacis. Mounds which might have given cover had been removed to the last stone, hollow roads filled up, houses pulled down, olive-groves and vineyards stubbed up to the roots, so as to give a perfectly smooth and featureless ascent up to the line of redoubts. Greatly to Wellington's credit (as may be incidentally re-marked) compensation was paid on a liberal scale to all owners of dwellings, mills, fruit-trees, &c., for the havoc made by these necessary pieces of demolition. The result was a complete clearance of cover. 'We have spared neither house, garden, vineyard, olive-trees, woods, or private property of any description,' wrote the officer in charge of the works to his chief at the end of the preparations: ' the only blind to the fire of the works now standing anywhere is that beautiful avenue of old trees in the pass of Torres Vedras. The Juiz da Fora and the inhabitants pleaded with me so hard for the latest moment, lest they might be cut down unnecessarily, that I have consented to defer it till the day before the troops march in. As I have trustworthy men with axes in readiness on the spot, there is no doubt of their being felled in time. The pine woods on the Torres heights are already down, and formed into abattis [1].'

It was not necessary, or indeed possible, to slope into a glacis the whole of the ground in front of each of the lines of defences. In many places other methods of making it impassable were used. At the north-western front of the first line, between Torres Vedras and the sea, for nearly six miles, a long marsh had been created : the river Zizandre had been dammed up, and had filled the whole of the narrow bottom in which it flows. 'It has overflowed its banks, and in a short time more than half the valley has become so complete a bog that no reward can induce any of the peasantry to pass over it [2],' wrote the officer who had carried out the experiment. Nor was it possible for the enemy to attempt to drain the bog, for four [3] redoubts furnished with heavy guns, and placed on dominating points of the hillside, commanded the bottom so completely that it was impossible for any party to approach it with safety. Yet the redoubts were out of the range of field-guns on the slopes beyond the Zizandre : only guns of position could have touched them, and Masséna had none such with him. Two

---

[1] Major Jones to Col. Fletcher, the chief engineer, then absent on a visit to Wellington's head quarters. See Jones, *Lines of Torres Vedras*, p. 187.

[2] Jones, *Lines*, p. 26.

[3] Afterwards, when Masséna had arrived, increased to sixteen redoubts with seventy-five guns. See Jones, p. 113.

similar inundations on a smaller scale had been caused at the other end of the Lines, by damming up the Alhandra and Alverca streams, each of which spread out in a marsh a mile broad, reaching to the foot of the heights above the Tagus, and could only be passed on the narrow paved high-road from Santarem to Lisbon.

In other places a very different method of making the Lines unapproachable had been adopted. Where the heights were very steep, but not absolutely inaccessible—a dangerous thing to the defence, for here 'dead ground,' unsearchable by the cannon of the redoubts above, must almost necessarily occur,—the slope had been cut or blasted away in bands, so as to make absolute precipices on a small scale.   At one point above Alhandra [1] this was done on a front of full 2,000 yards.   Even this was not the last precaution taken : at several places ravines ran deep into the line, and up them columns, more or less under cover, might possibly have penetrated.   Such ravines, therefore, were stuffed, at chosen points, by a broad abattis or entanglement, mainly composed of olive-trees with all their chief boughs remaining, dragged together and interlaced for a depth of many yards. Such a structure could not be crawled through, nor could it be hewn down without an infinite waste of time and labour ; nor, on the other hand, did it afford any cover, since grape or musketry could play perfectly well through it.   The chief of these traps was that laid across the long ravine above the village of Arruda, down the bottom of which flows one of the winter torrents which fall eastward into the Tagus.

It was fortunate that Portugal was a well-wooded country : there are regions where it would be impossible to procure the immense amount of timber that was lavished on the accessories of the redoubts.   All, as has been already mentioned, were palisaded ; many had in addition abattis or entanglements thrown up in front of them, some way down the hillside, so as to detain the advancing enemy under fire as long as possible.

The works were divided into eight sections, the first line

[1] Jones, *Lines*, p. 173. 'An extent of upwards of 2,000 yards on the left has been so cut and blasted along its summit as to give a continuous scarp, everywhere exceeding 10 feet in height, and covered for its whole length by both musketry and cannon.'

composed of four, the second line of three, while the eighth
consisted of the inner retrenchment for purposes of embarkation,
at the extreme southern point of the peninsula.   Of the outer
or secondary line the three sections were :

(1) A front of five miles from the Tagus at Alhandra along
the crest of a steep but not very lofty ridge, as far as the great
ravine that overlooks the village of Arruda.   This front was
elaborately fortified, as it blocks the great road, in the flat by
the waterside, which forms the easiest approach to Lisbon from
the north.   In the five miles there were ultimately constructed
no less than 23 redoubts with 96 guns.   Two thousand yards of
hillside in one place had been scarped into a precipice ; a mile
by the side of the Tagus had been inundated.   The one considerable gap in the line, the ravine at the head of the valley of
Calandrix, had been choked by one of the great *abattis* above
described.   The redoubts required a garrison of 6,000 men.

(2) The second section, from the ravine above Arruda to the
left of the steep Monte Agraça, formed somewhat of a salient
angle : it had a front in all of some four and a half miles, which
included the most lofty and defensible part of the back-bone
range of the Lisbon peninsula.   One of the four great paved
roads entering the capital from the north, however, passes over
the shoulder of these heights, and they were therefore very
heavily fortified from the first, the large redoubt for 1,600 men
on the top of Monte Agraça being one of the original outer
works ordered for construction in Wellington's earliest notes of
October 1809.   There were in all seven redoubts mounting 55
guns and requiring a garrison of 3,000 men on this fraction of
the lines.

(3) Quite different in character was the front of eight miles
from the left of Monte Agraça to the pass of Runa, overlooking
the upper valley of the Zizandre and the village of Sobral.   The
fortification of this line had not entered into Wellington's
original plan, and there were only two redoubts upon it when
Masséna appeared before it in October 1810.   Such defence as
there was consisted in the fact that the dominating Monte Agraça
redoubts overlooked it on the right, and that the two small
works just mentioned commanded the main high-road from
Sobral to Cabeça de Montechique, which goes through its centre.

But there was a clear possibility that the enemy might make a push up the valley and the high-road, by the village of Zibreira, and this was indeed the most probable point of attack in the whole 29 miles of front for the enemy to select.   When, at the last moment, the British Commander-in-Chief determined to hold the outer lines, and not merely to fall back after having used them for a temporary defence, he had to cram this point with troops, and to construct new works upon it as quickly as possible.   Four divisions, therefore, more than 20,000 men, were concentrated here.   Wellington's own head quarters were established at the hamlet of Pero Negro, on the slope above the high-road, and a very large redoubt was thrown up on the Portello hill, above Zibreira, with several smaller ones further to the right, to connect it with the Monte Agraça works. Sobral, the village at the foot of the heights, was held as an outpost, but abandoned when Masséna pushed forward to the front, as it was too far advanced to the north to be treated as an integral part of the position.   But the French, when they had carried Sobral with difficulty, looked at the main line behind it, and refused to attempt any further advance.   The hillside was as formidable as the Bussaco heights from which they had only recently been repulsed : it was full of troops and growing in strength every moment as the earthworks continued to arise.

(4) The fourth section of the outer or northern front was that from the gorge of the Zizandre (or the pass of Runa, as it is sometimes called) to the sea.   It was about twelve miles long, but of this space six miles and more was covered by the impassable bog formed by the obstructed Zizandre, and another mile was formed by the formidable entrenched camp of San Vincente, above the town of Torres Vedras, the most complete and self-sufficing of all the works in the peninsula.   This stronghold lay outside the main line, beyond the river, covering the bridge and the paved *chaussée* from Leiria to Lisbon, the only carriage-road on the western side of the Lines [1].   It was one of

---

[1] By an astonishing blunder the camp of Torres Vedras is placed by Napier in his map (and apparently in his text also) *south* of the river Zizandre, on the main line of heights, while in reality it was a great *tête-du-pont* covering the only passage from north to south over the stream and its bogs.

the earliest of the fortifications commenced by Wellington's engineers, having been started on November 8, 1809, and was placed in such a conspicuous point, and planned on such a large scale, that it attracted public attention more than any other part of the works, and gave its name to the whole in popular parlance [1]. The whole front on both sides of Torres Vedras and its great fort was so strong and inaccessible as to offer little temptation to the invader to select it as a point of serious attack, all the more so because troops brought opposite to it would be completely cut off from any left in front of the eastern and central part of the lines. For the geography of the peninsula at this point is peculiar: north of the gorge of the Zizandre the great back-bone range, the Serra de Barregudo and the Serra de Monte Junta, extends for a distance of fifteen miles, without being crossed by a single road practicable for horses, much less for wheeled vehicles. There are nothing but goat-tracks across the heights. If, therefore, any considerable body of troops had been sent to observe or contain the western section of the lines, it would have been separated by two days' march from the rest of the army, and liable to be crushed, ere succoured, by the defenders of Lisbon, who had good cross-roads across the peninsula, by which they could transfer themselves from point to point under the protection of their works. As a matter of fact, nothing but flying parties of French horse ever appeared in this direction. Masséna had not troops to spare for any secondary attack, more especially for one on such an unpromising part of the Lines. Wellington had foreseen this when he distributed his field army behind the various sections of the front: to support the garrisons of the twelve miles of redoubts about Torres Vedras he only placed one division, while there were three behind the eastern section, and more than four in the partially entrenched central part [2].

Passing on to the second line of defence, from Quintella on the Tagus to the mouth of the Rio São Lourenço on the

[1] See note to that effect in Jones, p. 21.

[2] The third division (Picton) only, behind Torres Vedras. Behind the Alhandra–Arruda section were the 2nd (Hill), Hamilton's Portuguese, and the Light Division; in the central part the 1st, 4th, 5th, 6th Divisions and three unattached Portuguese brigades (Pack, Coleman, and Al. Campbell).

Atlantic, we find three sections of defence, which, unlike those of the outer line, were all completed by September 1810, and had no central gap. (1) There was over a mile of impassable inundation at the eastern end, between Quintella and Alverca. Above the first-named village was an isolated hill, which was all fortress, for no less than six redoubts had been placed upon it, to enfilade the high-road across the inundated lower ground. Then came the Serra de Serves, three miles of lofty and difficult hills, which had been scarped into almost perfect inaccessibility. In a sudden dip west of this range was the pass of Bucellas, through which runs one of the three great high-roads that enter Lisbon. It was easily defensible, as it lies between two high and steep mountain-sides, and is only a couple of hundred yards broad. Redoubts were placed so as to rake it from end to end, and to flank it on both sides. The *chaussée* itself was blocked with successive abattis, and the viaduct leading up to it was mined.

(2) The second section of the inner line extended from the pass of Bucellas to the Park of Mafra, a front of over six miles. The eastern part of this was formed by the towering heights of the Cabeça de Montechique, the most dominating mountain-summit in the whole peninsula, almost steep enough to defend itself without fortification ; but three redoubts nevertheless had been reared upon its summit. But from the pass of Montechique, at the left side of the summit, down to Mafra the ground was less well marked, and here the *chaussée* from Sobral and Zibreira crossed the range. Much fortification, therefore, was lavished on these four miles, along which there were nine strong redoubts, connected with each other in the rear by a military road passing along the southern crest of the heights. There was a second and formidable ridge behind this line, where further defence could be offered in the unlikely event of the enemy forcing his way up the high-road.

(3) From Mafra to the sea, nearly ten miles, there was for the most part a well-marked line of heights protected in front by the ravine of the river of São Lourenço, a deep, rugged, and in many cases inaccessible cleft, only crossed by a single road, that from Torres Vedras to Mafra. Nevertheless, six redoubts were reared, to cover this, and the few other points where the ravine

was passable. The eastern part of this section, that along the wall of the Royal Park (Tapada) of Mafra, was its weakest portion, and for two miles at this point the British engineers set all their ingenuity to work. The outlying heights called the Serra de Chypre, in front of the park, were covered by four redoubts, and turned into a first defence. The wall of the Tapada itself was loopholed and furnished with a banquette. The important road which passes its foot was obstructed with cuts, enfiladed by the artillery of several works, and stockaded at more than one point. There was another group of redoubts along the south end of the Torres Vedras road, at the village of Morugueira ; and finally Mafra town, in the rear of all, was turned into a defensive post by means of trenches and barricades. Altogether, what was by nature the weakest point in the southern lines was made by art one of the strongest. This too, in spite of the fact that, being approachable only from Torres Vedras, it was on the whole not a probable front on which to expect an attack.

A mere mention must suffice for the eighth section of the defensive works, the semicircle at St. Julian's and Oyeras which was intended to protect the embarkation of the army if the worst should come. It was strongly entrenched, and could be held by a very few battalions, while the rest were utilizing the numerous and solid piers alongside of which the fleet of transports was to be moored.

Having described the Lines, it remains that we should describe the garrison set to guard them, detailing separately each element, regular and irregular. The forces at the disposition of Wellington were materially increased at the moment of his arrival within the Lines. On October 8 he found at his disposition a brigade of three battalions newly arrived at Lisbon, the 1/50th, 1/71st, and 1/92nd, all old Corunna regiments which had served in the Walcheren expedition, and were still none too healthy from their long sojourn in the deadly marshes of Zeeland. There had also landed about the same time the 94th regiment, and the Brunswick Oels Light Infantry, a foreign battalion raised from the refugees who had fought under the Duke of Brunswick in the abortive North German insurrection of 1809. Moreover, two battalions—the

2/30th and 2/44th—had just been sent to Lisbon from Cadiz, where General Graham now thought that the British contingent was larger than was absolutely necessary. The 1/4th and 1/23rd came out a little later, and do not appear in the fortnighty 'general state' of the army till November 15. Thus the army was swelled by nine battalions, or some 6,500 men [1]. No cavalry, however, had arrived.

Wellington used these new arrivals to form a new 6th Division of infantry, and to complete to full strength the 5th Division, which had hitherto possessed only one British brigade. He did not, however, keep the lately landed units together : acting on the principle which he always followed, of mixing veteran acclimatized battalions with new arrivals, he formed the new 6th Division by adding Campbell's brigade, taken from Cole's 4th Division, to two Portuguese regiments the 8th and the Lusitanian Legion, both of which had been hitherto attached to the 5th Division, and had served with Leith at Bussaco. In the 4th Division, Campbell's brigade was replaced by that of Pakenham, taken from Spencer's 1st Division, while compensation was made to Spencer, by giving him the newly landed 1/50th, 1/71st, and 1/92nd, as a new brigade under Erskine. The 5th Division under Leith got three more of the fresh arrivals, the 1/4th, 2/30th, and 2/44th as its second brigade. The 94th was given to Picton's second brigade,—which had hitherto consisted of only 2⅓ battalions,—to raise it to average brigade-strength. The Brunswick Oels Jägers, being a light corps, were partly divided up into separate companies and told off to different brigades (as the 5/60th, a similar unit, had already been), though the head quarters and six companies joined Pakenham's brigade in the 4th Division. But when the 1/23rd, the last of the reinforcements, came out, it also joined Pakenham, while the Brunswickers were transferred to the Light Division—where they did not long abide [2].

Even after allowing for the trifling losses at Bussaco, the British field army in Portugal was now far larger than it had

---

[1] About 5,800 rank and file, with 250 officers and 350 sergeants and drummers, by mid-winter return.

[2] For all these changes see Atkinson's admirable ' Composition of the British Army in the Peninsula,' printed in the *English Historical Review.*

ever been before, the gross total of troops in the Lines amounting to 42,000 men, of whom about 7,000 were sick or detached, and 35,000 were present under arms. This figure does not include the two battalions of marines who guarded St. Julian's and the lines around it at the mouth of the Tagus.

Of Portuguese regulars, Wellington had now under his hand the 24,000 men who had fought at Bussaco, plus the 1,400 cavalry under Fane and the brigade under Bradford (now consisting of five battalions)[1] which had been guarding the position behind the Alva on the day of the battle, together with the reserve artillery of Lisbon. The total made 27,500 men, of whom 24,500 were with the colours and 3,000 sick in hospital.

Of militia there were three brigades and four isolated units more within the Lines—the Southern Beira brigade of Lecor, three regiments[2], the Northern Estremaduran brigade of Miranda, also three regiments[3], and the Lisbon local brigade of five regiments[4] with two stray units from the north[5], and two from the south[6]. The numbers of all the regiments ran very low, owing to the way in which they had been neglected and under-fed by their government, since they were called out nine months before; many had died, and far more had deserted. The thirteen corps did not between them supply more than 8,200 men present under arms, with 1,000 sick in hospital. In addition there were 3,200 artillerymen improvised from the ranks of the infantry militia or the Ordenança, making altogether 12,400 troops of the 'second line.'

As to the Ordenança who had taken refuge in and about Lisbon with their families, when the whole population of south-

---

[1] The 12th and 13th line regiments and the 5th Caçadores, not much over 2,500 bayonets in all.

[2] Idanda, Castello Branco, Covilhão.

[3] Thomar, Leiria, Santarem ; the fourth battalion (Tondella) was in garrison at Peniche, as was also a considerable body of dépôt troops from the line, half-trained recruits, &c.

[4] 1, 2, 3, and 4 of Lisbon, and Torres Vedras.

[5] Feira and Vizeu, properly belonging to Trant's corps, but somehow separated from it.

[6] Setubal and Alcaçer do Sul.

western Beira and northern Estremadura retired within the
Lines, it is impossible to obtain any figures, save that they
supplied the bulk of the 3,000 volunteer artillerymen just
mentioned above, and that the picked men of the Ordenança of
the capital itself had been organized into two battalions of
'Atiradores Nacionales' of about 450 men each. The whole may
have amounted to any number from 20,000 up to 40,000 men,
of whom about two-thirds were armed with muskets, the rest,
those from the remoter districts, having still nothing better
than pikes. As most of them were scattered with their
families in the villages where they had taken refuge, or the
camps of huts which they had formed in sheltered situations,
they could hardly be considered to be in a state of mobilization,
and certainly were of no use either for garrisoning forts or for
employment in the line of battle.

Lastly, in calculating the forces which Wellington accumulated
within the Lines, we must mention the two Spanish divisions
from the Army of Estremadura. Hearing that all was quiet
for the moment on the frontier of Andalusia, the British
Commander had asked the Marquis of La Romana, whether, in
accordance with a promise made so long ago as July, he could
spare any troops to assist in the holding back of the main French
army of invasion. The Marquis, with a liberality of which the
Cadiz Regency would have disapproved, if its leave had been
asked, replied that he would bring up his two reserve divisions.
Leaving Ballasteros on the Andalusian border, and another
division under Imas at Badajoz, in addition to the garrison and
Madden's Portuguese cavalry, he marched for Aldea Gallega and
Lisbon with the troops of La Carrera [1] and Charles O'Donnell [2],
about 8,000 men. On October 25th he had arrived at the cantonments behind Mafra, on the second line of defence, which
his ally had requested him to occupy. Wellington defended
the bringing up of these troops by the plea 'that he did not
think himself justified in not bringing into his positions all the
force which was at his disposal' [3]. But it is doubtful whether the

---

[1] Who had now resigned the command of the cavalry, and gone back to
his old infantry division.

[2] The 'Vanguard' and 2nd Division of his army.

[3] *Dispatches*, vi. p. 544.

advantage of getting 8,000 Spanish troops within the Lines justified the danger incurred in Estremadura, when it was possible that Soult might send out Mortier at any moment to attack the depleted army that covered the approach to Badajoz. Napoleon thought that he should have done so, and when he heard of the arrival of La Romana at Lisbon, wrote to censure the Duke of Dalmatia in the fiercest strain[1]. 'It was a shame and a scandal that he had retired to Seville : the 5th Corps had orders to be always at La Romana's heels, and to prevent him from moving into Portugal, so that the news of its return to Seville roused the Emperor's surprise and anger.' There can be no doubt that Napoleon did well to be angry. The balance of affairs in Andalusia tended to stand at an equipoise precisely because La Romana's army was strong enough to keep the 5th Corps employed. When 8,000 men had been withdrawn by the Marquis to the Lisbon lines, Mortier was in a position to sweep all before him as far as the gates of Badajoz, or to execute a raid into the Alemtejo if that course seemed preferable. But Soult did not send his lieutenant on this errand on his own initiative, but waited till he received direct orders to do so from Paris. By that time it was too late, and neither the disaster of the Gebora nor even the fall of Badajoz had any influence on the course of events in Portugal. Masséna was forced to retreat before a single patrol from the Army of Andalusia had got into touch with his outposts. What might have happened if Soult had launched his blow at Badajoz in October, and had appeared on the left bank of the Lower Tagus in December, it is impossible to say. Probably Wellington would have found some means of averting disaster, but it is unquestionable that his task of defence would have been made far more difficult.

For the full realization of the meaning of the Lines of Torres Vedras there are two general facts which must be remembered. Firstly, they were garrisoned by troops which formed no part of the field army. Wellington's sixty thousand regulars were not frittered away in the garrisoning of redoubts, but were held in masses behind the lines, ready to reinforce any threatened point, and to deliver a pitched battle in the open, if the head of the

---

[1] *Correspondance*, xxi. pp. 273, 295.

LINES OF TORRES VEDRAS

Defensive Works shown thus:- ●

50 Metres between contours

B.V.Darbishire, Oxford, 1907

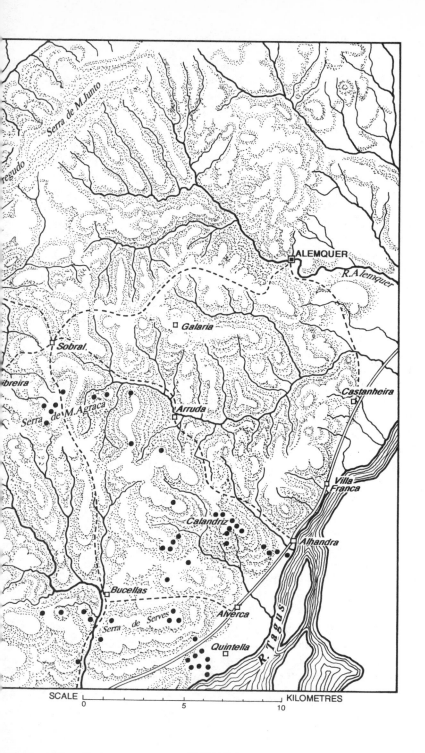

SCALE |___|___|___|___|___|___|___|___|___|___| KILOMETRES
      0   5   10

French army were thrust through the defences at some weak section. The generals of the seventeenth and eighteenth centuries, who so often built lines, and were so easily evicted from them, suffered disaster because they drew out their armies in one attenuated thread, and were therefore weak at every point, and always inferior to the assailant at the place where he made his assault. Wellington's army was (with the exception of the 3rd Division at Torres Vedras) gathered in two solid masses, one facing Sobral, on the heights between Monte Agraça and Runa, the second and smaller behind Alhandra. The one could reach the other in half a day's march, for the roads behind and parallel to the lines had been put in good repair.

The whole of this vast system of redoubts was to be held by the troops of the second line, and by them only. There were altogether some 20,000 men of the second line in the fortifications, composed of (1) the 8,000 (afterwards raised to 11,000) militia infantry. (2) Of about 800 Portuguese regular artillery, aided by over 2,000 gunners picked from the militia and Ordenança, trained by the regulars and incorporated with them. (3) Of some 250 British artillery-men from the batteries which had been lying in reserve at Lisbon. (4) Of picked companies of the Lisbon Ordenança (atiradores) drilled into a state of discipline not much worse than that of the militia. (5) Of the landing force of 2,000 British marines, partly from the fleet, partly brought specially from England to garrison the proposed lines of embarkation at St. Julian's. (6) Of the dépôts, convalescents and recruits of the eight Line regiments of infantry raised from Lisbon and Southern Estremadura—about 4,000 strong.

In all, therefore, there were about 20,000 men, mostly troops of secondary quality, or 28,000 if the Spanish auxiliaries are counted, ready to man the Lines, without a man being withdrawn from the ranks of the field army. The outer lines were calculated to require about 18,000 men for the redoubts, the inner ones 14,000, but clearly both did not require to be manned at once. If the outer line were broken, the garrison-troops from the intact parts of it could fall back on the second. Meanwhile the field army would be engaging any French columns that might have broken through, and there would be ample time to arrange for the manning of the second and stronger front. But it must be repeated once more that it was not on the passive defence of the redoubts by their garrisons that Wellington reckoned for success, but on the fighting of the field army, who would tackle the columns of attack that had committed themselves to the assault of the section—whichever it might be—that Masséna might select as his objective. All criticism based on general principles concerning the weakness of long extended lines falls to the ground, when it is remembered that Wellington had his army massed for a pitched battle in and behind his defences, not strung out on an interminable front.

The last point on which stress must be laid is that the most careful arrangements for the transmission of orders and intelligence from end to end of the Lines had been made. There were five signal-stations, with semaphores worked by seamen on (1) the redoubt No. 30 near the Atlantic, (2) the great redoubt of Torres Vedras, (3) the Monte de Socorro above Wellington's head quarters at Pero Negro, (4) the summit of the Monte Agraça, (5) the hill behind Alhandra on the Tagus. After some practice it was found that a message could be sent from one end to the other of the 29 miles in *seven* minutes, and from No. 3, the head quarters semaphore, to either end of the Lines in *four* minutes. There was a similar line of four semaphores on the second, or main, series of defences. Military roads had been opened behind both the fronts, so that troops could be moved along the shortest possible line. On the other hand, it was fortunate that there existed no cross-road from sea to sea *outside* the Lines, which could be of any practical use to the invader. The only route of this sort, that from Alemquer by Sobral to Runa, was commanded for the whole length from Sobral to Runa by the British heights, whose foot it hugs, while from Sobral to Alemquer it is separated from the Lines by the steep and pathless ridge of Galaria, across which nothing on wheels could pass. Nevertheless, here lay the invaders' best chance—corps placed on this road, and screened by the ridge, could be moved for some distance to left or right unseen from the Lines. The road, however, was bad, rocky, and narrow : it is marked as the ' Calgada Arruinada ' or ' ruined road ' in contemporary maps. The other

paved road in this direction, that from Sobral to Arruda and
Alhandra, passed through the line of ground occupied by the
British at two points, and was under fire from the redoubts at
short range for the rest of its course: it was absolutely impracticable.

It only remains to be added that the navy had been utilized
for auxiliary service : not only were its marines under orders to
man the St. Julian's lines, but its seamen had fitted out all the
gun-boats in the Lisbon arsenal.   A flotilla of great strength
infested the Tagus estuary, and by the fire of its heavy guns
prevented the French from approaching the shore, or endeavouring to build boats at the mouths of its creeks.   If any attacks
had been made upon either of the extreme ends of the Lines, the
columns delivering them would have been under fire from the
sea throughout their operations.   But, as we shall see, the French
never contemplated this : the one temptation which Masséna
felt was to assault, far inland, the gap in front of Sobral between
the Monte Agraça and the Serra de Socorro.   And there, as we
shall see, at the critical moment, prudence got the better of
ambition, and the invader turned back foiled.   The high-water
mark of French conquest in Europe was reached on the knoll by
Sobral on the wet and gusty 14th of October, 1810.

SECTION XXI: CHAPTER V

On the night of October 10, when Craufurd made his hasty retreat to Sobral, and went within the Lines, Montbrun had his head quarters at Alemquer, where he kept Taupin's infantry brigade, and Lamotte's and Sainte-Croix's cavalry. Pierre Soult's light horse felt towards their left, in the direction of the Tagus, and occupied Carregado, where they failed to find any British outposts, Hill's corps having been withdrawn behind the brook which enters the Tagus near Castanheira. The main body of the army was far to the rear, in one vast column : Ney's and Reynier's corps lay that night in and about Alcoentre : Junot's bivouacked around the convent of Nossa Senhora de Maxeira, a short distance to the south of Alcoentre. All the troops were terribly fatigued by three days' movement in torrential rain, and had no more marching-power left in them.

It was only on the following morning (October 11) that Montbrun discovered the Lines. His cavalry had been ordered to move forward on the two roads across which they lay. Pierre Soult therefore pushed for Villafranca, on the high road which skirts the Tagus ; he found Hill's outlying pickets at Villafranca, drove them out of the town, and on passing it came in sight of the line of redoubts and scarped hillside above Alhandra, which was manned by the Portuguese militia and backed by Hill's British infantry. It was impossible to advance further, so the brigadier, leaving an advanced post in Villafranca, drew back his three regiments to Castanheira, and sent his report to Montbrun.

That general himself, with the main body of his cavalry, had followed the rough road from Alemquer to Lisbon. He drove in some British dragoon pickets, and then arrived in front of the village of Sobral, which he found occupied by the infantry

outposts of Spencer's division. He did not attempt to push
further that day, as his flanking reconnaissance had come in
sight of the sections of the Lines behind Arruda and behind
Zibreira, where redoubts and solid lines of infantry were visible.
Sobral itself was clearly not held in force, nor did it form
an integral part of the British position. But Montbrun feared
to attack it, when he had only a single brigade of infantry
to the front, while many thousands of British troops might
issue from the Lines to overwhelm him if he committed himself
to a serious attack. The village on its knoll was left alone for
the present, though it was tempting to contemplate the seizure
of a point which lay so far forward—less than two miles from
the front of Wellington's chosen position. But Montbrun
contented himself with sending back word to Masséna that he
had come upon a continuous line of fortifications stretching
from the Tagus bank to some point westward, which was not
yet discovered. For his furthest reconnaissances towards Runa
and the Upper Zizandre had found the enemy in front of them,
however far they pushed.

Meanwhile Masséna's tired infantry of the main body had
made hardly any movement: the 2nd and 6th Corps still lay
about Alcoentre. Junot alone with the 8th Corps advanced
as far as Moinho de Cubo, half way between Alcoentre and
Alemquer. Thus Wellington was given a whole day more
to arrange his troops in their positions along the Lines. On
this morning he was rather under the impression that the
French attack would be directed upon Alhandra and Hill's
corps, which, he observed, would be a 'tough job, defended as
all the entrances of the valleys are by redoubts, and the villages
by abattis[1].' Moreover, the French 'positively could not' get
guns up to attack the line west of Hill, since, in the existing
state of the weather, no cannon could leave the paved roads,
and the only path of that description leading from the Sobral
direction to the Tagus bank ran through Arruda, where
Craufurd and the Light Division were now comfortably installed. Considering it likely, therefore, that Masséna would
bring a heavy attacking force, by circuitous roads from the rear,
to Villafranca, in order to make a frontal attack on Hill along

[1] *Dispatches*, vi. 502, to Craufurd.

the high-road by the Tagus, Wellington warned Craufurd and
Spencer to be ready to move in eastward to the assistance of
the extreme right wing of the Lines. In the afternoon, however, he discovered that the force in front of Sobral (Montbrun)
seemed much larger than that in front of Alhandra (Pierre
Soult), and showed more signs of making wide-spreading reconnaissances. He therefore drew up an alternative scheme, by
which, in the event of an attack on Spencer's front at Zibreira,
Cole's and Campbell's (the new 6th) divisions were to support
the threatened point, and even Picton was to come in from
the distant Torres Vedras[1]. No French troops were reported
from this last direction, and De Grey's cavalry pickets from
Ramalhal (far outside the Lines) reported that not the smallest
party of the enemy's horse had been seen west of the Serra
de Barregudo or the Monte Junta[2].

On the 12th Montbrun made a movement which seemed
to justify Wellington's first idea, that Hill was to receive the
French attack. He moved Taupin's brigade, the only hostile
infantry which had yet been seen, southward from Alemquer
to Villafranca on the Tagus. This was done, however, only
because the whole 8th Corps was coming up on this day from
Moinho de Cubo by Alemquer to Sobral, which it reached in
the afternoon, replacing Taupin's small force. Its arrival was
at once reported to Wellington, who saw that his second theory
of the intention of the enemy, not his first, had been correct,
and transferred his main attention to the side of Sobral. That
village, by some extraordinary blunder on the part of Sir Brent
Spencer, had been evacuated by the pickets of the 1st Division
during the night of the 11th–12th[3]. They were put back
into it, by the special orders of the Commander-in-Chief, in

---

[1] Wellington to Spencer, afternoon of Oct. 11, *Dispatches*, vi. 505.

[2] Wellington to Craufurd, same day, *Dispatches*, vi. 504.

[3] Wellington to Chas. Stuart, *Dispatches*, vi. 506. D'Urban's invaluable
diary has the note. 'Oct. 11 : 'Tis difficult to account for all this, which
must be vexatious to the Commander-in-Chief, who, aware of the importance
of the heights in front of Sobral, must have wished to keep them for the
present. . . . Oct. 12 : In the morning the enemy was no more to be seen,
and what we should never have given up, we were fortunately permitted
to re-occupy. But at nightfall the French, with about six battalions, retook the height and town of Sobral.'

the early morning, for Wellington wished to hold it as long as was safe, on account of the fine view obtainable from its knoll over the routes from Alemquer by which the enemy must approach. Hence, when Junot's advanced guard came up in the afternoon, there was a collision at Sobral. The troops of Clausel finally succeeded in expelling the British outposts, which belonged to Erskine's and Löwe's brigade, from the village. The casualties were few on both sides—nineteen men only were lost by the British [1]. The retiring pickets did not fall back into the Lines, but clung to the other side of the ravine which separates Sobral from the lower slopes of Monte Agraça. They were only 300 yards from the village.

While this skirmish was in progress the main body of the French were at last set in motion from Alcoentre. The 6th Corps advanced this day (October 12) to Moinho de Cubo and Otta ; the 2nd Corps, taking a road more to the east, so as to lean towards the Tagus, arrived at Carregado. Junot's corps was encamped behind Sobral, Clausel's division having its advanced posts (Brigade Ménard) in the village, while Solignac lay two miles to the rear. The weather was still abominable, and all the movements were accomplished with great fatigue and delay.

On this afternoon the French army suffered the loss of its most brilliant and energetic cavalry officer. General Sainte-Croix, while exploring the Tagus bank, north of Villefranca, in search of deserted boats, was cut in two by a cannon shot from a British gunboat which was watching his cavalry from the estuary. He was held to be the only officer, except Colonel Pelet, who had any personal influence with Masséna [2], and as that influence was always exerted on the side of daring action, it is probable that the many French diarists who deplore his death are right in considering that it may have had some positive effect on the conduct of the campaign [3].

[1] Of the nineteen casualties, nine belonged to the newly-landed 71st, four to the German Legion, six to the company of the 5/60th attached to Erskine. See Return in Record Office.

[2] Sainte-Croix had been the Marshal's chief-of-the-staff during the Wagram campaign, and was generally reputed to have been responsible for some of the boldest moves made by Masséna's army during that period.

[3] That Fririon is correct in dating Sainte-Croix's death on the 12th, and Delagrave and others wrong in placing it on the 16th, is proved by an

On the night of the 12th–13th Wellington had become convinced, and rightly, that the great mass of Junot's corps, visible behind Sobral, constituted the main danger to his position. He therefore drew in troops from his right, even calling down from Torres Vedras Picton, in whose front no enemy was yet visible. From Monte Agraça to the Portello redoubts he put in line four British divisions—Spencer, Cole, Picton, and Campbell, along with Pack's independent Portuguese brigade; this last was placed in the great redoubt on Monte Agraça, which dominated Sobral and all the lower hills. In reserve were two more divisions—the 5th under Leith, and a temporary Portuguese division consisting of the brigades of Coleman and Alex. Campbell. Altogether 30,000 men were concentrated on this comparatively short front of about four miles, besides the militia and artillery who garrisoned the minor forts [1]. Junot, whose corps did not now muster more than 12,000 men, did wisely to refrain from making any serious attack. He was not, however, wholly quiescent : attempting to extend his troops more to the right, to the west of Sobral, along the undulating ground in the direction of the Upper Zizandre, he got into touch with the outlying pickets of Cole's division, which stood beyond those of Spencer and Picton in the British line. The first attack fell on the light companies of the 7th Fusiliers and the newly-arrived Brunswick Oels battalion. When they were driven in, Cole fed his fighting-line with the light companies of Hervey's [late Collins's] Portuguese brigade. Finding his voltigeurs outnumbered, Junot, in a similar fashion, sent up Gratien's brigade from his second division to reinforce his advance. Hence there ensued

entry in D'Urban's diary of Oct. 15, stating that it had just been discovered that the general killed in front of Alhandra was called Sainte-Croix. Clearly then he was dead before the 16th.

[1] For his dispositions for resisting the suspected attack see *Dispatches*, vi. pp. 507–9 of Oct. 13. The line running from right to left was (1) Pack's Portuguese in the great redoubt facing Sobral, (2) 1st Division between the redoubt and Zibreira, (3) Picton touching Spencer's left, (4) Cole touching Picton's left, (5) Campbell (new 6th Division) on Cole's left, reaching to the Portello redoubts. Each of these divisions had one brigade in reserve. A separate general reserve was formed by Leith behind the right, and Coleman's and Alex. Campbell's Portuguese behind the left.

some sharp skirmishing, which lasted several hours, till Cole drew back his outpost line from the lower plateaux north of Sobral to the foot of his fighting-position, on the heights below the Portello redoubts. Junot had thus gained a mile of ground, but not ground that was of any service to him for a regular attack on the Lines, since it was merely part of the rolling upland that was dominated by Wellington's main position. The 4th Division lost twenty-five British and a much larger number of Portuguese in this long bicker. Hervey the Portuguese brigadier was wounded. The French casualties were probably a little the larger [1].

On the same afternoon Reynier, with somewhat over a battalion of infantry, made a detailed reconnaissance of Hill's position in front of Alhandra. He pressed in close enough to draw the fire of the nearer redoubts, but halted when he had realized the strength of the line opposite him, and reported to Masséna that he considered the right wing of the allied position hopelessly impracticable for an attack.

Next morning (October 14) the French Commander-in-Chief came up in person from the rear. It is astonishing that he had made no earlier attempt to judge with his own eye of the strength of Wellington's line of defence. He arrived at Sobral in time to witness a bitter skirmish, the most important of all

[1] I find in the note to Gachot's excellent editions of Delagrave's *Campagne de Portugal* that the losses of the French on this day were 157 men, those of the allies 139. The last statement, one sufficiently probable in itself, cannot be verified from any British source that I have found : Wellington, annexed to the document on page 511 of vol. vi of the *Dispatches*, gives the loss of Cole's British brigades in detail—they amount to twenty-five men only. But he does not give details of Hervey's Portuguese, though he mentions that the brigadier was wounded, and that the two regiments (Nos. 11 and 23 of the Line) distinguished themselves. They may well have lost the 124 men mentioned by Gachot, but I have no proof of it. Vere's usually accurate ' Marches of the 4th Division ' gives no figures for this day, nor does D'Urban's *Diary*. Wellington remarks that ' the attack of this day on General Cole's pickets near Sobral was without much effect.' It is certain, however, that the British lost a little ground in front of the heights. Martinien's *Liste des officiers tués et blessés*, which I so often find of use, shows that Junot's corps lost two officers killed and seven wounded. This, at the usual average, would imply 150–180 casualties.

the engagements that took place during the crucial days of the campaign of 1810. Spencer's outposts, as has been already mentioned, had on the 12th retired only some 200 or 300 yards from Sobral, and had taken up their position on the other side of the ravine that divides that village from the lower slopes of the Monte Agraça. Across the high-road the main picket, furnished by the 71st regiment, had thrown up a barricade. Junot considered this lodgement, so close to his line, as a thing that ought not to be permitted. Accordingly he brought up his artillery, which had only arrived from the rear on the previous night, to the front of Sobral, and, after cannonading the barricade for a short time, sent against it the *compagnies d'élite* of the 19th of the Line, supported by other troops of Ménard's brigade. The first rush of the attack carried the barricade and the line of stone walls on each side of it. But the whole of the 71st was ready to sustain the pickets, and with a fierce rush swept the assailants back across the barricade, down the slope, and into the outer houses of Sobral. From thence, of course, they had to retire, as a whole division was fronting them ; but they resumed their old position without being pursued.

Junot refused to renew his attack, and Masséna, who had arrived while the skirmish was in progress, did not direct him to go forward again. It was clear that there was a very strong force in front of the 8th Corps, and that the redoubts visible along the Monte Agraça on the one hand and the Portello heights on the other were of the most formidable description. Masséna's senior aide-de-camp and chief confidant, Pelet [1], thus describes the psychological situation : ' On arriving at Sobral, instead of the " undulating accessible plateaux " that we had been told to expect, we saw steeply scarped mountains and deep ravines, a road-passage only a few paces broad, and on each side walls of rock crowned with everything that could be accomplished in the way of field fortifications garnished with artillery ; then at last it was plainly demonstrated to us that we could not attack the Lines of Montechique with the 35,000 or 36,000 men [2] that

---

[1] For his position and character, see p. 209 of this volume.

[2] This figure is, of course, a ludicrous exaggeration. Masséna had still more than 50,000 men. Even on Jan. 1, 1811, after suffering two months

still remained of the army. For, even if we had forced some point of the Lines, we should not have had enough men left to seize and occupy Lisbon. . . . It was clear that we must wait for reinforcements[1].' Another eye-witness, Junot's aide-de-camp Delagrave, in his *Memoir on the Campaign of 1810–11*, expresses the same view in his single sentence, explaining that 'the prince, seeing that the enemy was better prepared and stronger than had been believed, put an end to the combat, and on each side the troops took up once more their original positions[2].' The loss in this combat—insignificant enough in itself, but decisive in that it revealed to Masséna the uselessness of a further advance—was 67 on the British side, about 120 on that of the French[3].

After putting a stop to the combat of Sobral, Masséna rode away eastward, along the slopes of the upland that faces the Monte Agraça, and as far as the knoll facing Arruda in the front of the Light Division. Here he pressed so near the British front that a single shot was fired at his escort from the redoubt No. 120 to warn him to trespass no further. He saluted the battery by lifting his hat to it, and went up the hill out of range[4]. Some of his aides-de-camp continued the

more of untold privation, the Army of Portugal was still 44,000 strong, plus sick and men detached.

[1] Pelet's *Appendice sur la Guerre d'Espagne*, p. 323 of vol. xxi of *Victoires et Conquêtes*.

[2] Delagrave, p. 100.

[3] Of the sixty-seven British casualties, thirty-eight were in the 71st, the rest in the neighbouring brigades of the 1st Division. Noël—who had charge of the battery at Sobral, estimates the French loss at 120—very probably the correct one, as Martinien's lists show one officer killed and six wounded, all in Ménard's brigade. This should mean 120–150 casualties. Delagrave gives the higher figure of 200 killed and wounded, probably an overstatement.

[4] Masséna was clearly seen from the British Lines. Leith Hay, a staff-officer of the 5th Division, noted ' a crowd of officers on horseback, dragoons with led horses, and all the cortége of a general-in-chief' (*Narrative*, p. 249), and saw the Marshal dismount by the windmill above Sobral. He was watching from Pack's redoubt, on the hill just opposite, through his telescope, about 2,000 yards from the French front. It is Jones who, on p. 40 of his *Lines of Torres Vedras*, gives the anecdote about the Marshal's salute.

exploration till they touched Reynier's vedettes near Villa-franca, but the Marshal himself returned to his head quarters at Alemquer to think over the situation.   There some sort of a council of war was held that same night : Junot, it is said, urged the Chief to try the effect of a bold dash at the English army arrayed in front of Sobral.   But he was talked down by Ney and Reynier, who argued that such an attack would be insane, considering the weakness of their corps and the strength of Wellington's fortifications.   Without doubt they were right : even if Masséna had brought his whole three corps to bear on Sobral, he had 10,000 men less than at Bussaco, and Wellington 10,000 men more, leaving the garrisons of the forts out of the question.   The allies had 30,000 bayonets concentrated on the threatened point, and could have brought up Hill, Craufurd, and Hamilton's and Le Cor's Portuguese—20,000 men more—from the east end of the Lines, the moment that it was clear that Reynier was no longer in front of them.   The position, owing to the forts, was far stronger than Bussaco, and the French cavalry would have been as useless on October 15 as it had been on September 27.   The report which Foy drew up for Masséna and presented to the Emperor gives the whole gist of the matter : ' The Marshal Prince of Essling has come to the conclusion that he would compromise the army of His Majesty if he were to attack in force lines so formidable, defended by 30,000 English and 30,000 Portuguese, aided by 50,000 armed peasants [1].'

An open assault on the Sobral position was now, indeed, the thing that the British most desired.   Wellington wrote, with his usual ironical moderation, to his trusted lieutenant, Crau-furd, that ' he thought his arrangements had now made the position tolerably secure [2].'   Among these last arrangements, it may be remarked, was the drawing back of the 71st and the light companies of the 1st Division from the barricades on the near side of the ravine of Sobral.   They were moved a few hundred yards to the rear, nearer to Zibreira.   This was pro-bably intended to encourage the French to sally out from Sobral up the road, where everything was now in order to receive them.

---

[1] See Foy's *Vie Militaire*, Appendix, p. 343.
[2] Wellington to Craufurd, *Dispatches*, vi. p. 517.

Their advance was hourly expected ; D'Urban, Beresford's Chief of the Staff, wrote gleefully on October 15, 'Each individual division has now more than sufficient troops to occupy the space allotted to it, and the overplus forms a first reserve for each respectively. If the force thus posted beats the attacking enemy, of which there can be little doubt, our telegraphic communications will bring down Craufurd from Arruda and Hill from Alhandra on to their flank—and the affair will be complete. There is much appearance that the enemy *will* attack this position with his whole force—Alhandra is far too strong for him. He cannot well retire, and it is hoped that his distress for provisions will compel him to bring matters to a speedy decision [1].'

But both the cautious Commander-in-Chief and the eager head of the Portuguese Staff were mistaken in estimating the position. They had judged wrongly the character of Masséna, and his psychological position of the moment. He would not attack ; indeed, after October 14 he seems never to have had the least intention of doing so. The lesson of Bussaco had not been lost, and he was no longer prepared to assail, with a light heart, the Anglo-Portuguese Army posted ready to receive him in a strong position. Probably the energetic statement of Ney and Reynier that they dared not risk their men—that the troops would be demoralized if ordered to advance for a second slaughter —also had its effect on the Marshal. But Masséna was proud and obstinate, and if he could not go forward, he shrank, for the moment, from going back. On October 15 began the one phase of the campaign which the British, from general down to subaltern, had least expected. The French army began to show signs of intending to settle down in front of the Lines, as if for a blockade. After a few more attempts to feel the front of the Lines about Arruda and the valley of Calandriz, which were so feeble that they did not even drive in Craufurd's outposts, the enemy began to fortify the front of his position with field-works, and sent away the whole of his cavalry to the rear—a sufficient sign that his offensive power was spent.

Masséna's first dream of masking the Lines by a close blockade was absolutely impracticable, considering the present state of his supplies. The troops were already living on the gleanings of

[1] D'Urban's *Journal*, under Oct. 15.

the hastily-evacuated villages of the Lisbon Peninsula, which
could not last them for long, and would not even have sufficed
for a week's consumption if Wellington's decrees had been
properly carried out.   If he was to feed his army from the thin
resources left behind by the Portuguese, Masséna would soon
find it necessary to spread it far and wide ; since, if he kept it
concentrated in front of Wellington, it would soon go to pieces,
exposed in bivouacs to the November rains, and forced to draw
its nourishment by marauding from afar.   It seems from the
instructions which he gave to Foy at the end of the second week
of his stay in front of Lisbon, that the Marshal actually contemplated clinging to his present advanced position till he should
receive reinforcements.   He hoped that the 9th Corps would
come up to his aid from Old Castile, and that Mortier and the
5th Corps would join him from Andalusia.   But these were
mere hypotheses : he was not in touch with either Drouet or
Mortier.   Indeed, he had been cut off from all communication
with his colleagues since the day that he crossed the Mondego.
The 9th Corps, as a matter of fact, was only at Valladolid, and
showed no signs of moving on.   Mortier had retired to the
mountains in front of Seville, after his successes over the army
of La Romana in September.   Almeida was in a state of close
blockade by Silveira's detachments from beyond the Douro.
Ciudad Rodrigo was in hardly better case, being strictly watched
by Julian Sanchez and his mounted guerrilleros, so that no one
could get to or from it without a very strong escort.   Gardanne's
regiment of dragoons, left behind by Masséna, was worn out in
the effort to keep open the road between Rodrigo and Salamanca [1].   From the Army neither Almeida nor Rodrigo received
a word of news from the 18th of September to the 15th of
November.   So effectually was the road closed, that rumours
were current of such divers characters as that Masséna had forced
the English to embark, and that he had been completely foiled,
and was marching back to Spain via Castello Branco.   Paris
was hardly better informed : the only news that the Emperor
got was that dribbled out, four or five weeks later, by the

---

[1] For the miseries and dangers of life in Rodrigo, see the *Memoirs* of the
Duchesse D'Abrantes.   Her letter to Junot, intercepted by Wellington,
tells the same tale : it is to be found in D'Urban's collection of documents.

English papers [1]. Hence came ludicrous notices in the *Moniteur*, of which the worst was one published on November 28, which stated that Coimbra had been occupied by Masséna without a battle, that the army on October 1 had only 200 sick and 500 wounded since it had left Almeida, and that no general or colonel had been killed or even hurt since the invasion began! And this after twelve such officers had fallen at Bussaco. That battle, we may remark, was presented ultimately to French readers as ' a demonstration executed by the brigades of Simon and Graindorge in order to mask the great flank-march of the Prince of Essling. But they had gone beyond their instructions, and brought on a combat in which 200 men had been killed and 1,200 wounded.' Fririon, the historian of the campaign, cannot restrain himself from adding, 'This is how history was written at that time ; it was by reports of this lying description that an attempt was made to calm anxious families. Did no one reflect that, by deceiving them in this way, the government made enemies of all those who trusted for a time in the exactitude of the *Bulletins*, and lost their illusion soon after, when they learnt the melancholy ends of their sons and their brothers [2] ? '

The dearth of news from the front was not Masséna's own fault. He had sent back several aides-de-camp to find their way to Almeida, but all had either been captured by the Ordenança or forced to turn back. The best known of these was the young Mascarenhas, one of the Portuguese traitors on the Marshal's staff. He started from Coimbra on October 3, with the Bussaco dispatch, disguised as a shepherd, but was detected by a band of Ordenança, and sent a prisoner to Lisbon. The Regency had him tried by court-martial, and as he was caught without a uniform, he was condemned as a spy as well as a traitor, and executed by the garotte in December [3].

There was a perfect cordon of Portuguese militia and irregulars round Masséna's rear in October and November. J. Wilson had come down to Espinhal, and had his outposts in Leiria ; Trant had returned to Coimbra. They were in touch, by means of the Estrada Nova and the garrison of Abrantes, with the Ordenança

---

[1] See *Correspondance*, vol. xxi. pp. 262, 280, 338, &c.
[2] See Fririon, pp. 57-8.
[3] See above, p. 277.

of Castello Branco, and a Spanish detachment of three battalions under Carlos D'España, which La Romana had sent to Villa Velha, at the same time that he took his two divisions under La Carrera and Charles O'Donnell within the Lines. On the side of the Atlantic the garrison of Peniche had sent out a force of 300 men to Obidos, under Captain Fenwick, and these joined hands with De Gray's cavalry at Ramalhal, in front of Torres Vedras. A few French parties which crossed the Monte Junta to raid towards the sea coast were cut off either by Fenwick or by the dragoons. But Masséna never sent any serious detachment in this direction.

For just one month (October 14—November 14) Masséna maintained his position in front of the Lines. The 8th Corps had thrown up some earthworks on, and to the flanks of, the hill of Sobral, thus assuming a defensive instead of an offensive position. The 2nd Corps went back to Carregado, but left strong detachments in Villafranca. By the dispositions of October 16 the 6th Corps remained with its main body at Otta, far to the rear, and an advanced guard at Alemquer. Ney was so placed that he could succour either of the other corps if they were attacked. A brigade of Loison's division was pushed forward to the hill opposite Arruda[1]: in face of this last Craufurd was adorning the front of his line with a luxury of abattis, entanglements, and pitfalls, which would have made the hillside inaccessible to even the most alert and vigorous person moving alone. Formed troops could not have got past the first two or three traps.

But the most significant part of Masséna's arrangements was to be found in his rear : Montbrun's cavalry reserve went back to Santarem ; thither also went the reserve artillery on the 17th, and the hospitals on the 20th of October. At the same time each of the corps was directed to send to Santarem all smiths, carpenters, and other artificers that could be found in its ranks. They were told to report to General Eblé, the officer commanding the artillery, who had received from the Marshal a special mission—the construction of boats and pontoons sufficient to bridge the Tagus or the Zezere. For, if he were starved out in Estremadura, Masséna had it in his mind that he might find

---

[1] Ferey's brigade, which had already faced Craufurd at Bussaco.

it convenient either to cross into the Alemtejo, or to force
a way across the Zezere into the Castello Branco district, in the
hope of opening communication with Spain via Zarza and
Alcantara.   Montbrun's cavalry explored northward and eastward, seeking for likely spots at which the Tagus might be
bridged, and on the other side reconnoitring the line of the
Zezere, to see how it was held.   Not a boat could be found on
the greater river ; at Chamusca a daring party of fifty men
swam its broad current, for a dash at some barks which were
visible on the other side, but all were found to have had their
bottoms carefully knocked out and to be filled with sand.
Dejean, the officer who explored as far as Punhete on the Zezere,
found all the bridges broken, and the garrison of Abrantes
watching the fords, with strong detachments at Punhete and
Martinchel.

Eblé found at Santarem that he had to create a pontoon
equipage with no materials at all to work from.   There was
raw iron in the bars and balconies of houses, and raw timber
in their floors and rafters, but nothing else.   His smiths
had to start on the weary task of forging saws and hammers,
his carpenters had to turn housebreakers—in the technical
sense—to obtain planks and joists.   His task was hard, and
would clearly take many weeks before it could be properly
accomplished.

Meanwhile time was all-important to Masséna, for every day
the country between Santarem and the Lines grew barer and
yet more bare, as the foragers of the three French corps worked
their will upon it.   The men were already going into hospital
by thousands, and dying there.   Junot's conscript battalions,
unsheltered from the rain in their bleak bivouac above Sobral,
suffered most—Ney's and Reynier's men were (for the most part)
housed if not fed.   The Army, which had 65,000 men on leaving
Almeida, and 55,000 after the loss of Coimbra, had dwindled
down to 50,000 effective sabres and bayonets by the month of
November [1].

Wellington was already pondering on the possibility of taking

[1] According to *Fririon*, p. 98, the morning state of Nov. 1 showed only
46,591 men effective.   But the figures of that officer are always a little
lower than what I have found in the official documents.

the offensive. He had received hundreds of deserters during the last few weeks [1], and knew by their means of the miserable condition of the enemy—of the fact that the cavalry had nearly all been sent to the rear, and of the attempt that was being made to create a bridge-equipage at Santarem [2]. His dispatches of October 27 and November 3 to Lord Liverpool treat at length of the advantages and disadvantages of assailing the French in their present position [3]. He sets forth the strength of his own army—29,000 British troops present with the colours, after deducting sick and men detached, 24,000 Portuguese effective, and 5,000 of La Romana's Spaniards, making a total of 58,615. He refuses to contemplate the use of the militia, infantry or artillery, in the field ; considering their behaviour at Bussaco and elsewhere, ' I should deceive myself if I could expect, or your Lordship if I should state, that any advantage would be derived from their assistance in an offensive operation against the enemy.' On the other hand, he estimates Masséna's fighting force at 55,000 men—a slight miscalculation, for there were only 50,000 effective at this moment, and of these 4,000 cavalry and one brigade of infantry were at Santarem and other distant places, from which they could not have been withdrawn for a battle suddenly forced upon their main corps. Masséna could really have put no more than 44,000 men in line within twenty-four hours of an alarm. Wellington then proceeds to argue that he must make a frontal attack, for if he drew a very large force out of the Lines, in order to assail the enemy's flank by a wide encircling march, ' the inevitable consequence of attempting such a manœuvre would be to open some one or other of the great roads to Lisbon, and to our shipping, of which the enemy would take immediate advantage to attain his object.' Accordingly ' we must carry their positions by main force, and in the course of the operation I must draw the army out of their cantonments, and expose men and horses to the inclemencies of the weather at this time of the year.' Moreover, if Masséna were defeated, it would cause Soult to evacuate Granada, raise the

[1] The first morning note of D'Urban's diary in November is nearly always ' more deserters arrived.'

[2] See Wellington to Lord Liverpool, *Dispatches*, vi. 554.

[3] See especially the longer dispatch of Nov. 3, on pp. 582-3 ibid.

siege of Cadiz, and come with 50,000 men to aid the army of
Portugal. ' So if I should succeed in forcing Masséna's positions,
it would become a question whether I should be able to maintain my own, in case the enemy should march another army into
this country.' Blake and the garrison of Cadiz, when freed from
Soult's presence, would certainly do nothing to help the general
cause of the Allies. They would neither come to Portugal, nor
be able to make a serious advance on Madrid, so as to draw off
Soult in that direction. He therefore concludes, that ' When
I observe how small the superiority of numbers is in my favour,
and know that the position will be in favour of the enemy, I am
of opinion that I act in conformity with the intentions of His
Majesty's Government in waiting for the result of what is going
on, and in incurring no extraordinary risk.' What he calls ' the
safe game' is to keep on the strict defensive, hoping that the
enemy's distress for provisions, and the operations of the militia
in his rear, may cause him either to make a desperate attack on
the Lines—in which he will be repulsed with awful loss—or else
to make such large detachments, to clear off the corps of Wilson,
Trant, and the rest, that it will become easy and safe to attack
the remaining army in its present position.

Here, as when we considered the reasons which determined
Wellington to evacuate the Coimbra country at the end of September, we are bound to recognize that he adopted an attitude
of caution which he would not have assumed in 1812 and 1813,
when he had thoroughly proved his army. The temptations to
assail Junot's isolated and advanced position at Sobral were
enormous. The 8th Corps had been thrust forward into a re-
entering angle of the British lines, in which it could be attacked
from the left flank as well as from the front. It was wasting
away daily from its privations, and had apparently not more
than 10,000 bayonets left—the cavalry of the corps (Sainte-
Croix's old division) had been sent off to Santarem, save one
regiment. To sustain Junot the 6th Corps could eventually be
used, but only one brigade of it (that of Ferey) was in the first
line, and this depleted unit, which had been so thoroughly
routed at Bussaco, had its old enemy, Craufurd's Light Division,
in its front. Of the rest of the 6th Corps, one division was at
Alemquer, eleven miles behind Sobral, the other at Otta, six

miles behind Alemquer [1]. It would have taken the one four or five hours, the other nearly the whole of a short November day, to assemble and to come up. Reynier could not quit Hill's front without freeing the latter's two strong divisions for action. Meanwhile Wellington had disposable, in Junot's immediate front, the divisions of Spencer, Cole, Leith, and Alex. Campbell [Picton had been sent back to Torres Vedras], plus the Portuguese brigades of Pack, Coleman, and A. Campbell, with La Romana's Spaniards also, if he should choose to employ them— this, too, after leaving Craufurd to look after Ferey, and Hill to keep Reynier in check. It is impossible not to conclude that a sudden frontal and flank attack on Sobral with 30,000 men must have enveloped and crushed the 8th Corps. Though its position was good, its supports were too far off; Ney could not have come up to Junot's aid, before he was overwhelmed. Masséna was uneasy about this possibility of disaster, and had issued orders on October 29 that if Junot and Ferey were attacked, they were to fall back on Alemquer, while Ney was to bring up his reserves to that same place, and Reynier to abandon his position in front of Alhandra and march on Alemquer also [2]. But the weak point of this arrangement was, that if Junot had been attacked at dawn, both in front and flank, by an overwhelming force, he could never have got back to Alemquer, and must have been cut off and battered to pieces close in the rear of Sobral. The English frontal attack—Spencer, Leith, and Pack—would have started at a distance of less than a mile from his position : Cole and Campbell on the flank had only two miles to cover. Both columns had a down-hill march before them till the line of rising ground about Sobral was reached. How could the 8th Corps have got away ? Even an orderly retreat, with a fighting rearguard, would have been impossible.

But if Junot's 10,000 men had been destroyed behind Sobral, Wellington would then have been in the position to push in between Ney and Reynier, whose columns would just have been beginning to near Alemquer. He might easily have driven them

---

[1] Loison, to whom Ferey's brigade belonged, had gone to the rear with his other brigade.

[2] The whole dispatch may be found in Fririon, pp. 96–7. That officer quite saw the danger of the position : see his comments on pp. 99–100.

apart, and have forced them to retire on Santarem or some such distant point, in order to complete their junction. Even had they succeeded in joining, Masséna would have had a demoralized army of little over 30,000 men remaining. It is certain that he must have refused to fight, and have started on a disastrous retreat either by Castello Branco, or more likely by Thomar. For the latter direction would have brought him to his base at Almeida—the former would have taken him through an almost uninhabited country, to a part of Spain, the mid-Tagus, where no French army was ready to receive or succour him.

It is impossible, therefore, to doubt that Wellington had a great opportunity before him. Yet it is easy to see why he refused to take it. A mere victory of the second class—the thrusting of Junot out of his positions, not followed by the complete annihilation of the 8th Corps—would have done no more for him than he himself stated in the above-quoted dispatch of November 3. If Junot got away with the main body of his troops, and joined Ney and Reynier, and if their united army took up a defensive position at Santarem or elsewhere, Masséna might still hang on to Portugal, till Soult brought up to his aid the whole Army of Andalusia, or great reinforcements arrived from Castile. Any chance—a fog, heavy rain, the rashness or stupidity of some subordinate—might prevent the complete and instantaneous success of the attack on Sobral. These things being taken into consideration, Wellington resolved to lie still in the Lines, and to let the weapon of starvation play for some time longer on the French. He expected them to retire within a few days from sheer necessity, or else to deliver the much desired attack on his impregnable position.

Masséna had found that the preparation of his bridge equipage at Santarem would be a long business. He knew that his numbers were shrinking every day in the most appalling fashion, not only from deaths and invaliding, but from desertion. Yet he stood still for a fortnight longer than his adversary had expected, and meanwhile made a last desperate appeal for help to the Emperor. He had guessed that all his previous attempts to communicate with Spain had failed because his messengers had been sent without a sufficient escort, and had fallen by the way. Accordingly, he told off a body of more than 500 men to bear his next letter, and gave the command of them to an officer of well-known intelligence and resource—Foy, who had served in all the three Portuguese campaigns, Junot's of 1808, Soult's of 1809, and this last of his own. Moreover, it was known that Napoleon had confidence in his ability, though he was an old Republican, and had actually been one of the few who had refused to sign the address which was drawn up to ask the First Consul to declare himself Emperor in 1804. Foy was given a whole battalion of infantry—the 4th of the 47th of the Line— with 120 mounted men. He was told to avoid the main roads, to cross the Zezere, pass north of Castello Branco, and to try to reach Spain by way of Sabugal or Penamacor. This was obviously a difficult task, since the Ordenança were known to be abroad, even in this rugged and deserted region. To cover Foy's start, Montbrun marched, with a brigade of dragoons and a couple of battalions of infantry, to make a demonstration against Abrantes, and draw the attention of its garrison from the upper Zezere. Montbrun forced the passage of the river at Punhete, after a sharp skirmish, and established his vanguard on the further side. He thus attracted to himself all the forces which Lobo, the governor of Abrantes, could spare outside his walls. Meanwhile (October 31) Foy passed the Zezere higher up, at an unguarded ford, and marched by Cardigos and Sobreira Formosa along the Castello Branco road. But he abandoned it before reaching that town, and turned north, crossing the Serra de Moradal by Fundão and Belmonte. From thence he reached Sabugal, and finally Ciudad Rodrigo on November 8. He had been unmolested save by a body of Ordenança, who cut off some of his stragglers. The passage of his column, whose strength was exaggerated by rumour, caused Carlos D'España to burn the bridge of Villa Velha, under the impression that Foy intended to seize it, and open up communication southward with Soult. He and Lobo reported to Wellington that Foy and Montbrun were the van of a great force, which was about to overrun and occupy the Castello Branco country [1]. But Masséna's messenger had no other object than to reach Castile with as great rapidity as possible, and without fighting.

[1] Wellington also, on Lobo's report, thought (*Dispatches*, vi. 604) that Foy's and Montbrun's object had been to seize the bridge of Villa Velha.

Arrived at Rodrigo, Foy gave over his escort to General Gardanne, with orders to him to collect all the convalescents of the Army of Portugal, and to draw out the garrison of Rodrigo and Almeida, if Drouet was now in condition to take charge of these fortresses. This should give him a force of 6,000 men, with which he was ordered to cut his way to join the main army, to whom he was to bring a convoy of ammunition, which was running desperately low at the front. How badly Gardanne executed his charge we shall presently see.

Foy meanwhile, with a fresh dragoon escort, rode for Salamanca and Valladolid, at which last place he was disgusted to find Drouet and the bulk of the 9th Corps, whom he had expected to meet at Rodrigo [1]. He met the general, and passed on to him Masséna's request that he would collect the whole of his 16,000 men, and march on Almeida, and from thence down the Mondego to Coimbra, after which he was to open up communication with the main army by Leiria or Thomar. Drouet, assuming some of the airs of a commander-in-chief, did not show the eagerness to carry out these directions which Foy had hoped to find.

From Valladolid Foy rode straight through by post, braving guerrilla bands and swollen rivers, through Burgos and Bayonne to Paris, which he reached on the night of November 21. On the next day he delivered his dispatches to the Emperor, and was put through two hours of sharp cross-questioning by his master. The notes of this conversation, taken down the same afternoon by the general, are one of the most interesting documents for the study of Napoleon's psychology. Striding up and down his study, pouring out strings of queries, rapid judgements, rebukes and laudations, even anecdotes and screeds of political philosophy, the Emperor presented a wonderful picture of restless and far-reaching intellectual activity. Foy put in his excuses and explanations in the gaps of the Emperor's tirades. 'Why the devil did Masséna thrust himself into that muddle [2] at Bussaco? Even in a plain country columns do not break through lines, unless they are supported by a superior artillery fire.' 'And the disgrace at Coimbra, where he has let his

---

[1] Only part of Claparéde's division had as yet even reached Salamanca. Foy to Massena, Nov. 8, from Rodrigo.   [2] échauffourée.

hospitals be taken by 1,500 ragged rascals! To lose your
hospitals is as disgraceful as to lose your flags! In a regularly
organized country—England, for example—Masséna would have
gone to the scaffold for that job. The English are full of
courage and honour: they defend themselves well. Masséna
and Ney did not know them, but Reynier, whom they had
beaten twice or thrice [Alexandria and Maida], ought to
know them! Wellington has behaved like a clever man: his
total desolation of the kingdom of Portugal is the result of
systematic measures splendidly concerted. I could not do that
myself, for all my power. Why did not Masséna stop at
Coimbra, after Bussaco?' 'Because,' faltered Foy, 'supposing
he had done so, Your Majesty would have reproached him by
saying "If you had only pushed straight on Lisbon the English
would have embarked."' 'Very possible, indeed,' replied the
Emperor, breaking into a broad smile. 'Well, I wanted to drive
them into the sea : I have failed. All right ; then I will have a
regular campaign in Portugal, and use them up. I can wear
them down in the nature of things, because England cannot
compete in mere numbers with me.' Then followed an excursus
into the characters of French generals—Junot, Ney, Soult
especially. Then a curious confession that he had made a
miscalculation in taking up the Spanish war: 'I thought the
system easier to change than it has proved in that country,
with its corrupt minister, its feeble king, and its shameless,
dissolute queen. But for all that, I don't repent of what I did ;
I had to smash up that nation: sooner or later they would
have done me a bad turn.'

Then comes the Emperor's conclusion upon the present state
of affairs. 'Masséna must take Abrantes—Elvas would be of
no good to us. The only way to get Wellington to make a
forward move will be to force him to try to raise the siege
of Abrantes. As long as Masséna stays in position opposite
Lisbon, nothing is lost ; he is still a terror to the English, and
keeps the offensive. If he retreats, I fear great disaster for him.
But why did he not take up some regular plan of operations ?
The very day after he reconnoitred the Lisbon lines, it was
clear that he would never attack them. I will send immediate
orders for the 5th Corps [Mortier] to invade the Alemtejo.

Will they be obeyed ? At that distance only those who choose
carry out my directions. [A hint at Soult's selfish policy.]
I tremble lest Masséna may call Drouet down to him, and then
get his communications cut again. By communications I mean
sure points, at two or three marches distance, properly garrisoned
and provisioned, where convoys can rest and be safe. An army
without open communications loses heart and gets demoralized.
. . . All the hope of the English is in that army of Wellington's! If we could destroy it, it would be a terrible blow to
them.'

The Emperor, pleased with Foy's intelligent explanations
of the situation, created him a general of division, and told
him to rest for a month, and then return to Portugal. He sent
for him to administer a second catechism on the 24th, and then
condescended to explain his view of the situation, and his orders
for the future. He quite approved of Masséna's resolve to
hold out in front of the Lines, and had already given Drouet
directions to assemble his corps at Almeida, and open up communications with the Army of Portugal—in fact, the order to do
so had been sent off as early as November 3, and its bearer must
have crossed Foy somewhere on the road [1]. Soult had also been
ordered, two days before Masséna's appeal came to hand, to
create a diversion in the direction of Spanish Estremadura [2].
He was now sent a sharp reproof for having done nothing, and
more especially for having allowed La Romana to slip away
with two divisions to Lisbon unmolested [3]. But it seems clear
that no orders to concentrate his whole army and invade the
Alemtejo were sent him, and these were the only measures that
could have helped Masséna. Napoleon's *obiter dictum* that it
would be no use to besiege and capture Elvas shows a mis-
apprehension of the situation. A mere demonstration in
Spanish Estremadura might call back La Romana, but would
not help the Army of Portugal to any appreciable extent. It
was not La Romana's 8,000 men who formed the strength

---

[1] This is the order in *Correspondance*, 17,097. It goes on to give Drouet
detailed orders as to what he should do ' aussitôt que les Anglais seront
rembarqués.'

[2] This had been sent off the day before Foy arrived, Nov. 20, it is *Correspondance*, 17,146.   [3] *Correspondance*, 17,172, dated Nov. 28.

of the defence of Lisbon. Wellington could have spared them without harm, and, indeed, sent them away long before Masséna quitted Portugal.

It may be added that (as facts were to show ere long) the mere sending up of Drouet to the front was not nearly sufficient to put Masséna in a position to incommode Wellington, more especially when the 9th Corps was told to drop detachments at short intervals at every stage after Almeida. By following these orders, indeed, Drouet brought to the main army a mere 6,000 men on December 26, having left the rest of his corps beyond the Mondego. His arrival was of absolutely no use to the Prince of Essling. The one thing which could have saved Masséna was the arrival, not of a small field force such as Drouet or Mortier commanded, but of a large army, on the Lower Tagus, and on its southern side. Such an army, as the disposition of the French troops in Spain then stood, could only have been produced if Soult had consented to abandon Granada, raise the siege of Cadiz, and march with the greater part of the Army of Andalusia into the Alemtejo, masking Badajoz and Elvas, and leaving a division or two in Seville to keep Blake and the Spanish troops from Cadiz in check. But the Duke of Dalmatia could never be induced to abandon two-thirds of his Andalusian viceroyalty, in order to execute a movement whose results, if successful, would mainly redound to the glory of Masséna. Nothing short of a definite and peremptory order from Paris would have made him call in Victor and Sebastiani, and evacuate Eastern and Southern Andalusia. Such an order the Emperor did not send. His dispatch of Dec. 4 only ordered that a corps of 10,000 men should advance to the Tagus in the direction of Villa Velha and Montalvão, to communicate with Masséna [1]. Soult undertook instead a blow at Badajoz, in January, with a force of 20,000 men, while leaving Cadiz still blockaded and Granada still held. Napoleon, therefore, must take the blame of the final failure of the invasion of Portugal. As has been shown above, from his own words, he was conscious that he was too far from the scene of operation, and that mere ordinary directions to his lieutenants might not be carried out with zeal. 'Je donne

[1] Berthier to Soult, Dec. 4, 1810.

l'ordre.   L'exécutera-t-on?   De si loin obéit qui veut [1].'   But
if this were so, it was surely necessary either that he should go
to Spain in person, or else—the more obvious alternative—that
he should appoint a real Commander-in-Chief in the Peninsula,
who should have authority to order all the other marshals and
generals to obey his directions, without malingering or appeals
to Paris.   Napoleon had deliberately created a divided authority
beyond the Pyrenees when he set up his military governments,
and instructed Suchet, Kellermann, and the other governors
to report directly to himself, and to pay no attention to commands emanating from Madrid [2].   King Joseph, as a central
source of orders, had been reduced to a nullity by this ill-
conceived decree.   Even over the troops not included in the
new viceroyalties he had no practical authority.   Not he and
his chief of the staff, but Masséna, ought to have been entrusted
with a full and autocratic power of command over all the
armies of Spain, if a true unity of purpose was to be achieved.

This necessary arrangement the Emperor utterly refused to
carry out : he sent rebukes to Drouet for hesitating to obey the
orders of the Prince of Essling, and he jested at the absurd
conduct of Ney and Junot in conducting themselves like independent generals [3].   But these officers were in command of
troops definitely allotted to the Army of Portugal.   Over the
other generals of Spain he refused to allow Masséna any
control, and he continued to send them his own ever-tardy
instructions, which had often ceased to be appropriate long
before the dispatch had reached its destination.   If we seek
the reasons of this unwise persistence in his old methods, we
find that they were two.   The first was his secret, but only half-
disguised, intention to annex all the Spanish provinces north of
the Ebro to France, an insane resolve which led him to keep
Suchet and Macdonald in Aragon and Catalonia, as well as
the governors of Navarre and Biscay, out of the control of any
central authority that he might set up in Spain.   The second
was his jealousy of entrusting the vast army south of the Ebro,

---

[1] See above, p. 458.

[2] See pp. 201 and 284 above.

[3] See the above-quoted conversation with Foy, in the latter's *Vie Militaire*,
p. 109.

far more than 250,000 men at the moment, to any single
commander. He remembered Soult's absurd strivings after
royalty in Portugal; he knew that Masséna, though the best
of soldiers, was false, selfish, and ambitious; and he refused
to hand over to either of them a full control over the whole
of the forces in the Peninsula. It was even better, in his
estimation, to leave King Joseph a shadow of power, than to
take the risk of giving over-much authority to one of the two
able, but not wholly trustworthy, marshals to whom he must
otherwise have entrusted it.

The war in Portugal, therefore, went on as a mere section
of the great contest in the Peninsula; the other and less
important episodes were not made wholly subordinate to it.
And if this system continued Wellington was free from any
real danger. He knew it himself; he studied diligently both
the political position and the details of the emplacement of
the imperial armies in the Peninsula. He was fortunate enough
to secure whole budgets of French dispatches captured by the
Ordenança [1], and all that he read confirmed him in his conclusion. 'I calculate,' he writes on October 27, 'that a
reinforcement of 15,000 men would not now give the enemy
so good an army as they had at Bussaco. He lost 2,000 killed
or taken there: Trant took 5,000 at Coimbra: above 1,000
prisoners have gone through this army: many have been killed
by the peasantry. They cannot have less than 4,000 sick [2], after
the march they have made, and the weather to which they are
exposed. The deserters tell us that almost every one is sick.
From this statement you may judge of the diminution of their
numbers; and you will see that I have not much reason to
apprehend anything from [Drouet's] "*quinze beaux bataillons*
which fought at Essling" [3], and which cannot be here before the
middle of November. I do not think I have much to apprehend even if Mortier is added to them. However, we shall see

[1] See for example those noted in *Dispatches*, vi. 545, and a whole series
copied out in D'Urban's journal in October and November, 1810.

[2] A most modest estimate, for the returns of sick for the second half of
October in a document at the *Archives de la Guerre* give a total of 10,897
men in hospital.

[3] An allusion to a phrase in one of the captured dispatches.

how *that* will be. . . . All the accounts which I receive of the
distresses of the enemy for want of provisions would tend to a
belief that their army cannot remain long in the position in
which it is placed, and it is astonishing that they have been
able to remain here so long as this [1].' That they have succeeded
in staying even a fortnight in front of the Lines is, he adds,
entirely the fault of the Portuguese government, for not carrying
out thoroughly the work of devastation. But, for the reasons
stated on an earlier page, Wellington was resolved not to take
the offensive, even against a foe whose ranks were beginning to
grow thin. Famine should do the work, and no lives should be
wasted.

There remained only one danger: it was just possible that
Soult, even though Masséna had not yet suffered any disaster
great enough to make the evacuation of Eastern Andalusia
imperative, might send Mortier and some additional divisions
of his other corps to Spanish Estremadura, and make a dash
at the Lower Tagus. Masséna's boat-building at Santarem,
of which every deserter spoke, might be intended to give him
the materials for a bridge by which he might communicate
across the Lower Tagus with Soult. Wellington accordingly
resolved to keep a strict watch beyond the Tagus, and to have
a flying force ready, which could hinder the construction of a
bridge or a bridge head. With this object on November 2
he sent over the Tagus General Fane, with his 1,500 Portuguese
horse, a battalion of Caçadores, and a few guns. All the North
Alemtejo Ordenança were called out to watch the river banks,
and to lend what small assistance they could to the cavalry.
Fane discovered the French dockyard at Santarem, and tried
to fire it with rockets on November 13. He failed, but the
mere appearance of his little force on the further bank of the
Tagus had some good effect, since it warned Masséna that an
attempt to pass the broad river would not be unopposed, and
therefore made him more chary of attempting it. Fane, being
in touch with Abrantes on his right hand and with Lisbon
on his left, now formed, as it were, a section of the blockading
screen which was thrown round the whole French army.

Wellington had miscalculated the time which the French could

[1]. Wellington to Liverpool, October 27, pp. 545 and 555 of vol. vi.

afford to spend in front of the Lines, without suffering actual starvation, by about a fortnight. On November 10 Masséna gave orders for the evacuation of his whole position, and a general retreat on Santarem, because it had become absolutely impossible to stay any longer on the ground facing Zibreira and Alhandra, unless the whole army was to perish. The report from the 8th Corps may suffice to give in a few words the condition of affairs, 'General Clausel wishes to observe that during the daytime he cannot count on any other troops save those actually guarding the outpost line. The majority of the men are absent on raids to the rear, to seek for maize and cattle. The last detachment which came back to camp had been nine days away. Generals and soldiers agree in stating that for some time it has only been possible to collect a little corn with extreme difficulty. For eight days the troops have been living on polenta (boiled maize flour) alone, and of this they have received only half a ration. During the last four days the 1st Division has received only one ration of meat, which amounted to six ounces of goat's-flesh. If the corps had to make a retreat, it would have to abandon its sick and wounded for want of carts, which the intendant-generals will not furnish [1].' The condition of the 2nd and 6th Corps was only so far better that they had to send their foragers a less distance, when seeking for the scanty store which could still be gleaned from the hidden granaries of the Portuguese.

But Masséna had no intention of retiring on Spain when he began to issue orders for a general movement to the rear. Profoundly sensible of the difficulties of a November retreat through the mountains, trusting that he might block the British army by maintaining a bold attitude in its front, and still hoping that large reinforcements might reach him ere long from Drouet and Mortier, he had resolved only to evacuate the Lisbon peninsula, and to retire no further than to the flat and fertile lands between Santarem and the Zezere. In the Plain of Golegão, as it is sometimes called, he hoped to feed his army for many weeks more, for the region was still comparatively full of resources, since it had only been exploited as yet by the garrison

[1] Fririon's confidential report to Masséna, night of 8th–9th of November.

of Santarem and the flying columns which had marched to the
Zezere.   It was now his cherished hope that Wellington might
follow him into the plainland, abandoning his defensive system,
and consenting to give battle in the open.   The English might
even be induced to attack the French army when it should have
taken up a new and a strong position.   In somewhat rash
confidence the Marshal professed himself certain of the result,
even with his depleted army of under 50,000 men, if Wellington
would consent to fight.   At the worst, if starved out again or
beaten in the field, he would retreat on Spain by Castello
Branco, for which purpose he had sent up the greater part of
his boat-train from Santarem to build a bridge over the Zezere.
He had also pushed part of Loison's brigade of infantry across
that river at Punhete, and was holding with it a point suitable
for a *tête-du-pont*.   A regiment of dragoons was attached to this
force : it skirmished not unfrequently with parties sent out to
reconnoitre from Abrantes, but with no serious result.   For
General Lobo, the governor, had no intention of coming out
with a large detachment, in order to push the French advanced
guard back over the river.   He had been ordered to keep to the
defensive, and only sent out occasional reconnaissances to see
whether the enemy were still in position.

Loison's troops were now no longer the only large force which
had quitted the army in front of the Lines.   Not only was
Montbrun, with the main body of the cavalry, watching the
roads from the north, but six battalions of infantry had been
sent up from the 6th Corps on November 8 to occupy Torres
Novas and Thomar.   If Wellington had attacked the enemy
behind Sobral on any day after that date, he would have found
Ney short of fourteen battalions [1] out of the thirty-four which
formed his corps.   There would have been only 10,000 infantry
ready to support Junot in the direction of Alemquer.   But this
fact, of course, was unknown to the English general, who had
already made up his mind not to take the offensive.   If it had
come to his knowledge, he might have attacked, even at the last

---

[1] Viz. 39th (3 batts.) and 69th (3 batts.) of Marchand's division at
Thomar and Torres Novas, with Loison's 66th (3 batts.), 82nd (2 batts.),
and 26th (3 batts.).   It will be remembered that Reynier was, at the
same time, minus the 4/47th, sent as escort with Foy to Ciudad Rodrigo.

moment, with an enormous probability of inflicting on the enemy not the mere repulse that he disliked to contemplate—on account of its ulterior effects—but a crushing defeat, which might have hurled them out of Portugal.

On November 10 Masséna ordered the hospitals of the 6th and 8th Corps at Alemquer, and of the 2nd Corps at Azambuja, to be sent off to Santarem. At the same time the intendants of the commissariat were ordered to direct to the rear the meagre store of provisions which was in their possession, loaded on the much depleted transport train which still survived. On the 13th the reserve parks and the artillery train of each corps were ordered to follow. On the 14th, at eight o'clock in the evening, the infantry, many of whom lay in contact with the British lines, acted on their marching directions. Ney's main body, which was out of sight of Wellington, was to move first; then Junot and Ferey's brigade, whose movement was most perilous—for if their departure were discovered while they were on the hither side of the defile of Alemquer, they ran a great risk of being enveloped and destroyed. Reynier was to maintain his position at Villafranca and Carregado, until it was reported to him that Junot and his corps had passed Alemquer and reached Moinho de Cubo. For if the 2nd Corps had gone off at an early hour, and its departure had been discovered, Hill might have marched from Alhandra on Alemquer quickly enough to intercept Junot at that point; and if Junot were being pursued at the moment by the troops from his immediate front, the whole 8th Corps might have been cut off.

On the night of the 14th, when the movement was commencing, Masséna was favoured with the greatest piece of luck which had come to him since the explosion of Almeida. A fog began to rise in the small hours, and had become dense by the early morning. It caused some difficulty to the retiring troops, and dragoons had to be placed at every cross road to point out the right direction to the infantry columns [1]. But it had the all-important result of permitting the British outposts to see nothing at dawn. The limit visible to them was less than 100 yards. It was only at ten o'clock in the morning of the 15th that the mists were suddenly rolled up by an east wind, and that the

---

[1] Delagrave, p. 123 and note.

nearer outposts could see that the French sentinels in front of them had disappeared. The first alarm was given by Campbell's 6th Division [1]. The news spread along the whole line from west to east, and reached the Commander-in-Chief, who ascended the hill in front of Sobral a few minutes later [2]. The ingenuity of the enemy in concealing his departure had been great. Ferey's brigade, in front of Arruda, had erected a well-designed line of dummy sentinels before the Light Division, which were not discovered to be men of straw, topped with old shakos and bound to poles, till the fog rolled off on the 15th [3].

Meanwhile the French had accomplished the first stage of their retreat absolutely unmolested. Ney had retreated as far as Alcoentre; Junot had passed the defile of Alemquer, and passed through Moinho de Cubo to Aveira de Cima. Reynier, who had waited till Junot was in safety before he withdrew at eight in the morning, reached Cartaxo before the day ended. The first and most difficult stage of the retreat had been finished without a shot being fired. What would have happened had the night of the 14th been clear and starry, and the morning sun had shone out on the 15th, so that Junot would have been detected as he was passing Alemquer, and Reynier would have been visible still in line of battle behind Villafranca, the French diarists of the campaign prefer not to contemplate. Yet they mostly continued to speak of Wellington as a mediocre general, who had all the luck on his side.

On the night of the 15th the British Commander-in-Chief had to draw his deductions from the facts before him. Three things were possible : Masséna might have been so thoroughly starved out and broken in spirit, that he might be intending to retire on Spain, either via Thomar and the Mondego, or by his new bridge on the Zezere and the route of Castello Branco. Or he might be proposing to cross the Tagus by means of the boats and pontoons still remaining at Santarem, to seek unwasted fields in the Alemtejo and a junction with Mortier. Or, again, he might merely be abandoning a position that was no longer tenable, in order to take up a new one—perhaps at Santarem, perhaps at

---

[1] Londonderry, ii. pp. 51–2.

[2] His first dispatch, that to Craufurd, is dated at 10.20.

[3] See Leach's *Diary*, p. 178.

Thomar, but very possibly at and about Abrantes, whose siege
he might be contemplating [1].

On the whole Wellington thought it probable that the last-
named plan was the one which Masséna intended to adopt. A
retreat on Spain would not only be difficult and dangerous, but
inconsistent with the Marshal's obstinate and courageous temper.
It was much more likely that he would endeavour to hold out
in Portugal, and meanwhile to cover his partial discomfiture by
a bold stroke, such as the siege of Abrantes, which would still
give an offensive air to his movements, and would also throw on
the British army the responsibility of relieving the fortress.
Such a course, it will be remembered, was what Napoleon recommended to Foy [2].   'There is still a chance that the enemy may
take up and try to keep a position at Santarem,' wrote Wellington
to Fane on the night of the 15th, 'endeavouring to keep his rear
open, and to get a communication with Ciudad Rodrigo across
the Zezere.'   But he was inclined to think that Abrantes was
Masséna's goal.   He therefore directed Fane to transfer his
cavalry to the point opposite Abrantes on the south bank of the
Tagus, and requested Carlos d'España to enter the place and
strengthen the garrison.   He intended to pass over Hill's two
divisions to strengthen Fane, and for that purpose directed
Admiral Berkeley to prepare all the boats of the fleet to ferry
Hill across to Salvaterra, on the south bank of the Tagus, from
whence his force could join Fane, and either reinforce Abrantes,
by means of its bridge of boats, or join in the pursuit of Masséna
if he were about (an unlikely chance) to retire on Spain by way
of his bridge over the Zezere [3] and Castello Branco.

Meanwhile all was still uncertain, and it was Wellington's first
task to find out what roads the enemy had taken in his retreat.
He did not on the 15th order his whole army to leave the Lines
in headlong pursuit.   Only Spencer, Craufurd, and Hill were

[1] Wellington to Fane, Nov. 15 : ' The enemy retreated last night.   He
intends either to retire across the Zezere into Spain, or across the Tagus
into Spain, or across the Zezere to attack Abrantes.   The last is possible,
as I last night received an account that on the 9th they had a considerable
reinforcement coming on the frontier at Beira Alta.'

[2] See p. 457 above.

[3] All from the orders issued at 10.30 in the morning ' from the hill in
front of Sobral '.   *Dispatches,* vi. 623.

directed to march that afternoon. The former, with a cavalry regiment out in his front, occupied Sobral, and pushed its vanguard forward to Alemquer by the high road. The second left Arruda, climbed the low hills in front of him, where Ferey had been encamped for the last month, and felt his way to Alemquer, by the bad road which his immediate adversary had taken eighteen hours before. Hill followed the great *chaussée* along the Tagus bank, by Villafranca and Castanheira, and reached Carregado before dark. He was warned to be in readiness to cross the river, by means of Admiral Berkeley's boats, at the earliest possible moment, in case the French should have built a bridge at Santarem to enable them to cross into the Alemtejo.[1]

The advancing troops found the French camps, and the villages where the more fortunate battalions had been quartered under cover, in the most dreadful condition. 'The Alemquer road was covered with horses, mules, and asses which had perished from want of forage. We passed many French soldiers lying dead by the road-side, whose appearance indicated that disease and want of food had carried them off. Every house in every town or village was thoroughly ransacked.'[2] 'Alemquer had been entirely sacked, the windows and doors torn down and burnt, as well as most of the furniture ; china, pier-glasses, and chandeliers all dashed to pieces with the objectless fury of savages. They had left many miserable fellows behind, who were too ill to march : these were, of course, put to death by the Portuguese whenever we happened to miss finding them out. We found several peasants whom the French had murdered and left upon the road, and also several French killed by the Portuguese. It was a dreadful sight to see so many fine towns and villages sacked, and without a creature in them.'[3]

On the 15th none of the enemy had been seen save the dead and the abandoned sick. The traces of their retreat, however, showed that all had gone off by the roads towards Santarem. On the 16th Wellington moved more troops out of the Lines, to support Hill, Craufurd, and Spencer, in the event of the enemy

---

[1] All from the orders issued at 10.30 in the morning ' from the hill in front of Sobral'. *Dispatches,* vi. 623.

[2] Leach's *Journal,* p. 179.

[3] George Simmons's *Journal,* pp. 121–2.

showing fight. Slade's horse followed Spencer, Pack's Portuguese followed Craufurd; Picton, Leith, Cole, and Campbell were left in the Lines, which Wellington still disliked to leave wholly unguarded while he was not yet certain of the ultimate intentions of the French. The advanced guard picked up about 300 prisoners this day—partly marauders, partly debilitated men who could not keep up with their regiments during a second stage of hard marching. Next day (November 17) it was evident that the enemy was being overtaken : Anson's cavalry brigade, which had reached the front on the preceding night, cut up a number of small parties of the French rearguard—the 16th Light Dragoons alone captured two officers and 78 men, not stragglers, but belated pickets and convoy guards. One of their exploits was long remembered—Sergeant Baxter, with five men only, came on an infantry outpost of 50 men, who had stacked their arms and were cooking. Bursting in upon them, he captured an officer and 41 men, though some of the Frenchmen had got to their muskets and wounded one of his troopers.[1]

On the afternoon of the 17th the enemy's rearguard was at last discovered, drawn up on a heath outside the village of Cartaxo. It consisted of one of Reynier's divisions, which Craufurd was preparing to attack, when the Commander-in-Chief came up, and refused him leave to begin the combat, because neither Hill nor Spencer was within supporting distance of him. Opinions differed as to whether an attack would have led to a repulse by superior numbers, or to the capture of the French division, which had a bridge and a long causeway—a most dangerous defile—in its rear[2]. Probably Craufurd was not in quite sufficient strength to be certain of success : he had but six strong battalions[3], a battery, and the 16th Light Dragoons in

---

[1] For a full description of the doings of the 16th on this day, see Tomkinson, pp. 59-60.

[2] Leach thinks, with William Napier (iii. 41), that Wellington acted wisely in refusing Craufurd leave to attack (p. 180). Tomkinson, another eye-witness, thinks that an opportunity was missed (pp. 60, 61).

[3] Having now received the Brunswick Oels Jägers, the Light Division was six battalions strong, not its usual five. Its strength about this time was some 4,000 bayonets. Merle's division was about 5,000 strong : it had dwindled to 4,200 effectives before December was out. Thus the English and Caçadore battalions averaged 650 men, the French 450 only,

his company. The enemy had the eleven weak battalions of Merle's division, and two regiments of cavalry : probably 1,000 bayonets and 300 sabres in all more than Craufurd could command. But an attack made with vigour, when half the French had begun to retire across the defile, might have had considerable results. Merle's division was, however, allowed to retire unmolested in the evening, while the Light Division took up quarters for the night at Cartaxo. Reynier drew back the whole of his corps next morning to the environs of Santarem, which he had been directed to defend. Meanwhile the 8th Corps had reached Pernes with one division, and Alcanhede with the other and its cavalry : these were the points at which Junot had been ordered to stay his retreat. The bulk of the 6th Corps was at Thomar, but Loison's division had been kept in the neighbourhood of the Zezere [1], and part of Marchand's infantry and Ney's corps-cavalry were at Cabaços. The retreat was thus ended, for Masséna was in possession of the new ground on which he intended to maintain himself for the winter, and he was prepared to accept a defensive battle if Wellington should push him any further. His left flank near the Tagus (Reynier's corps) was advanced : his right flank (Junot's corps) much ' refused.' Ney was forming the central reserve.

Unfortunately for himself the British Commander-in-Chief received, on the night of the 17th, confusing intelligence, which led him to the false conclusion that the enemy was still retiring, and was aiming either for Abrantes or for the borders of Spain. This news was sent by Fane, who from the other bank of the Tagus had observed French columns and convoys marching eastward from Santarem towards the Zezere [2], and wrongly inferred that the main army was making for this direction, and that only a rearguard had been left in Santarem. He was also influenced by the fact, reported from Abrantes, that Masséna had cast a second bridge over the Zezere near

so that the strength was not very unequal. But only 2,500 of Craufurd's troops were British.

[1] There its main body was now joined by Ferey's brigade, which had been detached for some weeks.

[2] Probably Ferey's brigade marching to join Loison and trains following it, and certainly Reynier's trains which he had sent off towards Golegão. See *Dispatches*, vi. 629.

Punhete, as if to give him a quicker chance of passing that river. In consequence of this news, Wellington directed Hill to cross the Tagus at Vallada with his own division, Hamilton's Portuguese, and the 13th Light Dragoons, in order to strengthen Abrantes if it were assailed, or to fall on the flank of the French, if they were merely passing that fortress on their retreat to Spain. Thus he deprived himself of 14,000 men on the right bank of the Tagus, where alone troops were really needed. To make up for Hill's absence, Leith's and Cole's divisions were called out of the Lines, where they had rested till this moment (18th November)[1]. But they were two marches off, and Wellington had for the moment in his front line only Craufurd, Spencer, Pack's Portuguese, and Slade's and Anson's cavalry, a force of some 16,000 men. Reynier was in his immediate front at Santarem, with 13,000 men of all arms. Junot's corps at Alcanhede and Pernes was twelve miles away, and about 11,000 strong: the greater part of his men could have been brought up in half a day's march. Ney was too distant to come up in less than 24 hours, and then only with half his corps, as Loison and one of Marchand's brigades were far away. But if Wellington had attacked Santarem on the 19th the Duke of Elchingen would have appeared next morning.

Craufurd was as strongly convinced as his chief that there was nothing in front of him but a rearguard on the night of the 18th, and he even doubted whether the last of the French would not withdraw at midnight. It was this that induced him to make the curious personal exploration mentioned by Napier (iii. 63)[2], when, followed by a single sergeant only, he pushed

---

[1] *The Diary of the Marches of the 4th Division*, by its Assistant Quarter-Master, Charles Vere, settles the date. For Leith's start on the same morning, see Leith-Hay's *Narrative*, i. p. 269.

[2] Napier, however, dates the General's escapade wrongly. It took place on the night of the 18th–19th, where it is duly related in the diary of George Simmons (p. 117), and not on the 21st as Napier implies. I have a copy of Delagrave's *Campagne de Portugal*, which once belonged to Napier ; he has written a sarcastic note on the bottom of page 111, commenting on the ridiculous account of the event which appeared in the French narratives. He adds that the sergeant's name was McCurry, and that ' the sergeant had sense enough to hold his tongue, but Craufurd spoke out, and so drew the fire of the enemy's picket.'

along the causeway in the small hours of the morning, ran into
the French picket, and escaped as if by miracle the volley that
was fired at him.   The picket reported to Reynier that they had
been seriously attacked, had killed three of their assailants, and
had heard the groans of wounded dragged away by the survivors.
Craufurd and his sergeant retired, thoroughly convinced that
the causeway had not been evacuated.

It was undoubtedly fortunate for the British Commander-in-
Chief that his habitual caution prevented him from making
a serious attack on the force at Santarem, under the impression
that it was a mere rearguard, left behind to detain him while
the enemy's main body was pushing for Abrantes.   Reynier's
position was very formidable.   The town of Santarem, surrounded
by an old mediaeval wall, stands on a lofty height above the
Tagus, with a narrow suburb—where the French dockyard
had been established—along the lower edge of the hill.   But
this was only the third and last line of the defensive position.
In front of it lay low alluvial ground, inundated by the rain
which had been falling during the last fortnight, and barely
passable save by the *chaussée* from Lisbon.   The plain was cut
in two by the Rio Mayor, a deep muddy stream at this time
of the year, and to reach Santarem a narrow bridge over this
obstacle had to be passed.   Just where the *chaussée* leaves the
marsh, to climb towards the town, was a long knoll, completely
commanding the road : on this Reynier had placed a battery
with infantry supports.   This force must be driven in by the
British, and the only practicable way to reach it was by forcing
a passage along the causeway, for the marsh between the road
and the Tagus turned out, when explored, to be practically
inaccessible to formed troops, though individuals might wade
through it in a few places.   Behind the advanced French knoll
were the foot-hills of the lofty ridge on which Santarem lies.
The enemy were visible upon it, working hard at the construction of a line of *abattis* from the olive-trees which cover its
slopes.   Behind this, again, was the town itself, hastily prepared
for defence.

On the morning of November 19th the British advanced
guard was on the edge of the swampy plain ; Craufurd's Light
Division occupied the near end of the long bridge over the Rio

Mayor, and skirmished with the French outposts, who refused to retire from the further side. Spencer came up more to the left, and further inland, Pack's Portuguese reached the upper course of the Rio Mayor. Neither Leith nor Cole had yet arrived at the front, so that the force available for an attack was no more than 16,000 men. Nevertheless, Wellington, still hoping that he had only a rearguard in front of him, made dispositions for a demonstration against the enemy's front, which was to be turned into a real attack if he showed want of strength. Craufurd was directed to advance across the swamp near the Tagus, if he found it practicable. Pack was to cross the upper Rio Mayor, and turn the hostile right. Spencer was formed at the entrance of the bridge and causeway, and ordered to charge up the *chaussée* at the French centre, and the battery commanding the road, so soon as he should see that the flanking divisions were making good progress. Fortunately for Wellington the attack was never delivered : more rain during the night had made the marsh so waterlogged that Craufurd, who had crossed the Rio Mayor by a narrow wooden bridge near Valle, came to a stand in the slush, though a few of his skirmishers pushed far enough forward to engage the enemy's pickets on the other side. Pack's Portuguese on the left flank got across the river with much difficulty, but their guns were absolutely stuck in the mud far to the rear, and the brigadier sent back word to Wellington that he should advance no further without special orders. The 1st Division had not yet begun to move. Thereupon the Commander-in-Chief called back both Craufurd and Pack, and gave up his plan. It is clear that he had nourished some intention of attacking in earnest, for he wrote to Hill that afternoon : ' I did not attack Santarem this morning, as the artillery of the left wing (Pack) had lost its way, and I am rather glad that I did not attack, as the enemy have there undoubtedly a very strong post, and we must endeavour to turn it. And if they [the main body] have not retired across the Zezere or towards the Alva, they must be too strong for us here.'

It is obvious that both Wellington's and Masséna's strategy on the 18th and 19th November is exposed to criticism. Why had the British General only 16,000 men to the front on these days, when he was risking a general action with the French ? One of two courses must have been adopted by the enemy : either he must be marching hard for the Zezere, and intending to retire into Spain, or he must be merely changing his ground, and proposing to fight at Santarem, or in front of Abrantes, or elsewhere. In either case it was strange tactics for Wellington to take the field with 16,000 men (deducting Hill on the other side of the Tagus), while he left Leith and Cole two or three marches behind, and still kept the divisions of Picton, Campbell, and Le Cor, and the unattached Portuguese brigade of Coleman and Alex. Campbell—20,000 men—unmoved within the Lines. For if the enemy was flying, there was no need to leave such a force of regulars to guard positions which the French could not be intending to attack. While if the other hypothesis was correct, and Masséna, with an army which Wellington still reckoned at 50,000 men, was in a fighting mood, and ready to give battle if he saw an advantageous opportunity, it was still more inexcusable to leave behind 20,000 men, who would be wanted for the decisive struggle.

On the other hand, the French Marshal was taking a terrible risk also. Supposing Wellington had been leading his whole force—deducting Hill—for a resolute attack on the Santarem positions, which was the most probable course for him to adopt, he might have had not only the 16,000 men that he had actually brought forward, but Leith and Cole with 11,000 more, and Picton and the other 20,000 men left in the Lines, a force, if the cavalry be thrown in, of full 50,000 sabres and bayonets. If Wellington had left Craufurd and Pack to block the marshy southern exit from Santarem, which was as difficult for Reynier as for his adversaries, he might have thrown 40,000 men into the empty space of twelve miles between Reynier and Junot, have driven away the latter's 11,000 men, and surrounded Reynier's 13,000 in Santarem. Ney could not have got up in time to prevent this. The 2nd Corps would either have had to surrender, for it had hardly any food, or to cut its way out with disastrous losses [1].

---

[1] The emplacement of the Anglo-Portuguese army is given as follows by Beresford's Quarter-Master-General, D'Urban, on the night of the 18th-19th, showing its complete dislocation :—

Reynier saw this perfectly, and was in an agony of mind on the 18th and 19th. He wrote urgent appeals to Masséna, for permission to abandon Santarem on the former day, pointing out that if his front was practically inaccessible, because of the swamps, his right might be turned by the upper Rio Mayor, where he had only a single regiment in observation, to face what might be an overwhelming strength of British troops, who might be preparing to cut in between him and Junot. He sent all his train, sick, and wounded to Golegão [1], and besought leave to follow them. When he received a peremptory reply, to the effect that he was to hold Santarem to the last, he came to the conclusion that he was to be sacrificed in order to allow the other two corps to escape unmolested. When Pack advanced on the 19th he sent the report that he was turned by 10,000 British troops—Pack had but 3,000 Portuguese—and that Clausel with Junot's nearest division was too far off to succour him. He prepared to suffer a disaster, and to die fighting [2]. He ordered his troops to surround Santarem, in rear as well as in front, with a double line of *abattis*, and continued to strengthen and repair its old walls.

Nothing, therefore, could exceed Reynier's relief when Pack and Craufurd halted, and Spencer did not move at all, after the firing had begun upon the 19th. On the next morning the British army was still stationary, save that a cavalry reconnaissance, pushed northward from Pack's position on the upper Rio Mayor, discovered Junot's outposts in the direction of Alcanhede and Pernes, and reported to Wellington that the enemy was in strength, with all arms, in this direction. Leith's

Light Division, Pack, and Slade's and Anson's cavalry—before Santarem.

1st Division—Cartaxo.

2nd Division—passing the Tagus at Vallada.

5th Division—Alemquer.

4th Division—Sobral.

6th Division—Ribaldeira (in the Lines).

3rd Division, and Coleman's and Alex. Campbell's Portuguese—Torres Vedras.

Le Cor's Division—Alhandra (in the Lines).

[1] It was their march, visible from the other side of the Tagus, which helped to deceive Fane as to the general movements of the French army.

[2] See Delagrave, 128–30, and Gachot's excellent notes thereon.

division came up this morning, raising the British force to
21,000 men, but this, as the Commander-in-Chief now saw, was
not sufficient to enable him to deal with two corps d'armée, of
which one was in an inaccessible position and now stockaded up
to the eyes. He halted, and sent, very tardily, orders for Cole
to join in haste, and for Campbell's division to come up from the
Lines. But even thus he was too weak to strike. Hill was
now at Almeirim, half way to Abrantes on the other side of the
Tagus. Fane had actually entered Abrantes, and sent news
that the enemy was making no forward movement from the
Zezere. Thus at last Wellington discovered that he must
have practically the whole French army in his front, while his
own forces were in a state of terrible dispersion.

On the 21st he wrote a dispatch to Lord Liverpool which
shows that he had given up all intention of pushing Masséna
further. 'Although the enemy have moved large bodies of
troops eastward from Santarem, I have not heard that any large
body has crossed the Zezere. . . . Their army being collected
between Santarem and the Zezere, they are in a situation to be
able to maintain themselves in their strong position till the
reinforcements, which I know are on the frontier, can join them.
For this reason, and because I am unwilling to expose to the
inclemencies of the weather a larger body of troops than is
absolutely necessary to press upon the enemy's rear, and to
support my advanced guard, I have kept in reserve a considerable proportion of the allied army—some of them still in their
cantonments in the Lines, our fortified position. I have ordered
General Hill to halt the head of his corps at Chamusca [on the
other side of the Tagus, fifteen miles south of Abrantes] till
the enemy's movements have been decided. . . . The rain, which
has been very heavy since the 15th, has so completely filled the
rivulets and destroyed the roads, that I have hitherto found it
impossible to dislodge the enemy from his position at Santarem,
by movements through the hills on his right flank. Possibly
the bad state of the roads has also been the cause of his
remaining at Santarem so long. . . . The enemy's army may be
reinforced, and they may again induce me to think it expedient,
in the existing state of affairs in the Peninsula, to resume my
positions [the Lines]. But I do not believe that they have it

in their power to bring such a force against us as to render the contest a matter of doubt [1].'

In a supplementary dispatch, dated the same day, Wellington adds: 'At first I thought the enemy were off, and I am not quite certain yet that they are not going. . . . I am convinced that there is no man in his senses, who has ever passed a winter in Portugal, who would not recommend them to go now, rather than to endeavour to maintain themselves upon the Zezere during the winter, or than attack our position, whatever may be the strength of their reinforcements.'

There were, indeed, men in the French camp who advised Masséna to continue his retreat, but he had no intention of taking up a timid policy after braving so many passed dangers. He had resolved to maintain himself between Santarem and the Zezere, and to call down Drouet and other reinforcements [2], in the hope that, ere the winter was over, the Emperor might find means to strengthen him to a force which, with the co-operation of Soult from Andalusia, would enable him finally to resume the offensive, and make a second and more formidable attack upon the Lines. In adopting this resolve he was, though as yet he knew it not, carrying out the instructions which the Emperor was at this very moment (November 22) dictating to Foy at Paris. But Wellington had not written at random when he reminded Lord Liverpool of the terrors of a Portuguese winter, and in the end the Prince of Essling was forced to begin on the 1st of March, with under 40,000 men of his original force, the retreat which he might have commenced on November 20 with over 50,000 [3].

The scheme for starving out the French, which Wellington had devised early in 1810, and begun to execute in September, was now transferred to a different area. Masséna had been able to endure for a month in front of the Lisbon Lines : the question now was whether he would be able to live so long in the land between the Rio Mayor and the Zezere. Wellington could not be sure of his data, in calculating the day when exhaustion would once more compel the French to shift their

---

[1] Wellington to Liverpool, Nov. 26, 1810.

[2] Notably the column of Gardanne, of which we shall speak presently.

[3] Including sick in each case, and excluding reinforcements received later.

ground. It was only certain that the plain of Golegão, and the Thomar–Torres Novas country, had not been devastated by the Portuguese government even with the same energy that they had displayed in the Lisbon Peninsula. And there, as the British Commander-in-Chief complained, not half the necessary work had been done. Yet something had certainly been accomplished; the population had nearly all been withdrawn, the mills destroyed, the corn buried or sent over the Tagus. Trusting to these facts, and to the rains and frosts of the oncoming winter, Wellington hoped that Masséna would finally be reduced to a disastrous retreat by sheer privation. 'Though it is certainly astonishing that the enemy have been able to remain in this country so long, and it is an extraordinary instance of what a French army can do [1].'

Resolved to take no further offensive action, and to let famine do its work, Wellington, on November 24, gave orders for the army to draw back and go into winter quarters, leaving only Craufurd and Pack in touch with the enemy in front of Santarem, and Spencer in support of them at Cartaxo. Of the other divisions, Hill remained behind the Tagus at Chamusca and Almeirim, with his own troops and Hamilton's Portuguese. Picton and the 3rd Division retained their old post at Torres Vedras, with Coleman and Alex. Campbell's Portuguese near them. Cole remained at Azambuja, in rear of Spencer. Leith was sent back to Alcoentre, Campbell's 6th Division was placed at Alemquer, behind Leith. Le Cor's Portuguese stayed at Alhandra, within the Lines.

'The army thus placed,' writes D'Urban, the Quarter-Master-General, on this day, 'at once takes care of Abrantes (by means of Hill), observes the enemy at Santarem (with Craufurd and Pack), has a division on the higher Rio Mayor road to turn the enemy's right, if this become expedient (Leith's to wit), and still "appuis" itself on the Lines, its retreat into which is secured by its echelloned position. Means are ready to pass General Hill back to the right bank of the Tagus, with such celerity, that his divisions can be counted upon for the order of march or battle on this side of the river as certainly as if he were already there [2].'

[1] *Dispatches*, vii. 59.　　　[2] D'Urban's *Diary*, under Nov. 24.

Masséna, on the other hand, also remained nearly quiescent for many days, the only important change which he made in the cantonments of his army being that he moved in Clausel's division closer to Santarem, to fill the dangerous gap between the 2nd and 8th Corps, which had existed on November 18. On the 22nd and 23rd he pushed forward, against Pack's Portuguese and Anson's light cavalry, a considerable force, consisting of Clausel's whole division and six squadrons from the 8th Corps, and General Pierre Soult with two cavalry regiments and three battalions from the 2nd Corps. After some lively but bloodless skirmishing, the allied troops retired behind the Rio Mayor, evacuating the village of Calares beyond the stream, and drawing in their cavalry pickets, which had hitherto held some ground on the further bank. This affair confirmed Wellington in his conclusion that nearly the whole French army was now concentrated on the Santarem–Pernes line, and made him more reluctant than ever to take the offensive.

Meanwhile Montbrun's cavalry, supported by small detachments from the infantry of Ney's corps, had pressed somewhat further to the north, in order to occupy a broader tract of land from which the army might feed itself, a task that grew harder every day. From his head quarters at Ourem and from Cabaços, on the Thomar–Coimbra road, he continued to send out strong reconnaissances in every direction, of which some occasionally pushed as far as Leiria on the road towards Coimbra, and others scoured the left bank of the lower Zezere and the Nabao. The limit of their excursions was fixed by the fact that Wilson's brigade of Portuguese militia still lay at Espinhal, and, though it was reduced by desertion and sickness to 1,500 men, was reported to Montbrun as a serious force, with which he had better not meddle. Trant's troops at Coimbra—a weak militia division—were also estimated at much over their real strength. It was not till later that sheer starvation drove the French further afield, and revealed to them the weakness of the *cordon* of inferior troops which hemmed them in upon the northern side.

The blockade of the French army, therefore, remained still unbroken, and its communication with the north was as absolutely interrupted in the end of November as in the beginning of October. One attempt to break through the screen of Portuguese irregulars had been made in November, but of its failure Masséna had as yet no knowledge. When Foy reached Rodrigo, on his way to Paris, he had handed over his escort of one battalion of infantry and 120 horsemen to General Gardanne, who was ordered to strengthen them with all the convalescents of the Army of Portugal, and with the garrisons of Almeida and Rodrigo also, if these last had now been relieved by troops of Drouet's 9th Corps. At the head of 6,000 men, as Masséna calculated, he could cut his way to join the main army, escorting a great train of munitions, of which both the artillery and the infantry at the front were lamentably in need. Gardanne could not gather in the Almeida garrison, as that place was still blockaded by Silveira's Portuguese. But with the two battalions from Rodrigo, added to Foy's late escort, and a mass of convalescents, he had collected some 5,000 men by November 20 [1], the day on which he marched by the Sabugal–Belmonte–Fundão route towards Punhete and the lower Zezere. He was cursed with dreadful weather, followed and harassed by all the Ordenança of the Castello Branco country, hampered by his heavy convoy, and much troubled by the disorderly convalescents, who were largely professional malingerers. But he got as far as Cardigos on the Sobreira–Formosa road, only fifteen miles from Punhete, where Loison was awaiting him on the Zezere. Here he was brought to a stand (November 27) by the flooded and bridgeless stream of the Codes. No news had reached him from Masséna, while he was assured by Portuguese deserters, who probably were sent out to deceive him by the governor of Abrantes, that the Marshal had not only evacuated his position before the Lines, but was retreating on Spain via the Mondego. They added that Hill had just reached Abrantes with 10,000 men, and was about to march against him. Thereupon Gardanne hastily turned back, reached Penamacor by forced marches on

---

[1] Belmas's figures (i. 137) given here must be about correct, not the 2,000 of Fririon, and *Victoires et Conquêtes*. For the two Rodrigo battalions were 1,500 strong, Foy's escort 600, and Gardanne took with him some of his own dragoon regiment, beside the convalescents.

November 29, and from thence retired to Rodrigo, having lost 400 men and 300 horses by disease and fatigue during his ill-conducted expedition. If he had pushed forward fifteen miles further on the 28th, he would have got into touch with Loison, and reached Masséna's head quarters in safety. Wellington, not without reason, professed himself unable to comprehend this strange march and countermarch. 'I do not exactly understand this movement [1],' and 'if this march was ordered by superior authority, and was connected with any other arrangements, it had every appearance of, and was attended by all the consequences of, a precipitate and forced retreat [2].'

Here, then, we leave Masséna and his army, cantoned in the space between the Rio Mayor and the Zezere, still destitute of news from France, and still entirely ignorant whether or no any endeavour was being made to relieve them. Of their further doings during the three months that ended on March 1, 1811, we shall tell elsewhere. Suffice it to say that, despite many dangers and risks, Wellington's scheme of starvation was played out to the end, and achieved complete success. Of the privation and losses that the French suffered, and the atrocities that they committed, of the difficulties of the British Commander-in-Chief —with an obstinate enemy still in front of him, a factious Regency and a half-starved population behind him in Lisbon, and a disquieting prospect that Soult might take a hand in the game—the fourth volume of this work will give full details.

[1] *Dispatches*, vii. p. 20, to Craufurd.
[2] Ibid., p. 36, to Lord Liverpool.

SECTION XXII

END OF THE YEAR 1810

CHAPTER I

OPERATIONS IN THE NORTH AND EAST

While tracing the all-important Campaign of Portugal, down to the deadlock in front of Santarem, which began about the 20th of November, 1810, and was to endure till the 1st of March in the succeeding year, we have been obliged to leave untouched events, civil and military, in many other parts of the Peninsula during the autumn. Only the Andalusian campaigns have been carried down to November : in Northern Spain we have traced the course of affairs no further than September[1] : in Eastern Spain no further than August[2]. Moreover, little has been said of the general effect on the French occupation caused by the division of supreme authority which Napoleon sanctioned in the spring[3], or of the importance of the long-deferred meeting of the Spanish Cortes, which assembled at Cadiz in the autumn. With these points we must deal before proceeding to narrate the campaigns of 1811.

The survey of the military operations, none of which were particularly important, must precede the summary of the political situation, with regard to King Joseph on the one side and the Cortes on the other. For the acts of the King and the Cortes had an influence extending far beyond the months in which they began, and were, indeed, main factors in the Peninsular struggle for years to come. But the doings of the armies in Galicia and Asturias on the one flank, in Catalonia and Valencia on the other, can easily be dismissed in a few pages : they were but preliminaries to the greater operations in the spring of 1811.

We may first turn to the north-west. When Masséna

[1] See pp. 270–1.   [2] See pp. 200–1 and 315–16.   [3] See pp. 312–14.

plunged into Portugal in September 1810, and was lost to the sight of his colleagues and subordinates for nearly three months, the situation left behind him was as follows :—Leon and Old Castille, as far as the Galician foot-hills and the Cantabrian sierras, were held down by Serras and Kellermann with some 12,000 men—a force none too great for the task that lay before them. The latter general had charge of the provinces of Valladolid, Toro, and Palencia, as one of the ' military governors ' recently appointed by the Emperor. He gave himself absurd airs of independent authority, and took little more heed of the orders of Masséna than of those of King Joseph, for whom he showed a supreme contempt. General Serras's troops were more definitely part of the Army of Portugal. They were in charge of the provinces of Zamora, Leon, and Salamanca, thus covering Kellermann's government on the outer flank, and taking care of the borders both of Galicia on the Spanish and of Tras-os-Montes on the Portuguese side. To cover this long front Serras had only eleven battalions [1], and two provisional regiments of dragoons—some 9,000 men. Out of this force he had to find garrisons for Astorga, Leon, Benevente, Zamora, and several smaller places. Kellermann, who was intended to serve as a reserve for Serras, as well as to guard the central depôts at Valladolid, had only two regiments of dragoons (part of his original division) and three infantry battalions, making 3,000 men in all [2]. Both of them were directed to keep in close touch with Bonnet, who, at the head of his old troops, the four regiments which never came south of the Cantabrian hills till the Salamanca campaign [3], kept a precarious hold on Central and Eastern Asturias with 9,000 men.

There were also present in the circumscription of Serras's and Kellermann's command the garrison of Ciudad Rodrigo (two battalions) and Gardanne's five squadrons of dragoons, which

---

[1] Viz. 113th Line (2 batts.), 4th of the Vistula (2 batts.), one battalion each of the 12th Léger and 32nd and 58th Line, four ' provisional battalions ' (Nos. 2, 4, 5, 7), and two provisional regiments of dragoons. Total on Sept. 15, 9,524 men, of whom 1,000 were cavalry.

[2] Two Swiss battalions, one battalion of the Garde de Paris, and the 5th and 17th dragoons. Total, 1,300 cavalry and 1,700 infantry.

[3] Line regiments (each of 4 batts.), Nos. 118, 119, 120, 122, and a squadron of the 21st Chasseurs, 9,298 men.

Masséna had left behind, in the vain hope that they would keep the line clear between Almeida and Salamanca. This force added 2,500 men to the total of the French troops in Leon.

If the French were left rather weak in this direction, the same was not the case in the region further east. From Burgos to the Bidassoa the country-side was full of troops in the latter half of September, when the Army of Portugal had gone westward. In the Government of Burgos were the two infantry divisions of the Young Guard, under Roguet and Dumoustier, with their two cavalry regiments, making 11,464 sabres and bayonets. Navarre was occupied by 8,733 men, Biscay by 8,085. The little province of Santander was held by three provisional battalions 3,500 strong. But this permanent garrison, making over 31,000 men, was at the moment supplemented by Drouet's 9th Corps, for whose arrival at the front Masséna had waited so long and so vainly. On September 15 its commander, its head quarters, and Claparéde's division, were at Vittoria : Couroux's division and the cavalry brigade of Fournier were echelloned between Vittoria and Bayonne. The whole corps mustered over 18,000 sabres and bayonets. Fifty thousand men, therefore, adding the permanent garrisons to the advancing corps of Drouet, were between Burgos and Bayonne, and there were yet a few more troops to come forward from the interior of France, for Caffarelli was bringing up another division, which had the official title of the 'Division of Reserve of the Army of Spain,' and consisted of four provisional regiments of infantry and two cavalry regiments, with a strength of 8,000 men [1]. It was ordered to be at Bayonne by October 20, and formed the nucleus of the force which in the next year was styled the ' Army of the North '.

Without counting this last unit, which was only in process of formation in September, Napoleon had between the Galician frontier and Bayonne no less than 72,000 men [2]. What had

---

[1] See *Correspondance*, xxi. 106. On Sept. 13, the date of the dispatch creating Caffarelli's division, one of its regiments was forming at Limoges, another at Blois, another at Bordeaux, the fourth at Orleans.

[2] Viz. Kellermann, 3,000 ; Serras, 9,000 ; Bonnet, 8,000 ; Young Guard, 11,500 ; Biscay, 8,000 ; Navarre, 8,500 ; Santander, 3,500 ; 9th Corps, 18,000 ; Masséna's Garrisons, 2,500.

his enemies to oppose to this formidable host, whose strength was considerably greater than that of the force with which Masséna invaded Portugal ? Of regularly organized troops the number of Spaniards and Portuguese opposed to them was absolutely insignificant. Silveira in the Tras-os-Montes had six regiments of militia and one of the line—this last being the 24th, the absconding garrison of Almeida. The whole made under 7,000 men, including an incomplete cavalry regiment. Mahy in Galicia had recruited up the depleted divisions which La Romana had left with him in the spring to a strength of 12,000 men, mostly raw and untrustworthy; for the best regiments had been destroyed at the siege of Astorga. The remains of the army of Asturias, which had suffered so many defeats at the hands of Bonnet during the spring and summer, consisted of about 6,000 men, of whom half, under Barcena and Losada, were holding the western end of the province, behind the Navia river, with head quarters at Castropol, while the rest lurked in the higher valleys of the Cantabrian Sierra, rendering Bonnet's communication with Serras in Leon insecure, and sometimes descending to the coast, to make a sudden attack on one of the small garrisons which linked the French garrison in Oviedo with that at Santander. Of these roving bands the chief leader was the adventurous Porlier, the *Marquesito* [1], as the Asturians called him, who won a well-deserved reputation for his perseverance and never-failing courage. The 25,000 men of Silveira, Mahy, and the Asturian army were the only regular troops opposed to the 75,000 French in Northern Spain. How came it, then, that the enemy was held in check, and never succeeded in pushing on to the support of Masséna any force save the two divisions of Drouet ? The answer is simple : the French garrisons were fixed down to their positions partly because of Napoleon's entire lack of naval power, partly because of the unceasing activity of the guerrilleros, who were far more busy in 1810 than at any preceding time. As to the first-named cause, it may be said that the 20,000 French in Asturias, Santander, and Biscay were paralysed by the existence of a small Anglo-Spanish squadron based on Corunna and Ferrol. As long as this existed, every small port along the whole

[1] As being nephew to the Marquis of La Romana.

northern coast of Spain had to be garrisoned, under penalty of a possible descent from the sea, which might cut the road from Oviedo to San Sebastian at any one of a hundred points, and provide arms and stores for the guerrilla bands of the mountains. Many such expeditions were carried out with more or less success in 1810. The first and most prosperous of them took place in July, when Porlier, putting his free corps of some 1,000 men on transports, and convoyed by the British commodore Mends, with a couple of frigates, came ashore near the important harbour of Santona, drove out the small garrison, and then coasted along in the direction of Biscay, destroying shore-batteries and capturing as many as 200 men at one point and another. Of the peasantry of the coast, some enlisted in Porlier's band, others took to the hills on their own account, when they had been furnished with muskets from the ships. The Marquesito repeated his raid in August, but this time stopped on shore, and put himself at the head of the local insurgents, who made so strong a head in the country about Potes and the upper Pisuerga, that Serras marched against him with almost the whole of his division [1], and spent September in hunting him along the sides of the sierras. But though aided by troops lent by Bonnet, and by detachments from Burgos, the French general could never catch the adroit partisan, who, when too hard pressed, returned to the central mountains of the Asturias.

Pleased with the exploits of Porlier, the Cadiz Regency resolved to keep up the game, and sent up to Corunna Colonel Renovales, the officer who had for so long made head against Suchet in the mountains of Aragon [2]. He was authorized to requisition a brigade from Mahy's army, and the more sea-worthy ships from the arsenal of Ferrol. Applications for naval assistance had also been made to the British Admiralty, and Sir Home Popham came, with four frigates and a battalion of marines, to assist in a systematic raid along the coasts of Asturias and Biscay. The joint expedition started from Corunna on October 14, with a landing force of 1,200 Spanish and 800 British bayonets on board. On the 16th it drew in to

[1] See pp. 270–1.   [2] See pp. 10–11.

land near the important harbour of Gijon, where Bonnet kept a force of 700 men, who depended for their succour on the main body of his division at Oviedo. But the French general chanced to be hunting Porlier further to the east, and had left the Asturian capital almost ungarrisoned. Hence, when Porlier unexpectedly appeared before Gijon on the inland side, having eluded his pursuer, and the ships threw the landing force ashore, the French battalion had to fly. Several ships, both privateers and merchantmen, with a considerable amount of military stores, fell into the hands of Porlier and Renovales. This exploit drew down on them the whole French force in the Asturias, for Bonnet concentrated every man and musket on Gijon. But the Anglo-Spanish squadron, having thus drawn him westward, sailed in the opposite direction, and, after threatening Santona, was about to touch at Vivero, when it was scattered by a hurricane from the Bay of Biscay. A Spanish frigate and brig, an English brig, and several gunboats and transports were dashed on the rocky coast, and lost with all hands. This disaster, which cost 800 lives, compelled Renovales to return to Corunna (November 2). But the raid had not been useless ; it had compelled Bonnet to evacuate many posts, distracted the garrisons of Santander and Biscay, and even induced Caffarelli to march down to the coast with his newly-arrived division, the 'Reserve of the Army of Spain.' Serras, too, had drawn up the greater part of his scattered division to the north-west, thus leaving the borders of Galicia and the Tras-os-Montes hardly watched. This enabled Mahy to send down troops into the plain of Leon, and to establish something like a blockade around Astorga. But all the operations of the Captain-General of Galicia were feeble and tentative. He passed among his countrymen as an easy-going man, destitute of energy or initiative [1]. Silveira, in the Tras-os-Montes, a more active but a more dangerous man to entrust with troops, took advantage of Serras's absence to cross the Douro, invest Almeida, and cut the communication between that place and Ciudad Rodrigo [2].

Such was the effect of the sea-power, even when it was used sparingly and by unskilful hands. The raids along the northern

[1] See for this verdict both Arteche and Toreno.   [2] See p. 447.

coast had kept Bonnet and the troops in Santander and Biscay
fully employed; they had distracted Serras, Caffarelli, and even
the garrisons of the province of Burgos. They had saved Mahy
and Silveira from attack, and had lighted up a blaze of insurrection in the western hills of Cantabria which, thanks
to the energy of Porlier and his colleague Louga, was never
extinguished.

Meanwhile the mass of French troops between Burgos and
Pampeluna—the 9th Corps, the Young Guard Divisions, and
the garrison in Navarre—had been 'contained' by an enemy of
a different sort. Here the influence of the British naval supremacy was little felt : it was due to the energy of Spaniards alone
that the 38,000 men under Drouet, Roguet and Dumoustier, and
Reille were prevented during the months of September, October,
and November from doing anything to help Masséna. Old
Castile, Navarre, and the lands of the Upper Ebro, were kept in
a constant turmoil by a score of guerrillero chiefs, of whom
the elder Mina was the leading figure. We have already had
occasion to speak of the exploits of his relative, 'the Student'
as he was called, to distinguish him from his uncle, and have
noted his final capture by Suchet [1]. Francisco Espoy y Mina
had rallied the relics of his nephew's band, and began his long
career of raids and countermarches in April 1810. His central
place of refuge was the rough country on the borders of Navarre
and Aragon, where he kept his main depôt at the head of the
valley of Roncal; but he often ranged as far afield as Biscay
and the provinces of Soria and Burgos. Almost from his first
appearance he obtained a mastery over the other chiefs who
operated on both sides of the Upper Ebro, having won his place
by the summary process of seizing and shooting one Echeverria,
'who,' as he writes, 'was the terror of the villages of Navarre,
which he oppressed and plundered in a thousand ways, till they
complained to me concerning him. I arrested him at Estella on
June 13, 1810, caused him to be shot with three of his principal
accomplices, and incorporated his band (600 foot and 200 horse)
with my own men [2].' Mina was the special enemy of Reille,

[1] See p. 286.
[2] See Mina's *Extracto de su Vida*, published in London, during his
exile, in 1825.

then commanding in Navarre, but he also attracted the attention of Drouet, one of whose divisions was entirely absorbed in
hunting him during the autumn of 1810. This was the main
cause of the non-appearance of the 9th Corps at Rodrigo and
Salamanca, when Masséna was so anxiously awaiting its arrival.
Mina's lot during this period was no enviable one: he was beset
on all sides by flying columns, and was often forced to bid his
band disperse and lurk in small parties in the mountains, till the
enemy should have passed on. Sometimes he was lurking, with
seven companions only, in a cave or a gorge: at another he
would be found with 3,000 men, attacking large convoys, or even
surprising one of the blockhouses with which the French tried
to cover his whole sphere of activity. The Regency, admiring
his perseverance, gave him, in September, the title of ' Colonel
and Commandant-General of all the Guerrilleros of Navarre.'
He asserts with pride, in his memoir, that he was at one and the
same time being hunted by Dorsenne, commanding at Burgos,
Reille from Navarre, Caffarrelli and his ' division of Reserve of
the Army of Spain,' by D'Agoult, Governor of Pampeluna,
Roguet, commanding the Young Guard, and Paris, one of
Suchet's brigadiers from the Army of Aragon. Yet none of the
six generals, though they had 18,000 men marching through
his special district, succeeded in catching him, or destroying any
appreciable fraction of his band.

There is no exaggeration in this ; his services were invaluable
during the campaign of Portugal, since he was wearing out a
French force of five times his own strength in fruitless marches,
under winter rains, and over roads that had become all but
impassable. The archives of the French War Office show lists
of officers by the dozen killed or wounded ' dans une reconnaissance en Navarre,' or ' dans une rencontre avec les bandes de
Mina,' or ' en combat près de Pampelune,' during the later
months of 1810. Wellington owed him no small gratitude, and
expressed it to him in 1813, when he entrusted him with much
responsible work during the Campaign of the Pyrenees. The
suffering inflicted on the provinces of the Upper Ebro by Mina's
activity was of course terrible: the French destroyed every
village that sheltered him or furnished him with recruits, and
were wont to shoot every prisoner from his band that they

caught, till he began to retaliate by corresponding or greater numbers of executions from the considerable number of prisoners in his hands. In 1811 this barbarous system was in full swing on both sides, but it was put to an end by mutual agreement in 1812. In addition to the woes that Navarre and its neighbours suffered under the French martial law, and by the monstrous requisitions imposed upon them to feed the mass of troops forming the flying columns, they had also to maintain the patriotic bands. Mina declares that he always took rations for his men, but avoided levying money contributions on the peasantry, depending on his booty, the rents of national and ecclesiastical property, on which he laid hands, on fines inflicted on 'bad Spaniards,' i.e. those who had done anything to help his pursuers, and on ' the custom-houses which I established upon the very frontier of France ; for I laid under contribution even the French custom-house at Irun, on the Bidassoa, which engaged to deliver, and actually paid to my delegates, 100 gold ounces (about £320) per month.' By this strange secret agreement private goods passing Irun and the other frontier posts were guaranteed against capture in the district which Mina's bands infested [1].

Eastward of Mina's sphere of activity the guerrilleros were more numerous but less powerful. Among the chief of them was Julian Sanchez, who, with a mounted band of 300 to 500 lancers—infantry would have been easily caught in the plain of Leon—busied himself in cutting the communication between Salamanca, Ciudad Rodrigo, Zamora, and Valladolid, and was Kellermann's chief tormentor. He was in regular communication with Wellington, and sent him many captured dispatches and useful pieces of information. In Old Castile the priest Geronimo Merino, generally known as ' El Cura,' was the most famous and most active among many leaders. It was his band, aided by that of Tapia, also a cleric, which on July 10, 1810, fought a most daring and desperate action at Almazan, near Soria, with two French battalions of marines, who were marching, the one to join Masséna the other to join Soult. It cost the enemy no less than 13 officers *hors de combat*, as the Paris

---

[1] Mina's *Breve Extracto*, p. 39.

archives show [1], and over 200 men, though the guerrilleros were
finally beaten off. In October he surprised and captured an
enormous convoy of corn and munitions of war, whose loss put
the French garrison of Burgos in considerable straits for some
weeks. He waged with Dorsenne the same horrible contest of
retaliation in the shooting of prisoners which Mina was at the
same time carrying on with the generals in Navarre. There
were many other bands in Old Castile, those of Abril, Tenderin,
Saornil, Principe, and others, of whom some are accused by their
own colleagues of being more harmful to the country-side than
to the French, from their reckless and miscellaneous plundering,
and their refusal to combine for any systematic action [2]. Yet
even the worst of them contributed to distract the activity of
the French garrisons, and to retard the communication of dispatches and the march of isolated detachments. Under the
easy excuse that it was dangerous to move any small body of
men along the high-roads, the French commanders of every
small town or blockhouse detained for weeks, and even months,
drafts on their way to the south or the west, with the result that
the number of recruits received at Madrid, Seville, or Salamanca
never bore any proper proportion to the total that had crossed
the Bidassoa.

Northward from Old Castile, on the skirts of the mountains
of Santander and Biscay, the dominating personality among the
guerrilleros was Louga, who afterwards rose to some distinction
as a commander of regular troops. His special task was the
cutting of the communications between Burgos and Bilbao, and
Bilbao and Santander ; but he often co-operated with Porlier,
when that restless partisan made one of his descents from the
Asturian mountains, either on to the coast region or on the
southern skirts of the Cantabrian sierras.

On the whole, there were probably never more than 20,000
guerrilleros in arms at once, in the whole region between the
Sierra de Guadarrama and the shore of the Bay of Biscay. They
never succeeded in beating any French force more than two or

---

[1] Martinien's lists show seven officers hit in the 44th Equipage de
Marine, which joined Masséna in the next month, and six in the Bataillon
D'Espagne, which was on its way to Cadiz.

[2] See Arteche, ix. 241.

three battalions strong, and were being continually hunted from
corner to corner.   Yet, despite their weakness in the open field,
their intestine quarrels, their frequent oppression of the country-
side, and their ferocity, they rendered good service to Spain, and
incidentally to Great Britain and to all Europe, by pinning
down to the soil twice their own numbers of good French troops.
Any one who has read the dispatches of the commandants of
Napoleon's ' military governments,' or the diaries of the officers
who served in Reille's or Dorsenne's or Caffarelli's flying columns,
will recognize a remarkable likeness between the situation of
affairs in Northern Spain during 1810 and 1811 and that in
South Africa during 1900 and 1901.   Lightly moving guerrilla
bands, unhampered by a base to defend or a train to weigh them
down, and well served as to intelligence by the residents of the
country-side, can paralyse the action of an infinitely larger
number of regular troops.

In the north-east of Spain, where the French were engaged
not with mere scattered bands of guerrilleros, but with two
regular armies, O'Donnell's Catalans and Caro's Valencians, the
fortune of war took no decisive turn during the autumn of 1810,
though one dreadful blow to the Spanish cause—the loss of
Tortosa—was to fall in the winter which followed.

We left Suchet in August 1810, established in his newly-
conquered positions at Lerida and Mequinenza, master of all the
plainland of Aragon, as well as of a strip of Western Catalonia,
and only waiting for the co-operation of Macdonald and the
7th Corps to recommence his operations [1].   That co-operation,
however, was long denied him.   The Emperor's last general
orders, which had reached Suchet in June, briefly prescribed to
him that the conquest of the city and kingdom of Valencia was
his final object, but that he must first break the Spanish line by
capturing Tortosa, the great fortress of the Lower Ebro, and
Tarragona, the main stronghold of Southern Catalonia [2].   For
both these latter operations he was to count on the aid of Macdonald and the Army of Catalonia [3].   Relying on this support,
Suchet, after less than a month had elapsed since the capture of
Mequinenza, had pushed his advanced guard down the Ebro,

[1] See pp. 300-9.   [2] *Correspondance* under May 29.
[3] *Correspondance* under Sept. 16.

till it was at the very gates of Tortosa. One detachment even
passed the town, and seized the ferry of Amposta, the only
passage of the Ebro near its mouth, actually cutting the great
road from Tarragona to Valencia, and only leaving the bridge
of Tortosa itself open, for the linking of the operations of Caro
and O'Donnell. Meanwhile Suchet was preparing his siege-train
at Mequinenza, and waiting for a rise in the Ebro, which would
commence to become navigable with the arrival of the autumn
rains, in order to ship his guns down-stream to their destined
goal. He was at the same time making the land route to Tortosa
passable, by repairing the old military road from Caspe to Mora
and Tivisa, which had been constructed during the wars of the
Spanish Succession, but had long ago fallen into ruin.

Suchet was quite aware that by thrusting a comparatively
small force—he had only brought up 12,000 men—into the near
neighbourhood of Tortosa, he was risking the danger of being
attacked at once by the Army of Valencia from the south and
O'Donnell's Catalans from the north. But he trusted that Macdonald and the 7th Corps would keep the latter—the more formidable enemy—employed, while he had a well-founded contempt
for the generalship of Caro, who had always proved himself the
most incompetent and timid of commanders. But Macdonald
arrived late, having been forced to spend the whole summer, as
has been already related [1], in his triple revictualling of Barcelona,
and meanwhile the Valencian army came to the front. Its
leading division, under Bassecourt, threatened Morella, on
Suchet's flank, early in August, hoping to draw him away to
defend this outpost. But a single brigade under Montmarie
sufficed to turn back the Valencian detachment, and Suchet
kept his positions. O'Donnell meanwhile, vainly hoping for
solid help from Caro, had joined the division of his army which
was kept at Falcet [2], and after threatening Suchet's head
quarters at Mora on July 30, so as to distract his attention,
suddenly turned aside and entered Tortosa with 2,500 men.
Calling out all the troops available for a sortie, he issued from
the town on August 3, and beat up the outposts of the division
under Laval, which was in observation before his gates. But
though the Catalans fought fiercely, and drove in the first

[1] See p. 311.   [2] See p. 313.

French line, they were not strong enough to push the enemy
away from Tortosa.   O'Donnell should have brought a heavier
force if he intended to accomplish his end.   Shortly after he
returned to Tarragona, whither he was called by the movements
of Macdonald.

Some days later than he had covenanted, Caro came up to
Vinaros, on the coast-road from Valencia, and to San Mateo
on the parallel inland road, with his whole army, including the
force which Bassecourt had been commanding.   It consisted of
no more than 10,000 ill-organized troops of the Line, who had
been joined by nearly as many unregimented peasants in loose
guerrilla bands.   The whole mass was far from being formidable,
as Suchet knew.   Wherefore the French general, cutting down
to the smallest possible figure the containing troops left before
Tortosa, and at his head quarters at Mora, marched with eleven
battalions and a cavalry regiment—only 6,000 men in all—to
meet the Valencians.   He drove their advanced cavalry from
Vinaros, and advanced against their positions at Calig and
Cervera del Maestre.   Caro at once ordered a precipitate
retreat, and did not stop till he had placed thirty miles between
himself and the enemy.   His obvious terror and dismay at
the approach of the French roused such anger that he was
summoned to give up the command by his own officers, and
obeyed without hesitation [1].   He fled by sea to Majorca,
knowing, it is said, that he would have been torn to pieces
if he had shown his face before the populace at Valencia, over
which he had exercised a sort of dictatorship for more than
a year.   Suchet, unable to catch such an evasive enemy, and
regarding the routed army as a negligible quantity, returned
to Mora, where he received the news that the long-expected
Macdonald was at last about to appear (August 20).

The Duke of Tarentum had thrown the third and last of his
great convoys into Barcelona on the 18th of August, having
brought with him as its escort the French division of his army,
which was now commanded by Frére [2], and the Italian divisions

[1] For details see Arteche, ix. 267, Schepeler, iv. 659-60, and Suchet's
Mémoires, vol. i. p. 193.   The dictator's own brother, General Juan Caro,
was one of those who deposed him.

[2] Vice Souham, wounded at Vich, and Augereau recalled.

of Severoli and Pignatelli. He had left behind him General
Baraguay d'Hilliers, in the position which Reille had been
wont to hold, as the defender of the Ampurdam and Northern
Catalonia as far as Hostalrich. Eighteen thousand men were
told off for this task, including all the German brigades; but
after garrisoning Gerona, Rosas, Figueras, and Hostalrich,
d'Hilliers had no great field-force left, and found full employment in warding off the raids of Manso, Rovira, and the other
miquelete leaders upon the communication between Gerona and
Perpignan. Nearly 10,000 men had also been left in Barcelona,
including many sick, and the three divisions with which Macdonald marched to join Suchet did not exceed 16,000 sabres
and bayonets, though the whole force of the 7th Corps was
reckoned at over 50,000 men.

On August 13 Macdonald forced the Pass of Ordal, after
some skirmishing with the somatenes, and entered the plain
of Tarragona. It was the news of his approach to the Catalan
capital which brought O'Donnell back in haste from Tortosa.
He concentrated the greater part of his troops, on the hypothesis that the 7th Corps might be intending to lay siege to the
place. He brought down Campoverde's division from the north to
join those of Ibarrola, Sarsfield, and the Baron de Eroles, which
were already on the spot. It soon became known, however,
to the Spaniards that Macdonald could not be bent on siege
operations, for he was bringing with him neither the heavy
artillery nor the enormous train of provisions that would be
required in such a case. He marched past Reus and Valls to
Momblanch, skirmishing all the way with O'Donnell's detachments, and thence to Lerida, which he reached on August 29.
There he found Suchet awaiting him for a conference. The
orders from Paris, on which both were acting, seemed to
prescribe that Tortosa and Tarragona should both be attacked [1].
But the General and the Marshal agreed that their joint
strength was not more than enough for one siege at a time.
They agreed that the 3rd Corps should undertake the leaguer
of Tortosa, and ' the containing' of the Valencian army, while
the 7th should cover these operations by keeping O'Donnell and

---

[1] See Suchet's *Mémoires*, i. 196–7, and the dispatch from Napoleon's
Correspondance of July 25, 1810.

the Catalans fully employed.   Suchet therefore drew his detachments southward from Lerida and the plains of the Segre,
handing over all that tract to Macdonald.   From this fertile
region alone could the Marshal have fed his corps, Central
Catalonia being barren, and so overrun by O'Donnell's detachments that it was impossible to forage freely within its bounds.
Suchet undertook to provide for his own corps during the
siege of Tortosa by bringing up stores from Saragossa and the
valley of the Ebro, via Mequinenza.   Macdonald lent him,
meanwhile, the weakest of his three divisions, 2,500 Neapolitans under Pignatelli, who were to escort the siege-train for
Tortosa along the Ebro, when the autumn rains made the river
navigable from Mequinenza to the sea.

While Suchet was moving southward and making ready for
the siege, the Duke of Tarentum established himself with head
quarters at Cervera on the Barcelona–Lerida road, and brigades
at Lerida, Agramunt, and Tarrega, all in the plain ; he was
ready to fall upon O'Donnell's flank if the Catalans should
make any attempt to succour Tortosa, by marching from
Tarragona along the roads parallel to the sea coast.   Meanwhile he had completely lost touch both with the garrison
of Barcelona and with Baraguay d'Hilliers in the Ampurdam.
This was the regular state of things during the Catalan war ;
for if the French left detachments to guard a line of communication, they were invariably cut off by the enemy ; while, if
they did not, the roads were blocked and no information came
through.   So vigorous were the somatenes at this moment, that
small parties moving from Tarrega to Cervera,—places only
twelve miles apart, and in the middle of the cantonments of
the 7th Corps,—were not unfrequently waylaid and destroyed.
Macdonald, despite his well-known humanity, was forced to
burn villages, and shoot roadside assassins caught red-handed.
He lay in the position which he had taken up on September
4–6 for the greater part of that month and the succeeding
October, concentrating at intervals a part of his forces for an
expedition into the hills, when the Catalans pressed him too
closely.   At the commencement of his sojourn in the plains, he
sent Severoli with an Italian brigade to collect provisions in the
valley of the Noguera Palleresa.   This raid led to dreadful

1

2

3

Dollar of Ferdinand VII
struck at Lima

Portuguese Cruzado Novo
of the Regent João

Double Vintem of the Regent
João (copper)

4

Gold Dollar of Charles IIII

5

6

7

Dollar of Charles IIII counter-marked
with head of George III and current
both in Spain and Great Britain

The 'Military Guinea' struck for
the Peninsular Army in 1813

Dollar of Ferdinand VII
struck at Mexico 1810

COINS CURRENT IN SPAIN AND PORTUGAL IN 1808–14

ravaging of the country-side, but Severoli returned with no
spoil and many wounded. He had pushed his advance as far
as Talarn, skirmishing the whole way, and driving the somatenes before him, but could accomplish nothing save the burning
of poor villages evacuated by their inhabitants. A week later
other expeditions scoured the mountain sides eastward, with
little more success[1].

Meanwhile, though Macdonald imagined that he was not only
protecting Suchet's northern flank, but also attracting the
attention of O'Donnell to himself, the enterprising Spanish
general had contrived an unwelcome surprise for him. He
knew that he was not strong enough to fight the 7th Corps
in the open field, nor even to face Suchet by making another
attempt to relieve Tortosa—which place, for the moment, was
in no immediate danger. He therefore resolved to draw
Macdonald from his present position, by a blow at the corner
of Catalonia where the French were weakest.

The Marshal considered that Baraguay d'Hilliers was perfectly safe in the northern region which he garrisoned, since no
regular Spanish force was now in arms in that direction.
O'Donnell resolved to undeceive him. Leaving the two divisions
of Obispo and Eroles to block the road from Macdonald's post
at Cervera to Barcelona, with orders to retire into Tarragona
if hard pressed, he ordered a third division, that of Campoverde, to prepare for a forced march to the north. At the
same time a force, consisting of the British frigate *Cambrian*
and the Spanish frigate *Diana*, convoying a few transports
with 500 men on board for disembarkation, sailed from Tarragona, for a destination which was kept secret to the last
moment. The troops were under Doyle, the British com-
missioner in Catalonia; Captain Fane of the *Cambrian* was
senior naval officer.

O'Donnell's march was perilous: he had to pass close to the
front of the garrisons of Barcelona, Hostalrich, and Gerona,
through a most difficult and mountainous country, without
giving any signs of his presence; for, if his movement were
discovered, Baraguay d'Hilliers might concentrate his scattered
brigades, and crush him by force of numbers. The march, how-

---

[1] For details see Vacani, iv. pp. 307–8.

ever, was carried out with complete success, and on September 13 O'Donnell lay with 6,000 infantry and 400 horse at Vidreras, south of Gerona, while the naval force was hovering off Palamos, the nearest point on the coast. The rough region between Gerona and the sea was at this moment occupied by half Rouyer's division of troops of the Confederation of the Rhine, under Schwartz—the ever-unlucky general whose name was connected with the disasters of Bruch [1] and Manresa [2]. He had with him four weak battalions of the 5th (Anhalt–Lippe) and 6th (Schwartzburg–Waldeck–Reuss) regiments, and a squadron of cuirassiers : a force which, owing to the sickliness of the autumn season, did not amount to much more than 1,500 men in all. But he was so close to Gerona [3], where lay Rouyer's other two regiments, and some French troops, that he was not considered in any danger by his superiors. Schwartz's main duty was to prevent any communication between the somatenes of the inland and the cruisers which were always passing up and down the coast. Provoked by a recent raid at Bagur, on September 10, where an English landing-party had stormed one of his coast batteries, and captured the garrison of 50 men, Schwartz had just strengthened all his posts along the shore. He had only 700 men at his head quarters at La Bispal; the rest were dispersed between Bagur, San Feliu, Palamos, and the connecting post at Calonje. On the morning of the fourteenth he was stricken with horror when his outposts informed him that they had been driven in by Spanish infantry and cavalry in overwhelming force. He sent orders, too late, for his troops on the coast to concentrate, and prepared to fall back on Gerona with his whole force. But his messenger had hardly gone when he was attacked by O'Donnell, who drove him into the indefensible castle of La Bispal, which was commanded by a neighbouring hill and the church tower of the village. After losing some men shot down from these points of vantage, Schwartz surrendered at nightfall, when the Spaniards were preparing to storm his refuge. His defence cannot have been very desperate, as he had lost only one officer and four men killed, and three officers and sixteen men wounded.

[1] See vol. i. p. 311.　　　　[2] See this vol. p. 295.
[3] Only about eighteen miles distant.

But this was only part of the disaster which befell the German brigade that day: by a careful timing of the attacks Doyle and Fane stormed Palamos with the landing-force at the same moment that La Bispal was being attacked, while Colonel Fleires, with a detachment of O'Donnell's land troops, surprised San Feliu, and Colonel Aldea with another cut off the companies at Calonje. In all the Spaniards captured on that day one general, two colonels, fifty-six officers, and 1,183 rank and file, with seventeen guns. Schwartz's brigade was absolutely destroyed; only a few stragglers reached Gerona, from which no help had been sent, because O'Donnell had turned loose all the somatenes of the region to demonstrate against the place [1].

Without waiting for Rouyer and Baraguay d'Hilliers to assemble their forces, O'Donnell departed from the scene of his exploits without delay. He himself, having received a severe wound in the foot, embarked with the prisoners on board Fane's ships and returned to Tarragona. Campoverde, with the land-force, retired hastily past Gerona to the mountains of the north, retook Puycerda, beat up the outposts of the French garrison of Montlouis on the frontier of Cerdagne, and raised some contributions on the other side of the Pyrenees. From thence he descended the Segre, and established himself at Cardona and Calaf, facing Macdonald's northern flank.

So thoroughly had the main body of the 7th Corps lost touch with the troops left behind at Gerona and in the Ampurdam, that the news of the disaster of La Bispal only reached Macdonald, via France and Saragossa, more than a fortnight after it had happened. It alarmed him for the safety of the north, but did not suffice to draw him away from Suchet, as O'Donnell had hoped. The news that the Spanish raiding division had disappeared from the neighbourhood of Gerona encouraged him to remain in his present position, which alone made the siege of Tortosa possible. Presently he was informed that a considerable force had appeared in his own sphere of operations—this being the same division of Campoverde which had done all the mischief in the north. He therefore marched

---

[1] The best narrative of Schwartz's disaster may be found in the diary of the Lippe-Bückeburg officer Barkhausen, one of the prisoners, pp. 110-15.

on October 18, with two French and two Italian brigades, to attack this new enemy.   On the next day he occupied Solsona, where the Junta of Upper Catalonia had hitherto been sitting. The place was found deserted by its inhabitants, and was plundered; its great cathedral was burnt—either by accident or design.   On the twenty-first, however, when the Marshal came in front of Cardona, he found the town, the inaccessible castle above it, and the neighbouring heights, manned by Campo-verde's division, strengthened by several thousand somatenes of the district.   The Italian general Eugenio marched straight at the position, with Salme's French brigade in support, despising his enemy, and not waiting for the Commander-in-Chief and the reserves.   He met with a sharp repulse, for the Spaniards charged his columns just as they drew near the crest, and hurled them down with loss.   Macdonald refused to throw in all his troops, and contented himself with bringing off the routed brigade.   He then returned to Solsona and Cervera, much harassed in his retreat by the somatenes.   It is curious that he did not press the combat further, as he had a large superiority of numbers over the Catalan division, and had not lost much more than 100 men in the first clash [1].   But the position was formidable, and the Marshal more than once in this campaign showed himself averse to taking risks.   Perhaps, also, he may have already made up his mind to return to the east and abandon Suchet, since it was at about this time that more disquieting information from Baraguay d'Hilliers reached him by way of France.

This new budget of troubles contained two main items.   The first was that the August supplies thrown into Barcelona were nearly exhausted, and that the town urgently required revictualling.   The second was that it was impossible to send on the necessary convoys, because of the extreme activity of the somatenes, and the inadequate number of troops left in Northern Catalonia.   One considerable train of waggons had been captured and destroyed near La Junquera, on the very frontier of France, by the Baron de Eroles, who had now taken up the

---

[1] Martinien's invaluable lists show only three Italian and one French officer hurt, which agrees well enough with Vacani's estimate of 80 to 100 *hors de combat.*

command of the northern insurgents. Another was standing
fast at Gerona for want of sufficient escort, a third had been
collected at Perpignan, but dared not start. So pressing was
the need for the relief of Barcelona, that Macdonald made
up his mind that he must break up from his present cantonments
—even at the risk of making the siege of Tortosa impossible—
and transfer himself to the north-east.

Accordingly, on November 4, he commenced a toilsome march
by way of Calaf, Manresa, and Hostalrich to Gerona, where he
arrived in safety on the 10th. Campoverde followed him, for
some way, by parallel paths along the mountains, but never
dared to strike, the strength of the 7th Corps when it marched in
a mass being too great for him. It is probable that the Marshal
would have had more trouble if O'Donnell had been in the field,
but that enterprising general was not yet healed of the wound
which he had received at La Bispal. It had gangrened, and he
had been sent to Majorca by his physicians, who declared that
a complete cessation from military work was the only chance
of saving his life. The interim command was turned over in
November to the senior Lieutenant-General in Catalonia,
Miguel Iranzo, a very poor substitute for the hard-fighting
Spanish-Irish general.

Macdonald, having joined Baràguay d'Hilliers, had now an
imposing mass of troops under his hand. Moreover, he got
back the services of his old divisional generals Souham and
Pino, who arrived from sick leave, and took over charge of the
divisions lately in the charge of Frère and Severoli. A great
draft from France and Italy had rejoined in their company.
The Marshal was therefore able to collect the fractions of the
great convoy destined for Barcelona, and to conduct it to that
city after a slow and cautious march on November 25. He
then changed the battalions in the garrison of Barcelona, where
he left both Pino and Souham, sent back to the Ampurdam
the troops he had borrowed from Baraguay d'Hilliers, as escort
for the returning convoy, and marched for the second time
to join Suchet; moving by way of Momblanch, he got once
more into touch with the Army of Aragon at Falcet, near
Mora, on December 12.

Thus the campaign came back, at midwinter, to the same

aspect that it had shown in the first days of September. It has
been the wont of military critics to throw the blame for the
lost three months on Macdonald [1]. But this seems unfair : it is
true that he was absent from the post which he had promised
to hold, for the protection of Suchet's rear, from November 4
to December 13. But why had so little been done to forward
the siege of Tortosa during the time from September 4 to
November 4—two whole months—while the Marshal was in
the covenanted position, and actually carrying out his promise
to contain the Catalans, and leave Suchet's hands free for the
actual prosecution of the projected siege ? The commander
of the Army of Aragon had been given two of the best
campaigning months of the year—September and October—
and had no enemy about him save the ever-unlucky Valencian
army, the local somatenes of the Lower Ebro, and the scattered
bands of Villacampa in the hills of Upper Aragon. It was only
sixty miles from his base at Mequinenza, where his siege-train
had been collected months before, to the walls of Tortosa,
and he had brought up his field army before that place as
early as August. No doubt the country between Mequinenza
and Tortosa is rough, and its roads execrable, while water-
transport along the Ebro was rendered more difficult than usual
by a rather dry autumn, which kept the river low. But twenty-
six heavy siege-guns were got down to Xerta, only ten miles
from Tortosa, as early as September 5, during a lucky flood,
while a considerable number more were pushed to the front
during the same month, by the land route, formed by Suchet's
new military road from Caspe to Mora. It seems, therefore,
that Suchet's inactivity in September and October can be
explained neither by laying blame on Macdonald, nor by
exaggerating the difficulties of transport. If, as he wrote
himself, ' Notre corps d'armée se trouvait enchaîné sur le bas
Ebre, sans pouvoir agir, et son chef n'avait d'espoir que dans
une crue d'eau et dans le secours des circonstances [2],' he was
himself responsible for his failure, either from over-caution or
because he had undertaken a task beyond his means. The real
cause of his two months' delay was the vigorous action of the

_____
[1] See especially Napier, iii. 199.
[2] Suchet, *Mémoires*, i. 205.

enemy. There was no danger from the disorganized Valencian army, which only made a feeble attempt on November 26-27 to beat up the small force under General Musnier, which lay at Uldecona to cover the blockade of Tortosa from the south; the attack, led by Bassecourt, was driven off with ease. The real opponents of Suchet were the irregular forces of the Catalans, and the Aragonese insurgents in his rear. The former, though few in numbers, since Macdonald was attracting their main attention, attacked every convoy that tried to float down the gorge of the Ebro, and sometimes with success. On the 15th of September they captured a whole battalion of Pigna-telli's Neapolitans, which was acting as guard to some boats. On other occasions they took or destroyed smaller or greater portions of flotillas carrying guns or stores to Xerta, where the siege park was being collected. But Villacampa's Aragonese gave even greater trouble; from his lair in the Sierra de Albaracin that enterprising partisan made countless descents upon Suchet's rear, and so molested the garrisons of Upper Aragon, that the French general had repeatedly to send back troops from his main body to clear the roads behind him. Villacampa was beaten whenever he tried to fight large bodies, even though he was aided by a General Carbajal, whom the Regency had sent from Cadiz with money and arms, to stir up a general revolt in the Teruel-Montalban region. The Polish General Chlopiski, detached in haste from the blockade of Tortosa, broke the forces of Carbajal and Villacampa in two successive engagements at Alventosa, on the borders of Valencia (October 31), and Fuensanta, near Teruel (November 11). The insurrection died down, Villacampa retired into his mountains, and Chlopiski returned to the main army. But only a few days later Suchet had to cope with a new danger: Macdonald having taken himself off to Gerona, the Catalans were at last able to detach regular troops to reinforce the somatenes of the Lower Ebro. A brigade under General Garcia Navarro came up to Falcet, opposite Mora, and formed the nucleus of a raiding force, which beset the whole left bank of the Ebro, and made its navigation almost impossible. Suchet had to detach against it seven battalions under Abbé and Habert, who attacked Navarro's entrenched camp at Falcet on

November 12, and stormed it.   The Spanish general, who showed distinguished personal courage, and charged valiantly at the head of his reserves, was taken prisoner with some 300 men.   The somatenes fled to the hills again, and the regulars retired to Reus, near Tarragona, where they were out of Suchet's sphere of operations.   It was just after this combat that the unfortunate Army of Valencia made the useless diversion of which we have already spoken [1].   It, at least, kept Suchet busy for a few days.   By the time that it was over, the greater part of the remaining siege-material was ready at Xerta, the water-carriage down the Ebro having become easy since Garcia Navarro's defeat.   When, therefore, Macdonald's arrival at Momblanch was reported at Suchet's head quarters, and an adequate covering-force was once more placed between him and the Catalan army in the direction of Tarragona, the actual leaguer of Tortosa could at length begin.   It lasted, short though it was, till the New Year of 1811 had come, and must, therefore, be described not here but in the fourth volume of this work.

Thus six months had elapsed between the fall of Lerida and the commencement of the next stage of the French advance in Eastern Spain.   If it is asked why the delay was so long, the answer is easy: it was due not, as some have maintained, to Suchet's slowness or to Macdonald's caution, but solely to the splendid activity displayed by Henry O'Donnell, a general often beaten but never dismayed, and to the tenacity of the Catalans, who never gave up hope, and were still to hold their own, after a hundred disasters, till the tide of success in the Peninsula at last turned back in 1812–13.

[1] See previous page.

SECTION XXII: CHAPTER II

KING JOSEPH AND THE CORTES

It only remains that we should deal shortly with the higher politics of Spain during the last months of 1810—the troubles of King Joseph, and the complications caused by the meeting of the Cortes at Cadiz.

Of the growing friction between the King and the commanders of the 'military governments' created by the Emperor in February, we have already spoken [1]. Joseph did well to be angry when his dispatches to Saragossa or Barcelona were deliberately disregarded by his brother's special orders. But things became worse, when he was not merely ignored, but openly contemned. A few examples may suffice. In the early summer a brigade sent out by Marshal Ney raided the province of Avila, which was not included in any of the military governments, raised requisitions there, and—what was still more insulting—seized and carried off the treasure in the offices of the civil intendant-general of the province [2]. Joseph wrote to Paris that 'the Emperor cannot be desirous that his own brother—however unworthy—should be openly humiliated and insulted; that he asked for justice, and abstained from any further comment' [3]. Napoleon replied by placing Avila in the block of provinces allotted to the Army of Portugal, and withdrew it for the time from the King's authority. It was soon after that he created Kellermann's new 'military government' of Valladolid, thus taking another region from under the direct authority of Joseph. Some months later Kellermann asserted the complete independence of his viceroyalty, by causing the

---

[1] See pp. 201–2 and 316. [2] See p. 242.

[3] Joseph to Napoleon. Ducasse's *Correspondance du Roi Joseph,* vii. 278–9. The Emperor gave Avila back to the King in September, see Nap. *Correspondance,* xxi. 126.

judges of the high-court of Old Castille, which sat at Valladolid, to take a new oath of allegiance to the Emperor of the French, as if they had ceased to be subjects of the kingdom of Spain [1]. Soult, too, continued, as has been shown before, to cut off all revenues which the King might have received from Andalusia, and Joseph's financial position became even worse than it had been in 1809 [2].

The summary of his complaints, containing a declaration that he wished to surrender his crown to the Emperor, was drawn up as the autumn drew near ; it deserves a record ; it is absolutely reasonable, and confines itself to hard facts. ' Since Your Majesty withdraws Andalusia from my sphere of command, and orders that the revenues of that province should be devoted exclusively to military expenses, I have no choice left but to throw up the game. In the actual state of affairs in Spain the general who commands each province is a king therein. The whole revenues of the province will never suffice to keep him ; for what he calls his " absolute necessities " have never been formally stated, and as the revenues rise he augments his " necessities." Hence it results that any province under the command of a general is useless for my budget. From Andalusia alone I hoped to get a certain surplus, after all military expenses had been paid. But its command is given over to a general who would never recognize my authority ; and with the command, he gets the administrative and governmental rights. Thus I have been stripped of the only region which could have given me a sufficient maintenance. I am reduced to Madrid [i. e. New Castile], which yields 800,000 francs per mensem, while the indispensable expenses of the central government amount to 4,000,000 francs per mensem. I have around me the wrecks of what was once a great national administration, with a guard, the depôts and hospital of the army, a garrison, a royal household, a ministry, a council of state, and the refugees from the rebel provinces. This state of affairs could not endure for two months longer, even if my honour, and the consciousness of what is due to me, would allow me to remain

[1] See Miot de Melito's Diary, Sept. 8, 1810.
[2] Joseph to Napoleon, Aug. 25, 1810. Ducasse, vii. 321, and ibid., p. 332 of Sept. 12.

in this humiliating position.   Since the Army of Andalusia has
been taken from me, what am I ?   The manager of the hospitals
and magazines of Madrid, the head jailer of the central depôt of
prisoners ! '   Joseph then states his conditions.   If he is allowed
(1) to have a real control over the whole army ; (2) to send
back to France officers, of whatever rank, notoriously guilty
of maladministration ; (3) to reassure his Spanish partisans as
to rumours current concerning his own forced abdication and
the dismemberment of the monarchy ; (4) to issue what proclamations he pleases to his subjects, without being placed under
a sort of censorship, he will retain his crown, and pledge himself to reduce all Spain, and ' make the country as profitable to
the interests of France as it is now detrimental.'   If not, he
must consider the question of retiring across the Pyrenees and
surrendering his crown [1].

Napoleon could not give any such promises, and for good
reasons : he rightly distrusted his brother's military ability,
and knew that—whatever was the title given to Joseph—men
like Soult or Masséna would disregard his orders.   Apparently
he considered that a conflict of authorities in Spain, such as had
been existing for the last six months, was at least better than
the concentration of power in the hands of one indifferent
commander-in-chief.   It is doubtful whether he did not err
in his conclusion.   Almost anything was better than the
existing anarchy, tempered by orders, six weeks late, from
Paris.   But a second, and a more fatal, objection to granting
Joseph's conditions was that the ' rumours current concerning the
dismemberment of the Spanish monarchy ' were absolutely true.
Napoleon was at this moment at the very height of his wild
craze for adding alien and heterogeneous provinces to the
French Empire, in the supposed interest of the Continental
System.   It was in 1810 that he declared Holland and the
Valais, Hamburg and Bremen, Oldenburg and Dalmatia,
integral parts of his dominions.   And Northern Spain was
destined to suffer the same fate.   Mina and Rovira, Eroles and
Manso, were to wake some morning to find themselves French
subjects !   On October 12 the Emperor wrote to Berthier :
' You will inform General Caffarelli, in strict confidence, that

[1] Joseph to Napoleon, Aug. 9, Ducasse, vii. 307.

my intention is that Biscay shall be united to France. He must not speak of this intention, but he must act with full knowledge of it. Make the same private communication to General Reille about Navarre[1].' Aragon, or at least the portion of it north of the Ebro, and Catalonia were to suffer the same fate. Already justice was administered there in the name of the Emperor, not in that of the King of Spain, and a coinage was being struck at Barcelona which no longer bore the name of 'Joseph Napoleon King of Spain and the Indies[2].'

The line of argument which Napoleon adopted with regard to this proposed annexation is very curious. His directions to his Foreign Minister, Champagny, run as follows[3]: 'Herewith I send you back the Spanish documents with six observations, which are to serve as the base for negotiation. But it is important that you should broach the matter gently. You must first state clearly what are my opinions on the Convention of Bayonne [viz. that the Emperor regards his guarantee of the integrity of Spain as out of date and cancelled]. Then speak of Portugal[4], and next of the expense that this country [Spain] costs me. Then let the Spanish envoys have time to reflect, and only after an interval of some days tell them that I must have the left bank of the Ebro, as an indemnity for the money and all else that Spain has cost me down to this hour. I think that, as in all negotiations, we must not show ourselves too much in a hurry.' The mention of Portugal means that the Emperor contemplated making his brother a present of the Lusitanian realm, where Spain was hated only one degree less than France, as a compensation for Catalonia and the rest. On the same morning that Mina found himself a Frenchman, all

---

[1] *Correspondance*, xxi. p. 213.

[2] For a specimen, see the plate of coins in vol. ii, facing p. 478.

[3] Napoleon to Champagny, Sept. 9, 1810.

[4] I cannot find anywhere any authority for Napier's strange statement (iii. p. 261) that it was Almenara, and not Napoleon, who started the idea that Portugal should be exchanged for the Ebro Province. The nearest thing to it is that ' M. d'Almenara déclare formellement qu'il ne consente à aucune cession de territoire espagnol, que cette compensation [Portugal] ne soit pas stipulée et garantie ; mais comme il est dans l'intention formelle du roi de ne pas consentir à aucun démembrement, même avec une compensation plus avantageuse, il n'aurait jamais ratifié un pareil traité.' Ducasse, *Correspondance*, vii. 190.

the Ordenança of the Beira hills were to discover that they were Castilians ! Mad disregard of national feeling could go no further.

A letter to the French ambassador at Madrid explained at much greater length the Emperor's reasons for breaking the oath that he had sworn to his brother at Bayonne, when he named him King of Spain. 'When the promise was made, His Majesty had supposed that he had rallied to his cause the majority of the Spanish nation. This has proved not to be the case : the whole people took arms, the new king had to fly from Madrid, and was only restored by French bayonets. Since then he has hardly rallied a recruit to his cause ; it is not the King's own levies that have fought the rebels : it is the 400,000 French sent across the Pyrenees who have conquered every province. Therefore all these regions belong not to the King, but to the Emperor, by plain right of conquest. He intends, for this reason, to regard the Treaty of Bayonne as null ; it has never been ratified by the Spanish nation. One only chance remains to the King : let him prevail upon the newly-assembled Cortes at Cadiz to acknowledge him as their sovereign, and to break with England. If that can be done, the Emperor may revert to his first intentions, and ratify the Treaty of Bayonne, except that he must insist on a " rectification of frontiers sufficient to give him certain indispensable positions " ' —presumably San Sebastian, Pampeluna, Figueras, Rosas, &c.[1]

The mere first rumour of his brother's intentions, transmitted by Almenara and the Duke of Santa-Fé, his ambassadors ordinary and extraordinary at Paris, drove Joseph to despair. 'The Spanish nation,' he wrote [2], 'is more compact in its opinions, its prejudices, its national egotism, than any other people of Europe. There are no Catholics and Protestants here, no new and old Spaniards ; and they will all suffer themselves to be hewn in pieces rather than allow the realm to be dismembered. What would the inhabitants of the counties round London say if they were menaced with being declared no longer English ? What would Provençals or Languedocians say if they were told

[1] Napoleon to Laforest, ambassador at Madrid, Nov. 7.
[2] Joseph to the Queen of Spain, Oct. 12. Ducasse, *Correspondance*, vii. 355.

that they were to cease to be Frenchmen ? My only chance here is to be authorized to announce that the promise that Spain should not be dismembered will be kept. If that is granted, and the generals who have misbehaved are recalled to France, all may be repaired. If not, the only honourable course for me is to retire into private life, as my conscience bids me, and honour demands.' On November 18, after having received more formal news of the Emperor's intentions from his envoys, Joseph declared that the die was cast : he would return to his castle of Mortefontaine, or to any other provincial abode in France that he could afford to purchase, as soon as his brother's resolve was made public.

Yet the crisis never came to a head. The annexation of the Ebro provinces was never published, though private assurances of their impending fate were laid before the Spanish ministers and the King. What caused the Emperor to hesitate, when all was prepared ? The answer may be found in his dispatch to Laforest on November 7 : ' I need hardly warn you,' he writes, ' that these insinuations (the ultimatum to the King) are to be made only on condition that the French army has entered Lisbon, and that the English have taken to their ships.'   And again, 'The Emperor is acting in sincerity : if in reality the capture of Lisbon, and an offer from the cabinet of Madrid, might possibly decide the rebels to treat, His Majesty might consent, &c., &c.' It was the Lines of Torres Vedras which saved King Joseph from abdication and Spain from dismember-ment. The evacuation of Portugal by Wellington was the indispensable preliminary to the carrying out of the great annexation scheme : its completion was deferred till the ominous silence of Masséna should be ended by a triumphant dispatch proclaiming the capture of Lisbon. Since that dispatch never came, Napoleon kept postponing his ultimatum. Then followed the news, delivered at Paris by Foy on November 21, showing that Masséna had been brought to a standstill. Even then the Emperor's plan was kept back, not abandoned. It was not till the Army of Portugal had recoiled in despair and disarray to the banks of the Coa that Napoleon abandoned his cherished scheme, and consented to treat with his brother on reasonable terms. But Joseph's visit to Paris in the spring of 1811 and its consequences belong to another chapter of this history. It must suffice here to point out that he spent all the winter of 1810–11 in a state of mental anguish, expecting every day to be forced to publish his abdication [1], and, meanwhile, living a life of shifts and worries—selling his last silver plate to feed his courtiers [2], and exchanging an endless correspondence of remonstrances and insinuations with Soult and the commanders of the 'military governments' of the North [3]. Even from the military point of view he did not consider himself safe; the Empecinado and other guerrillero chiefs carried their incursions up to the very gates of Madrid; and La Mancha, from which, by the Emperor's orders, much cavalry had been withdrawn for the benefit of Soult [4], was frequently raided by detachments from Blake's Army of Murcia. 'A chaque instant du jour et de la nuit,' wrote the unhappy sovereign, 'je suis exposé à monter à cheval pour défendre ma vie contre les bandes exaspérées des insurgés, qui entourent Madrid : cette ville est aux avant-postes [5].'

Meanwhile, the other government which claimed to be the legal representative of Spanish nationality was even more truly 'aux avant-postes.' The Cortes had assembled at Cadiz, where the booming of the French cannon was perpetually heard, and where an occasional shell from Villantroys' celebrated mortars would plump harmlessly into the sand of the Peninsula or the outskirts of the town itself. The Cortes had opened its sessions on September 24, though less than half its members had assembled. The difficulty of collecting them had been very great, since all had to arrive by sea, and many had to come from regions very remote, such as Asturias, Galicia, or Catalonia. The assembly could not be called satisfactory or repre-

[1] See his letters to his wife in December 1810 and January 1811, about his brother's 'mauvaises dispositions à mon égard.'

[2] He writes that at his most splendid State banquets nothing but china is now to be seen on his table.

[3] The question of the Consuls and Soult (mentioned in an earlier chapter) crops up again in Joseph to Berthier, Nov. 28.

[4] Napoleon to Berthier, Oct. 4, orders Digeon's brigade of Lahoussaye's dragoons to cross the Sierra Morena, thus leaving the king only four regiments of French cavalry in New Castile.

[5] Ducasse, *Correspondance*, vii. p. 361.

sentative. The scheme drawn up for its election by the commission that had sat in the preceding winter was complicated. There was to be a deputy for every 50,000 souls
throughout Spain; but the form of selection was indirect:
the villages chose each one primary elector; the primary
electors met at the chief town of the district to choose a second
body of secondary electors; the secondary electors chose a
final committee for the whole province (*Junta provincial
electoral*) and these last, aided by the Governor, Archbishop,
and Intendant of the province, nominated the deputies. But
this complicated system could only work in the regions which
were in the hands of the patriots. Only Valencia, Murcia,
Estremadura, the Balearic Isles, and Galicia were wholly free
at the moment. In Catalonia the capital, Barcelona, and
large tracts of the country were occupied by the French. In
the Asturias three-quarters of the province were held down
by Bonnet. The two Castiles, Andalusia (excepting Cadiz),
Biscay, Navarre, Leon, and Aragon were entirely or almost
entirely in the hands of the enemy. The delegates supposed
to represent them were either chosen in hole-and-corner
meetings of insurgent juntas lurking in some remote fastness,
or—where even this semblance of local election was not possible
—by nomination by the Regency, or in wholly casual assemblies
of the natives of those districts who chanced to be in Cadiz at
the time. The representatives of Madrid, for example, were
chosen in this fashion by the body of exiles from that city
meeting in the spacious courtyard of a large public building [1].
The result of this informal and irregular method of choice was
that many provinces purported to be represented by deputies
who had no real local influence therein, but had chanced to
commend themselves to the insurgent juntas, or to the persons
—in some cases a mere handful—who happened to have fled
from that particular region to Cadiz. It is said that the very
names, and much more the persons, of a good many of the
deputies were absolutely unknown to their supposed constituents.
Most of all was this the case with the members of the Cortes
who were supposed to represent Spanish America. It had
been decreed by the late Central Junta that the colonies formed

[1] Argüelles, *Cortes de Cadiz*, p. 160.

an integral part of the Spanish monarchy, and were therefore entitled to representation. But the modest number of twenty-six members allotted to them were elected at Cadiz, by a committee of Americans nominated by the Regency from those who happened to be resident in that town. Most of the deputies were out of touch with the people beyond the seas, of whom they were theoretically the delegates.

This fact was specially unfortunate when the first symptoms of discontent and sedition in Buenos Ayres, Mexico, and the Caraccas had begun to show themselves. Though few realized it as yet, the insurrection of Spanish America was just about to break forth. The least foreseen of all the results of Napoleon's aggressions in Old Spain was that the colonies, which had been called upon to take their part in the national war against the French, and had been promised a share in the administration of the empire, should accept the show of freedom and equality that was offered in a serious spirit. The Americans demanded that they should no longer be treated as subjects and tributaries of the mother country, but recognized as possessing rights and interests of their own, which must be taken into consideration when the general governance of the dominions of Ferdinand VII was in question. And these rights and interests included not only a claim to such self-government as other Spanish provinces possessed, but a demand that their commercial and economic needs should no longer be subordinated to the convenience of the mother country. The colonies could not see why the monopoly of all their trade should be left in the hands of the merchants of Old Spain. They wished to traffic on their own account with Great Britain and the United States. This claim was one which no inhabitant of Old Spain could view with equanimity. The monopoly of South American commerce had always been believed to be the most essential item in the greatness of the realm. It had been preserved almost as strictly in the eighteenth century as in the seventeenth or sixteenth. The old *Asiento*, which gave Great Britain a minute share in that commerce, had been conceived to be a humiliation and a disgrace to the king who granted it. Spain had fought more than once to preserve the American monopoly—it is only necessary to allude to the war of

'Jenkins's Ear' to show what she was prepared to face in its defence.

And now, when the mother country was in such desperate straits, the questions of American self-government and American trade were raised in the crudest form. Great Britain had provoked the distrust of her Spanish allies by many of her acts, even when they were done in good faith and with no ulterior motive. But the most irritating of all was the request, which had been already made more than once in a tentative fashion, for a measure of free trade with South America. Wellington had recommended that the point should not be pressed, when Spain was in her extremity; but it was inevitable that since nearly all British subjects, and nearly all Americans, were desirous to see the old barriers removed, the question should crop up again and again. The opening of the American trade was the only return that Spain could make for the aid that Great Britain had now been giving her for more than two years of war. When Canning in 1809 wrote that 'in questions of commerce any proper occasion must be used to recommend a more enlarged and liberal policy than has hitherto been acted upon in Spain,' it is easy to see what was in his mind. The ministers in power in 1810 were mostly of the same opinion. But to ask for free trade with America in the year when Hidalgo was making his first rising in Mexico, and the *cabildos* on the Rio de la Plata were quietly substituting municipal self-government for the ancient autocratic rule of their viceroys, was to provoke acute suspicion. In 1806–7 Great Britain had backed Miranda and other colonial separatists, either with the hope of getting a footing for herself in South America, or at least with that of establishing republics which would grant her all the commercial privileges that she asked. The successive Spanish governments of 1808–10 could never convince themselves that the scheme had been completely dropped, and mistook British demands for open trade with America for a desire to sever the discontented colonies from their mother country. The most unpopular act of the Regency of 1810 was their decree of May 7, issued, as all Spaniards held, in base subservience to their allies, which had granted England and Portugal a certain limited right of exchanging their products with the colonies, on paying the heavy customs-due of ten and a half or fifteen and a half per cent.[1] So great was the cry raised against it in Cadiz that the Regency was cowardly enough to cancel it on June 22, under the pretext that it had not been ratified in a session at which all its members were present!

But it was not the American question alone which lay as a source of danger before the newly-assembled Cortes, nor was it the American deputies alone who misrepresented their constituents. Speaking in general, it may be said that the whole assembly showed a disproportionate number of liberals, when the relative numbers of the democratic and the conservative parties throughout Spain were taken into consideration. The events of the next ten years were to show that the *Serviles*, as their opponents called them, were really in a majority in the whole country-side and in many towns. If that had not been so, Ferdinand VII could not have restored autocratic government with such ease when the Peninsular War was over. Reactionaries of the blackest dye, who would have liked to restore the Inquisition, and would have put back the press into the shackles which it had endured before 1807, were probably in a clear majority in the nation. The clerical interest was in many ways the mainstay of the War of Independence, and the clergy, with very few exceptions, would gladly have gone back to the system of the eighteenth century[2]. The majority of the old official class sympathized with them, and the peasantry were almost everywhere under their control. On the other hand, the Liberals, if all shades of them were reckoned together, had a clear majority in the Cortes, both because the regions which were properly represented in that assembly chanced to be those in which they were most numerous, and because they had secured a disproportionate number of the seats belonging to the lost provinces, which had been filled up by more or less fictitious elections within the walls of Cadiz. That town itself was the least conservative place in Spain, and the refugees who had served as electors because they happened to be on the

---

[1] For details see Schepeler, iii. p. 691. The goods must also be carried in Spanish vessels, so the grant was not a very liberal one !

[2] Liberal clergy of the type of the journalist Blanco-White (Leucadio Doblado) were rare exceptions.

spot, were not drawn from the bulk of the population—were neither priests nor peasants,—but mainly came from those sections of the upper and middle classes where liberal opinions had made more progress.

The Cortes on the whole was a democratic body: Spain, on the whole, was reactionary. The number of those who hated Napoleon because they regarded him as the enemy of the Church, the jailer of the Pope, and the breaker-up of old laws, was much greater than that of those who hated him because he was the embodiment of autocracy, and the foe of all free self-government. Intense national pride was common to both parties, and all could unite against a foe whose aim was the dismemberment of Spain. But the union was made difficult by the fact that men who had imbibed, more or less consciously, some of the 'Principles of 1789' had to co-operate with men who looked back on the régime of Philip II as a Golden Age. ' I can see no prospect of Liberty behind the crowd of priests who everywhere stand foremost to take the lead of our patriots. I cannot look for any direct advantage from the feeling which prompts the present resistance to Napoleon, as it arises chiefly from an inveterate attachment to the religious system whence our present degradation takes source. If the course of events enables us to attempt a political reform, it will be by grafting the feeble shoots of Liberty upon the stock of Catholicism, an experiment which has hitherto, and must ever, prove abortive' wrote a desponding Liberal [1]. How could the writer of such words and his friends work cordially in company with such fanatics as the Estremaduran deputy who, in one of the earlier sessions of the Cortes, proposed the astonishing motion that, in spite of all that had happened since 1807, 'the Inquisition remains in full possession of its ancient authority, and can make free use of all the powers which it has ever enjoyed in the past [2].' There were others who objected to the use of the dangerous word 'constitution,' and even to the phrase *las leyes de España*, as implying an authority independent of the crown [3].

[1] Doblado's Letters, p. 392.

[2] Motion by one Francisco Maria Riesco, deputy, and formerly Inquisitor, at Llerena in Estremadura. Arguëlles's *Las Cortes de Cadix*, p. 209.

[3] See below, p. 520.

When it is remembered that the form in which the Cortes had been summoned was new and experimental, that the elections had been—even according to that form—irregular, that no single member was accustomed to parliamentary usages, that the parties represented in it held views of the most divergent kinds, the wonder is not that the assembly displayed many weaknesses, but that it did no worse. Observers of a pessimistic frame of mind had feared that it would break up altogether after a few stormy sittings. 'It was too full,' wrote the regent Lardizabal, ' of youths, and of men who yesterday were mere adventurers, without any practice in command, knowledge of business, or experience of the world. Whole provinces were represented by deputies whom they had not chosen, and were expected to conform to a constitution, and to accept sweeping reforms, made by men to whom they had given no mandate, faculty, or authority to take such changes into consideration. For neither the Regency, nor even the King, had the legal right to nominate deputies: no one could choose them save the provinces or cities which were integral parts of the nation, and no one could claim to represent a province save the men to whom that same province had given powers, and instructions to act in conformity with its wishes.'

This motley assembly, so many of whose members were of doubtful legitimacy, held its opening session on September 24, 1810. The meeting-place was not within the walls of Cadiz itself, but in the large suburban town of La Isla, in the centre of the great island of Leon, which forms the outwork of the city. It was hoped that the six miles which separated its sitting-place from Cadiz would prevent interruption by popular demonstrations, such as had been so pernicious to the French chamber during the Revolution. The Cortes had as their home the large but bare theatre of San Fernando, which had been roughly fitted up with benches and tribunes. After high mass had been celebrated by the old Cardinal Bourbon, the only male member of the royal family who was not in captivity [1], the Regency declared the session opened, and then withdrew, after

[1] He was of the same branch as the Countess of Chinchon, Godoy's wife, being son of Luis, youngest child of Philip V, by a quasi-morganatic marriage with a lady of the name of Vallabriga.

a brief speech by the Senior Regent, the Bishop of Orense, who bade the assembly constitute itself in due form and elect its president and secretaries.

This was done with no delay; the president chosen was a Catalan, Ramón Lazaro de Dou, while the two secretaries were Evaristo Perez de Castro and Manuel Lujan. Both of them were well known to entertain Liberal opinions, and their choice marked the predominance of their party in the Cortes. Sitting till midnight was long past, the assembly passed six decrees drawn up by Muñoz Torrero, one of the few clerical deputies who held Liberal views, and Manuel Lujan. By these the Cortes declared itself in possession of supreme power in the State, but resolved that, of the three branches of authority— the legislative, the executive, and the judicial—it intended to take only the first-named under its own charge, handing over the executive to the late Regency, and the judicial to the ordinary courts of law. The Regency should be responsible to the Cortes for all its acts of administration, and liable to be called to account. It was ordered to make an instant oath of obedience to the assembly, ' recognizing the sovereignty of the nation represented by the deputies of this general and extraordinary Cortes.' This Castaños and the other regents did with an ill grace, all save the Bishop of Orense, who misliked the oath, contending that its terms spoke of the nation as being sovereign in its own right, without consideration of the King's indefeasible majesty [1]. He would not swear, and so vacated his place. He did not lose much by his early dismissal, for on October 28 the Cortes abruptly deposed his four colleagues—Castaños, Lardizabal, Saavedra, and Escaño—and replaced them by a new Regency of three members. These were Joaquim Blake, that most unlucky of generals; Admiral Cisgar, then commanding the Carthagena squadron, who passed as an able administrator; and an obscure naval captain, Pedro Agar, of whom little was known save that he was American born, and might, therefore, theoretically represent the colonies. The

---

[1] ' Que la nación era soberana *con el rey,* desde luego prestaría el juramento pedido. Pero si se entendia que la nación era soberana *sin el rey,* y soberana de su mismo soberano, nunca se sometería á tal doctrina.' See more of his argument in Toreno, ii. 225.

change in regents was decidedly for the worse as far as character and ability went. Apparently the Cortes were jealous of an administration whose power was older than their own, and had not originally been created by them. They wished to have an executive more entirely dependent on themselves. Some of the Liberals pretended that the old regents were plotting to hold a sort of ' Pride's Purge' of the Cortes, and to restore themselves to power. But of this no proof was ever given [1]. Considering the difficult times which they had passed through, and their well-intentioned if rather feeble attempt to serve the state, Castaños and his colleagues deserved a better fate than arbitrary dismissal, without thanks, and with a tacit accusation of treason laid to their charge.

Between the time of the first assembly of the Cortes and the change in the Regency an infinite number of subjects had been dealt with. The Liberal majority, led by Agostin Argüelles, had decreed liberty of the Press in all political discussions, but very illogically refused it for discussions on matters of religion. They had abolished all feudal rights and privileges of nobility. They passed a decree of amnesty for all rebels in America who should lay down their arms, and proposed many projects for improving the position of the Colonies, few of which, unfortunately, happened to bear any relation to the chief grievances under which the South Americans conceived themselves to be labouring. The insurrection still went on, and, though the mother country was placed in such a desperate condition, troops were actually withdrawn from the Murcian army to sail with General Elio, who was directed to restore order at Buenos Ayres and in the provinces of the Rio de la Plata. Discussions continued, with much heat and a considerable amount of eloquence, on many other points, during the early days of the Junta. The subjects of debate were generally constitutional, occasionally financial. It was worthy to be observed that the two topics on which all the deputies rallied together were the question of opposition to the French, and the question of the defence of their own sovereign rights. Even the majority of

---

[1] Compare Toreno's insinuation against the Regent Lardizabal (ii. 213), to whom he ascribes a definite plot, with Arteche's defence and eulogy of the late Regency, ix. 109–11.

the *Serviles* would join with the Liberals whenever any doubt was raised with regard to the right of the Cortes to arrogate to itself the title of Majesty or the attributes of supreme power. When, for example, the Bishop of Orense refused to take the oath of obedience, several clericals of most reactionary views took part against him ; and when a few weeks later the Marqués del Palacio, named as a deputy-regent during the absence of Blake, also displayed reluctance to swear to the same form on similar grounds, he did not receive the report that he had expected from the reactionaries. Indeed, he was put under arrest for some time, without, as it seems, any attempt to protect him being made by the *Serviles*. Like the Bishop of Orense, he ended by swallowing his scruples and accepting the prescribed formula [1].

A similar desire to assert its own absolute supremacy impelled the Cortes to refuse to countenance two dynastic intrigues which came from different quarters. The eldest daughter of Charles IV, Carlotta, Princess of the Brazils and wife of the Regent João of Portugal, was the nearest of kin to Ferdinand VII who had escaped Napoleon's claws in 1808. She was of opinion that she had a good right to expect the Regency during her brother's captivity at Valençay, and her agents repeatedly urged her claims, both during the days of the first Regency and after the Cortes had assembled. Sousa-Holstein, the Portuguese ambassador, naturally lent them his aid, and she had Spanish partisans, though few of them were persons of good reputation. Yet, by constant persuasion and promises, Carlotta's representatives actually succeeded in inducing great numbers of the deputies to pledge themselves to push her interests. It is said that, at one time or another, a full half of the members had given the intriguers encouragement. But to do this, and to make a formal attempt to pass a decree conferring the Regency on her, were very different things. When overt action was urged by her agents, or their partisans in the Cortes, nothing came of the attempt. The assembly was naturally unwilling to surrender its own sovereignty, and to introduce a court and its intrigues into Cadiz. It must be added that João of Portugal had no liking for his wife's

[1] Toreno, ii. pp. 222–3.

scheme, that Wellington saw its disadvantages [1], and that the great bulk of the Spaniards would have resented the whole affair, as a Portuguese intrigue, if it had ever been laid before the nation as a definite proposal.

The second dynastic scheme which was running its course at this time was engineered by another branch of the Spanish royal house.   The restless and unscrupulous Queen Caroline of Sicily could not forget that if Carlotta of Portugal was the nearest relative of the captive King, yet her husband Ferdinand was his nearest male kinsman, save the princes in Napoleon's hands.   She availed herself of this fact to urge that one of her children would be a very suitable person to be entrusted with power in Spain, and thought of her younger son Prince Leopold as a possible candidate for the Regency.   But since he had not the necessary reputation or age, the Queen soon fell back upon her son-in-law Louis Philippe, Duke of Orleans, the exiled son of the infamous Philippe Égalité.   He had not only a good military record for his services at Jemappes and elsewhere in the early Belgian campaigns, but was universally known as a man of ability.   Unfortunately, he had fought on the Republican side in 1792—a thing hard to forget, and certain to cause suspicion : and his ability was always displayed for purposes of self-interest, and savoured of unscrupulousness.

Nevertheless, Orleans had already made overtures to the old Regency in the spring of 1810, and had been promised by them a command on the borders of Catalonia.   They had failed to keep the pledge, and he now appeared at Cadiz, and wished to present himself before the Cortes and plead his cause.   He took small profit thereby, for the assembly regarded him and his relatives as suspicious persons, refused to give him an audience when he presented himself before its doors, and politely but firmly insisted that he should return to Sicily in a few days—an order which he was forced to obey.   'Whether it was that he was a Frenchman, though a Bourbon, or whether it was that he had once been a Republican, though he had ceased to be one, or whether it was that he was a prince of

---

[1] See Wellington to Henry Wellesley, Nov. 4, 1810 :—'If the Princess of the Brazils be the person appointed regent, the Court will be inundated with intriguers of all nations, and attended by other evils.'

the royal house, and therefore distasteful to the newly-assembled Cortes, who were secretly inclined to democratic views, the majority viewed him with disfavour [1].'   On October 3 he set sail for Palermo.

At the end of 1810 we leave the Cortes still indulging in fiery constitutional debates, still busy in asserting its own supreme power, and curbing many attempts at self-assertion in the new Regency which it had created.   With the English government it was not on the best of terms : though it decreed the erection of a statue to George III as the friend and deliverer of Spain—a monument which (it need hardly be said) was never erected—it was very slow to seek or follow the advice of the allied power.   It clamoured for subsidies, but refused the opening of the South American trade—the only return that could be given for them.   Money in hard gold or silver Great Britain could no longer supply—for the years 1810–11 were those when the paper-issues of the Bank were our sole currency ; cash had almost disappeared, and could only be procured by offering six pounds or more in notes for five guineas.   But the Spaniards did not want paper, but gifts or loans in gold or silver.   They got no more of the precious metals—Great Britain had none to spare, and found it almost impossible even to procure dollars to pay Wellington's army in Portugal.   All that was given after 1809 was arms and munitions of war.

English observers in the Peninsula were not well pleased with the first months of the rule of the Cortes.   ' The natural course of all popular assemblies,' wrote Wellington to his brother, Henry Wellesley, now minister at Cadiz, ' and of the Spanish Cortes among others, is to adopt democratic principles, and to vest all the powers of the State in their own body.   This assembly must take care that they do not run in that tempting course, as the wishes of the nation are decidedly for monarchy. Inclination to any other form of government would immediately deprive them of the confidence of the people, and they would become a worse government, and more impotent, because more numerous, than the old Central Junta.'   A few weeks later he doubted whether even a Regency under Carlotta of

---

[1] See Galiano, quoted by Arteche, ix. 76.

Portugal, with all its disadvantages, would not be better than mere democracy [1].

Vaughan, on the spot at Cadiz, gave quite a different view of the situation, but one equally unfavourable to the Cortes as a governing power. ' It is full of priests, who (united with the Catalans) are for preserving the old routine, and adverse to everything that can give energy and vigour to the operation of government. Fanaticism and personal interest direct their opinions. . . . Be assured that the Cortes is, as at present constituted, anything but revolutionary or Jacobinical. . . . If there is not soon some new spirit infused into it, it will become an overgrown Junta, meddling with every paltry detail of police, and neglecting the safety of the country—and the Regency will be content to reign (very badly) over Cadiz and the Isla [2].'

There was much truth in both these verdicts, though Vaughan underrated the force of self-interest in driving a popular assembly to claim all power for itself, while Wellington underrated the dead-weight of clerical conservatism, which was the restraint upon that tendency. Both were right in asserting that, whatever the Cortes might be, the mass of the nation had no wish to set out on the path of Jacobinism. They both perceived the danger that the Cortes might turn itself into a constitutional debating society, and at the same time prevent any really efficient executive from being established. Such was its actual fate. Except that Spain now possessed a governing authority which, with all its faults, had infinitely more pretension to claim a legal mandate from the people than any of its predecessors, the situation was not greatly changed. From the military point of view, as we shall see in the next volume, the aspect of the Peninsula was in no degree improved. The same blunders that had marked the administration of the old Provincial Juntas, of the Supreme Central Junta, and of the first Regency, continued to exhibit themselves under the rule of the Cortes.

[1] Wellington to Henry Wellesley, from Cartaxo, Nov. 21, 1810.
[2] Charles Vaughan to Charles Stuart, Feb. 27, 1811.

APPENDICES

I

THE SPANISH FORCES AT THE SIEGE OF GERONA

The original garrison under the command of Alvarez consisted of the following units. The first column gives the strength on May 6, the second the number that remained on Dec. 11, 1809, the day of the surrender.

Regiment of Ultonia (three batts.) . . .	800	250
,, Borbon ,, . . .	1,300	360
Voluntarios de Barcelona, 2nd batt. . . .	1,125	378
1st battalion of the Miqueletes of Vich . .	600	250
1st & 2nd batts. ,, Gerona . .	1,120	380
Squadron of San Narciso	108	50
Regular Artillery	278	140
Men of the 2nd batt. of the Miqueletes of Gerona drafted into the artillery	240	100
Sailors drafted into the artillery . . .	130	90
Sappers	22	10
Total of the original garrison . . .	5,723	2,008

Reinforcements received August 17 :

Miquelete battalion of Cervera	500	320
Draft for the 1st battalion of Vich . . .	300	200
Draft for 2nd ,, Gerona . . .	100	50

Reinforcements brought in by Garcia Conde on Sept. 1 :

Regiment of Baza (2 batts.)	1,368	1,074
1st and 2nd Miqueletes of Talarn . . .	900	390
2nd Miqueletes of Vich	300	100
Picked companies of Santa Fé, Iliberia, Voluntarios de Tarragona	180	106
	3,648	2,240

Add 1,100 irregulars of the ' Crusade.' Losses unknown.
Of 9,371 men engaged first and last in the defence, only 4,248 survived.

II

THE FRENCH FORCES AT THE SIEGE OF GERONA

The following were the losses of the three divisions which conducted the siege of Gerona during its first three months, down to Sept. 15, 1809 :—

(1) REILLE's Original Siege Corps :

	Strength on June 1. Rank & file.	Strength on Sept. 15. Rank & file.	Losses.
Division Verdier :			
French Brigade :			
32nd Léger (one batt.)	846	489	357
16th Line (one batt.) .	730	324	406
2nd ,, ,,	490	205	285
56th ,, ,,	684	449	235
German Brigade :			
Würzburg (two batts.)	1,519	649	870
1st of Berg (two batts.)	1,310	705	605
2nd ,, ,,	1,313	604	709
Division Morio :			
2nd Westphalians (two batts.)	1,009	340	669
3rd ,, ,, ,,	1,446	491	955
4th ,, ,, ,,	832	534	298
4th Light Infantry (one batt.)	300	269	31
Division Lecchi :			
Velites of the Italian Guard	461	50	411
5th Italian Line (two batts.)	820	280	540
1st Neapolitans (two batts.)	765	172	593
2nd ,, ,, ,,	1,119	322	797
	13,644	5,883	7,761

Of these 6,666 were returned as sick or wounded, and 1,495 as dead or missing. Probably 300 were deserters.

The Artillery counted on the first date (June 1) :	Officers.	Men.
From the 7th corps	11	961
Siege-Train from France	36	1,362
The engineers and sappers were	12	314
The cavalry (28th chasseurs, and five squadrons of Italian horse) .	51	771
	110	3,408

Adding these figures to those of the infantry the total of the Siege Army was 17,162 men.

(2) The Covering Army, under St. Cyr in person, consisted on June 1 of the following troops :

Souham's Division :

	Men.
Brigade Bessières :	
1st Léger (three batts.)	1,965
3rd ,, (one batt.)	639
24th Dragoons (three squadrons)	597
Brigade Espert :	
42nd Line (three batts.)	2,406
67th ,, (one batt.)	644

Pino's Division :

Brigade Mazzuchelli :	
1st Italian Léger (three batts.)	1,359
4th Italian Line ,, ...	1,580
Brigade Fontane :	
2nd Italian Léger (three batts.)	1,507
6th Italian Line ,, ...	1,427
7th Italian ,, (one batt.)	477
Cavalry Brigade Palombini (Italian Chasseurs and Dragoons, six squadrons)	912

Chabot's Division :

7th Line (two batts.)	1,034
93rd ,, (one batt.)	687
3rd Provisional Chasseurs	498
Total of the Covering Army	15,732

On Dec. 31 the Siege Army showed 6,343 infantry, 2,390 engineers, artillery, &c. The Covering Army had still 11,666 men. But two battalions and some drafts had joined from France, so that the total loss was more than that indicated by these figures.

III

DEL PARQUE'S ARMY IN THE TAMAMES–ALBA DE TORMES CAMPAIGN, OCT.–NOV. 1809

MORNING STATE OF NOVEMBER 20

	Officers.	Men.
Vanguard Division, Major-General Martin de la Carrera :		
*Principe (three batts.), *Saragossa (three batts.), *1st of Catalonia, *2nd of Catalonia, *Gerona, *Barbastro, ‡Escolares de Leon, ‡Vittoria, ‡Monforte de Lemos, ‡Voluntarios de la Muerte, one battery field artillery	363	7,050

1st Division, Major-General Francisco Xavier Losada :
†Granaderos Provinciales de Galicia (two batts.), *Leon
(two batts.), *1st and 2nd of Aragon, *Voluntarios
de la Corona (two batts.), ‡Regimento del General,
‡1st and 2nd of La Union, ‡Betanzos (two batts.),
‡Orense, ‡Compaña de Guardias Nacionales, one
battery field artillery 351 7,985

2nd Division, Major-General Conde de Belveder :
*Rey (1st and 2nd batts.), *Zamora (1st and 2nd batts.),
*Seville (1st and 2nd batts.), *Toledo (1st and 3rd
batts.), *Hibernia (two batts.), *Voluntarios de
Navarra, ‡Santiago, ‡Lovera (two batts.), one battery
field artillery 344 6,415

3rd Division [Asturians], Major-General Francisco Ballasteros :
*Navarra (three batts.), *Princesa (two batts.), †Oviedo,
‡Covadonga, ‡Villaviciosa, ‡Candas y Luanco, Cas-
tropol, ‡Pravia, ‡Cangas de Tineo, ‡Grado, ‡Infiesto,
‡Lena, one battery field artillery 368 9,623

5th Division [Leonese], Brigadier-General Marquis de Castrofuerte :
‡Tiradores de Ciudad Rodrigo, ‡2nd of Ciudad Rodrigo,
‡Voluntarios de Fernando VII, †Leon, †Logroño,
†Toro, †Valladolid, one battery field artillery . . 245 5,912

Head-Quarters' Guard : Batallón del General . . . 40 897

[N.B.—The 4th Division, Galician troops under Mahy
about 7,000 strong, and the garrison of Ciudad
Rodrigo, 3,817 bayonets, were never brought up to
the front.]

Cavalry Division, the Prince of Anglona :
*Borbon, *Sagunto, ‡Granaderos de Llerena . . 83 1,053
(With only 868 horses.)
*Reyna, *Provisional Regiment[1], ‡Cazadores de Ciudad
Rodrigo (incomplete units, lately reformed), with one
horse-artillery battery 46 500

The artillerymen and a few companies of sappers are
included in the divisional totals.

Total 1,840 39,435

From this total of 41,275 men there were to be deducted, on Nov. 20,
sick 5,601, absent 1,573, detached (from the 5th Division) 1,279, so that
the total of efficients under arms was 32,822.

* Old line regiments. † Old militia regiments. ‡ New levies.
[1] This Provisional regiment received the name of '2nd of Algarve' in
December.

IV

FRENCH LOSSES AT TAMAMES, OCT. 18, 1809

The detailed return of the losses of the 6th Corps at Tamames has not been preserved. Marchand merely states that he lost 1,300 men. But the subjoined list of losses of officers, taken from Martinien's invaluable tables, shows sufficiently well which were the units that were hard hit :—

1st Division :	Killed.	Wounded.	2nd Division :	Killed.	Wounded.
Brigade Maucune :			Brigade Labassée :		
6th Léger . .	1	6	25th Léger .	3	8
69th Ligne . .	2	4	27th Ligne .	–	2
Brigade Marcognet :			59th Ligne .	–	3
39th Ligne . .	4	12	Cavalry :		
76th Ligne . .	7	15	15th Dragoons	–	2
	—	—	15th Chasseurs	1	1
	14	37	État-Major . .	–	2
Total 18 killed, 55 wounded.				4	18

At the average rate of 21 men hit per officer, which prevailed during the Peninsular War, this total of 73 officers ought to imply a total loss of about 1,533 men. But Marchand's 1,300 is probably correct.

V

THE PARTITION OF THE ARMY OF ESTREMADURA IN SEPTEMBER 1809

[N.B.—' bᵒⁿ' is Spanish contraction for *batallón*.]

The way in which the old army of Cuesta was divided in September 1809 has never been worked out ; nor has the composition of Areizaga's army of La Mancha, after it had been joined by the Estremaduran reinforcements, ever been reconstructed. A search in the Madrid War Office, in which I was assisted by the kindness of Captain Figueras, has produced the following two documents :—

(1) A list of Albuquerque's army without any figures of strength save the general total, as follows :

' Cuerpos que quedaron constituendo el Cuerpo de Ejercito de Estremadura, de 12,000 hombres. Oct. 1, 1809.

*Reales Guardias Walonas (4º batallon). [Late in garrison at Badajoz.]

‡Osuna (2 batallones).   [Late of Iglesias's Division.]

‡Velez Malaga (3 batallones).   ,,   ,,

‡Voluntarios Extrangeros (1 bᵒⁿ).   ,,   ,,

†Provincial de Burgos   ,,   ,,   ,,

‡Tiradores de Merida ,, [Late of Zayas's Division.]
†Provincial de Truxillo ,, ,, ,,
‡2ndo de Antequera ,, [Late of Portago's Division.]
†Provincial de Badajoz ,, ,, ,,
‡Leales de Fernando VII (2 bones). [Late in garrison at Badajoz.]
‡Voluntarios de Plasencia (1 bon) ,, ,,
‡Voluntarios de Zafra ,, ,, ,,
‡Voluntarios de La Serena ,, ,, ,,

Caballería—Comandante General el Brigadier Baron de Carondelet.

*Calatrava, *Villaviciosa, *Voluntarios de España, ‡Cazadores Perseguidores de Andalucia, ‡Cazadores de Sevilla.

*Borbon, ‡Cazadores de Llerena and *Sagunto have marched for Ciudad Rodrigo under the Prince of Anglona.

(2) A second document gives, as having marched under Eguia to join the Army of the Centre in La Mancha, the following corps :

*Real Marina (1º y 2º batallones). [Late of Bassecourt's Division.]
*Africa (3º bon). ,, ,,
*Murcia (1º y 2º bones). ,, ,,
*Reyna (1º bon). ,, ,,
*2ond de Mallorca (1º bon). [Late of Iglesias's Division.]
*Cantabria (1º, 2º, 3º bones). [Late of Zayas's Division.]
*Badajoz (1º, 2º bones). [Late of Portago's Division.]
†Provincial de Toledo (1 bon). ,, ,,
*Cazadores de Barbastro (1 bon). [Late of the Vanguard Division.]
*Voluntarios de Valencia (2º bon). ,, ,,
‡Tiradores de Estremadura (1 bon). ,, ,,
Provincial de Plasencia
                    Caballería

*Reales Carabineros, *Rey, *Reyna, *Infante, *Pavia, *Almanza, *1º y 2º Usares de Estremadura, ‡Cazadores de Madrid, ‡Cazadores de Toledo, ‡Carabineros y Lanceros de Estremadura.

30 piezas de Artillería.

This leaves unaccounted for, of Cuesta's old army, the following corps : *2º de Voluntarios de Cataluña, *Campo Mayor, ‡Cazadores de Valencia y Albuquerque, ‡Canarias, †Provincial de Guadix, *Irlanda (two batts.), *Jaen, ‡3º de Sevilla, ‡2º de Voluntarios de Madrid, ‡Voluntarios de la Corona, †Provincial de Siguenza, Granaderos Provinciales.

Of these Jaen, Corona, Madrid, and the grenadiers certainly went with Eguia to La Mancha. Irlanda went to Del Parque at Ciudad Rodrigo, 2º de Cataluña went to Cadiz to recruit. There are left Campo Mayor, Canarias, 3º de Sevilla, Provincial de Siguenza, Provincial de Guadix, Cazadores de Valencia y Albuquerque. Probably they formed the division of 6,000 men which the Junta is said to have deducted from the army of Estremadura for its own protection, and to have withdrawn to the borders of Andalusia in September. At any rate we find in November Campo

*Old regular units.   † Old militia units.   ‡ New levies.

Mayor, Canarias, and Provincial de Guadix serving again in the army of Albuquerque. But I cannot be sure that some of the others did not accompany Eguia (like Jaen and Corona), though not mentioned in the document no. 2.

VI

AREIZAGA'S ARMY IN THE OCAÑA CAMPAIGN

No detailed 'morning state' of this army has been preserved, but the names and gross totals of the divisions are on record in documents at the Madrid War Office. So far as I can make it out, the organization of the army must have been nearly as follows :—

INFANTRY DIVISION

	Officers.	Men.
Vanguard Division, General José Zayas :		
Voluntarios de Valencia, 2nd of Majorca, Provincial de Plasencia, Voluntarios de España, Granaderos Provinciales, Cantabria (seven batts.)	210	5,768
1st Division, General L. Lacy :		
Burgos, 1st of España, Provincial de Cordova, 1st of Loxa, Alcala, 1st of Seville, Provincial de Chinchilla (nine batts.)	328	7,420
2nd Division, General Gaspar Vigodet :		
Corona, Ordenes Militares, 1st of Guadix, Ronda, Alcazar, Ciudad Real (nine batts.) . . .	288	6,797
3rd Division, General P. Giron :		
1st and 2nd Spanish Guards, 2nd of Cordova, Bailen, Provincial de Jaen, Provincial de Toledo (eight batts.)	200	5,034
4th Division, General Francisco Castejon :		
1st of Malaga, 5th of Seville, 2nd of Loxa, Bujalance, Cazadores de Velez Malaga, Xeres, 3rd of Cordova (eight batts.)	236	6,151
5th Division, General T. Zerain :		
Cazadores de Barbastro, 2nd of España, 2nd of Seville, 2nd of Madrid, Provincial de Granada, 3rd Walloon Guards (seven batts.)	209	5,677
6th Division, General N. Jacomé :		
Badajos, Provincial de Malaga, Tiradores de Estremadura, Jaen, Provincial de Ecija (?), 4th of Seville (?), Alpujarras (?) (nine batts. ?)	312	7,325
7th Division, Brigadier-General F. Copons :		
Murcia, Real Marina, Africa, Reyna (six batts.) . .	197	4,927
Troops not included in any division :—Granaderos del General, Compaña de Buen Orden, Compañas Sueltas	—	778
	1,980	49,877

CAVALRY

Commanded by General Manuel Freire.

1st Division, Brigadier-General Juan Bernuy :
   Rey, Infante, Voluntarios de Madrid, Almanza, Carabineros
   y Lanceros de Estremadura .   .   .   .   .   .

2nd Division, Brigadier José Rivas :
   Cazadores de Toledo, Pavia, 1st and 2nd Hussars of Estremadura .   .   .   .   } 5,766

3rd Division, Brigadier Miguel March :
   Montesa, Reyna, Santiago, Principe, Cordova, Alcantara .

4th Division, Colonel V. Osorio :
   Cazadores de Granada, Granaderos de Fernando VII, Far-
   nesio, Lusitania, España. .   .   .   .   .

60 guns with artillerymen, about   1,500

Sappers, &c., no figures given, perhaps.   600

General Total 59,723

The materials from which the above organization has been reconstructed are : (1) Rolls of Venegas's army, before it was joined by Eguia's reinforcements. (2) Roll of the reinforcements led by Eguia (printed in Appendix No. V). (3) Gross totals of each division, without list of their component battalions, preserved in the Madrid War Office. (4) A morning state of the army taken on Dec. 1 : in this the divisions of Lacy and Zayas are amalgamated, and that of Jacomé has disappeared, its wrecks having been distributed among the remaining six divisions. (5) The regimental annals in the Conde de Clonard's great history of the Spanish army. Unfortunately this only serves for the regular regiments, there being no record of the fates of the militia battalions or the newly-raised volunteer regiments. I am specially uncertain about the Cavalry and the 6th Division (Jacomé), which seems to have been composed of those Estremaduran units which had not been organized as the 'Vanguard' and '7th Division.' But it almost certainly had some Andalusian regiments added. I mark them with a (?).

VII

THE FRENCH ARMY OF SPAIN ON JAN. 15, 1810

FROM A DOCUMENT IN THE ARCHIVES NATIONAUX AT PARIS

	Present under Arms.		De-tached.	Sick.	Prison-ers.	Total.
	Offi-cers.	Men.				
1st CORPS (MARSHAL VICTOR) :						
1st DIVISION (Ruffin) at Almagro :						
9th Léger, 24th Line, 96th Line (3 batts. each)	120	4,306	96	991	—	5,513
2nd DIVISION (Darricau) at Daymiel :						
16th Léger, 8th Line, 45th Line, 54th Line (2 batts. each) . . .	157	5,744	287	1,893	29	8,110
3rd DIVISION (Villatte) at Membrilla :						
27th Léger, 63rd Line, 94th Line, 95th Line (3 batts. each) . . .	215	6,124	156	589	3	7,087
LIGHT CAVALRY BRIGADE (Beaumont) at Villa-nueva de los Infantes :						
2nd Hussars, 5th Chas-seurs	45	778	254	27	23	1,127
DIVISION OF DRAGOONS (Latour-Maubourg) at El Moral :						
1st, 2nd, 4th, 9th, 14th, 26th Dragoons . . .	96	2,164	633	76	61	3,030
ARTILLERY AND TRAIN . .	33	1,747	252	144	2	2,178
DETACHMENTS on the march to join	4	1,019	—	—	—	1,023
ÉTAT-MAJOR	112	—	—	—	—	112
Corps Total	782	21,882	1,678	3,720	118	28,180
2nd CORPS (GENERAL HEUDELET, vice SOULT) :						
1st DIVISION (Merle) at Talavera :						
2nd Léger, 36th Line, 4th Léger, 15th Line (3 batts. each) . . .	231	5,718	238	660	—	6,847

| | Present under Arms. | | De-tached. | Sick. | Prison-ers. | Total. |
	Offi-cers.	Men.				
2nd Division (Heudelet) at Talavera : 17th Léger, 47th, 70th, 86th Line (3 batts. each), 31st Léger (4 batts.)	290	7,035	227	920	—	8,472
Light Cavalry Division (Soult) : 1st Hussars, 22nd Chasseurs, 8th Dragoons, Chasseurs Hanovriens	79	787	191	36	—	1,093
Division of Dragoons (Lahoussaye) : 17th, 18th, 19th, 27th Dragoons.	58	1,171	242	66	8	1,545
Artillery, Train, and Engineers	15	664	71	44	—	794
État-Major	79	—	—	—	—	79
Corps Total	752	15,375	969	1,726	8	18,830
3rd Corps (General Suchet) :						
1st Division (Laval) at Montreal : 14th and 44th Line, 2nd of the Vistula (2 batts. each) [3rd of the Vistula absent and not counted]	119	4,171	280	290	488	5,348
2nd Division (Musnier) at Alcañiz : 114th, 115th, 121st Line (3 batts. each), 1st of the Vistula (2 batts.)	203	6,970	212	813	267	8,465
3rd Division (Habert) at Fraga : 5th Léger, 116th Line (2 batts. each), 117th Line (3 batts.) . . .	136	4,193	8		—	4,757
Cavalry Brigade (Boussard) : 4th Hussars, 13th Cuirassiers	77	1,822	229	44	—	2,172
Artillery, Train, and Engineers	28	1,179	—	66	—	1,273

	Present under Arms.		De-tached.	Sick.	Prison-ers.	Total.
	Offi-cers.	Men.				
GARRISON TROOPS at Tu-dela, Saragossa, Jaca, &c., including the 3rd of the Vistula and 3 batts. of Chasseurs des Montagnes	132	4,030	187	186	—	4,535
ÉTAT-MAJOR	80	—	—	—	—	80
Corps Total	775	22,365	916	1,819	755	26,630
4th CORPS (GENERAL SEBASTIANI) :						
1st DIVISION :						
58th Line (3 batts.) . . [28th, 32nd, 75th Line left at Madrid] . . .	57 —	1,573 —	98 —	550 —	1 —	2,279 —
2nd DIVISION (Laval) :						
9 German batts. (absent at Segovia, on march to Bayonne with the prisoners of Ocaña) .	—	—	—	—	—	—
3rd DIVISION (Werlé) at Ocaña :						
4th, 7th, 9th Poles (2 batts. each)	130	4,679	112	1,177	50	6,148
LIGHT CAVALRY BRIGADE (Perreymond) at Ocaña :						
10th and 27th Chasseurs, and Polish Lancers .	62	1,289	390	89	109	1,939
DIVISION OF DRAGOONS (Milhaud) at Velez :						
5th, 12th, 16th, 20th, 21st Dragoons . . .	104	1,617	250	216	128	2,315
ARTILLERY, TRAIN, AND ENGINEERS	14	555	20	45	—	634
ÉTAT-MAJOR	45	—	—	—	—	45
Corps Total	412	9,713	870	2,077	288	13,360
5th CORPS (MARSHAL MORTIER) :						
1st DIVISION (Girard) at El Moral :						
34th, 40th, 64th, 88th Line (3 batts. each) .	201	6,839	228	1,683	—	8,951
2nd DIVISION (Gazan) at El Moral :						
21st and 28th Léger, 100th and 103rd Line (3 batts. each) . . .	219	6,414	212	1,432	10	8,287

	Present under Arms.		De-tached.	Sick.	Prison-ers.	Total.
	Offi-cers.	Men.				
CAVALRY DIVISION (Marisy) at Granatuela :						
10th Hussars, 21st Chasseurs, 13th and 22nd Dragoons.	81	1,458	391	411	11	2,352
ARTILLERY AND TRAIN . .	17	741	50	135	3	946
PROVISIONAL REGIMENT of 2 squadrons each of 13th and 22nd Dragoons, on march to join their corps	31	557	—	—	—	588
ÉTAT-MAJOR	54	—	—	—	—	54
Corps Total	603	16,009	881	3,661	24	21,178
6th CORPS (MARSHAL NEY) :						
1st DIVISION (Marchand) at Ledesma :						
6th Léger (2 batts.), 39th, 69th, 76th Line (3 batts. each) . . .	163	5,908	31	943	132	7,177
2nd DIVISION (Mermet) at Alba de Tormes :						
25th Léger (2 batts.), 27th and 59th Line (3 batts. each), 50th Line (2 batts.) . . .	201	6,656	10	714	4	7,585
3rd DIVISION (Loison) on the march :						
26th and 82nd Line (4 batts. each), 66th Line (3 batts.), Légion du Midi and Légion Hanovrienne (2 batts. each), 15th Léger, 32nd Léger (1 batt. each), 2 provisional batts.	302	11,948	543	1,652	142	14,587
CAVALRY DIVISION (Lorges):						
3rd Hussars, 15th Chasseurs, 15th, 25th Dragoons	108	2,314	60	132	2	2,616
ARTILLERY, TRAIN, ENGINEERS	24	1,120	6	78	2	1,230
DRAFTS, on the march from Bayonne to Salamanca .	156	5,636	506	—	—	6,298
ÉTAT-MAJOR	79	—	—	—	—	79
Corps Total	1,033	33,582	1,156	3,519	282	39,572

	Present under Arms.		De-tached.	Sick.	Prisoners.	Total.
	Officers.	Men.				
7th Corps (Marshal Augereau):						
1st Division (Souham) at Vich:						
1st Léger and 42nd Line (3 batts. each), 7th Line (2 batts.), 3rd Léger and 93rd Line (1 batt. each), 24th Dragoons, 3rd Provisional Chasseurs . .	169	5,213	397	2,627	57	8,463
2nd Division (Pino) at Massanet:						
Italians: 1st and 2nd Léger, 4th, 5th, 6th Line (2 batts. each), 7th Line (1 batt.), and Dragoons of Napoleon	238	6,346	201	2,409	93	9,287
3rd Division (Verdier) at Besalu, including the remains of Morio's and Lecchi's late divisions:						
French — 32nd Léger, 2nd, 16th, 56th Line (1 batt. each); Neapolitans—1st and 2nd Line (2 batts. each); Westphalians — 2nd, 3rd, and 4th Line (2 batts. each), 1st and 2nd of Berg, and Würzburg (2 batts. each), and Valais, Ducal Saxon, and La Tour d'Auvergne (1 batt. each), with 2nd Neapolitan Light Horse .	334	6,009	486	7,190	299	14,318
4th Division (Duhesme) at Barcelona:						
French — 7th Line (2 batts.), 37th and 112th Line (1 batt. each), 2nd Swiss (1 batt.), Chasseurs des Montagnes (1 batt.), 5th Italian Line (2 batts.), *Bataillon Départemental,* and 3rd Provisional Cuirassiers	240	5,971	33	2,056	87	8,387
Head-Quarters Guard (1 batt. French 67th) .	17	527	12	260	4	820
Artillery, Train, Engineers	44	1,346	43	708	27	2,168

	Present under Arms.		De-tached.	Sick.	Prison-ers.	Total.
	Offi-cers.	Men.				
DRAFTS marching from Perpignan to Barcelona .	32	1,608	—	—	—	1,640
DRAFTS at Perpignan, &c. .	127	6,125	—	—	—	6,252
ÉTAT-MAJOR	137	—	—	—	—	137
Corps Total	1,338	33,145	1,172	15,250	567	51,472
8th CORPS (GENERAL JUNOT) :						
1st DIVISION (Clausel) at Burgos : 22nd Line (4 batts.), 14th, 19th, 25th, 28th, 34th, 36th, 50th, 75th Line (1 batt. each) .	241	9,105	541	890	—	10,777
2nd DIVISION (Lagrange) at Burgos : 65th Line (4 batts.), 2nd, 4th, 12th, 15th Léger, 32nd, 46th, 58th, 121st, 122nd Line (1 batt. each)	195	8,688	668	701	91	10,343
3rd DIVISION (Solignac) at Burgos : 15th, 47th, 70th, 86th Line (2 batts. each), Régiment Irlandais, Régiment de Prusse (2 batts. each) . . .	135	6,925	573	398	43	8,074
CAVALRY DIVISION (Ste. Croix) : 3 provisional brigades of 2 squadrons each from 16 dragoon regiments	255	5,193	31	—	—	5,479
ARTILLERY, TRAIN, EN-GINEERS	30	1,614	4	62	—	1,710
DETACHMENTS forming gar-rison of Burgos . . .	12	714	4	132	4	866
ÉTAT-MAJOR	88	—	—	—	—	88
Corps Total	956	32,239	1,821	2,183	138	37,337
TOTAL OF THE EIGHT ARMY CORPS	6,651	184,310	9,463	33,955	2,180	236,559

TROOPS NOT FORMING PART OF THE EIGHT ARMY CORPS

	Present under Arms.		De-tached.	Sick.	Prison-ers.	Total.
	Offi-cers.	*Men.*				
(1) DIVISION DESSOLLES (Reserve) in march for Andalusia :						
12th Léger (4 batts.), 43rd, 51st, 55th Line (3 batts. each) . . .	229	8,125	1,277	960	50	10,641
(2) GOVERNMENT OF NAVARRE (Dufour) :						
Garrison entirely composed of drafts, depôts, and provisional units .	177	8,335	192	972	—	9,676
(3) GOVERNMENT OF BISCAY (Valentin) :						
One batt. each of 118th, 119th, 120th Line, 3 *régiments de marche,* and 6 ' *Bataillons auxiliaires* '	329	14,943	2,299	1,834	—	19,405
(4) PROVINCES OF VALLADOLID AND PALENCIA (Kellermann) :						
Kellermann's Division of Dragoons, 3rd, 6th, 10th, 11th	131	3,077	165	123	47	3,543
2nd, 3rd, 4th Swiss (1 batt. each), Garde de Paris	80	1,690	—	—	—	1,770
(5) PROVINCE OF SEGOVIA :						
Laval's German Division, detached from the 4th Corps. Nassau, Hesse, Baden, Holland (2 batts. each), Frankfurt (1 batt.), and Westphalian Chevaux-Légers, with French detachments garrisoning Segovia	204	4,203	1,730	3,371	231	9,739
(6) MADRID AND NEW CASTILE :						
1st DIVISION OF THE 4th CORPS :						
28th, 30th, 72nd Line (2 batts. each) . . .	125	4,123	90	1,710	35	6,083

	Present under Arms.		De-tached.	Sick.	Prison-ers.	Total.
	Offi-cers.	Men.				
CAVALRY BRIGADE :						
26th Chasseurs, 3rd Dutch Hussars . . .	41	765	208	50	32	1,096
ARTILLERY, ENGINEERS, TRAIN	49	1,472	83	107	—	1,711
PROVISIONAL BATTALIONS newly arrived at Madrid	77	4,784	—	37	91	4,989
ÉTAT-MAJOR AT MADRID .	38	—	—	—	—	38
Total in Madrid and New Castile	330	11,144	381	1,904	158	13,917
(7) **SANTANDER** (Bonnet) :						
118th, 119th, 120th, 122nd Line (3 batts. each)	225	6,839	—	646	232	7,972
(8) **IMPERIAL GUARD** :						
1st **DIVISION YOUNG GUARD** (Roguet) :						
4 Regiments of Infantry, 1st Provisional Regiment of Cavalry . .	190	6,424	76	299	—	6,989
2nd **DIVISION YOUNG GUARD** (Dumoustier) :						
4 Regiments of Infantry, 2nd Provisional Regiment of Cavalry . .	227	6,945	386	143	—	7,701
3rd Provisional Regiment of Cavalry . .	39	674	—	—	—	713
ARTILLERY, TRAIN, ENGINEERS	40	1,854	—	—	—	1,894
ÉTAT-MAJOR	8	—	—	—	—	8
Total Imperial Guard	504	15,897	462	442	—	17,305
(9) **TROOPS AT BAYONNE** or near it and on the march for Spain :						
Neuchâtel (1 batt.), Marines (2 batts.), 20 squadrons of Gendarmes, Artillery, Train, Engineers . .	357	12,939	318	47	—	13,661
(10) **ARRIÈRE - GARDE DE L'ARMÉE DE PORTUGAL** [troops designated for service, who have not yet marched],afterwards forming Drouet's 9th Corps.	267	16,148	—	—	—	16,415
Grand Total	9,484	287,650	16,287	44,254	2,898	360,603

Of whom 324,996 are actually in Spain, and of these 262,051 are ' Present under arms ' with the colours.

VIII

MASSÉNA'S ARMY OF PORTUGAL

ON SEPT. 15, 1810, JAN. 1, 1811, AND MARCH 15, 1811

From returns in the Archives Nationaux at Paris.

	On Sept. 15, 1810.		On Jan. 1, 1811.		On March 15, 1811.	
	Offi-cers.	*Men.*	*Offi-cers.*	*Men.*	*Offi-cers.*	*Men.*
2ND CORPS, General REYNIER.						
1st Division, General MERLE :						
Brigade Sarrut :						
2nd Léger (1st, 2nd, 3rd, 4th batts.)	77	2,281	52	1,670	54	1,343
36th Ligne (1st, 2nd, 3rd, 4th batts.)	82	1,994	54	1,226	73	1,163
Brigade Graindorge :						
4th Léger (1st, 2nd, 3rd, 4th batts.)	77	2,078	48	1,318	61	1,142
Divisional Total	236	6,353	154	4,214	188	3,648
2nd Division, General HEUDELET :						
Brigade Foy :						
17th Léger (1st, 2nd, 3rd batts.)	57	1,341	48	998	34	876
70th Ligne (1st, 2nd, 3rd, 4th batts.)	71	2,387	40	1,422	41	1,231
Brigade Arnaud :						
31st Léger (1st, 2nd, 3rd, 4th batts.)	57	1,711	44	1,641	54	1,620
47th Ligne (1st, 2nd, 3rd, 4th batts.)	76	2,387	64	1,461	59	1,541
Divisional Total	261	7,826	196	5,522	188	5,268
CavalryBrigade,GeneralP.SOULT:						
1st Hussars, 22nd Chasseurs, 8th Dragoons, Hanoverian Chasseurs	106	1,291	92	1,048	91	808
Artillery, Train, Engineers . .	25	1,554	33	1,251	*	*
État-Major	66	—	65	—	60	—
Grand Total of Corps	694	17,024	540	12,035	527	9,724

* Not stated separately. All the Artillery of the Army of Portugal is placed under one head in the return of March 15, and not distributed to the corps.

	On Sept. 15, 1810.		On Jan. 1, 1811.		On March 15, 1811.	
	Offi-cers.	Men.	Offi-cers.	Men.	Offi-cers.	Men.
6TH CORPS, Marshal NEY.						
1st Division, General MARCHAND :						
Brigade Maucune :						
6th Léger (1st, 2nd batts.) .	42	1,436	29	1,008	33	1,011
69th Ligne (1st, 2nd, 3rd batts.)	56	1,661	47	1,198	42	1,058
Brigade Marcognet :						
39th Ligne (1st, 2nd, 3rd batts.)	58	1,628	54	1,249	37	1,150
76th Ligne (1st, 2nd, 3rd batts.)	58	1,732	52	1,350	39	1,247
Divisional Total	214	6,457	182	4,805	151	4,466
2nd Division, General MERMET :						
Brigade Bardet :						
25th Léger (1st, 2nd batts.) .	37	1,678	39	1,363	37	1,275
27th Ligne (1st, 2nd, 3rd batts.)	59	1,827	59	1,550	32	1,185
Brigade Labassée :						
50th Ligne (1st, 2nd, 3rd batts.)	65	2,056	54	1,551	51	1,431
59th Ligne (1st, 2nd, 3rd batts.)	60	1,834	60	1,556	42	1,430
Divisional Total	221	7,395	212	6,040	162	5,321
3rd Division, General LOISON :						
Brigade Simon:						
26th Ligne (5th, 6th, 7th batts.)	64	1,561	46	989	47	1,077
Légion du Midi	18	546	17	363	15	397
Légion Hanovrienne (2 batts.)	29	1,129	19	611	23	698
Brigade Ferey :						
32nd Léger (2nd batt.). . .	20	393	14	243	18	262
66th Ligne (4th, 5th, 6th batts.)	68	1,762	42	1,353	44	1,316
82nd Ligne (4th and 6th batts.)[1]	40	1,196	25	733	36	801
Divisional Total	239	6,587	163	4,292	183	4,551
Cavalry Brigade, Gen. LAMOTTE : 3rd Hussars, 15th Chasseurs .	74	1,606	48	604	51	839
Artillery, Train, Engineers .	28	1,403	34	1,735[2]	*	*
État-Major	82	—	77	—	70	—
Grand total of Corps	858	23,448	716	17,476	617	15,177

[1] The 82nd had detached its 5th battalion, 575 strong, to form part of the garrison of Almeida.

[2] Some fractions of the general artillery reserve had been transferred to the corps since Sept. 15, hence the rise in numbers.

	On Sept. 15, 1810.		On Jan. 1, 1811.		On March 15, 1811.	
	Offi-cers.	Men.	Offi-cers.	Men.	Offi-cers.	Men.
8TH CORPS, General JUNOT, Duc d'Abrantès.						
1st Division, General CLAUSEL :						
Brigade Menard :						
19th Ligne (4th batt.) . . .	19	634	18	278	†	231
25th Ligne (4th batt.) . .	16	571	15	253	†	238
28th Ligne (4th batt.) . . .	17	442	19	324	†	250
34th Ligne (4th batt.) . . .	15	624	13	342	†	305
Brigade Taupin :						
15th Léger (4th batt.) . . .	21	813	17	485	18	501
46th Ligne (4th batt.) . . .	18	546	15	259	†	202
75th Ligne (4th batt.) . . .	19	532	16	233	†	178
Brigade Godard :						
22nd Ligne (1st, 2nd, 3rd, 4th batts.)	80	2,427	72	1,648	70	1,617
Divisional Total	205	6,589	185	3,822	88	3,522
2nd Division, General SOLIGNAC :						
Brigade Gratien :						
15th Ligne (1st, 2nd, 3rd batts.)[1]	63	1,262	58	925	62	906
86th Ligne (1st, 2nd, 3rd batts.)[2]	55	1,090	54	1,006	43	982
Brigade Thomières :						
65th Ligne (1st, 2nd, 3rd, 4th batts.)	82	2,680	80	1,951	65	1,555
Régiment Irlandais	37	971	23	525	21	462
Régiment de Prusse . . .	29	957	22	354	22	435
Divisional Total	266	6,960	237	4,761	213	4,340
Cavalry Division Gen. Ste. CROIX :						
1st, 2nd, 4th, 9th, 14th, 26th Dragoons, two squadrons of each	92	1,771	86	895	118	1,443
Artillery, Train, Engineers . .	17	964[2]	23	1,083[3]	*	*
État-Major	75	—	69	—	70	—
General Total of Corps	655	16,284	600	10,561	489	9,305

† By March 15 these six battalions had got so weak that their cadres had been sent back to France, and the remaining rank and file were being drafted into the regiments of the 2nd Corps.

[1] These regiments had detached their 4th battalions, 578 and 873 strong respectively, to form the garrison of Ciudad Rodrigo.

[2] Like the 6th Corps, the 8th had received part of the General Park of the army, and absorbed it.

[3] About 17 officers and 150 men had been drafted into the garrisons of Almeida and Rodrigo.

	On Sept. 15, 1810.		On Jan. 1, 1811.		On March 15, 1811.	
	Offi-cers.	Men.	Offi-cers.	Men.	Offi-cers.	Men.
RESERVE OF CAVALRY, General MONTBRUN.						
Brigade Lorcet : 3rd [1] and 6th Dragoons . .	52	1,040	51	793	51	733
Brigade Cavrois : 11th Dragoons [2]	27	634	28	557	28	551
Brigade Ornano: 15th and 25th Dragoons . .	57	1,369	57	1,178	58	1,014
Horse Artillery	6	294	4	162	*	*
Divisional Total	142	3,337	140	2,690	137	2,298
Artillery Reserve, Train, and Engineers not attached to any corps [3]	54	2,311	42	1,546	127	5,728 [4]
Gendarmerie	6	171	7	190	6	210
État-Major of the Army and officers not attached to any corps	66	—	60	—	62	—
Total of the whole Army	2,475	62,575	2,105	44,488	1,965	42,442

NOTE.—On Dec. 26 General Gardanne brought up to the front the 4/86th Line originally left at Ciudad Rodrigo, and some drafts, making in all 1,393 men ; these are counted in the figures of Jan. 1, 1811. On Feb. 5 General Foy brought up in a similar fashion 1,862 convalescents and drafts : these are counted in the figures of March 15, 1811.

The losses of the original 65,050 men who entered Portugal were therefore greater by 3,255 casualties than is shown in the table. The increase in the number of some regiments (e. g. 47th Line and Ste. Croix's Dragoons) between Jan. 1 and March 15 is thus explained. Of the original 65,000 only 40,000 remained, not 44,000, on March 15, 1811.

There is another ' return ' in the Archives Nationaux dated Sept. 27 where the figures are slightly lower than those given above, the total running to 62,538 effectives present instead of 65,050. The 2,500 men deficient represent the sick, stragglers, etc. between Sept. 15 and Sept. 27. The Second Corps for example returns 896 ' sick present' in addition to its 16,641 ' effectives present.' The 62,538 represent therefore the exact fighting-force at Bussaco.

[1] The 3rd Dragoons left one squadron, 157 men, at Almeida.
[2] The 10th Dragoons, the other regiments of this brigade, 718 strong, had been left at Ciudad Rodrigo under General Gardanne.
[3] About 300 artillerymen left at Ciudad Rodrigo and Almeida.
[4] This includes not only the original reserve artillery, park, &c., of the army, but the whole of the artillery of the three corps, which is not distributed among them in the return of March 15, 1811.

N.B.—No French return gives the 44th Equipage de Marine, which certainly marched with Masséna on Sept. 15. This naval battalion of 924 men should be added to the total.

IX

BRITISH LOSSES AT THE COMBAT OF THE COA, JULY 24, 1810

	Killed.		Wounded.		Missing.		Total.
	Officers.	Men.	Officers.	Men.	Officers.	Men.	
Staff . . .	—	—	1	—	—	—	1
1/43rd Foot .	3	15	10	86	—	15	129
1/52nd Foot .	—	1	2	16	—	3	22
1/95th Foot .	1	11	8	55	1	53	129
1st Portuguese Caçadores .	—	2	—	7	—	7	16
3rd ditto . .	—	2	1	24	—	2	29
Cavalry — 1st Hussars,K.G.L., and 16th Light Dragoons .	—	1	1	3	—	2	7
Total .	4	32	23	191	1	82	333

The total in the text, as in Wellington's dispatch, is wrong because of the omission of the 16 wounded of the 1/52nd who are inserted from the regimental returns, Wellington made out the total to be 317.

X

WELLINGTON'S ARMY AT BUSSACO, SEPT. 27, 1810
INFANTRY

1st Division, General Spencer :

	Officers.	Men.	
Stopford's Brigade :			
1st Coldstream Guards	24	790	
1st Scots Fusilier Guards	26	791	} 1,684
1 company 5/60th Foot	2	51	
Lord Blantyre's Brigade :			
24th Foot, 2nd batt.	30	338	
42nd ,, ...	23	391	} 1,516
61st ,, 1st ,, ...	36	648	
1 company 5/60th Foot	3	47	
Löwe's Brigade :			
1st Line batt. K.G.L.	28	510	
2nd ,, ,, ...	31	453	
5th ,, ,, ...	30	460	} 2,061
7th ,, ,, ...	24	429	
Detachment Light Batts. K.G.L. . . .	6	90	

Pakenham's Brigade :	Officers.	Men.	
7th Foot, 1st batt.	26	843	} 1,792
79th ,, ,, ...	38	885	

	Total of 1st Division	327	6,726	7,053

2nd Division, General HILL :

W. Stewart's Brigade :

3rd Foot, 1st batt.	32	826	
31st ,, 2nd ,, ...	27	384	
48th ,, ,, ...	27	454	} 2,247
66th ,, ,, ...	30	433	
1 company 5/60th Foot	1	33	

Inglis's Brigade :

29th Foot	31	430	
48th ,, 1st batt.	32	519	
57th ,, ,, ...	28	727	} 1,818
1 company 5/60th Foot	1	50	

Catlin Crawfurd's (Wilson's) Brigade :

28th Foot, 2nd batt.	32	522	
34th ,, ,, ...	36	617	
39th ,, ,, ...	27	394	} 1,672
1 company 5/60 Foot	2	42	

Hamilton's Portuguese Division attached to 2nd Division :

Archibald Campbell's Brigade :

4th Line Regiment (two batts.) . . .	—	1,164	} 2,250[1]
10th ,, ,, ,, . . .	—	1,086	

Fonseca's Brigade :

2nd Line Regiment (two batts.) . . .	—	1,317	} 2,690[1]
14th ,, ,, ,, . . .	—	1,373	

	Total of 2nd Division	306	10,371	10,677

3rd Division, General PICTON :

Mackinnon's Brigade :

45th Foot, 1st batt.	35	560	
74th ,, ,, ...	38	456	} 1,808
88th ,, ,, ...	40	679	

Lightburne's Brigade :

5th Foot, 2nd batt.	31	464	
83rd ,, 2nd ,, ...	43	461	} 1,160
90th ,, 5th ,, (three companies) . .	16	145	

Champlemond's (vice Harvey's) Portuguese Brigade :

9th Line Regiment (two batts.) . . .	—	1,234	} 1,775[1]
21st ,, ,, (one batt.) . . .	—	541	

	Total of 3rd Division	203	4,540	4,743

[1] In the Portuguese regiments the officers are counted in with the men.

4th Division, Major-General COLE :

Alex. Campbell's Brigade :	*Officers.*	*Men.*	
7th Foot, 2nd batt.	29	585	
11th ,, 1st ,, ...	42	920	2,109
53rd ,, 2nd ,, ...	25	448	
1 company 5/60th Foot.	2	58	
Kemmis's Brigade :			
27th Foot, 3rd batt.	34	785	
40th ,, 1st ,, ...	48	1,007	2,448
97th ,, ...	27	493	
1 company 5/60th Foot.	4	50	
Collins's Portuguese Brigade :			
11th Line (two batts.)	—	1,438	2,843[1]
23rd ,, ,, ...	—	1,405	
Total of 4th Division	211	7,189	7,400

5th Division, General LEITH :

Barnes's Brigade :			
1st Foot, 3rd batt.	35	733	
9th ,, 1st ,, ...	30	585	1,879
38th ,, 2nd ,, ...	29	467	
Spry's Portuguese Brigade :			
3rd Line (two batts.)	—	1,134	
15th ,, ,, ...	—	905	2,619[1]
Thomar Militia (attached)	—	580	
Lusitanian Legion (three batts.), Baron Eben[2].	—	1,646	2,807[1]
8th Line (two batts.), Colonel Douglas . .	—	1,161	
Total of 5th Division	94	7,211	7,305

Light Division, Brigadier-General CRAUFURD :

Beckwith's Brigade :			
43rd Foot, 1st batt.	40	804	
95th ,, ,, (four companies) . .	12	384	1,896[1]
3rd Portuguese Caçadores	—	656	
Barclay's Brigade :			
52nd Foot, 1st batt.	29	946	
95th ,, ,, (four companies) . .	12	358	1,891[1]
1st Portuguese Caçadores	—	546	
Total of Light Division	93	3,694	3,787

[1] In the Portuguese regiments the officers are counted in with the men.

[2] Leith in his report (Wellington, *Supplementary Dispatches*, vi. 636) gives the above brigading. The Portuguese official list of troops present (given by Soriano da Luz, iii) puts Eben as commanding an imperfect brigade, consisting of the 8th Line only, while the Lusitanian legion is given as a separate force under Lieut.-Col. Grant.

Independent Brigades of Portuguese Infantry :

1st Brigade, Brig.-Gen. D. Pack : *Officers. Men.*

	Officers	Men	
1st Line Regiment (two batts.)	—	1,089	
16th ,, ,, ,,	—	1,130	} 2,769
4th batt. Caçadores	—	550	

5th Brigade, Brig.-Gen. A. Campbell :

6th Line Regiment (two batts.)	—	1,317	
18th ,, ,, ,,	—	1,386	} 3,249
6th batt. Caçadores	—	546	

6th Brigade, Brig.-Gen. Coleman :

7th Line Regiment (two batts.)	—	815	
19th ,, ,, ,,	—	1,124	} 2,345
2nd batt. Caçadores	—	406	

Total of Independent Portuguese Brigades   8,363

CAVALRY

	Officers	Men
4th Dragoons (two squadrons)	15	195

ARTILLERY

British { Horse	18	314	
British { Field	37	663	
K.G.L. Field	19	299	
Portuguese	—	[1] 880 [2]	
Total Artillery	74	2,156	2,230

ENGINEERS	24	19	43
WAGGON TRAIN	25	397	422
STAFF CORPS	1	40	41

GENERAL TOTAL

	British.	Portuguese.	Total.
Infantry	24,777	24,549	49,326
Cavalry	210	—	210
Artillery	1,350	880	2,230
Engineers	43	—	43
Waggon Train	422	—	422
Staff Corps	41	—	41
Total present at Bussaco	26,843	25,429	52,272

[1] In the Portuguese regiments the officers are counted in with the men.

[2] This figure includes two batteries not present, but detached with Lecor's division beyond the Nundego. The totals can not be distinguished.

N.B.—It may be convenient to give here the list of the units of Wellington's field army which were *not* present at the battle of Bussaco ; these were :—

BRITISH CAVALRY :

	Officers.	Men.	
De Grey's Brigade :			
3rd Dragoon Guards	18	392	620
4th Dragoons (two squadrons) . . .	14	196	
(Near Mealhada.)			
Slade's Brigade :			
1st Dragoons	20	513	967
14th Light Dragoons	17	417	
Anson's Brigade :			
16th Light Dragoons	23	440	902
1st Hussars, K.G.L.	19	420	
(Both near Mealhada.)			
Fane's Brigade :			
13th Light Dragoons	29	401	430

PORTUGUESE CAVALRY (under Fane) :

1st Regiment	—	422	1,450
4th ,, ...	—	451	
7th ,, ...	—	223	
10th ,, ...	—	354	

(All beyond the Alva in the direction of Chamusca, &c.)

LECOR'S Portuguese Division :

Bradford's Brigade :			
12th Line Regiment (two batts.) . . .	—	1,277	2,811
13th ,, ,, ,, : . .	—	1,078	
5th batt. Caçadores	—	456	
Militia Brigade :			
Three regiments (Idanha, Castello Branco, Covilhão)	— ? 2,000	2,000	
		4,811	

(At and about Ponte de Murcella, and behind the Alva.)

In garrison at Lisbon, 88th Foot, 2nd batt.		
In march for Lisbon, 58th ,, ,,	68	1,086
At Raiva, 1 comp. K.G.L.		
Sick	—	6,565
' On command '	—	2,220

Of the remaining Portuguese regiments Nos. 5 and 17 were at Elvas, No. 20 at Cadiz, No. 22 at Abrantes, No. 24 had been taken prisoner at Almeida. These are not part of the field army.

The total of the fractions of the field army not present at Bussaco was 9,180.

XI

MASSÉNA'S ORDERS FOR BUSSACO

Moura, 26 7ᵇʳᵉ 1810.

Demain le 27 7ᵇʳᵉ l'armée attaquera les hauteurs en avant de Moura occupées par l'armée ennemie.

Le 2ⁿᵈ Corps attaquera la droite de l'armée ennemie : il tentera à cet effet de couper la ligne, en gravissant un des points de la montagne le plus accessible. Il y arrivera par une ou deux colonnes, en se faisant précéder par des tirailleurs. Une fois arrivé sur le sommet du point qu'il aura décidé d'attaquer, il se formera en colonne serrée, et descendra par la crête de la montagne sur le chemin de Coimbre. Le point où il devra s'arrêter est le Couvent de *Bussaco.* Il aura soin de se former une réserve, pour se soutenir au besoin. Son artillerie sera disposée de manière à pouvoir contrebattre celle de l'ennemi, et à lui servir de point d'appui.

Le 6ᵐᵉ Corps attaquera par les deux chemins qui conduisent sur la route de Coimbre ; une de ses divisions formera sa réserve, et son artillerie sera placée par différentes positions, pour pouvoir le soutenir au besoin. M. le Maréchal Ney disposera ses deux colonnes d'attaque de manière à donner quand le Général Reynier sera maître des hauteurs, et qu'il marchera sur le Couvent de *Bussaco.* Ce sera à M. le Maréchal Ney à presser son attaque s'il voit que l'ennemi s'avance pour faire un mouvement sur le Général Reynier, ou pour faire un mouvement de retraite (*sic*).[1] M. le Maréchal est trop pénétré de l'à-propos de son mouvement pour qu'on le lui détermine. Il se fera précéder par ses tirailleurs. Arrivé sur la crête de la montagne il se mettra en bataille pour l'ensemble des mouvements ultérieurs de l'armée.

Le 8ᵐᵉ Corps se rassemblera en arrière de Moura à 6 heures du matin. Il y prendra position, et fera des dispositions pour soutenir au besoin les corps d'armée attaquants, et pour marcher lui-même à l'ennemi.

Son artillerie sera placée de manière à arrêter l'ennemi s'il faisait un mouvement en avant.

La réserve de Cavalerie sera placée sur la route de Coimbre, en arrière et au centre du 8ᵐᵉ Corps.

Le Maréchal Prince d'Essling : Signé MASSÉNA.

Copie conforme : Le Gén. de division B. N. Fririon.
Pour son Excellence M. le duc d'Abrantès.

---

[1] A strange phrase. How could the enemy 'advance in order to make movement of retreat'?

XII

LOSSES AT BUSSACO
ENGLISH AND PORTUGUESE

	Killed.		Wounded.		Missing.		Total.
	Officers.	Men.	Officers.	Men.	Officers.	Men.	
1st DIVISION (Spencer):							
Stopford's Brigade :							
1st Coldstream Guards .	—	—	—	—	—	—	
1/3rd Guards	—	—	—	2	—	—	2
Blantyre's Brigade :							
24th Foot, 2nd Batt. . .	—	—	1	—	—	—	1
42nd ,, ,, . .	—	—	—	6	—	—	6
61st ,, 1st ,, . .	—	—	—	—	—	—	
Löwe's Brigade :							
1st Line batt. K.G.L. .	—	3	1	5	—	—	9
2nd ,, ,, ,, .	—	1	1	6	—	1	9
5th ,, ,, ,, .	—	1	—	9	—	—	10
7th ,, ,, ,, .	—	—	—	9	—	—	9
Light Companies . .	—	1	—	11	—	3	15
Pakenham's Brigade :							
7th Foot, 1st batt. . .	—	1	1	22	—	—	24
79th ,, ,, . .	—	7	1	41	1	6	56
Divisional Loss	—	14	5	111	1	10	141
2nd DIVISION (Hill). No Losses whatever.							
3rd DIVISION (Picton):							
Mackinnon's Brigade :							
45th Foot, 1st batt. . .	3	22	4	109	—	12	150
74th ,, . .	1	6	1	21	—	2	31
88th ,, ,, . .	1	30	8	94	—	1	134
Lightburne's Brigade :							
5th Foot, 2nd batt. . .	—	1	—	7	—	—	8
60th ,, 5th ,, . .	—	3	5	16	—	5	29 [1]
83rd ,, 2nd ,, . .	—	—	1	4	—	—	5
Champlemond's Portuguese Brigade :							
9th Line (two batts.) . .	—	5	1	23	—	—	29
21st ,, (one batt.) . .	2	13	5	67	—	—	87
Divisional Loss	7	80	25	341	—	20	473
4th DIVISION (Cole). No Losses whatever.							
5th DIVISION (Leith):							
Barnes's Brigade :							
1st Foot, 3rd batt. . .	—	—	—	—	—	—	—
9th ,, 1st ,, . .	—	5	1	18	—	—	24
38th ,, 2nd ,, . .	—	5	1	17	—	—	23

[1] The greater part of the losses of this battalion were in the companies attached to other brigades, but the total is inserted here.

	Killed.		Wounded.		Missing.		Total.
	Offi-cers.	Men.	Offi-cers.	Men.	Offi-cers.	Men.	
Spry's Portuguese Brigade : 3rd and 15th Line.	No losses whatever.						
Lusitanian Legion.	No losses whatever.						
Portuguese 8th Line : two batts.	1	29	3	102	—	9	144
Divisional Loss	1	39	5	137	—	9	191
LIGHT DIVISION (Craufurd) :							
43rd Foot, 1st batt. . .	—	—	—	8	—	—	8
52nd ,, ,, . .	—	3	3	10	—	—	16
95th ,, ,, . .	—	9	—	32	—	—	41
1st Caçadores	—	2	—	20	—	1	23
3rd ,, ...	—	10	3	76	—	—	89
Divisional Loss	—	24	6	146	—	1	177
Pack's Portuguese Brigade : 1st Line (two batts.) . .	1	4	2	32	—	—	39
16th ,, ,, . .	1	2	2	26	—	2	33
4th Caçadores	1	9	4	52	—	—	66
Coleman's Portuguese Brigade : 7th Line (two batts.) . .	—	—	—	3	—	—	3
19th ,, ,, . .	—	8	1	28	—	—	37
2nd Caçadores	—	6	—	30	—	7	43
A. Campbell's Portuguese Brigade : 6th Line (two batts.) . .	—	—	—	—	—	—	—
18th ,, ,, . .	—	—	—	—	—	—	—
6th Caçadores	—	1	1	20	—	1	23
Total	3	30	10	191	—	10	244
ARTILLERY : British	—	1	—	7	—	—	8
K.G.L.	—	—	—	3	—	—	3
Portuguese	—	1	—	8	—	—	9
Total	—	2	—	18	—	—	20
GENERAL STAFF	—	—	6	—	—	—	
Grand Total	11	189	57	944	1	50	1252
[of whom British . .	5	99	34	457	1	30	626 [1]
,, Portuguese	6	90	23	487	—	20	626 [1]

[1] An extraordinary coincidence in the total losses of the two nations !

XIII

FRENCH LOSSES AT BUSSACO

	Killed or prisoners.		Wounded.		Total.
	Officers.	Men.	Officers.	Men.	
2ND CORPS.					
MERLE's Division					
Sarrut's Brigade :					
2nd Léger	2	81	16	209	308
36th Ligne	6	178	22	277	483
Graindorge's Brigade :					
4th Léger	11	118	9	110	248
Artillery	—	—	—	2	2
Divisional Total	19	377	47	598	1,041
HEUDELET's Division :					
Foy's Brigade :					
17th Léger	2	60	20	271	353
70th Ligne	6	54	11	246	317
Arnaud's Brigade :					
31st Léger.	3	67	7	219	296
47th Ligne	—	—	3	3	6
Artillery	—	—	—	6	6
Divisional Total	11	181	41	745	978
Corps Troops :					
Engineers	—	1	—	2	3
Train	—	1	—	—	1
Grand Total	30	560	88	1,345	2,023

[Signed : BARBOT, Saldere, Oct. 1.]

This return from the *Archives du Ministère de la Guerre* omits the État-Major, which had one officer killed and four wounded, and the Cavalry, which, though in reserve, had some slight losses, for Martinien's *Liste des Officiers* shows that the 8th Dragoons and the 1st Hussars had each one officer wounded, and that Pierre Soult, the general commanding the brigade, was also hit; probably ten or a dozen casualties among the men are implied. But the casualties must have been very few in the mounted arm. Fririon, Masséna's chief of the Staff, says that the prisoners of the second corps came to 15 officers and 349 rank and file, many of them wounded. If so, the killed must have amounted to 15 officers and 211 men.

	Killed.		Wounded.		Total.
	Officers.	Men.	Officers.	Men.	
6TH CORPS.					
MARCHAND's Division :					
Maucune's Brigade :					
6th Léger	2	70	12	281	365
69th Ligne	2	44	18	416	480
Marcognet's Brigade :					
39th Ligne	—	19	3	213	235
76th Ligne	—	7	3	83	93
Divisional Total	4	140	36	939	1173
MERMET's Division :					
Bardet's Brigade :					
25th Léger	—	3	—	20	23
27th Ligne . . .	—	—	1	—	1
Labassée's Brigade :					
(50th, 59th) no losses .	—	—	—	—	—
Divisional Total	—	3	1	20	24
LOISON's Division :					
Simon's Brigade :					
26th Ligne	6	37	15	225	283
Légion du Midi . . .	1	32	5	273	311
Légion Hanovrienne .	4	26	5	182	217
Ferey's Brigade :					
32nd Léger	2	13	3	95	113
66th Ligne	5	15	15	123	158
82nd Ligne	3	18	4	145	170
Divisional Total	21	141	47	104 3	1252
ÉTAT-MAJOR :	—	—	7	—	7
Grand Total	25	284	91	2,056	2456

No return from the Artillery, part of which was engaged beside Moura, and must have had a few casualties, like that of the 2nd Corps.

8TH CORPS. Junot's corps having been in reserve, we should not have expected to find any casualties, but Martinien's lists show a few officers— five in all—hit, in the 28th and 86th Ligne, besides an aide-de-camp of Clausel wounded. This must mean that the corps caught a few stray shells when it was brought up to cover the retreat of Ney's routed divisions. It would be a minimum to estimate the losses at sixty. Three of Masséna's *adjoints de l'État-Major,* and an officer from the Grand Park, are also mentioned as wounded in Martinien's lists.

The total of the French losses therefore must have been quite 4,600 killed, wounded, and missing. The return accounts for no prisoners from the 6th Corps. But General Simon was certainly captured, and he is not likely to have been the *sole* prisoner.

XIV

WELLINGTON'S ARMY WITHIN THE LINES OF TORRES VEDRAS. MORNING STATE OF NOV. 1, 1810

1. BRITISH TROOPS (effective, without sick or detached)

	Officers.	Men.	Total.
CAVALRY DIVISION (STAPLETON COTTON) :			
De Grey's Brigade : 3rd Dragoon Guards and 4th Dragoons	51	753	804
Slade's Brigade : 1st Dragoons and 14th Light Dragoons	40	858	898
Anson's Brigade : 16th Light Dragoons and 1st Hussars K.G.L.	39	769	808
Unbrigaded : 13th Light Dragoons . . .	23	300	323
Total Cavalry .	153	2,680	2,833

INFANTRY

	Officers.	Men.	Total.
1st DIVISION (SPENCER) :			
Stopford's Brigade : 1st Coldstream Guards, 1st Scots Fusilier Guards, and one company 5/60th Foot .	61	1,624	1,685
Cameron's Brigade : 2/24th, 2/42nd, 1/79th Foot, and one company 5/60th	101	1,438	1,539
Erskine's Brigade : 1/50th, 1/71st, 1/92nd Foot, and one company 5/60th Foot	108	1,935	2,043
Löwe's Brigade : 1st, 2nd, 5th, 7th Line battalion K.G.L., and a light company K.G.L. . .	120	1,561	1,681
Divisional Total .	390	6,558	6,948
2nd DIVISION (HILL) :			
Colborne's Brigade : 1/3rd, 2/31st, 2/48th, 2/66th Foot, and one company 5/60th	138	1,967	2,105
Houghton's Brigade : 29th, 1/48th, 1/57th, and one company 5/60th Foot	97	1,560	1,657
Lumley's Brigade : 2/28th, 2/34th, 2/39th, and one company 5/60th Foot	94	1,395	1,489
Divisional Total .	329	4,922	5,251
3rd DIVISION (PICTON) :			
Mackinnon's Brigade : 1/45th, 1/74th, 1/88th Foot	117	1,564	1,681
Colville's Brigade : 2/5th, 2/83rd, 94th, and three companies 5/60th Foot	122	1,533	1,655
Divisional Total .	239	3,097	3,336

	Officers.	Men.	Total.
4th Division (Cole):			
Kemmis's Brigade : 2/27th, 1/40th, 97th, and one company of 5/60th Foot	118	2,454	2,572
Pakenham's Brigade : 1/7th, 1/61st Foot, and Brunswick-Oels Jägers	125	2,095	2,220
Divisional Total .	243	4,549	4,792
5th Division (Leith):			
Hay's Brigade : 3/1st, 1/9th, 2/38th Foot . .	89	1,958	2,047
Dunlop's Brigade : 2/30th, 2/44th Foot . .	56	1,126	1,182
Divisional Total .	145	3,084	3,229
6th Division (Alex. Campbell):			
Only one Brigade ; 2/7th, 1/11th, 2/53rd Foot, and one company 5/60th Foot	101	1,847	1,948
Divisional Total .	101	1,847	1,948
Light Division (Craufurd):			
Beckwith's Brigade : 1/43rd, and companies of the 1st and 2nd 95th	56	1,427	1,483
2nd Brigade : 1/52nd and companies of 1/95th .	52	1,230	1,282
Divisional Total .	108	2,657	2,765
Infantry Unattached to any Division :			
2/58th, 2/88th Foot, and one company K.G.L. .	64	874	938
General Total of Infantry	1,619	27,588	29,207
British Artillery (Horse)	18	304	322
,, ,, (Foot)	48	797	845
K.G.L. Artillery	19	328	347
Total Artillery .	85	1,429	1,514
Engineers	24	19	43
Train	24	398	422
Staff Corps	3	37	40
Total Effective Strength of the British Troops on Nov. 1, 1810 :			
Cavalry	153	2,680	2,833
Infantry	1,619	27,588	29,207
Artillery	85	1,429	1,514
Other Corps	51	454	505
Grand Total	1,908	32,151	34,059

The army had at the same time 9,213 men in hospital, and 2,628 men detached, who are not counted in the above total.

N.B.—Wellington, as it will be noted on page 451, says that he had only 29,000 British sabres and bayonets ready to take the offensive at this date. This appears to be an under-estimate ; but it must be remembered that he (according to his custom) only counts rank and file, omitting officers. Moreover, the two battalions not brigaded, 2/58th and 2/88th, forming the garrison of the Lisbon forts, the gunners (about 200) in the forts, and the Train (as non-combatant) are also omitted in his calculation, so that 29,000 is not far out.

II. PORTUGUESE TROOPS (effective, without sick or detached)

FROM A RETURN OF OCT. 29, 1810

	Officers & Men Present.
INFANTRY OF THE LINE :	
1st Brigade (Pack) : 1st and 16th Line, 4th Caçadores	2,267
2nd Brigade [1] (Fonseca) : 2nd and 14th Line	2,414
3rd Brigade [2] (Spry) : 3rd and 15th Line	2,163
4th Brigade [1] (Arch. Campbell) : 4th and 10th Line	2,407
5th Brigade (A. Campbell) : 6th and 18th Line and 6th Caçadores	2,442
6th Brigade (Coleman) : 7th and 19th Line, and 2nd Caçadores	2,196
7th Brigade [3] (Baron Eben) : 8th Line, 1st and 2nd Lusitanian Legion	2,083
8th Brigade [4] (Sutton, vice Champlemond) : 9th and 21st Line	1,961
9th Brigade [5] (Collins, vice Harvey) : 11th and 23rd Line	2,535
1st and 3rd Caçadores, attached to Light Division	964
12th Line [6], attached to Lecor's Militia Division	1,213
Total Regular Infantry	22,645

REGULAR CAVALRY (FANE'S DIVISION) :	
1st, 4th, 7th, 10th Regiments	1,193
REGULAR ARTILLERY (9 batteries)	701
Total Regulars of all Arms	24,539

N.B.—The Portuguese regulars had, over and above these 24,539 officers and men present with the colours, 3,011 men sick and detached.

[1] These two brigades, forming Hamilton's division, were always acting with Hill's British Division.
[2] Forming part of Leith's 5th Division.
[3] Forming part of Alex. Campbell's 6th Division.
[4] Forming part of Picton's 3rd Division.
[5] Forming part of Cole's 4th Division.
[6] This regiment, with the 13th Line, formed Bradford's brigade of Lecor's Portuguese division. But the 13th was absent, in garrison at Abrantes.

Officers & Men Present.

MILITIA AND EMBODIED ORDENANÇA :

(1) Lecor's Division (Alhandra Forts) : Regiments of Santarem, Idanha, Castello Branco, Covilhão, and Feira. [12th Line, counted above, was also attached][1] 2,616

(2) At Bucellas Forts : Regiments of Lisbon (Termo), Thomar, Torres Vedras 1,907

(3) In the Forts facing Sobral : Atiradores Nacionaes (embodied Ordenança), 2 batts. 761

(4) In Torres Vedras Forts ; Regiments of Lisbon (E.), Lisbon (W.), Setubal, Alcaçer do Sul 2,231

(5) At Mafra Forts : Regiment of Vizeu 691

Militia Artillery [composed of cadres from the regular artillery filled with Volunteers from the Militia and embodied Ordenança] 2,886

Total Militia, &c. . 11,092

The Militia and embodied Ordenança had, over and above these 11,092 officers and men present with the colours, 1,267 sick and detached.

DEPÔT TROOPS :

The depôts of the Line and Militia contained, on Oct. 29, 6,470 more or less trained recruits, who had not yet joined their corps, but all did so before Dec. 1, and 530 sick. I have on page 434 reckoned the amount of these available on Oct. 15 at 3,000 men. Besides these 6,470 men there was at Peniche, outside the lines and in Masséna's rear, a general depôt of recruits, containing several thousand men who were not yet trained. Of these no account, of course, is taken here.

III. SPANISH TROOPS WITHIN THE LINES

VANGUARD DIVISION OF THE ARMY OF ESTREMADURA (LA CARRERA) :

Principe (2 batts.), 1st and 2nd of Catalonia (1 batt. each), Vittoria (1 batt.)—about 2,500

[N.B.—One battalion of Principe, and Volunteers of Gerona, belonging to this division, remained behind at Badajoz.]

2nd DIVISION (CHARLES O'DONNELL) :

Zamora (2 batts.), Rey (2 batts.), Toledo (2 batts.), Hibernia (2 batts.), Princesa (2 batts.), 2nd of Seville (1 batt.)—about 5,500

[N.B.—Fernando VII, Voluntarios de Navarra, and Tiradores de Castilla, belonging to this division, remained behind in Estremadura, at Badajoz and elsewhere.]

Total . 8,000

---

[1] The 5th Caçadores, which had formed part of Bradford's brigade and Lecor's division, was in October and November outside the lines, on the south side of the Tagus, observing Santarem, and under the orders of the Cavalry-General Fane.

These numbers are probably a little overstated ; on Feb. 1 the whole Vanguard, including the battalions left behind, had only 2,687 effectives, and the whole 2nd Division, including the four battalions left in Estremadura, only 5,108. It is probable that the wastage of the Spanish troops when inside the Lines was not large, and that on Nov. 1 the whole of La Romana's sixteen battalions did not make 7,000 men.

TOTAL OF REGULAR TROOPS IN THE LINES

BRITISH	34,059
PORTUGUESE	24,539
SPANISH	8,000
Total .	66,598

Add Portuguese Militia and embodied Ordenança, 11,092 strong, and the total of organized troops in the Lines makes 77,690.

XV

THE BRITISH AND PORTUGUESE ARTILLERY IN THE CAMPAIGN OF 1810

To match the list of the Artillery units in Wellington's army which the late Colonel F. A. Whinyates was so good as to compile for me for the year 1809, and which forms Appendix XI of my second volume, I have compiled, with the invaluable aid of Major John H. Leslie, R.A., who is responsible for all the British section, the following appendix to cover the year 1810.

ROYAL HORSE ARTILLERY.

Two troops served in the Bussaco campaign, viz. :—

A Troop, Captain H. D. Ross, which had arrived in Portugal in July 1809. [Present designation, ' A Battery,' R.H.A.]

I Troop, Captain R. Bull, which had arrived in August 1809. [Present designation, ' I Battery,' R.H.A.]

There was also present in Lisbon the skeleton of D Troop, Captain G. Lefebure. [Present designation, ' V Battery,' R.H.A.] But this unit had suffered from perils of the sea: a transport carrying part of its officers and men had been driven ashore on Ireland ; and the portion which arrived in March 1810, being incomplete and almost horseless, was not sent to the front. It lent some men to the other two R.H.A. batteries : the rest were employed in the Lisbon Forts.

ROYAL FOOT ARTILLERY [1].

Two batteries served in the Bussaco campaign, viz. :—

[1] The companies of the battalions R.A. were not numbered in 1810, but only designated by their captains' names. The numbers here given, for purposes of easier identification, are those given to these companies when numeration was introduced about 1822.

6th Company, 7th battalion, Captain G. Thompson, which had arrived
in March 1809. [Present designation, 18th Battery, R.F.A.]

7th Company, 8th battalion, Captain R. Lawson, which had arrived
in September 1808. [Present designation, 87th Battery, R.F.A.]

There were also present in the Peninsula, but not in the Bussaco
campaign :—

1st Company, 4th battalion, Captain J. Hawker [now 72nd Company,
R.G.A.].

10th Company, 8th battalion, Captain P. Meadows [an extinct unit].

Both of which arrived at Lisbon in October 1810, and waited in the
Torres Vedras Lines for the retiring army, having come too late for the
field operations.   Also

1st Company, 8th battalion, Bt.-Major A. Bredin [now 27th Battery,
R.F.A.].

2nd Company, 1st battalion, 2nd Captain H. Baynes [now 2nd Battery,
R.F.A.].

10th Company, 5th battalion, Captain F. Glubb [now 48th Company,
R.G.A.].

All of which had arrived in 1808–9.   But Baynes's battery had not taken
the field since Talavera, and Bredin's and Glubb's [both incomplete] had
not gone to the front in 1809 or in 1810.   They had all lain within the
Lines since the winter of 1809–10.

In addition there were five batteries with Graham's force at Cadiz.

8th Company, 5th battalion, Captain H. Owen [now 60th Company,
R.G.A.].

6th Company, 9th battalion, Captain P. J. Hughes [an extinct unit].

6th Company, 10th battalion, Captain W. Roberts [now 63rd Company,
R.G.A.].

4th Company, 10th battalion, Captain R. H. Birch [1] [now 21st Company,
R.G.A.].

5th Company, 10th battalion, Captain W. H. Shenley [now 11th
Company, R.G.A.].

King's German Legion Artillery.

2nd Company, Captain C. von Rettberg [arrived August 1808].

4th Company, Captain A. Cleeves [arrived August 1808].

Both present at Bussaco.   In the 1809 campaign they had been commanded respectively by Captains A. Tieling and H. L. Heise.

Portuguese Artillery.

The Portuguese Artillery force consisted of four regiments of about
1,200 men each, from which batteries were formed from time to time for
field service, or garrison service indifferently.

In the Bussaco campaign there took part the following units, which were
present at the battle :—

[1] Captain Birch commanded this company from June 1810 to July 1812,
vice Captain Alex. Dickson, employed with the Portuguese army.

1st Regiment, two batteries under Major Alex. Dickson, both of 6-pounders, viz. those of Captain Pedro de Rozierres and Captain João da Cunha Preto.

2nd Regiment, two batteries under Major V. von Arentschildt, viz. those of Captain João Porfirio da Silva and Captain Jacinto P. M. Freire, both of 3-pounders.

4th Regiment, one battery commanded by Captain Antonio de Sousa Passos (6-pounders).

There were also at the front, but not engaged at Bussaco, two more batteries, which were with Lecor's division behind the Alva, on the Ponte Murcella position—viz. one of 9-pounders, captainless till Oct. 1, when it came under the command of Captain Wilhelm Braun, and one of 3-pounders. The former joined Dickson's division on Sept. 28 ; the latter joined Arentschildt's division.

Two more field batteries joined the army at the Lines after its retreat : that of Captain Francisco Cypriano Pinto (6-pounders) was allotted to Dickson's division ; the other (no captain, 9-pounders) joined Arentschildt's command.

The rest of the Artillery at Lisbon was utilized as garrison-artillery for the Lines, receiving into its ranks an immense proportion of half-trained volunteers from the Militia and Ordenança, so that the whole can hardly be considered as forming part of the regular army. I have reckoned it into the militia force in the preceding table. The districts served by this artillery, the commanders of the districts, and the number of effective men in each were on Nov. 15, 1810 :—

	Regulars.	Militia-volunteers.	Total.
Alhandra Forts—Major João C. Pinto	258	182	440
Bucellas Forts—Colonel Romão de Arriada	218	847	1,065
Monte Agraça Forts—Major J. J. da Cruz	150	300	450
Torres Vedras Forts—Captain F. J. V. Barreiros	150	248	398
Mafra Forts—Major Caetano P. Xavier	233	305	538
	1,009	1,882	2,891

Adding these to the 701 men of the nine field batteries we get 3,592 in all, of whom 1,710 were regulars.

The officer in command of the whole Portuguese artillery was Marechal de Campo J. A. da Roza. Colonel Romão de Arriada commanded the 1st Regiment.

The 4th Regiment of the Portuguese artillery, that of the Oporto district, furnished only one battery (that of Captain Passos) to the army of Wellington, the rest of it being either serving with Silveira's army in the north, or with Trant, or doing garrison duty at Oporto. This regiment had also contributed to the lost garrison of Almeida.

The 3rd Regiment supplied no men to the field army or the garrison of the Torres Vedras Lines, being absorbed in garrisoning Abrantes, Elvas, Campo Mayor, and the other places on the frontier south of the Tagus.

INDEX

OTHER
NAPOLEONIC BOOKS
Published by Greenhill Books

Military Maxims of Napoleon
Edited and with Introduction and Commentary
by David G. Chandler

On the Napoleonic Wars: Collected Essays
by David G. Chandler

The Campaign of 1812 in Russia
by General Carl von Clausewitz
Introduction by George F. Nafziger

Life in Napoleon's Army:
The Memoirs of Captain Elzéar Blaze
Commentary by Lt. Gen. Charles Napier
Introduction by Philip Haythornthwaite

KEVIN F. KILEY
Artillery of the Napoleonic Wars, 1792–1815

F. LORAINE PETRE:
Napoleon's Campaign in Poland, 1806–1807

Napoleon's Conquest of Prussia, 1806

EDWARD RYAN
Napoleon's Shield and Guardian:
The Unconquerable General Daumesnil

JAC WELLER:
Wellington at Waterloo

Adventures with the Connaught Rangers,
1809–1814
by William Grattan